Frommer's®
Bahamas

Our Bahamas

by Darwin Porter & Danforth Prince

THE BAHAMAS ARCHIPELAGO STRETCHES FROM SOUTH FLORIDA almost to Haiti, comprising more than 700 islands. And the experiences that await you are as diverse as the islands themselves. On Paradise Island, you can order "surf and turf" from a tuxedo-clad waiter; buy Bulgari gems; partake of Las Vegas–style gambling; or sail on a James Bond–style yacht (many 007 films used Nassau and Paradise Island as backdrops). The waters off New Providence Island are dense with gardens of elkhorn coral and the sea floor is a graveyard of shipwrecks that draw boatloads of scuba divers.

Personally, we prefer the tranquil, less developed side of The Bahamas—from the underwater caverns of Lucayan National Park to Bimini's raffish End of the World Bar. If you move south from the megaresorts on Nassau and Paradise Island, you'll discover the Out Islands; here, virtually unchanged, is the kind of natural setting that Columbus and his crew first spotted in the 15th century. If you dream of lying under a sheltering palm tree on a deserted beach with talcum-fine sands, these are the islands to visit—some of them so underpopulated, electricity has yet to arrive.

The photos we've chosen reflect the best of these islands, whether you prefer action, relaxation, or a little of both.

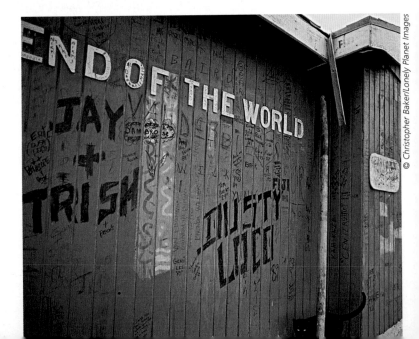

© Christopher Baker/Lonely Planet Images

Bimini's **END OF THE WORLD BAR (left)**, with its sand floor and a back door that opens to the harbor, boasts a storied past; Adam Clayton Powell, the legendary congressman from Harlem, was a fixture here in the 1960s. These days, when the fishing is done, beer-bellied fishermen—each looking like a clone of another former patron, Ernest Hemingway—arrive with their suntanned dates to drink the night away.

Breathtaking **PINK SANDS BEACH (above)** is our favorite in The Bahamas. Its pristine beauty stretches for 5km (3 miles) along Harbour Island's eastern flank. In the wild pirate days, long past, "Calico Jack" Rackham—The Bahamas' most notorious freebooter—raced along this beach clad only in a red kerchief. These days you'll find tranquillity in the beach's northern bird sanctuary and pleasant swimming conditions.

Beginning at 3am on the day after Christmas, revelers in elaborate costumes celebrate **JUNKANOO**. The raucous street parade is an ancient ritual of African heritage that still lives on in The Bahamas and is a symbol of national pride. Some **JUNKANOO MASKS (above)** cover an entire face. This masked man joins stilt, street, and acrobatic dancers, along with clowns and monsters—perhaps a "fly" with red-and-chartreuse eyes and 2.7m (9ft.) wings. The **KING OF JUNKANOO (right)** wears an elaborate headdress, a caparison vest, and a giant hoop skirt made from cardboard and decorated with thin strips of crepe paper meticulously glued on. Part jive, part shuffle, and all dazzling gymnastics, parade participants dance to the syncopated beat of blowing bugles, tin whistles, clanking cowbells, conch shells, and Goombay drums (goat skins stretched over wooden frames).

Take a stroll through Nassau's vast bustling **STRAW MARKET (right),** which dates from 1901, and you'll find all sorts of items made from the top of thatch palm—baskets with colorful embroidery, handbags, hats, tablemats, and even dolls.

The hub of market life from the Out Islands, Potter's Cay lies under the Paradise Island Bridge. **QUEENIE (below)** sells island staples such as papaya, bananas, coconuts, and pineapples. Fishing boats arrive at Potter's Cay, too, to unload their catch of the day, especially snapper and grouper—two mainstays of the Bahamian diet—and the "sexy conch," which Bahamian men view as an aphrodisiac.

The 5.6ha (14-acre) sprawling "water city" at the Atlantis Paradise Island Resort & Casino justifies the resort's hype that "An ocean runs through it." The aquarium here is touted as the largest marine habitat in the world, with more than 100 species of tropical fish, some 14,000 in all. Take a stroll through this Plexiglas walkway at **MARINE PARK (left)**, which provides a unique perspective to see marine life from down below as fish swim overhead.

Paying homage to the "lost continent" of Atlantis, the $850 million, 2,349-room **ATLANTIS PARADISE ISLAND RESORT & CASINO (above)** is a fantasy megaresort. It stands across from Nassau on Paradise Island, the poshest destination in The Bahamas. Atlantis, with a Disney-style replica of a Mayan temple, is not just a resort, but also a water park with marine life, underwater caves, waterfalls, blue lagoons, and a walk-through aquarium.

Built in 1838, this red-and-white banded **LIGHTHOUSE (left)** on Elbow Cay in the Abacos is one of the last hand-turned, kerosene-fueled beacons in The Bahamas. Climb 36m (120 ft.) to the top for a view of dazzling land- and seascapes. Local residents have repeatedly tried to destroy the lighthouse, hoping that ships near Hope Town would wreck on the reefs and they could salvage the profitable cargoes.

"THE CLOISTERS," (below) were once part of a 14th-century monastery near Lourdes, France. Newspaper baron William Randolph Hearst purchased the remains but when dismantled, they were not labeled. Paradise Island developer, Huntington Hartford, grandson of the founder of A&P, hired architects to reassemble the stones; the project took more than a year to complete.

The **HORSE-DRAWN SURREY (above)** is still the most romantic way to travel about Nassau. Drivers await passengers in the heart of Rawson Square and tell a colorful living history of Nassau—of all the blood, gore, lore, and legend. You'll pass the grounds of the 1859 Royal Victoria Hotel, once home to a man who inspired Margaret Mitchell to create the character of Rhett Butler in *Gone With the Wind*.

On October 12, 1492, Columbus landed on this frontier island, 122km (200 miles) southeast of Nassau. He named it San Salvador. In 1956, scholar Ruth Durlacher Wolper Malvin placed a lonely cross—known now as the **COLUMBUS MONUMENT (right)**—at what is believed, though disputed, to be the spot where Columbus made landfall.

PINK FLAMINGOS (left)—the graceful national birds of The Bahamas—strike elegant poses in the remote nature reserve of the Inagua National Park. The Romans killed these birds for their tongues—considered the greatest of all delicacies—but they are protected today and are no longer an endangered species. Every spring, flamingos flock to Great Inagua, the most southerly and the third-largest island of The Bahamas, to mate.

At the 16ha (40-acre) **LUCAYAN NATIONAL PARK (above)** on Grand Bahama Island, a wooden path winds through terrain that islanders call the "bush country." Along with rare birds, flora, and fauna, the park's environment ranges from dune-covered beaches to Golden Rock Creek, fed by what is touted as the world's largest underground freshwater cavern system. Bones, pottery, and other artifacts prove that this was a former stomping ground of the Lucayans, who came here to drink from the freshwater springs.

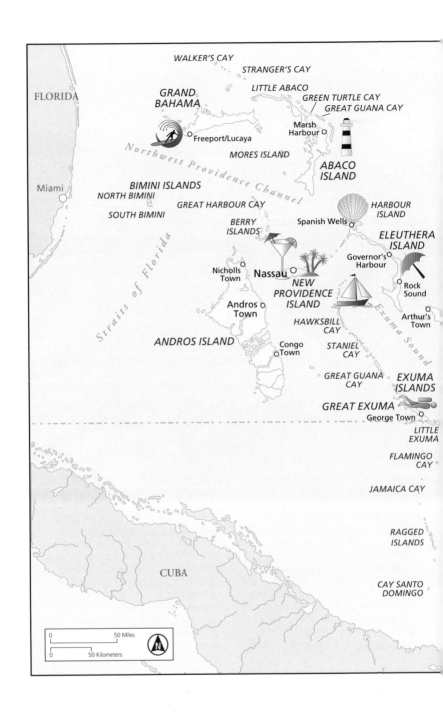

The Best Sun & Sand in the Bahamas

 Cable Beach

 Cabbage Beach

 Xanadu Beach

 Tahiti Beach

 Pink Sands Beach

 Ten Bay Beach

 Saddle Cay

 Stocking Island

 Cat Island's Beaches

CAT ISLAND

Cockburn Town   SAN SALVADOR

ATLANTIC OCEAN

Stella Maris   RUM CAY

Tropic of Cancer

LONG ISLAND

Deadman's Cay

CROOKED ISLAND

ACKLINS ISLAND   MAYAGUANA ISLAND

NORTH CAICOS

PINE CAY   MIDDLE CAICOS

PROVIDENCIALES   Grace Bay   EAST CAICOS

LITTLE INAGUA   CAICOS ISLANDS   GRAND TURK ISLAND

SOUTH CAICOS

TURKS AND CAICOS ISLANDS   SALT CAY   TURKS ISLANDS

GREAT INAGUA

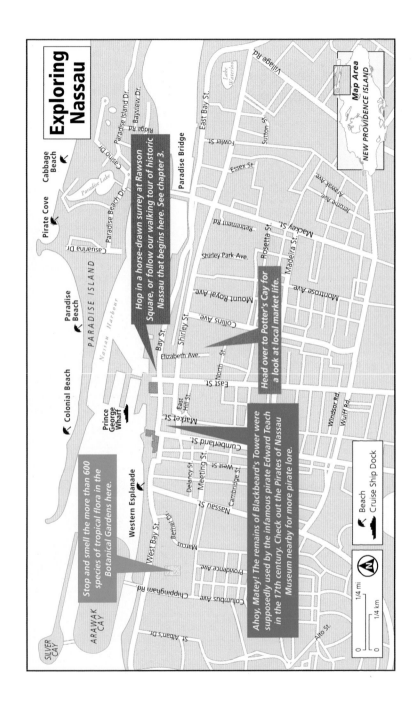

Exploring Nassau

Map Area

NEW PROVIDENCE ISLAND

Stop and smell the more than 600 species of tropical flora in the Botanical Gardens here.

Hop in a horse-drawn surrey at Rawson Square, or follow our walking tour of historic Nassau that begins here. See chapter 3.

Head over to Potter's Cay for a look at local market life.

Ahoy, Matey! The remains of Blackbeard's Tower were supposedly used by the infamous pirate Edward Teach in the 17th century. Check out the Pirates of Nassau Museum nearby for more pirate lore.

Beach
Cruise Ship Dock

1/4 mi
1/4 km

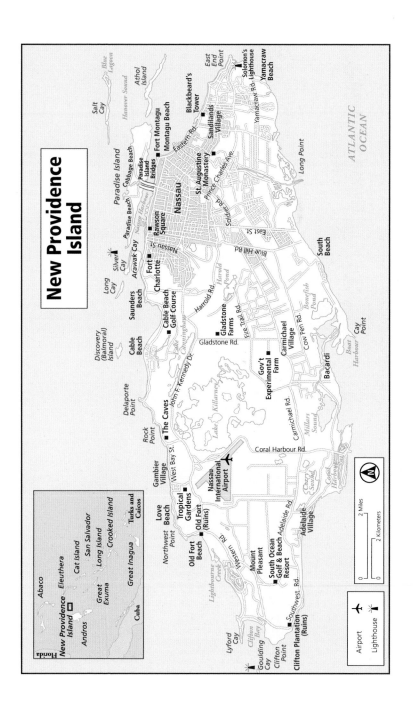

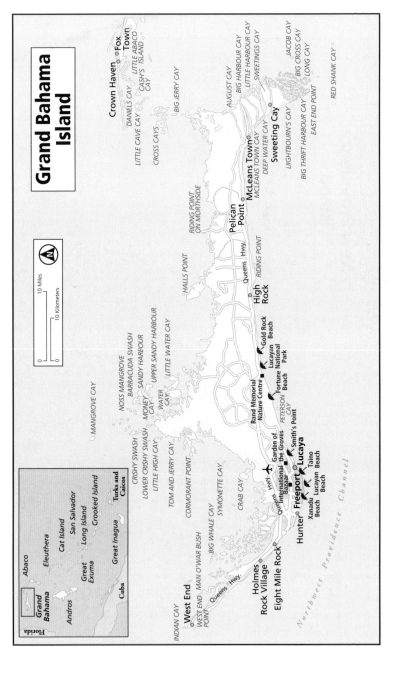

Frommer's®

Bahamas

2009

by Darwin Porter & Danforth Prince

Here's what the critics say about Frommer's:

"Amazingly easy to use. Very portable, very complete."
—*Booklist*

"Detailed, accurate, and easy-to-read information for all price ranges."
—*Glamour Magazine*

"Hotel information is close to encyclopedic."
—*Des Moines Sunday Register*

"Frommer's Guides have a way of giving you a real feel for a place."
—*Knight Ridder Newspapers*

WILEY

Wiley Publishing, Inc.

Published by:

Wiley Publishing, Inc.
111 River St.
Hoboken, NJ 07030-5774

ISBN: 978-0-470-28550-3

Editor: Avital Binshtock
Production Editor: Michael Brumitt
Cartographer: Guy Ruggiero
Photo Editor: Richard Fox
Anniversary Logo Design: Richard Pacifico
Production by Wiley Indianapolis Composition Services

Front cover photo: Snorkeling in the blue waters of The Bahamas
Back cover photo: Providence Island: Colorful architecture

For information on our other products and services or to obtain technical support, please contact our Customer Care Department within the U.S. at 800/762-2974, outside the U.S. at 317/572-3993 or fax 317/572-4002.

Wiley also publishes its books in a variety of electronic formats. Some content that appears in print may not be available in electronic formats.

Manufactured in the United States of America

5 4 3 2 1

Contents

List of Maps

An Invitation to the Reader

In researching this book, we discovered many wonderful places—hotels, restaurants, shops, and more. We're sure you'll find others. Please tell us about them, so we can share the information with your fellow travelers in upcoming editions. If you were disappointed with a recommendation, we'd love to know that, too. Please write to:

Frommer's Bahamas 2009
Wiley Publishing, Inc. • 111 River St. • Hoboken, NJ 07030-5774

An Additional Note

Please be advised that travel information is subject to change at any time—and this is especially true of prices. We therefore suggest that you write or call ahead for confirmation when making your travel plans. The authors, editors, and publisher cannot be held responsible for the experiences of readers while traveling. Your safety is important to us, however, so we encourage you to stay alert and be aware of your surroundings. Keep a close eye on cameras, purses, and wallets, all favorite targets of thieves and pickpockets.

About the Authors

As a team of veteran travel writers, **Darwin Porter** and **Danforth Prince** have produced dozens of titles for Frommer's, including best-selling guides to Europe, the Caribbean, and parts of the U.S. Porter, a film critic, columnist, and radio broadcaster, is also a noted biographer of Hollywood celebrities, having garnered critical acclaim for chronicling the lives of Marlon Brando, Katharine Hepburn, Howard Hughes, and Michael Jackson, among others. Prince has worked at the Paris bureau of the *New York Times* and is currently the president of Blood Moon Productions and other media-related firms. In 2008, Porter and Prince collaborated on the release of their newest book about Hollywood, sexuality, and sin as filtered through 85 years of celebrity excess, *Hollywood Babylon—It's Back!*

Other Great Guides for Your Trip:

Frommer's Portable Bahamas
Frommer's Caribbean 2009
Frommer's Caribbean Cruises & Ports of Call
Frommer's Caribbean Ports of Call

Frommer's Star Ratings, Icons & Abbreviations

Every hotel, restaurant, and attraction listing in this guide has been ranked for quality, value, service, amenities, and special features using a **star-rating system.** In country, state, and regional guides, we also rate towns and regions to help you narrow down your choices and budget your time accordingly. Hotels and restaurants are rated on a scale of zero (recommended) to three stars (exceptional). Attractions, shopping, nightlife, towns, and regions are rated according to the following scale: zero stars (recommended), one star (highly recommended), two stars (very highly recommended), and three stars (must-see).

In addition to the star-rating system, we also use **seven feature icons** that point you to the great deals, in-the-know advice, and unique experiences that separate travelers from tourists. Throughout the book, look for:

Finds	Special finds—those places only insiders know about
Fun Fact	Fun facts—details that make travelers more informed and their trips more fun
Kids	Best bets for kids and advice for the whole family
Moments	Special moments—those experiences that memories are made of
Overrated	Places or experiences not worth your time or money
Tips	Insider tips—great ways to save time and money
Value	Great values—where to get the best deals

The following **abbreviations** are used for credit cards:

AE	American Express	DISC	Discover	V	Visa
DC	Diners Club	MC	MasterCard		

Frommers.com

Now that you have this guidebook to help you plan a great trip, visit our website at **www.frommers.com** for additional travel information on more than 4,000 destinations. We update features regularly to give you instant access to the most current trip-planning information available. At Frommers.com, you'll find scoops on the best airfares, lodging rates, and car rental bargains. You can even book your travel online through our reliable travel booking partners. Other popular features include:

- Online updates of our most popular guidebooks
- Vacation sweepstakes and contest giveaways
- Newsletters highlighting the hottest travel trends
- Podcasts, interactive maps, and up-to-the-minute events listings
- Opinionated blog entries by Arthur Frommer himself
- Online travel message boards with featured travel discussions

What's New in The Bahamas

Big changes may be in store for The Bahamas, but don't expect them to be implemented on any pre-announced schedule. Life in the islands simply operates on its own time.

The exception to that rule is the fabulous Atlantis sprawl on Paradise Island. Its developers have set about achieving their goal within a relatively short period of time and seem determined to keep developing until they run out of space.

NEW PROVIDENCE ISLAND (NASSAU/CABLE BEACH) Between now and 2012 (or who knows when), Cable Beach's shoreline strip is expected to undergo a building boom. It's taken a bit of time to get started, but plans call for Cable Beach to one day be so enticingly developed that it will give Paradise Island's mammoth resorts a run for their money.

On the drawing board are plans for marinas, a redesigned golf course, and even new "lakes." How much of that will happen by the time you visit just can't be predicted.

In a development that's actually happened, **Compass Point** (© **876/946-1958** or 242/327-4500) made a comeback on New Providence Island's Love Beach (west of Cable Beach). It was closed for a long time, but its brightly painted wooden cottages are back in business, welcoming visitors who shun big resorts in favor of more island-style lodgings.

And at last, New Providence Island has a worthy B&B. It's **A Stone's Throw Away** (© **242/327-7030**), 13 miles west of Nassau's center. French and Belgian owners brought continental sophistication to the charming little 10-unit enclave with luxuriously furnished bedrooms.

PARADISE ISLAND The latest hotel development in the sprawling Atlantis compound is **The Reef** (© **800/ATLANTIS** [285-2684] or 242/363-3000), a condo complex where even the smallest unit is a one-bedroom apartment. An expensive but beguiling beacon of luxury living, it also offers modern kitchens for those wanting to do their own cooking and is the resort's tallest building, permeated with an Atlantis theme.

The newest restaurant to open is **Bobby Flay's Mesa Grill** (© **242/363-3000**), on the Cove Hotel's lobby level. It features American Southwestern cuisine—we're talking cornmeal tamales, hot sauce, grilled steaks, and chile relleno.

GRAND BAHAMA ISLAND (FREEPORT/LUCAYA) The **Ocean Reef Yacht Club** (© **242/373-2468**) has opened near the Port Lucaya area, offering town house-style accommodations in a marina-style resort that rents condos with one, two, or three bedrooms, and has become a particular favorite of yachters.

THE ABACOS At Great Guana Cay in the Abacos, the amusingly named **Flip Flops on the Beach** (© **800/222-2646**) has been inaugurated with only four units. Each of these is either a one- or two-bedroom cottage, opening onto one of the country's best sandy beaches. Guests often have picnic lunches at tables on the beach, making use of a charcoal grill for nighttime barbecues.

BIMINI The first real luxury resort to have emerged on the island in years, **Bimini Bay Resort** (© 242/347-2900) may one day have a casino. Right now, it offers the comfort of a tropical condo with rattan furnishings and modern kitchens. There's also a good restaurant, called **Casa Lyon,** on-site, plus a 136-slip marina.

THE EXUMAS Near George Town, the **February Point Resort Estates** (© 877/839-4253) rents luxury villas while its owners are away. This is the most upscale resort community in The Bahamas. Guests enjoy the good life on an 32-hectare (80-acre) peninsula overlooking tiny cays and virgin beaches. Rentals come with two, three, four, or even five well-furnished bedrooms.

In other George Town developments, the old Peace & Plenty Beach Inn has been reborn as **Exuma Beach Inn** (© 242/336-2251). Bedrooms are attractively decorated with such touches as Italian tiles and marble vanities. Private balconies overlook scenic Elizabeth Harbour.

CAT ISLAND This sleepy island in the southern Bahamas is seeing some development with the opening of **Island Hopp-Inn** (© 242/342-2100), an all-suite resort with panoramic views of the Atlantic. Its spacious suites, large enough for three or four guests, are furnished in a tropical style with four-poster beds, rattan furnishings, and well-equipped kitchens.

Six new villas, each with a well-equipped kitchen and one or two bedrooms, are available at **Sammy T's Beach Resort** (© 242/354-6009). There are also many recreational facilities here, including an outdoor pool and a fitness center.

The Best of The Bahamas

If you've decided that The Bahamas sounds like the perfect place to relax, feel free to start unwinding right now, because we've done all the legwork for you. Below you'll find our carefully compiled lists of the best that The Bahamas has to offer, from beaches and dive sites to resorts, restaurants, and sightseeing—and nearly everything else you'll want to see and do.

1 The Best Beaches

- **Cable Beach** (New Providence Island) The glittering shoreline of Cable Beach proffers easy access to shops, casinos, restaurants, watersports, and bars. It's a sandy 6.5km-long (4-mile) strip, with a great array of facilities and activities. See p. 93.
- **Cabbage Beach** (Paradise Island) Think Vegas in the Tropics. It seems as though most of the sunbathers dozing on the sands here are recovering from the previous evening's partying, and it's likely to be crowded near the mega-hotels, but you can find more solitude on the beach's northwestern extension (Paradise Beach), which is accessible only by boat or on foot. Lined with palms, sea grapes, and casuarinas, the sands are broad and stretch for at least 3km (2 miles). See p. 131.
- **Xanadu Beach** (Grand Bahama Island) Grand Bahama has 97km (60 miles) of sandy shoreline, but Xanadu Beach is most convenient to Freeport's resort hotels, several of which offer shuttle service here. There's more than a kilometer of white sand and (usually) gentle surf. Don't expect to have Xanadu to yourself, but if you want more quiet and

privacy, try any of the beaches that stretch from Xanadu for many miles in either direction. See p. 160.
- **Tahiti Beach** (Hope Town, the Abacos) Since this beach is so isolated at the far end of Elbow Cay Island, you can be sure that only a handful of people will ever visit these cool waters and white sands. The crowds stay away because you can't drive here; you have to walk or ride a rented bike along sand and gravel paths from Hope Town. You can also charter a boat to reach the beach—which isn't too hard, since the Abacos are the country's sailing capital. See p. 211.
- **Pink Sands Beach** (Harbour Island) Running the entire length of the island's eastern side, these pale-pink sands stretch for 5km (3 miles) past a handful of low-rise hotels and private villas. A coral reef protects the shore from breakers, making for some of the safest swimming in The Bahamas. See p. 243.
- **Ten Bay Beach** (Eleuthera) Ten Bay Beach lies a short drive south of Palmetto Point, just north of Savannah Sound. Once upon a time, the exclusive Cotton Bay Club chose to build a hotel here because of the fabulous

The Bahamas' Best Beaches

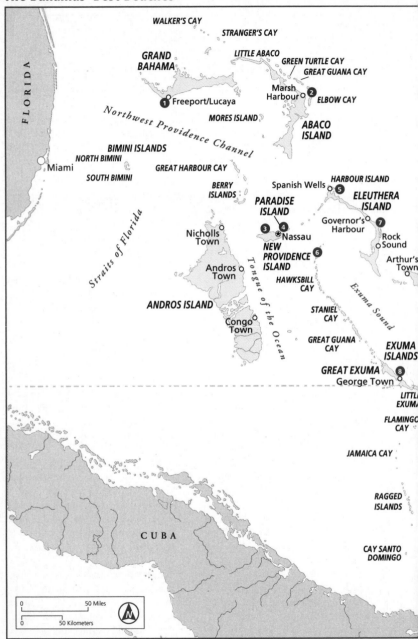

A T L A N T I C

O C E A N

CAT ISLAND
9

Cockburn **SAN SALVADOR**
Town

Stella **RUM CAY**
Maris

Tropic of Cancer

**LONG
ISLAND**

Deadman's Cay

**CROOKED
ISLAND**

**ACKLINS
ISLAND**

**MAYAGUANA
ISLAND**

**TURKS AND CAICOS
ISLANDS**
NORTH (U.K.)
CAICOS
PINE CAY MIDDLE CAICOS
PROVIDENCIALES EAST CAICOS
Grace GRAND
Bay CAICOS TURK
LITTLE INAGUA ISLANDS SOUTH ISLAND
CAICOS
SALT
GREAT INAGUA CAY TURKS
ISLANDS

scenery. There may not be facilities here now, but since the hotel closed, the white sands and turquoise waters here have been more idyllic and private than ever. See p. 234.

- **Saddle Cay** (the Exumas) Most of the Exumas are oval-shaped islands strung end to end like links in a 209km (130-mile) chain. One notable exception is Saddle Cay, with its horseshoe-shaped curve near the Exumas' northern tip. It can be reached only by boat but offers an unspoiled setting without a trace of the modern world—and plenty of other cays and islets where you can play Robinson Crusoe for a few hours, if you like. See p. 258.

- **Stocking Island** (the Exumas) One of the finest white sandy beaches in The Bahamas lies off Elizabeth Harbour, the archipelago's main harbor, which is close to the little capital of George Town. You can reach Stocking Island easily by boat from Elizabeth Harbour, and the sands of this offshore island are rarely crowded; snorkelers and divers love to explore its gin-clear waters. In addition to its beach of powdery white sand, the island is known for its blue holes, coral gardens, and undersea caves. See p. 265.

- **Cat Island** The white beaches ringing this island are pristine, opening onto crystal-clear waters and lined with coconut palms, palmettos, and casuarina trees—and best of all, you'll practically have the place to yourself. One of our favorite beaches here, near Old Bight, has a beautiful, lazy curve of white sand. Another fabulous one lies 5km (3 miles) north of New Bight, at the Fernandez Bay Village resort. This curvy beach is set against another backdrop of casuarinas and is unusually tranquil. Another good shoreline here is the long, sandy stretch that opens onto Hawk's Nest Resort & Marina on the southwestern side. None of the Cat Island beaches has any facilities (bring everything you need from your hotel), but they do offer peace, quiet, and seclusion. See "Cat Island," in chapter 11.

2 The Best Diving

- **New Providence Island** Many ships have sunk near Nassau in the past 300 years, and all the dive outfitters here know the most scenic wreck sites. Other underwater attractions are gardens of elkhorn coral and dozens of reefs packed with life. The most spectacular dive site is the **Shark Wall,** 16km (10 miles) off New Providence's southwest coast; it's blessed with incredible, colorful sea life and the healthiest coral offshore. You'll even get to swim with sharks (not as bait, of course). See p. 97.

- **Grand Bahama Island** The island is ringed with reefs, and dive sites are plentiful, including the **Wall,** the **Caves** (site of a long-ago disaster known as Theo's Wreck), and **Treasure Reef.** Other popular dive sites include **Spit City** (yes, that's right), **Ben Blue Hole,** and the **Rose Garden** (no one knows how this one got its name). What makes Grand Bahama Island a cut above the others is the presence of a world-class dive operator, **UNEXSO** (the Underwater Explorer Society; ⓒ **800/992-DIVE** [3483] or 242/373-1244; www. unexso.com). See p. 164.

- **Andros** Marine life abounds in the barrier reef off the coast of Andros, which is one of the world's largest and a famous destination for divers. The reef plunges 1,800m (5,906 ft.) to a narrow drop-off known as the

Tongue of the Ocean. You can also explore mysterious blue holes, formed when subterranean caves filled with seawater, causing their ceilings to collapse and expose clear, deep pools. See p. 185 and 195.

- **Bimini** Although Bimini is most famous for its game fishing, it boasts excellent diving, too. Five kilometers (3 miles) of offshore reefs attract millions of colorful fish. Even snorkelers can see black coral gardens, blue holes, and an odd configuration on the sea floor that is allegedly part of the lost continent of Atlantis (a fun legend, at any rate). Divers can check out the wreck of a motorized yacht, the *Sapona* (owned by Henry Ford), which sank in shallow waters off the coast in 1929. See p. 181.

- **Harbour Island** (Eleuthera) In addition to lovely coral and an array of colorful fish, divers can enjoy some unique experiences here, such as the **Current Cut,** an exciting underwater gully that carries you on a swiftly flowing underwater current for 10 minutes. Four wrecked ships also lie nearby, at depths of less than 12m (39 ft.), including a barge that was transporting the engine of a steam locomotive in 1865, reportedly after the American Confederacy sold it to raise cash for its war effort. See p. 243.

- **Long Island** (The Southern Bahamas) Snorkeling is spectacular on virtually all sides of this island. But experienced divers venturing into deeper waters offshore can visit underwater cages to feed swarms of mako, bull, and reef sharks. Dive sites abound, including the Arawak "green

hole," a blue hole of incomprehensible depth. See p. 286.

- **Lucayan National Park** This park on Grand Bahama Island is the site of a 9.5km-long (6-mile) underground freshwater cave system, the longest of its type in the world. The largest cave contains spiral staircases that lead visitors into a freshwater world inhabited by shrimp, mosquito fish, fruit bats, freshwater eels, and a species of crustacean *(Spelionectes lucayensis)* that has never been documented elsewhere. On the 16-hectare (40-acre) preserve are examples of the island's five ecosystems—pine forests, rocky coppice, mangrove swamps, whiteland coppice, and sand dunes. Pause to sunbathe on a lovely stretch of sandy beach or hike along paths accented by orchids, hummingbirds, and barn owls. See p. 166.

- **Pelican Cays Land and Sea Park** Known for its undersea caves, seemingly endless coral reefs, and abundant plant and marine life, this park, 13km (8 miles) north of Cherokee Sound at Great Abaco Island, is a highlight for scuba divers. See p. 205.

- **Exuma Cays Land and Sea Park** A major attraction, this park is the first of its kind anywhere on the planet. The 35km-long (22-mile), 13km-wide (8-mile) natural preserve attracts scuba divers to its 453 sq. km (175 sq. miles) of sea gardens with spectacular reefs, flora, and fauna. Inaugurated in 1958, it lies some 35km (22 miles) northwest of Staniel Cay and 64km (40 miles) southeast of Nassau; it's only accessible by boat. See p. 272.

3 The Best Snorkeling

- **New Providence and Paradise islands** The waters that ring densely populated New Providence Island and nearby Paradise Island are

easy to explore. Most people head for the **Rose Island Reefs**, the **Gambier Deep Reef**, the **Booby Rock Channel,** the **Goulding Reef Cays,** and some easily seen, well-known underwater wrecks that lie in shallow water. Virtually every hotel on the island offers equipment and can book you onto a snorkel cruise to sites farther offshore. See p. 96 and 132.

- **Grand Bahama Island** Resort hotels can hook you up with snorkeling excursions, such as the ones offered by **Ocean Motion Water Sports Ltd.** (© 242/374-2425; www. oceanmotionbahamas.com), the best snorkeling outfitter, which can also connect you with a number of other watersports, from banana-boating to water-skiing. The clear water around Grand Bahama is wonderful for snorkeling because it has a rich marine life. Snorkelers are fond of exploring **Ben's Cave,** a stunning cavern that's part of Lucayan Caves, as well as the coral beds at places like **Silver Point Reef** and **Gold Rock.** See p. 164.

- **Bimini** Snorkelers are enthralled with the black coral gardens that are easily accessible from shore and the colorful marine life around the island. Sometimes when conditions are right, snorkelers can frolic with a pod of spotted dolphins. Off North Bimini, snorkelers are attracted to a cluster of huge flat rocks that jut from 6 to 9m (20–30 ft.) out of the water at **Paradise Point.** The most imaginative snorkelers claim that these rocks, which seem hand-hewn, were part of a road system that once traversed the lost continent of Atlantis. See p. 181.

- **Long Island** (The Southern Bahamas) Shallow bays and sandy beaches offer many possibilities for snorkeling, and the staffs at both major resorts will direct you to the finest conditions near their stretches of beach. The island's southern end is especially dramatic because of its unique sea cliffs. Many east-coast beach coves also offer fantastic snorkeling opportunities. See p. 286.

- **Elbow Cay** With its 209km (130-mile) string of beautiful cays and some of The Bahamas' best beaches, the Abacos are ideal for snorkeling, especially in the waters off **Elbow Cay.** Visibility is often excellent because the cay lies close to the Gulf Stream's cleansing waters. **Mermaid Beach,** a particularly colorful reef, is another favorite. **Froggies Out Island Adventures** (© 242/366-0431; www. froggiesabaco.com) provides equipment and the best snorkeling advice. See p. 207.

- **Stocking Island** George Town is the capital of the Exumas, which is celebrated for its crystal-clear waters so beloved by yachties. From George Town, Stocking Island lies across Elizabeth Harbour, which is only 1.6km (1 mile) away. Stocking Island is a long, thin barrier island that attracts snorkelers who explore its blue holes (ocean pools of fresh water floating on heavier saltwater). The island is also ringed with undersea caves and coral gardens in stunning colors. You'll find that Stocking Island has some of the Southern Bahamas's most gorgeous beaches. See p. 265.

- **San Salvador** Following in the wake of Columbus, snorkelers find a rich paradise on this relatively undiscovered island, with its unspoiled, unpopulated kilometers of beaches ideal for swimming, shelling, and close-in snorkeling (snorkeling close to shore). A week's stay is enough time to become acquainted with only some of the possibilities, including **Bamboo Point, Fernandez Bay,** and **Long Bay,** all within a few kilometers of Cockburn (the main village) on the island's west side. At San Salvador's southern tip are some of our favorite places for snorkeling, **Sandy Point** and nearby **Grotto Bay.** See chapter 11.

4 The Best Fishing

- **New Providence Island** The waters around New Providence teem with game fish. In-the-know fishermen long ago learned the best months to pursue their catch: November to February for wahoo found in the reefs, June and July for blue marlin, and May to August for the oceanic bonito and blackfin tuna. Nassau, in particular, is ideal for sportfishing. Most boat charters allow passengers to start fishing within 15 minutes after leaving the dock. The best outfitter is **Born Free Charters** (*(C)* **242/393-4144**); anchoring and bottom-fishing are also options. See p. 95.

- **Grand Bahama Island** The tropical waters along Grand Bahama lure anglers in search of "the big one" because its waters are home to some of the biggest game fish on earth. Off the coast, the clear waters are good hunting grounds for snapper, grouper, yellowtail, wahoo, barracuda, and kingfish. Many fishermen catch dolphin (the mahimahi kind, not Flipper). And Deep Water Cay is a fishing hot spot. The best outfitter is **Reef Tours, Ltd.** (*(C)* **242/ 373-5880**). See p. 162.

- **Green Turtle Cay** The deep-sea fishing possibilities off the coast of this cay draw anglers from all over the world. An abundance of giant game fish as well as tropical fish live in these beautiful waters. Both dedicated fisherman and more casual anglers come to the little island seeking yellowfin tuna, a few dolphinfish, and big-game wahoo, among other catches. Green Turtle Cay also has some of the best fishing guides in The Bahamas, weather-beaten men who've spent a lifetime fishing the surrounding waters. The best place to hook up with one of these guides is **Green Turtle Club** (*(C)* **242/365-4271**). See p. 223.

- **Treasure Cay** In the Abacos, some of the best fishing grounds are in the sea bordering this remote island. At **Treasure Cay Marina** (*(C)* **242/365-8250**), fishermen from all over the world hire experienced skippers to take them out in their search for barracuda, grouper, yellowtail, snapper, tuna, marlin, dolphinfish, and wahoo. Deep-sea, bottom-, and drift fishing are yours for the asking. The cay's own bonefish flats are just a short boat cruise from the marina. See p. 218.

- **The Exumas** Anglers from all over America descend on this beautiful archipelago for deep-sea fishing or bottom-fishing. Fishermen hunt for kingfish, wahoo, dolphinfish, tuna, and bonito in the deepest waters off the coastline. Many visitors also fly here just to go bonefishing. Among other outfitters who can hook you up with fishing outings is **Club Peace & Plenty** (*(C)* **800/525-2210** or 242/ 336-2551), which rents the necessary equipment and can arrange for experienced guides to accompany you. See p. 263.

5 The Best Sailing

- **Marsh Harbour and Hope Town** (the Abacos) Known among yachters for their many anchorages, sheltered coves, and plentiful marine facilities, the Abacos are considered one of the most perfect sailing areas in the world. You can charter boats of all shapes and sizes for a week or longer, with or without a crew. See "The Active Vacation Planner," in chapter 3, and p. 204 and 211 in chapter 8.

- **The Exumas** Yachties head to these beautiful sailing waters to see some of the country's most dramatic coastal scenery. **The Family Island Regatta,** the most popular boating spectacle in The Bahamas, is held here annually. Most of the recreational boating happens in the government-protected **Exumas Cays Land and Sea Park,** an area of splendid sea gardens and rainbow-hued coral reefs that stretches south from Wax Cay to Conch Cay. You can rent motorboats at **Minns Water Sports** (© 242/336-3483) in George Town. See p. 256.

- **New Providence Island** Although sailing in the waters off New Providence isn't the equal of those yachting favorites the Exumas and the Abacos, boaters can still find many delights. More organized boating excursions are offered in New Providence than anywhere else in The Bahamas, especially by outfitters such as **Barefoot Sailing Cruises** (© 242/393-0820; www.barefootsailingcruises.com) and **Majestic Tours Ltd.** (© 242/322-2606). You can also choose from an array of sunset cruises, such as the ones **Flying Cloud** (© 242/363-4430) offers aboard its fleet of catamarans. The most popular—and the most scenic—trip is sailing to tranquil **Rose Island,** 13km (8 miles) east of the center of Nassau and reached after sailing past several small uninhabited cays. In addition, **Blue Lagoon Island,** 4.8km (3 miles) northeast of Paradise Island, is a magnet for boaters, offering seven white-sand beaches with seaside hammocks. The drawback to this island, however, is that cruise-ship passengers flock here and many beach buffs like to come on day trips. See p. 94.

- **Grand Bahama Island** On the beautiful waters off this large island, you can go sailing aboard *Ocean Wonder* (© 242/373-5880), which is supposedly the world's largest twin-diesel-engine glass-bottom boat. This vessel offers the best and most panoramic picture of underwater life off the coast of Grand Bahama—a view most often reserved for scuba divers. You can also sail aboard *Bahama Mama,* a two-deck 22m catamaran, on its "Robinson Crusoe Beach Party." The catamaran also sails at sunset on a booze cruise. **Superior Watersports** (© 242/373-7863; www.superiorwatersports.com) operates this catamaran. See p. 165.

- **Marsh Harbour** One of the finest anchorages in the Out Islands is in Marsh Harbour, called "The Boating Capital of The Bahamas." **The Moorings** (© 888/952-8420 or 242/367-4000; www.moorings.com), one of the world's leading charter sailboat outfitters, rents boats to sail the Abacos' waters. Passengers discover white-sand beaches and snug anchorages on uninhabited cays. Sailing here is one of the great experiences of visiting The Bahamas. See p. 201.

6 The Best Golf Courses

- **Cable Beach** The main draw is the 18-hole **Cable Beach Golf Course** (© 242/677-4175; www.radisson-cablebeach.com/golf.html). The oldest golf course in The Bahamas, this par-71 green was the private retreat of British expatriates in the 1930s. Today it's managed by a corporate namesake of Arnold Palmer and owned by Cable Beach casino marketers. Small ponds and water traps heighten the challenge, amid more than 6,453 yards of well-maintained greens and fairways. See p. 96.

- **Paradise Island** Tom Weiskopf designed **Ocean Club Golf Club** (℃ **242/363-3000;** www.oneandonly resorts.com), an 18-hole, par-72 course, and it's a stunner. With challenges that include the world's largest sand trap and water hazards (mainly the Atlantic Ocean) on three sides, the course has received praise from Jack Nicklaus and Gary Player. For the best panoramic ocean view—good enough to take your mind off your game—play the par-3 14th hole. See p. 132.

- **Grand Lucaya, Grand Bahama Island** The Lucayan Country Club now boasts two separate golf courses. Designed by Robert Trent Jones, Jr., **The Reef Course** (℃ **242/373-2004;** www.ourlucaya.com) opened in 2000. The Bahamian press called it a bit like a Scottish course, "but a lot

warmer." The sandy course has links-style greens. the **Lucayan Course** (℃ **242/373-2003;** www.ourlucaya. com), is a well-respected, renovated tree-lined course originally laid out in 1964. Both courses have 18 holes and a par of 72. Though they aren't immediately adjacent, shuttle buses carry golfers from one course to the other at frequent intervals. See p. 163.

- **The Exumas** At long last, the Southern Bahamas has a world-class golf course: The **Four Seasons Resort Emerald Bay Golf Club** (℃ **242/ 366-6800;** www.fourseasons.com) opens onto Emerald Bay's waters. The par-72, 18-hole course was designed by Greg Norman, who created six oceanfront holes. The course is challenging yet not daunting, so it appeals to golfers of various skill levels. See p. 266.

7 The Best Tennis Facilities

- **Paradise Island** Well-heeled tennis buffs check into the **One&Only Ocean Club** (℃ **242/363-2501;** www.oneandonlyresorts.com). Many visitors go there just for tennis, which can be played day or night on their nine Har-Tru courts. Guests booked into the club's cabanas and villas can practically roll out of bed onto the courts (tennis is free for them). Although beginners and intermediate players are welcome, the courts are often filled with first-class competitors. The tennis complex at **Atlantis**

(℃ **242/363-3000;** www.atlantis. com) is more accessible to the general public, with six courts (three clay and three concrete), some lit for night games. See p. 120 and 132.

- **Grand Bahama Island** Freeport is another top choice for tennis buffs. The island's best tennis is at the **Ace Tennis Center** at the **Westin & Sheraton at Our Lucaya Resorts,** Royal Palm Way (℃ **242/350-5294**), with four courts, including one that's grass. See p. 165.

8 The Best Honeymoon Resorts

- **Sandals Royal Bahamian Hotel & Spa** (Cable Beach, New Providence Island; ℃ **800/SANDALS** or 242/ 327-6400; www.sandals.com) is one branch of a Jamaica-based chain of

couples-only, all-inclusive hotels that are favorites among honeymooners. This one is more upscale than many of its Jamaican counterparts and offers 27 secluded honeymoon suites with semiprivate plunge pools. Staff members lend their experience and talent to on-site wedding celebrations; Sandals will provide everything from a preacher to flowers, as well as champagne and a cake. It's more expensive than most Sandals resorts, but you can usually get better prices than the official rack rates through a travel agent or a package deal. See p. 80.

- The **One&Only Ocean Club** (Paradise Island; ℂ **888/528-7157** in the U.S. only, or 242/363-2501; www. oneandonlyresorts.com) is elegant, low-key, low-rise, and exclusive. Guests include many older honeymoon couples. With waterfalls, fountains, reflecting pools, and a stone gazebo, its formal terraced gardens were inspired by the club's founder (an heir to the A&P fortune) and are The Bahamas' most impressive. At the center is a French cloister, with carvings from the 12th century. See p. 120.

- **Old Bahama Bay** (Grand Bahama Island; ℂ **800/444-9469** or 242/350-3500; www.oldbahamabay.com) is perfect for honeymooners seeking a hideaway in a boutique-style hotel with cottages adjacent to a marina. The casinos, entertainment, shopping, and dining of Freeport/Lucaya are 40km (25 miles) away, so it's ideal for quiet luxury, solitude, and romance. See p. 152.

- **Kamalame Cay** (Staniard Creek, Andros; ℂ **242/368-6281;** www. kamalame.com) requires deep pockets; it's one of the most exclusive resorts in the Out Islands, a perfect honeymoon retreat for the couple wanting to escape casinos and resorts. With its 5km (3 miles) of white-sand beaches in both directions, this pocket of posh specializes in luxury and comfort. And don't worry if

you've already taken your honeymoon; this is the perfect place to take a second one, or even a third. See p. 189.

- Romantics appreciate the **Green Turtle Club** (Green Turtle Cay, the Abacos; ℂ **242/365-4271;** www.green turtleclub.com) for its winning combination of yachting atmosphere and well-manicured comfort. It's small (31 rooms) and civilized in an understated way. The charming, clapboard-covered village of New Plymouth is nearby, accessible by motor launch or, even better, a 45-minute walk across windswept scrublands. See p. 221.

- **Abaco Inn** (Elbow Cay, The Abacos; ℂ **800/468-8799** or 242/366-0133; www.abacoinn.com) provides barefoot elegance and romance in the sands. This sophisticated little hideaway is one of the gems of the Abacos. Luxury villa suites with sunrise and sunset views are the way to go. You and your loved one should seek out a hammock in the gardens. See p. 208.

- **The Bluff House Beach Hotel** (Green Turtle Cay, the Abacos; ℂ **800/745-4911** or 242/365-4247; www.bluffhouse.com) was named for its location atop a 24m (79-ft.) cliff towering over a pink-sand beach. Its 4.8 hectares (12 acres) front the Sea of Abaco on one side and the harbor of White Sound on the other. The accommodations are very private, with a rustic, seafaring decor that has its own elegance. In addition to rooms, the hotel offers beach and hillside villas, and colonial suites with private balconies that overlook the water. See p. 220.

- **Pink Sands** (Harbour Island, Eleuthera; ℂ **800/407-4776** or 242/333-2030; www.pinksandsresort. com) allows for a spectacular getaway at an elite, 11-hectare (27-acre) beachfront estate owned by Chris Blackwell, the founder of Island Records. Its location on a 5km (3-mile) stretch of private pink sand, sheltered by a barrier reef, is just one of its assets. You can ask for a bedroom that evokes an upscale bordello in Shanghai to put you in a romantic mood, and you can also enjoy the best meals on the island. See p. 245.

• **Stella Maris Resort Club** (Long Island, the Southern Bahamas; ℂ **800/426-0466,** 242/338-2051, or 954/359-8238; www.stellamaris resort.com) is right on the Atlantic, built on the grounds of an old plantation, and has become a Long Island social hub. Sailing is important here, as are diving and getting away from it all. Many of the guests hail from Germany, lending the place a European flair. The sleepy island itself is one of The Bahamas' most beautiful, and honeymooners fit into the grand scheme of things perfectly. See p. 288.

9 The Best Family Vacations

• A family could spend their entire vacation at **Sheraton Cable Beach Resort** (Cable Beach, New Providence Island; ℂ **800/325-3535** or 242/327-6000; www.sheraton.com). On the grounds of this vast resort is a pool area that features the most lavish artificial waterfall this side of Tahiti; a health club at the nearby Crystal Palace that welcomes guests and their children; Camp Junkanoo, with supervised play for kids of ages 3 through 12; and a long list of in-house activities that includes dancing lessons. Major changes and redevelopment are planned. See p. 82.

• **Atlantis Paradise Island Resort & Casino** (Paradise Island; ℂ **800/ ATLANTIS** [285-2684] in the U.S., or 242/363-3000; www.atlantis.com) is one of the world's largest hotel complexes, with endless rows of shops and watersports galore. Both children and adults will enjoy the 5.6-hectare (14-acre) sea world with water slides, a lagoon, white sandy beaches, and underground grottoes, plus an underwater viewing tunnel and 240m (787 ft.) of cascading waterfalls. Its children's menus and innovative, creative

children's programs are the best in The Bahamas and perhaps even in the Caribbean. See p. 116.

• **Best Western Castaways Resort & Suites** (Grand Bahama Island; ℂ **800/780-7234** in the U.S., or 242/352-6682; www.bestwestern. com) is a good choice for families on a budget. The pagoda-capped lobby is set a very short walk from the ice-cream stands, souvenir shops, and fountains of the International Bazaar. Children under 12 stay free, and the in-house lounge presents limbo and fire-eating shows several evenings a month. The hotel also offers a babysitting service and a free shuttle to Williams Town Beach. See p. 143.

• **Regatta Point** (George Town, Great Exuma; ℂ **800/688-0309** in the U.S. or 242/336-2206; www.regatta pointbahamas.com) offers efficiency apartments at moderate prices. On a palm-grove cay, it's family-friendly and has its own little beach. Bikes are available and Sunfish boats can be rented. There's also a grocery store nearby where you can pick up supplies. Many units are suitable for families of four or five. See p. 263.

10 The Best Places to Get Away from It All

- **Green Turtle Club** (Green Turtle Cay, the Abacos; ℂ 242/365-4271; www.greenturtleclub.com), secluded and private, is a sailing retreat that consists of tasteful one- to three-bedroom villas with full kitchens. It opens onto a small private beach with a 35-slip marina, which is one of the archipelago's most complete yachting facilities. Many rooms open to the pool, and the dining room is decorated in Queen Anne style. See p. 221.

- **Rock House Hotel** (Harbour Island, off the coast of Eleuthera; ℂ 242/333-2053; www.rockhousebahamas.com) is a glamorous and stylish inn—really, a glorified B&B. This posh little hideaway is drawing more and more of the glitterati to its shores. Set on a low bluff above the harbor, it is tranquillity itself. No one will find you if you decide to hide out in its whimsically decorated bedrooms. See p. 246.

- **Club Med–Columbus Isle** (San Salvador, the Southern Bahamas; ℂ 800/CLUB-MED or 242/331-2000; www.clubmed.com): This was the first large resort to be built on one of The Bahamas' most isolated islands, site of Columbus's first landfall in the New World. It's unusually luxurious, and unusually isolated, for a Club Med, and it occupies a gorgeous beach. The sheer difficulty of reaching it adds to the get-away-from-it-all mystique. See p. 281.

- **Fernandez Bay Village**'s (Cat Island, the Southern Bahamas; ℂ 800/940-1905, 242/342-2018, or 954/474-4821; www.fernandezbayvillage.com) dozen stone-and-timber villas are the closest thing to urban congestion Cat Island ever sees. There's a funky, thatch-roofed beach bar that'll make you feel like you're in the South Pacific—a great place to enjoy a cold beer each afternoon after you leave the stunning sands and turquoise waters behind for the day. There's only one phone at the entire resort, and your bathroom shower will probably open to a view of the sky. See p. 277.

11 The Best Restaurants

- **Sun and . . .** (Nassau, New Providence Island; ℂ 242/393-1205) has made a comeback after being closed for many years. Once again, it is the leading independent choice on New Providence, serving a finely honed international cuisine. It's a throwback to Nassau in its grand heyday. Originally built in the 1930s as a private residence, it lies in an upscale residential neighborhood east of Nassau's center. See p. 86.

- **Moso** (in the Wyndham Nassau Resort, Cable Beach, New Providence Island; ℂ 242/327-6200) is the island's best Asian restaurant. Its well-trained staff has learned the secrets of the cuisines of the Far East, and they dispense an array of some of the best-known and tastiest dishes, including teriyaki specialties. See p. 90.

- **Nobu** (Atlantis, Paradise Island; ℂ 242/363-3000) brings a member of this celebrated chain to The Bahamas. It's the island's most-talked-about—and arguably its best, attracting a string of celebrities. The setting is glamorous, and the cuisine is top-rated, prepared with either market-fresh ingredients or exotic imported ingredients. See p. 128.

- **Dune** (in the One&Only Ocean Club, Paradise Island; © 242/363-2501, ext. 64739) is the most cutting-edge restaurant in Paradise Island and Nassau. It's the creation of French-born restaurant guru Jean-Georges Vongerichten, the moving force behind several of New York City's top dining spots. Every dish served here is something special—from shrimp dusted with orange powder to chicken and coconut milk soup with shiitake cakes. See p. 127.

- **Bahamian Club** (Paradise Island; © 242/363-3000), a notch down from the superb Dune, is still one of The Bahamas' leading restaurants and our favorite at the sprawling mega-resort of Atlantis. Strictly upscale, it presents superb French and international cuisine against a backdrop evoking the British Colonial era. See p. 125.

- Head to **Mangoes Restaurant** (Marsh Harbour, the Abacos; © 242/367-2957) for the best and most authentic Bahamian food in the Abaco chain. Visiting yachties and locals flock to this welcoming spot for its fine cuisine. Order a conch burger for lunch and then return in the evening for the catch of the day—straight from the sea and grilled to your specifications. The namesake mango sauce really dresses up a plate of grilled pork tenderloin. See p. 203.

- **The Landing** (Harbour Island, Eleuthera; © 242/333-2707; www.harbourislandlanding.com), an attractive restaurant at the ferry dock, has awakened Eleuthera's sleepy taste buds. Brenda Barry and daughter Tracy feed you well from a choice of international cuisines, often prepared from recipes gathered during their world travels. Under mature trees in their garden, you feast on delicious pasta dishes, freshly made gazpacho, pan-fried grouper, or warm duck salad. See p. 248.

- **Rock House Restaurant** (Harbour Island, Eleuthera; © 242/333-2053; www.rockhousebahamas.com), in the Rock House Hotel on increasingly chic Harbour Island, serves superb international cuisine. Its hip bodega aura evokes Miami, but it's thoroughly grounded on the island. At lunch, you can get a rock lobster sandwich; at night, the chefs display their culinary prowess with an array of satisfying dishes. See p. 251.

12 The Best Nightlife

- **Cable Beach** has a lot more splash and excitement than Nassau, its neighbor on New Providence Island. Wandering around Cable Beach is also much safer than exploring Nassau's back streets at night. The main attraction is the **Wyndham Nassau Resort & Crystal Palace Casino** (© 242/327-6200; www.wyndhamnassauresort.com), with an 800-seat theater known for staging glitzy extravaganzas and a gaming room that will make you think you're smack-dab in the middle of Vegas. One of the largest casinos in the islands, the Crystal Palace features 750 slot machines, 51 blackjack tables, nine roulette wheels, seven craps tables, and a baccarat table (we think the Paradise Island casino has more class, though). Despite all the glitter, you can still find cozy bars and nooks throughout the resort, if you'd prefer a tranquil evening. See p. 112.

- **Paradise Island** provides the flashiest nightlife in all of The Bahamas, hands down. Not even nearby Nassau and Cable Beach can come close. Nearly all of the action takes place at the incredible **Atlantis Paradise**

Island Resort & Casino (© 242/363-3000; www.atlantis.com), where you'll find high rollers from Vegas and Atlantic City alongside grandmothers from Iowa who play the slots when the family isn't looking. It's all gloss, glitter, and showbiz, with good gambling (though savvy locals say your odds of beating the house are better in Vegas). For a quieter night out, you can also find intimate bars, discos, a comedy club, and lots more in this sprawling behemoth of a hotel. See p. 135.

- **Lucaya,** on Grand Bahama Island, also offers gambling action that's less elaborate than the venues listed above. It happens on the Isle of Capri casino at the **Westin & Sheraton at Our Lucaya Resorts,** Royal Palm Way (© 877/OUR-LUCAYA or 242/373-1333; www.ourlucaya.com). The facility also operates a bar and restaurant. See p. 169.

2

The Bahamas in Depth

After George Washington visited The Bahamas, he wrote that they were "Isles of Perpetual June." Today, the 760-mile-long chain of islands, cays, and reefs is rightfully known as the playground of the Western world. The northernmost island is Grand Bahama, whose western point is about 75 miles almost due east of Palm Beach, Florida. The southernmost is Great Inagua, some 60 miles northeast of Cuba and less than 100 miles north of Haiti. (Henri Christophe, the onetime self-proclaimed Haitian king, supposedly built a summer palace here in the early 19th century.)

There are 700 of these islands, many of which bear the name "cay," pronounced *key.* ("Cay" is Spanish for "small island.") Some, such as Andros, Grand Bahama, Great Abaco, Eleuthera, Cat Island, and Long Island, are fairly large, while others are tiny enough to seem crowded if more than two people visit at a time.

Rising out of the Bahama Banks, a 70,000-square-mile area of shoals and broad elevations of the sea floor where the water is relatively shallow, The Bahamas are flat, low-lying islands. Some rise no more than 10 feet above sea level at the highest point, with Mount Alvernia on Cat Island holding the height record at just above 200 feet.

In most places, the warm, shallow water is so clear that it allows an easy view of the bottom, though cuts and channels are deep. The Tongue of the Ocean between Andros and the Exumas, for example, goes thousands of feet down.

1 The Bahamas Today

The Bahamas is one of the Atlantic's most geographically complicated nations. A coral-based archipelago, its hundreds of islands, cays, and rocky outcroppings became politically independent in 1973 after centuries of colonial rule.

Great Britain actually granted The Bahamas internal self-rule in 1964 and the fledgling nation adopted its own constitution but chose not to sever its ties with its motherland. It has remained in the Commonwealth, with the British monarch as its head of state. In the British tradition, The Bahamas has a two-house Parliament, a ministerial cabinet headed by a prime minister, and an independent judiciary. The queen appoints a Bahamian governor-general to represent the Crown.

As The Bahamas moves deeper into the millennium, the government and various investors continue to pump money into the tourism infrastructure, especially on Paradise Island, across from Nassau, and toward Cable Beach, which adjoins Nassau. Cruise-ship tourism continues to increase, and the upscale crowd is coming back after abandoning The Bahamas for many years in favor of other Caribbean islands such as St. Barts and Anguilla.

When Hubert Ingraham became prime minister in 1992, he launched the country down the long road toward regaining its market share of tourism, which, under Prime Minister Lynden Pindling, had seen a rapid decline. Polls revealed that some first-time visitors vowed never to return to

The Bahamas under the administration of the notorious Pindling, whose government had taken over a number of hotels and failed to maintain them properly.

When Ingraham took office, however, he wisely recognized that the government wasn't meant to be in the hospitality business and turned many properties back over to the professionals. Tourism in the post-Pindling era is booming again; more than 1.6 million visitors from all over the world now flock here annually. In Nassau, it's easy to see where the government's money is being spent: on widened roads, repaved sidewalks, underground phone cables, massive landscaping projects, a cleanup campaign, and additional police officers walking the beat to cut down on crime.

Perry Gladstone Christie, prime minister from 2002 to 2007, continued to carry out those same policies to better Nassau. Ingraham was reelected to the position in 2007.

Unlike Haiti and Jamaica, The Bahamas has remained politically stable and made the transition from white-minority rule to black-majority rule with relatively little tension.

Economic conditions have slowly improved here as well. There's not the wretched poverty in Nassau that there is in, say, Kingston, Jamaica—though many poor residents do still live on New Providence Island's Over-the-Hill section, an area to which few tourists venture (although the neighborhood is gritty and fascinating).

The biggest changes have occurred in the hotel sector. Developers vastly expanded the Atlantis resort on Paradise Island, turning it into a virtual water world. In addition, Hilton has developed the decaying old British Colonial in Nassau, restoring it to life. And Grand Bahama Island is in an interesting state of flux as hotels along the entire Lucayan strip get upgraded.

If there's a downside to this boom, it's the emphasis on mega-hotels and casinos—and the corresponding de-emphasis on the Out Islands, which include the Abacos, Andros, Bimini, Cat Island, the Exumas, Long Island, and San Salvador. Large resort chains, with the exception of Four Seasons and Club Med, have ignored these islands; most continue to slumber away in relative seclusion and poverty. Other than the Four Seasons mega-resort that opened in the Exumas, development has been minor. Little change in this Out Islands–versus–the–rest situation is anticipated soon, except for Eleuthera, which will have several new boutique hotels in the near future.

There's another important trend to note in The Bahamas: The government and many citizens here have awakened to eco-tourism. More than any government in the Caribbean except perhaps Bonaire, this nation has started to try to protect its ecology. Government, private companies, and environmental groups have drawn up a national framework of priorities to protect the islands. One of their first goals was to save the nearly extinct West Indian flamingo. Today, about 60,000 flamingos inhabit Great Inagua Island. Other programs aim to prevent the extinction of the green turtle, the white-crowned pigeon, the Bahamian parrot, and the New Providence iguana.

Although tourism and the environment are bouncing back, many problems remain for this archipelago nation. While some Bahamians seem among the friendliest and most hospitable people in the world, others—particularly those in the tourist industry—can be downright hostile. To counter this, the government is working to train its citizens to be more helpful, courteous, and efficient. Sometimes this training has been taken to heart; at other times, however, it clearly has not. Service with a smile is not assured in The Bahamas.

Drug smuggling also remains a serious problem, and, regrettably, there seems to be no immediate solution. Because the country is so close to U.S. shores, it is often used as a temporary depot for drugs shipped from South America to Florida. The Bahamas developed a tradition of catering to the illicit habits of U.S. citizens as well; during the heyday of Prohibition, many Bahamians grew rich smuggling rum into America. Things have improved, but you'll still see stories in the newspapers about floating bales of marijuana turning up just off The Bahamas' coastline.

Though this illicit trade rarely affects the casual tourist, it's important to know that it exists—so don't agree to carry any packages to or from the U.S. for a stranger, or you could end up taking a much longer vacation than you had ever imagined.

2 Looking Back at The Bahamas

HISTORY

THE EARLY YEARS   After Columbus made his first landfall somewhere in The Bahamas, Ponce de León voyaged here in 1513 looking for the legendary Fountain of Youth. This journey, incidentally, led to the European discovery of Florida and the Gulf Stream—but not the magic fountain. Ponce de León's historian described the waters of the Little Bahama Bank, just north of Grand Bahama, as *bajamar* (pronounced "bahamar," Spanish for shallow water). This seems to be a reasonable source of The Bahamas' name.

It was Columbus, landing on October 12, 1492, who met the island residents, Arawak Indians called Lucayans. He renamed an island, called Guanahani by its native inhabitants, to San Salvador. Over the years, there has been much dispute as to just which island this was. Long ago, it was decided that the discoverer's first landfall in the New World was a place known as Watling Island—the modern-day San Salvador. Recent claims, however, place the first landing on Samana Cay, 65 miles southeast of what's now called San Salvador. In 1986, *National Geographic* propounded and supported this island as being the place where Columbus made landfall.

The Lucayans Columbus encountered are believed to have come to the islands in about the 8th century A.D. from the Greater Antilles (but originally from South America); they were seeking refuge from the savage Caribs then living in the Lesser Antilles. The Lucayans were peaceful people. They welcomed the Spaniards and taught them a skill soon shared with the

Dateline

- **700s** Lucayans, seeking refuge from the cannibalistic Caribs, emigrate to The Bahamas from the Greater Antilles.
- **1492** Columbus makes his first landfall in the New World, most likely in San Salvador, although some historians dispute this.
- **1513** Ponce de León searches for the Fountain of Youth and discovers the Gulf Stream instead.
- **1629** England claims The Bahamas.
- **1640s** First Western settlements are established, as the Company of Eleutherian Adventurers arrive.
- **1656** New Providence Island (site of Nassau) is settled.
- **1717** King George I orders Capt. Woodes Rogers, the first royal governor, to chase the pirates out of Nassau.
- **1776** The fledgling U.S. Navy captures Nassau but soon departs.
- **1782** The British Crown Colony surrenders The Bahamas to Spain, which rules it for almost a year.

continues

entire seagoing world: how to make hammocks from heavy cotton cloth.

The Spanish, who claimed the Bahamian islands for their king and queen, did not repay the Lucayans kindly. Finding neither gold nor silver mines nor fertile soil, the conquistadors cleared the islands of their inhabitants, taking some 40,000 doomed Lucayans to other islands in New Spain to work in mines or dive for pearls. References to the islands first discovered by Columbus are almost nil after that time for about the next 135 years.

THE COMING OF THE ENGLISH
England formally claimed The Bahamas in 1629. No settlement took place, however, until the 1640s, when religious disputes arose in Bermuda and England. English and Bermudian settlers sailed to an island called Cigatoo, changed the name to Eleuthera (from the Greek word for freedom), and launched a tough battle for survival. Many became discouraged and went back to Bermuda, but a few hardy souls hung on, living on the products of the sea—fish, ambergris, and shipwreck salvage.

Other people from Bermuda and England followed and New Providence Island was settled in 1656. They planted cotton, tobacco, and sugarcane, and established Charles Towne, honoring Charles II, at the harbor.

PIRATES & PRIVATEERS The promising agricultural economy was short-lived. Several governors of that era were corrupt, and soon the islands became a refuge for English, Dutch, and French buccaneers who plundered the ships of Spain, the country that controlled the seas. The Spaniards responded by repeatedly ravaging New Providence for revenge, causing many of the settlers to leave. The remainder apparently found the pirates a good source of income. Privateers, a slightly more respectable type of freebooter (they had their sovereign's permission to prey on enemy ships), also found The Bahamas' many islets, tricky shoals, and secret harbors to be good hiding places on ships sailing between the New and Old Worlds.

Late in the 17th century, Charles Towne's name was changed to Nassau to honor King William III, then on the British throne, who also had the title of Prince of Nassau. But the change in nomenclature didn't ease the troubled capital, as some 1,000 pirates still called New Providence home.

Finally, the appeals of merchants and law-abiding islanders for Crown control were heard, and in 1717, the lord proprietors turned over the government of The Bahamas, both civil and military, to King George I, who commissioned

- **1783** Spain signs the Peace of Versailles, ceding The Bahamas to Britain.
- **1834** The United Kingdom Emancipation Act frees slaves throughout the British Empire.
- **1861–65** U.S. Civil War brings prosperity to The Bahamas by way of blockade-running. Nassau becomes a vital supply base for the Confederacy.
- **1919** The Bahamas revive from an economic slump by rum-running during America's Prohibition years.
- **1933** The American repeal of Prohibition causes an economic collapse on the islands.
- **1940** The Duke of Windsor, after renouncing England's throne, is named governor of The Bahamas as war rages in Europe.
- **1964** Sir Roland Symonette becomes the country's first premier. The Bahamas are granted internal self-government.
- **1967** Lynden Pindling is named premier in a close election.
- **1968** African-Bahamians assume control of their government.

Capt. Woodes Rogers as the first royal governor.

Rogers seized hundreds of the lawless pirates. Some were sent to England to be tried. Eight were hanged. Others received the king's pardon, promising thereafter to lead law-abiding lives. Rogers was later given authority to set up a representative assembly, the precursor of today's Parliament. Despite such interruptions as the capture of Nassau by the fledgling U.S. Navy in 1776 (over in a few days) and the surrender of the Crown Colony to Spain in 1782 (of almost a year's duration), the government of The Bahamas since Rogers's time has been conducted in an orderly fashion. The Spanish matter was settled in early 1783 in the Peace of Versailles, when Spain permanently ceded The Bahamas to Britain, ending some 300 years of disputed ownership.

LOYALISTS, BLOCKADE-RUNNERS & BOOTLEGGERS

After the American Revolution, several thousand Loyalists from the former colonies emigrated to The Bahamas. Some of these, especially southerners, brought their black slaves with them and tried their luck at planting sea-island cotton in the Out Islands, as the islands other than New Providence were called. Growing cotton was not a success; the plants fell prey to the chenille bug, but by then, the former Deep South planters had learned to fish, grow vegetables, and provide for their families and servants in other ways.

The first white settlers of The Bahamas had also brought slaves with them, but with the United Kingdom Emancipation Act of 1834, the slaves were freed and the government compensated the former owners for their "property loss." It was a fairly peaceful transition, though it was many years before any real equality was seen.

The Civil War in America brought a transient prosperity to The Bahamas through blockade-running. Nassau became a vital base for the Confederacy, with vessels taking manufactured goods into the Carolinas, and bringing out cotton. The Union's victory ended blockade-running and plunged Nassau into economic depression.

The next real boom the islanders enjoyed was engendered by U.S. Prohibition. As with the blockade-runners—but this time with faster boats and more of them—rum-runners churned the waters between The Bahamas and the southeastern states. From the passage of the 18th Amendment in 1919 to repeal of that law in 1933, Nassau, Bimini, and Grand Bahama served as bases for running contraband alcoholic beverages across the Gulf Stream to assuage the Americans' thirst.

- **1972** Bahamians vote for total independence from Britain.
- **1973** On July 9, the Union Jack in New Providence is lowered for the last time, ending more than 3 centuries of British rule.
- **1992** After 25 years in power, Prime Minister Pindling goes down in defeat.
- Ingraham, campaigning against corruption and recession, replaces him.
- **2002** Perry Gladstone Christie defeats Ingraham to become prime minister.
- **2007** Hubert Ingraham returns to power as prime minister.

Ceaseless battles were waged between the U.S. Coast Guard and this new generation of freebooters. When the U.S. repealed Prohibition, it dealt another shattering blow to the Bahamian economy.

THE WAR YEARS   On August 17, 1940, the Duke and Duchess of Windsor arrived in Nassau, following his appointment as governor of the colony. The duke had abdicated as King Edward VIII to marry the woman he loved, a divorced American named Mrs. Simpson. The people of The Bahamas were shocked that such a once-powerful figure had been assigned the post of governing their impoverished colony, which was viewed as a "backwater" of the British Empire. The duke set about trying to make The Bahamas self-sufficient and providing more employment.

World War II healed the wounds of the bootlegging days, as The Bahamas served as an Atlantic air and sea station. From this, the country inherited two airports built for U.S. Air Force use during hostilities with the Germans. The islands were of strategic importance when Nazi submarines intruded into Atlantic coastal and Caribbean waters. Today U.S. missile-tracking stations still exist on some of the outlying islands.

THE POSTWAR YEARS   In the post–World War II years, party politics developed in The Bahamas as independence from Britain seemed more possible. In 1967, Lynden Pindling became premier after winning a close election.

He stayed in power until 1992 in an administration filled with scandal and graft. He was finally defeated in 1992 by Hubert Ingraham (discussed earlier). Perry Gladstone Christie then defeated Ingraham and was prime minister from 2002 until 2007, when Ingraham was returned to power.

During the election of 1972, the Bahamian people opted for total independence. The Bahamas agreed to be a part of the British Commonwealth, presided over by Queen Elizabeth II. Her future appointed representatives would only be a governor-general holding a ritualized position with mostly symbolic power.

The Commonwealth of The Bahamas came into being in 1973, making it the world's 143rd sovereign state. Its government was to be ministerial with a bicameral legislature and headed by a prime minister and an independent judiciary. The end to centuries of colonial rule was actually signaled in 1964, when The Bahamas was granted internal self-government pending drafting of a constitution, which was adopted in 1969. By choice, the island nation did not completely sever its ties with Great Britain, preferring to remain in the Commonwealth of Nations with the British monarch as its head of state.

3 Architecture & Crafts

ARCHITECTURE   The unique geography and history of The Bahamas contributed to a distinctive architectural style—**the Bahamian clapboard house**—that is today one of the most broadly copied in the Tropics. But it wasn't until the early 19th century that this design began to become perfected and standardized.

The earliest clapboard-sided houses were usually angled to receive the trade winds. Large window openings and high ceilings increased airflow, while awning-style push-out shutters shaded windows and helped direct breezes indoors even during rainstorms. Unlike larger and more impressive houses, where foundations were massive edifices of coral, brick, or stone, the first floors of Bahamian cottages were elevated on low stilts or light masonry pilings to further allow air to circulate. Raising the building also served the function of keeping the floor joists, beams, and planking above floodwaters during a hurricane surge.

Ruggedly built of timbers whose ends were often pegged (not nailed) together and pinned to stone pilings several feet above ground, Bahamian-style clapboard houses survived when many rigid stone-built structures collapsed during hurricanes. Modern engineers affirm that these structures' flexibility increases their stability in high winds.

Some of the best-preserved and most charming examples of the Bahamian cottage style can be found in Harbour Island, off the coast of Eleuthera, and, to a lesser extent, at Spanish Wells and Green Turtle Cay.

CRAFTS   The most prevalent craft in The Bahamas is the weaving of **straw goods.** So widespread is this activity that the largest assemblage of saleable objects in the archipelago—Nassau's Straw Market—was named after this ancient art form. In its open-air stalls, you'll find every imaginable kind of basket, hat, purse, tropical furniture, and souvenir.

At their best, the objects are gracefully woven concoctions of palm fronds or palmetto leaves crafted into patterns bearing such old-fashioned names as shark's tooth, Jacob's ladder, Bahama Mama, peas 'n' grits, lace-edge, and fish gill. At their worst, the objects are almost unbearably touristy, amusing but tasteless souvenirs.

The finest straw work is said to come, incidentally, from the Out Islands, with Long Island producing some of the best. So tightly woven are hats from Long Island that they can function for short periods as water buckets.

The second-most-important craft in the islands is **wood carving.** Local art critics consider the best wooden carvings those that are intuitively inspired by the flora, fauna, and images of the islands. The worst ones tend to be crafted specifically for a fast buck at the tourist market. Your eye and intuition will tell you which is which.

Interestingly, The Bahamas does not produce clay from any natural source, so any terra-cotta object you find will almost certainly have been produced from foreign-bought materials and inspired by the pottery traditions of other places. Ceramics in The Bahamas tend to be reserved for formally trained sculptors who promote their work as fine art.

4 The Lay of the Land

With more than 700 islands and some 2,000 cays, The Bahamas spreads over 100,000 square miles of the Atlantic Ocean and encompasses countless natural attractions, including underwater reefs that stretch 760 miles from the Abacos in the northeast to Long Island in the southeast.

The Bahamas is the largest oceanic archipelago nation in the tropical Atlantic Ocean, with miles of crystal-clear waters rich in fish and other marine resources.

Although New Providence is heavily populated, the rest of the Out Islands, including Grand Bahama, have relatively small populations. Unlike Puerto Rico, Jamaica, Barbados, and other Caribbean island nations, The Bahamas has large areas of undeveloped natural land. The islands also have the most extensive ocean-hole and limestone cave systems in the world.

The Bahamas' approximately 900 square miles of coral reefs include the world's third-largest barrier reef, off the coast of Andros. Reef marine life includes green moray eels, cinnamon clownfish, and Nassau grouper. The Bahamas was one of the first Caribbean countries to outlaw long-line fishing, recognizing it as a threat to regional ecology.

Another act of Parliament, the Wild Birds Protection Act, was passed to ensure the survival of all bird species throughout The Bahamas. Great Inagua Island is home to more than 60,000 pink flamingos, Bahamian parrots, and much of the world's population of reddish egrets. These birds live in the government-protected 287-square-mile Inagua National Park.

These islands are also home to more than 1,370 plant species and some 13 endemic mammal species, the majority of them bats. Other resident mammals include wild pigs, donkeys, raccoons, and the Abaco wild horse. Whales and dolphins, including the humpback and blue whales and the spotted dolphin, are in the seas around the islands.

The **Bahamas National Trust** administers 12 national parks and protected areas covering more than 240,000 acres. Its headquarters, which is home to one of the Western Hemisphere's finest collections of wild palms, is on Nassau at The Retreat on Village Road (© **242/393-1317**). Volunteers help arrange visits to the islands' national parks, the best of which are previewed below.

Eco-tourism highlights of The Bahamas include:

- **Inagua National Park** Located on Great Inagua Island in the Southern Bahamas, this park is internationally famous as the site of the world's largest colony of wild West Indian flamingos. In Bahamian dialect, these birds are sometimes called *fillymingos* or *flamingas*.

- **Union Creek Reserve** This 7-square-mile enclosed tidal creek on Great Inagua serves as a captive breeding research site at which to study giant sea turtles, with special emphasis on the endangered green turtle. In the distant past, the waters around Green Turtle Cay in the Abacos teemed with prehistoric-looking green turtles. However, because they were a valuable food source, they were overhunted and their population diminished greatly.

- **Exuma Cays Land and Sea Park** This park is the first of its kind anywhere on the planet and is a major attraction of The Bahamas. The 22-mile-long, 8-mile-wide natural preserve encompasses 175 square miles of sea gardens with spectacular reefs, flora, and fauna. Inaugurated in 1958, it lies some 22 miles northwest of Staniel Cay (40 miles southeast of Nassau) and is accessible only by boat. The Exumas provide one of the world's most colorful yachting grounds. Its nearest rivals in the Caribbean are the British Virgin Islands and the Grenadines.

For more information, contact the **Ecotourism Association of Grand Bahama** (© **242/373-2485**).

ISLANDS IN BRIEF

The most developed islands for tourism in The Bahamas are **New Providence,** site of Cable Beach and Nassau (the capital); **Paradise Island;** and **Grand Bahama,** home of Freeport and Lucaya. If you're after glitz, gambling, bustling restaurants, nightclubs, and a beach-party scene, these big three islands are where you'll want to be. Package deals are easily found.

Set sail (or hop on a short commuter flight) for one of the **Out Islands,** such as Andros, the Exumas, or the Abacos, and you'll find fewer crowds—and often lower prices, too. Though some of the Out Islands are accessible mainly (or only) by boat, it's still worth your while to make the trip if you like the idea of having an entire beach to yourself. These are really the places to get away from it all.

NEW PROVIDENCE ISLAND (NASSAU/CABLE BEACH)
New Providence isn't the largest Bahamian island, but it's the nation's historic heart, with a strong maritime tradition and the country's largest population (125,000). It offers groves of palms and casuarinas; sandy, flat soil; the closest thing in The Bahamas to urban sprawl; and superb anchorages sheltered from rough seas by nearby Paradise Island. New Providence also has the country's busiest airport and is dotted with hundreds of villas owned by foreign investors. Its two major resort areas are Cable Beach and Nassau.

Cable Beach is a glittering beachfront strip of hotels, restaurants, and casinos; only Paradise Island has been more developed. Its center is the Marriott Resort & Crystal Palace Casino. Often, deciding between Cable Beach and Paradise Island isn't so much a choice of which island you prefer as a choice of which hotel you prefer. But it's easy to sample both, since it takes only about 30 minutes to drive between the two.

Nassau, the Bahamian capital, isn't on a great stretch of shoreline and doesn't have as many first-rate hotels as either Paradise Island or Cable Beach—with the exception of the British Colonial Hilton, which has a small private beach. The main advantages of Nassau are its colonial charm and lower price point. Its hotels may not be ideally located, but they are relatively inexpensive, sometimes even during the winter high season. You can base yourself here and commute easily to the beaches at Paradise Island or Cable Beach. Some travelers even prefer Nassau

because it's the seat of Bahamian culture and history—not to mention the shopping mecca of The Bahamas.

PARADISE ISLAND
If high-rise hotels and glittering casinos are what you want, alongside some of the best beaches in The Bahamas, there is no better choice than Paradise Island, directly off Nassau's coast. It has the best food, entertainment, hotels, and terrific beaches and casinos. Its major drawbacks are that it's expensive and often overcrowded. With its colorful history but unremarkable architecture, Paradise Island remains one of the most intensely marketed pieces of real estate in the world. The sands and shoals of the long, narrow island protect Nassau's wharves and piers, which rise across a narrow channel only 180m (591 ft.) away.

Owners of the 277-hectare (684-acre) island have included brokerage mogul Joseph Lynch (of Merrill Lynch) and Huntington Hartford (heir to the A&P supermarket fortune). More recent investors have included Merv Griffin. The island today is a carefully landscaped residential and commercial complex with good beaches, lots of glitter (some of it tasteful, some of it way too over-the-top), and many diversions.

GRAND BAHAMA ISLAND (FREEPORT/LUCAYA)
The island's name derives from the Spanish term *gran bajamar* (great shallows), which refers to the shallow reefs and sandbars that, over the centuries, have destroyed everything from Spanish galleons to English clippers on these shores. Thanks to the development schemes of U.S. financiers such as Howard Hughes, Grand Bahama boasts a well-developed tourist infrastructure. Casinos, beaches, and restaurants are now plentiful.

Grand Bahama's **Freeport/Lucaya** resort area is another popular destination for American tourists, though it has a lot more tackiness than Paradise Island or

Beaches 101: Paradise Island, Cable Beach & Others

In The Bahamas, the issue about public access to beaches is a hot and controversial subject. Recognizing this, the government has made efforts to intersperse public beaches near private ones, where access would otherwise be impeded. Although mega-resorts restrict nonguests from having easy access to their individual beaches, there are so many public beaches on New Providence Island and Paradise Island that all a beach lover has to do is stop the car at, or walk to, many of the unmarked, unnamed beaches that flank these islands.

If you stay in one of the large beachfront resorts, just head for the ocean via the sand in front the resort. But here are a few details that will come in handy if your accommodation isn't oceanfront, or if you want to explore another beach:

Cabbage Beach 𝕽𝕽 On Paradise Island, this is the real showcase, with broad, white sands that stretch for at least 3km (2 miles). Casuarinas, palms, and sea grapes border it. While it's likely to be crowded in winter, you can find a little more elbowroom by walking to its northwestern stretch. You can reach Paradise Island from downtown Nassau by walking over the bridge, taking a taxi, or boarding a ferryboat at Prince George Dock. Cabbage Beach does not have public facilities, but if you patronize one of the handful of bars and restaurants nearby, you can use their restrooms.

Cable Beach 𝕽𝕽 No particular beach is actually called Cable Beach, yet this is New Providence Island's most popular beachfront destination. This 6.5km (4-mile) stretch of resorts and white-sand beaches in the central northern coast has calypso music floating to the sand from hotel pool patios while vendors make their way between sunblock-slathered bodies. There are no public toilets here because guests of the resorts use their hotel's restrooms. If you're not a hotel guest or customer, you're not supposed to use the facilities. The Cable Beach resorts begin 4.8km (3 miles) west of downtown Nassau.

Caves Beach On the north shore, past Cable Beach, Caves Beach, which has soft sands, lies some 11km (6¾ miles) west of Nassau. It stands near Rock Point, right before the turnoff along Blake Road that leads to the airport.

Cable Beach. The compensation for that is a lower price tag on just about everything. Freeport/Lucaya offers plenty of opportunities for fine dining, entertainment, and gambling.

This island, especially popular with families, also offers the best hiking in The Bahamas and some of the finest sandy beaches. Its golf courses attract players from all over the globe and host major tournaments several times a year. You'll find some of the world's best diving here, as well as UNEXSO, the internationally famous diving school.

BIMINI One of The Bahamas' smallest destinations, Bimini is close enough to Miami (just 81km/50 miles) to be distinctly separate from the archipelago's other islands.

Since visitors often don't know of this beach, it's a good spot at which to escape the hordes. There are no toilets or changing facilities.

Delaporte Beach Just west of the busiest section of Cable Beach, Delaporte Beach is a public-access beach where you can go to escape the crowds. It opens onto clear waters and boasts white sands, although it has no facilities.

Goodman's Bay This public beach lies east of Cable Beach on the way toward Nassau's center. Goodman's Bay and Saunders Beach (see below) often host local fundraising cookouts, at which vendors sell fish, chicken, conch, peas 'n' rice, or macaroni and cheese. People swim and socialize to blaring reggae and calypso music. To find out when one of these beach parties is happening, ask the staff at your hotel or pick up a local newspaper. There is a playground here, too, and toilet facilities.

Paradise Beach 🏖🏖 This beach, on Paradise Island, is one of the best in the entire area. White and sandy, it's dotted with *chikees* (thatched huts), which are perfect when you've had too much sun. Mainly used by guests of the Atlantis resort (see p. 132), it lies at the island's far western tip. If you're not a guest, access is difficult. If you're staying at a hotel in Nassau and want to come to Paradise Island for a day at the beach, it's better to go to Cabbage Beach (see above).

Saunders Beach East of Cable Beach, this is where many islanders go on the weekends. To reach it, take West Bay Street from Nassau toward Coral Island. The beach is across from Fort Charlotte, just west of Arawak Cay. Like Goodman's Bay (see above), it often hosts local fundraising cookouts that are open to the public, which can be a lot of fun. There are no public facilities.

Western Esplanade (also called **Junkanoo Beach**) If you're staying at a hotel in downtown Nassau, such as the British Colonial Hilton (see p. 76), this is a good beach to patronize close to town. The narrow strip of sand is convenient to Nassau and has toilets, changing facilities, and a snack bar.

Bimini is actually a pair of islands with a total area of 23 sq. km (9 sq. miles); smaller North Bimini is better developed than South Bimini. Luxurious yachts and fishing boats are always docked at both islands' marinas. Throughout Bimini, there's a slightly run-down Florida-resort atmosphere mingled with some small-town charm (think old-time Key West, before the cruise-ship crowds ruined it).

Sportfishing here is among the best in the world. Once the setting for Ernest Hemingway's *Islands in the Stream* (see below), Bimini attracts big-game fishers for big-league fishing tournaments. If you'd like to follow in the footsteps of such famous anglers as Zane Grey and Howard Hughes, this is your island. In addition, the scuba diving here ranks among the country's very best.

THE BERRY ISLANDS Between Nassau and Florida's coast, these 30-odd islands—which comprise only about 77 sq. km (30 sq. miles) of land—attract devoted yachters and fishermen. This series of islets, cays, and rows of barely submerged rocks has extremely limited tourist facilities and is geared mostly toward well-heeled anglers, many of whom hail from Florida. Most of the full-time population (about 700 people) lives on Great Harbour. These islands are a lot classier and more charming than Bimini.

ANDROS Made up of two islands connected by a series of canals and cays called *bights,* Andros makes up the largest landmass in The Bahamas. It attracts divers, fishing enthusiasts, and sightseers.

Most of the island is uninhabited and unexplored. Its main villages are Nicholl's Town, Andros Town, and Congo Town; all are accessible by frequent boat and plane connections from Miami and Nassau. Lodging options range from large resorts to small, plain guesthouses that cater mainly to fishermen.

The world's third-largest barrier reef lies off the coast of Andros, and divers come from all over the world to explore it. The reef plunges 1,800m (5,906 ft.) at a narrow drop-off known as the Tongue of the Ocean. Bonefishing here is among the best on earth, as is the marlin and bluefin tuna fishing.

Known as the "Big Yard," the central portion of Northern Andros is mostly a dense forest of mahogany and pine where more than 50 orchid varieties bloom. In Southern Andros, there's a 103-sq.-km (40-sq.-mile) forest and mangrove swamp worth exploring. Any hotel concierge can arrange for a local guide to give you a tour of either of these natural attractions.

THE ABACOS This cluster of islands and islets is a mecca for yachters and other boaters who flock here year-round—particularly in July, when the Regatta Time in Abaco race is held at the Green Turtle Yacht Club. For centuries, residents of the Abacos have built boats, although tourism is now the main industry.

With the exception of Eleuthera's Harbour Island, you'll find more New England charm here than anywhere else in The Bahamas. Loyalists who left after the American Revolution settled here and built Cape Cod-style clapboard houses with white picket fences. The best places to experience this old-fashioned charm are Green Turtle Cay and Elbow Cay, which are accessible from Marsh Harbour. Marsh Harbour itself has an international airport and a shopping center, although its hotels aren't as good as those on Green Turtle Cay and Elbow Cay.

Many of the Abacos are undeveloped and uninhabited. For the best of both worlds, visitors can stay on either Walker's, Green Turtle, or Treasure cay, and then charter a boat to tour the more remote areas.

ELEUTHERA Long and slender, this most historic of the Out Islands (the first English settlers arrived here in 1648) is actually a string of islands that includes Spanish Wells and chic Harbour Island. The length of the island (177km/ 110 miles) and the distances between Eleuthera's communities require access via three airports. Frequent flights connect Eleuthera to Nassau, which lies about 97 km (60 miles) east. Eleuthera is similar to the Abacos; visitors are drawn to the fabulous secluded beaches and miles of barrier reef.

Gregory Town is the island chain's pineapple capital. A bit farther south is **Surfer's Beach,** one of the best surfing spots in The Bahamas. Several accommodations are available in this sleepy, slightly budget-oriented section of Eleuthera. The region's only major resort is the Club Med at Governor's Harbour; other inns are more basic.

At the southern end of the island, **Rock Sound** is in a slump, waiting to see whether the fabled Cotton Bay Club will ever reopen.

Off the coast, **Harbour Island** offers excellent hotels and food, and pastel-colored houses that evoke Cape Cod, right down to their picket fences. The beaches here are famed for their sand tinged pink by crushed coral and shells. **Spanish Wells,** another offshore island near Eleuthera, has extremely limited accommodations, and the residents—descendants of long-ago Loyalists—aren't very welcoming to visitors.

THE EXUMAS   Just 56km (35 miles) southeast of Nassau, this 588km-long (365-mile) string of islands and cays—most of them uninhabited—is the great yachting hub of The Bahamas, rivaling (some say surpassing) the Abacos. These waters, some of the country's prettiest, are also ideal for fishing. Many secluded beaches open onto tranquil cays. Daily flights service the Exumas from Nassau, Miami, and Atlanta.

The Exumas' commercial center is **George Town** on **Great Exuma,** while the **Exuma Cays Land and Sea Park** (see p. 272)—protected by The Bahamas National Trust—comprises much of the coastline. The park is accessible only by boat and is one of the major natural wonders and sightseeing destinations of The Bahamas, with abundant undersea life, reefs, blue holes, and shipwrecks. Portions of the James Bond thriller *Thunderball* were filmed at **Staniel Cay.** Each April, George Town hosts the inter-island Family Island Regatta, a major yachting event. A big new Four Seasons resort and golf course officially opened in late 2004 at **Emerald Bay** in Great Exuma, bringing a new type of crowd here. The Four Seasons offers a deep-water marina with 125 state-of-the-art slips for ocean-going yachts, along with a dock master. A few good inns are also on Great Exuma, mainly in George Town, and the locals are very hospitable. You'll feel like you practically have the archipelago to yourself.

5 The Bahamas in Popular Culture: Books, Film & Music

LITERATURE

The greatest literary figure inspired by The Bahamas was not Bahamian at all. He was Ernest Hemingway, a through-and-through American. The Bahamas figured in some of his fiction, notably *Islands in the Stream.* Hemingway preferred Bimini because of its fishing, and he was the first person the locals had seen land a bluefin tuna on rod and reel. "Papa," as he was known, stayed at Helen Duncombe's Compleat Angler Hotel (see p. 180).

Hemingway went to Bimini first in 1934 on his boat, *Pilar,* bringing writer John Dos Passos, among others, with him. He was also there in 1937, working on revisions for his manuscript *To Have and*

Have Not. But the Bahamians remember him mainly for *Islands in the Stream.* No writer before or since has captured in fiction the seedy charm of Bimini's Alice Town.

There are no Hemingways anymore, but novelists still use The Bahamas as a backdrop for their fiction. Instead of fishing, however, there is usually a drug-scene theme. Typical of this genre is D. C. Poyer's *Bahama Blue.* Poyer, also the author of *Hatteras Blue,* obviously loves the sea but hates the drug runners who use it. In his book, the hero sets off to make a 400-foot dive to recover 50 tons of cocaine off the coast. It's a thriller, and certainly evocative of the '90s in The Bahamas.

OTHER BOOKS   *Grand Bahama* (Caribbean Macmillan) by Peter Barratt, a town planner in charge of developing Freeport on Grand Bahama, writes of how a barren pine-covered island became a major tourist center.

Photographer-writer Hans W. Hannau prepared *The Bahama Islands in Full Color* (Argos, Inc.), a large pictorial volume with 68 color photographs. Somewhat of a coffee-table book, it does contain 76 pages of text with much general information about The Bahamas.

The *Yachtsman's Guide to The Bahamas* (Tropic Island Publishers), a thoroughly researched, annually revised guide, is essential for visitors contemplating boat tours.

RELIGION & FOLKLORE   Daniel J. Crowley's *I Could Talk Old-Story Good: Creativity in Bahamian Folklore* (University of California Press, Berkeley) and Leslie Higgs's *Bush Medicine in The Bahamas* (Nassau Guardian) are both recommended.

FICTION   For insight into Bahamian life, read Desmond Bagley's *Bahama Crisis* (HarperCollins), Ernest Hemingway's *Islands in the Stream* (Charles Scribner & Sons), or Dennis Ryan's *Bahamas: In a White Coming On* (Dorrance & Co.).

TRAVEL   *Isles of Eden: Life in the Southern Family Islands of The Bahamas* (Benjamin) by Harvey Lloyd, with a foreword by former prime minister Lynden Pindling, describes the island people who live in this rarely visited archipelago which stretches 90 miles southeast of Nassau all the way to Haiti. Lloyd blends unusual island photography with social commentary, history, and personal recollections.

HISTORY   From Columbus to today's historians, many authors have found the history of The Bahamas rich in material. Sample on the following reads:

The Story of The Bahamas (Macmillan Education Ltd.) by Paul Albury, a 294-page book that's the best of its kind, relates these islands' checkered past—from pirates to shipwreckers to rumrunners. Robert H. Fuson's *The Log of Christopher Columbus* (International Marine Publishing) presents the words of the explorer himself having the first impressions of The Bahamas ever recorded by a European. From his 1492 log comes the following: "I made sail and saw so many islands that I could not decide where to go first."

MUSIC

The Bahamas maintains great pride in its original musical idioms, often comparing their vitality to the more famous musical traditions of Jamaica, Puerto Rico, and Trinidad. Other than the spirituals whose roots were shared by slaves in colonial North America, by far the most famous musical products of the archipelago are Goombay and its closely linked sibling, Junkanoo.

GOOMBAY   Goombay music is an art form whose melodies and body movements are always accompanied by the beat of goatskin drums and, when available, the liberal consumption of rum. Goombay is a musical combination of Africa's tribal heritage (especially that of the Egungun sect of the Yoruba tribe) mingled with the Native American and British colonial influences of the New World. Although its appeal quickly spread to other islands, its traditions remain strongest within The Bahamas.

The most outlandish moments of the Goombay world occur the day following Christmas (Boxing Day). Dancers outfit themselves in masquerade costumes whose bizarre accessories and glittering colors evoke the plumage of jungle birds. Once dismissed by the British colonials as the pastime of hooligans, Goombay is now the most widespread and broad-based celebratory motif in The Bahamas, richly encouraged by the island's political and business elite. Goombay musicians and dancers are almost always male, celebrating a tradition whereby men and boys from the same family pass on the rhythms and dance techniques from generation to generation. Goombay is the Bantu word for "rhythm" while also referring to a type of African drum.

Today, Goombay has a gentle, rolling rhythm, a melody produced either by a piano, a guitar, or a saxophone, and the enthusiastic inclusion of bongos, maracas, and rhythm ("click") sticks. Lyrics, unlike the words that accompany reggae, are rarely politicized, dealing instead with topics that might have been referred to in another day as "saucy." Eventually, the sounds of Goombay would be commercialized and adapted into the louder and more strident musical form known as Junkanoo.

JUNKANOO   Until the 1940s, Junkanoo referred almost exclusively to the yuletide procession wherein revelers in elaborate costumes paraded down main streets accompanied solely by percussion music. (During the days of slavery, Christmas was the most important of the four annual holidays granted to slaves, and the one that merited the most exuberant celebrations.) The rhythms of Junkanoo became hypnotic, growing with the spectators' enthusiasm and the dancers' uninhibited movements. Essential to the tradition were the use of cowbells, traditional drums, and whistles.

Theories differ as to the origins of Junkanoo's name, but possible explanations include a Creole-pidgin derivation of French-speaking Haiti's term *gens inconnus,* which means "unknown people"—a reference to the masked dancers. Around World War II, Bahamian musicians fleshed out the yuletide Junkanoo parade's percussion rhythms with piano, electric bass, and guitar. This sparked the beginning of its development

into what is today, The Bahamas' most prevalent musical form.

RECORDINGS   One of the best-selling albums in Bahamian history is the privately produced *An Evening with Ronnie.* Composer of more hit singles than almost any other Bahamian star, Ronnie Butler's album contains renditions of "Burma Road," "Crow Calypso," and "Native Woman." Tony McKay emigrated to New York and New Orleans after becoming an international sensation with his Junkanoo music. His best-selling records include *Rushing through the Crowd* and *Reincarnation.*

The internationally acknowledged Baha Men (formerly High Voltage) reinterprets Goombay songs from the mid–20th century in *Junkanoo.* Of special interest are their Junkanoo adaptations of classic Goombay songs by such stars as George Symonette and Blind Blake. Some of the best Junkanoo stars on the Bahamian scene are members of the group K.B., whose folk renditions of Out Island values have led to such blockbusting singles as "She Fat," a romantic ode to the allure of overweight women. You'll find it on K.B.'s album *Kickin' Bahamian.*

The well-known Eddie Minnis survives exclusively on the sales of his paintings and records. His album *Discovery,* produced for the Bahamian quincentennial, features melodies and lyrics inspired by the folk idioms of the Exumas and Eleuthera. He has also produced other albums, all of which are available at record stores in Nassau.

The Bahamas has always inspired some of the Atlantic's most fervent religiosity. The country's most popular interpreter of gospel music is a Freeport-based group called the Cooling Waters, whose releases have approached the top of the religious-song charts in The Bahamas *and* the U.S.

One of the most important groups of all is King Eric and his Knights, whose leader is considered one of the patriarchs of Bahamian music. He composed an album, *Island Boy,* whose best-selling single, "Once Is Not Enough," later became the country's theme song.

FILMS

The lush look of The Bahamas makes it a favorite with film crews. Among the films shot here were the James Bond movies *Dr. No, Never Say Never Again,* and *Thunderball.* Clifton Wall, off New Providence, is a dramatic sea wall near a dozen shallow and deep sites. One wreck here formed the backdrop for *Never Say Never Again.* The film crew sunk a 110-foot freighter that had been seized by the Bahamian government as a dope runner. Considered The Bahamas' most photogenic wreck site, it was also used in the movie *Wet Gold* and in several TV commercials. A few hundred yards away are the ruins of an airplane prop used in *Thunderball.* The movie's famous speargun sequence was shot at Thunderball Reef.

Parts of other films have also been shot in The Bahamas, including *Splash!* and *Cocoon.* Also, *Islands in the Stream,* starring George C. Scott and Claire Bloom, is based on the Hemingway novel about a sculptor living in isolation in The Bahamas.

6 Eating & Drinking in The Bahamas

There is a bona fide Bahamian cuisine, but you'll have to leave the first-class hotels to find it. If you want to dine on authentic Bahamian food, look for the word "BAHAMIAN" in caps beside the restaurant reviews in this guide. When you see the word "INTERNATIONAL," know that this is typical fare likely to be offered anywhere, especially at a resort in Florida.

In some remote places, especially the Out Islands, Bahamian food is the only type of cuisine offered. Of course, the major restaurants have continental chefs, but elsewhere, especially at little local restaurants, you eat as the Bahamians eat.

Cuisine, sad to say, is not one of the most compelling reasons to come to The Bahamas. You can fare much better on the mainland, especially in Florida. Except for some notable exceptions (see "The Best Restaurants," in chapter 1), many restaurants serve fairly routine international fare of the surf-and-turf variety. Local seafood dishes consist mainly of grouper and conch. In the Out Islands, you'll likely get one or the other every night. More exotic fish is often flown in frozen from Miami, as is most meat and poultry.

The best restaurants are in Nassau, Cable Beach, Paradise Island, and, to a lesser extent, Freeport/Lucaya. That doesn't mean you can't eat satisfactorily elsewhere in The Bahamas. You can, but chances are you won't be collecting recipes.

THE CUISINE

SOUP Bahamian fish chowder can be prepared in any number of ways. Old-time chefs tell us that it's best when made with grouper. To that, they add celery, onions, tomatoes, and an array of flavorings that might include A1 sauce (or Worcestershire, or both), along with thyme, cooking sherry, a bit of dark rum, and lime juice.

Increasingly rare these days, turtle soup was for years a mainstay of the Out Islands. It and other turtle dishes still appear on some menus despite turtles' status as endangered species. If you have alternatives, choose another dish.

CONCH The national food of The Bahamas is conch (pronounced "konk"). This mollusk's firm white meat is enjoyed throughout the islands. Actually, it tastes somewhat bland, at least until Bahamian chefs get their hands on it. Locals eat it as a snack (usually served at happy hours in taverns and bars), as a main dish, as a salad, or as an hors d'oeuvre.

Some people think it tastes like abalone because it does not have a fishy taste like halibut, but a chewy consistency, which means that a chef pounded it to tenderize it. Every cook has a different recipe for making conch chowder. A popular version includes tomatoes, potatoes, sweet peppers, onions, carrots, salt pork or bacon, bay leaf, thyme, and (of course) salt and pepper.

Conch fritters, shaped like balls, are served with hot sauce and are made with finely minced sweet peppers, onions, and tomato paste, among other ingredients. They are deep-fried in oil.

Conch salad is another local favorite, and it, too, has many variations. Essentially, it is uncooked conch marinated in Old Sour (a hot pepper sauce) to break down its tissues and add extra flavor. This tangy dish is served with diced small red (or green) peppers and chopped onion.

Cracked conch (or fried conch, as the old-timers call it) is prepared like a breaded veal cutlet. Pounded hard and dipped in batter, it is then sautéed. Conch is also served steamed, in Creole sauce, curried, "scorched," creamed on toast, and stewed. Instead of conch chowder, you might get conch soup. You'll also see "conch burgers" on menus.

SEAFOOD The most elegant item you'll see on nearly any menu in The Bahamas is the local spiny lobster. A tropical cousin of the Maine lobster, it is also called crayfish or rock lobster. Only the tail is eaten, however, and it's not as sweet as the Maine species. You get fresh lobster only in season, from the first of April until the end of August. Otherwise it's frozen.

Bahamian lobster, in spite of its cost, is not always prepared well. Sometimes a cook leaves it in the oven too long and the meat becomes tough and chewy. But when prepared right, like it is at Nassau's famed Graycliff restaurant, it is perfection and worth the exorbitant cost.

The Bahamian lobster lends itself to any international recipe for lobster, including Newburg or Thermidor. A typical local preparation is to curry it with lime juice and fresh coconut, among other ingredients.

After conch, grouper is the second-most-consumed fish in The Bahamas. It's served in a number of ways, often batter-dipped or sautéed, and called "fingers" because of the way it's sliced. The fish can also come steamed and served in a spicy Creole sauce. Sometimes it comes dressed in a sauce of dry white wine, mushrooms, onions, and thyme. Because the fish has a mild taste, the other ingredients' extra flavor is needed.

Baked bonefish is also common, and it's very simple to prepare. The bonefish is split in half and seasoned with a hot pepper sauce (Old Sour) and salt, and then popped into the oven.

Baked crab is one of The Bahamas' best-known dishes. A chef mixes eggs and the meat of either land or sea crabs with seasonings and bread crumbs. The crabs are then replaced in their shells and baked.

PEAS 'N' RICE & JOHNNYCAKE If mashed potatoes are still the "national starch" of America, then peas 'n' rice fulfills that role in The Bahamas. Peas 'n' rice, like mashed potatoes, can be prepared in a number of ways. One popular method is to cook pigeon peas (which grow in pods on small trees) or black-eyed peas with salt pork, tomatoes, celery, uncooked rice, thyme, green pepper, onion, salt, pepper, and whatever special touch a chef wants to add. When it's served as a side dish, Bahamians often sprinkle hot sauce over the concoction.

Johnnycake, another famed Bahamian dish, dates from the early settlers, who were often simple and poor. They survived mainly on a diet of fish and rice, supplemented by johnnycake, a pan-cooked bread made with butter, milk, flour, sugar, salt, and baking powder. (Originally it was called "Journey Cake," which was eventually corrupted to "johnnycake.") Fishermen could make this simple bread on the decks of their vessels: They'd build a fire in a box that had been filled with sand to keep the flames from spreading to the craft.

TROPICAL FRUITS Bahamians are especially fond of fruits, and they make inventive dishes out of them, including soursop ice cream and sapodilla pudding. Guavas are used to make their famous guava duff dessert. The islanders also grow and enjoy melons, pineapples, passion fruit, and mangoes.

Their most famous fruit is the papaya, which is called "pawpaw" or "melon tree." It's made into a dessert or chutney or eaten for breakfast in its natural state. It's also used in many lunch and dinner recipes. An old Bahamian custom of using papaya as a meat tenderizer has, at least since the 1970s, invaded North American kitchens. Papaya is also used to make fruity tropical drinks, such as the Bahama Mama shake. And if you see it

for sale in a local food store, take home some "Goombay" marmalade, which is made with papaya, pineapple, and green ginger.

RUM, LIQUEURS & SPECIALTY DRINKS Although rum came north from Cuba and Jamaica, Bahamians quickly adopted it as their national alcoholic beverage. Using their imagination, they invented several local drinks, including the Yellow Bird, the Bahama Mama, and the Goombay Smash.

The Yellow Bird is made with crème de banana liqueur, Vat 19 rum, orange juice, pineapple juice, apricot brandy, and Galliano. A Bahama Mama has Vat 19, citrus juice (perhaps pineapple too), bitters, a dash of nutmeg, crème de cassis, and a hint of grenadine. The Goombay Smash usually consists of coconut rum, pineapple juice, lemon juice, Triple Sec, Vat 19, and a dash of simple syrup.

Nearly every bartender in the islands has a personal version of Planter's Punch. A classic recipe is to make it with lime juice, sugar, and Vat 19, plus a dash of bitters. It's usually served with a cherry and an orange slice. If you want a typically Bahamian liqueur, try Nassau Royale. It is used to make an increasingly popular drink, the C. C. Rider, which includes Canadian Club, apricot brandy, and pineapple juice.

3

Planning Your Trip to The Bahamas

You can be in The Bahamas after a quick 35-minute jet hop from Miami. And it's never been easier to take advantage of great package deals that can make these islands a terrific value.

1 Visitor Information

The two best sources to try before you leave home are your travel agent and **The Bahamas Tourist Office** nearest you. Visit the nation's official tourism office at www.bahamas.com, or call ✆ **800/ BAHAMAS** (224-2627) or 242/302-2000. You can also walk in at these branch offices:

Chicago: 8600 W. Bryn Mawr Ave., Suite 820, North Chicago, IL 60631 (✆ **773/867-3877**)

Plantation: 1200 S. Pine Island Rd., Suite 750 & 770, Plantation, FL 33324 (✆ **954/236-9292**)

Los Angeles: 11400 West Olympic Blvd., Suite 200, Los Angeles, CA 90064 (✆ **800/439-6993** or 310/ 312-9544)

New York: 60 E. 42 St., Suite 1850, New York, NY 10165 (✆ **212/758-2777**)

Texas: 3102 Oak Lawn Ave., Suite 700, Dallas, TX 75219 (✆ **214/560-2280**)

Toronto: 6725 Airport Rd., Suite 202, Mississauga, ON L4V 1V2 (✆ **800/ 667-3777** or 905/672-9017)

United Kingdom: 10 Chesterfield St., London W1J 5JL (✆ **020/7355-0800**)

You may also want to contact the U.S. State Department for background bulletins, which supply up-to-date information on crime, health concerns, import restrictions, and other travel matters. Call ✆ **888/407-4747** or visit www.travel. state.gov.

A travel agent can be a great source of information. Make sure your agent is a member of the American Society of Travel Agents (ASTA). If you get poor service from an ASTA agent, you can write to the ASTA Consumer Affairs Department, 1101 King St., Alexandria, VA 22314 (✆ **800/440-ASTA** [440-2782] or 703/739-2782; www.astanet.com).

SEARCHING THE WEB

Bahamas websites include:

The Bahamas Ministry of Tourism (www.bahamas.com or www.tourism bahamas.org): Official tourism site.

The Bahamas Out Islands Promotion Board (www.myoutislands.com): Focuses on remote isles.

Bahamas Tourist Guide (www.inter knowledge.com/bahamas): Travelers' opinions.
Bahamas Vacation Guide (www. bahamasvg.com): Service listings.
Nassau/Paradise Island Promotion Board (www.nassauparadiseisland. com): Service listings.

MAPS

As you emerge at one of the major airports, including those of Nassau (New Providence) and Freeport (Grand Bahama Island), you can pick up island maps that are good for routine touring around those islands. However, if you plan to do extensive touring in the Out Islands, you should go first to a bookstore in either Nassau or Freeport and ask for a copy of *Atlas of The Bahamas.* It provides touring routes (outlined in red) through all the major Out Islands. Once you arrive on these remote islands, it may be hard to obtain maps.

2 Entry Requirements

ENTRY REQUIREMENTS
PASSPORTS

To enter The Bahamas, **citizens of Britain** and **Canada** coming in as visitors *must* bring a passport to demonstrate proof of citizenship. Under new Homeland Security regulations that started December 31, 2005, **U.S. travelers** were required to have a valid passport to reenter the United States by January 1, 2008.

Onward or return tickets must be shown to immigration officials in The Bahamas. Citizens of other countries, including Australia, Ireland, and New Zealand, should carry a valid passport.

For information about how to get a passport, go to "Passports" in the "Fast Facts" section of the appendix. The websites listed provide downloadable passport applications as well as the current fees for processing passport applications. For an up-to-date, country-by-country listing of passport requirements around the world, go to the "Foreign Entry Requirement" Web page of the U.S. State Department at **http://travel.state.gov**.

VISAS

The Commonwealth of The Bahamas does not require visas. On entry to The Bahamas, you'll be given an immigration card to complete and sign. The card has a carbon copy that you must keep until departure, at which time it must be turned in. You'll also have to pay a departure tax before you can exit the country (see "Taxes," under "Fast Facts: The Bahamas," in the appendix).

MEDICAL REQUIREMENTS

For information on medical requirements and recommendations, see "Health," later in this chapter.

CUSTOMS
WHAT YOU CAN BRING INTO THE BAHAMAS

Bahamian Customs allows you to bring in 200 cigarettes, or 50 cigars, or 1 pound of tobacco, plus 1 quart of spirits (hard liquor). You can also bring in items classified as "personal effects" and all the money you wish.

WHAT YOU CAN TAKE HOME FROM THE BAHAMAS

Visitors leaving Nassau or Freeport/ Lucaya for most U.S. destinations clear U.S. Customs & Border Protection before departing The Bahamas. Charter companies can make special arrangements with the Nassau or Freeport flight services and U.S. Customs & Border Protection for pre-clearance. No further formalities are required upon arrival in the United States once the pre-clearance has taken place in Nassau or Freeport.

Collect receipts for all purchases you make in The Bahamas. *Note:* If a merchant suggests giving you a false receipt, misstating the value of the goods, beware—the merchant might be an informer to U.S. Customs. You must also declare all gifts received while abroad.

If you purchased an item during an earlier trip abroad, carry proof that you have already paid Customs duty on the item at the time of your previous reentry. To be extra careful, compile a list of expensive carry-on items and ask a U.S. Customs agent to stamp your list at the airport before your departure.

U.S. Citizens

For specifics on what you can bring back and the corresponding fees, download the invaluable free pamphlet *Know Before You Go* online at **www.cbp.gov**. (Click on "Travel" and then click on "Know Before You Go.") Or contact the **U.S. Customs & Border Protection (CBP)**, 1300 Pennsylvania Ave. NW, Washington, DC 20229 (*(C)* **877/287-8667**), and request the pamphlet.

Canadian Citizens

For a clear summary of Canadian rules, write for the booklet *I Declare,* issued by the **Canada Border Services Agency** (*(C)* **800/461-9999** in Canada, or 204/983-3500; www.cbsa-asfc.gc.ca).

U.K. Citizens

For information, contact **HM Revenue & Customs** at *(C)* **0845/010-9000** (from outside the U.K., 02920/501-261), or consult their website at **www.hmrc. gov.uk**.

Australian Citizens

A helpful brochure available from Australian consulates or Customs offices is *Know Before You Go.* For more information, call the **Australian Customs Service** at *(C)* **1300/363-263,** or log on to **www.customs.gov.au**.

New Zealand Citizens

Most questions are answered in a free pamphlet available at New Zealand consulates and Customs offices: *New Zealand Customs Guide for Travellers, Notice no. 4.* For more information, contact **New Zealand Customs Service,** The Customhouse, 17–21 Whitmore St., Box 2218, Wellington (*(C)* **04/473-6099** or 0800/428-786; www.customs.govt.nz).

---

3 When to Go

THE WEATHER

The temperature in The Bahamas averages between 75°F and 85°F (24°C–29°C) in both winter and summer, although it can get chilly in the early morning and at night. The Bahamian winter is usually like a perpetual late spring—naturally, the high season for North Americans rushing to escape snow and ice. Summer brings broiling hot sun and humidity. There's a much greater chance of rain during the summer and fall.

THE HURRICANE SEASON

The curse of Bahamian weather, the hurricane season, lasts (officially) from June 1 to November 30. But there is no cause for panic. More tropical cyclones pound the U.S. mainland than The Bahamas.

Hurricanes are actually fairly infrequent here, and when one does come, satellite forecasts generally give adequate advance warning so that precautions can be taken.

If you're heading for The Bahamas during the hurricane season, you might want to visit the National Weather Service at www.nws.noaa.gov.

For an online 10-day forecast, check the Weather Channel at www.weather. com.

THE "SEASON"

In The Bahamas, hotels charge their highest prices during the peak winter period from mid-December to mid-April, when visitors fleeing from cold north winds flock to the islands. Winter is the driest season.

Average Temperatures & Rainfall (in.) in The Bahamas

Month	Jan	Feb	Mar	Apr	May	June	July	Aug	Sept	Oct	Nov	Dec
Temp. °F	70	70	72	75	77	80	81	82	81	78	74	71
Temp. °C	21	21	22	24	25	27	27	28	27	26	23	22
Rainfall (in.)	1.9	1.6	1.4	1.9	4.8	9.2	6.1	6.3	7.5	8.3	2.3	1.5

Note that these numbers are daily averages, so expect temperatures to climb significantly higher in the noonday sun and to cool off a good deal in the evening.

If you plan to visit during the winter, try to make reservations at least 2 to 3 months in advance. At some hotels, it's impossible to book accommodations for Christmas and the month of February without even more lead time.

SAVING MONEY IN THE OFF SEASON

The Bahamas is a year-round destination. The islands' "off season" runs from late spring to late fall, when tolerable temperatures (see "The Weather," above) prevail throughout most of the region. Trade winds ensure comfortable days and nights, even in accommodations without air-conditioning. Although the noonday sun may raise temperatures to uncomfortable levels, cool breezes usually make the morning, late afternoon, and evening more pleasant here than in many parts of the U.S. mainland.

Dollar for dollar, you'll spend less money by renting a summer house or fully equipped unit in The Bahamas than you would on Cape Cod, Fire Island, Laguna Beach, or the coast of Maine.

The off season—roughly from mid-April to mid-December (rate schedules vary from hotel to hotel)—amounts to a summer sale. In most cases, hotel rates are slashed from 20% to a startling 60%. It's a bonanza for cost-conscious travelers, especially families who like to go on vacations together. In the chapters ahead, we'll spell out in dollars the specific amounts hotels charge during the off season.

OTHER OFF-SEASON ADVANTAGES

Although The Bahamas may appear inviting in the winter to those who live in northern climates, your trip may be more enjoyable if you go in the off season. Here's why:

- After the winter hordes have left, a less hurried way of life prevails.
- Swimming pools and beaches are less crowded—perhaps not crowded at all.
- To survive, resort boutiques often feature summer sales.
- You can often appear without a reservation at a top restaurant and get a table for dinner.
- The endless waiting game is over: no waiting for a rented car, no long wait for a golf course tee time, and quicker access to tennis courts and watersports.
- The atmosphere is more cosmopolitan than it is in winter, mainly because of the influx of Europeans.
- Some package-tour fares are as much as 20% lower, and individual excursion fares may be reduced from 5% to 10%.
- Accommodations and flights are much easier to book.
- Summer is an excellent time for family travel, which is not always possible during the winter season.
- Finally, the best Bahamian attractions—sea, sand, surf, and lots of sunshine—remain absolutely undiminished.

Avoiding Spring Break

Throughout March and into mid-April, it's spring-break season in the Caribbean for vacationing college and high-school students. Expect beach parties, sports events, and musical entertainment; if the idea of hundreds of partying fraternity kids doesn't appeal to you, beware. When you make your reservations, ask if your hotel is planning to host any big groups of kids.

OFF-SEASON DISADVANTAGES

Let's not paint too rosy a picture. Although the advantages of off-season travel far outweigh the disadvantages, there are nevertheless some drawbacks to traveling here in summer:

- You might be staying at a construction site. Hoteliers save their major renovations until the off season. You may wake up to the sound of hammers.
- Single tourists find the dating scene better in winter when there are more visitors, especially unattached ones.
- Services are often reduced. In the peak of winter, everything is fully operational. But in summer, many programs (such as watersports) might be curtailed in spite of fine weather.

THE BAHAMAS CALENDAR OF EVENTS

For specific events, you can call your nearest branch of **The Bahamas Tourist Office** (see "Visitor Information," earlier) at ℂ **800/ BAHAMAS** (224-2627) or check their website at **www.bahamas.com**.

January

Junkanoo. This Mardi Gras–style festival begins 2 or 3 hours before dawn on New Year's Day. Throngs of cavorting, costumed figures prance through Nassau, Freeport/Lucaya, and the Out Islands. Jubilant men, women, and children wear elaborate headdresses and festive apparel as they celebrate their African heritage with music and dance. Mini-Junkanoos, in which visitors can participate, are regular events. Local tourist offices will advise the best locations to see the festivities.

New Year's Day Sailing Regatta, Nassau and Paradise Island. Three dozen or more sailing sloops, ranging from 5 to 8.5m (16–28 ft.), converge off Montagu Bay in a battle for bragging rights. For information, call ℂ **242/ 394-0445.**

Annual Bahamas Wahoo Championships, Berry Islands. Anglers try to bait one of the fastest fish in the ocean, reaching speeds up to 70 mph. For information, call ℂ **305/234-7386** or visit www.bahamaswahoo.com. Mid-January.

February

The Mid-Winter Wahoo, Bimini. The Bimini Big Game Resort & Marina draws Hemingway look-alikes and other anglers to this winter event that is heavily attended by Floridians. For more information, call ℂ **800/ 737-1007** or contact the tournament director, at the Bimini Tourist Office at ℂ **242/347-3529;** www.bimini. bahamas.com. Early February.

Farmer's Cay Festival. This festival is a rendezvous for yachtsmen cruising the Exuma Islands and a homecoming for the people of Farmer's Cay, Exuma. Boat excursions will depart Nassau at Potter's Cay for the festival at 8pm on Friday, and then return to Nassau at 8pm on Saturday from the Farmer's Cay Dock. For information, contact

Terry Bain in Little Farmer's Cay, Exuma, at ✆ **242/355-4006**, or the Exuma Tourist Office at ✆ **242/336-2430**. First Friday and Saturday in February.

March

Bacardi Billfish Tournament, Freeport. A weeklong tournament attracting the who's who of deep-sea fishing. Headquarters is the Port Lucaya Resort & Yacht Club. For more information, call ✆ **242/373-9090** or visit www.portlucayamarina.com. Mid-March.

April

Bahamas Family Island Regatta, George Town, the Exumas. Featuring Bahamian craft sloops, these celebrated boat races are held in Elizabeth Harbour. There's also a variety of onshore activities, including basketball, a skipper's party, and a Junkanoo parade. Call ✆ **242/524-2841** or check www.georgetowncruisingregatta.org for exact dates and information. Usually third week of April.

Bahamas Billfish Championship. This annual event is divided into four competitions, taking place at four different venues and times, spanning April to June. Anglers can fish any and all of the tournaments taking place at Marsh Harbour (third week of Apr), Harbour Island (first week of May), Spanish Cay (mid-May), and Treasure Cay (first week to second week of June). Since dates vary, contact the **Bahamas Billfish Championship** at Two Oakland Blvd., Suite 195, Hollywood, FL 33020 (✆ **866/920-5577** or 954/920-5577; www.bahamasbillfish.com). April to June.

Bahamas White Marlin Open, the Abacos. This rendezvous off Abaco draws anglers seeking an action-packed billfish tournament. The headquarters

is the Treasure Cay Resort & Marina. For more information, call ✆ **800/275-2260** or 954/920-7877, or visit www.bahamaswhitemarlinopen.com. Dates vary.

May

Long Island Regatta, Salt Pond, Long Island. This event sees some 40 to 50 sailing sloops from throughout The Bahamas compete in three classes for trophies and cash prizes. Onshore, dancing to indigenous "rake 'n' scrape" music, sporting events, and local food specialties for sale make for a carnival-like atmosphere. For more information, call ✆ **242/324-6294**. Late May.

June

Eleuthera Pineapple Festival, Gregory Town, Eleuthera. This celebration devoted to the island's succulent pineapple features a Junkanoo parade, craft displays, dancing, a pineapple recipe contest, tours of pineapple farms, and a "pineathalon"—a .5km (⅓-mile) swim, 5.5km (3½-mile) run, and 6.5km (4-mile) bike ride. For more information, call ✆ **242/332-2142**. First week of June.

Bahamas Summer Boating Fling/Flotilla. Boating enthusiasts and yachters make the 1-day crossing from Florida to The Bahamas (Port Lucaya's marina on Grand Bahama Island) in a flotilla of boats guided by a lead boat. All "flings" depart from the Radisson Bahia Mar Resort & Yacht Center in Fort Lauderdale. For more information, contact the **Bahamas Tourism Center** in Florida at ✆ **800/327-7678** or 954/236-9292. End of June to beginning of August.

July

Annual Racing Time in Abaco, Marsh Harbour. This weeklong regatta features a series of sailboat races in the Sea of Abaco. Onshore festivities include nightly entertainment, cocktail parties, beach picnics, cultural activities, and a grand finale party. For registration forms and information, contact the Abaco Tourist Office at © 242/367-3067. Early July.

Independence Week. Independence celebrations are marked throughout the islands by festivities, parades, and fireworks. It all culminates on Independence Day. July 10.

August

Emancipation Day. The first Monday in August commemorates the emancipation of slaves in 1834. A highlight of this holiday is an early morning "Junkanoo Rushout" starting at 4am in Fox Hill Village in Nassau, followed by an afternoon of "cookouts," cultural events such as climbing a greased pole, and the plaiting of the Maypole. First Monday in August.

Cat Island Regatta, Southern Bahamas. Sleepy Cat Island comes alive in the weekend of festive events, including sloop races, live "rake 'n' scrape" bands, quadrille dancing, old-fashioned contests and games, and local cuisine. Contact the **Regatta Desk** at © 242/502-0600 in Nassau. Early August.

September

All Abaco Sailing Regatta. Local sailing sloops rendezvous at Treasure Cay Harbour for a series of championship races and onshore festivities. Contact the **Regatta Desk** in Nassau at © 242/502-0600 or in Abaco at © 242/367-3067. Late September.

October

Discovery Day. The New World landing of Christopher Columbus, traditionally said to be the island of San Salvador, is celebrated throughout The Bahamas. Naturally, San Salvador has a parade every year on October 12.

North Eleuthera Sailing Regatta. Native sailing sloops take to the waters of North Eleuthera, Harbour Island, and Spanish Wells in a weekend of championship races. For information, contact the **Eleuthera Tourist Office** at © 242/332-2142. Mid-October.

Great Bahamas Seafood and Heritage Festival, Heritage Village, Arawak Cay. A cultural affair, this festival held in October showcases authentic Bahamian cuisine, traditional music, and storytelling. For more information, exact times, and schedule of events, contact the **Ministry of Tourism** at © 242/302-2000.

November

Guy Fawkes Day. The best celebrations are in Nassau. Nighttime parades through the streets are held on many of the islands, culminating in the hanging and burning of Guy Fawkes, an effigy of the British malefactor who was involved in the Gunpowder Plot of 1605 in London. It usually takes place around November 5, but check with island tourist offices.

Bimini Big Game Fishing Club All Wahoo Tournament. Anglers take up the tough challenge of baiting one of the fastest fishes in the ocean. Headquarters is the Bimini Sands Resort & Marina. For information, contact © 242/373-3500, or visit www.bahamaswahoo.com. Mid-November.

Annual One Bahamas Music & Heritage Festival. This 3-day celebration is staged at both Nassau and Paradise Island to celebrate national unity. Highlights include concerts featuring top Bahamian performing artists, "fun walks," and other activities. For details, contact the **Nassau/Paradise Island Office** at the Ministry of Tourism, (©) **242/302-2000.** Last week of November.

December

Junkanoo Boxing Day. High-energy Junkanoo parades and celebrations are held throughout the islands on December 26. Many of these activities are repeated on New Year's Day (see "January," above). December 26.

Lying off the east coast of Florida, the archipelago of The Bahamas is the easiest and most convenient foreign destination you can fly to unless you live close to the Canadian or Mexican borders.

Nassau is the busiest and most popular point of entry (this is where you'll fly if you're staying on Paradise Island). From here, you can make connections to many of the more remote Out Islands. If you're headed for one of the Out Islands, refer to the "Getting There" section that appears at the beginning of each island's coverage later in this book for details. Freeport, on Grand Bahama, also has its own airport, which is served by flights from the U.S. mainland, too.

Flight time to Nassau from Miami is about 35 minutes; from New York, 2½ hours; from Atlanta, 2 hours and 5 minutes; from Philadelphia, 2 hours and 45 minutes; from Charlotte, 2 hours and 10 minutes; from central Florida, 1 hour and 10 minutes; and from Toronto, 3 hours.

THE MAJOR AIRLINES

From the U.S. mainland, about a half-dozen carriers fly nonstop to the country's major point of entry and busiest airline hub, **Lynden Pindling International Airport** ((©) **242/377-1759**). Some also fly to the archipelago's second-most-populous city of Freeport. Only a handful (see below) fly directly to any of the Out Islands.

American Airlines ((©) **800/433-7300;** www.aa.com) has several flights per day from Miami to Nassau, as well as four daily flights from Fort Lauderdale to Nassau. In addition, the carrier flies three times daily from Miami to Freeport. It also offers three flights daily from Miami to George Town and one flight daily from Miami to Marsh Harbour.

Delta ((©) **800/221-1212;** www.delta. com) has several connections to The Bahamas, with service from Atlanta, Orlando, and New York's LaGuardia.

(Tips) New Security Measures

Because of increased security measures, the Transportation Security Administration has made changes to the prohibited items list. All liquids and gels—including shampoo, toothpaste, perfume, hair gel, suntan lotion, and all other items with similar consistency—are limited on carry-on baggage and the security checkpoint. Pack these items in your checked baggage. Carrying liquids of any sort to the screening checkpoint will cause you delays and will most likely result in the item being confiscated.

With the ever-changing security measures, we recommend that you check the **Transportation Security Administration's** website, **www.tsa.gov,** as near to your departure date as possible to make sure that no other restrictions have been imposed.

The national airline of The Bahamas, **Bahamasair** (② **800/222-4262** or 242/ 377-8451; www.bahamasair.com), flies to The Bahamas from Miami and Fort Lauderdale, landing at either Nassau (with seven nonstop flights daily) or Freeport (with two nonstop flights daily).

US Airways (② **800/428-4322;** www. usairways.com) offers daily direct flights to Nassau from Philadelphia and Charlotte, North Carolina.

JetBlue (② **800/JET-BLUE** [538-2583]; www.jetblue.com) has one direct flight daily to Nassau, from JFK in New York.

Other carriers include **Continental Airlines** (② **800/231-0856;** www. continental.com), which has greatly expanded its link to The Bahamas through South Florida through its regional affiliate, Gulfstream International. Continental operates flights between Fort Lauderdale and Andros Town on Andros, with four round-trip flights each week. The airline also offers daily service from Fort Lauderdale to both George Town and Governor's Harbour. In addition, it maintains frequent links between Fort Lauderdale, Freeport, Marsh Harbour, North Eleuthera, and Treasure Cay. **Twin Air** (② **954/359-8266;** www.flytwinair.com) flies from Fort Lauderdale three times a week to Rock Sound and Governor's Harbour, and four times a week to North Eleuthera.

Air Canada (② **888/247-2262;** www. aircanada.com) is the only carrier offering scheduled service to Nassau from Canada. Direct flights from Toronto and Montreal leave daily; other flights from Toronto and Montreal, as well as other Canadian cities, make connections in the U.S.

British travelers opt for transatlantic passage aboard **British Airways** (② **800/ AIR-WAYS** [247-9297] in the U.S. or 0870/850-9850 in the U.K.; www.

britishairways.com), which offers four weekly direct flights from London to Nassau. The airline also has at least one flight daily to Miami. From here, many connections are available to Nassau and many other points within the archipelago on several carriers.

FLYING TO THE OUT ISLANDS

Many frequent visitors to The Bahamas do everything they can to avoid the congestion, inconvenience, and uncertain connections of the Nassau International Airport. A couple of U.S.-based airlines offer service directly to some of the Out Islands. **American Eagle** (② **800/433-7300;** www.aa.com) offers frequent service from Miami International Airport to the Abacos, Eleuthera, and the Exumas. **US Airways** (② **800/428-4322;** www. usairways.com) flies nonstop every day from Fort Lauderdale to Eleuthera, usually making stops at both Governor's Harbour and North Eleuthera. US Airways also flies every day from West Palm Beach to the Abacos, stopping in both Treasure Cay and Marsh Harbour.

Chalk's International Airlines (② **877/924-2557;** www.flychalks.com) operates 17-passenger amphibious aircraft that take off and land in waters near the company's portside terminals. From the Florida mainland, a nonstop flight departs for Bimini from Fort Lauderdale International Airport. The flight then continues on to Paradise Island. There's also a one-stop flight from Fort Lauderdale International Airport to Bimini. (The airline also offers charter flights to virtually anywhere in The Bahamas.)

GETTING AROUND

If your final destination is Paradise Island, Freeport, or Nassau (Cable Beach) and you plan to fly, you'll have little trouble reaching your destination. However, if you're heading for one of the Out Islands, you face more exotic choices, not only of airplanes, but also of other means of transport, including a mail boat, the traditional connecting link in days of yore.

As mentioned, each section on one of the Out Island chains has specific transportation information, but here's a general overview.

BY PLANE

The national airline of The Bahamas, **Bahamasair** (© **800/222-4262;** www. bahamasair.com), serves 19 airports on 12 Bahamian islands, including Abaco, Andros, Cat Island, Eleuthera, Long Island, and San Salvador. Many of the Out Islands have either airports or airstrips, or are within a short ferry ride's distance of one. You can usually make connections to these smaller islands from Nassau.

BY RENTAL CAR

Many travelers don't really need to rent a car in The Bahamas, especially those who are coming for a few days of soaking in the sun at their resort's own beach. In Nassau and Freeport, you can easily rely on public transportation or taxis. In some of the Out Islands, there are a few car-rental companies, but most rental cars are unusually expensive and in poor condition (the roads are often in the same bad state as the rental cars).

Most visitors need transportation only from the airport to their hotel; perhaps you can arrange an island tour later, and an expensive private car won't be necessary. Your hotel can always arrange a taxi for you if you want to venture out.

You may decide that you want a car to explore beyond the tourist areas of New Providence Island, and you're very likely to want one on Grand Bahama Island.

Just remember: Road rules are much the same as those in the U.S., but you *drive on the left.*

For the Out Islands, turn to the relevant "Getting Around" sections of the chapters that follow to determine if you'll want a car (you may want one to explore on Eleuthera or Great Abaco Island); perhaps you'll stay put at your resort but rent a car for only 1 day of exploring.

The major U.S. car-rental companies operate in The Bahamas, but not on all the remote islands. We always prefer to do business with one of the major firms if they're present because you can call ahead and reserve from home via a toll-free number, they tend to offer better-maintained vehicles, and it's easier to resolve any disputes after the fact. Call **Budget** (© **800/472-3325;** www.budget.com), **Hertz** (© **800/654-3001;** www.hertz. com), **Dollar** (© **800/800-3665;** www. dollarcar.com), or **Avis** (© **800/331-1084;** www.avis.com). Budget rents in Nassau and Paradise Island. Liability insurance is compulsory.

"Petrol" is easily available in Nassau and Freeport, though quite expensive. In the Out Islands, where the cost of gasoline is likely to vary from island to island, you should plan your itinerary based on where you'll be able to get fuel. The major towns of the islands have service stations. You should have no problems on New Providence or Grand Bahama Island unless you start out with a nearly empty tank.

Visitors may drive with their home driver's license for up to 3 months. For longer stays, you'll need to secure a Bahamian driver's license.

BY TAXI

Once you've reached your destination, you'll find that taxis are plentiful in the Nassau/Cable Beach/Paradise Island area and in the Freeport/Lucaya area on Grand Bahama Island. These cabs, for the most part, are metered—but they take cash only, no credit cards. See "Getting Around" in the chapters on each island that follow for further details.

In the Out Islands, however, it's not so easy. In general, taxi service is available at all air terminals, at least if those air

Moments Slow Boat to the Out Islands

Delivering goats, chickens, hardware, and food staples along with the mail, Bahamian mail boats greatly improve the quality of life for the scattered communities of the Out Islands. You can book passage aboard these vessels to at least 17 different remote islands. All 30 boats leave from Nassau, and the round-trip takes a full day. For more information, consult an office of **The Bahamas Tourist Office** (see "Visitor Information," earlier) or the dock master at the Nassau piers at *©* **242/326-9781** or 326-9772.

terminals have "port of entry" status. They can also be hailed at most marinas.

Taxis are usually shared, often with the local residents. Out Island taxis aren't metered, so you must negotiate the fare before you get in. (Expect to pay a rate of around US$20/£10 per hour.) Cars are often old and badly maintained, so be prepared for a bumpy ride over some rough roads if you've selected a particularly remote hotel.

BY MAIL BOAT

Before the advent of better airline connections, the traditional way of exploring the Out Islands—in fact, about the only way unless you had your own vessel—was by mail boat. This service is still available, but it's recommended only for those who have lots of time and a sense of adventure. You may ride with cases of rum, oil drums, live chickens, or even an occasional piano.

The boats—19 of them composing the "Post Office Navy" under the direction of the Bahamian Chief of Transportation—are often fancifully colored, high-sided, and somewhat clumsy in appearance, but the little motor vessels chug along, serving the 30 inhabited islands of The Bahamas. Schedules can be thrown off by weather and other causes, but most mornings mail boats depart from Potter's Cay (under the Paradise Island Bridge in Nassau) or from Prince George Wharf. The voyages last from 4½ hours to most of a day, sometimes even overnight. Check the schedule of the particular boat

you wish to travel on with the skipper at the dock in Nassau.

This is a cheap way to go: The typical fare from Nassau to Marsh Harbour is US$55 (£28) per person, one-way. Many of the boats offer two classes of passenger accommodations, first and second. In first class, you get a bunk bed; in second, you may be entitled only to deck space. (Actually, the bunk beds are usually reserved for the seasick, but first-class passengers on larger boats sit in a reasonably comfortable enclosed cabin.)

For information about mail boats to the Out Islands, contact the **Dock Masters Office** in Nassau, under the Paradise Island Bridge on Potter's Cay (*©* **242/393-1064**).

BY CHARTERED BOAT

For those who can afford it, this is the most luxurious way to see The Bahamas. On your private boat, you can island-hop at your convenience. Well-equipped marinas are on every major island and many cays. There are designated ports of entry at Great Abaco (Marsh Harbor), Andros, the Berry Islands, Bimini, Cat Cay, Eleuthera, Great Exuma, Grand Bahama Island (Freeport/Lucaya), Great Inagua, New Providence (Nassau), Ragged Island, and San Salvador.

Vessels must check with Customs at the first port of entry and receive a cruising clearance permit to The Bahamas. Carry it with you and return it at the official port of departure.

Yachtsman's Guide to The Bahamas (Tropical Island Publishers) covers the entire Bahamas. Copies are available at major marine outlets and bookstores, and by mail direct from the publisher for US$40 (£20), plus postage: Tropical Island Publishers, P.O. Box 12, Adelphia, NJ 07710 (© **877/923-9653;** www.yachtsmansguide.com).

Experienced sailors with a sea-wise crew can charter **"bareboat"** (a fully equipped boat with no crew). You're on your own, and you'll have to prove you can handle it before you're allowed to take out such a craft. You may want to take along an experienced yachter familiar with local waters, which may be tricky in some places.

Most yachts are rented on a weekly basis. Contact **Abaco Bahamas Charters** (© **800/626-5690** or 242/366-0151; www.abacocharters.com) or the **Moorings** (© **888/952-8420** or 727/535-1446; www.moorings.com).

5 Money & Costs

It's always advisable to bring money in a variety of forms on a vacation: a mix of cash, credit cards, and traveler's checks. You should also exchange enough petty cash to cover airport incidentals, tipping, and transportation to your hotel before you leave home, or withdraw money upon arrival at an airport ATM.

In many international destinations, ATMs offer the best exchange rates. Avoid exchanging money at commercial exchange bureaus and hotels, which often have the highest transaction fees.

CURRENCY

The currency is the **Bahamian dollar (B$1),** pegged to the U.S. dollar so that they're always equivalent. (In fact, U.S. dollars are accepted widely throughout The Bahamas.) There is no restriction on bringing foreign currency into The Bahamas. Most large hotels and stores accept traveler's checks, but you may have trouble using a personal check. It's a good idea to exchange enough money to cover airport incidentals and transportation to your hotel before you leave home.

Be sure to carry some small bills or loose change when traveling. Petty cash will come in handy for tipping and public transportation. Consider keeping the change separate from your larger bills so that it's readily accessible and you'll be less of a target for theft. In general, prices are about the same as in urban America, but they are less expensive than costs in the U.K. Food is often more expensive, however, since so much of it has to be imported.

ATMs

The easiest way to get cash away from home is from an ATM (automated teller machine). The **Cirrus** (© **800/424-7787;** www.mastercard.com) and **PLUS** (© **800/843-7587;** www.visa.com) networks span the globe; look at the back of your bank card to see which network you're on and then call or check online for ATM locations at your destination. Know your personal identification number (PIN) and your daily withdrawal limit. Ask your card carrier if your current PIN works in The Bahamas, particularly in the Out Islands. Every card is different, but some need a four-digit rather than a six-digit PIN to withdraw cash abroad.

Many banks impose a fee every time a card is used at a different bank's ATM, and that fee can be higher for international transactions (up to US$5/£2.50 or more) than for domestic ones (rarely more than US$1.50/75p). On top of this, the bank from which you withdraw cash may charge its own fee. To compare

The Bahamian & U.S. Dollars vs. the British Pound, the Euro & the Canadian Dollar

The chart inserted below reflects the figures in the paragraphs above, but because international currency ratios can and almost certainly will change prior to your arrival in The Bahamas, you should confirm up-to-date currency rates before your departure.

US$/B$	UK£	Euro	C$	US$/B$	UK£	Euro	C$
1	0.50	1.45	1.00	75	37.50	108.75	75.00
2	1.00	2.90	2.00	100	50.00	145.00	100.00
3	1.50	4.35	3.00	125	62.50	181.25	125.00
4	2.00	5.80	4.00	150	75.00	217.50	150.00
5	2.50	7.25	5.00	175	87.50	253.75	175.00
6	3.00	8.70	6.00	200	100.00	290.00	200.00
7	3.50	10.15	7.00	225	112.50	326.25	225.00
8	4.00	11.60	8.00	250	125.00	362.50	250.00
9	4.50	13.05	9.00	275	137.50	398.75	275.00
10	5.00	14.50	10.00	300	150.00	435.00	300.00
15	7.50	21.75	15.00	350	175.00	507.50	350.00
20	10.00	29.00	20.00	400	200.00	580.00	400.00
25	12.50	36.25	25.00	500	250.00	725.00	500.00
50	25.00	72.50	50.00	1,000	500.00	1,450.00	1,000.00

banks' ATM fees within the U.S., use **www.bankrate.com**. For international withdrawal fees, ask your bank.

You can also get cash advances on your credit card at an ATM. Credit card companies do try to protect themselves from theft by limiting the funds someone can withdraw outside their home country, so notify your credit card company before you leave home. And keep in mind that you'll pay interest from the moment of your withdrawal, even if you pay your monthly bills on time.

On New Providence Island and Paradise Island, there are plenty of ATMs, including one at the Nassau International Airport. There are far fewer ATMs on Grand Bahama Island (Freeport/Lucaya), but those that are here are strategically located—including ones at the airport and the casino (of course).

Very few ATMs are in the Out Islands. If you must have cash on your Out Island trip, make arrangements before you leave Nassau or Freeport; outside of Freeport, we counted just seven ATMs in the entire remaining Out Islands, including the one at the post office in Marsh Harbour. This situation is fluid, however, and more ATMs may be added in the future.

CREDIT CARDS

Credit cards are another safe way to carry money, but their use has become more difficult, especially in The Bahamas. They also provide a convenient record of all your expenses, and they generally offer relatively good exchange rates. You can usually withdraw cash advances from your credit cards at banks or ATMs, provided you know your PIN. Keep in mind that you'll pay interest from the moment

What Things Cost in Nassau/Paradise Island	US/B$	UK£
Taxi from airport to Paradise Island	30.00	15.00
Taxi from airport to Nassau Center	22.00	11.00
Average bus fare	1.00	.50
Ferry between Nassau and Paradise Island	4.00	2.00
Moped rentals at Bowcar Scooter	60.00	30.00
Double room at One&Only Ocean Club (very expensive)	765.00	382.50
Double room at British Colonial (expensive)	269.00	134.50
Double room at Orange Hill Beach Inn (moderate)	125.00	62.50
Double room at Quality Inn Junkanoo Beach Nassau (inexpensive)	111.00	55.50
Two-tank dive at Bahamas Divers	99.00	49.50
18 holes at Ocean Club Golf Club	260.00	130.00
1 hour of tennis at Atlantis	20.00	10.00
Lunch at Poop Deck (moderate)	24.00	12.00
Lunch at Café Skans (inexpensive)	12.00	6.00
Dinner at Sun and . . . (expensive)	70.00	35.00
Dinner at Taj Mahal (moderate)	36.00	18.00
Dinner at Travellers Rest (inexpensive)	28.00	14.00
Admission to Ardastra Gardens	15.00	7.50
Tickets to Rain Forest Theater	32.00–40.00	16.00–20.00

of your withdrawal, even if you pay your monthly bills on time. Also, note that many banks now assess a 1% to 3% "transaction fee" on **all** charges you incur abroad (whether you're using the local currency or your native currency).

There is almost no difference in the acceptance of a debit or a standard credit card.

Chip and PIN represent a change in the way that credit and debit cards are used. The program is designed to cut down on the fraudulent use of credit cards. More and more banks are issuing customers Chip and PIN versions of their debit or credit cards. In the future, more and more vendors will be asking for a four-digit personal identification number,

or PIN, which will be entered into a keypad near the cash register. In some cases, a waiter will bring a hand-held model to your table to verify your credit card.

Warning: Some establishments in The Bahamas might not accept your credit card unless you have a computer chip imbedded in it. The reason? To cut down on credit card fraud.

More and more places in The Bahamas are moving from the magnetic-strip credit card to the new chip-and-PIN system.

In the changeover in technology, some retailers have falsely concluded that they can no longer take swipe cards, or can't take signature cards that don't have PINs any more.

For the time being, both the new and old cards are used in shops, hotels, and restaurants regardless of whether they have the old credit and debit card machines or the new chip-and-PIN machines installed.

TRAVELER'S CHECKS

You can buy traveler's checks at most banks. They are offered in denominations of US$20, US$50, US$100, US$500, and sometimes US$1,000. Generally, you'll pay a service charge ranging from 1% to 4%.

The most popular traveler's checks are offered by **American Express** (© 800/ 528-4800 or 221-7282 for cardholders—this number accepts collect calls, offers service in several foreign languages, and exempts Amex gold and platinum cardholders from the 1% fee), **Visa** (© 800/732-1322; AAA members can obtain Visa checks for a US$9.95 fee— for checks up to US$1,500—at most AAA offices or by calling © 866/339-3378), and **MasterCard** (© 800/223-9920).

Be sure to keep a record of the traveler's checks' serial numbers separate from your checks in the event that they are stolen or lost. You'll get a refund faster if you know the numbers.

American Express, Thomas Cook, Visa, and **MasterCard** offer **foreign currency traveler's checks,** useful if you're traveling to one country or to the euro zone; they're accepted at locations where dollar checks may not be.

Another option is the new prepaid traveler's check cards, reloadable cards that work much like debit cards but aren't linked to your checking account. The **American Express Travelers Cheque Card,** for example, requires a minimum deposit, sets a maximum balance, and has a one-time issuance fee of US$15. You can withdraw money from an ATM (for a fee of US$2.50 per transaction, not including bank fees), and the funds can be purchased in dollars, euros, or pounds. If you lose the card, your available funds will be refunded within 24 hours.

6 Health

STAYING HEALTHY

We list **hospital** and **emergency numbers** under "Fast Facts," in each chapter. Even on the remotest island, you'll find, if not a hospital, a local medicine man (or woman, in many cases). Many Bahamians are fond of herbal remedies. But you don't need to rely on these primitive treatments, as most resorts have either hospitals or clinics on-site.

The major health risk here is not tropical disease, as it is in some Caribbean islands, but rather the bad luck of ingesting a bad piece of shellfish, exotic fruit, or too many rum punches. If your body is not accustomed to some of these foods or they haven't been cleaned properly, you may suffer diarrhea. If you tend to have digestive problems, then drink bottled water and avoid ice, unpasteurized milk, and uncooked food such as fresh salads. However, fresh food served in hotels is usually safe to eat.

The Bahamas has excellent medical facilities. Physicians and surgeons in private practice are readily available in Nassau, Cable Beach, and Freeport/ Lucaya. A dozen or so health centers are in the Out Islands. Medical personnel hold satellite clinics periodically in small settlements, and there are about 35 other clinics, adding up to a total of approximately 50 health facilities throughout the outlying islands. (We've listed the names and telephone numbers of specific clinics in the individual island coverage that follows throughout this book.) If intensive or urgent care is required, patients are

Healthy Travels to You

The following government websites offer health-related travel advice:

- **Australia:** www.dfat.gov.au/travel
- **Canada:** www.hc-sc.gc.ca/index_e.html
- **U.K.:** www.dh.gov.uk
- **U.S.:** www.cdc.gov/travel

brought by the Emergency Flight Service to **Princess Margaret Hospital** (② 242/322-2861) on Shirley Street, Nassau. Some of the big resort hotels have in-house physicians or can quickly secure one for you.

There is also a government-operated hospital, **Rand Memorial** (② 242/352-6735), on East Atlantic Drive, Freeport, and several government-operated clinics on Grand Bahama Island. Nassau and Freeport/Lucaya also have private hospitals.

Dentists are plentiful in Nassau, somewhat less so on Grand Bahama. You'll find dentists on Great Abaco Island, at Marsh Harbour, at Treasure Cay, and on Eleuthera. There aren't dentists on some of the remote islands, especially those in the Southern Bahamas, but hotel staff should know where to send you for emergencies.

Contact the **International Association for Medical Assistance to Travellers** (**IAMAT;** ② 716/754-4883, or 416/652-0137 in Canada; **www.iamat.org**) for tips on travel and health concerns in the countries you're visiting, and for lists of local English-speaking doctors. The United States **Centers for Disease Control and Prevention** (② 800/311-3435 or 404/498-1515; www.cdc.gov) provides up-to-date information on health hazards by region or country and offers tips on food safety. The website **www.tripprep.com**, sponsored by a consortium of travel medicine practitioners, may also offer helpful advice on traveling abroad. You can find listings of reliable clinics overseas at the **International Society of Travel Medicine** (www.istm.org).

COMMON AILMENTS

EXPOSURE TO THE SUN Getting too much sun can be a real issue in The Bahamas. You must, of course, take the usual precautions you would anywhere against sunburn and sunstroke. Your time in the sun should be wisely limited for the first few days until you become accustomed to the more intense rays of the Bahamian sun. Also bring and use strong UVA/UVB sunblock products.

WHAT TO DO IF YOU GET SICK AWAY FROM HOME

In most cases, your existing health plan will provide the coverage you need. But double-check; you may want to buy **travel medical insurance** instead (see the section on insurance in the appendix). Bring your insurance ID card with you wherever you travel.

We list **hospitals** and **emergency numbers** under "Fast Facts" in each chapter.

If you suffer from a chronic illness, consult your doctor before your departure. Pack **prescription medications** in your carry-on luggage, and carry them in their original containers, with pharmacy labels—otherwise, they won't make it through airport security. Carry the generic name of prescription medicines, in case a local pharmacist doesn't know the brand name.

For travel abroad, you may have to pay medical costs upfront and be reimbursed later. See "Medical Insurance," under "Insurance," in the appendix.

7 Safety

STAYING SAFE

When going to Nassau (New Providence), Cable Beach, Paradise Island, or Freeport/Lucaya, exercise the same caution you would if visiting Miami. Whatever you do, if people peddling drugs approach you, steer clear of them.

Crime is increasing, and visitors should use caution and good judgment when visiting The Bahamas. While most criminal incidents take place in a part of Nassau not usually frequented by tourists (the "Over-the-Hill" area south of downtown), crime and violence have moved into more upscale tourist and residential areas.

Women, especially, should take caution if walking alone on the streets of Nassau after dark, particularly if those streets appear to be deserted.

In the last year, the U.S. Embassy has received several reports of sexual assaults, including some against teenage girls. Most assaults have been perpetrated against intoxicated young women, some of whom were reportedly drugged. To minimize the potential for sexual assault, the embassy recommends that young women stay in groups, consume alcohol in moderation, and not accept rides or drinks from strangers.

Pickpockets (often foreigners) work the crowded casino floors of both Paradise Beach and Cable Beach. See that your wallet, money, and valuables are well secured.

Travelers should avoid walking alone after dark or in isolated areas, and avoid placing themselves in situations in which they are alone with strangers. Be cautious on deserted areas of beaches at all hours. Don't leave valuables such as cameras and purses lying unattended on the beach while you go for a swim.

If you're driving a rental car, always make sure your car door is locked, and never leave possessions in view.

Hotel guests should always lock their doors and should never leave valuables unattended, especially on beaches. Visitors should store passport/identity documents, airline tickets, credit cards, and extra cash in hotel safes. Avoid wearing expensive jewelry, particularly Rolex watches, which criminals have specifically targeted. Use only clearly marked taxis and make a note of the license plate number for your records.

You're less likely to be mugged or robbed in the Out Islands, where life is generally more peaceful. There are some hotels there that, even today, don't have locks on the doors.

The loss or theft of a passport overseas should be reported to the local police and the nearest embassy or consulate. A lost or stolen birth certificate and/or driver's license generally cannot be replaced outside the United States. U.S. citizens may refer to the Department of State's pamphlets, *A Safe Trip Abroad* and *Tips for Travelers to the Caribbean,* for ways to promote a trouble-free journey. The pamphlets are available by mail from the Superintendent of Documents, U.S. Government Printing Office, Washington, DC 20402; via the Internet at www.gpoaccess.gov/index.html; or via the Bureau of Consular Affairs home page at www.travel.state.gov.

8 Specialized Travel Resources

TRAVELERS WITH DISABILITIES

A disability should not stop anyone from traveling to the Bahamian islands. Because these islands are relatively flat, it is fairly easy to get around, even for persons with disabilities.

Many travel agencies offer customized tours and itineraries for travelers with disabilities. Among them are **Flying Wheels Travel** (☎ 507/451-5005; www.flyingwheelstravel.com), **Access-Able Travel Source** (☎ 303/232-2979; www.access-able.com), and **Accessible Journeys** (☎ 800/846-4537 or 610/521-0339; www.disabilitytravel.com).

Organizations that offer assistance to travelers with disabilities include **Moss-Rehab** (☎ 800/225-5667; www.mossresourcenet.org), the **American Foundation for the Blind** (AFB; ☎ 800/232-5463 or 212/502-7600; www.afb.org), and **SATH** (Society for Accessible Travel & Hospitality; ☎ 212/447-7284; www.sath.org). **AirAmbulanceCard.com** (☎ 877/424-7633) is partnered with SATH and allows you to preselect top hospitals in case of an emergency.

Also check out the quarterly magazine *Emerging Horizons* (www.emerginghorizons.com) and *Open World* magazine, published by SATH.

TIPS FOR BRITISH TRAVELERS WITH DISABILITIES Contact the Royal Association for Disability and Rehabilitation (RADAR), Unit 12, City Forum, 250 City Rd., London, EC1V 8AF (☎ 020/7250-3222; www.radar.org.uk).

For more on organizations that offer resources to travelers with disabilities, go to www.frommers.com.

GAY & LESBIAN TRAVELERS

Generally speaking, The Bahamas isn't a gay-friendly destination. Think twice before choosing to vacation here. Although many gay people visit or live here, the country has very strict antihomosexual laws. Relations between homosexuals, even when between consenting adults, are subject to criminal sanctions carrying prison terms. If you would like to make visiting gay beaches, bars, or clubs part of your vacation, consider South Miami Beach, Key West, or Puerto Rico instead.

Of course, the big resorts welcome one and all, even if forced to do so. For many years, the all-inclusive Sandals Royal Bahamian on Cable Beach refused to accept same-sex couples and booked only heterosexual guests. However, rights groups in Canada and Great Britain lobbied successfully, and the Sandals people found they could no longer advertise their resorts, and their discriminatory policies, in those countries. As a result, Sandals capitulated and ended its previous ban. However, gay and lesbian couples looking for a carefree holiday should seriously consider whether they want to spend their hard-earned dollars in a resort like Sandals that did not voluntarily end its ban against homosexuals until forced to do so by more liberal and far-sighted governments.

Single gays and gay couples should travel here with great discretion. If you're intent on visiting, the **International Gay & Lesbian Travel Association** (IGLTA; ☎ 954/776-2626; www.iglta.org) is the trade association for the gay and lesbian travel industry, and offers an online directory of gay- and lesbian-friendly travel businesses; go to their website and click on "Members."

Many agencies offer tours and travel itineraries specifically for gay and lesbian travelers. Among them are **Above and**

Beyond Tours (© 800/397-2681; www.abovebeyondtours.com), **Now, Voyager** (© 800/255-6951; www.nowvoyager.com), and **Olivia Cruises & Resorts** (© 800/631-6277; www.olivia.com).

Gay.com Travel (© 415/834-6500; www.gay.com/travel or www.outandabout.com) is an excellent online successor to the popular *Out & About* print magazine. It provides regularly updated information about gay-owned, gay-oriented, and gay-friendly lodging, dining, sightseeing, nightlife, and shopping establishments in every important destination worldwide.

The following travel guides are available at many bookstores, or you can order them from any online bookseller: *Spartacus International Gay Guide* (Bruno Gmünder Verlag; www.spartacusworld.com/gayguide) and *Odysseus: The International Gay Travel Planner* (Odysseus Enterprises Ltd.); and the *Damron* guides (www.damron.com), with separate annual books for gay men and lesbians. For more gay and lesbian travel resources, go to www.frommers.com.

SENIOR TRAVEL

In The Bahamas, the standard adult rate usually applies to everyone over 21 years of age. The careful, frugal travel shopper, however, might find some deals if arrangements are made before you go.

Members of **AARP** (formerly known as the American Association of Retired Persons), 601 E St. NW, Washington, DC 20049 (© 888/687-2277; www.aarp.org), get discounts on hotels, airfares, and car rentals. AARP offers members a range of benefits, including *AARP The Magazine* and a monthly newsletter. Anyone over 50 can join.

Many reliable agencies and organizations target the 50-plus market. **Elderhostel** (© 800/454-5768; www.elderhostel.org) arranges study programs for those aged 55 and over.

Recommended publications offering travel resources and discounts for seniors include the quarterly magazine *Travel 50 & Beyond* (www.travel50andbeyond.com); *Travel Unlimited: Uncommon Adventures for the Mature Traveler* (Avalon); *101 Tips for Mature Travelers,* available from Grand Circle Travel (© 800/959-0405 or 617/350-7500; www.gct.com); and *Unbelievably Good Deals and Great Adventures That You Absolutely Can't Get Unless You're Over 50* (McGraw-Hill), by Joan Rattner Heilman. For more information and resources about travel for seniors, go to www.frommers.com.

FAMILY TRAVEL

The Bahamas is one of the top family-vacation destinations in North America. The smallest toddlers can spend blissful hours on sandy beaches and in the shallow seawater, or in swimming pools constructed with them in mind. There's no end to the fascinating pursuits offered for older children, ranging from boat rides to shell collecting, to horseback riding, hiking, or even dancing. Some children are old enough to learn to snorkel and to explore an underwater wonderland. Some resorts will even teach kids to swim or windsurf.

Most families with kids head for New Providence (Nassau), Paradise Island, or Grand Bahama Island (Freeport). Look for our "Kids" icon, indicating attractions, restaurants, or hotels and resorts that are especially family-friendly. See also "The Best Family Vacations," in chapter 1, for additional recommendations.

Every country's regulations differ, but in general, children traveling abroad should have plenty of documentation on hand, particularly if they're traveling with someone other than their own parents (in which case a notarized form letter from a parent is often required).

For details on entry requirements for children traveling abroad, go to the U.S. State Department website (http://travel.state.gov).

Recommended family travel websites include **TravelwithYourKids.com, Family Travel Forum** (www.familytravelforum.com), **Family Travel Network** (www.familytravelnetwork.com), and **Family Travel Files** (www.thefamilytravelfiles.com). For a list of more family-friendly travel resources, turn to the experts at www.frommers.com.

WOMEN TRAVELERS

Should a woman travel alone to The Bahamas? Opinions and reports vary. A woman traveling alone in such countries as Jamaica faces certain dangers, and safety is often an issue. Women traveling alone in The Bahamas rarely encounter aggressive, potentially dangerous behavior from males and are usually treated with respect. However, some Bahamian men may assume that a woman traveling alone is doing so in order to find a male partner. To avoid such unwanted attention, dress a bit conservatively and don't go wandering the streets of Nassau unescorted at night. It's always advisable to wear a cover-up to your swimsuit when leaving the beach and heading into town. For additional details, see "Staying Safe," above.

Women Welcome Women World Wide (5W; © 01494/465441; www.womenwelcomewomen.org.uk) works to foster international friendships by enabling women of different countries to visit one another (men can come along on the trips; they just can't join the club). It's a big, active organization, with more than 3,500 members from all walks of life in some 70 countries.

Also check out the award-winning website **Journeywoman** (www.journeywoman.com), a "real life" women's travel-information network where you can sign up for a free e-mail newsletter and get advice on everything from etiquette to safety; or the travel guide *Safety and Security for Women Who Travel,* by Sheila Swan and Peter Laufer (Travelers' Tales, Inc.), offering common-sense tips on safe travel. For general travel resources for women, go to www.frommers.com.

AFRICAN-AMERICAN TRAVELERS

Black Travel Online (www.blacktravelonline.com) posts news on upcoming events and includes links to articles and travel-booking sites. **Soul of America** (www.soulofamerica.com) is a comprehensive website, with travel tips, event and family-reunion postings, and sections on historically black beach resorts and active vacations.

Agencies and organizations that provide resources for black travelers include **Rodgers Travel (© 800/825-1775;** www.rodgerstravel.com) and the **African American Association of Innkeepers International (© 877/422-5777;** www.africanamericaninns.com). For more information, check out the following collections and guides: *Go Girl: The Black Woman's Book of Travel & Adventure* (Eighth Mountain Press), a compilation of travel essays by writers including Jill Nelson and Audre Lorde; *The African-American Travel Guide,* by Wayne Robinson (Hunter Publishing; www.hunterpublishing.com); *Steppin' Out,* by Carla Labat (Avalon); and *Pathfinders Travel (© 215/438-2140;* www.pathfinderstravel.com), which includes articles on everything from Rio de Janeiro to Ghana, as well as information on upcoming ski, diving, golf, and tennis trips.

SINGLE TRAVELERS

Single tourists often find the dating scene better in The Bahamas during the winter when there are more visitors, especially unattached ones.

Frommers.com: The Complete Travel Resource

For an excellent travel-planning resource, we highly recommend **Frommers. com** (www.frommers.com), which *PC Magazine* named the best travel website. We're a little biased, of course, but we guarantee that you'll find its travel tips, reviews, monthly vacation giveaways, bookstore, and online-booking capabilities thoroughly indispensable.

On package vacations, single travelers are often hit with a "single supplement" to the base price. To avoid it, you can agree to room with other single travelers or find a compatible roommate before you go, from one of the many roommate-locator agencies.

TravelChums (www.travelchums.com) is an Internet-only travel-companion matching service with elements of an online-personals-type site, hosted by the respected New York–based Shaw Guides travel service. Many reputable tour companies offer singles-only trips.

For more information, check out Eleanor Berman's guide *Traveling Solo: Advice and Ideas for More Than 250 Great Vacations* (Globe Pequot), with advice on traveling alone, either solo or as part of a group tour. For more information on traveling single, go to www. frommers.com.

9 Sustainable Tourism

Sustainable tourism is conscientious travel. It means being careful in the environments you explore, and respecting the communities you visit. Two overlapping components of sustainable travel are **ecotourism** and **ethical tourism**. The **International Ecotourism Society (TIES)** defines eco-tourism as responsible travel to natural areas that conserves the environment and improves the well-being of local people. TIES suggests that eco-tourists follow these principles:

- Minimize environmental impact.
- Build environmental and cultural awareness and respect.
- Provide positive experiences for both visitors and hosts.
- Provide direct financial benefits for conservation and for local people.
- Raise sensitivity to host countries' political, environmental, and social climates.
- Support international human rights and labor agreements.

You can find some eco-friendly travel tips and statistics, as well as touring companies and associations—listed by destination under "Travel Choice"—at the TIES website, www.ecotourism.org. Also check out **Ecotravel.com,** which lets you search for sustainable touring companies in several categories (water-based, land-based, spiritually oriented, and so on).

While much of the focus of ecotourism is about reducing impacts on the natural environment, ethical tourism concentrates on ways to preserve and enhance local economies and communities, regardless of location. You can embrace ethical tourism by staying at a locally owned hotel or shopping at a store that employs local workers and sells locally produced goods.

Responsible Travel (www.responsible travel.com) is a great source of sustainable travel ideas; the site is run by a spokesperson for ethical tourism in the travel industry. **Sustainable Travel International** (www.sustainabletravelinternational.org) promotes ethical tourism practices and manages an extensive directory of sustainable properties and tour operators around the world.

In the U.K., **Tourism Concern** (www.tourismconcern.org.uk) works to reduce social and environmental problems connected to tourism. The **Association of Independent Tour Operators** (AITO; www.aito.co.uk) is a group of specialist operators leading the field in making holidays sustainable.

Volunteer travel has become popular among those who want to venture beyond the standard group-tour experience to learn languages, interact with locals, and make a positive difference while on vacation. Volunteer travel usually doesn't require special skills—just a willingness to work hard—and programs vary in length from a few days to a number of weeks. Some programs provide free housing and food, but many require volunteers to pay for travel expenses, which can add up quickly.

For general info on volunteer travel, visit **www.volunteerabroad.org** and **www.idealist.org**.

Before you commit to a volunteer program, it's important to make sure any money you're giving is truly going back to the local community, and that the work you'll be doing will be a good fit for you. **International Volunteer Programs Association** (www.volunteerinternational.org) has a helpful list of questions to ask to determine the intentions and the nature of a volunteer program.

10 Packages for the Independent Traveler

Before you search for the lowest airfare on your own (see earlier in this chapter), you may want to consider booking your flight as part of a package deal—a way to travel independently but pay group rates.

A package tour is not an escorted tour, in which you're led around by a guide. Except by cruise ships visiting certain islands, the option of being escorted around six or so Bahamian islands on an escorted tour does not exist.

Package tours are simply a way to buy the airfare, accommodations, and other elements of your trip (such as car rentals, airport transfers, and sometimes even activities) at the same time and often at discounted prices.

One good source of package deals is the airlines themselves. Most major airlines offer air/land packages, including **American Airlines Vacations** (© 800/321-2121; www.aavacations.com), **Delta Vacations** (© 800/654-6559; www.deltavacations.com), **Continental Airlines Vacations** (© 800/301-3800; www.covacations.com), and **United Vacations** (© 888/854-3899; www.unitedvacations.com). Several big **online travel agencies**—Expedia, Travelocity, Orbitz, Site59, and Lastminute.com—also do a brisk business in packages.

Liberty Travel (© **888/271-1584;** www.libertytravel.com) is one of the biggest packagers in the U.S. Northeast, and it usually boasts a full-page ad in Sunday papers. There's also **TourScan, Inc.,** 1051 Boston Post Rd., Darien, CT 06820 (© **800/962-2080** in the U.S.; www.tourscan.com), which researches the best-value vacation at each hotel and condo.

For British travelers, package tours to The Bahamas can be booked through **Kuoni Travel,** Kuoni House, Dorking, Surrey RH5 4AZ (© **01306/744-444;** www.kuoni.co.uk), which offers both land and air packages to destinations such as Nassau and Freeport, and to some places in the Out Islands. They also offer packages for self-catering villas on Paradise Island.

For an all-inclusive package, **Just-A-Vacation, Inc.,** 15501 Ebbynside Ct., Bowie, MD 20716 (🕾 **301/559-0510;** www.justavacation.com), specializes in all-inclusive resorts on the islands of The Bahamas, plus other destinations in the Caribbean, including Barbados, Jamaica, Aruba, St. Lucia, and Antigua. **Club Med** (🕾 **888/WEB-CLUB** [932-2582]; www.clubmed.com) has various all-inclusive options throughout the Caribbean and The Bahamas.

Travel packages are also listed in the travel section of your local Sunday newspaper. Or check ads in the national travel magazines, such as *Arthur Frommer's Budget Travel Magazine, Travel + Leisure, National Geographic Traveler,* and *Condé Nast Traveler.*

11 The Active Vacation Planner

The more than 700 islands in the Bahamian archipelago (fewer than 30 of which are inhabited) are surrounded by warm, clear waters—ideal for fishing, sailing, and scuba diving. (Detailed recommendations and the costs of these activities are previewed under the individual destinations listings.) The country's perfect weather and its many cooperative local entrepreneurs allow easy access to more than 30 sports throughout the islands.

WATERSPORTS

FISHING   The shallow waters between the hundreds of cays and islands of The Bahamas are some of the most fertile fishing grounds in the world. Even waters where marine traffic is relatively congested have yielded impressive catches in the past, although overfishing has depleted schools of fish, especially big-game fish. Grouper, billfish, wahoo, tuna, and dozens of other species thrive in Bahamian waters, and dozens of charter boats are available for deep-sea fishing.

Frontiers International (🕾 **800/245-1950** or 724/935-1577; www.frontiers trvl.com) features fly- and spin-fishing tours of The Bahamas and is a specialist in saltwater-fishing destinations. In addition, reef fishing, either from small boats or from shorelines, is popular everywhere, with grouper, snapper, and barracuda being the most commonly caught species.

Specialists and serious amateurs of the sport often head for any of the following destinations.

The island of **Bimini** is known as the "Big-Game Fishing Capital of the World." Here anglers can hunt for the increasingly elusive swordfish, sailfish, and marlin. For tournament listings, see the "Bahamas Calendar of Events," earlier in this chapter. Bimini maintains its own Hall of Fame, where proud anglers have their catches honored. World records for the size of catches don't seem to last long here; they are usually quickly surpassed.

Walker's Cay in the Abacos and **Chub Cay** in the Berry Islands are famous for both deep-sea and shore fishing. Some anglers return to these cays year after year. Grouper, jacks, and snapper are plentiful. Even spearfishing without scuba gear is common and popular.

Andros boasts the world's best bonefishing. Bonefish (also known as "gray fox") are medium-size fish that feed in shallow, well-lit waters. Known as some of the most tenacious fish in the world, they struggle ferociously against anglers who pride themselves on using light lines from shallow-draft boats. **Andros Island Bonefish Club** in North Andros (🕾 **242/368-5167;** www.androsbonefishing.com) specializes in fishing adventures off some of the most remote and sparsely populated coastlines in the country.

SAILING The Bahamas is one of the top yachting destinations in the Atlantic. Its more than 700 islands and well-developed marinas provide a spectacular and practical backdrop for sailing enthusiasts. For a listing of frequent regattas, see the "Bahamas Calendar of Events," earlier in this chapter. The mini archipelago of the **Abacos** is called "The Sailing Capital of the World." You might think it deserves the title until you've sailed the **Exumas,** which we think are even better.

Don't be dismayed if you don't own a yacht. All sizes and types of crafts, from dinghies to blue-water cruisers, are available for charter, and crew and captain are optional for experienced sailors. If your dreams involve experiencing the seagoing life for an afternoon or less, many hotels offer sightseeing cruises aboard catamarans or glass-bottom boats, often with the opportunity to snorkel or swim in the wide-open sea.

The Abacos have many marinas. The best arrangements for boating can be made at **Abaco Bahamas Charters** (© 800/626-5690 or 242/366-0151; www.abacocharters.com) and at the **Moorings** (© 888/952-8420 or 727/535-1446; www.moorings.com). In the Exumas it's difficult to rent boats because most yachters arrive with their own.

SCUBA DIVING The unusual marine topography of The Bahamas offers an astonishing variety of options for divers. Throughout the more than 700 islands are innumerable reefs, drop-offs, coral gardens, caves, and shipwrecks. In many locations, you may feel that you are the first human ever to explore the site. Since fewer than 30 of the Bahamian islands are inhabited, you can usually dive in pristine and uncrowded splendor.

Andros Island boasts the third-largest barrier reef in the world. Chub Cay, in the Berry Islands, and Riding Rock, San Salvador, also offer premium spots to take a plunge in an underwater world teeming with aquatic life. The intricate layout of the Exumas includes virtually every type of underwater dive site, very few of which have ever been explored. The Abacos, famous for yachting, and the extensive reefs off the coast of Freeport are also fabulous dive sites.

Freeport, incidentally, is home to the country's most famous and complete diving operation, **UNEXSO** (© 800/992-DIVE or 242/373-1244; www.unexso.com). It offers a 5.2m-deep (17-ft.) swimming pool where divers can work toward certification, and the popular "Dolphin Experience," in which visitors are allowed to pet, swim, snorkel, and dive with these remarkable animals.

You can easily learn to dive for the first time in The Bahamas. Lots of Bahamian hotels offer resort courses for novices, usually enabling a beginner to dive with a guide after several hours of instruction. You'll probably start out in the swimming pool for your initial instruction and then go out with a guide from the beach. A license (called a certification card, or "C" card) proving the successful completion of a designated program of scuba study is legally required for solo divers. Many resort hotels and dive shops offer the necessary 5-day training course. Participants who successfully complete the courses are awarded certifications by diving organizations such as PADI or NAUI.

For useful information, check out the website of the Professional Association of Diving Instructors (PADI) at www.padi.com. You'll find a description of the best dive sites and a list of PADI-certified dive operators. *Rodale's Scuba Diving Magazine* also has a helpful website at www.scubadiving.com. Both sites list dive-package specials and display gorgeous color photos of some of the most beautiful dive spots in the world.

SEA KAYAKING If you want to explore the pristine Exumas National Land and Sea Park, a spectacular natural area consisting of 365 mostly uninhabited cays that may be more impressive than anything in the Caribbean, **Ibis Tours** is your best bet. They'll take you on sea-kayaking itineraries that allow lots of time to enjoy the area's white-sand beaches and numerous reefs. You can also snorkel along the way. An 8-day trip leaving from Nassau costs US$1,795 (£898). For more information, contact Ibis (© **914/409-5961;** www.ibistours.com).

OTHER ACTIVITIES

BIKE & SCOOTER RENTALS Most biking or scooter riding is done either on New Providence Island (Nassau) or on Grand Bahama Island; both have relatively flat terrain. Biking is best on Grand Bahama Island because it's bigger, with better roads and more places to go. Getting around New Providence Island is relatively easy once you're out of the congestion of Nassau and Cable Beach. In Nassau many hotels will rent you a bike or motor scooter.

On Grand Bahama Island, you can rent bikes at most big hotels (see chapter 6 for phone numbers and addresses of hotels). You can also rent motor scooters starting at about US$60 (£30) per day. The tourist office at Freeport/Lucaya will outline on a map the best biking routes.

In the Out Islands, roads are usually too bumpy and potholed for much serious biking or scooter riding. Bike-rental places are almost nonexistent unless your hotel has some vehicles.

GOLF The richest pickings are on Grand Bahama Island. The **Reef Course** is the first new golf course to open in The Bahamas since 1969. Designed by Robert Trent Jones, Jr., it features water along 13 of its 18 holes. The oldest course on Grand Bahama Island is the **Lucayan Golf Course,** a wooded course with elevated greens and numerous water hazards designed for precision golf. See chapter 6 for details, and also refer to "The Best Golf Courses," in chapter 1.

Quality golf in The Bahamas, however, is not restricted to Grand Bahama Island. The **Cable Beach Golf Course** is the oldest golf course in the country. The widely publicized **Ocean Club Golf Club** has unusual obstacles—a lion's den and a windmill—which have challenged the skill of both Gary Player and Jack Nicklaus. It also boasts the world's largest sand trap. See chapters 4 and 5 for more information, and also refer to "The Best Golf Courses," in chapter 1.

A spectacular Greg Norman–designed course opened in Great Exuma, part of the massive new **Four Seasons** resort. See chapter 10.

Golf is also available at a course in the Abacos at the **Treasure Cay Golf Club.** The design is challenging, with many panoramic water views and water obstacles. See chapter 8 for more information.

HIKING The Bahamas isn't the greatest destination for serious hikers. The best hiking is on Grand Bahama Island, especially in **Lucayan National Park,** which spreads across 16 hectares (40 acres) and is some 32km (20 miles) from Lucaya. A large map at the entrance to the park outlines the trails. The park is laced with trails and elevated walkways. The highlight of the park is what may be the largest underground cave system in the world, some 11km (6¾ miles) long. Spiral steps let you descend into an eerie underground world.

Also on Grand Bahama Island, the **Rand Memorial Nature Centre** is the second-best place for hiking. It offers some 40 wooded hectares (99 acres) that you can explore on your own or with a tour guide. A .8km (.5 mile) stretch of winding trails acquaints you with the flora and fauna that call Grand Bahama home, everything from a native boa constrictor to the Cuban emerald hummingbird, whose favorite food is the nectar of the hibiscus.

HORSEBACK RIDING The best riding possibilities are at **Pinetree Stables** on Grand Bahama Island (© **242/373-3600** or 305/433-4809; www.pinetree-stables.com). Its escorted eco-tour trail rides are especially interesting. Rides are offered two times a day Tuesday through Sunday; be sure to book rides a few days in advance. See chapter 6 for more information.

Virtually the only place on New Providence Island (Nassau) that offers horseback riding is **Windsor Equestrian Centre & Happy Trails Stables,** Coral Harbour (© **242/362-1820;** www.windsorequestriancentre.com), which features both morning and afternoon trail rides and requires a reservation. These tours include transportation to and from your hotel. The trail rides are guided through the woods and along the beach. See chapter 4 for more information.

Horseback riding is hardly a passion on the other islands.

TENNIS Most tennis courts are part of large resorts and are usually free for the use of registered guests during the day. Charges are imposed to light the courts at night. Nonguests are welcome but are charged a player's fee; they should call in advance to reserve. Larger resorts usually offer on-site pro shops and professional instructors. Court surfaces range from clay or asphalt to such technologically advanced substances as Flexipave and Har-Tru.

New Providence, with more than 80 tennis courts, wins points for offering the greatest number of choices. At least 21 of these lie on Paradise Island. See chapter 5. After New Providence, Grand Bahama has the largest number of courts available for play—almost 40 in all. See chapter 6. Within the Out Islands, tennis courts are available on the Berry Islands, the Abacos, Eleuthera, and the Exumas. See chapters 7, 8, 9, and 10 for more information.

12 Staying Connected

TELEPHONES

Please refer to "Telephones," under "Fast Facts," in the appendix.

Toll-free numbers: Numbers beginning with 08 and followed by 00 are toll-free. But be careful. Numbers that begin with 08 followed by 36 carry a .35€ (50¢/25p) surcharge per minute.

In lieu of the cybercafes that exist in most cities today, in The Bahamas you may have to rely on the good graces of your hotel to get your e-mail, especially in the Out Islands.

CELLPHONES

The three letters that define much of the world's wireless capabilities are GSM (Global System for Mobiles), a big, seamless network that makes for easy cross-border cellphone use in countries worldwide. In general reception is good. In the U.S., T-Mobile, AT&T Wireless,

and Cingular use this quasi-universal system; in Canada, Microcell and some Rogers customers use GSM; and all Europeans and most Australians use GSM.

For many, **renting** a phone is a good idea. While you can rent a phone from any number of overseas sites, including kiosks at airports and at car-rental agencies, we suggest renting the phone before you leave home. North Americans can rent one before leaving home from **InTouch USA** (© **800/872-7626** or 703/222-7161; www.intouchglobal.com) or **Roadpost** (© **888/290-1616** or 905/272-5665; www.roadpost.com). InTouch will also, for free, advise you on whether your existing phone will work overseas.

Buying a phone can be economically attractive, as many nations have cheap prepaid phone systems. Once you arrive

Online Traveler's Toolbox

Veteran travelers usually carry some essential items to make their trips easier. Following is a selection of handy online tools to bookmark and use.

- **Airplane Food** (www.airlinemeals.net)
- **Airplane Seating** (www.seatguru.com and www.airlinequality.com)
- **Foreign Languages for Travelers** (www.travlang.com)
- **Maps** (www.mapquest.com)
- **Time and Date** (www.timeanddate.com)
- **Travel Warnings** (http://travel.state.gov, www.fco.gov.uk/travel, or www. voyage.gc.ca)
- **Universal Currency Converter** (www.xe.com/ucc)
- **Visa ATM Locator** (www.visa.com), **MasterCard ATM Locator** (www. mastercard.com)
- **Weather** (www.intellicast.com and www.weather.com)

at your destination, stop by a local cell-phone shop and get the cheapest package; you'll probably pay less than US$100 for a phone and a starter calling card. Local calls may be as low as 10¢ per minute, and in many countries incoming calls are free.

Wilderness adventurers might consider renting a **satellite phone ("satphone").** It's different from a cellphone in that it connects to satellites and works where there's no cellular signal or ground-based tower. You can rent satellite phones from Roadpost (see above). InTouch USA (see above) offers a wider range of satphones but at higher rates. Per-minute call charges can be even cheaper than roaming charges with a regular cellphone, but the phone itself is more expensive. Satphones are outrageously expensive to buy, so don't even think about it.

INTERNET & E-MAIL
WITH YOUR OWN COMPUTER

More and more hotels, cafes, and retailers are signing on as Wi-Fi (wireless fidelity) "hot spots." Mac owners have their own networking technology: Apple AirPort. **T-Mobile Hotspot** (www.t-mobile.com/ hotspot or www.t-mobile.co.uk) serves up wireless connections at coffee shops nationwide. **Boingo** (www.boingo.com) and **Wayport** (www.wayport.com) have set up networks in airports and high-class hotel lobbies. iPass providers (see below) also give you access to a few hundred wireless hotel lobby setups.

For dial-up access, most business-class hotels offer dataports for laptop modems. In addition, major Internet service providers (ISPs) have **local access numbers** around the world, allowing you to go online by placing a local call. The **iPass** network also has dial-up numbers around the world. You'll have to sign up with an iPass provider, who will then tell you how to set up your computer for your destination(s). For a list of iPass providers, go to www.ipass.com and click on "Individuals Buy Now." One solid provider is **i2Roam** (© **866/811-6209** or 920/233-5863; www.i2roam.com).

Wherever you go, bring a **connection kit** of the right power and phone adapters, a spare phone cord, and a spare Ethernet network cable—or find out whether your hotel supplies them to guests.

WITHOUT YOUR OWN COMPUTER

To find cybercafes check **www.cyber captive.com** and **www.cybercafe.com**.

Aside from formal cybercafes, most **public libraries** have Internet access. Avoid **hotel business centers** unless you're willing to pay exorbitant rates.

Most major airports now have **Internet kiosks** scattered throughout their gates. These give you basic Web access for a per-minute fee that's usually higher than cybercafe prices.

13 Tips on Accommodations

The Bahamas offers a wide selection of accommodations, ranging from small private guesthouses to large luxury resorts. Hotels vary in size and facilities, from deluxe (offering room service, sports, swimming pools, entertainment, and so on) to fairly simple inns.

There are package deals galore, and they are always cheaper than "rack rates." (A rack rate is what an individual pays if he or she literally walks in from the street. These are the rates we've listed in the chapters that follow, though you can almost always do better—especially at the big resorts.) It's sometimes good to go to a reliable travel agent to find out what, if anything, is available in the way of a land-and-air package before booking a particular accommodation. See section 10, "Packages for the Independent Traveler," earlier in this chapter, for details on a number of companies that usually offer good-value packages to The Bahamas.

There is no rigid classification of hotel properties in the islands. The label "deluxe" is often used (or misused) when "first class" might have been a more appropriate term. "First class" itself often isn't. For that and other reasons, we've presented fairly detailed descriptions of the properties so that you'll get an idea of what to expect. However, even in the deluxe and first-class resorts and hotels, don't expect top-rate service and efficiency. When you go to turn on the shower, sometimes you get water and sometimes you don't. You may even experience power failures.

The winter season in The Bahamas runs roughly from the middle of December to the middle of April, and hotels charge their highest prices during this peak period. Winter is generally the dry season in the islands, but there can be heavy rainfall regardless of the time of year. During the winter months, make reservations 2 months in advance if you can. You can't

What the Hotel Symbols Mean

As you're shopping around for your hotel, you may see the following terms used:

- **AP (American Plan):** Includes three meals a day (sometimes called full board or full pension).
- **EP (European Plan):** Includes only the room—no meals.
- **CP (Continental Plan):** Includes continental breakfast of juice, coffee, bread, and jam.
- **MAP (Modified American Plan):** Sometimes called half-board or half-pension, this room rate includes breakfast and dinner (or lunch instead of dinner, if you prefer).

book early enough if you want to travel over Christmas or in February.

The off season in The Bahamas—roughly from mid-April to mid-December (although this varies from hotel to hotel)—amounts to a sale. In most cases, hotel rates are slashed a startling 20% to 60%. It's a bonanza for cost-conscious travelers, especially for families who can travel in the summer. Be prepared for very strong sun, though, plus a higher chance of rain. Also note that hurricane season runs through summer and fall.

MAP VS. AP, OR DO YOU WANT TO GO EP?

All Bahamian resorts offer a **European Plan (EP)** rate, which means that you pay for the price of a room. That leaves you free to dine around at night at various other resorts or restaurants without restriction. Another plan preferred by many is the **Continental Plan (CP),** which means you get a continental breakfast of juice, coffee, bread, and jam included in a set price. This plan is preferred by those who don't like to look around for a place to eat breakfast.

Another major option is the **Modified American Plan (MAP),** which includes breakfast and one main meal of the day, either lunch or dinner. The final choice is the **American Plan (AP),** which includes breakfast, lunch, and dinner. At certain resorts you will save money by booking on either the MAP or AP because discounts are granted. If you dine a la carte often for lunch and dinner, your dining costs will be much higher than if you stay on the MAP or AP.

Dining at your hotel at night cuts down on transportation costs. Taxis especially are expensive. Nonetheless, if dining out and having many different culinary experiences is your idea of a vacation and you're willing to pay the higher price, avoid AP plans or at least make sure the hotel where you're staying has more than one dining room.

One option is to ask if your hotel has a dine-around plan. You might still keep costs in check, but you can avoid a culinary rut by taking your meals in some other restaurants if your hotel has such a plan. Such plans are rare in The Bahamas, which does not specialize in all-inclusive resorts the way that Jamaica or some other islands do.

Before booking a room, check with a good travel agent or investigate on your own what you are likely to save by booking on a dining plan. Under certain circumstances in winter, you might not have a choice if MAP is dictated as a requirement for staying there. It pays to investigate, of course.

THE RIGHT ROOM AT THE RIGHT PRICE

Ask detailed questions when booking a room. Specify your likes and dislikes. There are several logistics of getting the right room in a hotel. In general, back rooms cost less than oceanfront rooms, and lower rooms cost less than upper-floor units. If budget is a major consideration with you, opt for the cheaper rooms. You won't have a great view, but you'll save your money for something else. Just make sure that it isn't next to the all-night drummers.

Of course, all first-class or deluxe resorts feature air-conditioning, but many Bahamian inns do not, especially in the Out Islands. Cooling might be by ceiling fans or, in more modest places, the breeze from an open window, which also brings the mosquitoes. If sleeping in a climate-controlled environment is important to your vacation, check this out in advance.

If you're being your own travel agent, it pays to shop around by calling the local number given for a hotel and its toll-free number, if it has one. You can check online and call a travel agent to see where you can obtain the best price.

Another tip: Ask if you can get an upgrade or a free night's stay if you stay an extra few days. If you're traveling during the "shoulder" periods (between low and high season), you can sometimes get a substantial reduction by delaying your travel plans by a week or 10 days. For example, a US$300 (£150) room booked on April 12 might be lowered to US$180 (£90) by April 17, as mid-April marks the beginning of the low season in The Bahamas.

Transfers from the airports or the cruise dock are included in some hotel bookings, most often in a package plan but usually not in ordinary bookings. This is true of first-class and deluxe resorts, but rarely of medium-priced or budget accommodations. Always ascertain whether transfers (which can be expensive) are included.

When using the facilities at a resort, make sure that you know exactly what is free and what costs money. For example, swimming in the pool is nearly always free, but you might be charged for use of a tennis court. Nearly all watersports cost extra, unless you're booked on some special plan such as a scuba package. Some resorts seem to charge every time you breathe and might end up costing more than a deluxe hotel that includes most everything in the price.

Some hotels are right on the beach. Others involve transfers to the beach by taxi or bus, so factor in transportation costs, which can mount quickly if you stay 5 days to a week.

THE ALL-INCLUSIVES

A hugely popular option in Jamaica, the all-inclusive-resort hotel concept finally has a foothold in The Bahamas. At these resorts, everything is included—sometimes even drinks. You get your room and all meals, plus entertainment and many watersports (although some cost extra).

Some people find the cost of this all-inclusive holiday cheaper than if they'd paid individually for each item, and some simply appreciate knowing in advance what their final bill will be.

The first all-inclusive resort hotel in The Bahamas was **Club Med** (© 888/ **WEB-CLUB** [932-2582]; www.club med.com) on Paradise Island. This is not a swinging-singles kind of place; it's popular with everybody, from honeymooners to families with kids along. There's another mammoth Club Med at Governor's Harbour on Eleuthera. Families with kids like it a lot here, and the resort also attracts scuba divers. There's a third branch in San Salvador, in the Southern Bahamas, which has more of a luxurious hideaway atmosphere.

The biggest all-inclusive of them all, **Sandals** (© 888/SANDALS [726-3257]; www.sandals.com), came to The Bahamas in 1995 on Cable Beach. This Jamaican company is now walking its sandals across the Caribbean, in Ocho Rios, Montego Bay, and Negril. The most famous of the all-inclusives (but not necessarily the best) ended its ban against same-sex couples. See chapter 4 for details on these resorts.

RENTAL VILLAS & VACATION HOMES

You might rent a big villa, a good-size apartment in someone's condo, or even a small beach cottage (more accurately called a cabana).

Private apartments come with or without maid service (ask upfront exactly what to expect). This is a more no-frills option than villas and condos. The apartments may not be in buildings with swimming pools, and they may not have a front desk to help you.

Many cottages or cabanas ideally open onto a beach, although others may be clustered around a communal swimming pool. Most of them are fairly simple, containing only a plain bedroom plus a small kitchen and bathroom. In the peak winter season, reservations should be made at least 5 or 6 months in advance.

Hideaways Aficionado (© **877/843-4433** in the U.S., or 603/430-4433; www.hideaways.com) publishes *Hideaways Life,* a 24-page pictorial directory of home rentals throughout the world, with full descriptions so you know what you're renting. Rentals range from cottages to staffed villas, to whole islands! On most rentals, you deal directly with owners. At condos and small resorts, Hideaways offers member discounts. Other services include specialty cruises, yacht charters, airline ticketing, car rentals, and hotel reservations. Annual membership costs US$185 (£93).

Sometimes local tourist offices will also advise you on vacation-home rentals if you write or call them directly.

THE BAHAMIAN GUESTHOUSE

Many Bahamians stay at a guesthouse when traveling in their own islands. In The Bahamas, however, the term *guesthouse* can mean anything. Sometimes so-called guesthouses are really like simple motels built around swimming pools. Others are small individual cottages with their own kitchenettes, constructed around a main building in which you'll often find a bar and restaurant serving local food.

4

New Providence
(Nassau/Cable Beach)

One million visitors a year make New Providence Island, including Nassau, adjoining Cable Beach, and Paradise Island (which is covered separately in chapter 5) their vacation destination. This is the center of all The Bahamas' action: the best shopping, the best entertainment, the most historic attractions, and some of the best beaches.

The capital of The Bahamas, the historic city of Nassau is a 35-minute flight from Miami. Despite the development and modern hotels, a laid-back tropical atmosphere still pervades the city, so it still offers a good dose of colonial charm. The commercial and banking hub of The Bahamas, as well as a mecca for shoppers, Nassau lies on the north side of New Providence, which is 34km (21 miles) long and 11km (6¾ miles) wide at its greatest point.

Cable Beach, a stretch of sand just west of the city, is lined with luxury resorts—in fact, the Nassau/Cable Beach area has the largest tourist infrastructure in The Bahamas, though Paradise Island wrangles for that spot with another concentration of luxury lodgings. If you want to stay right on the sand, don't choose a hotel in downtown Nassau; head for Cable Beach or Paradise Island. Although you can easily reach the beach from a base in Nassau, it won't be right outside your window.

Nearby Nassau/Cable Beach are an array of watersports, golf, tennis, and plenty of duty-free shops—not to mention those fine powdery beaches. In addition, Paradise Island's resorts, restaurants, and beaches (described in the next chapter), are just a short distance away. Paradise Island, which lies just opposite Nassau, is connected to New Providence Island by a toll bridge. For northbound traffic (that is, from New Providence Island to Paradise Island), the bridge costs US$1 (50p) for cars or taxis and is free for pedestrians. Southbound traffic for all vehicles is free. There's also frequent ferry and water-taxi service between Nassau and Paradise Island.

As the sun goes down, Cable Beach and Paradise Island heat up, offering fine dining, glitzy casinos, cabaret shows, moonlight cruises, dance clubs, and romantic evening strolls. (Though you should probably confine the evening stroll to Cable Beach or Paradise Island, and not the streets of downtown Nassau, which can be dangerous at night.)

The shops might draw a lot more business than the museums, but no city in The Bahamas is as rich in history as Nassau. You can climb up the Queen's Staircase to Fort Fincastle. These 66 steps are said to have been cut in the sandstone cliffs by slaves in the 1790s. Other Nassau attractions include Ardastra Gardens, which feature 2 hectares (5 acres) of landscaping and more than 300 exotic birds, mammals, and reptiles. Most popular are the trained pink flamingos that march for audiences daily to their trainer's commands.

It's surprising that Nassau has retained its overlay of British colonial charm despite its proximity to Florida and the

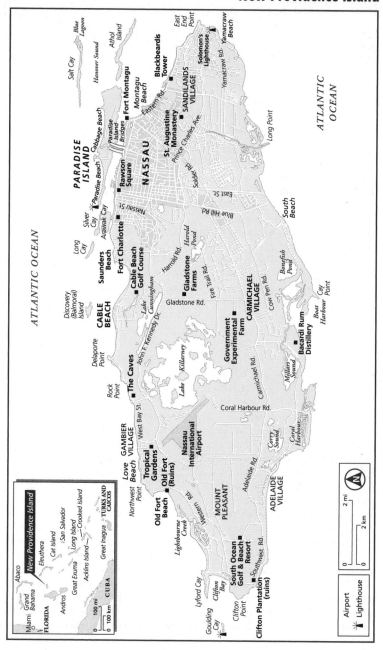

New Providence Island

ATLANTIC OCEAN

ATLANTIC OCEAN

Salt Cay

Blue Lagoon

Athol Island

Hanover Sound

East End Point

Yamacraw Beach

Solomon's Lighthouse

Yamacraw Rd.

Blackbeard's Tower

Fort Montagu

Montagu Beach

SANDILANDS VILLAGE

Eastern Rd.

St. Augustine Monastery

Prince Charles Ave.

NASSAU

PARADISE ISLAND

Cabbage Beach

Paradise Island Bridges

Paradise Beach

Rawson Square

Soldier Rd.

Long Point

Silver Cay

Arawak Cay

Nassau St.

East St.

Long Cay

Fort Charlotte

Saunders Beach

Cable Beach Golf Course

Blue Hill Rd.

Harrold Rd.

Harold Pond

South Beach

Discovery (Balmoral) Island

CABLE BEACH

Gladstone Farms

Fire Trail Rd.

Harrold Rd.

Cunningham

Gladstone Rd.

CARMICHAEL VILLAGE

Cow Pen Rd.

Bonefish Pond

Delaporte Point

The Caves

Lake Cunningham

John F. Kennedy Dr.

Lake Killarney

Government Experimental Farm

Cay Point

Bacardi Rum Distillery

Boat Harbour

Rock Point

Carmichael Rd.

Millars Sound

West Bay St.

Coral Harbour Rd.

Coral Harbour

GAMBIER VILLAGE

Love Beach

Tropical Gardens

Old Fort (Ruins)

Northwest Point

Old Fort Beach

Nassau International Airport

Adelaide Rd.

Corry Sound

Adelaide Village

MOUNT PLEASANT

Western Rd.

Lighthourne Creek

South Ocean Golf & Beach Resort

Southwest Rd.

Lyford Cay

Clifton Bay

Clifton Point

Clifton Plantation (ruins)

Goulding Cay

New Providence Island

Abaco

Grand Bahama

Miami

FLORIDA

Eleuthera

Cat Island

San Salvador

Andros

Great Exuma

Long Island

Crooked Island

Acklins Island

TURKS AND CAICOS

Great Inagua

CUBA

0   100 km
0   100 mi

ATLANTIC OCEAN

N

0   2 mi
0   2 km

Airport

Lighthouse

massive influx of North American business. It still hasn't become completely Americanized, despite new development, traffic, and cruise-ship crowds. Stately old homes and public buildings still stand proudly among the modern high-rises and bland government buildings. Tropical foliage lines streets on which horse-drawn surreys trot by, carrying visitors enjoying leisurely tours. Police officers in white starched jackets and dome-shaped pith helmets direct traffic on the main streets, as they have long done. This could almost be England—but for the weather, that is, and for the staunch and sometimes defiant presence of a deeply entrenched sense of Bahamian nationalism.

1 Orientation

ARRIVING

BY PLANE   Planes land at Nassau's **Lynden Pindling International Airport** (© **242/377-1759**), 13km (8 miles) west of Nassau, in the pine forests beside Lake Killarney.

No bus service goes from the airport to Cable Beach, Nassau, or Paradise Island. Your hotel may provide **airport transfers** if you've made arrangements in advance; these are often included in package deals. You'll find any number of **car-rental** offices here (p. 70), though we don't really think you need one.

If you don't have a lift arranged, take a **taxi** to your hotel. From the airport to the center of Nassau, expect to pay around US$22 (£11); from the airport to Cable Beach, US$15 (£7.50); and from the airport to Paradise Island, US$28 (£14), a rate which includes the bridge toll for passage between New Providence and Paradise islands. Drivers expect to be tipped 15%, and some will remind you should you "forget." You don't need to stop at a currency exchange before departing the airport: U.S. dollars are fine for these (and any other) transactions.

BY CRUISE SHIP   Nassau has spent millions of dollars expanding its port so that a number of cruise ships can come into port at once. Sounds great in theory. Practically speaking, however, facilities in Nassau, Cable Beach, and Paradise Island become extremely overcrowded as soon as the big boats dock. You'll have to stake out your space on the beach, and you'll find downtown streets, shops, and attractions overrun with visitors every day you're in port.

Cruise ships dock near Rawson Square, the heart of the city and the shopping area, and this is the best place to begin a tour of Nassau. Unless you want to go to one of the beach strips along Cable Beach or Paradise Island, you won't need a taxi. You can go on a shopping expedition near where you dock: The Straw Market is nearby, at Market Plaza; Bay Street, the main shopping artery, is also close; and the Nassau International Bazaar is at the intersection of Woodes Rogers Walk and Charlotte Street.

The government has added **Festival Place** (© **242/322-7680**) to the Prince George dock (where cruise ships arrive). Designed as a welcome point and service center for cruise-ship visitors, it's a multicolored structure with about 45 shops selling sundries, gift items, duty-free luxury goods, and Bahamian-themed arts, crafts, and souvenirs. There's also a tourist information booth (© **242/323-3182** or 323-3183) and various snack bars and cafes. You can lounge and have a daiquiri while you listen to the live calypso entertainment, or get your hair braided. This mall-like facility is open daily 8am to 8pm, but if cruise ships are in port, closing may be extended to as late as 10pm. From a point nearby, you can catch a ride by horse and surrey, or take a water taxi across the channel to Paradise Island (p. 114).

Favorite New Providence Experiences

Listening to the sounds of Goombay. At some local joint, you can enjoy an intoxicating beat and such island favorites as Andros-born Elon Moxey's "Catch the Crab," and K.B.'s "Civil Servants" (a satire on The Bahamas' sometimes pervasive governmental bureaucracy). Deeply ingrained in the Bahamian musical psyche is a song that eventually became a huge international hit, "Funky Nassau." Older, more nostalgic tunes include "Goin' Down Burma Road," "Get Involved," and "John B. Sail."

Riding in a horse-drawn surrey. If you'd like to see Nassau as the Duke of Windsor did when he was governor, consider this archaic but charming form of transportation. It's elegant, romantic, and nostalgic. Surreys await passengers at Rawson Square, in the exact center of Nassau.

Taking a glass-bottom boat ride. Right in the middle of Nassau's harbor, numerous boats wait to take you through the colorful sea gardens off New Providence Island. In the teeming reefs, you'll meet all sorts of sea creatures that inhabit this underwater wonderland.

Spending a day on Blue Lagoon Island. It's like an old Hollywood fantasy of a tropical island. Located off the Paradise Island's eastern end, Blue Lagoon Island boasts seven sandy beaches. Boats from the Ferryboat Docks take you there and back.

VISITOR INFORMATION

The Bahamas Ministry of Tourism maintains a **tourist information booth** at Nassau International Airport in the arrivals terminal (© **242/377-6806;** www.bahamas. com). Hours are from 9am to 10pm daily.

Information can also be obtained from the Information Desk at the **Ministry of Tourism's Office,** Bolam House, George Street (© **242/302-2000**), which is open Monday to Friday 9am to 5pm. You can also get guidance from the tourist information booth at Festival Place (© **242/323-3182** or 323-3183), where the cruise ships dock. This kiosk is usually open daily from 7:45am to 6pm.

THE LAY OF THE LAND

Most of Nassau's hotels are city hotels and are not on the water. To stay right on the sands, choose a hotel in Cable Beach (described later in this chapter) or on Paradise Island (see chapter 5).

Rawson Square is the heart of Nassau, positioned just a short walk from **Prince George Wharf,** where the big cruise ships, many of them originating in Florida, berth. Here you'll see the Churchill Building, which contains the offices of the Bahamian prime minister, along with other government ministries.

Busy **Bay Street,** the main shopping artery, begins on the south side of Rawson Square. This was the turf of the infamous Bay Street Boys, a group of rich, white Bahamians who once controlled political and economic activity on New Providence.

On the opposite side of Rawson Square is **Parliament Square,** with its government houses, House of Assembly, and statue of a youthful Queen Victoria. These are Georgian and Neo-Georgian buildings, some from the late 1700s.

The courthouse is separated by a little square from the **Nassau Public Library and Museum,** which opens onto Bank Lane. It was the former Nassau Gaol (jail). South of the library, across Shirley Street, are the remains of the **Royal Victoria Hotel,** which opened the same year the American Civil War began (1861) and hosted many a blockade runner and Confederate spy.

A walk down Parliament Street leads to the **post office.** Philatelists may want to stop in because some Bahamian stamps are true collectors' items.

Moving southward, farther away from the water, Elizabeth Avenue takes you to the **Queen's Staircase.** One of the major landmarks of Nassau, it climbs to Bennet's Hill and Fort Fincastle.

If you return to Bay Street, you'll discover the oversized tent which contains the **Straw Market,** a handicrafts emporium where you can buy all sorts of souvenirs.

2 Getting Around

BY TAXI
You can easily rely on taxis and skip renting a car. The rates for New Providence, including Nassau, are set by the government. Although working meters are required in all taxis, some of them don't work. Consequently, the government has established a well-defined roster of rates for passage between the airport and various points around the island. When you get in, the fixed rate is US$3 (£1.50), plus 40¢ (20p) for each additional quarter-mile. Each passenger over 2 years old pays an extra US$3 (£1.50). For sightseeing purposes, taxis can also be hired at the hourly rate of US$45 (£23) for a five-passenger cab. Luggage is carried at a surcharge of US$1 (50p) extra per piece, although the first two pieces are free. To call a cab, dial © **242/323-5111.** It's easy to get a taxi at the airport or at any of the big hotels.

BY CAR
You really don't need to rent a car. It's a lot easier to rely on taxis when you're ready to leave the beach and do some exploring.

However, if you choose to drive (perhaps for a day of touring the whole island), some of the biggest U.S. car-rental companies maintain branches at the airport, in downtown Nassau, at Cable Beach, and on Paradise Island. The market leader is **Avis** (© **800/331-1212** or 242/377-7121; www.avis.com), which also maintains a downtown office at Bay Street and Cumberland Street across from the British Colonial Hotel (© **242/326-6380**). **Budget Rent-a-Car** (© **800/527-0700** or 242/377-9000; www.budgetrentacar.com) has a desk at the airport and a branch downtown on Shirley Street (© **242/323-7191**). **Dollar/Thrifty Rent-a-Car** (© **800/800-3665** or 242/ 377-8300; www.dollar.com) also has a desk at the airport, and another one at the British Colonial Hilton (© **242/325-3716**). Finally, **Hertz** (© **800/654-3131;** www.hertz.com) is only at the airport.

Remember: Drive on the left!

BY BUS
The least expensive means of transport is by any of the buses (some locals refer to them as "jitneys") that make runs from downtown Nassau to outposts all over New Providence. The fare is US$1 (50p), and exact change, in coins or with a dollar bill,

Tips **On Your Own Sturdy Feet**

This is the only way to see Old Nassau, unless you rent a horse and carriage. All the major attractions and principal stores are within walking distance. You can even walk to Cable Beach or Paradise Island, although it's a hike in the hot sun.

Confine your walking to the daytime, and beware of the occasional pickpocket and purse snatcher. In the evening, avoid walking the streets of downtown Nassau, where, from time to time, muggings have been reported.

is required. The jitneys operate daily from 6:30am to 7pm. Buses to the Cable Beach area and points west of that include the much-used **no. 10,** the **10A,** and **"the Western bus."**

They depart from the corner of Bay Street and George Street, and stop at various clearly designated spots along Bay Street. Buses headed to the eastern (mostly residential and rarely accessed by short-term visitors) part of New Providence Island depart from the Frederick Street North depot.

BY BOAT

Water taxis operate daily from 9am to 6pm at 20-minute intervals between Paradise Island and Prince George Wharf.

An alternative service involves **ferryboats,** which link the wharves at the end of Casuarina Drive on Paradise Island to Rawson Square, which lies across the channel on New Providence Island. The ferry operates daily from 9:30am to 4:15pm, with departures every half-hour from both sides of the harbor.

Both the ferryboats and the water taxis charge the same fixed rate: US$3 (£1.50) per person, each way, for passage across the channel.

BY MOPED

Lots of visitors like to rent mopeds to explore the island. Unless you're an experienced rider, stay on quiet roads until you feel at ease. (Don't start out in all the congestion on Bay St.) Some hotels maintain rental kiosks on their premises. If yours doesn't, try **Bowcar Scooter Rental** (© 242/328-7300) at Festival Place, near the cruise-ship dock. That company rents mopeds at a rate of US$60 (£30) per day. Included in the rental price are insurance and mandatory helmets for both drivers and passengers. Mopeds are rented daily between 8am and 5pm.

FAST FACTS: New Providence

American Express The local representative is **Destinations,** 303 Shirley St., between Charlotte and Parliament streets, Nassau (© 242/322-2931). Hours are Monday to Friday 9am to 5pm.

ATMs Major banks with ATMs in Nassau include the **Royal Bank of Canada** (© 242/322-8700), **Bank of Nova Scotia** (© 242/356-1517), and the **First Caribbean Bank** (© 242/356-8000). Some accept cards only in the **Cirrus** network (© 800/424-7787), while others take only **PLUS** (© 800/843-7587). ATMs at the Paradise Island and Cable Beach casinos dispense quick cash. Be aware that, whereas ATM machines within large hotels and casinos tend to dispense U.S. dollars, ATM machines within banks and at the airport dispense Bahamian dollars. Since both U.S. and Bahamian currencies are readily accepted anywhere, it's not a crucial issue, but it's a good idea to read the information on the individual ATM machine before proceeding with your transaction.

Babysitting Hotel staff can help you hire an experienced sitter. Expect to pay between US$10 and US$15 (£5–£7.50) per hour, plus US$3 (£1.50) per hour for each additional child.

Climate See "When to Go," in chapter 3.

Dentist The **Princess Margaret Hospital** on Sands Road (© 242/322-2861) has a dental department.

Doctor For the best service, go to the **Princess Margaret Hospital** on Sands Road (© 242/322-2861).

Drugstores Try **Lowes Pharmacy,** Palm Dale, in downtown Nassau (© 242/322-8594), open Monday to Saturday 8am to 6:30pm, which also maintains three other branches—one in the Harbour Bay Shopping Center (© 242/393-4813), open Monday to Saturday 8am to 8:30pm and Sunday 9am to 5pm; another in the **Town Center Mall** (© 242/325-6482), open Monday to Saturday 9:30am to 8pm; and an additional outlet on Soldier Road (© 242/394-6312), open Monday to Saturday 8am to 8pm. Nassau has no late-night pharmacies.

Embassies & Consulates See "Fast Facts: The Bahamas," in the appendix.

Emergencies Call © **911** or 919.

Eyeglass Repair The **Optique Shoppe,** 22 Parliament St. at the corner of Shirley Street (© 242/322-3910), is convenient to the center of Nassau. Hours are Monday to Friday 9am to 5pm and Saturday 9am to noon.

Hospitals The government-operated **Princess Margaret Hospital** on Sands Road (© 242/322-2861) is one of the country's major hospitals. The privately owned **Doctors Hospital,** 1 Collins Ave. (© 242/322-8411), is the region's most modern private healthcare facility.

Hot Lines For help or assistance of any kind, call © **242/326-HELP** (326-4357).

Internet Access Check out **Cyberjack** at the **Mall on Marathon Road** (© 242/394-6254), where you can get online from your own laptop or log on to one of their computers. The cost is 15¢ (8p) per minute. Most of the larger hotels also offer guests Internet access for a fee. Payable by credit card, the fee can in some cases be as high as 50¢ (25p) per minute of use, which can add up quickly if you're an addictive Web surfer.

Laundry & Dry Cleaning **Superwash** (© 242/323-4018), at the corner of Nassau Street and Boyd Road, offers coin-operated machines; it's open 24 hours a day, 7 days a week. Drop-off service is available for a small additional fee. In the same building is the **New Oriental Dry Cleaner** (© 242/323-7249).

Newspapers & Magazines The *Tribune Daily* and the *Nassau Guardian,* both published in the morning, are the country's two competing daily newspapers. At your hotel and visitor information stations, you can find various helpful magazines, brochures, and booklets.

Photographic Needs The largest camera store in Nassau is **John Bull** (© 242/322-4253), on Bay Street, 3 blocks west of Rawson Square. It maintains four additional branches scattered at heavily visited tourist sites across New Providence and Paradise Island. Each of these outlets also sells perfume, watches, and jewelry.

Police Dial © **911** or 919.

Post Office & Postage The **Nassau General Post Office,** at the top of Parliament Street on East Hill Street (© 242/322-3344), is open Monday to Friday 9am to 5pm and on Saturday 8:30am to 12:30pm. Note that you can also buy stamps from most postcard kiosks. A postcard sent airmail to the U.S. or Canada costs 50¢ (25p); a letter to the same destinations costs 65¢ (35p) per half-ounce.

Safety Avoid walking along lonely side streets in downtown Nassau at night, when robberies and muggings sometimes occur. Because the local government is particularly punitive against crimes against tourists, most visitors from outside The Bahamas are never affected—but it's always better to be safe than sorry. Cable Beach and Paradise Island tend to be safer than downtown Nassau after dark.

Taxes There is no sales tax on any purchase made within The Bahamas, though there is a 12% hotel tax. Visitors leaving The Bahamas each pay a US$20 (£10) departure tax, a tariff which isn't immediately obvious, since it's automatically included in the price of any airline or cruise-ship ticket.

3 Where to Stay

In the hotel descriptions that follow, we've listed regular room prices, or "rack rates," but these are simply for ease of comparison. They are likely to be accurate for smaller properties, but you can almost always get a better price than what's listed below at the larger hotels and resorts.

Read the section entitled "Packages for the Independent Traveler" in chapter 3, before booking a hotel separately from your airfare. If you do book your own reservations, always inquire about honeymoon specials, golf packages, summer weeks, and other potential discounts. In many cases, too, a travel agent can get you a package deal that would be cheaper than these official rates.

Hotels add a 12% tax to your rate. Sometimes this is quoted in advance as part of the net price; other times, it's added as an unexpected afterthought to your final bill. When you are quoted a rate, always ask if the tax is included. Many hotels also add a 15% service charge to your bill. Be sure to ask about these charges in advance so you won't be shocked when you receive the final tab.

Taxes and service charges are not included in the hotel reviews below, which lead off with a selection of hotels within the heart of Nassau, followed by accommodations in Cable Beach. Most visitors prefer to stay at Cable Beach since the resorts here are right on the sand. But you can stay in Nassau and commute to the beaches at Cable Beach or Paradise Island; it's cheaper but less convenient. Those who prefer the ambience of Old Nassau's historic district and being near the best shops may decide to stay in town.

Where to Stay & Dine in Nassau

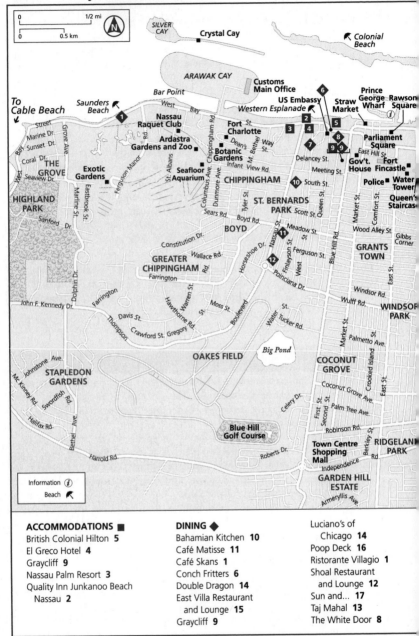

ACCOMMODATIONS ■
British Colonial Hilton **5**
El Greco Hotel **4**
Graycliff **9**
Nassau Palm Resort **3**
Quality Inn Junkanoo Beach
  Nassau **2**

DINING ◆
Bahamian Kitchen **10**
Café Matisse **11**
Café Skans **1**
Conch Fritters **6**
Double Dragon **14**
East Villa Restaurant
  and Lounge **15**
Graycliff **9**

Luciano's of
  Chicago **14**
Poop Deck **16**
Ristorante Villagio **1**
Shoal Restaurant
  and Lounge **12**
Sun and... **17**
Taj Mahal **13**
The White Door **8**

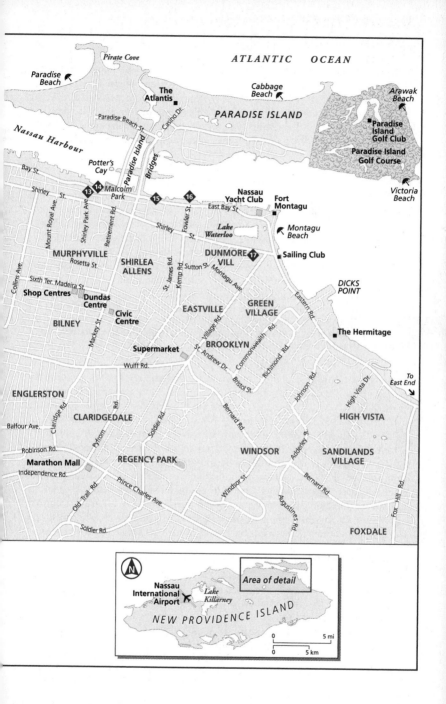

ATLANTIC OCEAN

Pirate Cove

Paradise
Beach

The
Atlantis

Cabbage
Beach

PARADISE ISLAND

Arawak
Beach

Paradise
Island
Golf Club

Paradise Island
Golf Course

Nassau Harbour

Paradise Beach St.

Casino Dr.

Paradise Island

Bridges

Potter's
Cay

Bay St.

Shirley   St.

Mount Royal Ave.

Shirley Park Ave.

Retirement Rd.

13 **14** Malcolm
Park

15   **16**

**Nassau
Yacht Club**

**Fort
Montagu**

East Bay St.

Montagu
Beach

Shirley   St.

Fowler St.

*Lake
Waterloo*

Victoria
Beach

MURPHYVILLE

Rosetta St.

Collins Ave.

SHIRLEA
ALLENS

St. James Rd.

Kemp Rd.

Sutton St.

**DUNMORE
VILL** **17**

Montagu Ave.

Sailing Club

*DICKS
POINT*

Sixth Ter. Madeira St.

Shop Centres

**Dundas
Centre**

**Civic
Centre**

Mackey St.

BILNEY

EASTVILLE

Village Rd.

GREEN
VILLAGE

Commonwealth   Rd.

Richmond Rd.

Eastern Rd.

■ **The Hermitage**

Supermarket

BROOKLYN

St. Andrew Dr.

Bristol St.

Wulff Rd.

Johnson Rd.

High Vista Dr.

To
East End

ENGLERSTON

Claridge Rd.

Rd.

CLARIDGEDALE

Soldier Rd.

Bernard Rd.

HIGH VISTA

Balfour Ave.

Pyfrom Rd.

Robinson Rd.

Marathon Mall

Independence Rd.

REGENCY PARK

Old Trail Rd.

Prince Charles Ave.

Soldier Rd.

Windsor St.

WINDSOR

Adderley St.

Augustine's Rd.

Bernard Rd.

SANDILANDS
VILLAGE

Fox Hill Rd.

FOXDALE

N

**Nassau
International
Airport** ✈

*Lake
Killarney*

Area of detail

NEW PROVIDENCE ISLAND

0		5 mi
0		5 km

NASSAU
EXPENSIVE

British Colonial Hilton 🐦🐦   In the restored British Colonial Hilton, there's a palpable air of the long-ago days when The Bahamas was firmly within Britain's political and social orbit. This landmark seven-story structure has seen its share of ups and downs over the years. Plush and glamorous when it was built in 1900, it burned to the ground in 1920 and was rebuilt 3 years later before deteriorating into a flophouse. Between 1996 and 1999, a Canadian entrepreneur poured US$68 million into its restoration.

Don't expect the glitz and glitter of Cable Beach or Paradise Island here—the Hilton is after business travelers rather than the casino crowd. It also lacks the aristocratic credentials of Graycliff (see below). Nonetheless, it's a dignified and friendly, but rather sedate, hotel with a discreetly upscale decor (no Disney-style themes or gimmicks). Bedrooms are a bit on the small side but capped with crown moldings and accessorized with tile or stone-sheathed bathrooms with tub/showers. The staff, incidentally, is well-trained, motivated, upbeat, and hardworking. There's a small beach a few steps away, but it's not very appealing, as it's on the narrow channel separating New Providence from Paradise Island, with no wave action at all.

1 Bay St., Nassau, The Bahamas. © 800/HILTONS (445-8667) in the U.S. and Canada, or 242/322-3301. Fax 242/302-9010. www.hilton.com. 291 units. Winter US$269–US$389 (£135–£195) double, US$509–US$1,400 (£255–£700) suite; off-season US$214–US$369 (£107–£185) double, US$429–US$1,400 (£215–£700) suite. AE, DC, DISC, MC, V. Bus: 10. **Amenities:** 2 restaurants; 2 bars; outdoor pool; health club; full-service spa; tour desk; business center; secretarial service; room service; babysitting; laundry service; dry cleaning. *In room:* A/C, TV, Wi-Fi, minibar, coffeemaker, hair dryer, iron, trouser press, safe.

Graycliff 🐦   Now in a kind of nostalgic decay, Graycliff remains the grande dame of downtown Nassau hotels even though her tiara is a bit tarnished and her age is showing. In spite of its drawbacks, this place still has its devotees, especially among older visitors. Originally an 18th-century private home reflecting Georgian colonial architecture, it's now an intimate inn with old-fashioned atmosphere. Even though it's not on the beach, people who can afford to stay anywhere sometimes choose Graycliff because it epitomizes the old-world style and grace that evokes Nassau back in the days when the duke and duchess of Windsor were in residence. Churchill, of course, can no longer be seen paddling around in the swimming pool with a cigar in his mouth, and the Beatles are long gone, but the three-story Graycliff marches onward without the visiting celebs who today head for Paradise Island. Beach lovers usually go by taxi to either nearby Goodman's Bay or the Western Esplanade Beach, nearly adjacent to Arawak Cay.

The historic garden rooms in the main house are large and individually decorated with antiques, though the better units are the more modern garden rooms. The Yellow Bird, Hibiscus, and Pool cottages are ideal choices, but the most luxurious accommodation of all is the Mandarino Suite, which sports Asian decor, a king-size bed, an oversize bathroom, and a private balcony overlooking the swimming pool. Bathrooms are spacious, with tub/showers, deluxe toiletries, and robes.

8–12 W. Hill St., Nassau, The Bahamas. © 800/476-0446, 242/302-9150 or 326-6188. Fax 242/326-6188. www.graycliff.com. 20 units. Winter US$375–US$425 (£188–£213) double, US$475–US$700 (£238–£350) cottage; off-season US$325–US$370 (£163–£185) double, US$425–US$575 (£213–£288) cottage. AE, MC, V. Bus: 10 or 21A. **Amenities:** 2 restaurants; 2 bars; 2 outdoor pools; spa; Jacuzzi; sauna; room service; massage; babysitting; laundry service; dry cleaning. *In room:* A/C, TV, Wi-Fi, minibar, hair dryer, iron, safe.

MODERATE

Nassau Palm Resort *(Value* A short walk west of downtown Nassau, within a cluster of other cost-conscious hotels that include both the El Greco (p. 77) and the Quality Inn, this hotel lies across busy West Bay Street from the relatively narrow confines of Junkanoo Beach (which is also known as Lighthouse Beach or the Western Esplanade). Though not as fine or dramatic as Cable Beach, a few miles west, it's a safe urban beach with tranquil waters and a lot of shells. This place is a good value for those who don't demand particularly attentive service and who don't want to pay the higher prices charged by the more deluxe and better-accessorized hotels along Cable Beach. Bedrooms are outfitted in a standardized motel style, most with a view of Nassau Harbour, and come with extras you don't always find in a moderately priced choice, such as alarm clocks, two-line phones, and a working desk. All have relatively well-maintained bathrooms containing tub/showers.

There's a bar and two restaurants within a few steps of the hotel itself and several other places to eat and drink within a 5-minute walk.

W. Bay St., Nassau, The Bahamas. © **242/356-0000.** Fax 242/323-1408. www.nassau-hotels.com. 183 units. Winter US$98 (£49) double, US$135 (£68) suite; off-season US$89 (£45) double, US$95 (£48) suite. AE, DISC, MC, V. Bus: 10 or 17. **Amenities:** 2 restaurants; 2 bars; 2 outdoor pools; health club; spa; salon; room service; laundry service; dry cleaning; nonsmoking rooms; rooms for those w/limited mobility. *In room:* A/C, TV, Wi-Fi, fridge, coffeemaker, hair dryer, iron, safe.

INEXPENSIVE

El Greco Hotel This hotel is across the street from Junkanoo Beach/Lighthouse Beach/The Western Esplanade and a short walk from Arawak Cay's sometimes raucous nightlife. It's also a quick walk from the shops and restaurants of downtown Nassau. El Greco is a well-managed bargain choice that attracts many European travelers. The Greek owners and staff genuinely seem to care about their guests—in fact, the two-story hotel seems more like a small European B&B than your typical Bahamian hotel.

The midsize rooms aren't that exciting, but they're clean and comfortable, with decent beds and small tile bathrooms with tub/showers. Bedrooms have a bright decor—a sort of Mediterranean motif, each with two ceiling fans and carpeted floors. Accommodations are built around a courtyard that encompasses bougainvillea-draped statues that were crafted in the Italian baroque style. There's no restaurant on-site, but you can walk to many places nearby for meals.

W. Bay St., Nassau, The Bahamas. © **242/325-1121.** Fax 242/325-1124. 27 units, Winter US$140 (£70) double, US$160–US$220 (£80–£110) suite; off-season US$120 (£60) double, US$140–US$190 (£70–£95) suite. AE, MC, V. Free parking. Bus: 10. **Amenities:** Bar; pool; babysitting. *In room:* A/C, TV.

Quality Inn Junkanoo Beach Nassau This no-nonsense, efficiently designed, green-fronted hotel rises prominently across West Bay Street's sometimes busy traffic, from the narrow sands known variously as Junkanoo Beach, Lighthouse Beach, Long Wharf, and the Western Esplanade. Partly because of its compact rooms, it's the least desirable, and also the least expensive, of the also-recommended hotels (the Nassau Palm and the El Greco) that lie nearby within this congested downtown neighborhood. But during the peak of winter, when other competitors might be more expensive or sold out completely, it offers comfortable, unpretentious lodgings in a six-story venue that might be appealing if you don't expect tons of amenities or superlative service.

W. Bay and Nassau sts., Nassau, The Bahamas. ✆ **242/322-1515.** Fax 242/322-1514. www.choicehotels.com. 63 units. Year-round US$111–US$129 (£56–£65) double. AE, DC, MC, V. Bus: 10 or 16. **Amenities:** Bar; outdoor pool; business center; dry-cleaning service; nonsmoking rooms; rooms for those w/limited mobility. *In room:* A/C, TV, beverage maker, hair dryer, iron, safe.

CABLE BEACH

Cable Beach has always figured high in the consciousness of The Bahamas. Since Atlantis premiered on Paradise Island, Cable Beach has flourished, and occasionally suffered, in the shadow of its more dramatic counterpart.

Cable Beach derived its name from the underwater telephone and telegraph cable that brought electronic communications from the outside world. For years, it was a rural outpost of New Providence Island, flanked by private homes and a desirable shoreline that was a destination for local residents. Its first major touristic boost came with the construction of the old Ambassador Beach Hotel, now the site of Breezes Bahamas. In the 1980s, a building boom added the string of condos, timeshares, and hotels, all designed to serve the holiday needs of sun-seekers and casinogoers, that have defined the area's appearance ever since. The district boasts a wide variety of restaurants and sports facilities, lots of glitz and glitter, and one of the country's two biggest casinos (in terms of square footage).

In 2005, a consortium of major-league investors, coalescing under the Baha Mar logo, pinpointed Cable Beach as the eventual site of one of the Atlantic's most far-reaching resort developments. In 2007, they inaugurated a plan that will radically alter the present landscape of Cable Beach, adding to the overall competitiveness of Nassau in general and its northern seafront in particular. Expect big changes between 2009 and 2012, when a multitiered redevelopment program presumably will alter the status of Cable Beach as what might—if all phases of the redevelopment are completed as planned—become one of the world's most talked-about casino and resort destinations. The project's investors also own and operate Cable Beach Resorts and Crystal Palace Casino.

Major infrastructure changes will include a revised layout of West Bay Street, one of New Providence Island's busiest traffic arteries, to direct traffic away from building sites for as many as four additional name-brand hotels. The overall vision will include dredging new lakes and marinas, creating water traps for a thoroughly redesigned golf course, demolishing some older buildings within the Cable Beach compound, and extensively enlarging the existing casino.

The project also calls for constructing a new string of resort hotels, each of which will cater to a different resort market. A W hotel, for example, will accent avant-garde design and, it's hoped, attract a youthful, trend-setting clientele. Another property will offer more conservative—and probably somewhat plusher—comforts geared to the *haute bourgeoisie.* And serious gamblers looking for Las Vegas flash will gravitate toward a new incarnation of a Caesar's Palace. The makeover melee will also include intelligent reuse of some of the existing structures, including a radical rethinking of the Wyndham and Sheraton properties, which, in their present incarnations, are recommended in "Where to Stay in Cable Beach," below.

Even in its current form, Cable Beach has many loyal fans, some of whom think Paradise Island is too expensive, too snobbish, too contrived, too artificial, and too derivative of a Disney-inspired theme park. Stay tuned for further developments—and expect endless delays; at press time, government officials were complaining that the massive project wasn't moving at its anticipated rate.

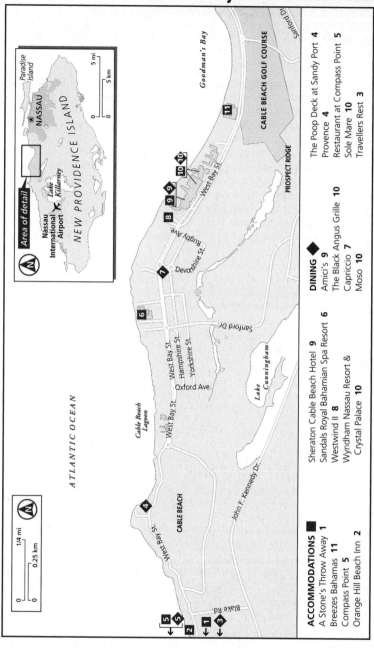

ACCOMMODATIONS ■

A Stone's Throw Away **1**
Breezes Bahamas **11**
Compass Point **5**
Orange Hill Beach Inn **2**
Sheraton Cable Beach Hotel **9**
Sandals Royal Bahamian Spa Resort **6**
Westwind II **8**
Wyndham Nassau Resort &
Crystal Palace **10**

DINING ◆

Amici's **9**
The Black Angus Grille **10**
Capriccio **7**
Moso **10**
The Poop Deck at Sandy Port **4**
Provence **4**
Restaurant at Compass Point **5**
Sole Mare **10**
Travellers Rest **3**

ATLANTIC OCEAN

Cable Beach Lagoon

CABLE BEACH

West Bay St.
Blake Rd.
Oxford Ave.
West Bay St.
Hampshire St.
Yorkshire St.
Sanford Dr.
Lake Cunningham
John F. Kennedy Dr.
Devonshire St.
Rugby Ave.
West Bay St.
Goodman's Bay
CABLE BEACH GOLF COURSE
PROSPECT RIDGE
Sanford Dr.

Area of detail

NEW PROVIDENCE ISLAND

Paradise Island
NASSAU
Nassau International Airport
Lake Killarney

5 mi
5 km

1/4 mi
0.25 km

WHERE TO STAY IN CABLE BEACH
VERY EXPENSIVE

Breezes Bahamas ⓐ   In 1996, SuperClubs, an all-inclusive chain which competes successfully with Sandals Royal Bahamian (see below), spent US$125 million transforming a tired old relic—the Ambassador Beach Hotel—into this all-inclusive resort. Today, its biggest competitor is the nearby Sandals, which is more imposing, more elegant, more stylish, more expensive, and more upscale. Rowdier and more raucous, however, and located on a prime 450m (1,476-ft.) beachfront along Cable Beach, Breezes attracts a more middle-of-the-road crowd; it's unpretentious and more affordable (though it isn't exactly cheap, and we think it's a bit overpriced for what it is). This U-shaped beachfront resort has two wings of rooms plus a main clubhouse facing a large, sometimes overcrowded terrace with a swimming pool that serves as the social centerpiece. Couples and single travelers are equally accepted here, and the rate includes everything—the room, meals, snacks, unlimited wine (not the finest) with lunch and dinner, even premium-brand liquor at the bars, plus activities and airport transfers. The air-conditioned guest rooms contain pastel-painted furniture with Formica tops. Accommodations are not as luxurious as those at Sandals, but rates are deliberately lower.

Diners can sample unremarkable international fare at the food court, although the Italian restaurant serves better food. A beachside grill and snacks are available throughout the day. Entertainment includes a high-energy disco, a piano bar, and a nightclub. Karaoke is inevitable, but the professional Junkanoo live shows, which are presented every Saturday night, are more entertaining, and local bands often perform.

Cable Beach, Nassau, The Bahamas. ⓒ **800/GO-SUPER** (467-8737) or 242/327-5356. Fax 242/327-5155. www.superclubs.com. 391 units. Year-round US$333–US$413 (£167–£207) per person per night, double occupancy; US$600–US$750 (£300–£375) per person per night, double occupancy, suite. Rates include all meals, drinks, tips, airport transfers, and most activities. AE, DISC, MC, V. Free parking. Bus: 10. No children under 14 year-round; no one under 18, unless accompanied by an adult 21 or older, Mar–May. **Amenities:** 5 restaurants; 5 bars; 3 outdoor pools; 3 tennis courts; health club; watersports equipment; laundry service; nonsmoking rooms; rooms for those w/limited mobility. *In room:* A/C, TV, coffeemaker, hair dryer, iron, safe.

Sandals Royal Bahamian Hotel & Spa ⓐⓐⓐ   This all-inclusive property is the most upscale Sandals resort in the world. It's shockingly expensive, though you can often get special promotional rates that make it more reasonable. The property originated as a very posh hotel, the Balmoral Beach, in the 1940s. In 1996, the Jamaica-based Sandals chain poured US$20 million into renovating and expanding the resort, and additional upgrades have been ongoing ever since. Everywhere, you'll find trappings of Edwardian England in the tropics: manicured gardens, rich cove moldings, neoclassical/Palladian architectural themes, plus hidden courtyards tastefully accentuated with sculptures. The resort is located on a beach a short walk west of Cable Beach's more glittery mega-hotels.

A favorite for honeymoon getaways, Sandals offers well-furnished and often elegant rooms, all classified as suites and positioned within either the resort's core Manor House or the 1998 Windsor Building. Others, including some of the most upscale and expensive, occupy outlying villas known collectively as the Royal Village. The villas are preferable because of their rigorously secluded settings and easy access to nearby semiprivate plunge pools. Bedrooms, regardless of their location, have thick cove moldings, formal English furniture, and tub/shower bathrooms loaded with perfumed soaps and cosmetics. The rooms that face the ocean offer small curved terraces with ornate iron railings and views of an offshore sand spit, Sandals Key.

Moments Junkanoo Festivals

No Bahamian celebration is as raucous as Junkanoo. Its special rituals origi-nated during the colonial days of slavery, when African-born newcomers could legally drink and enjoy themselves only on certain strictly predeter-mined days of the year. In how it's celebrated, the **Junkanoo festival** closely resembles Carnaval in Rio and Mardi Gras in New Orleans. Its major differ-ence lies in the costumes and the timing (the major Junkanoo celebrations occur the day after Christmas, a legacy of the English celebration of Boxing Day on Dec 26, and New Year's Day). On a more touristy note, a 2-month festival, the **Junkanoo Summer Festival** (© **242/302-2085;** www.bahamas.com), takes place in June and July every year.

In the old days, Junkanoo costumes were crafted from crepe paper, often in primary colors, stretched over wire frames. One sinister offshoot of the celebrations was that Junkanoo costumes and masks were used to conceal the identity of anyone seeking vengeance on a white person, or on another slave. Today, locals have more money to spend on costumes and Junkanoo festivals than they did in the past. The finest costumes can cost up to US$15,000 (£7,500) and are sometimes sponsored by local bazaars, lotteries, church groups, and charity auctions. Everyday folks from all walks of Bahamian life join in, often with homemade costumes that are sensuous or humorous. The best time and place to observe Junkanoo is New Year's Day in Nassau, when throngs of cavorting, music-making, and costumed figures prance through the streets. Find yourself a good viewing position on Bay Street. Less elaborate celebrations take place in major towns on the other islands, including Freeport on Grand Bahama Island.

Bahamian and international fare is offered in generous portions in the property's restaurants. In addition to spectacular buffets, the options include white-glove service and continental dishes in the **Baccarat Dining Room.** The two latest additions include **Kimonos,** offering Japanese cuisine, and **Casanova,** specializing in Italian fare. Other choices include **Arizona** for Southwestern-style grilled specialties, and **Spices** for upscale buffets three times a day. The pool here is one of Nassau's most appealing, with touches of both Vegas and ancient Rome (outdoor murals and repli-cas of ancient Roman columns jut skyward above the water). Complimentary shuttle service goes to the casino and nightlife options at the nearby Wyndham Crystal Palace complex, and concierge service is provided for residents of the resort's higher-priced accommodations.

W. Bay St., Cable Beach, Nassau, The Bahamas. © **800/SANDALS** (726-3257) or 242/327-6400. Fax 242/327-6961. www.sandals.com. 403 units. Winter US$1,800–US$4,000 (£900–£2,000) per couple for 2 days; off-season US$1,600–US$3,800 (£800–£1,900) per couple for 2 days. Rates include all meals, drinks, and activities. AE, DISC, MC, V. Free parking. Bus: 10. Couples only; no children allowed. **Amenities:** 9 restaurants; 9 bars; 6 outdoor pools; 2 tennis courts; health club; full-service spa; watersports equipment; nonsmoking rooms; rooms for those w/limited mobility. _In room:_ A/C, TV, coffeemaker, hair dryer, iron, safe.

The Art of Massage

The Red Lane Spa at Sandals Royal Bahamian Hotel & Spa in Nassau has repeatedly made the top 10 list of spa resorts in the *Condé Nast Traveler* reader's choice survey. The decor features walls and floors of Italian Satumia stone, rich mahogany doors, and a collection of pre-Raphaelite prints in gilded frames. One service offered, Massage Duet, allows couples to learn the art of massage from a professional so that they can practice on each other in the comfort of their hotel room.

EXPENSIVE

Sheraton Cable Beach Resort ⰻ ⟨Kids⟩   Prominently visible in the center of Cable Beach (its best asset) is this seven-story high-rise, connected by a shopping arcade to Crystal Palace Casino. The nearby Wyndham Nassau Resort (p. 83) is glitzier and has better and more exclusive and extensive facilities, but the Sheraton is still one of the most desirable choices for families. Because many of its bedrooms contain two double beds, its accommodations are usually suitable for a family of four. Painted pale beige, the property has an Aztec-inspired facade of sharp angles and strongly defined horizontal lines, with prominent balconies. The edifice, which forms a horseshoe-shaped curve around a landscaped beachfront garden, is big, brassy, and the beneficiary of an US$82-million (£41 million) renovation.

You'll think of Vegas when you see the rows of fountains in front, the acres of marble sheathing inside, the four-story lobby with towering windows, and the hotel's propensity for hosting large wedding parties, often with groups of participants flown in from the U.S. Big enough to get lost in, but with plenty of intimate nooks, this hotel offers an extensive array of things to do.

Bedrooms are modern and comfortable, reflecting a lighthearted and somewhat whimsical interpretation of Tommy Bahama style, replete with dark-stained wood furniture, white walls, and monochromatic, understated colors completely devoid of the floral prints of yesteryear. Big windows open onto views of either the garden or the beach. Units are equipped with one king-size bed or two doubles, along with phones with voice mail.

The hotel contains three restaurants, the most glamorous of which is Amici (p. 90), serving traditional Italian cuisine in a two-story garden setting. The Outdoor Grill serves a Caribbean-flavored continental breakfast and lunch buffets.

W. Bay St., Cable Beach, Nassau, The Bahamas. ⓒ 800/325-3535 or 242/327-6000. Fax 242/327-6987. www.sheraton.com/cablebeach. 694 units. Feb–Apr US$269–US$390 (£135–£195) double; May–Aug US$249–US$600 (£125–£300) double; Sept–Jan US$219–US$540 (£110–£270) double. AE, MC, V. Free parking. Bus: 10. **Amenities:** 4 restaurants; 3 bars; 3 outdoor pools; 2 tennis courts; gym; shopping arcade; salon; room service; babysitting; laundry service; dry cleaning; rooms for those w/limited mobility. *In room:* A/C, TV, Wi-Fi, coffeemaker, hair dryer, iron, safe.

Westwind II Club ⟨Kids⟩   Set on the western edge of Cable Beach's hotel strip, 9.5km (6 miles) from the center of Nassau, the Westwind II is a cluster of two-story buildings that contain two-bedroom, two-bathroom timeshare units, each with a full kitchen (there's a grocery store nearby). The size and facilities of these units make them ideal for traveling families, and the accommodations, when they're not occupied by their investor-owners, are available to the public. All the diversions of the mega-hotels are nearby and easily reached, but in the complex itself, you can enjoy a low-key, quiet atmosphere and privacy. (A masonry wall separates the compound from the street traffic.) Each unit has pleasant decor that includes white tiled floors, rattan furniture, and a balcony or a terrace. Since units are identical, price differences are based on whether the units face the beach, the pool, or the garden. The manicured grounds feature palms, flowering hibiscus shrubs, and seasonal flowerbeds. Don't stay here if you expect any of the luxuries or facilities of the nearby Wyndham Nassau Resort (see below). Westwind II is more for self-sufficient, do-it-yourself types.

W. Bay St., Cable Beach, Nassau, The Bahamas. (℃) **866/369-5921** or 242/327-7019. Fax 262/327-7529. www. westwind2.com. 54 units. Winter US$247–US$315 (£124–£158) double; off-season US$194–US$263 (£97–£132) double. MC, V. Bus: 10. **Amenities:** Bar; 2 pools; 2 tennis courts; babysitting; coin-operated laundry; rooms for those w/limited mobility. *In room:* A/C, TV, Wi-Fi, kitchen, fridge, coffeemaker, iron.

Wyndham Nassau Resort & Crystal Palace Casino *(Kids)*   This big, flashy mega-resort on the lovely sands of Cable Beach is so vast and all-encompassing that some of its guests never even venture into Nassau during their stay on the island. The futuristic-looking complex incorporates three high-rise towers, a futuristic central core illuminated with sunlight streaming through massive greenhouse-style translucent domes, and a cluster of beachfront gazebos—all linked with arcades, covered passageways, and mini-pavilions. Guest rooms come in several different price brackets, ranging from standard island view to ocean vista, each with private balconies. Corner suites with lots of space are the way to go, complete with wraparound balconies and king-size beds looking out onto the water through floor-to-ceiling glass.

As noted in our introduction to Cable Beach (p. 89), this hotel will be the carefully planned centerpiece—predicted for 2011—of a radical expansion of the hotel lineup along Cable Beach.

Aside from a massive casino, one of the two largest in The Bahamas, the complex contains a wide array of dining and drinking facilities. Three of its restaurants are among New Providence's best (see "Where to Dine," below). Appealingly experimental, and a particular favorite of ours, is Moso (p. 90), an enclave of hip that assembles onto one menu the best dishes from around Asia and the Pacific Rim. Even if you're not a guest of the hotel, you might want to avail yourself of the drinking and dining options or the casino action here.

W. Bay St., Cable Beach, Nassau, The Bahamas. (℃) **800/222-7466** in the U.S., or 242/327-6200. Fax 954/915-2929. www.wyndhamnassauresort.com. 542 units. Winter US$229–US$419 (£115–£210) double, US$439–US$1,000 (£220–£500) suite; off-season US$229–US$289 (£115–£145) double, US$439–US$1,000 (£220–£500) suite. AE, DC, MC, V. Free self-parking, valet parking US$5 (£2.50). Bus: 10. **Amenities:** 6 restaurants; 1 bar; outdoor pool; nearby golf course; health club; Jacuzzi; sauna; business center; room service; massage facilities; babysitting; laundry service; dry cleaning; nonsmoking rooms; rooms for those w/limited mobility. *In room:* A/C, TV, fridge, coffeemaker, hair dryer, iron, safe.

MODERATE

Orange Hill Beach Inn *(Finds)*   This hotel, set on 1.4 landscaped hillside hectares (3½ acres), lies about 13km (8 miles) west of Nassau and 1.5km (1 mile) east of Love Beach, which has great snorkeling. It's perfect for those wanting to escape the crowds and stay in a quieter part of New Providence; it's easy to catch a cab or jitney to Cable Beach or downtown Nassau. The welcoming owners, Judy and Danny Lowe, an Irish-Bahamian team, jokingly refer to the place as "Fawlty Towers Nassau."

Originally built as a private home in the 1920s, this place became a hotel in 1979 after the Lowes added more rooms and a swimming pool. Lodgings come in a variety of sizes, though most are small. The bathrooms are also small, but well maintained. Each room has a balcony or patio, and some have kitchenettes. Many of the guests are

Europeans, especially during summer. Recent renovations included updated furniture in the rooms and upgraded bathrooms.

On-site is a bar serving sandwiches and salads throughout the day, and a restaurant that offers simple but good dinners. Diving excursions to the rich marine fauna along New Providence's southwestern coast are among the most popular activities here, and the hotel provides free regular jitney service to and from local grocery stores, a fact that's much appreciated by clients who prepare their meals within their kitchenettes.

W. Bay St., just west of Blake Rd., Nassau, The Bahamas. ✆ **888/399-3698** or 242/327-7157. Fax 242/327-5186. www.orangehill.com. 32 units. Winter US$125 (£63) double, US$150 (£75) w/kitchenette; off-season US$125 (£63) double, US$129 (£65) w/kitchenette. MC, V. Free parking. Bus: 10. **Amenities:** Restaurant; bar; outdoor pool; laundry service and coin-operated laundry; rooms for those w/limited mobility. *In room:* A/C, TV, Wi-Fi, kitchenette (in some).

WEST OF CABLE BEACH
EXPENSIVE

Compass Point 🐟🐟   This whimsical, offbeat resort is self-consciously funky and out-of-the-way, positioned within a brightly painted compound of vernacular wooden cottages. The island's most westerly resort, directly beside Love Beach, several minutes' drive west from Cable Beach, is the closest thing to Jamaica in The Bahamas. In fact, it's associated with the Jamaica-based chain of hotels (Island Outposts) owned by Christopher Blackwell, the music-industry entrepreneur who discovered and promoted Bob Marley's talent. Accommodations are within airy, old-fashioned brightly painted cottages, each simply but artfully furnished, island-style, in a manner that encourages barefoot living if not altogether nudity. Prices vary according to the unit's view and the size, and whether or not it's raised on stilts above the rocky landscape on which the resort sits (units on stilts get more breezes and better views).

West Bay St., Gambier, Nassau. ✆ **876/946-1958** or 242/327-4500. Fax 242/327-9904. www.compasspointhotel. com. 18 units. Summer US$300 (£150) studio for 2, US$380 (£190) 1-bedroom apt for 2, US$400 (£200) 2-bedroom apt for 4; winter US$270 (£135) studio for 2, US$300 (£150) 1-bedroom apt for 2, US$400 (£200) 2-bedroom apt for 4. AE, MC, V. Bus: 10. **Amenities:** Restaurant; bar; pool. *In room:* A/C, TV, fridge, hair dryer, safe.

A Stone's Throw Away 🐟🐟 *Finds*   At last, New Providence has a gourmet-level B&B, a secluded hideaway conceived by French and Belgian owners, 13 miles west of Nassau. This boutique hotel is for discerning visitors and has already been discovered by some celebrities (though, for privacy's sake, management doesn't name names). Surrounded by verandas, the colonial-style inn's public rooms evoke an old plantation home. On the ground floor, guest rooms open into gardens and a pool area, while the upper two floors provide panoramic lake views. Bedrooms are luxuriously furnished with high-density towels, Egyptian cotton sheets, Indonesian teak beds, and mahogany antiques. The property's staff serves three meals a day, including finely honed continental dinners.

Tropical Garden Rd. and W. Bay St., Gambier, New Providence, The Bahamas. ✆ **242/327-7030**. www.astonesthrow away.com. 10 units. Nov–May US$200–US$290 (£100–£145) double, US$290 (£145) suite; off-season US$175–US$235 (£88–£118) double, US$235 (£118) suite. AE, MC, V. **Amenities:** Restaurant; bar; beachfront; outdoor pool; room service; nonsmoking rooms. *In room:* A/C, TV, Wi-Fi, minibar.

4 Where to Dine

NASSAU

Nassau restaurants open and close often. Even if reservations aren't required, it's a good idea to call first just to find out that a place is still in business, and that the hours listed haven't changed. European and American cuisine are relatively easy to find.

Surprisingly, it used to be difficult to find Bahamian cuisine, but in recent years, more restaurants have begun to offer authentic island fare.

EXPENSIVE

Graycliff 🦈🦈 CONTINENTAL   Part of the Graycliff hotel, an antiques-filled colonial mansion located in Nassau's commercial core (opposite the Government House), this deeply entrenched, long-enduring restaurant retains a history and an almost palpable sense of nostalgia for the old days of The Bahamas as a colonial outpost of Britain, despite sweeping changes in both the government and the society at large. The chefs use local Bahamian products whenever available and turn them into old-fashioned cuisine that still appeals to tradition-minded visitors, many of whom return here year after year. Try dishes, neither completely traditional nor regional, such as grouper soup in puff pastry, and plump, juicy pheasant cooked with pineapples grown on Eleuthera. Lobster is another specialty, and it comes one half in beurre blanc and the other with a sauce prepared from the head of the lobster. Other options include escargots, foie gras, and *tournedos d'agneau* (lamb). The pricey wine list is usually praised as one of the finest in the country, with more than 200,000 bottles. This hotel and restaurant are managed by the same entrepreneurs who run a cigar-making facility; as such, their collection of Bahama-derived cigars is the world's most comprehensive.

Graycliff Hotel, W. Hill St. © 242/322-2796. Reservations required. Jacket advised for men. Main courses US$24–US$38 (£12–£19) lunch, US$38–US$64 (£19–£32) dinner. AE, MC, V. Mon–Fri noon–3pm; daily 6:30–10pm. Bus: 10, 10A, or 21A.

Humidor Churrascaria 🦈 BRAZILIAN   Brazilian *rodizio*, the art of grilling large amounts of chicken, sausage, pork, and beef, has finally come to Nassau within this annex of the fabled Graycliff Hotel. Set within the same building as Graycliff's cigar factory and shop, within a generously proportioned, high-ceilinged enclave that's vaguely reminiscent of the long-ago British regime, it's fun, colorful, and filling. A staff wearing yellow, gaucho-inspired shirts invites you to the salad bar and then makes endless runs from the grill to your plate with skewers of assorted grilled meats—plus occasional *raciones* of grilled pineapple—as part of a ritual that evokes South America's pampas and plains. The only option available is the set-price dinner noted below. Vegetarians or the not-terribly-hungry can easily make do with a meal composed entirely from the salad bar.

12 West Hill St. © 242/302-9150. Reservations required. Set-price, all-you-can-eat *churrasco* dinner US$40 (£20). Access to salad bar without any *churrasco* US$25 (£13). AE, MC, V. Mon–Sat 6:30–10pm. Bus: 10, 10A, or 21A.

Ristorante Villagio 🦈🦈 TUSCAN/CONTINENTAL   One of the island's most appealing restaurants lies 3.2km (2 miles) west of Cable Beach, close enough to the posh and gated residential enclave of Lyford Cay to ensure a steady flow of upscale locals. Set within an ochre-colored enclave of shopping and office buildings known as Caves Village at Caves Point, it's posh, a bit dilettantish, and charming. There's a cozy dining room with an open-to-view kitchen, elaborate French Empire-style crystal chandeliers, a wall with display cases devoted to a collection of colorful Murano glass, and the kind of thick-legged rustic furniture that might have been pulled out of a farmhouse in Tuscany. Even better is a sprawling covered terrace whose furniture—wrought-iron tables and deep-upholstered sofas and armchairs—seems appropriate for someone's private library. Menu items are savory and artful; the lemongrass-poached lobster salad is fabulous, as are the *trenette* pasta with seafood, the clam linguini, and the Angus beef with arugula. Veal cutlets Milanese are served with hazelnut sauce. Also delicious are the slices of black sea bass atop a bed of truffle-studded creamed potatoes, bacon-braised organic leeks, and wild mushrooms; and very slow-roasted Norfolk duckling steeped in sherry, onions, and olives, and served over braised cabbage and pancetta ham. Staff here manages to combine some almost cliché-ridden, slightly dotty English supervisors and a rather hip Bahamian and international staff.

In 2007, the same managers established a nearby, somewhat less formal bistro, **Mangos,** within the same shopping compound, where food is only a bit less expensive, but where service can be excruciatingly slow and serving errors are frequent.

At Caves Point, W. Bay St. at Blake Rd. © 242/327-0965. Reservations recommended. Main courses US$32–US$75 (£16–£38). Tues–Sat 6–9:30pm. Bus: Western.

Sun and . . . ✸✸ INTERNATIONAL   For nearly 30 years, through good and bad times, this restaurant has been a prominent culinary landmark in Nassau, the best of a core of locally owned restaurants valiantly holding their own against daunting competition from better-funded restaurants within the island's mega-resorts. Today, under the hardworking leadership of Belgium-born owner-chef Ronny Deryckere and his wife, Esther, it's more of an inner sanctum than ever, occupying the premises of what was originally built in the 1930s as a private residence, Red Mill House, within an upscale, mostly residential neighborhood east of downtown Nassau. You might want a drink within the bar area, which is a distinctly separate entity all its own, before heading into one of several dining rooms, each of them arranged around a central courtyard containing tropical plants, shrubs, and a swimming pool. Some of the dishes emerging from the kitchens of this place are unique to New Providence and Paradise Island: Examples include sweetbreads, prepared either with white wine and mushroom sauce or with a demi-glacé and cognac; the best Roquefort salad in town; an absolutely fabulous version of steak tartare, served with *pommes frites;* and grilled octopus with chopped onions and olive tapenade. Of special note is the Bahamian fisher's platter, composed of artfully prepared fish that was entirely caught from local waters. If there's a moment during the dinner when you're not otherwise occupied, check out the photos lining the walls depicting clients of yesteryear, including those of Frank Sinatra, Bob Hope, Richard Widmark, and the Duke of Windsor.

Lakeview Rd. at E. Shirley St. © 242/393-1205. Reservations required. Lunch platters US$11–US$19 (£5.50–£9.50); dinner main courses US$35–US$60 (£18–£30). AE, DC, MC, V. Tues–Sun 11:30am–3pm and 6:30–10pm. Closed Sun June–Sept.

MODERATE

Café Matisse ✸ INTERNATIONAL/ITALIAN   Set directly behind Parliament House, in a mustard-beige-colored building built a century ago as a private home, this restaurant is on everybody's short list of downtown Nassau favorites. It serves well-prepared Italian and international cuisine to businesspeople, workers from nearby government offices, and all kinds of dealmakers. There are dining areas within an enclosed courtyard, as well as on two floors of the interior, which is decorated with colorful Matisse prints. It's run by the sophisticated Bahamian-Italian team of Greg and Gabriella Curry, who prepare menu items that include calamari with spicy chili-flavored jam, served with tomatoes and fresh mozzarella cheese; a mixed grill of seafood; grilled filet of local grouper served with a light tomato-caper sauce; spaghetti with lobster; grilled rack of lamb with gravy; a perfect filet mignon in a green-peppercorn sauce; and a zesty curried shrimp with rice.

Bank Lane at Bay St., just north of Parliament Sq. © 242/356-7012. Reservations recommended. Main courses US$17–US$28 (£8.50–£14) lunch, US$23–US$46 (£12–£23) dinner. AE, DISC, MC, V. Tues–Sat noon–3pm and 6–10pm. Bus: 17 or 21.

East Villa Restaurant and Lounge CHINESE/BAHAMIAN   You might imagine yourself in 1980s Hong Kong in this well-designed modern house across the road from the Nassau Yacht Club headquarters, a short drive east of downtown Nassau's commercial core. It's somewhat upscale and completely devoid of the sense of bureaucracy associated with restaurants in some of the island's larger resorts. Sometimes attracting affluent Florida yachters to its dimly lit precinct, its aquariums bubble in a simple but tasteful contemporary setting. Zesty Szechuan flavors appear on the menu, but less spicy Cantonese alternatives exist, including sweet-and-sour chicken and steamed vegetables with cashews and water chestnuts. Lobster tail in the spicy Chinese style is one of our favorites. Dishes can be ordered mild, medium, or zesty hot. On the Bahamian side of the menu, cracked conch, Bahamian lobster tail, grilled steaks, and pan-fried grouper cutlets with scallops are highlights.

E. Bay St. © 242/393-3377. Reservations required. Main courses US$13–US$24 (£6.50–£12) lunch, US$18–US$38 (£9–£19) dinner. AE, MC, V. Sun–Fri noon–3pm; daily 6–10pm. Bus: 9A, 9B, 11, or 19.

Luciano's of Chicago ITALIAN/SEAFOOD/STEAK   One of Nassau's best upscale restaurants lies within a low-slung, red-painted building. The Nassau branch of a successful franchise that originated in Chicago, it emphasizes stiff drinks, two-fisted portions, and macho charm. Many visitors prefer the terrace that has tables and pergolas positioned for a view of the towers and glittering lights of Atlantis just across the water. In addition to the terrace, there's a smoothly upscale dining room, air-conditioned and outfitted in tones of beige and brown. The menu includes a tempting roster of two-fisted steaks, a romaine salad topped with basil-and-garlic-marinated sweet peppers, pot-roasted and marinated chicken served with sautéed garlic and *kalamata* olives, and country-style rigatoni with sweet Italian sausage, pancetta ham, and a light tomato-flavored cream sauce. A soup that's particularly successful is made from escarole, white beans, and Italian sausage.

E. Bay St., just before the northbound entrance to the Paradise Island Bridge. © 242/323-7770. Reservations recommended. Main courses US$15–US$35 (£7.50–£18) lunch, US$20–US$50 (£10–£25) dinner. AE, DC, DISC, MC, V. Mon–Fri 11:30am–3pm; daily 6–10pm. Bus: 10.

Poop Deck BAHAMIAN/SEAFOOD   Raffish and informal, this is the older (and original) version of a restaurant that has expanded with another branch at Cable Beach. This original is less touristy, hosting a clientele of sailors, yachtspeople, and workers from the nearby marinas and boatyards. Many of them find perches on the second-floor open-air terrace, which overlooks the harbor and Paradise Island. If you like dining with a view, you won't find a better place than this in the heart of Nassau. At lunch, order conch chowder (perfectly seasoned) or a juicy beef burger. The waiters are friendly, the crowd is convivial, and the festivities continue into the evening, usually with lots of drinking. Native grouper fingers served with peas 'n' rice is the Bahamian soul-food dish. Two of the best seafood selections are the fresh lobster and the stuffed mushrooms with crabmeat. The creamy linguine with crisp garlic bread is another fine choice.

Nassau Yacht Haven Marina, E. Bay St. © 242/393-8175. Reservations recommended for dinner, not necessary at lunch. Main courses US$13–US$19 (£6.50–£9.50) lunch, US$19–US$30 (£9.50–£15) dinner. AE, DC, DISC, MC, V. Daily noon–4:30pm and 5–10:30pm. For the branch at the Nassau Yacht Haven: Bus 10, 19, or 23. For the branch on W. Bay St.: Bus 10 or "the Western bus."

Shoal Restaurant and Lounge 🅡 *Value* BAHAMIAN   Many of our good friends in Nassau swear that this is one of the best joints for authentic local food. We rank it near the top for a dining venue that's utterly without glamour but which serves sensible down-home food at a spot that's far removed from the typical tourist path. After all, where else can you get a good bowl of okra soup these days? This may or may not be your fantasy, but to a Bahamian, it's like pot liquor and turnip greens with corn bread are to a Southerner. Many diners follow an inaugural bowl of soup (either split pea or the above-mentioned okra) with more conch, either cracked or perhaps curried. But you can also order some unusual dishes, such as Bahamian-style curried mutton with native spices and herbs, stewed oxtail, or braised short ribs. Peas 'n' rice almost automatically accompanies virtually everything served here.

Nassau St. near the Poinciana Dr. intersection. 🅒 242/323-4400. Main courses US$9.50–US$17 (£4.75–£8.50). AE, DISC, MC, V. Sun–Thurs 7:30am–10pm; Fri 7:30am–10:30pm; Sat 6am–10pm. Bus: 16.

Taj Mahal NORTHERN INDIAN   This is Nassau's best and most frequently recommended Indian restaurant. Within a room lined with Indian art and artifacts, you'll dine on a wide range of savory and zesty Punjabi, tandoori, and curried dishes. Some of the best choices are the lamb selections, though concessions to local culture, like curried or tandoori-style conch, have begun cropping up on the menu. If you don't know what to order, consider a tandoori mixed platter, which, with a side dish or two, might satisfy two diners. All of the *korma* dishes, which combine lamb, chicken, beef, or vegetables in a creamy curry sauce, are very successful. Takeout meals are also available.

48 Parliament St. at Bay St. 🅒 242/356-3004. Reservations recommended. Main courses US$18–US$38 (£9–£19). AE, MC, V. Daily noon–3pm and 6:30–11pm. Bus: 10 or 17.

INEXPENSIVE

Bahamian Kitchen *Value* *Kids* BAHAMIAN/INTERNATIONAL   Located next to Trinity Church, within one of downtown's most congested neighborhoods, this is one of the best places for good Bahamian food at modest prices. Solid, unpretentious, and decent, it evokes the kind of restaurant you might find on a remote Bahamian Out Island. Down-home dishes include Bahamian-style lobster, fried red snapper, conch salad, stewed fish, curried chicken, okra soup, and pea soup and dumplings. Most dishes are served with peas 'n' rice. You can also order such old-fashioned Bahamian fare as stewed fish and corned beef and grits, all served with johnnycake. If you'd like to introduce your kids to Bahamian cuisine, this is an ideal choice. There's takeout service, which is great if you're planning a picnic.

Trinity Place, off Market St. 🅒 242/325-0702. Lunch and dinner main courses US$12–US$45 (£6–£23). AE, MC, V. Mon–Sat noon–10pm. Bus: 10.

Café Skans *Value* GREEK/AMERICAN/BAHAMIAN   Owned and operated by a hardworking Greek family, this is a straightforward, Formica-clad diner with an open kitchen, offering flavorful food that's served without fanfare in generous portions. Set in the midst of Nassau's densest concentration of shops, it attracts local residents and office workers from the government buildings nearby. Menu items include Bahamian fried or barbecued chicken, conch chowder, bean soup with dumplings, souvlakia or gyros in pita bread, burgers, steaks, and various seafood platters. This is where workaday Nassau comes for breakfast.

Bay St., near the corner of Market St. 🅒 242/322-2486. Reservations not accepted. Breakfast US$4–US$11 (£2–£5.50); sandwiches US$6–US$12 (£3–£6); main-course platters US$6–US$19 (£3–£9.50). MC, V. Daily 8am–6pm. Bus: 10 or 17.

Conch Fritters Bar & Grill BAHAMIAN/INTERNATIONAL   A true local hang-out with real island atmosphere, this lighthearted, family-friendly restaurant changes its focus several times throughout the day. Lunches and dinners are high-volume, high-turnover affairs mitigated by attentive staff. Guests invariably include older diners and parents with young children in tow. Food choices are standard but still quite good, including cracked conch, fried shrimp, grilled salmon, blackened rib-eye steak, burgers, sandwiches, and six different versions of chicken, including a combination platter with barbecued ribs. Specialty drinks from the always-active bar include the Goombay Smash. Musicians perform Thursday to Saturday 7 until 10pm.

Marlborough St. (across from the British Colonial Hilton). ℭ 242/323-8801. Burgers, sandwiches, and platters US$10–US$36 (£5–£18). AE, MC, V. Daily 11am–11pm (until midnight Fri–Sat). Bus: 10.

Double Dragon CANTONESE/SZECHUAN   The chefs at this unpretentious eatery hail from the province of Canton in mainland China, so that locale inspires most of the food here. You'll find it within an unscenic, raffish-looking waterfront neighborhood a short drive east of downtown Nassau. If you've ever really wondered about the differences between Cantonese and Szechuan cuisine, a quick look at the menu here will highlight them. Lobster, chicken, or beef, for example, can be prepared Cantonese style, with mild black-bean or ginger sauce; or in spicier Szechuan formats of red peppers, chilis, and garlic. Honey-garlic chicken and orange-flavored shrimp are always popular and succulent. Overall, this place is a fine choice if you're eager for a change from grouper and burgers.

E. Bay St. btw. Mackey St. and Williams Court. ℭ 242/393-5718. Main courses US$10–US$23 (£5–£12). AE, DISC, MC, V. Mon–Thurs noon–10pm; Fri noon–11pm; Sat 4–11pm; Sun 5–10pm. Bus: 10 or 19.

CABLE BEACH
VERY EXPENSIVE

The Black Angus Grille ℱ STEAKS/SEAFOOD   This is a truly excellent steakhouse that's positioned amid a cluster of dining options immediately above Cable Beach's Crystal Palace Casino. Relaxed but macho-looking and undeniably upscale, it's Cable Beach's most consistently busy restaurant—a function of its good food and, according to its manager, of the predilection of gamblers for juicy, carnivorous steaks after a nerve-jangling session at the gaming tables. Early in 2007, management spent a small fortune upgrading the decor, adding an intricately crafted paneled ceiling and generally improving a dark, slightly overcrowded venue that might have appealed to Frank Sinatra and the Rat Pack.

Steaks are well-prepared—succulent, juicy, and cooked to your specifications. There's prime rib, filet mignon, pepper steak, grilled tuna with a white bean salad, blackened conch filet, Caesar salad, different preparations of seafood, and an array of dessert soufflés that include versions with chocolate, praline, and orange. **Hint:** If you're absolutely fixated on steak, this is indeed a seductive culinary venue. But immediately adjacent to the Black Angus are two other restaurants, the all-Italian Sole Mare (p. 89), with equivalently priced and, frankly, much more creative food. There's also the less expensive yet highly imaginative nouvelle-Asian Moso (p. 90), which we also prefer.

In the Wyndham Nassau Resort, upstairs from the Crystal Palace Casino, W. Bay St. ℭ 242/327-6200. Reservations recommended. Main courses US$26–US$60 (£13–£30). AE, DC, DISC, MC, V. Daily 6–11pm. Bus: 10.

Sole Mare ℱℱ NORTHERN ITALIAN   This is our top choice for elegant and stylish dining along Cable Beach, and it also serves the island's best northern Italian cuisine. The chefs are well-trained, intuitive, and inventive, as shown by intensely creative dishes that crop up at regular intervals such as lobster macaroni paired with an herb-infused version of lamb-loin souvlakia, or deep-fried calamari stuffed with fresh herbs and feta cheese. The fresh fish of the day is the keynote of many a delectable meal here. A number of other ingredients have to be imported from the U.S., but the chefs still work their magic with them. A meal might begin with Castilian-style garlic soup, or jumbo shrimp sautéed in ouzo, and reach a high point with either a *piperade* (Basque stew) of lobster or a filet of halibut prepared lyonnaise style with cream, minced onions, and scalloped potatoes. The restaurant offers three flavors of dessert soufflés: The one we prefer is prepared with sweet Marsala wine and fresh strawberries.

In the Wyndham Nassau Resort & Crystal Palace Casino, W. Bay St. ℂ 242/327-6200. Reservations required. Main courses US$28–US$49 (£14–£25). AE, DC, DISC, MC, V. Tues–Wed and Fri–Sun 6–11pm (hours and opening days vary with the season and resort occupancy; call ahead). Bus: 10.

EXPENSIVE

Amici ✿ ITALIAN   Following a radical renovation and upgrade in 2007, this highly recommended restaurant works hard to maintain its status as a culinary showcase for the flavorful and savory Italian cuisine that many guests crave after too long an exposure to an all-Bahamian diet. Set within the Sheraton directly astride Cable Beach, it includes spinning ceiling fans, a big-windowed beach view, and the kind of dark-stained wooden furniture you might expect in a trattoria in Italy. Popular and long-enduring dishes here include scampi cocktails, Caesar salads, fettuccine alfredo, Florentine-style breast of chicken on a bed of spinach, spicy shrimp, and braised pork shank with olive oil, hot peppers, and angel-hair pasta.

Sheraton Cable Beach Resort, W. Bay St. ℂ 242/327-6000. Main courses US$23–US$48 (£12–£24). AE, DC, DISC, MC, V. Daily 6–10:30pm. Bus: 10.

Capriccio ITALIAN/INTERNATIONAL   Set beside a prominent roundabout, about .5km (⅓ mile) west of the mega-hotels of Cable Beach, this restaurant lies within a much-weathered, faux-baroque Italian building with Corinthian columns and an outdoor terrace. Inside, it's a lot less formal, outfitted like an upscale lunch-eonette, but with lots of exposed granite, busy espresso machines, and kindly Bahamian staff who understand Italian culinary nuance. At lunch, you get pretty ordinary fare such as fresh salads, sandwiches, and a few hot platters like cracked conch. But the cooks shine at night, offering dishes such as chicken breast with sage and wine sauce, veal cutlets served Milanese-style or with Marsala sauce, spaghetti with pesto and pine nuts, and seafood platters.

W. Bay St. ℂ 242/327-8547. Reservations recommended. Lunch items US$6–US$24 (£3–£12); dinner main courses US$15–US$32 (£7.50–£16). MC, V. Mon–Sat 11am–10pm; Sun 5–10pm. Bus: 10 or 17.

Moso ✿✿ ASIAN   This is the island's newest and most experimental restaurant. There are many good and intriguing things about it: It deliberately prices meals several notches below the rates charged by other restaurants in the same resort. You'll quickly get the sense that this is a hipster kind of place serving hipster cuisine—in fact, every dish you've ever liked from every Asian menu you've ever looked at all seems to have found its way onto the menu here. Each member of this restaurant's Bahamian waitstaff spent several months studying the preparation and context of Asian food and Asian culture, and they'll guide you through a menu composed of many different small and medium-size dishes. These you'll compose into combinations that don't necessarily follow Western dining rituals. The best menu items include aromatic crispy duck; Mongolian-style chicken and beef hot pot; fresh tofu stir-fried with minced pork, garlic, and chili; seared ahi tuna *tataki* with *yazu* lemon sauce; and a succulent blend of octopus and local conch with cucumbers in rice vinegar. You can also order meticulously carved portions of chicken breast, shrimp, pork tenderloin, filet mignon, lobster tail, salmon, or mahimahi prepared in any of three different ways: Cantonese, Sichuan dry-rubbed, or teriyaki-style.

Wyndham Nassau Resort, upstairs from the Crystal Palace Casino, W. Bay St. ✆ 242/327-6200. Reservations recommended. Small plates US$6–US$13 (£3–£6.50); main courses US$14–US$39 (£7–£20). AE, DC, DISC, MC, V. Thurs–Mon 6–10:30pm (opening days may vary). Bar daily 6pm–1am. Bus: 10.

The Poop Deck at Sandy Port INTERNATIONAL/SEAFOOD   This is one of the three most imposing, desirable restaurants west of Cable Beach, convenient for the owners of the many upscale villas and condos, including Lyford Cay, that occupy New Providence's western edge. It's set within a peach-colored concrete building that's highly visible from West Bay Street. Despite the rosy exterior, it's a bit sterile-looking inside. This simple island restaurant evolved from a roughneck bar that occupied this site during the early 1970s. Lunch is usually devoted to well-prepared burgers, pastas, sandwiches, and salads. Dinners are more substantial, featuring filet mignon, seafood and steak combos, cracked conch, fried shrimp, and fresh fish. The house drink is a Bacardi Splish-Splash, an enticing blend of Bacardi Select, Nassau Royal Liqueur, pineapple juice, cream, and sugar-cane syrup.

Poop Deck Dr., off W. Bay St. ✆ 242/327-DECK (327-3325). Reservations recommended. Main courses US$13–US$19 (£6.50–£9.50) lunch, US$19–US$33 (£9.50–£17) dinner. AE, DISC, MC, V. Tues–Sat noon–10:30pm; Sun noon–10pm. Bus: 10, or "the Western bus."

Provence ✿ MEDITERRANEAN   Nassau's best dishes that feature the sunny cuisine of southern France are showcased within this restaurant that's outfitted in cheerful tones of yellow. Lying near West Bay Street's western terminus, it's extremely popular with well-heeled locals (some of whom aren't particularly enchanted with the island's blockbuster casino hotels and their eateries). Decor includes big-windowed sea views and oil paintings of landscapes that conjure up the Mediterranean coast. Provence prepares its *cuisine du soleil* with superb simplicity—Atlantic salmon with citrus butter, for example—so as not to mar the natural flavor. Other dishes are heavily spiced, such as the rib-eye steak in a fire-breathing pepper sauce. The chefs also turn out a delightful bouillabaisse evocative of the type served in Marseille. Daily seafood specials are featured—our favorite being the pan-seared sea bass, or else you might order the black grouper filet. Everybody seems to like the lobster cocktails and the rack of lamb.

Old Town Sandy Port. ✆ 242/327-0985. Reservations required. Lunch main courses US$9–US$25 (£4.50–£13); dinner main courses US$27–US$48 (£14–£24). AE, DISC, MC, V. Mon–Fri 11:30am–3pm; Mon–Sat 6–10:30pm. Bus: 10, or "the Western bus."

WEST OF CABLE BEACH

The Restaurant at Compass Point ✿ BAHAMIAN   Dining here might remind anyone who experienced the '60s of how they felt after ingesting one of those hallucinogenic brownies during their college years. The ceiling is orange, the bar is a study in marine blues, the view sweeps out over the sea, and everywhere you'll be reminded of the vivid Junkanoo, or reggae, colors of the West Indies. Anyhow, it's a charming and somewhat out-of-the-way retreat from the densely populated urban scenes of downtown Nassau and nearby Cable Beach. Lunches are simple and uncomplicated

> (Tips) **Ingredients for the Island's Best Picnics**
>
> If you're keen on organizing a picnic and want to assemble your provisions, consider heading about 3km (2 miles) west of Cable Beach. Within a shopping complex known as the Caves Village Shopping Centre, you'll find the **Gourmet Market** (② 242/327-1067), the island's most upscale grocery store. Functioning like a magnet for villa owners within the nearby exclusive gated community of Lyford Cay, it offers fruits, fish, cheeses, wines, and pastries. And yes, they'll make sandwiches and even assemble, with or without strong guidance from you, picnic meals to go. It's open Monday to Saturday from 9am to 6:30pm, Sunday from 7am to 1:30pm.

affairs, with turkey club sandwiches, meal-size salads, and burgers. Dinners are more elaborate and steeped in West Indian tradition, focusing on dishes which include cracked conch and pan-fried grouper with peas, rice, and plantain. Try the lobster stir-fried with mango and goat peppers. Because of its position facing the setting sun, the bar is well-known as a spot from which to look for the elusive "green flash," and if that's your aim, the bartender can explain this to you and prepare a bright-yellow Compass Bliss.

Compass Point Resort, W. Bay St., Gambier, Nassau. ② 242/327-4500. Reservations recommended. Lunch platters US$11–US$19 (£5.50–£9.50); dinner main courses US$18–US$55 (£9–£28). AE, MC, V. Daily 11am–11pm (last order). Bar closes at midnight. Bus 10 from Nassau and Cable Beach.

Travellers Rest ⓡ ⓥalue BAHAMIAN/SEAFOOD   Set in an isolated spot about 2.5km (1½ miles) west of Cable Beach's mega-hotels, this restaurant feels far away from it all. Its owners will make you feel like you're dining on a remote Out Island. Travellers Rest is set in a cozy cement-sided house that stands in a grove of sea-grape and palm trees facing the ocean. Because of its location close to the airport, clients whose flights are delayed sometimes opt to chill out here until their flight departs. The restaurant was established by Winnipeg-born Joan Hannah in 1972 and since then has fed ordinary as well as famous folks like Stevie Wonder, Gladys Knight, Julio Iglesias, Eric Clapton, and Rosa Parks. Dine outside, but if it's rainy (highly unlikely), go inside the tavern, with its small bar decorated with local paintings. In this laid-back atmosphere, you can feast on well-prepared grouper fingers, barbecued ribs, curried chicken, steamed or cracked conch, or minced crayfish. Finish with guava cake, the best on the island. The conch salad served on the weekends is said to increase men's virility.

W. Bay St., near Gambier (14km/8¾ miles west of the center of Nassau). ② 242/327-7633. Main courses US$12–US$29 (£6–£15) lunch, US$14–US$42 (£7–£21) dinner. AE, DISC, MC, V. Daily noon–10pm. Bus: 10, or "the Western bus."

5 Beaches, Watersports & Other Outdoor Pursuits

One of the great sports centers of the world, Nassau and the islands that surround it are marvelous places for swimming, sunning, snorkeling, scuba diving, boating, water-skiing, and deep-sea fishing, as well as playing tennis and golf.

You can learn more about available activities by calling **The Bahamas Sports Tourist Office** (© 800/422-4262 or 954/236-9292) from anywhere in the continental U.S. Call Monday through Friday from 9am to 5pm, Eastern Standard Time (EST). Or write the center at 1200 South Pine Island Rd., Suite 750, Plantation, FL 33324.

HITTING THE BEACH

In The Bahamas, as in Puerto Rico, the issue regarding public access to beaches is a hot and controversial subject. Recognizing this, the government has made efforts to intersperse public beaches with easy access between more private beaches where access may be impeded. Although mega-resorts discourage nonresidents from accessing their individual beaches, there are so many local public beaches that all you'd have to do is drive or walk to any of the many unmarked, unnamed beaches.

Anyway, most people stay in one of the large beachfront resorts which have the ocean meeting the sand right outside of their doors. For those hoping to explore more of the coast, here's a list of recommended beaches that are absolutely accessible to the public:

Cable Beach 🏖🏖   No particular beach is actually called Cable Beach, yet this is the most popular stretch of sand on New Providence Island. Instead of an actual beach, Cable Beach is the name given to a string of resorts and beaches in the center of New Providence's northern coast, attracting the most visitors. This beachfront offers 6.5km (4 miles) of soft, white sand, with many different types of food, restaurants, snack bars, and watersports offered by the hotels lining the waterfront. Calypso music floats to the sand from hotel pool patios where vacationers play musical chairs and see how low they can limbo. Vendors wend their way between sunscreen-slathered bodies selling armloads of shell jewelry, T-shirts, beach cover-ups, and fresh coconuts for sipping the sweet "water" straight from the shell. Others offer hair-braiding services or sign up visitors for water-skiing, jet-skiing, and banana boat rides. Kiosks advertise parasailing, scuba diving, and snorkeling trips, as well as party cruises to offshore islands. Waters can be rough and reefy, but then calm and clear a little farther along the shore. There are no public toilets here because guests of the resorts use their hotel facilities. If you're not a hotel guest and not a customer, you're not supposed to use the facilities. Cable Beach resorts begin 4.8km (3 miles) west of downtown Nassau, and even though they line much of this long swath of beach, there are various sections where public access is available without crossing through private hotel grounds.

Caves Beach   On the north shore, past the Cable Beach hotels, Caves Beach is 11km (6¾ miles) southwest of Nassau. It stands near Rock Point, right before the turnoff along Blake Road that leads to the airport. Since visitors often don't know of this place, it's a good spot to escape the hordes. It's also an attractive beach with soft sands. There are no toilets or changing facilities.

Delaporte Beach   Just west of Cable Beach's busiest section is this public-access beach where you can escape the crowds. It opens onto clear waters and boasts white sands, although it has neither facilities nor toilets.

Goodman's Bay   This public beach lies east of Cable Beach on the way toward Nassau's center. Goodman's Bay and Saunders Beach (see below) often host local fundraising cookouts, during which vendors sell fish, chicken, conch, peas 'n' rice, and macaroni and cheese. People swim and socialize to blaring reggae and calypso tunes. To find out when one of these beach parties is happening, ask your hotel's staff or pick up a local newspaper. There's a playground, plus toilet facilities.

Finds **A Beach for Lovers**

Continuing west along West Bay Street, you reach **Love Beach,** across from Sea Gardens, a nice stretch of sand lying east of Northwest Point. Love Beach, although not big, is a special favorite of lovers (hence the name). The snorkeling is superb, too. It's technically private, but no one bothers visitors, even though locals fervently hope it won't become overrun like Cable Beach.

Old Fort Beach *Finds*   To escape the crowds on weekdays, we often head here, a 15-minute drive west of Nassau International Airport (take W. Bay St. toward Lyford Cay). This lovely beach opens onto Old Fort Bay's turquoise waters, near western New Providence. The least developed of the island's beaches, it attracts many homeowners from swanky Lyford Cay nearby. In winter, it can be quite windy, but in summer, it's as calm as the Caribbean.

Saunders Beach   East of Cable Beach, this is where many islanders go on the weekends. To reach it, take West Bay Street from Nassau toward Coral Island. This beach lies across from Fort Charlotte, just west of Arawak Cay. Like Goodman's Bay (see above), it often hosts local fundraising cookouts open to the public. These can be a lot of fun. There are no public facilities.

Western Esplanade   If you're staying at a hotel in downtown Nassau, such as the British Colonial, this is a good beach to patronize close to town. On this narrow strip of sand convenient to Nassau, you'll find toilets, changing facilities, and a snack bar. It's also known as Junkanoo Beach.

BIKING

A half-day bicycle tour with **Bahamas Outdoors Ltd.** (© 242/362-1574; www.bahamasoutdoors.com) takes you on a 5km (3-mile) bike ride along scenic forest and shoreline trails in the Coral Harbour area on the island's southwestern coast. New Providence resident Carolyn Wardle, an expert in the region's ecology, bird life, and history, provides tutelage and ongoing commentary. The itinerary follows a series of easy trails, usually on hard-packed earth, along seashores and through pink forests. En route, you'll see sleepy Adelaide Village (settled by freed slaves in the 1830s) and views, with the naked eye or aided by binoculars, of local birds. Shorts and a T-shirt are the recommended attire, and tours rarely include more than a half-dozen participants at a time; most are morning events that rarely last more than 4 hours. The cost is around US$70 (£35) per person.

If you'd like to go it alone, know that some of the major hotels on Paradise Beach and Cable Beach rent bikes to their guests. You can bike along Cable Beach or along the beachfront at Paradise Island, but roads through downtown Nassau are too narrow and traffic is too congested to make the ride genuinely pleasant or even particularly safe.

BOAT CRUISES

A number of operators offer cruises from the harbors around New Providence, with trips ranging from daytime voyages for snorkeling, picnicking, sunning, and swimming, to sunset and moonlight cruises.

Barefoot Sailing Cruises, Bay Shore Marina, on East Bay Street (② **242/393-0820;** www.barefootsailingcruises.com), operates the 41-foot *Wind Dance,* which leaves for all-day cruises involving many sailing and snorkeling possibilities. This is your best bet if you're seeking a more romantic cruise and don't want 100 people aboard. The cruises usually stop at Rose Island, a charming, picture-perfect spot with an uncrowded beach and palm trees. You can also sail on a ketch, the 56-foot *Riding High.* Cruise options are plentiful, including sailing, snorkeling, and exploring for US$65 (£33) per person for a half-day and US$99 (£50) for a full day. A 2-hour sunset cruise, departing between 5 and 8pm two to three times a week, depending on the season, the weather, and advance bookings, costs US$55 (£28) per person.

Flying Cloud, Paradise Island West Dock (② **242/363-4430**), is a twin-hulled sailing catamaran carrying 50 people for day and sunset trips. It's a good bet for those who want a more intimate cruise and shy away from the heavy volume carried aboard the Majestic Tours catamarans (see below). Snorkeling equipment is included in the cost, which is US$60 (£30) per person for a half-day charter. A 2½-hour sunset cruise also goes for US$60 (£30). Evening bookings are on Monday, Wednesday, and Friday. On Sunday, a 5-hour cruise leaves at 10am and costs US$75 (£38) per person.

Majestic Tours Ltd., Hillside Manor (② **242/322-2606;** www.majesticholidays.com), will book 3-hour cruises on two of the biggest catamarans in the Atlantic, offering views of the water, sun, sand, and outlying reefs. This is the biggest and most professionally run of the cruise boats, and it's an affordable option, but we find that there are just too many other passengers aboard. An onboard cash bar keeps the drinks flowing. The *Yellow Bird* is suitable for up to 110 passengers and departs from Prince George's Dock in downtown Nassau, just behind the Straw Market; ask for the exact departure point when you make your reservation. The cost is US$54 (£27) per adult, half-price for children under 10 years, and snorkeling equipment is included. The tour lasts 4 hours and includes lunch and drinks. The outfitter has also added another boat, the *Robinson Crusoe,* which holds 200 passengers. On Wednesday, Friday, and Sunday, cruises run from 10am to 4:30pm, costing US$55 (£28) for adults and half-price for children 10 and under. Sunset dinner cruises (7–10pm on Tues and Fri) cost US$61 (£31) per adult, again half-price for children.

FISHING

Fishing choices are plentiful: You can troll for wahoo, tuna, and marlin in the deep sea, or cast in the shallows for snapper, grouper, and yellowtail. Anchoring and bottom-fishing are calmer options. May to August are the best months to catch oceanic bonito and the blackfin tuna, June and July for blue marlin, and November through February for the wahoo found in reefy areas. Arrangements for fishing trips can be made at any of the big hotels, but unfortunately, there's a hefty price tag.

One of the most reliable companies, **Born Free Charters** (② **242/393-4144;** www.bornfreefishing.com) maintains a fleet of three vessels, each between 11 and 14m long, that can seat six comfortably. You can rent them for a half-day (US$600–US$800/£300–£400) or a full day (US$1,200–US$1,600/£600–£800). Each additional person pays US$50 (£25). We recommend this company because it offers so many types of fishing and gives lots of leeway regarding where you want to fish and how much time you want to spend.

Occasionally, boat owners will configure themselves and their boats as businesses for deep-sea fishing. Unless you're dealing with a genuinely experienced guide, however, your fishing trip may or may not be a success. **John Pratt** has emerged over the years as one of the most consistently reliable deep-sea fishermen. He maintains a 14m fishing boat, making it available for full- or half-day deep-sea fishing excursions. It docks every night at the island's largest marina, the 150-slip **Nassau Yacht Haven,** on East Bay Street (✆ **242/393-8173** or 422-0364), where a member of the staff will direct you. Alternatively, you can call ✆ **242/422-0364** to speak to Mr. Pratt directly. It takes about 20 minutes of boat travel to reach an offshore point where dolphin and wahoo may or may not be biting, depending on a raft of complicated seasonable factors. These trips need to be booked several weeks in advance.

GOLF

Some of the country's best golfing is in Nassau and on nearby Paradise Island. Although "dormant," or storm-damaged, courses on the extreme western end of New Providence might one day be rejuvenated, at press time, the only functioning golf course on New Providence Island that was open to nonmembers was the **Cable Beach Golf Course** ★★ on West Bay Street, Cable Beach (✆ **242/677-4175**). An intricately designed 18-hole, 6,453-yard, par-71 championship golf course, it benefited from a major redesign between 2000 and 2003. The makeover reshaped the fairways, repositioned putting greens, and introduced new hazards and water-lined holes throughout two-thirds of its layout. Better year-round playing conditions were ensured by introducing a salt-tolerant grass (paspalum) that is greener, firmer, and more upright, withstanding the salty breezes and tropical heat while providing a premium putting surface. The alterations were overseen by veteran designer Fred M. Settle, Jr.

Many of the players who tee off are guests of hotels on Cable Beach. Between November and April, greens fees cost US$110 (£55) for guests of the Sheraton or Wyndham hotels, or US$180 (£90) for people staying anywhere else. In the off-season (May–Oct), residents of the Wyndham or Sheraton properties pay US$90 (£45); people staying at other venues pay US$120 (£60). Greens fees include the use of an electric golf cart.

By 2010, the Cable Beach course may have gravitated into the orbit of Baha Mar Resorts. As such, it will eventually benefit from massive amounts of capital available for additional improvements and reconfigurations; it might become more Disney-esque and lavish, but work likely won't begin until late 2009, and it will remain closed for a full 2 years after that. Stay tuned.

HORSEBACK RIDING

Windsor Equestrian Centre & Happy Trails Stables, Coral Harbour, on the southwest shore (✆ **242/362-1820;** www.bahamahorse.com), offers a 90-minute horseback trail ride, which is limited to a maximum of eight riders at a time, for US$110 (£55) per person. The price includes free transportation to and from your hotel. The stables are signposted from the Nassau International Airport, which is 3km (2 miles) away. Children must be 12 or older, riders must weigh less than 91kg (201 lb.), and reservations are required.

SNORKELING, SCUBA DIVING & UNDERWATER WALKS

There's great snorkeling off most of the New Providence shores, especially **Love Beach.** Most hotels and resorts will rent or loan snorkeling equipment to guests. Several of the companies mentioned above under "Boat Cruises" (p. 94) also offer snorkel trips. Also see "Easy Side Trips to Nearby Islands," later in this chapter, for descriptions of additional snorkeling excursions.

Our favorite site for snorkeling is **Goulding Cay,** off the island's western tip. Underwater, you'll find a field of hard corals, especially the elegant elkhorn. The clear waters here and shallow coral heads make it ideal for filmmakers. In fact, it's been featured in many films, from a number of James Bond movies to *20,000 Leagues Under the Sea.* More elkhorn coral is found to the south at **Southwest Reef,** which also shelters stunning star coral in water less than 2.4m (8 ft.) deep. To the north is **Fish Hotel,** which is not much on coral but graced with large schools of fish, especially red snapper, jacks, and grunts.

There are more dive sites around New Providence than you can see in one visit, but a few of our favorites follow: **Shark Wall** ꞏꞏ, 16km (10 miles) off the coast, is the most intriguing. Others include the **Rose Island Reefs,** the **Southwest Reef, Razorback,** and **Booby Rock Reef.** Dive outfitters can also lead you to many old shipwrecks off the coast, along with caves and cliffs. Wrecks include *Mahoney* and *Alcora,* plus the wreck featured in the James Bond film *Never Say Never Again.* Divers can also explore the airplane propeller used in another Bond film, *Thunderball.* All dive outfitters take you to one or more of these sites.

Bahamas Divers, on East Bay Street (ℂ **800/398-3483** in the U.S. or 242/ 393-5644; www.bahamadivers.com), offers packages that include a half-day of snorkeling at offshore reefs for US$45 (£23) per person, and a half-day scuba trip with experienced certified divers for between US$65 (£33) and US$119 (£60), depending on the destination. Half-day excursions for certified divers to deeper outlying reefs, drop-offs, and blue holes can be arranged, usually for US$99 (£50) for a two-tank dive and US$65 (£33) for a one-tank dive. Novice divers sometimes sign up for a carefully supervised course which includes instruction with scuba equipment in a swimming pool, followed by a shallow shorefront dive accompanied by an instructor, also for US$99 (£50) per person.

Participants receive free transportation from their hotel to the boats. Children must be 10 or older, and reservations are required, especially during the holiday season.

Stuart Cove's Dive Bahamas, on Southwest Bay Street, South Ocean (ℂ **800/ 879-9832** in the U.S. or 242/362-4171; www.stuartcove.com), is about 10 minutes from top dive sites, including the coral reefs, wrecks, and the underwater airplane structure featured in James Bond thrillers. For the island's most exciting underwater adventure, divers head to the *Caribe Breeze* **wreck,** depicted in the film *Open Water.* Here the staff feeds reef sharks some 15m (49 ft.) below the water; from a position of safety, divers in full scuba gear witness the show. Steep sea walls and the Porpoise Pen Reefs (named for Flipper) are also on the diving agenda. A two-tank dive in the morning costs US$99 (£50); an all-day program goes for US$150 (£75). All prices for boat dives include tanks, weights, and belts. An open-water certification course starts at US$950 (£475). Bring along two friends, and the price drops to US$490 (£245) per person. Three-hour escorted boat snorkeling trips cost US$55 (£28) each; children under 12 are included for US$30 (£15) each.

A special feature is a series of shark-dive experiences priced from US$145 (£73). At **Shark Arena,** divers kneel while a dive master feeds the toothsome predators off a long pole. On the **Shark Buoy** dive at a depth of about 9m (30 ft.), sharks swim among divers while the dive master feeds them.

6 Seeing the Sights

Most of Nassau can be explored on foot, beginning at Rawson Square in the center, where Bahamian fishers unload a variety of produce and fish—crates of mangoes, oranges, tomatoes, and limes, plus lots of crimson-lipped conch. To experience this slice of Bahamian life, go any morning Monday through Saturday before noon.

The best way to see some of Nassau's major public buildings is to take our walking tour (p. 103), which will give you not only an overview of the historic highlights, but also an overall feel for the city. After that, concentrate on specific sights you'd like to take in; Ardastra Gardens and Coral Island Bahamas are notable options.

THE TOP ATTRACTIONS

Ardastra Gardens, Zoo & Conservation Center ❧   The main attraction of the Ardastra Gardens, almost 2 hectares (5 acres) of lush tropical plants about 1.5km (1 mile) west of downtown Nassau near Fort Charlotte, is the parading flock of **pink flamingos.** The Caribbean flamingo, national bird of The Bahamas, had almost disappeared by the early 1940s but was brought back to significant numbers through the efforts of the National Trust. They now flourish in the rookery on Great Inagua. A flock of these exotic feathered creatures has been trained to march in drill formation, responding to human commands with long-legged precision and discipline. The flamingos perform daily at 10:30am, 2:10pm, and 4:10pm.

⟨Finds⟩ To Market, to Market at Potter's Cay

One of the liveliest places in Nassau during the day is **Potter's Cay,** a native market that thrives beneath the Paradise Island Bridge. From the Out Islands, fishing boats and heavily laden sloops arrive early in the morning to unload the day's catch. Spiny lobster is the most expensive seafood, but grouper reigns supreme along with fresh crab, jack, and mackerel.

If grouper is king, then "sweet, sexy conch," as the locals say, is queen. Vendors make the freshest conch salad right on the spot; if you haven't eaten the delicacy before, this is the place to try it.

What we don't like to see are fishmongers chopping up sea turtles, a highly endangered species. However, the vendors are not of the politically correct sort, and they're more interested in catering to the Bahamians' life-long love of turtle flesh than they are in preserving the species for future generations.

Not just fish is sold here. Sloops from the Out Islands also bring in cartons of freshly harvested vegetables, including the fiery hot peppers so beloved by locals, along with an array of luscious exotic fruits. *Tip:* Many of these vendors have a wicked sense of humor and will offer you a taste of tamarind, claiming it's the "sweetest taste on God's earth." Invariably, tricked visitors spit it out: The taste is horrendously offensive.

You can also see mail boats leaving and coming to this quay. Watching their frenetic departure or arrival is one of the island's more amusing scenes.

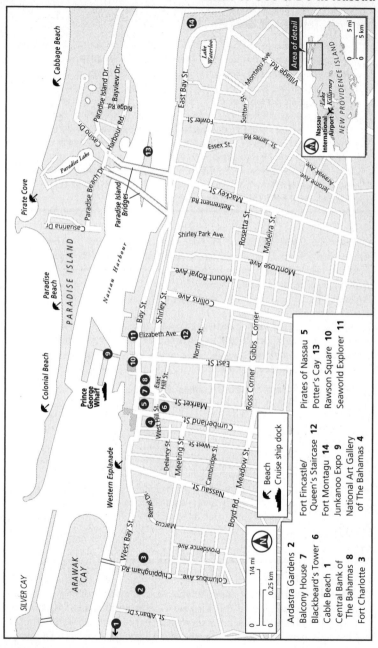

Ardastra Gardens **2**
Balcony House **7**
Blackbeard's Tower **6**
Cable Beach **1**
Central Bank of
  The Bahamas **8**
Fort Charlotte **3**

Fort Fincastle/
  Queen's Staircase **12**
Fort Montagu **14**
Junkanoo Expo **9**
National Art Gallery
  of The Bahamas **4**

Pirates of Nassau **5**
Potter's Cay **13**
Rawson Square **10**
Seaworld Explorer **11**

Beach
Cruise ship dock

Finds The Secret Garden

The Retreat, Village Road (℃ **242/393-1317**), on the southern outskirts of downtown Nassau, is the home of The Bahamas National Trust. A clapboard-sided green-and-white building, it was originally conceived as the homestead of the Langlois family and purchased from them by the National Trust in 1925. Whereas there's nothing of particular interest inside the house (it contains mostly workaday offices), its gardens are worth a visit. They consist of 4.4 hectares (11 acres) of the most unspoiled greens on New Providence and con-tain about 200 species of exotic palm trees. The grounds, which are for the most part flat, can be navigated with a map available on-site. A gift shop sells books and memorabilia approved by and associated with the National Trust. Visit Monday to Friday from 9am to 5pm; admission costs US$2 (£1) for adults and US$1 (50p) for children and students.

Other exotic wildlife here include boa constrictors (very tame), macaws, kinkajous (honey bears) from Central and South America, peacocks and peahens, capuchin monkeys, iguanas, lemurs, margays, brown-headed tamarins (monkeys), and a croco-dile. There are also numerous waterfowl in Swan Lake, including black swans from Australia and several species of wild ducks. Parrot feedings take place at 11am, 1:30pm, and 3:30pm.

You can get a good look at Ardastra's flora by walking along the signposted paths. Many of the more interesting and exotic trees bear plaques listing their names.

Chippingham Rd. ℃ 242/323-5806. www.ardastra.com. Admission US$15 (£7.50) adults, US$7.50 (£3.75) children 4–12, 3 and under free. Daily 9am–4:30pm. Bus: 10.

National Art Gallery of The Bahamas ℛ At long last, this archipelago nation has a showcase in which to display the works of its talented artists. In a restored 18th-century building in the center of Nassau, the gallery features Bahamian art, which, as an entity, has existed for only 50 years. Museum curators claim that the present collection is only the nucleus of a larger, long-range strategy to beef up the present number of works. Most of the paintings on exhibit are divided into a historical and a contemporary collection. Pioneering Bahamian artists are honored, as are younger and more modern painters. Among island artists, Amos Ferguson is one of the most acclaimed. His somewhat naïve yet sophisticated technique is at its best in the paint-ing *Snowbirds;* he used house paint on cardboard to create a remarkable portrait. Maxwell Taylor and Antonius Roberts are two other heavily featured Bahamian painters.

Villa Doyle, W. Hill St. in downtown Nassau. ℃ 242/328-5800. www.nagb.org.bs. Admission US$5 (£2.50) adults, US$3 (£1.50) seniors and students, free for children 12 and under. Tues–Sat 10am–4pm. Bus: 10.

Seaworld Explorer ℛ If you're curious about life below the waves but aren't a strong swimmer, hop aboard this 45-person submarine. Tours last 90 minutes and include 45 to 55 minutes of actual underwater travel at depths of about 3.5m (11 ft.). Big windows allow big views of a protected ecology zone offshore from Paradise Island Airport. The remainder of the time is devoted to an above-water tour of landmarks on either side of the channel that separates Nassau from Paradise Island.

W. Bay St. at Elizabeth Ave. © 242/356-2548. Reservations required. Tours US$45 (£23) adults, US$25 (£13) children 2–12. Tours Tues, Wed, Fri, and Sat at 9:30am, 11:30am, and 1:30pm year-round; additional departure at 1:30pm Dec–June. Bus: 10.

MORE ATTRACTIONS

Balcony House   This landmark house's original design exemplifies late-18th-century Southeast American architecture. The pink two-story structure is named for its overhanging and much-photographed balcony. Restored in the 1990s, the house has been returned to its original design, recapturing a historic period. The mahogany staircase inside is thought to have been salvaged from a wrecked ship in the 1800s. At press time, the house was closed for renovations but might, by the time of your visit, have reopened. Call in advance before you go.

Trinity Place and Market St. © 242/302-2621. Free admission, but donation advised. Mon–Wed and Fri 9:30am–1pm and 2–4:30pm; Thurs 10am–1pm. Bus: 10.

Blackbeard's Tower   These crumbling remains of a watchtower are said to have been used by the infamous pirate Edward Teach in the 17th century. The ruins are only mildly interesting—there isn't much trace of buccaneering. What's interesting is the view: With a little imagination, you can almost see Blackbeard, who also purportedly lived here (though this is hardly well documented), peering out at unsuspecting ships.

Yamacraw Hill Rd. (8km/5 miles east of Fort Montagu). No phone. Free admission. Daily 24 hr. Reachable by jitney.

Central Bank of The Bahamas   The nerve center that governs the archipelago's financial transactions is also the venue for a year-round cycle of temporary exhibitions of paintings that represent the nation's multifaceted artistic talent. The cornerstone of the building was laid by Prince Charles on July 9, 1973, when the country became independent from Britain. Queen Elizabeth II officially inaugurated the bank in February 1975.

Trinity Place and Frederick St. © 242/322-2193. Free admission. Mon–Fri 9:30am–4:30pm. Bus: 10.

Meet the Bahamians

The **People-to-People Program,** established by the Ministry of Tourism, provides an opportunity for visitors to learn more about the culture of The Bahamas by interacting with the Bahamians themselves. The program matches visitors, often entire families, with more than 1,500 Bahamian volunteers of similar ages and interests for a day or evening activity, which could include boating, fishing, shopping at the local outdoor market, enjoying a back-street tour, or, more often, visiting them in their home for a traditional meal of peas 'n' rice, fried fish, and guava duff. These encounters have resulted in lasting friendships between visitors and locals. Philip Archer, a program volunteer for more than 18 years, has received hundreds of invitations to visit families from different countries. Celebrating its 30th anniversary in 2007, the People-to-People Program has expanded beyond Nassau to Abaco, Bimini, Eleuthera, Grand Bahama Island, and San Salvador. To participate in the program in Nassau/Paradise Island and the Out Islands, e-mail peopletopeople@bahamas.com. To participate in the program on Grand Bahama Island, e-mail peopletopeople@gbmot.com.

Finds **Going Over the Hill**

Few visitors make the trip anymore, but it used to be a tradition to go over the Hill to Nassau's most colorful area. **"Over-the-Hill"** is the actual name of this poor residential district, where descendants of former slaves built compact, rainbow-hued houses, leaving the most desirable lands around the harbor to the rich folk. This, not the historic core of Nassau around Rawson Square, is truly the heart of Bahamian-African culture.

The thump of the Junkanoo-Goombay drum can be heard here almost any time of the day or night. The area never sleeps, or so it is said. Certainly not on Sunday morning, when you can drive by the churches and hear hell and damnation promised loudly to all sinners and backsliders.

This fascinating part of Nassau begins .5km (⅓ mile) south of Blue Hill Road, which starts at the exclusive Graycliff hotel. But once you're "Over-the-Hill," you're a long way from the hotel's vintage wine and expensive Cuban cigars. Some people—usually savvy store owners from abroad—come here to buy local handicrafts from individual vendors. The area can be explored on foot (during the day *only*), but many visitors prefer to drive. *Note:* This area is well worth a visit, but keep your eyes open; most of Nassau's criminal incidents happen in this part of town.

Fort Charlotte   Begun in 1787, Fort Charlotte is the largest of Nassau's three major defense buildings, built with plenty of dungeons. It used to command the western harbor. Named after King George III's consort, it was built by Gov. Lord Dunmore, who was also the last royal governor of New York and Virginia. Its 42 cannons (only seven remain on-site) never fired a shot—at least, not at an invader. Within the complex are underground passages, which can be viewed during a free tour (guides are very happy to accept a tip).

Off W. Bay St. on Chippingham Rd. ℂ **242/325-9186.** Admission US$5 (£2.50). Daily 8am–4pm. Bus: 10.

Fort Fincastle   Reached by climbing the Queen's Staircase, this fort was constructed in 1793 by Lord Dunmore, the royal governor. You can take an elevator ride to the top and walk on the observation floor (a 38m-high/125-ft. water tower and lighthouse) for a panoramic view of the harbor. The tower is New Providence's highest point. This fort's so-called bow is patterned like a Mississippi paddle-wheel steamer; it was built to defend Nassau against a possible invasion, though no shot was ever fired.

Though the ruins hardly compete with the view, you can walk around on your own. Be wary, however, of the very persistent young men who will try to show you around; they'll try to hustle you, but you really don't need a guide to see some old cannons.

Elizabeth Ave. No phone. Free admission. Mon–Sat 8am–5pm. Bus: 10 or 17.

Fort Montagu   Built in 1741, this fort—the island's oldest—stands guard at the eastern entrance to Nassau's harbor. The Americans captured it in 1776 during the Revolutionary War. Less interesting than Fort Charlotte and Fort Fincastle (p. 102), the ruins of this place are mainly for fort buffs. Regrettably, it can be visited only from the outside, but many visitors find the nearby park, with well-maintained lawns, plenty of shade, and vendors peddling local handicrafts, more interesting than the fort itself.

Eastern Rd. No regular hours. Bus: 10 or 17.

Junkanoo Expo   This museum is dedicated to Junkanoo—the colorful, musical, and surreal festival that takes place on December 26 when Nassau explodes into sounds, festivities, celebrations, and a sea of masks. It is the Bahamian equivalent of the famous Mardi Gras in New Orleans. If you can't visit Nassau for Junkanoo, seeing this exhibition is the next best thing. You'll get a good idea of the lavish costumes and floats that the revelers use during this annual celebration. The bright colors and costume designs are impressive, if for no other reason than their sheer size. Some of the costumes are nearly as big as one of the small parade floats—but the difference is that only one person wears and carries each one. The Expo is in an old Customs warehouse at the entrance to the Nassau wharf and includes a souvenir boutique selling a variety of Junkanoo handicrafts and paintings.

Prince George Wharf, Festival Place. ℰ **242/356-2731.** Admission US$2 (£1). Mon–Sat 10am–4pm. Bus: 10.

Pirates of Nassau *(Kids)*   This museum, which opened in 2003, celebrates the dubious "golden age of piracy" (1690–1720). Nassau was once a bustling, robust town in which buccaneers grew rich from gold and other goods plundered at sea. Known as a paradise for pirates, it also attracted various rogues and the wild women who flooded into the port to entertain them—for a price, of course. The museum re-creates those bawdy, lusty days in exhibits illustrating pirate lore. You can walk through the belly of a pirate ship (the *Revenge*) as you hear "pirates" plan their next attack, smell the dampness of a dungeon, and even hear the final prayer of an ill-fated victim before he walks the gangplank. It's fairly cheesy but fun for kids. Exhibits also tell the saga of Capt. Woodes Rogers, who was sent by the English crown to suppress pirates in the Caribbean.

Marlborough and George sts. ℰ **242/356-3759.** www.pirates-of-nassau.com. Admission US$12 (£6) adults, US$6 (£3) children 3–17, free for children 2 and under (1 child gets in free). Mon–Sat 9am–6pm; Sun 9am–noon. Bus: 10.

WALKING TOUR   **HISTORIC NASSAU**

Start:	Rawson Square.
Finish:	Prince George Wharf.
Time:	2 hours.
Best Times:	Monday through Saturday between 10am and 4pm.
Worst Times:	Sunday, when many places are closed and lots of cruise ships are in port.

Begin your tour at:

❶ Rawson Square

The center of Nassau, Rawson Square lies directly inland from Prince George Wharf, where many of the big cruise ships dock. Everyone seems to pass through this crossroads, from the prime minister, to bankers and local attorneys, to cruise-ship passengers, to shoppers from Paradise Island, to Junkanoo bands. On the square is the Churchill Building, used by the prime minister and some government ministries. Look for the statue of Sir Milo Butler, a former shopkeeper who became the first governor of The Bahamas after Britain granted its independence in 1973.

Across Rawson Square is:

❷ Parliament Square

A statue of a youthful Queen Victoria dominates the square. To the right of it stand more Bahamian government office buildings, and to the left is the House of Assembly, the New World's oldest governing body in continuous session. In the building behind the statue, the Senate meets; this is a less influential body than the House of Assembly. Some of these Georgian-style buildings date from the late 1700s and early 1800s. Immediately south of Parliament Square, in a Georgian-inspired building between Parliament Street and Bank Lane, is the Supreme Court. The bewigged and begowned judges here, looking very British, interpret Bahamian law and dispense high-authority justice.

TAKE A BREAK
If you'd like to relax, try **Café Matisse**, Bank Lane and Bay Street, behind Parliament Square (📞 242/356-7012). The house specialty is pizza topped with fresh local seafood. Lunch is served Tuesday to Sunday noon to 3pm.

The Supreme Court building stands next to the:

❸ Nassau Public Library and Museum

This 1797 building was once the Nassau Gaol (jail) and became the public library in 1873. Chances are, you will have seen greater libraries. But what's amusing here is that the small prison cells are now lined with books. Another item of interest is the library's collection of historic prints and old documents dating from colonial days. It's open to visitors Monday through Thursday from 10am to 8pm, Friday from 10am to 5pm, and Saturday from 10am to 4pm.

Across from the library on Shirley Street is the:

❹ Former site of the Royal Victoria Hotel

The hotel that once occupied this site was the haunt of Confederate spies, royalty, smugglers of all sorts, and ladies and gentlemen. The American journalist Horace Greeley pronounced it "the largest and most commodious hotel ever built in the Tropics," and many agreed with him. The hotel experienced its heyday during the American Civil War. At the Blockade Runners' Ball, some 300 guests reportedly consumed 350 magnums of champagne. Former guests have included two British prime ministers, Neville Chamberlain and his successor, Winston Churchill. Prince Albert, consort of Queen Victoria, also stayed here once. The hotel closed in 1971. After it was destroyed by fire, it was demolished and razed to the ground. Today, the site accommodates one of Nassau's showcase parking lots. Incidentally, the parking lot seems to be such a source of pride to the city that it is unlikely the Royal Victoria will ever be rebuilt, at least in that spot.

After imagining the former splendor of the Royal Victoria, head south along Parliament Street. At the end of it stands:

❺ Nassau General Post Office

If you're a collector, you may want to purchase colorful Bahamian stamps, which might be valuable in future years. You can also mail letters and packages here.

Walk east (right) on East Hill Street. Turn left onto East Street, then right onto Shirley Street, and head straight on Elizabeth Avenue. This will take you to the landmark:

❻ Queen's Staircase

This stairway, built in 1793 by slaves who cut the 66 steps out of sandstone cliffs, leads to Bennet's Hill.

These stairs provide access from Old Nassau's center to:

❼ Fort Fincastle

Lord Dunmore built this fort in 1793. Designed in the shape of a paddle-wheel

Walking Tour: Historic Nassau

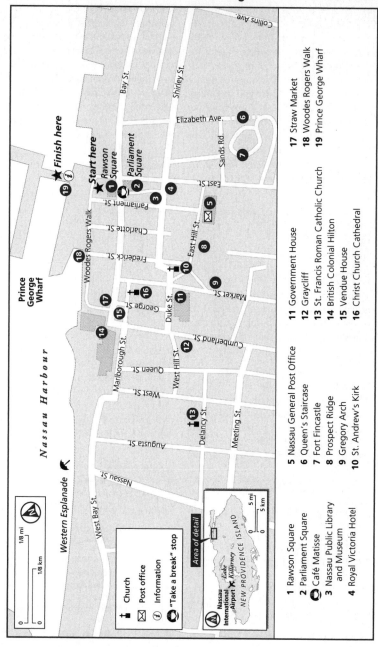

Start here — Rawson Square

Finish here

Prince George Wharf

Nassau Harbour

Western Esplanade

Area of detail

Nassau International Airport — Lake Killarney — NEW PROVIDENCE ISLAND

0 · 5 mi
0 · 5 km

Legend
- ✝ Church
- ☒ Post office
- (i) Information
- ☕ "Take a break" stop

0 — 1/8 mi
0 — 1/8 km

1 Rawson Square
2 Parliament Square
3 Café Matisse
4 Nassau Public Library and Museum
4 Royal Victoria Hotel

5 Nassau General Post Office
6 Queen's Staircase
7 Fort Fincastle
8 Prospect Ridge
9 Gregory Arch
10 St. Andrew's Kirk

11 Government House
12 Graycliff
13 St. Francis Roman Catholic Church
14 British Colonial Hilton
15 Vendue House
16 Christ Church Cathedral

17 Straw Market
18 Woodes Rogers Walk
19 Prince George Wharf

steamer, it was a place from which to look out for marauders who never came. It was eventually converted into a lighthouse because it occupied the highest point on the island. The tower rises more than 60m (197 ft.) above the sea, providing a panoramic view of Nassau and its harbor.

A small footpath leads down from the fort to Sands Road. Once you reach it, head west (left) until you approach East Street again, and then bear right. When you come to East Hill Street (again), go left because you will have returned to the post office.

Continue your westward trek along East Hill Street, which is the foothill of:

⑧ Prospect Ridge

This was the old dividing line between Nassau's rich and poor. The rich (usually white) people lived along the waterfront, often in beautiful mansions. Bahamians of African descent went over the hill to work in these rich homes during the day but returned to Prospect Ridge to their own homes (most often shanties) at night.

Near the end of East Hill Street, you come to:

⑨ Gregory Arch

This tunnel was cut through the hill in 1850. After it opened, working-class black Bahamians were happy to not have to go over the steep hill anymore; they could instead go through this arch to return home.

At the intersection with Market Street, turn right. On your right, you'll see:

⑩ St. Andrew's Kirk (Presbyterian)

Called simply "the Kirk," the church dates from 1810 but has seen many changes over the years. In 1864, it was enlarged, and a bell tower was added along with other architectural features. This church had the first non-Anglican parishioners in The Bahamas.

On a steep hill, rising to the west of Market Street, you see on your left:

⑪ Government House

This house is the official residence of the archipelago's governor-general, the queen's representative to The Bahamas. (The post today is largely ceremonial, as an elected prime minister does the actual governing.) This pink-and-white neoclassical mansion dates from the early 19th century. Poised on its front steps is a rather jaunty statue of Christopher Columbus.

Opposite the road from Government House on West Hill Street is:

⑫ Graycliff

A Georgian-style hotel and restaurant, this stomping ground of the rich and famous was constructed by Capt. John Howard Graysmith in the 1720s. In the 1920s, it achieved notoriety when it was run by Polly Leach, a pal of gangster Al Capone. Later, under royal ownership, it attracted such famous guests as Winston Churchill and the duke and duchess of Windsor.

Upon leaving Graycliff, you'll see, embedded in a hill, a plaque that commemorates the spot where Nassau's oldest church once stood.

On the corner of West Hill and West streets is Villa Doyle, the former home of William Henry Doyle, chief justice of the Bahamian Supreme Court in the late 1800s.

Opposite it stands:

⑬ St. Francis Roman Catholic Church

Constructed between 1885 and 1886, it was the country's first Catholic church. New York's archdiocese raised the funds to construct it.

Continue along West Street until you reach Marlborough. Walk the short block that leads to Queen Street and turn right, passing the American embassy. At the corner of Queen Street and Marlborough rises the:

⑭ British Colonial Hilton

Built in 1923, the nation's most famous hotel was once run by Sir Harry Oakes, who was at the time the most powerful man on the islands and a friend of the duke of Windsor. Oakes's murder in 1943, still unsolved, was called "the crime of the century." This historic location was the site of Fort Nassau, as well as the set for several James Bond thrillers. In 1999, it became a Hilton hotel.

One part of the hotel fronts George Street, where you'll find:

⓯ Vendue House

One of Nassau's oldest buildings, Vendue House was once called the Bourse (Stock Exchange) and was the site of many slave auctions. It is now a museum.

Not far from Vendue House on George Street is:

⓰ Christ Church Cathedral

Dating from 1837, this Gothic Episcopal cathedral is the venue of many important state ceremonies, including the opening of the Supreme Court, during which a procession of bewigged, robed judges emerges, followed by barristers, and accompanied by music from the police band.

Continue north on George Street to the Bay Street intersection.

⓱ Straw Market

The market—largely destroyed by a fire in fall 2001, and still not rebuilt—is now housed within a tentlike temporary structure that opens onto Bay Street (at George St., about 2 blocks from its original premises). It has long been a favorite of cruise-ship passengers. You'll find not only straw products, but all sorts of souvenirs and gifts as well. Bahamian women at the market weave traditional baskets and braid visitors' hair with beads. Hours are daily from 7am to around 8pm, though each individual vendor (there are around 200 of them) sets his or her own hours.

Continue north toward the water until you reach:

⓲ Woodes Rogers Walk

The walk was named for a former governor of the colony who was thrown into debtors' prison in London before coming back to Nassau as the royal governor. Head east on it for a panoramic view of the harbor, with its colorful mail and sponge boats. Markets sell vegetables, fish, and lots of conch.

The walk leads to:

⓳ Prince George Wharf

The wharf was constructed in the 1920s, the heyday of American Prohibition, to provide harbor space for hundreds of bootlegging craft defying the American blockade against liquor. Queen Elizabeth II's yacht, the HMS *Britannia,* has been a frequent visitor. Cruise ships also dock here.

ORGANIZED TOURS

There's a lot to see in Nassau. Many tour options can be customized to suit your taste and take you through the colorful historic city and outlying sights of interest.

Walking tours, arranged by the Ministry of Tourism, leave from the tourist information booth at Festival Place every day intermittently, and depending on demand, at 10am. Tours last an hour and include descriptions of some of the city's most venerable buildings, with commentaries on Nassau's history, customs, and traditions. The cost is US$10 (£5) per person for all ages. Call ⓒ **242-395-8382** to confirm that tours are running. Advance reservations are "helpful but not essential," according to a Ministry spokesperson.

Majestic Tours, Hillside Manor, Cumberland Street, Nassau (ⓒ **242/322-2606**), offers a number of trips, both night and day. A 2½-hour city-and-country tour leaves daily at 2pm, visiting major points of interest, including forts, the Queen's Staircase, the water tower, and the former site of the Straw Market (passing but not entering it). The tour costs US$45 (£23) per person. An extended city-and-country tour also

(Moments) Journeys into the Wilds

You can take a day off from the beach and join one of the wildlife tours offered by **Bahamas Outdoors** (© **242/362-1574** or 457-0329; www.bahamas outdoors.com). We highly recommend speaking to Carolyn Wardle, president of Bahamas Outdoors, for insight into the best of the island's remaining wildlife habitats. Born in Surrey, England, and a resident of New Providence for decades, Ms. Wardle, a passionate conservationist (she's a director of the Society for the Conservation and Study of Caribbean Birds), is well-known to residents of New Providence's more isolated regions. Armed with sturdy shoes, a Bahamas Outdoors T-shirt, sunglasses, a hat, and binoculars, she knows the island's wildlife habitats (forest, seashore, and freshwater ponds) better than anyone on the island. Consider signing on for a half-day tour, priced at US$59 (£30) per person, or a full-day tour, at US$99 (£50) per person. Tours rarely include more than a half-dozen participants and can be conducted either in a vehicle (with frequent stops along the way for closer observation) or on an all-terrain bike. Depending on your stated preferences, the focus of your island tour could include birds, native flora and fauna, butterflies, national parks, historic sites, or—best of all—a combination of all of them. Access to binoculars and a battered collection of field guides is included in the price of any tour. The full-day tours also include a picnic lunch.

It's advisable to make advance reservations at least a day in advance. Most tours begin in front of the tour participants' hotel at whatever time was prearranged. Bird-watching tours tend to begin earlier (around 7am) than biking and/or historic and nature tours, which begin just a bit later.

leaves daily at 2pm and includes the Ardastra Gardens. The charge is US$55 (£28) per person, half-price for children 12 and under. Combination tours depart Tuesday through Thursday at 10am and combine all the sights you see on the first tour listed above, plus the Retreat Gardens and lunch. They cost US$65 (£33) per person, half-price for children. Many hotels have a Majestic Tours Hospitality Desk in the lobby, for information about these tours, as well as for reservations and tickets. Other hotels have brochures and tell you where to sign up.

EASY SIDE TRIPS TO NEARBY ISLANDS

Remote **Rose Island** is a sliver of land poking out of the sea just northeast of Nassau's Prince George waterfront. Shelling is one of the lures of this little islet. If you want to escape the crowds of Nassau, you can take a boat, the *Robinson Crusoe*, which leaves Wednesday, Friday, and Sunday at 10am from Nassau and returns at 4:30pm. The cost is US$55 (£28) for adults, US$28 (£14) for children ages 5 through 11, and free for kids under 5. You can relax in a hammock, snorkel among the coral reefs, and enjoy the white-sand beach before and after your sizzling barbecue lunch with unlimited white wine (included in the price). Bookings for this island retreat trip are available through **Majestic Tours** (© **242/322-2606;** www.majesticholidays.com).

If you want to see the Exuma island chain on a daylong excursion, try the **Fantastic Exuma Powerboat Adventure.** The name may sound silly, but the trip provides an excellent overview of the area. The boat departs Nassau Harbour at 9am and arrives in the Exuma Cays about an hour later. There are several stops, with snorkeling at a private cay (Ship Channel), visiting the iguanas on Allan's Cay, feeding stingrays along the shore, and enjoying a barbecue lunch. A full bar is available all day, and the drinks are included in the cost, which is US$190 (£95) per adult and US$120 (£60) for children 2 through 12. Transportation from a participant's hotel to the port of embarkation is included in the price. The experience finishes around 5pm. For more information and prices, contact **Powerboat Adventures (© 242/363-1466;** www. powerboatadventures.com).

7 Shopping

Today, Nassau's shopping options are more upscale than they have been in decades past. Swanky jewelers and a burgeoning fashion scene have appeared. There are still plenty of T-shirts claiming that "It's Better in The Bahamas," but you can also find platinum watches and diamond jewelry.

The range of goods is staggering; in the midst of all the junk souvenirs, you'll find an increasing array of china, crystal, watches, and clothing from such names as Bally, Herend, Lalique, Baccarat, and Ferragamo.

But can you really save money compared to what you would pay stateside? The answer is "yes" on some items, "no" on others. To figure out what's a bargain and what's not, you've got to know the price of everything back in your hometown, turning yourself into a sort of human price calculator.

Don't try to bargain with the salespeople in Nassau stores as you would do with merchants at the local market. The price marked is the price you must pay if you buy, though you won't be pressed to make a purchase. The salespeople here are courteous and helpful in most cases.

There are no import duties on 11 categories of luxury goods, including china, crystal, fine linens, jewelry, leather goods, photographic equipment, watches, and fragrances. Antiques, of course, are exempt from import duty worldwide. But even though prices are "duty-free," you can still end up spending more on an item in The Bahamas than you would back home; it's a tricky situation.

If you're contemplating a major purchase, such as a good Swiss watch or expensive perfume, it's best to do some research in your local discount outlets or online before making a serious purchase in The Bahamas. While the alleged 30% to 50% discount off stateside prices might apply in some cases, it's not true in others. Certain cameras and electronic equipment, we have discovered, are listed in The Bahamas at, say, 20% or more below the manufacturer's "suggested retail price." That sounds good, except the manufacturer's suggested price might be a lot higher than what you'd actually pay, so this tricky wording might mean that you're not getting the discount you think you are. Some shoppers even take along department-store catalogs from the U.S. or print out online buying guides to determine if they are indeed getting a bargain; it's not a bad idea.

A lot of price-fixing seems to be going on in Nassau. For example, a bottle of Chanel perfume is likely to sell for pretty much the same price anywhere, regardless of the store.

How much you can take home depends on your country of origin. For details about this, plus Customs requirements for some other countries, refer to "Entry Requirements & Customs," in chapter 3.

The principal shopping areas are **Bay Street** and its side streets downtown, as well as the shops in the arcades of hotels. Not many street numbers are used along Bay Street; just look for store signs.

BRASS & COPPER

Brass and Leather Shop   With two branches on Charlotte Street, this shop offers English brass, handbags, luggage, briefcases, attachés, belts, scarves, and ties from such designers as Furla, Tumi, HCL, and others. If you look and select carefully, you can find some good buys here. 12 Charlotte St., between Bay and Shirley sts. ℂ **242/322-3806**.

CIGARS

Remember, U.S. citizens are prohibited from bringing Cuban cigars back home because of the trade embargo. If you buy them, enjoy them in The Bahamas.

Graycliff Cigar Company ℛ   In 1994, an emigrant businessman from Lake Como, Italy, moved to Nassau to supervise his investment, the Graycliff Hotel, and liked it so much there that he decided to stay. Eventually, he established the country's best-known and most respected cigar factory. It employs about 16 mostly Cuban-expatriate cigar rollers, who, within full view, use non-Cuban tobacco to create 10 different styles of sought-after cigars. These are sold on the premises and priced around US$5.25 to US$22 (£2.65–£11) each, depending on quality. There's also a 16-inch "big bamboo," priced at US$50 (£25), that makes whoever smokes it look almost like a caricature, and which is guaranteed to get its consumer very, very high. Best of all, these cigars, crafted with the finest techniques, are completely legal to import back into the U.S. Open Mon–Sat 9am–6pm. 12 West Hill St. ℂ **242/302-9150**.

CRYSTAL, CHINA & GEMS

Solomon's Mines   Evoking the title of a 1950s MGM flick, this is one grand shopping adventure. This flagship store, with many branches, is one of the largest duty-free retailers in the Caribbean, a tradition since 1908. Entering the store is like making a shopping trip to London or Paris. The amount of merchandise is staggering, from a US$50,000 (£25,000) Patek Philippe watch to one of the largest collections of Herend china in the West. Most prices on timepieces, china, jewelry, crystal, Herend, Baccarat, Ferragamo, Bally, Lalique, and other names are discounted 15% to 30%—and some of the merchandise and oddities here are not available in the U.S., such as the stunning African diamonds. The selections of Italian, French, and American fragrances and skin-care products are the best in the archipelago. Bay St. (ℂ **242/356-6920**); Charlotte and Bay sts. (ℂ **242/325-7554**).

FASHION

Cole's of Nassau   This boutique offers the most extensive selection of designer fashions in Nassau. Women can find everything from swimwear to formal gowns, from sportswear to hosiery. Cole's also sells gift items, sterling-silver designer and costume jewelry, hats, shoes, bags, scarves, and belts. Parliament St. ℂ **242/322-8393**.

Fendi   This is Nassau's only outlet for the well-crafted Italian-inspired accessories made by this famous luxe-goods company. With handbags, luggage, shoes, watches, wallets, and portfolios to choose from, the selection may well solve some of your gift-giving quandaries. Charlotte St. at Bay St. ℂ **242/322-6300**.

HANDICRAFTS

Sea Grape Boutique   This is one of the island's genuinely fine gift shops, with an inventory of exotic decorative items that you'll probably find fascinating. It includes jewelry crafted from fossilized coral, sometimes with sharks' teeth embedded inside, and clothing that's well suited to the sometimes-steamy climate. W. Bay St. (next to Travellers Restaurant). ℂ 242/327-1308.

JEWELRY

Colombian Emeralds   Famous around the Caribbean, this international outlet is not limited to emeralds, although its selection of that stone is the best in The Bahamas. You'll find an impressive display of diamonds, as well as other precious gems. The gold jewelry here sells for about half the price it does stateside, and many of the gems are discounted 20% to 30%. Ask about their "cybershopping" program. Bay St. ℂ 242/326-1661.

John Bull   The jewelry department here offers classic selections from Tiffany & Co., cultured pearls from Mikimoto, the creations of David Yurman and Carrera y Carrera, Greek and Roman coin jewelry, and Spanish gold and silver pieces. It's the best name in the business. The store also features a wide selection of watches, cameras, perfumes, cosmetics, leather goods, and accessories. It is one of the country's best places to buy a Gucci or Cartier watch. Bay St. ℂ 242/322-4253.

LEATHER

In addition to the stores mentioned below, another good source for leather goods is the **Brass and Leather Shop,** described under "Brass & Copper," p. 110.

Gucci   This shop, opposite Rawson Square, is the best place to buy leather goods in Nassau. The wide selection includes handbags, wallets, luggage, briefcases, gift items, scarves, ties, eveningwear for men and women, umbrellas, shoes, sandals, watches, and perfume, all by Italy's famous producer of luxury items. Saffrey Sq., Bay St., corner of Bank Lane. ℂ 242/325-0561.

Leather Masters   This well-known retail outlet carries an internationally known collection of leather bags, luggage, and accessories by Ted Lapidus, Lanvin, Lancel of Paris, Etienne Aigner of Germany, and I Santi of Italy, plus luggage by Piel and Travel Pro. Non-leather items include pens, lighters, watches by Colibri, silk scarves, neckties, and cigar accessories. 8 Parliament St. ℂ 242/322-7597.

LINENS

The Linen Shop   This is Nassau's best outlet for linens, selling beautifully embroidered bedding, Irish handkerchiefs, and tablecloths. Look also for the most exquisite children's clothing and christening gowns in town. In the Ironmongery Building, Bay St., near Charlotte St. ℂ 242/322-4266.

MAPS

Balmain Antiques   This place offers a wide and varied assortment of 19th-century etchings, engravings, and maps, many of them antique, and all of them reasonably priced. Other outlets have minor displays of these collectibles, but this outlet has the finest. Some items are 400 years old. It's usually best to discuss your interests with Mr. Ramsey, the owner, so he can direct you to the proper drawers. His specialties include The Bahamas, Civil War-era America, and the history of African-descended peoples.

He also has a collection of military historical items. The shop also features a selection of primitive Haitian art. You'll find the shop on the second floor of the Mason's Building on Bay Street. 🕿 242/323-7421.

MARKETS

The **Nassau International Bazaar** consists of some 30 shops selling international goods in a new arcade. A pleasant place for browsing, the million dollar complex sells goods from around the globe. The bazaar runs from Bay Street down to the waterfront (near Prince George Wharf). With cobbled alleyways and garreted storefronts, it looks like a European village.

Prince George Plaza, on Bay Street, is popular with cruise-ship passengers. Many fine shops (Gucci, for example) occupy space here. When you get tired of shopping, dine at the open-air rooftop restaurant that overlooks Bay Street.

PERFUMES & COSMETICS

Nassau has several good perfume outlets, notably **John Bull** and **Little Switzerland,** which also stock a lot of non-perfume merchandise.

The Beauty Spot   The country's largest cosmetic shop, this outlet sells duty-free cosmetics by Lancôme, Chanel, YSL, Elizabeth Arden, Estée Lauder, Clinique, Christian Dior, and Biotherm, among others. It also operates facial salons. Bay and Frederick sts. 🕿 242/322-5930.

The Perfume Bar   This little gem has exclusive rights to market Boucheron. It also stocks the Clarins line (though not exclusively). Bay St. 🕿 242/322-7216.

The Perfume Shop   In the heart of Nassau, within walking distance of the cruise ships, the Perfume Shop offers duty-free savings on world-famous perfumes. Women can treat themselves to a flacon of Eternity or Chanel. For men, the selection includes Drakkar Noir, Polo, and Obsession. Bay and Frederick sts. 🕿 242/322-2375.

8 New Providence After Dark

Gone are the days when tuxedo-clad gentlemen and elegantly gowned ladies drank and danced the night away at such famous nightclubs as the Yellow Bird and the Big Bamboo. You can still find dancing, along with limbo and calypso, but for most visitors, the major attraction is gambling.

Cultural entertainment in Nassau is limited, however. The chief center for this is the **Dundas Center for the Performing Arts,** which sometimes stages ballets, plays, and musicals. Call 🕿 242/393-3728 to find out what's scheduled during your visit.

ROLLING THE DICE

As another option, you can easily head over to Paradise Island and drop into the massive, spectacular casino in **Atlantis.** For more information about that, see chapter 5.

Wyndham Nassau Resort & Crystal Palace Casino   This dazzling casino is the only one on New Providence Island and is now run by the Wyndham Nassau Resort. Thanks to constant improvements, and the management's willingness to restock it with some of the world's most up-to-date games and slot machines, it stacks up well against the other major casinos of the Caribbean. Incorporating more than 3,252 sq. m (35,004 sq. ft.) into its flashy-looking premises, it's animated, bustling, and filled with the serious business of people having fun with their money and temptations. The gaming room features hundreds of slot machines—only a few of which resemble the low-tech, one-armed bandits that were in vogue 20 years ago. You'll find blackjack tables, roulette wheels, craps tables, a baccarat table, and a sophisticated electronic link to Las Vegas that provides odds on most of the world's major sporting events. There's also a serious commitment to poker. W. Bay St., Cable Beach. ✆ 242/327-6200.

THE CLUB & MUSIC SCENE

Club Fluid   Set within a two-story building in downtown Nassau, this basement-level nightclub features a baby-blue-and-white interior, dozens of mirrors that are much appreciated by narcissists, two bars, and a dance floor. It attracts an animated crowd of local residents, most of them between 20 and 45, who groove to the reggae, soca, hip-hop, and R&B music. It's open Wednesday to Saturday from 9pm to 2am. W. Bay St., near the corner of Frederick St. ✆ 242/356-4691. Cover US$10–US$25 (£5–£13).

Rain Forest Theater   Accessible directly from Crystal Palace Casino on Cable Beach, this 800-seat theater is a major nightlife attraction. Revues tend to be small-scale, relatively restrained, and very definitely on the safe and family-friendly side of the great cultural divide. Fake palm trees on each side and touches of glitter set the scene for the onstage entertainment. Hours vary with the season, the act, and the number of guests booked into the hotel at the time. Billboards located prominently throughout the hotel hawk whoever is headlining at the moment. In the Crystal Palace Casino, W. Bay St., Cable Beach. ✆ 242/327-6200. US$32–US$40 (£16–£20) per person. Drinks are extra.

THE BAR SCENE

Charlie's on the Beach/Cocktails 7 Dreams   The focus within this sparsely decorated club is local gossip, calypso and reggae music, and stiff drinks, all of which make for a high-energy night out in Nassau. The setting is a simple warehouse-like structure a few blocks west of the British Colonial Hilton, though management warns that during some particularly active weekends (including spring break), the entire venue might move, for the short term, to a larger, as-yet-undetermined location. Open only Wednesday and Friday to Sunday 9pm to 4am. W. Bay St. near Long Wharf Beach. ✆ 242/328-3745. Free admission or US$15 (£7.50) cover, depending on the night.

5

Paradise Island

Located 180m (591 ft.) off Nassau's north shore, Paradise Island is a favorite vacation spot for East Coast Americans fleeing their icy winters for the stunning white sands of Paradise Beach. In addition to its gorgeous strands, the island boasts beautiful foliage, including brilliant red hibiscus and a grove of casuarina trees sweeping down to form a tropical arcade.

Now the priciest piece of real estate in The Bahamas, this island once served as a farm for Nassau and was known as Hog Island. Purchased for US$294 (£147) by William Sayle in the 17th century, it cost A&P grocery-chain heir Huntington Hartford US$11 million in 1960. He renamed the 6.5km-long (4-mile) sliver of land Paradise before selling his interest in it. Long a retreat for millionaires, the island underwent a massive building boom in the 1980s. Its old Bahamian charm is now gone forever, lost to the high-rises, condos, second homes of the wintering wealthy, and gambling casino that have taken over. The island's centerpiece is the mammoth Atlantis Paradise Island Resort & Casino, which has become a nightlife mecca and a sightseeing attraction in its own right.

For those who want top hotels, casino action, Vegas-type revues, fabulous beaches, and a posh address, Paradise Island is the place. It's sleeker and more upscale than Cable Beach, its closest rival. True, Paradise Island is overbuilt and overly commercialized, but its natural beauty still makes it a choice vacation spot, perfect for a quick 3- or 4-day getaway.

Note that we treat Paradise Island as a separate entity in this guide, but it is actually part of New Providence, connected by a bridge. You can travel between the two on foot, by boat, or by car. It's easy to stay in Nassau or Cable Beach and come over to enjoy Paradise Island's beaches, restaurants, attractions, and casino. You can also stay on Paradise Island and head over to Nassau for a day of sightseeing and shopping. So view this section as a companion to chapter 4, and refer to chapter 4 for transportation details, nearby sights, and a wider array of sports and recreation choices.

1 Orientation

ARRIVING

Most visitors to Paradise Island arrive in Nassau and commute to Paradise Island by ground transport.

When you arrive at the Lynden Pindling International Airport (also known as **Nassau International Airport;** see chapter 4 for information on flying into Nassau), you won't find bus service to take you to Paradise Island. Many package deals include hotel transfers from the airport. Otherwise, if you're not renting a car, you'll need to take a taxi. Taxis in Nassau are metered and take cash only, no credit cards. It will usually cost you US$30 (£15) to go by cab from the airport to your hotel. The driver will also ask you to pay the northbound one-way US$1 (50p) bridge toll, a charge that will be added onto your metered fare at the end of the ride.

VISITOR INFORMATION

Paradise Island does not have a tourist office, so refer to the tourist facilities in downtown Nassau (see "Orientation," at the beginning of chapter 4). The concierge or guest-services staff at your hotel can also give you information about local attractions.

ISLAND LAYOUT

Paradise Island's finest beaches lie on the Atlantic (northern) coastline, while the docks, wharves, and marinas are on the southern side. Most of the island's largest and glossiest hotels and restaurants, as well as the casino and a lagoon with landscaped borders, lie west and north of the roundabout. The area east of the roundabout is less congested, with only a handful of smaller hotels, a golf course, the Versailles Gardens, the cloister, the airport, and many of the island's privately owned villas.

2 Getting Around

You don't need to rent a car here. Most visitors walk around Paradise Island's most densely developed sections and hire a taxi for the occasional longer haul.

The most popular way to reach nearby Nassau is to **walk across the toll bridge.** There is no charge for pedestrians.

To tour Paradise Island or New Providence by **taxi,** make arrangements with either a taxi driver or your hotel's reception desk. Taxis wait at the entrances to all the major hotels. The hourly rate is about US$60 (£30) in cars or small vans.

If you are without a car and don't want to take a taxi or walk, you can take a **ferry** to Nassau, which leaves from the dock on Casino Drive every 30 minutes; the 10-minute ride costs US$4 (£2) one-way. Quicker and easier than a taxi, the ferry deposits you right at Prince George Wharf, in downtown Nassau. Daily service runs from 9am to 6pm.

Water taxis also operate between Paradise Island and Nassau's Prince George Wharf. They depart daily from 8:30am to 6pm at 20-minute intervals. Round-trip fare is US$6 (£3) per person.

If you are a guest at one of the properties associated with Atlantis (p. 116), hop aboard one of the complimentary shuttle buses for drop-offs at any of the resort's accommodations. They depart from the Lynden Pindling International Airport at 30-minute intervals every day between 7am and 11pm, costing US$6 (£3) per person round-trip. Atlantis guests can also take a complimentary tour of the island, which departs daily at noon.

Unlike New Providence, no public buses are allowed on Paradise Island.

3 Where to Stay

In the off-season (mid-Apr to mid-Dec), prices are slashed by at least 20%—and perhaps a lot more, though the weather isn't as ideal. But because Paradise Island's summer business has increased dramatically, you'll never see some of the 60% reductions that you might find at a cheaper property in the Greater Nassau area. Paradise Island doesn't have to lower its rates to attract summer business. For inexpensive accommodations, refer to the recommendations we list for New Providence Island in chapter 4. Paradise Island isn't cheap!

Where to Stay & Dine on Paradise Island

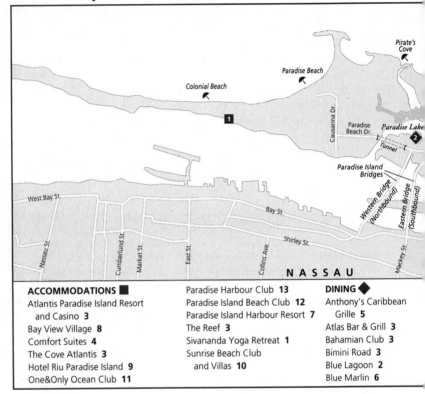

ACCOMMODATIONS ■

Atlantis Paradise Island Resort
  and Casino **3**
Bay View Village **8**
Comfort Suites **4**
The Cove Atlantis **3**
Hotel Riu Paradise Island **9**
One&Only Ocean Club **11**

Paradise Harbour Club **13**
Paradise Island Beach Club **12**
Paradise Island Harbour Resort **7**
The Reef **3**
Sivananda Yoga Retreat **1**
Sunrise Beach Club
  and Villas **10**

DINING ◆

Anthony's Caribbean
  Grille **5**
Atlas Bar & Grill **3**
Bahamian Club **3**
Bimini Road **3**
Blue Lagoon **2**
Blue Marlin **6**

VERY EXPENSIVE

Atlantis Paradise Island Resort & Casino ✦✦✦ *Kids*   This creatively designed mega-resort, the biggest in The Bahamas, functions as a vacation destination and theme park in its own right. A blockbuster in every sense of the word, it contains the most creative interiors, the most intriguing aesthetics, and the most elaborate waterscapes of any hotel in the country. It's the most recent incarnation of a resort that originated in the early days of Paradise Island's tourism industry, passing through rocky and sometimes less glamorous days before reaching its startling incarnation as a destination that appeals to adults (its gambling facilities are the largest in The Bahamas) and to ecologists—its focus on protecting marine life adds a welcome dose of "save the planet" to an otherwise relentlessly consumerist theme, and dozens of waterways crisscross the flat, sandy terrain on which the resort sits.

Atlantis also exerts a potent lure for children, and the child that remains within many of us, thanks to its evocation of a "Lost Continent" whose replicated ruins evoke—you guessed it—Atlantis.

But whereas the newest buildings manage to conjure science fiction and ancient mythology at the same time (no easy feat), its older buildings still retain a whiff of the old Merv Griffin days of the 1980s. But thanks to skillful landscaping and the

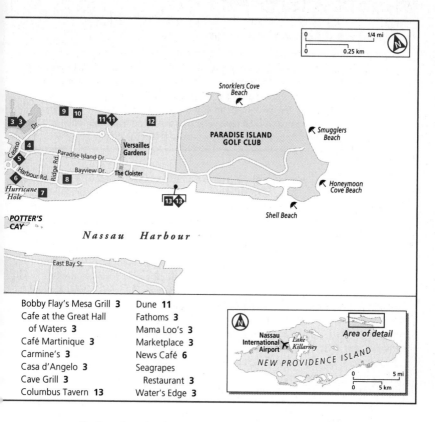

presence of miles of canals whose currents carry swimmers with flotation devices on meandering runs down mythical rivers, no one seems to notice.

The entire sprawling compound opens onto a long stretch of sandy beach with a sheltered marina. Think Vegas in the Tropics, with a mythological theme and an interconnected series of lagoons, lakes, rivers, waterfalls, and water tubes thrown in, and you'll get the picture. One advantage to the place is that there's a lot of visual distraction and high-energy, upbeat stimulation; the downside is that it's huge, impersonal, and at times downright bureaucratic. The service from the sometimes bored staff just can't keep up with the number of guests here.

Overall, however, it's an appropriate (albeit rather expensive) choice for a family vacation, since the price includes direct access to endless numbers of watery gimmicks. Children's programs are comprehensive and well choreographed, and many parents simply turn their kids loose onto the extensive grounds, understanding that a battalion of lifeguards and supervisors keep the show rolling and the safety levels up to par. Singles and young couples who want a lot of razzle-dazzle appreciate the place, too, though some people find it over-the-top, too expensive, and too firmly mired in the limitations of its own "lost continent" theme.

(Tips Recent Changes at Atlantis

Several months prior to the release of this edition, Atlantis completed a new phase of development which, to some extent, redefined the mega-resort's present layout. These included the opening of a 400-unit **condominium complex** whose units are rented to hotel guests according to the whims and priorities of each individual owner. The new **Dolphin Cay** has at least 28 resident dolphins. Furthermore, the **convention facilities** were improved and massively enlarged to a whopping total of more than 27,870 sq. m (299,990 sq. ft.)

The place, which is owned by Kerzner International, a global investment company that originated in South Africa, offers so many sports, dining, and entertainment options that many guests never venture off the property during their entire vacation. It's expensive, but for your money, you'll find yourself neck-deep amid many of the diversions you might expect from a theme park. And if you opt for one of the resort's less plush accommodations, especially within the Beach Tower, the sticker shock won't seem as severe.

Accommodations retain distinctly different levels of opulence, based, for the most part, on where they're located. The most opulent and expensive accommodations lie in semi-secluded annexes whose facilities are not open to the hotel's more general clientele. These include The **One&Only Ocean Club** and **The Cove,** a 600-unit, all-suite hotel-within-a-hotel which opened in 2007. Both pockets of heightened posh were conceived and designed as separate and semi-independent components within the resort, and each is described in separate recommendations below.

As this resort has expanded, lodgings within its central core are emerging as its less expensive accommodations. And of those accommodations, the plushest lie within the **Royal Towers**—the tallest and most imaginative edifice in The Bahamas. You'll get the feeling that an army of designers labored long and hard over the interior decors, replete as they are with decorative replicas of seahorses, winged dragons, and huge conch shells sprouting from cornices and rooflines. Rooms in the Royal Towers' **Imperial Club** come with a personal concierge and upgraded amenities.

In a category all its own is the newest hotel on the block, **The Reef,** a condo complex whose one-, two-, and three-bedroom units, each with full kitchen, are rented out as hotel accommodations according to a complicated schedule that's clearly understood by investors before they buy.

Less posh and less plush are rooms within the **Coral Tower,** and least expensive of the entire lot are accommodations within the still-serviceable but older **Beach Tower,** with a floor plan shaped like an airplane propeller, dating back to the dimly remembered 1980s. But even in the older, least expensive sections, accommodations are comfortable, well-accessorized, and available with the understanding that occupants still get full access to the sprawling water parks that are otherwise accessible only on a limited basis to nonresidents. Most units sport a balcony or terrace with water views, individually controlled air-conditioning, in-room movies, and voice mail and modem access, plus roomy bathrooms with tubs and showers.

The most deluxe accommodation anywhere within the Atlantis fiefdom is the **Bridge Suite,** an architectural oddity that, several stories above ground level, links the two spires of the Royal Towers. It rents for US$25,000 (£12,500) per night and, over the course of its celebrated history, was occupied by Michael Jordan for a time.

Any old hotel might feature tropical gardens, but Atlantis goes one better by featuring the world's largest collection of outdoor open-air marine habitats, each of them aesthetically stunning. A few of these were conceived for snorkelers and swimmers, but most were designed so that guests could observe the marine life from catwalks above and from glassed-in underwater viewing tunnels. Even folks who don't stay here, including thousands of cruise-ship passengers, can take part in orchestrated tours. These jaunts include 11 different exhibition lagoons, containing millions of gallons of water and at least 200 species of tropical fish. On-site marine habitats include a separate lagoon for sharks, for dolphins, and for stingrays, and individual habitats for lobsters, piranhas, and underwater exotica.

Swimmers can meander along an underwater snorkeling trail called **Paradise Lagoon** to explore a five-story replica of an ancient ziggurat-shaped Mayan temple, the sides of which incorporate water slides with slippery, wet, and wild runs, including an 18m (59-ft.) nearly vertical drop. Riders emerge from the sculpted mouths of giant Mayan gods like human sacrifices as they race giddily down the course of the water slide.

In 2007, additional water attractions, known collectively as **Aquaventure,** were added, bringing the surface area devoted to water features to 123 acres. The most visible monument within Aquaventure is a mythical-looking building, the **Power Tower,** site of another set of even more imaginative water slides, each skillfully landscaped into the surrounding vegetation. Aquaventure's labyrinth of meandering streams and waterfalls is accessible, without charge, for guests staying at Atlantis. Nonresidents, however, are strictly barred from entering unless they buy a day pass, which costs US$150 (£75) for adults, US$120 (£60) for children aged 4 to 12, and nothing for kids under age 4. Day-pass holders get access to all marine habitats, water slides, beach and pool facilities, and Aquaventure.

One major entertainment venue within the Paradise Island layout that's open, without charge, to the general public is **Marina Village,** inspired by an old Bahamian harborfront with a string of clapboard-sided houses (think historic Key West, Florida, but with a lot more money). Flanking a marina that draws some of the world's most spectacular yachts, it's self-enclosed and has dozens of shops, bars, and restaurants, replete with gazebos and live musicians.

The focal point of Atlantis's extravagance is the massive **Paradise Island Casino,** the best-designed and most imaginatively conceived casino in The Bahamas. Set over a lagoon's watery depths, it contains three bars and two restaurants.

Within the diverse and scattered elements of this extended resort, you'll find some 40 separate food and beverage outlets, some of which open, close, and are reconfigured at sometimes dizzying rates. None of them comes cheap: You should expect to pay a lot to dine or drink in the resort. For detailed descriptions of its most worthy eateries, see "Where to Dine" and "Paradise Island After Dark," later in this chapter.

Casino Dr., Paradise Island, The Bahamas. (C) 800/ATLANTIS (285-2684) in the U.S., or 242/363-3000. Fax 242/363-6300. www.atlantis.com. 2,900 units. Rates in Beach Towers, Coral Towers, and Royal Towers: Winter US$495–US$795 (£248–£398) double, from US$940 (£470) suite; off-season US$340–US$650 (£170–£325) double, from US$680 (£340) suite. Package deals available. AE, DC, DISC, MC, V. Self-parking US$12 (£6) per day, valet parking US$15 (£7.50) per day. **Amenities:** 20 restaurants; 18 lounges and clubs; 17 outdoor pools interspersed w/123 acres of waterscape; golf course; 5 tennis courts; health club; spa; sauna; watersports; children's programs (ages 3–12); salon; room service; massage; babysitting; laundry service; dry cleaning; nonsmoking rooms; rooms for those w/limited mobility. In room: A/C, TV, minibar, hair dryer, iron, safe.

Tips **Not a Registered Guest?**

Guided tours of the resort are available to those not staying overnight. Called "Discover Atlantis," the hour-long affair costs US$30 (£15) per person, with kids under 12 getting in for half that. If you sign up, know that some of the resort's most intriguing areas remain off-limits to everyone except registered guests. Despite that, there's a lot to see on this tour. But in the end, the experience is rather tightly choreographed, not permitting free time to float down the lazy rivers. If anything, it's meant to pique your interest in Atlantis and up your motivation to return one day as a registered guest. For more information, call © 242/363-3000. Besides the tour, the general public has access to the **casino, nightclubs,** and Marina Village's **shops** and **restaurants.**

The Cove 🐠🐠🐠   Housed within a handsome, turquoise-and-coral-colored tower whose fanciful detailing matches the resort's mythical theme, this hotel was configured as a semiprivate hideaway. Don't expect anything conventional about this place: It's partially (but not completely) devoted to an adult-oriented venue that takes pains to dilute a growing perception that Atlantis has placed too heavy an emphasis on family fun. Inaugurated in 2007, it boasts an avant-garde design that combines the best of minimalist Japan and ultra-high-end postmodern Florida. Every unit is luxurious, high-tech, and larger than you might have expected, with step-down living rooms, personal butlers, and every imaginable electronic and service-related amenity. Whereas one of the two pools reserved only for guests of The Cove is family-friendly, the adults-only social centerpiece is a 2,700-sq.-m (29,063-sq.-ft.) rectangular "ultrapool" which is strictly off-limits to anyone under 18. It's ringed by 20 private cabanas, which can be rented by the day for sybaritic adults seeking seclusion from the younger crowds. On the lobby level, there's a branch of Bobby Flay's Mesa Grill. Immediately adjacent to The Cove, and open to any Atlantis guest or day-pass holder, is Mandara Spa, whose design was inspired by the architecture of Bali, with rampant use of stone, bamboo, and tropical hardwoods.

Casino Dr., Paradise Island, The Bahamas. © **800/ATLANTIS** (285-2684) in the U.S., or 242/363-3000. Fax 242/363-6300. www.atlantis.com. 600 suites. Winter US$745–US$1,510 (£373–£755) suite; off-season US$600–US$1,175 (£300–£588) suite. **Amenities:** 2 restaurants; 2 bars; casino access; 3 pools; access to an 18-hole golf course; access to 5 tennis courts; health club; steam room; shuttle service; room service; babysitting; laundry service; dry cleaning; nonsmoking rooms. *In room:* A/C, TV, minibar, hair dryer, iron, safe, butler service.

One&Only Ocean Club 🐠🐠🐠   Tranquil, secluded, and intimate, this is Paradise Island's most exclusive address, with sky-high prices to accompany the refined ambience and pampering service (the best in The Bahamas). Although it's owned by the same entity that controls the much larger Atlantis, huge efforts are expended to separate it from the clients at the less personalized, more family-oriented mega-resort. In fact, though Atlantis's facilities are available to the residents here, that same privilege does not extend in the opposite direction. As such, you'll find a boutique-style hotel with a highly visible security force that, to a large degree, is cloistered from the much splashier venue nearby.

The spacious and elegantly furnished rooms are comfortable, with king-size beds, gilt-framed mirrors, and dark-wood armoires. The marble bathrooms are massive, each containing a bidet, twin basins, a tub, and a shower.

Proudly Remaining Adult at Atlantis

Faced with increasing numbers of families with children, and with the perception that its acres of water slides and canals are a glorified summer camp for the children of parents who can afford it, there's an awareness that Atlantis needs quiet corners where grown-ups can be grown-ups.

If you fall into that category we advise that you check into either **The Cove, The Reef,** the **One&Only Ocean Club,** or one of the more upscale rooms within the **Royal Towers.** None of those venues officially restricts children, but the Beach and Coral towers tend to house the greatest numbers of foursomes—usually a nuclear family with their offspring or festive 20-somethings on reprieve from their lives in the frigid north.

If you've opted for lodgings within The Cove, spend time at the **adult-only swimming pool;** its staffers are hip, and 20 cabanas await you and your significant other.

On your first night at Atlantis, go for drinks and dinner at **Nobu.** We find the Asian food here delicious and fascinating—enough so that most well-adjusted North American kids will find it bizarre. The pre-dinner scene at the bar, where women look foxier than in the glaring sun of a Bahamian noon, is definitely not for children. Awaken, too, to the nocturnal charms of **Aura,** the appealingly permissive nightclub where celeb-gazing is something of an art form.

Finally, book a long session at **Mandara Spa.** If you see anyone inside who's under 18, it's likely they're in line to inherit a very substantial fortune. Otherwise, even though adults adore it, it's not the sort of place teeny-boppers necessarily crave.

The resort's real heart and soul lays in the surrounding gardens, designed by the island's former owner, Huntington Hartford II, heir to the A&P grocery fortune. This resort, in fact, was once the site of his private home. The formal gardens surround a rebuilt medieval French cloister set on 14 hectares (35 acres) of manicured lawns. Graceful 12th-century arcades are visible at the crest of a hill, across a stretch of terraced waterfalls, fountains, a stone gazebo, and rose gardens. Larger-than-life statues dot the vine-covered niches on either side of the gardens. Begin your tour of the gardens at the large swimming pool, which feeds a series of reflecting pools that stretch out toward the cloister.

A new addition is the kid-friendly pool, replete with aqua toys and a waterfall.

This is also one of the best-developed tennis resorts in The Bahamas, and the white-sand beach adjacent to the hotel is the finest in the area.

What could arguably be called Paradise Island's best dining is at the resort's Dune restaurant (p. 127), a creation of culinary legend Jean-Georges Vongerichten.

Ocean Club Dr., Paradise Island, The Bahamas. (C) **888/528-7157** in the U.S., or 242/363-2501. Fax 242/363-2424. www.oneandonlyresorts.com. 106 units, 3 private villas. Winter US$765–US$1,560 (£383–£780) double, from US$1,460 (£730) suite, from US$9,000 (£4,500) villa; off-season US$490–US$1,190 (£245–£595) double, from US$805 (£403) suite, from US$7,000 (£3,500) villa. AE, MC, V. Free parking. **Amenities:** 2 restaurants; 3 bars; 2 pools; 18-hole golf course; 6 tennis courts; health club; spa; steam room; shuttle to Atlantis casino; room service; baby-sitting; laundry service; dry cleaning; nonsmoking rooms. *In room:* A/C, TV, free Wi-Fi, kitchens, minibar, hair dryer, iron, safe, butler service.

The Reef 𝒶𝒶𝒶   Inaugurated in 2007, and purpose-built as a condominium complex in which the smallest unit is a fully self-sufficient one-bedroom apartment, this (along with The Cove) is Atlantis's tallest building. It's also the most flamboyantly state-of-the-art, permeated with the theme that defines virtually everything else around it. Although its decor most closely matches accommodations within The Cove, its level of contemporary comfort surpasses everything else at Atlantis. Opt for a room here if you're entertaining a group of four or more, if having a spectacularly high-tech kitchen is important to you, or if you have so much money that cost is absolutely no object. All of Atlantis's diversions and distractions are open to short-term residents of The Reef, and some renters liked the place so much that they bought a unit.

Casino Dr., Paradise Island, The Bahamas. ℭ 800/ATLANTIS (285-2684) in the U.S., or 242/363-3000. Fax 242/363-6300. www.atlantis.com. 550 suites. Winter US$575–US$1,075 (£288–£538) double; off-season US$395–US$1,015 (£198–£508) double. **Amenities:** Unrestricted access to all Atlantis attractions and amenities. *In room:* A/C, TV, free Wi-Fi, kitchen, washing machine, clothes dryer, hair dryer, iron, safe, butler service.

EXPENSIVE
Hotel Riu Paradise Island 𝒶 *Kids*   In 2004, the Riu Hotels chain refurbished the old Sheraton Grand here into an all-inclusive mega-resort. Renovations included a pool enlargement, a restaurant addition, and room enhancements. Opening onto a 5km (3-mile) stretch of beach, and within walking distance from Atlantis, this 14-story ecru-colored high-rise offers some of Paradise Island's most comfortably appointed bedrooms. It's more understated than Atlantis, a lot cheaper, and more user-friendly and manageable in terms of size and layout. Your kids would likely be happier at Atlantis, but Riu is a viable runner-up for the family set. Guests can leave the shelter of the poolside terrace and settle almost immediately onto one of the waterside chaise longues on the beach.

Welcoming drinks are served while you relax on comfortable chairs in the lobby bar amid palm trees and tropical foliage. All the spacious accommodations here are deluxe and tastefully decorated. Many have spacious balconies that afford sweeping water views or luxurious terraces.

For an extra charge, you can skip the all-inclusive dinner fare and dine at Tengoku, a Japanese-themed restaurant. Other choices available to jaded buffetgoers include Atlantic Restaurant, which serves fine steaks and maintains a nonsmoking section, plus a terrace; and Sir Alexander, Riu's gourmet a la carte restaurant, featuring highly refined continental gourmet cuisine made with first-rate ingredients. Live entertainment is available 6 nights a week.

6307 Casino Dr., Paradise Island, The Bahamas. ℭ 888/666-8816 in the U.S., or 242/363-3500. Fax 242/363-3900. www.riu.com. 379 units. Winter US$548–US$574 (£274–£287) double, from US$700 (£350) suite; off-season US$512–US$538 (£256–£269) double, from US$592 (£296) suite. Rates are all-inclusive. AE, MC, V. **Amenities:** 4 restaurants; 3 bars; pool; tennis court; gym; spa; Jacuzzi; sauna; watersports; salon; massage; babysitting; laundry service; dry cleaning; nonsmoking rooms; rooms for those w/limited mobility. *In room:* A/C, ceiling fan, TV, minibar, hair dryer, safe.

Paradise Island Beach Club 𝒶   This timeshare complex is set near Paradise Island's eastern tip, adjacent to a relatively isolated strip of spectacular beachfront. Managed by Marriott, it's more of a self-catering condo complex than a full-fledged resort. Many guests cook at least some meals in their own kitchens and head elsewhere, often to bigger hotels, for restaurants, watersports, gambling, and entertainment. Views from the bedrooms are usually ocean panoramas. Overall, the setting is comfortable and cozy.

You'll feel like you have your own Florida apartment with easy beach access. Accommodations have two bedrooms (for a maximum of six persons), with wicker and rattan furnishings and nice touches that include double basins in each bathroom.

On the premises are both a round and a triangular swimming pool, with a pool bar that opens for breakfast and serves drinks throughout the day until 5pm. The entertainment of the island's more densely developed sections lies just a short walk away.

Ocean Ridge Dr., Paradise Island, The Bahamas. (✆ 242/363-2523. Fax 242/363-2130. www.pibc-bahamas.com. 44 units. Winter US$459 (£230) 2-bedroom apt; off-season US$359 (£180) 2-bedroom apt. AE, MC, V. **Amenities:** Pool bar; 2 pools; exercise room; salon; massage; coin-operated laundry service; rooms for those w/limited mobility. *In room:* A/C, TV, kitchen, hair dryer, iron, safe.

Paradise Island Harbour Resort 🐾 *Kids*   Adjacent to Nassau Harbour and opening onto a marina, this 12-floor property is all inclusive and a family favorite because of its Camp Paradise Kids Club. It has very little beach, though it does offer a man-made tanning beach. Management compensates with a spectacular outdoor, free-form swimming pool. Accommodations are spacious and decorated in an airy, tropical style with good maintenance. The resort attracts those seeking plenty of activities and bountiful food and drink.

Harbour Dr., Paradise Island, The Bahamas. (✆ 242/363-2561. Fax 242/363-1220. www.paradiseislandbahama.com. 246 units. Winter $239–$380 double, $500 suite for 2; off season $230–$317 double, $390–$450 suite for 2. Rates are all inclusive. AE, DC, DISC, MC, V. Amenities: 3 restaurants, 2 bars, outdoor pool, 2 tennis courts, health club, watersports, children's programs, car rental, massage, babysitting, nonsmoking rooms, rooms for those with limited mobility. In room: AC, TV, fridge, beverage maker, hair dryer, iron safe.

Sunrise Beach Club and Villas 🐾 *Kids*   This cluster of Spanish-style low-rise town houses occupies one of the most desirable stretches of beachfront. Midway between Hotel Riu and the One&Only Ocean Club, it's a short walk from the casino and a variety of sports and dining options. Accommodations are clustered within five groupings of red-roofed town houses, each with access to the resort's two swimming pools (one of which has a waterfall) and a simple snack bar. The hotel is usually full of Germans, Swiss, and Austrians, many of whom stay for several weeks. Guests can prepare their own meals because units have kitchens. Expect pastel colors, summery-looking furniture, and a private patio or veranda, plus king-size beds and floor-to-ceiling mirrored headboards, as well as average-size bathrooms with a tub and shower. The best units are the three-bedroom apartments, situated directly on the beach. This is a good bet for quieter families who want a more subdued, relaxed vacation, and to avoid the circus at Atlantis.

Paradise Island, The Bahamas. (✆ 800/451-6078 or 242/363-2234. Fax 242/363-2308. www.sunrisebeachclub.com. 100 units. Winter US$331–US$389 (£166–£195) 1-bedroom unit, US$579 (£290) 2-bedroom unit; off-season US$221–US$255 (£111–£128) double, US$463 (£232) 2-bedroom unit. AE, MC, V. Amenities: Bar; 2 pools; babysitting; coin-operated laundry; nonsmoking rooms; rooms for those w/limited mobility. *In room:* A/C, TV, kitchen, beverage maker, hair dryer, iron, safe.

MODERATE

Best Western Bay View Suites 🐾   More than 20 kinds of hibiscus and many varieties of bougainvillea beautify this 1.6-hectare (4-acre) condo complex. The accommodations here are near the geographic center of Paradise Island, only a 10-minute walk to either the harbor or Cabbage Beach (the complex has no beach of its own). The restaurants of Atlantis are only a few minutes away, but the modest Terrace restaurant here is nothing to be ashamed of. A shopping center is only 3 minutes away, and a full-time personal cook can be arranged on request.

An Offshore Yoga Retreat

Ex-Beatle George Harrison and a host of other yoga devotees over the years have checked into **Sivananda Ashramyoga Retreat,** which is reached only by boat from Paradise Island. For some 40 years, it's been completely removed from the rest of Paradise Island's frantic gambling, heady lifestyle, and high prices. Today, the retreat teaches the healing arts and spiritual practices.

Guest lecturers from all over the world come here to give seminars and practice meditation. When not devoting their time to yoga, guests rest on a lovely sandy beach, all part of a compound that reaches from Nassau Harbour to the Atlantic. It's mandatory for guests to attend two 2-hour meditation sessions, the first starting at 5am. Two 2-hour yoga classes are also required. But you're free daily from 10am to 4pm. A boat shuttles guests into Nassau so they can see its sights.

Participants are housed in the simple main house or in small one-room bungalows. Vegetarian meals are included in the rate of US$89 (£45) for a single, US$79 to US$89 (£40–£45) in a double, or US$69 (£35) in a three- or four-bed dormitory. Tent space is available for US$59 (£30) per night. For air-conditioned rooms, an extra daily charge of US$10 (£5) applies. The most desirable units, a dozen of them, front the beach. There are also 35 private single rooms, plus seven dormlike spaces. American Express, MasterCard, and Visa are accepted.

We particularly recommend rooms near the center of the resort because they are closest to the three swimming pools and laundry facilities. Each accommodation has its own kitchen with a dishwasher, plus a patio or balcony and daily maid service. Units come in a wide variety of sizes—the largest can hold up to six—and some open onto views of the harbor. Penthouse suites contain roof gardens with views of the harbor. Bedrooms come with king-, queen-, or twin-size beds. Rates are slightly less for weekly rentals.

Bayview Dr., Paradise Island, The Bahamas. © **800-WESTERN** (937-8376), 757-1357, or 242/363-2555. Fax 242/363-2370. www.bwbayviewsuites.com. 75 units. Winter US$247 (£124) 1-bedroom suite, US$425 (£213) town house (for 4), from US$496 (£248) villa; off-season US$195 (£98) 1-bedroom suite, US$335 (£168) town house (for 4), from US$345 (£173) villa. AE, DC, MC, V. **Amenities:** Lunch-only restaurant; bar; 3 pools; tennis court; babysitting; coin-operated laundry; nonsmoking rooms; rooms for those w/limited mobility. *In room:* A/C, TV, kitchen, coffeemaker, hair dryer, iron, safe.

Comfort Suites *(Value)*   A favorite with honeymooners and a good value, this three-story all-suite hotel is across the street from Atlantis and is a nice alternative to the behemoth. You get the splash and wonder, but don't have to stay when the cruise-ship crowds descend. Though Comfort Suites has its own pool bar and restaurant, guests are granted signing privileges at the nearby Atlantis for its drinking-and-dining spots, as well as the pool, beach, and sports facilities. Accommodations are priced by their views: over the island, the pool, or the garden. Medium-size bathrooms are stocked with beach towels and ample vanities. Bedrooms are standard motel size, with two double beds or one king.

Paradise Island Dr., Paradise Island, The Bahamas. © **877/424-6423** in the U.S. or Canada, or 242/363-3680. Fax 242/363-2588. www.comfortsuites.com. 227 units. Winter US$269–US$373 (£135–£187) double; off-season US$225–US$333 (£113–£167) double. Rates include continental breakfast. AE, DISC, MC, V. **Amenities:** Restaurant; bar; pool; tennis court; health club; babysitting; laundry service; coin-operated laundry; nonsmoking rooms; rooms for those w/limited mobility. *In room:* A/C, TV, fridge, beverage maker, hair dryer, iron, safe (in some).

INEXPENSIVE

Paradise Harbour Club & Marina   The noteworthy thing about this place is its sense of isolation despite being on heavily developed Paradise Island. Built in 1991 near the island's extreme eastern tip, it's just a few steps from the also-recommended Columbus Tavern (p. 130). It's pale pink, with rambling upper hallways, terra-cotta tile floors, and clean, well-organized bedrooms with tub/showers in the bathrooms. If available, opt for one of the top-floor accommodations so you can enjoy the view. Some of its quaint services, all free, include a water taxi to downtown Nassau, a beach shuttle (albeit in a golf cart), and use of snorkeling gear and bikes.

Paradise Island Dr., Paradise Island, The Bahamas. ℂ **242/363-2992**. Fax 242/363-2840. www.phc-bahamas.com. 23 units. Winter US$150 (£75) double, US$210 (£105) junior suite, US$275 (£138) 1-bedroom unit; off-season US$120 (£60) double, US$180 (£90) junior suite, US$250 (£125) 1-bedroom unit. MC, V. **Amenities:** Restaurant; bar; pool; exercise room; Jacuzzi; watersports; golf cart shuttle to the beach; room service; babysitting; coin-operated laundry; rooms for those w/limited mobility. *In room:* A/C, TV, kitchen (in some), minibar, coffeemaker, hair dryer, iron, safe (in some).

4 Where to Dine

Paradise Island offers an array of the most dazzling, and the most expensive, restaurants in The Bahamas. If you're on a strict budget, cross over the bridge into downtown Nassau, which has far more reasonably priced places to eat. Though pricey, meals on Paradise Island are often unimaginative—surf and turf appears on many a menu, so, unfortunately, you may not get what you pay for.

The greatest concentration of restaurants, all near the casino, is owned by Kerzner International. There are other good places outside this complex, however, including Dune at the One&Only Ocean Club.

EXPENSIVE

Bahamian Club ⋆⋆ STEAKS   With an upscale British colonial feel and an aura like that of an elegant and somewhat macho-looking country club, this is a big (but civilized) clubby spot, with spacious vistas, mirrors, gleaming mahogany, and forest-green walls. The excellent food is served in two-fisted portions. Meat is king here, all those old favorites from roasted prime rib to Cornish hen, plus the island's best T-bone, along with a selection of veal and lamb chops. The retro menu also features the inevitable Dover sole, lobster thermidor, and grilled salmon. All of these dishes are prepared with top-quality ingredients from the U.S. Appetizers also hearken back to the good old days, with fresh jumbo-shrimp cocktail, baby spinach salad with a blue-cheese dressing, and onion soup. Try the Bahamian conch chowder for some local flavor. Side dishes are excellent here, especially the penne with fresh tomato sauce and the roasted shiitake mushrooms. Proper attire is required—that means no jeans or sneakers.

In Atlantis's Coral Towers, Casino Dr. ℂ **242/363-3000**. Reservations required. Main courses US$38–US$55 (£19–£28). AE, DC, DISC, MC, V. Usually Wed–Mon 6–11pm, though days and hours may vary.

Blue Lagoon ⋆ SEAFOOD   Views of the harbor and Paradise Lake, along with music from a one-man band, complement a candlelit meal here—a nice escape from the casino's glitter and glitz. Many of the fish dishes, including stone crab claws and the Nassau conch chowder, are excellent. The ubiquitous broiled grouper almondine is on the menu, as are dishes such as steak au poivre with a brandy sauce and duck à l'orange. The chef even whips up a good Caesar salad for two. Yes, you've probably

> **Tips Hopping, Skipping & Jumping with Dining Hours**
>
> Restaurants here, especially in hotels, are not known for keeping fixed dining hours. Hours of operation can vary with the season and the hotel's occupancy level. Dining rooms—again, mainly in hotels—can open and close with no reason that's immediately obvious. If you're planning on going to a particular restaurant, call in advance even if reservations aren't required.

had better versions of these dishes elsewhere, but they are competently prepared, even though the meats are shipped in frozen.

In the Club Land'or, Paradise Dr. © **242/363-2400.** Reservations required. Main courses US$27–US$85 (£14–£43). AE, MC, V. Mon–Sat 5–10pm.

Bobby Flay's Mesa Grill 🎇 AMERICAN SOUTHWESTERN   In 2007, Atlantis carved this Southwestern-chic enclave out of a beachfront spot on the lobby level of The Cove, the "boutique" hotel within Atlantis. Don't presume that this is a down-home, greasy joint for chili, beer, and barbecue. It's actually rather haute, distinctly gourmet, and run by celebrity chef Bobby Flay, whose name is well-known to anyone who watches any food channel. Decor is distinctively southwestern, with lots of exposed wood and colors inspired by New Mexico's arid regions.

Begin a meal here with a shrimp-and-roasted-garlic cornmeal tamale with fresh corn and cilantro sauce or raw tuna nachos with mango hot sauce and avocado cream. Follow that with the 16-spice chicken or honey-glazed salmon. There are at least three succulent preparations of grilled steaks, and an excellent vegetarian option for a main course is the cornmeal-crusted chile relleno filled with goat cheese, wild mushrooms, and a smoked red-pepper sauce. Well-flavored side dishes include collard greens, sweet potato gratin, black-eyed peas with rice, and cilantro-pesto mashed potatoes. Children under 12 are discouraged from dining here

In The Cove. © **242/363-3000** ext. 59250. Main courses US$32–US$59 (£16–£30). Daily 7–10pm (last seating). AE, DC, MC, V.

Café at the Great Hall of Waters 🎇 *Kids* INTERNATIONAL   Speaking to us confidentially, an Atlantis staffer said that this was probably the resort's most under-appreciated dining spot. After a close second look, we've upgraded our evaluation of the place, recommending it highly to anyone except agoraphobics, who might be frightened by its soaring ceiling and relative lack of intimacy. If you would enjoy dining in a monumental setting surrounded with the most marine habitats of any restaurant in the world, this place is for you. You feel like an underwater diver as rainbow-hued fish float behind the huge plate-glass windows while rows of lobsters parade through the sand. There's a kids' menu, and little ones love taking walks along the edges of the marine habitats between courses. In such a watery setting, the food becomes almost secondary, although it's quite good. The chef imports top-quality ingredients for such dishes as rack of lamb with arugula pesto. Lobster is a specialty, as are versions of smoked salmon with lemongrass and jumbo lump Andros crab cakes. Desserts are uniformly delicious.

Royal Towers, Atlantis, Casino Dr. © **242/363-3000.** Reservations required. Main courses US$30–US$52 (£15–£26). AE, DC, MC, V. Thurs–Mon 7–11am, 11:30am–2:30pm, and 6–10pm, though days and hours may vary.

Café Martinique ✦✦✦ FRENCH   The most elegant and upscale restaurant on Paradise Island is within Atlantis's Marina Village. It occupies a replica of the kind of town house that might belong to a billionaire who happened to live in, say, Martinique and happened to have imported art and antiques from Belle Époque Paris. This mixture of haute Paris with a French Colonial twist is enormously appealing and especially visible, for example, within the wrought-iron birdcage elevator that brings you upstairs to the dining room. Begin your meal in the supremely comfortable bar area—the kind of place where Charles de Gaulle might have been fêted. The carved mahogany antiques are pure French Caribbean, the upholsteries scream upscale Paris, and the food items are luxe. In the tastefully posh dining area, masses of flowers, cheese, and dessert trolleys—not to mention the cuisine of superchef Jean-Georges Vongerichten—await your pleasure. This is one of the very few dining areas at Atlantis where men are asked to wear jackets; no one seems to object. Begin with such delectable items as caviar or smoked salmon. The main courses are limited, but each is sublime, especially the lobster thermidor and the Dover sole meunière. The restaurant is known for its grills, everything from prime rib for two to a succulent veal chop.

In Marina Village at Atlantis, Casino Dr. © 242/363-3000. Reservations required. Main courses US$32–US$79 (£16–£40). AE, DC, DISC, MC, V. Daily 6–11pm, though days and hours may vary.

Casa d'Angelo ✦ ITALIAN   Posh, richly upholstered, and lined with art and objects reflecting the tastes of old-world Italy, Paradise Island's premier Italian restaurant offers classic dishes prepared with skill, served with flair, and evocative of the kind of elegant manicured cuisine you'd expect from a top-notch Italian restaurant in Florida. Some of the best main courses include sautéed Fra Diavolo–style calamari and clams served over crostini; tuna carpaccio with spinach, olives, artichoke hearts, and orange sauce; risotto with porcini mushrooms, truffle oil, goat cheese, and thyme; wood oven-roasted free-range chicken with roasted garlic and Tuscan potatoes; and grilled swordfish steak with garlic, white wine, tomatoes, capers, black olives, onions, and fresh oregano.

In the Coral Tower at Atlantis, Casino Dr. © **242/363-3000.** Reservations required. Main courses US$32–US$60 (£16–£30). AE, DC, MC, V. Daily 6–10pm, though days and hours may vary.

Chopstix CANTONESE   Many people come here just to hang out in the bar. But if you're in the mood for a good Chinese meal, you'll be ushered to a table in a circular dining room, engaging and stylish, with a ceiling draped with fabric that evokes a richly decorated tent. The sophisticated decor seems to encourage both your sense of humor and your sense of camp; it suggests Shanghai during the British colonial age. Some of the island's best appetizers are served here—try the steamed shrimp dumplings or the Thai chicken spring rolls. This might be followed with wok-seared grouper with garlic sauce or coconut curry chicken with mango.

In the Coral Tower, Atlantis, Casino Dr. © **242/363-3000.** Reservations recommended. Main courses US$26–US$49 (£13–£25). AE, DC, DISC, MC, V. Tues–Sat 6–10pm, though days and hours may vary.

Dune ✦✦✦ INTERNATIONAL   One of Paradise Island's most cutting-edge restaurants is in the One&Only Ocean Club. It has a sweeping view of the ocean, a teakwood floor that evokes being aboard a yacht, very attentive service, and a gray-and-black decor that looks like it was plucked from a chic enclave in Milan. Near the restaurant's entrance is a thriving herb garden from which many of the culinary flavorings are derived. The chefs here invariably select the very finest ingredients, which are then handled with razor-sharp technique. Every dish has a special something, especially the shrimp dusted with orange powder and served with artichokes and arugula. A splendid choice is tuna spring rolls with soybean salsa. Also charming to the palate is a chicken and coconut-milk soup served with shiitake cakes. The goat cheese and watermelon salad is an unexpected delight. Grouper filet—that Bahamian standard—is at its savory best here when served with zesty tomato sauce.

In the One&Only Ocean Club, Ocean Club Dr. ℂ 242/363-2501, ext. 64739. Reservations required. Main courses US$22–US$40 (£11–£20) lunch, US$42–US$60 (£21–£30) dinner. AE, DC, DISC, MC, V. Daily 7–11am, noon–3pm, and 6–10:30pm, though days and hours may vary.

Fathoms ⚘ SEAFOOD   You'll feel as if you're dining under the sea in this very dark seafood palace. The grotto-themed decor, depending on your taste, might come off either mystical or a bit spooky. Illuminating its glossy, metallic interior and four enormous plate-glass windows, sunlight filters in through the watery marine habitats that surround the Dig, Atlantis's re-creation of an archaeological excavation.

At first you'll think the best appetizer is a selection of raw seasonal seafood. But then you're tempted by the blackened sashimi flavored with red ginger. The lobster gazpacho is terrific, and you can also dig into a bowl of steamy black mussels flavored with chardonnay, garlic, and tomato. The wood-grilled yellowtail comes perfectly cooked with a wasabi potato mash and caviar, and the grilled Atlantic salmon is extra inviting with its side of Parmesan garlic fries. Meat devotees will find a wide selection here. Save room for dessert, and make it a light, feathery soufflé—a different flavor is served every night.

In the Royal Towers, Atlantis, Casino Dr. ℂ 242/363-3000. Reservations recommended. Main courses US$27–US$50 (£14–£25). AE, DC, MC, V. Daily 5:30–10pm, though days and hours may vary.

Marketplace ⚘ *Value* BUFFET/INTERNATIONAL   Unless you're hopelessly jaded or blasé, you won't leave here without feeling amazed at how abundant and elaborate the buffets at a casino resort can really be. Decorated with old vases and terra-cotta tiles, this one evokes a sprawling market in which all the food just happens to be beautifully prepared, elegantly displayed, and showcased in breathtaking variety and quantity—making it the best buffet on Paradise Island. Before you start loading stuff onto your plate, browse your way past the various cooking stations and do some strategic planning. From fresh fruit to made-as-you-watch omelets, you can make breakfast as light or as heavy as you want. At lunch and dinner, you'll find everything from fresh seafood and made-to-order pastas to carved roast beef and lamb. No intimate affair, this place seats some 400 diners. Sit inside or on the patio overlooking a lagoon.

In the Royal Towers, Atlantis, Casino Dr. ℂ 242/363-3000. Reservations not needed. Breakfast buffets US$25 (£13) per person; lunch buffets US$30 (£15) per person; dinner buffets US$58 (£29) per person. AE, DC, MC, V. Daily 7–11am, noon–3pm, and 5:30–10pm.

Nobu ⚘⚘⚘ JAPANESE/ASIAN   It's the most talked-about, hip, and sought-after restaurant in Atlantis, thanks to a massive publicity push, avant-garde Asian food, and an association with an ongoing round of celebrities. It's the culinary statement of Japanese chef Nobu Matsuhisa, whose New York City branch caused a sensation among the glitterati there when it opened in the '90s. Don't expect a conventional meal here, as dishes appeal as much to the intellect as they do to the stomach. The kitchen staff is as finely tuned as their New York and London counterparts. Some diners prefer to start with Nobu's special cold dishes, including lobster seviche. But since conch is queen in The Bahamas, you might opt instead for conch seviche. The best appetizer we've sampled is the yellowtail sashimi with jalapeño. If you prefer your dishes spicy, try the rock shrimp tempura with a cream sauce or else Chilean sea bass with black-bean sauce. Many of the meals, such as a whole fish, emerge from a wood-fired oven. The tempura selection is vast, ranging from pumpkin to shiitake. Most patrons order sushi or sashimi, and the selection is wide, including some exotica such as live conch, sea urchins, or freshwater eel. Of course, you can also order well-prepared standards which include tuna, octopus, and salmon, as well as snow or king crab. If you want Paradise Island's most lavish and exotic menu, request the chef's signature fixed-price meal, which he calls "Chef's Choice Omakase Menu."

In Atlantis's casino, Casino Dr. (242/363-3000. Reservations required. Main courses US$18–US$70 (£9–£35); sushi or sashimi rolls US$4–US$15 (£2–£7.50); sushi or sashimi dinner US$55 (£28); chef's special menu US$150 (£75). AE, DC, DISC, MC, V. Daily 6–11pm.

Water's Edge *G* BUFFET/SEAFOOD   Frankly, we prefer the buffet at the Marketplace (p. 128), but if you're looking for a buffet venue where ongoing displays of seafood are the main appeal, this fits the bill. Three 4.5m (15-ft.) waterfalls splash into an artificial lagoon just outside the dining room's windows. Huge chandeliers illuminate the room, which has views of an open kitchen where a battalion of chefs create a nightly seafood buffet. And if you're in the mood for pasta and pizza, they're here, but for the most part garnished with (guess what?) seafood. Depending on the night, some dishes are better than others, but almost universally, the lavish displays of fresh shellfish from the raw bar will include 6-ounce lobster tails, stone crab claws, more shrimp than you can cope with, and, when they're in season, fresh raw oysters. The main problem here is that the food has a hard time competing with the ambience. If you've already sampled the Marketplace, you might have already had enough.

In the Coral Towers at Atlantis, Casino Dr. (242/363-3000. Reservations recommended. Seafood buffet US$58 (£29). AE, DC, DISC, MC, V. Daily 5:30–10pm.

MODERATE

Bimini Road *G* BAHAMIAN/INTERNATIONAL   The name refers to a mysterious underwater rock formation off the coast of Bimini that resembles a ruined triumphal boulevard (p. 8). Partly because of its relatively reasonable prices and partly because it showcases the cuisine of The Bahamas more proudly than any other restaurant at Atlantis, this eatery is among the most consistently popular and crowded dining spots. Some aspects of the place, especially the red leatherette banquettes and Formica tables, evoke a Goombay version of a brightly painted diner somewhere in the Out Islands. Yet a second glance reveals a sophisticated-looking and hysterically busy open kitchen (entertainment in its own right), and walls covered with tropical murals, some influenced by the Junkanoo festival (p. 39). The kitchen constantly churns out food items that include lobster and beef rib-eye. Start with specialties like the scorched conch salad or else Rum Bay boiled fish in a citrus broth. Other island favorites include the catch of the day, which can be grilled, blackened, or fried island-style. A tasty dish is chicken mojo—boneless breast with spices and a lime mojo sauce charcoal-roasted and served over native rice. The only problem with this place involves an inconvenient crowd of expectant diners who cluster, somewhat uncomfortably, near the entrance waiting for a table. A phone call in advance for information about wait times might help you avoid this inconvenience.

In the Marina Village at Atlantis, Casino Dr. (242/363-3000. Reservations accepted only for parties of 6 or more. Main courses US$24–US$40 (£12–£20). AE, DISC, MC, V. Daily noon–3pm and 6–11pm.

Carmine's ITALIAN   A lot of the signals that emanate from this place communicate "family." Here we're talking about a large, loud, and in-your-face Italian family who work out their emotional conflicts with gusto, verve, and platters piled high with an amazing amount of food. Set at Marina Village's most distant point from the casino, this is the local branch of a restaurant that will always be associated New York City's Little Italy or outer boroughs.

Even though it was custom-built, you'll get the idea that a team of decorators gentrified this boathouse, with its many square yards of mahogany bar tops, terra-cotta tiles, and monumental wine racks. This place prides itself on serving portions that could feed a party of four to six. As such, it's at its best when groups gather together to order several platters for collective consumption. If you're a single diner or a couple, head instead for other dining haunts such as Café Martinique or Bahamian Club.

In the Marina Village at Atlantis, Casino Dr. © 242/363-3000. Reservations accepted only for parties of 6 or more. Main courses US$30–US$38 (£15–£19). AE, DC, DISC, MC, V. Daily 6–11pm.

Columbus Tavern ⭐ *Finds* CONTINENTAL/BAHAMIAN   Far removed from the glitz and glamour of the casinos, this tavern seems relatively little known, even though Freddie Lightbourne of the Poop Deck restaurant has been running it for years. It deserves to be discovered because it serves good food at reasonable (for Paradise Island) prices. The tavern has clichéd nautical decor (don't come here for the setting), with tables placed both inside and outside overlooking the harbor. The bar is worth a visit in itself, with its long list of tropical drinks. Go local by starting off with the conch chowder. Even though it's imported frozen, the rack of lamb tastes flawless. You can also order tamarind chicken and a quite good grouper filet topped with a tantalizing lobster-and-shrimp sauce.

In the Paradise Harbour Club Resort, Paradise Island Dr. © 242/363-5923. Reservations required for dinner. Main courses US$11–US$32 (£5.50–£16) lunch, US$20–US$48 (£10–£24) dinner. AE, MC, V. Daily 8:30am–10pm.

INEXPENSIVE

Anthony's Caribbean Grill AMERICAN/CARIBBEAN   Its owners think of this place as an upscale version of Bennigan's or T.G.I. Friday's. But the decor is thoroughly Caribbean, thanks to psychedelic tropical colors, underwater sea themes, and jaunty maritime decorative touches. A bar dispenses everything from conventional mai tai to embarrassingly oversized 48-ounce "sparklers"—with a combination of rum, amaretto, vodka, and fruit punch that is about all most serious drinkers can handle. Menu items include burgers, barbecued or fried chicken, ribs with Caribbean barbecue sauce, several meal-size salads, and pizzas topped with everything from lobster to jerk chicken.

In the Paradise Island Shopping Center, at Paradise and Casino drives. © 242/363-3152. Lunch US$10–US$15 (£5–£7.50); dinner US$10–US$39 (£5–£20). AE, DISC, MC, V. Daily 7:30am–11pm.

Atlas Grill and Sports Bar BURGERS AND STEAKS   The blare of its dozen or so TVs competes with the jangling of slot machines here. This is the sports bar with the most elaborate array of viewing stations on Paradise Island. They're set up in two separate ovals, each of which rings, at different perimeters, an oval-shaped bar. Decor includes lots of primary colors and various statues depicting Atlas and his many macho struggles. What should you get here? Consider burgers with beer, burgers with scotch, or burgers with a soft drink.

In Atlantis's casino, Casino Dr. © 242/363-3000. Reservations not necessary. Main courses US$10–US$28 (£5–£14). AE, DC, MC, V. Daily 11am–4pm; Thurs–Sun 4pm–3am, though days and hours (especially at dinner) may vary.

News Café DELI   Low-key and not touristy, this spot has Formica-clad decor that's a far cry (and, to some, a welcome change) from the unrelenting glossiness of other parts of the island. This is where you'll find most of the island's construction workers, groundskeepers, and hotel staff having breakfast and lunch. The eatery maintains a stack of the day's newspapers, so you have something to read as you sip your morning cappuccino or latte. You can also stock up here on sandwiches for a beach picnic.

In the Hurricane Hole Plaza, Paradise Island. ℂ 242/363-4684. Reservations not accepted. Breakfast, lunch sandwiches, and platters US$7–US$12 (£3.50–£6); assorted coffees US$2–US$4 (£1–£2). AE, DC, DISC, MC, V. Daily 24 hr.

5 Beaches, Watersports & Other Outdoor Pursuits

Visitors interested in something more than lazing on the beach have only to ask hotel personnel to make the necessary arrangements. Guests at **Atlantis** (ℂ 242/363-3000), for example, have access to a surprising number of diversions without so much as leaving the hotel property. They can splash in private pools; play tennis, ping-pong, and shuffleboard; ride the waves; snorkel; or rent Sunfish, Sailfish, jet skis, banana boats, and catamarans from contractors located in kiosks.

HITTING THE BEACH

On Paradise Island, **Cabbage Beach** 🌴🌴 (also known as **West Beach**) is the real showcase. Its broad white sands stretch for at least 3km (2 miles). Casuarinas, palms, and sea grapes border it. It's likely to be crowded in winter, but you can find more elbowroom by walking to the beach's northwestern stretch. You can reach Paradise Island from downtown Nassau by walking over the bridge, taking a taxi, or boarding a ferryboat at Prince George Dock. Cabbage Beach does not have public restrooms, but if you patronize one of the handful of bars and restaurants nearby, they'll let you use their facilities. Note that during the construction of Atlantis's soon-to-come waterfront timeshare property, access to some sections of this beach might be off-limits.

Favorite Paradise Island Experiences

Sunset at the Cloister. Here, amid the reassembled remains of a 12th-century French stone monastery once owned by William Randolph Hearst, you can enjoy one of the most beautiful pink and mauve sunsets in all The Bahamas.

A Night at the Casino. Atlantis's casino—the only one on Paradise Island—is one of the world's most impressive and imaginatively decorated. Many visitors arrive on the island just to test their luck in this gaming destination. Once you're here, make it a point to check out the huge clusters of hand-blown glass arranged into amazing sculptures, conceived by American glass-blowing master Dale Chihuly. This casino contains at least four of his pieces, each one massive, hyper-fragile, awe-inspiring, and giving the impression of emanating their own light. Looking for a dining venue? The echoing interior passageway interconnecting the various parts of this widely flung resort is home to a medley of shops and restaurants, some of them among the finest in The Bahamas.

Our other favorite beach in this area is the white-sand **Paradise Beach** ✪✪, which is used mainly by guests of The Cove (p. 120), as it lies at the island's far western tip. If you're not a resident, access is difficult. If you're staying at a hotel in Nassau and want to come to Paradise Island for a day at the beach, it's better to go to Cabbage Beach (see above). However, sunsets viewed from the sands of Paradise Beach look particularly beautiful.

FISHING

Anglers can fish close to shore for grouper, dolphinfish, red snapper, crabs, even lobster. Farther out, in first-class fishing boats fitted with outriggers and fighting chairs, they troll for billfish or giant marlin.

The best way to pursue this pastime is to go to your hotel's activities desk, where an employee will set you up with a local charter operator for a half or full day of fishing. Also see "Beaches, Watersports & Other Outdoor Pursuits," in chapter 4.

GOLF

Ocean Club Golf Club ✪✪, on Paradise Island Drive (© **242/363-3000;** www. oneandonlyresorts.com), at the island's east end, is an 18-hole championship golf course designed by Tom Weiskopf that overlooks both the Atlantic Ocean and Nassau Harbour. Attracting every caliber of golfer, the par-72 course is known for its hole 17, which plays entirely along the scenic Snorkelers Cove. Greens fees, including use of a golf cart, cost US$260 (£130) per player for 18 holes of play, without reductions for guests at any individual hotels. Rental clubs and shoes are available.

Golfers seeking more variety will find one other course on New Providence Island (see "Beaches, Watersports & Other Outdoor Pursuits," in chapter 4).

SNORKELING & SCUBA DIVING

Bahama Divers, in the Yachthaven Marina on East Bay Street (© **242/393-5644;** www.bahamadivers.com), is the island's best all-around center for watersports, specializing in scuba diving and snorkeling. A two-tank morning dive goes for US$99 (£50), whereas a single-tank afternoon dive costs US$65 (£33). A half-day snorkeling trip is US$45 (£23), and dive packages are also offered.

For more scuba sites in the area, see "Snorkeling, Scuba Diving & Underwater Walks," in chapter 4.

TENNIS

No other hotel in The Bahamas pays as much attention to tennis as **One&Only Ocean Club,** Ocean Club Drive (© **242/363-2501**). It's the site of six Har-Tru courts, which go a long way toward evoking the days when Paradise Island was a lot more British-looking than it is today, and when tennis was a lot more widely played. Guests booked into the club's cabanas and villas can practically roll out of bed and onto the courts, which are often filled with first-class competitors, although beginners and intermediate players are welcome. Tennis is free for guests of the One&Only Ocean Club; access to the courts is forbidden to virtually everyone else. Guests of the Ocean Club can play with the resident tennis pro for US$75 (£38) per hour.

Other hotels with courts include **Atlantis** ✪ (© **242/363-3000**), with five hardsurface clay courts. Atlantis guests (nonguests are not admitted) pay US$20 (£10) per hour for access to the courts and can play with the organization's resident pro for an additional US$75 (£38) per hour. Ball rentals go for US$9.50 (£4.75) per hour, tennis racquets for another US$10 (£5) per hour. At least two major annual tennis championships are held at the Atlantis courts, drawing players from around Europe and the Americas.

6 Seeing the Sights

Most of the big hotels here maintain activity-packed calendars, especially for that occasional windy, rainy day that comes in winter. Similar to life aboard a large cruise ship, the resorts offer diversions (some of them age-specific) that include water-volleyball games, bingo, fish-feeding demonstrations, and movie screenings. And that doesn't include the disco parties for teens and preteens that tend to be scheduled for late afternoons or early evenings. To an increasing degree, hotels such as Atlantis have configured themselves as destinations in their own right.

Atlantis Paradise Island Resort & Casino 🏆🏆   Regardless of where you're staying—even if it's at New Providence's most remote hotel—you'll want to visit this lavish theme park, hotel, restaurant complex, casino, and entertainment center. It is, hands down, Paradise Island's biggest attraction. You could spend all day here—and all night, too—wandering through the shopping arcades, sampling the varied restaurants' international cuisine, or gambling at roulette wheels, slot machines, poker games, and blackjack tables. And once you're here, don't even think about leaving without a walk along the marina or a visit to The Dig, a theme-driven marine attraction that celebrates the eerie, tragic legend of the lost continent of Atlantis. During the day, you can wear casual clothes, but at night you should dress up a bit, especially to try one of the better restaurants.

The most crowded time to visit is between 9am and 5pm on days when cruise ships are berthed in the nearby harbor (usually every Tues, Fri, and Sat). The most crowded time to visit the casino is between 8 and 11pm any night of the week. There is no cover to enter: You pay just for what you eat, drink, and gamble away (and that could be considerable). Ironically, it's illegal for Bahamian citizens or residents to gamble. That restriction, however, most definitely does not apply to visitors from other countries. Except for the price of the liquor, entertainment within the bars—which usually includes live salsa, Goombay, and calypso music provided by local bands—is free.

Casino Dr. 🕿 242/363-3000. Free admission. Daily 24 hr.

The Cloister 🏆   Located in the Versailles Gardens of the One&Only Ocean Club, this 12th-century cloister built by Augustinian monks in southwestern France was reassembled here stone by stone. Huntington Hartford, the A&P heir, purchased the cloister from the estate of William Randolph Hearst. Regrettably, after the newspaper

---

⌒Finds Spa Serenity

The 2,323-sq.-m (25,005-sq.-ft.) **Mandara Spa** at Atlantis is a Zen-inspired enclave of calm and serenity designed to make guests feel like gods and goddesses. Services include exotic body scrubs and wrap treatments with names like Caribbean Coffee Scrub, Tropical Coconut Scrub, and Sunburn Cooler. Spa guests also get to take a dip in Poseidon's Thalassotherapy Pool, a beautiful open-air natural seawater pool. Prices, however, are not likely to encourage serenity.

⌒Moments A Special Place of Beauty

Paradise Island's loveliest spot is Ocean Club's **Versailles Gardens,** far removed from the glitz and faux glamour. Within its seven terraces, the sites of many a wedding, are statues of some of Huntington Hartford's favorite people, including Mephistopheles, Franklin D. Roosevelt, and Doctor Livingstone. The gardens are open anytime, day or night, and admission is free.

---

czar originally bought the cloister, it was hastily dismantled in France for shipment to The Bahamas. However, the parts had not been numbered—they all arrived unlabeled on Paradise Island. The reassembly of the complicated monument baffled most, and defied conventional methods of construction, until artist and sculptor Jean Castre-Manne set about doing it piece by piece. It took him 2 years, and what you see today presumably bears some similarity to the original. The gardens, which extend over the rise to Nassau Harbour, are filled with tropical flowers and classical statues. Though the monument retains a timeless beauty, recently erected buildings have encroached on either side, marring Hartford's original vision.

In the One&Only Ocean Club gardens, Ocean Club Dr. ℭ 242/363-2501. Free admission. Daily 24 hr.

7 Shopping

For serious shopping, cross over the Paradise Island Bridge into Nassau (see chapter 4). However, many of Nassau's major stores also have outlets on Paradise Island.

The Shops at the Atlantis (ℭ 242/363-3000) is the largest concentration of shops and boutiques on Paradise Island, rivaling anything else in The Bahamas in terms of size, selection, and style. The boutiques are subdivided into two different sections that include the well-appointed **Crystal Court Arcade** corridor that meanders between the Royal Tower and the Coral Tower, encompassing 3,252 sq. m (35,004 sq. ft.) of prime high-traffic retail space. The boutiques within the waterfront **Marina Village** are newer. An additional handful of emporiums is scattered randomly throughout other sections of the resort, as noted below. It's all about flagrantly conspicuous consumption that's sometimes fueled by the gaming frenzy in the nearby casino. So if you want to do more than browse, bring your platinum card and remain alert that in a high-ticket venue like this, maxing out your credit cards might happen sooner than you might ever have believed.

The resort contains two branches of **Colombian Emeralds** (one in the Marina Village, another within Atlantis Paradise Island's Beach Tower), where the colored gemstones far outnumber the relatively limited selection of diamonds. Individual purveyors include **Lalique,** the France-based purveyor of fine crystal and fashion accessories for men and women; **Cartier; Versace,** the late designer to the stars (this boutique also has a particularly charming homeware division); **Façonnable,** a youthful, sporty label for young and beautiful club-hoppers; **Bulgari,** producer of some of the world's most enviable jewels, as well as watches, giftware, and perfumes; and **Gucci** and **Ferragamo,** in case you forgot your best dancing shoes. For bathing suits, **Cole's of Nassau** sells swimwear by Gottex, Pucci, and Fernando Sanchez. Finally, **John Bull,** known for its Bay Street store in Nassau and as a pioneer seller of watches throughout The Bahamas, also has an interesting assortment of timepieces, jewelry, and designer accessories.

One of our favorite shops, **Doongalik Studios** (© 242/394-1886), in Marina Village, doesn't sell the predictably upscale roster of gemstones and fashion that you might have had your fill of by now. At press time, it's still the complex's only art gallery. Owned and operated by Jackson Burnside, the architect and art connoisseur who designed Marina Village, it's a bastion of authentic Bahamian culture within the glittering row of shops otherwise devoted to luxury goods. Come here for insight into who is creating contemporary art in The Bahamas. Oil paintings by locally famous artists (including John Cox, John Paul, Jessica Colebrooke, and Eddie Minnis) range from US$800 to US$2,500 (£400–£1,250) each. Prints—sometimes of works by the same artists—are priced between US$15 and US$100 (£7.50–£50) each. Sculptures can be especially interesting, with some crafted from gnarled driftwood.

8 Paradise Island After Dark

Paradise Island has the country's best nightlife, and most of it centers on Atlantis.

The Entertainment Centre at Atlantis Paradise Island ★★★   There's no other spot in The Bahamas, with the possible exception of the Crystal Palace complex on Cable Beach, with such a wide variety of after-dark attractions, and absolutely nothing that approaches its inspired brand of razzle-dazzle. Even if you stay in Nassau or Cable Beach, you'll want to drop in at this artfully decorated, self-contained temple to decadence, even if gambling isn't really your passion. Love it or hate it, this place is simply a jaw-dropper.

The **casino** is the most lavishly planned, most obviously themed venue of its kind this side of Vegas. Its managers claim that it's the only casino in the world built above a body of water. Designed in homage to the lost continent of Atlantis, it appears to have risen directly from the waters of the lagoon. The gaming area is centered on buildings representing a Temple of the Sun and a Temple of the Moon, with a painted replica of the zodiac chart overhead. Rising from key locations are four of the most elaborate sculptures in the world. Massive and complex, they were crafted by teams of artisans spearheaded by Dale Chihuly, the American-born master whose glass-blowing skills are heralded globally. Other than the decor, the casino's gaming tables, open daily from 10am to 4am, are the main attraction in this enormous place, and about a thousand whirring and clanging slot machines operate 24 hours a day.

Recent additions include a lineup of poker tables and the **Pegasus Race and Sports Book,** with an illuminated and computerized display that lists the odds for many of the world's upcoming sporting events. Thanks to instantaneous communications with a centralized betting facility in Las Vegas, the staff here will make odds on a staggering number of sports events, both professional and collegiate, as well as horse racing and greyhound racing. This facility also contains a mini-amphitheater with plush armchairs and views over a battery of TV screens, each displaying one of the sporting and/or racing events for which odds are being calculated and money is changing hands. Upstairs from the casino is **Aura,** a totally upscale nightclub experience that manages to attract a few local hipsters as well as Atlantis guests. Come anytime during casino hours for a drink. A sweaty, flirty crowd parties all night on the dance floor. The club gets going around 10pm nightly, with a cover charge of US$50 (£25) for females and US$100 (£50) for males, unless they're residents of Atlantis, in which case they enter without charge. (Note that the nonresidents' entrance charge is usually waived for women if they're hip or beautiful enough.) Drinks inside carry big-city price tags, usually hovering around US$17 (£8.50) for a scotch and soda. Ringing the casino are at least 3,252 sq. m (35,004 sq. ft.) of retail shopping space, with even more located nearby in the Marina Village (see "Shopping," above) and an impressive cluster of hideaway bars and restaurants.

Also in Atlantis, **Joker's Wild** (© 242/363-3000) is the only real comedy club in The Bahamas, with a talented company of funny people who work hard to make you laugh. Showtimes are Tuesday through Sunday at 9:30pm and there's a per-person cover charge of US$15 (£7.50) for everyone. At least two comedians appear on any given night, and most of them hail from either the U.S. or the U.K. Midway btw. Beach and Coral towers, on Casino Dr. © 242/363-3000.

THE BAR SCENE

Bimini Road   The joint is always jumping and is imbued with a Junkanoo theme and decorated by wall-size murals. At many bars at this sprawling resort, the bartenders seem to ignore you. Not here. They are a lively bunch, slinging drinks with names like the Fountain of Youth. A specialty is a sour-apple-flavored mixture known as Gussie Mae. The place is especially popular with yachties, who tie up at the nearby marina. A costumed dance troupe performs 4 nights a week (times vary), and live bands pump out island music for most of the night. Even patrons get in on the act with conga lines. The restaurant (p. 129) serves food daily from 11am to 10pm, including conch fritters and cracked lobster tail. Both of this establishment's bars (one on the outdoor terrace, the other indoors) are open 11am to 1:30am daily. Marina Village, Atlantis, Casino Dr. © 242/363-3000.

Dune Bar   This luxe dining room (p. 127) is also the setting for the island's most elegant and sophisticated lounge; it's becoming increasingly popular as a plush and appealing meeting spot for singles. The action centers around a translucent white marble bar skillfully illuminated from behind. The outdoor terrace can be undeniably romantic. At the One&Only Ocean Club, Ocean Club Dr. © 242/363-2501. Call for hours, which can vary.

Plato's Lounge   This is Atlantis's most popular bar, a sensual spot where you can escape the din of the slot machines and relax in an upscale environment that's flanked with replicas of Greek texts that might have been hand-lettered by Plato himself when he wrote about the fabled lost continent of Atlantis. Sofas are deep and comfortable. A pianist sets the mood during cocktail hour and early evening, and you'll invariably get the sense here that you're right in the heart of everything. In the sunlit hours, the site doubles as a cafe, serving pastries and snacks from 6am until 4pm. It's open until 1am nightly. Royal Towers, Atlantis, Casino Dr. © 242/363-3000.

Grand Bahama
(Freeport/Lucaya)

6

Fabulous beaches and relatively afford-able prices continue to make Grand Bahama Island a year-round destination. Weather also enhances its continued pop-ularity. Even though the island is in the Atlantic Ocean, the Gulf Stream's forever-warm waters make its beaches, particu-larly those at the western tip, desirable even in winter. The Little Bahama Bank protects the island from the storms that roar in from the northeast. Grand Bahama Island is also easy to get to, given that it's only 81km (50 miles) east of Palm Beach, Florida.

Despite some cutting-edge architec-tural development in the late 1990s near Lucaya Beach, the island may never return to its high-roller days of the '60s. In that era, everybody from Howard Hughes to Frank Sinatra and the Rat Pack showed up to feud, play, act out, maneuver, manipu-late, and overindulge.

However, recent improvements in Port Lucaya and massive redevelopment on the island's West End have brought a smile back to its face, which had grown wrinkled and tired in the late 20th cen-tury. But downtown Freeport is still blighted by the closure and continuing decay of a mega-resort that once flour-ished as its centerpiece, the Crowne Plaza. That scar has, regrettably, extended into the island's once-fabled shopping mall, the International Bazaar. Because of the lack of business and "the morgue"—that is, the sprawling, storm-damaged corpse of the nearby Crowne Plaza

Resort—the shopping area remains in a lackluster state of decline.

Still, Grand Bahama remains the most popular tourist destination in The Bahamas besides Paradise Island. It's just 81km (50 miles) and less than 30 minutes by air off the Florida coast, and is the northernmost and fourth-largest landmass in The Bahamas (118km/73 miles long and 6.5–13km/4–8 miles wide).

Freeport/Lucaya was once just a dream. Wallace Groves, a Virginia-born financier, saw the prospect of developing the island into a miniature Miami Beach. Almost overnight in the 1950s, the low-lying pine forest transformed into one of the world's major resorts. Today, although the island's center of gravity has firmly shifted from Freeport to Lucaya, Groves's dream has at least been partially realized.

The Lucaya district was developed 8 years after Freeport, as a coastal resort cen-ter, and has evolved into a blend of resi-dential and tourist facilities. As the two communities grew, their identities became almost indistinguishable. But elements of their original purposes still exist today. Freeport is the downtown area, attracting visitors with its commerce, industry, and resorts. Meanwhile, Lucaya is called the "Garden City" and pleases residents and vacationers alike with its fine beaches.

Grand Bahama is more than an Atlantic City clone, however. If you don't care for gambling or if shopping is not your scene, try one of the alternatives. You can commune with nature at plenty of quiet places, including the Rand Nature Centre. Lucayan National Park—with its underwater caves, forest trails, and secluded beach—is another major attraction. Just kilometers from Freeport/Lucaya are serene places where you can wander in a world of casuarina, palmetto, and pine trees. During the day, you can enjoy long stretches of beach, broken by inlets and fishing villages. Because the island is so big, most of it remains relatively unspoiled.

Reviews of Grand Bahama Island are definitely mixed. Some discerning travelers who could live anywhere have built homes here; others vow never to set foot on the island again, finding it, with the exception of Port Lucaya, tacky or uninspired. Judge for yourself.

1 Orientation

For a general discussion on traveling to The Bahamas, refer to chapter 3.

ARRIVING

A number of airlines fly to **Grand Bahama International Airport** from the continental U.S., including **American Airlines** (© 800/433-7300; www.aa.com) and **Bahamasair** (© 242/377-3218; www.bahamasair.com), both with daily flights from Miami. **Gulfstream Continental Connection** (© 800/231-0856; www.gulfstream air.com) flies to Freeport from Miami and West Palm Beach once daily, and from Fort Lauderdale five times daily. **US Airways** (© 800/428-4322; www.usairways.com) flies in once a day from Charlotte, North Carolina.

Competing airlines include **AirTran** (© 800/247-8726; www.airtran.com), flying nonstop from Atlanta (daily) as well as Baltimore (Thurs–Mon). **Delta Connection** (© 800/221-1212) flies daily from Atlanta.

Many visitors arrive in Nassau and then hop on one of the five daily Bahamasair flights to Freeport. These 30-minute hops run US$135 to US$235 (£68–£118) round-trip.

No buses run from the airport to the major hotel zones. But many hotels will provide airport transfers, especially if you've bought a package deal. If yours does not, no problem; **taxis** meet arriving flights and take you from the airport to one of the hotels in Freeport or Lucaya for about US$12 to US$26 (£6–£13). The ride shouldn't take more than about 10 minutes.

Discovery Cruise Line (© 800/937-4477 or 242/351-1339; www.discoverycruise line.com) offers daily passage between Fort Lauderdale and Grand Bahama. Frankly, the vessels making this 89km (55-mile) jaunt aren't the newest or glitziest, but they fit the bill with the requisite pool deck and bar, along with a casino, show lounge, and dining facilities. The trip from Florida takes about 5 hours, and you'll disembark very well fed. Round-trip fare costs between US$180 and US$250 (£90–£125) per person, and you can make reservations online.

VISITOR INFORMATION

Assistance and information are available at the **Grand Bahama Tourism Board,** located in the Fidelity Financial Centre, West Mall Drive at Poinciana Drive (© 242/350-8600). It's open Monday to Friday 9am to 5pm. That organization maintains three smaller information booths, each of which is open daily 9am to 5pm. They're located at **Freeport International Airport** (© 242/352-2052), at **Port Lucaya Marketplace** (© 242/373-8988), and at the cruise-ship docks adjacent to **Lucayan Harbour** (© 242/350-8600).

Grand Bahama Island

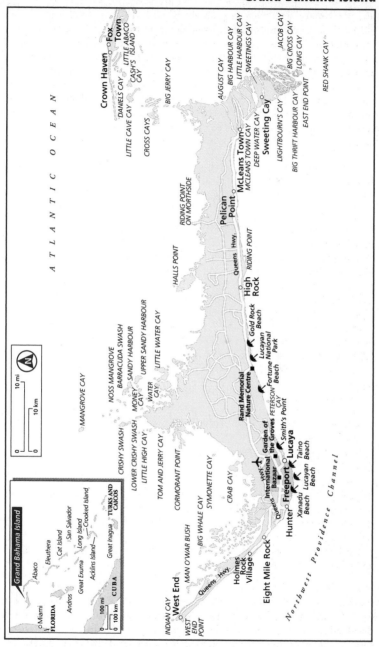

ISLAND LAYOUT

Other than the perhaps unexpected novelty of driving on the left, getting around Freeport/Lucaya is fairly easy because of the flat terrain. Although Freeport and Lucaya are frequently mentioned in the same breath, newcomers should note that **Freeport** is a landlocked collection of hotels and shops rising from the island's center, while the better-maintained and more appealing **Lucaya**, about 4km (2½ miles) away, is a bustling waterfront section of hotels, shops, and restaurants clustered next to a saltwater pond on the island's southern shore.

Freeport lies midway between Grand Bahama's northern and southern shores. Bisected by some of the island's largest roads, it was originally conceived as the site of the biggest hotels. Until a few years ago, the **International Bazaar** here was one of the country's most visited. Now in a dismaying state of disrepair, it's merely a theme-oriented retail mall that has seen better days. Immediately adjacent is the local **straw market,** where you can buy inexpensive souvenirs and Bahamian handicrafts.

To reach **Port Lucaya** from Freeport, head east from the International Bazaar along East Sunrise Highway, and then turn south at the intersection with Seahorse Road. The intersection—actually an oversize roundabout—is marked with a prominent stone marker that says PORT LUCAYA. From that roundabout, less than a mile later, you'll be in the heart of the Lucaya complex. Know in advance that the shops and restaurants on the marina side of Seahorse Road are identified as being within the "Port Lucaya" subdivision. Conversely, the Westin and the Sheraton hotels, their restaurants and shops, and the Isle of Capri Casino, all of which are clustered on the landward side of Seahorse Road, are identified as **"Our Lucaya."**

Port Lucaya's architectural centerpiece is **Count Basie Square,** named for the great entertainer who used to have a home on the island. A short walk east or west of the square will take you to most of the hotels, rising above the narrow strip of sand that separates the sea from a saltwater pond.

Life on Grand Bahama Island doesn't get more glamorous after you leave the Lucaya Complex. To the west of Freeport and Lucaya, the West Sunrise Highway passes grim and impersonal-looking industrial complexes that include The Bahamas Oil Refining Company. Once you pass the built-up waterfront sprawl of Freeport's western end, you can take Queen's Highway northwest all the way to **West End,** some 45km (28 miles) from Freeport's center. Along the way you pass the not-very-picturesque wharves of **Freeport Harbour,** where cruise ships dock. Just to the east lies **Hawksbill Creek,** a nondescript village that's home to some of the local port workers.

Much less explored is Grand Bahama's isolated **East End.** Its most distant tip lies about 72km (45 miles) from the center of Freeport and is reached via the **Grand Bahama Highway.** Despite its name, the route is bumpy and potholed in places and, along extensive stretches of its central area, is either blocked by piles of sand, rock, and fallen trees or is under construction. For access to the East End's most distant reaches from Freeport or Lucaya, allow about 2 hours of driving time. First you pass the **Rand Nature Centre,** about 5km (3 miles) east of Freeport. About 11km (6¾ miles) on is **Lucaya National Park,** and 8km (5 miles) farther lies the hamlet of **Free Town;** east of that is **High Rock,** known for its Emmanuel Baptist Church. From here, the road becomes considerably rougher until it ends in **MacLean's Town,** which celebrates Columbus Day with an annual conch-cracking contest. From here, you can take a water taxi across Runners Creek to the exclusive **Deep Water Cay Club,** which caters to serious anglers.

In Freeport/Lucaya, but especially on the rest of Grand Bahama Island, you will almost never find a street number on a hotel or a store. Sometimes in the more remote places, including sparsely populated areas on Lucaya's outskirts, you won't even find street signs. In lieu of numbers, locate places by their relation to hotels, beaches, or landmarks.

2 Getting Around

BY TAXI

The government sets the taxi rates, and the cabs are metered (or should be). Metered rates are US$3 (£1.50) for the first .3km (¼ mile) and 40¢ (20p) each additional 1.6km (1 mile). Additional passengers over the age of 2 are US$3 (£1.50) each. If there's no meter, agree on a price with the driver in advance. You can call for a taxi, though most cabs wait at the major hotels or the cruise dock to pick up passengers. One major dispatcher is **Freeport Taxi Company,** Logwood Road (© **242/352-6666**), open 24 hours. Another is **Grand Bahama Taxi Union,** at Freeport International Airport, Old Airport Road (© **242/352-7101**), also open 24 hours. *Note:* Typical taxi rates are as follows: From the cruise dock to: Xanadu Beach Hotel, US$17 (£8.50); Port Lucaya Marketplace, US$24 (£12); Flamingo Beach Resort, US$24 (£12); and Viva Fortuna Beach, US$29 (£15). From the airport to: Port Lucaya or Our Lucaya, US$19 (£9.50); Viva Fortuna, US$20 (£10); Royal Oasis, US$11 (£5.50); and Xanadu US$14 (£7).

BY BUS

Public bus service runs from the International Bazaar and downtown Freeport to Lucaya. Typical fare is US$1 (50p) for adults, 50¢ (25p) for children. Check with the Grand Bahama Tourism office (p. 138) for bus schedules; there is no number to call for information.

BY CAR

If you plan to confine your exploration to the center of Freeport with its International Bazaar and Lucaya with its beaches, you can rely on public transportation. However, if you'd like to explore the rest of the island (perhaps to find a more secluded beach), a rental car is the way to go. Terrain here is universally flat, a fact that's appreciated by drivers trying to conserve gasoline. Try **Avis** (© **800/331-1212** or 242/332-7666; www.avis.com) or **Hertz** (© **800/654-3131** or 242/352-9250; www.hertz.com). Both these companies maintain offices in small bungalows near Freeport International Airport. From inside the terminal, an employee of either company will contact a colleague, who will direct you to the curb outside the luggage pickup point. Then, someone will arrive in a company car or van to drive you to their pickup location.

One of the best companies is **Dollar Rent-a-Car,** Old Airport Road (© **800/800-3665** or 242/352-9325; www.dollar.com), which rents everything from a new Kia Sportage to a VW Jetta. Rates range from US$60 (£30) per day for a car with a manual transmission, or from US$65 (£33) for an automatic. Mileage is unlimited, but the collision damage waiver (CDW) costs another US$17 (£8.50) per day (US$350/£175 deductible). Remember to drive on the left as British rules apply.

BY SCOOTER

A scooter is a fun way to get around, as most of Grand Bahama is flat with well-paved roads. Scooters can be rented at most hotels or, for cruise-ship passengers, in the

Freeport Harbour area. You can also find dozens of stands along the roads in Freeport and Lucaya, and also in major parking lots, charging from US$40 to US$65 (£20–£33) per day. Helmets are required and provided by the outfitter.

ON FOOT

You can explore the center of Freeport or Lucaya on foot, but if you want to venture into the East End or West End, you'll need to rent a car, hire a taxi, or try Grand Bahama's erratic public transportation.

FAST FACTS: Grand Bahama

Banks In Freeport/Lucaya, banks are open from 9:30am to 3pm Monday to Thursday, and 9:30am to 4:30pm on Friday. Most banks here have **ATMs** that accept Visa, MasterCard, American Express, and any other bank or credit card on the Cirrus, Honor, Novus, and PLUS networks.

Currency Exchange Americans need not bother exchanging their money into Bahamian dollars because the currencies are on par. However, Canadians and Brits will need to convert their money, which can be done at local **banks** (see above) or at some **hotels,** though hotels tend to offer less favorable rates.

Doctors For the fastest and best service, head to **Rand Memorial Hospital** (see "Hospitals," below).

Drugstores For **prescriptions** and other pharmaceutical needs, go to Mini Mall, 1 West Mall, Explorer's Way, where you'll find **L.M.R. Drugs** (© 242/352-7327), next door to Burger King. Hours are Monday to Saturday 8am to 8pm and Sunday 8am to 3pm.

Embassies & Consulates See "Fast Facts: The Bahamas," in the appendix.

Emergencies For all emergencies, call © **911**, or dial **0** for the operator.

Eyeglass Repair The biggest specialist in eyeglasses and contact lenses is the **Optique Shoppe,** 7 Regent Centre, downtown Freeport (© **242/352-9073**).

Hospitals If you have a medical **emergency,** contact the government-operated, 90-bed **Rand Memorial Hospital,** East Atlantic Drive (© **242/352-6735** or 352-2689 for ambulance).

Information See "Visitor Information," above.

Laundry & Dry Cleaning Try **Jiffy Cleaners Number 3,** West Mall at Pioneer's Way (© **242/352-7079**), open Monday 8am to 1pm, Tuesday to Saturday 8am to 6pm.

Newspapers & Magazines The *Freeport News* is a morning paper published Monday through Saturday except holidays. Nassau's two dailies, the *Tribune* and the *Nassau Guardian,* are also available here, as are some New York and Miami papers, especially the *Miami Herald,* usually on the date of publication. American newsmagazines, such as *Time* and *Newsweek,* are flown in on the day of publication.

Police Dial © **911**.

Post Office The main post office (© **242/352-9371**) is on Explorer's Way in Freeport.

Safety Avoid walking or jogging along lonely roads. There are no particular danger zones, but stay alert: Grand Bahama is no stranger to drugs and crime.

Taxes All visitors leaving The Bahamas from Freeport must pay a departure tax, but because it's factored into the cost of your airline or cruise ticket, very few visitors even realize they're paying it. Hotel bills are saddled with a 12% tax regardless of room category. But other than that, to encourage shoppers, no other sales taxes are charged.

Taxis See "Getting Around," above.

Weather Grand Bahama, in the north of The Bahamas, has winter temperatures varying from about 60° to 75°F (16°–24°C) daily. Summer variations range from 78°F to the high 80s (26°C to the low 30s Celsius). In Freeport/Lucaya, phone © **915** for weather information.

3 Where to Stay

Your choices are in Freeport, near the Bahamia Casino and International Bazaar, or Lucaya, which is closer to the beach. *Remember:* In most cases, a resort levy of 8% and a 15% service charge will be added to your final bill. Be prepared, and ask if it's already included in the price you're quoted.

FREEPORT
EXPENSIVE

Island Seas Resort   A three-story timeshare property that's open to nonmembers, this resort, painted a tone of peach, opens onto a secluded beach positioned midway between downtown Freeport and Port Lucaya. Island Seas offers its own water fun with a pool, hot tub, and waterfall. Also on-site is a tiki-hut restaurant and bar. The location is convenient for the Port Lucaya Market and the Lucaya Golf and Country Club. Because they have individual owners, each condo is furnished with a decor that's different from that of its immediate neighbor. Floor plans include one or two bedrooms. Each contains a full bathroom with tub/shower, plus a full kitchen and balcony. Although technically they're not associated with the hotel, many watersports outfitters are located right on the beach.

William's Town, Freeport, Grand Bahama, The Bahamas. © **800/801-6884** or 242/373-1271. Fax 242/373-1275. www.islandseas.com. 197 units Year-round US$299 (£150) double, US$309 (£155) 2-bedroom unit. AE, DISC, MC, V. **Amenities:** Restaurant; bar; pool; tennis court; gym/exercise facilities; bike rentals; on-site car-rental kiosk; massage. *In room:* A/C, TV, fully equipped kitchen, iron, safe.

INEXPENSIVE

Best Western Castaways Resort & Suites *(Kids*   Castaways is a modest and unassuming hotel that's almost immediately adjacent to the International Bazaar in downtown Freeport. A mix of vacationers and business travelers stay here because of its clean, well-maintained motel-style rooms and moderate prices. Pink-walled, green-shuttered rooms surround a quartet of landscaped courtyards, creating shelter from the traffic outside. It's not on the water, but a free shuttle will take you to nearby Williams Town Beach. Surrounded by gardens, the four-story hotel has an indoor-outdoor garden lobby with a gift shop and kiosks selling island tours and watersports opportunities. Cheerful bedrooms are outfitted in basic motel style. The Flamingo

Where to Stay & Dine in Freeport/Lucaya

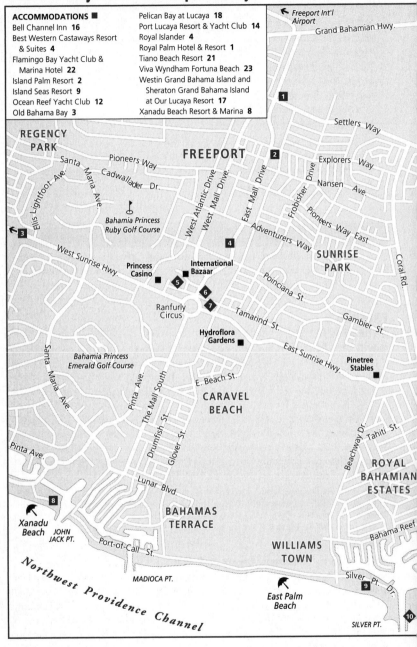

ACCOMMODATIONS ■

Bell Channel Inn **16**
Best Western Castaways Resort & Suites **4**
Flamingo Bay Yacht Club & Marina Hotel **22**
Island Palm Resort **2**
Island Seas Resort **9**
Ocean Reef Yacht Club **12**
Old Bahama Bay **3**
Pelican Bay at Lucaya **18**
Port Lucaya Resort & Yacht Club **14**
Royal Islander **4**
Royal Palm Hotel & Resort **1**
Tiano Beach Resort **21**
Viva Wyndham Fortuna Beach **23**
Westin Grand Bahama Island and Sheraton Grand Bahama Island at Our Lucaya Resort **17**
Xanadu Beach Resort & Marina **8**

Freeport Int'l Airport

Grand Bahamian Hwy.

Settlers Way

REGENCY PARK

FREEPORT

Explorers Way

Nansen Ave.

Santa Maria Ave.
Ellis Lightfoot Ave.

Pioneers Way

Cadwallader Dr.

West Atlantic Drive

West Mall Drive

East Mall Drive

Frobisher Drive

Pioneers Way East

Bahamia Princess Ruby Golf Course

West Sunrise Hwy.

Adventurers Way

SUNRISE PARK

Coral Rd.

Princess Casino

International Bazaar

Poinciana St.

Ranfurly Circus

Tamarind St.

Gambier St.

Hydroflora Gardens

East Sunrise Hwy.

Pinetree Stables

Santa Maria Ave.

Bahamia Princess Emerald Golf Course

Pinta Ave.

The Mall South

Drumfish St.

Glover St.

E. Beach St.

CARAVEL BEACH

Beachway Dr.

Tahiti St.

ROYAL BAHAMIAN ESTATES

Pinta Ave.

Lunar Blvd.

BAHAMAS TERRACE

Xanadu Beach

JOHN JACK PT.

Port-of-Call St.

WILLIAMS TOWN

Bahama Reef

Northwest Providence Channel

MADIOCA PT.

East Palm Beach

Silver Pt. Dr.

SILVER PT.

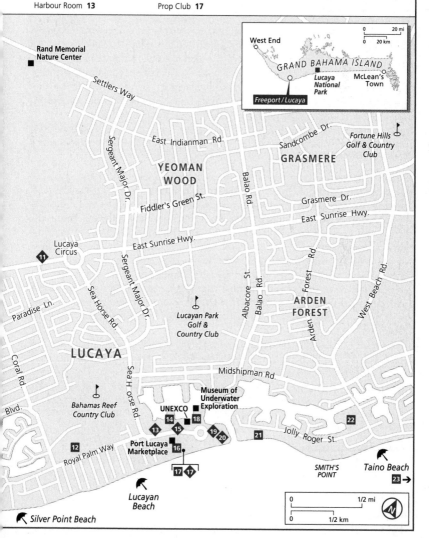

Restaurant presents Bahamian and American dishes daily from 7:30am to 10pm; it also serves one of the island's best breakfasts. There's a swimming pool area with a wide terrace and a pool bar serving sandwiches and cool drinks. A children's playground adjoins the pool.

E. Mall Dr., Freeport, Grand Bahama, The Bahamas. ⓒ 800/780-7234 or 242/352-6682. Fax 242/352-5087. www. bestwestern.com. 118 units. Winter US$155 (£78) double, US$185 (£93) suite; off-season US$135 (£68) double, US$150–US$160 (£75–£80) suite. Children under 12 stay free in parent's room. AE, MC, V. **Amenities:** Restaurant; 2 bars; pool; babysitting; self-service laundry; nonsmoking rooms; rooms for those w/limited mobility. *In room:* A/C, TV, hair dryer, iron, safe.

Island Palm Resort *(Value)*   Set within the commercial heart of Freeport, this simple three-story motel consists of four buildings separated by parking lots and greenery. An easy walk to virtually everything in town and 2km (1¼ miles) from the International Bazaar, it offers good value in no-frills, eminently serviceable rooms with well-kept bathrooms equipped with tub/showers. Complimentary shuttle service ferries anybody who's interested to nearby Williams Town Beach (also called Island Seas Beach), where you can jet-ski and snorkel at its sibling property, the Island Seas.

E. Mall Dr., Freeport, Grand Bahama, The Bahamas. ⓒ 242/352-8485. Fax 242/352-6640. 143 units. Winter US$89 (£45) double; off-season US$79 (£40) double. Extra person US$15 (£7.50). AE, DISC, MC, V. **Amenities:** Bar; pool; nonsmoking rooms; rooms for those w/limited mobility. *In room:* A/C, TV, Wi-Fi, minibar.

Royal Islander   This hotel was built during an unfortunate Disney-style period in Freeport's expansion during the early 1980s. Its improbable-looking pyramidal roofs inspired by a trio of Mayan pyramids were rendered somewhat less obvious in 2004 when they were covered with dark-gray metal. Interiors are tasteful and hospitable, with rooms arranged around a verdant courtyard that seems far removed from the busy traffic and sterile-looking landscape outside. Rooms on the street level have white-tile floors, while those upstairs have wall-to-wall carpeting. Bathrooms are on the small side, but have sinks and tub/showers. Throughout, the motif is Floridian tropical, with some pizzazz and rates that tend to be cheaper than the Best Western across the street. There's a family link between the owners of this place and the owners of the more opulent Xanadu (p. 151), so an hourly bus shuttles between here and there.

There's a coffee-shop-style snack bar and a small restaurant on the premises, but other than that, you'll have to wander a short distance, perhaps to the International Bazaar just across the street, to find diversions and dining.

E. Mall Dr., Freeport, Grand Bahama, The Bahamas. ⓒ 242/351-6000. Fax 242/351-3546. www.bahamasvacation guide.com/royalislander.html. 100 units. Year-round US$102 (£51). Children under 14 stay free in parent's room. AE, MC, V. **Amenities:** Restaurant; snack bar; bar; pool; Jacuzzi; children's playground; self-service laundry; nonsmoking rooms. *In room:* A/C, TV, safe.

Royal Palm Resort & Suites   Don't confuse this hotel with some of its competitors, whose names and amenities are roughly equivalent. The staff here commented to us about how often a taxi will arrive with passengers whose reservations are at other hotels with similar names; these include the Royal Islander, the Island Palm, and the relatively more expensive Island Seas. This particular choice is a well-maintained, cost-effective motel that's the closest property to the airport. It's set behind a hot-pink, two-story facade. Though inland from the beach, it provides an oasis of resort-style living, with its wings wrapping around a swimming pool. A radical renovation was completed in late 2005.

Rooms are suitable for up to four occupants each. Each is outfitted like you'd expect at a motel-style tropical resort—with tile floors, simple but tasteful furniture, and flower-patterned upholsteries. Although it's usually a bit more expensive than either the Royal Islander or the Island Palm, its repeat clientele—about 50% of whom are here for business reasons—don't seem to mind.

E. Mall at Settlers' Way, Freeport, The Bahamas. (© **888/790-5264** or 242/352-3462. Fax 242/352-5759. www.royal palmsuites.com. 48 units. US$129–US$149 (£65–£75) double. AE, DC, MC, V. **Amenities:** Restaurant; poolside bar (Conch Juice Corner); tennis court; children's playground; hourly shuttles to Xanadu Beach; Internet cafe; gift shop. *In room:* A/C, TV, kitchenette, fridge, microwave, coffeemaker, hair dryer.

LUCAYA
EXPENSIVE
Westin Grand Bahama Island at Our Lucaya Resort & Sheraton Grand Bahama Island at Our Lucaya Resort *(Kids)*   This massive US$400-million resort is one of the country's largest—and by far, it's the finest, most appealing, and best-accessorized property on Grand Bahama Island. The resort is set beside one of the best white strands in The Bahamas—Lucaya Beach. Although the area had been losing tourist business to Paradise Island, it got a big boost in 1999 when this sprawling metropolis opened its doors.

Guests of any of this resort's subdivisions usually get more than they bargained for. The first of the three sections was completed late in 1998 as the **Sheraton Grand Bahama Island at Our Lucaya Resort.** With a vague South Beach Art Deco design, it's laid out in a massive open-sided, stone-trimmed hexagon. About half of the rooms face the beach and the swimming pool; the other half look toward the gardens. The 513-room resort is contemporary but relaxed. Its developers have created a young vibe that draws many families. Bedrooms are whimsical and fun, thanks to fabric designs you'd expect on a loud, Elvis-era Hawaiian shirt and maple-veneered furniture, all put together with artful simplicity.

In 2000, two newer, more upscale, and more cutting-edge subdivisions opened immediately next door. The smaller and somewhat more private of the two is **Westin Lighthouse Pointe,** a 322-unit low-rise condo and timeshare complex that focuses on an adult clientele. Its larger counterpart—and the one we find more appealing—is the 536-unit **Westin Breakers Cay.** This grand 10-story, white-sided tower has edges that bend in a postmodern S-curve beside the beach. Each of this complex's three subsections stretches like pearls in a necklace along a narrow beach strip, allowing guests to drop in to any of the bars, restaurants, and gardens that flank its edges. Also on-site, in a two-story compound flanking the sea, **The Lanai** is composed of just 23 sprawling two-bedroom suites, each richly furnished and melding Colonial Caribbean style with 21st-century decor.

A complex this big contains an impressive array of restaurants, each with a different theme and ambience. The most interesting are reviewed under "Where to Dine," later in this chapter. Consistent with the broad themes, each of the subdivisions has a dramatic or unconventional swimming pool. For example, the Sheraton's pool seems to flow around a replica of a 19th-century sugar mill, complete with an aqueduct that might be worthy of ancient Rome. And the Westin is separated from the powder-white sands of Lucaya Beach by a trio of lap pools, each 15m (49 ft.) long and 1.2m (4 ft.) deep, with edges replicating the hotel's sinuous "S" shape. Lap swimmers especially appreciate these spans of water, each of which has a subtly different temperature. The pools culminate in a watery crescent whose infinity edge seems to merge directly into the Atlantic. In particular, the swim-up bar and hot tubs seem perfect for wedding celebrations after the ceremony.

A spa and fitness center, a quartet of tennis courts, a convention center, a state-of-the-art casino (called The **Isle of Capri,** it's the island's only one), and an upscale shopping mall have all also been added in recent years. There's also an increasing emphasis on golf, thanks to the opening of the spectacular **Reef Course** (p. 163). An innovative feature for tennis players is the **Fast Grand Slam of Tennis,** which features replicas of the world's best-known court surfaces—red clay at the French Open, manicured grass at Wimbledon, Rebound Ace at the Australian Open, and DecoTurf at the U.S. Open.

Children aged 2 to 12 can be amused and entertained throughout daylight hours every day at The Bahamas' best-run children's venue, **Camp Lucaya.**

Royal Palm Way, Lucaya, Grand Bahama, The Bahamas. (℃ 877/OUR-LUCAYA [687-5822]) in the U.S., or 242/373-1333. Sheraton fax 242/373-8804; Westin fax 242/350-5060. www.ourlucaya.com. 1,260 units. Sheraton year-round US$149–US$435 (£75–£218) double; US$450–US$700 (£225–£350) suite; US$30 (£15) extra per day for 3rd and 4th occupants. Westin Lighthouse Pointe or Breakers Cay year-round US$189–US$319 (£95–£160) double; from US$400 (£200) suite; US$30 (£15) extra per day for 3rd and 4th occupants. 2-bedroom Lanai suites US$1,400–US$1,700 (£700–£850) per night year-round for up to 6 occupants. AE, DC, DISC, MC, V. **Amenities:** 9 restaurants; 10 bars; 5 pools; 2 18-hole golf courses; 4 tennis courts; health club; spa; watersports equipment/rentals; children's programs; business center; salon; room service; babysitting; laundry service; dry cleaning; nonsmoking rooms; rooms for those w/limited mobility. *In room:* A/C, TV, Wi-Fi, kitchenette (in suites only), minibar, hair dryer, iron, safe.

MODERATE

Ocean Reef Yacht Club & Resort 𝒜   This marina-style resort offers town house-style accommodations with one, two, or three bedrooms, as well as two-bedroom suites, each with its own Jacuzzi. The resort caters mainly to yachties but welcomes all vacationers to its individually owned town houses and apartments, which are rented out when the owners are away. Opening onto a marina and the water, the tropically furnished club lies half a mile from a good beach and a 10-minute drive into Port Lucaya. Rental units come in various shapes and sizes, the least expensive being the narrow yet comfortable efficiency units. All accommodations have fully equipped kitchens or kitchenettes. Three meals a day are served at the outdoor **Groupers Bar & Grill;** the namesake grouper, of course, is a specialty, but so is Bahamian lobster.

Royal Palm Way, Port Lucaya, Grand Bahama, The Bahamas. (℃ 242/373-2468. www.oryc.com. 60 units. Winter US$135–US$150 (£68–£75) double; US$155–US$190 (£78–£95) 2-bedroom apt for 4; off-season US$110–US$130 (£55–£65) double, US$140–US$175 (£70–£88) 2-bedroom apt for 4. MC, V. **Amenities:** Restaurant; bar; 2 pools; bike rentals; dive shop; free shuttle service to beach; public Internet; laundry service. *In room:* A/C, TV, Jacuzzi in some.

Pelican Bay at Lucaya 𝒜𝒜   Here's a good choice for travelers with champagne tastes and beer budgets, a hotel with more architectural charm than any other small property on Grand Bahama. It's built on a peninsula jutting into a labyrinth of inland waterways, with moored yachts on several sides. Pelican Bay evokes a Danish or Dutch seaside village with rows of whimsically trimmed town houses, each painted a different color, and each overlooking the harbor. The hotel opened in 1996, expanded in 1999, and was refurbished in 2005 into the kind of venue you might expect to see in an upscale decorating magazine. Its location couldn't be better, immediately adjacent to Port Lucaya Marketplace, where restaurants and entertainment spots abound. Lucaya Beach, one of the best stretches of white sand on the island, is a 5-minute walk away. Taíno Beach, with equally good sands, lies immediately to the east, on the opposite side of a saltwater channel with hourly ferryboat service. UNEXSO, which provides some of the best dive facilities in The Bahamas, is next door. If that weren't enough, the extensive amenities of Our Lucaya (p. 154) are available for use.

Accommodations—especially suites—are about as stylish and high-fashion as you'll find on Grand Bahama Island, rivaled only by the Westin/Sheraton compound at Our Lucaya, located a very short walk away. Each has either a veranda or a balcony, usually with water views, and floors of buffed, tinted concrete with a scattering of rustic art objects and handicrafts from all over the world. The hotel has one main restaurant, the **Ferry House,** which specializes in imaginative international cuisine and serves lunch Monday to Saturday and dinner daily. The **Yellow Tail Pool Bar** offers drinks, salads, and sandwiches throughout the day.

Seahorse Rd., Lucaya, Grand Bahama, The Bahamas. ⓒ 800/852-3702 in the U.S., or 242/373-9550. Fax 242/373-9551. www.pelicanbayhotel.com. 183 units. Winter US$129–US$239 (£65–£120) double, US$369 (£185) suite; off-season US$129–US$229 (£65–£115) double, US$319 (£160) suite. Rates include breakfast. AE, MC, V. **Amenities:** Restaurant; bar; 3 pools; Jacuzzi; business center; babysitting; nonsmoking rooms. *In room:* A/C, TV, minibar (in suites), minifridge, coffeemaker, hair dryer, iron, safe.

Port Lucaya Resort & Yacht Club ⓖ   Comfortable, cost-conscious, unpretentious, and convenient, this resort opened in 1993 in the heart of Port Lucaya. Many guests are drawn to its nautical atmosphere and good location. It was designed as a compound of pastel-colored two-story structures that guests reach either on foot or (if they're transporting luggage) via golf cart after checking in. They're scattered in rows that wind around a horseshoe-shaped courtyard, very close to a marina and steps from the local restaurants, bars, shops, and nightlife. The guest-room wings separate the piers—home to some very expensive marine hardware—from a verdant central green space with a gazebo-style bar and a swimming pool. Although set inland on a waterway (Lucayan Harbour), this resort is an easy walk from Lucaya Beach, one of the island's finest, and Taíno Beach.

The medium-size rooms have tile floors and are attractively and comfortably furnished with rattan pieces and big wall mirrors. The rooms are divided into various categories, ranging from standard to deluxe, and open onto the marina, the Olympic-size swimming pool, or the well-landscaped garden. If you don't want to hear the sounds coming from the lively marketplace, request units 1–6, which are more tranquil and distanced from the noise. Bathrooms are tidy but not overly large, with tub/showers and a layout like you might find at a middle-bracket motel in Florida.

Bell Channel Bay Rd., Lucaya, Grand Bahama, The Bahamas. ⓒ 800/LUCAYA-1 (582-2921) or 242/373-6618. Fax 242/373-6652. www.portlucayaresort.com. 160 units. Winter US$112–US$162 (£56–£81) double, US$196–US$280 (£98–£140) suite; off-season US$90–US$134 (£45–£67) double, US$214–US$224 (£107–£112) suite. Extra person US$28 (£14) per day. Children 12 and under stay free in parent's room. AE, DISC, MC, V. **Amenities:** 2 bars; pool; Jacuzzi; babysitting; nonsmoking rooms. *In room:* A/C, TV, fridge available for US$10 (£5) extra per day, hair dryer, iron.

INEXPENSIVE

Bell Channel Inn Hotel   This is the best resort for scuba divers, lying as it does near the ocean. Much of it looks like a moderately priced motel in Florida. The inn offers its own full-service dive shop and a private boat. You don't come here for luxurious bedrooms, but each unit is spacious, well furnished, and comfortable. Most contain small refrigerators as well, and each comes with a private balcony with a view over the channel and Port Lucaya. The hotel operates free shuttle service to the beach and maintains a solar-heated pool. If you're a diver, ask about the various dive packages available when booking a room; some of the best dive sites lie only a 5- to 10-minute

---

Tips **Especially Fun Places for Kids**

The Westin and Sheraton at Our Lucaya resorts (p. 147)   Camp Lucaya (also known as the Westin Children's Camp) is the best-run, most-amenities-packed children's camp in The Bahamas, a full-service child-minding facility for infants to 12-year-olds. The camp is open only to children of guests at either the Sheraton or the Westin at Our Lucaya and is open daily year-round from 9am to 5pm. It includes a supervised children's pool and classes about Bahamian culture (politics, arts, ecosystems, and crafts). A day's involvement might include learning native dances, creating island-inspired art, coconut bowling, or exploring a garden reserved just for kids. The Marine Explorer's Club, co-sponsored by the Underwater Explorer Society (UNEXSO), offers ocean and marine experiences to youngsters, including an opportunity to go nose-to-nose with dolphins. For infants (age 2 and under), the staff imposes a 2-hour time limit for babysitting services. Children aged 3 to 12, however, can remain within the camp premises all day without charge, though parents are advised to check on their children periodically.

Viva Wyndham Fortuna Beach (p. 152)   This all-inclusive beachfront hotel, a 10-minute drive east of Port Lucaya (making it the island's most easterly resort), maintains its Kids Club exclusively for children aged 2 to 11. It provides sports, games, and lessons throughout the day, under the supervision of trained staff members who know when to get parents involved and when to let them slip away for pursuits of their own.

---

boat ride away. The on-site **Seafood Restaurant & Bar** specializes in preparing the fresh catch of the day.

Kings Rd., Lucaya, Grand Bahama, The Bahamas. © **242/373-1053.** Fax 242/373-2886. www.bellchannelinn.com. 32 units. US$85 (£43) double; US$107 (£54) triple; US$129 (£65) quad. AE, MC, V. **Amenities:** Restaurant; bar; outdoor pool; dive shop; Wi-Fi in lobby; babysitting; laundry service; nonsmoking rooms. *In room:* A/C, TV, fridge (in some), coffeemaker, hair dryer.

TAÍNO BEACH
MODERATE
Taíno Beach Resort *Kids*   This hotel lies across a saltwater canal from the grounds of the Westin and Sheraton at Our Lucaya. It's also located adjacent to Taíno Beach, the sister shore of the better-known Lucaya Beach. Enveloped by semitropical gardens, but without the posh and cutting-edge glamour of the Westin and Sheraton, it dates back to 1995, when construction began on what eventually evolved into a three-phase development. All the bedrooms are in concrete buildings, each painted a shade of coral. Units start with efficiencies, studios, and one-bedroom suites, and go up to elaborate villa and penthouse accommodations. The bedrooms are spacious, well furnished, and handsomely maintained, with a tub/shower in the efficiency rooms and a walk-in shower in the studios.

The quality and size of your accommodation and amenities depends on how much you want to pay. Penthouses (on the fourth floor) are multilevel studios with their own sun deck and private pool.

On the premises, two restaurants serve international cuisine; there's also a scattering of bars whose number (a maximum of five) varies with the occupancy level and the season.

The hotel maintains a ferry service ($2.50/£1.25 per person each way, free for infants under 2) that makes frequent trips across the canal to a dock associated with Our Lucaya. From there, the restaurants, shops, and bars of the Port Lucaya Marketplace and access to Grand Bahama's only casino, the Isle of Capri, are within a 10-minute walk.

Jolly Roger Dr., Taíno Beach, Lucaya, Grand Bahama, The Bahamas. © 888/311-7945 or 242/373-9354. Fax 242/373-4421. www.timetravelcorp.com. 157 units. Year-round US$125 (£63) efficiency, US$175 (£88) studio, US$225 (£113) penthouse. Children 12 and under stay free in parent's room. AE, MC, V. **Amenities:** Restaurant; pool bar; pool; tennis court; babysitting; laundry service; nonsmoking rooms (all); rooms for those w/limited mobility. *In room:* A/C, TV, Wi-Fi, beverage maker, hair dryer, iron.

INEXPENSIVE

Flamingo Bay Yacht Club & Marina Hotel   Unlike the Ritz Beach Resort (its nearby sibling on Taíno Beach), this hotel is set back from the water, about a 5-minute walk from a highly appealing length of white sand. Built of painted concrete, with three stories, it offers midsize, unpretentious, and uncomplicated bedrooms that are comfortable and attractively furnished in a Caribbean motif. Each has a well-maintained bathroom with tub/shower, and either two double beds or a king-size bed. Each comes with such extras as a microwave and toaster. From a nearby 20-slip marina, a water taxi runs hourly across a narrow saltwater canal to a pier operated by the Westin, from where it's a short walk to the Isle of Capri Casino and the center of Lucaya. The fee for transportation either way is US$2.50/£1.25 per person, free for infants under 2. Though amenities are sparse, customers are permitted to use the plentiful options at the Ritz Beach Resort.

Jolly Roger Dr., Taíno Beach, Lucaya, Grand Bahama, The Bahamas. © 800/824-6623 or 242/373-4677. Fax 242/373-4421. www.timetravelcorp.com. 58 units. Year-round US$90–US$130 (£45–£65) double. Children 12 and under stay free in parent's room. AE, DISC, MC, V. **Amenities:** Coin-operated laundry; nonsmoking rooms. *In room:* A/C, cable-connected TV, kitchenette, beverage maker, hair dryer, iron.

AT XANADU BEACH

Xanadu Beach Resort and Marina   Permeated with one of the most quirky and idiosyncratic histories of any hotel in The Bahamas, and now painted a cheerful shade of yellow, this hotel is radically different from the way it was when it housed the reclusive billionaire Howard Hughes. Xanadu soars triumphantly above a scrub-dotted landscape that's crisscrossed with canals, mysteriously upscale villas, and reminders of the hurricane damages of the past several years. You'll get the sense here of a brave and valiant hotel that has struggled to provide service and comfort to visitors, despite negative fortunes and a hotel scene that has shifted to an increasing degree away from Freeport and toward Port Lucaya. Much of Xanadu's allure is the result of the hard work and devotion of the Donato family. It benefited in 2005 from a big influx of cash that reconfigured the lobby area into a Spanish Baroque fantasy. Macho-looking and elegant, it evokes a private club where billionaires might feel at home. Bedrooms are comfortable and the nearby beach is alluring. Is the ghost of Howard Hughes still lurking in the penthouse? Perhaps. Members of the staff, particularly the charming, capable general manager, Ms. Toni Donato, have a lot to say about that.

Freeport, Grand Bahama, The Bahamas. © 888/790-5264 or 242/352-6783. Fax 242/352-5799. www.xanadubeach hotel.com. 186 units, plus 3 1-bedroom waterfront villas. Year-round US$155 (£78) double; US$209–US$450

(£105–£225) suite; US$485 (£243) villa per day for up to 4 occupants. AE, DC, MC, V. **Amenities:** Pool; 2 tennis courts; gym; watersports concessions; full-service PADI dive shop; gift shop; babysitting. *In room:* A/C, TV, Wi-Fi, mini-bar.

ON GRAND BAHAMA ISLAND'S WEST END
EXPENSIVE

Old Bahama Bay ★★   One of the most dramatic real-estate developments in The Bahamas lies at this outpost on the island's extreme western tip. Locals, educated and trained in the U.S., run this operation. Built on a site that in the early 1980s was the setting for the unsuccessful Jack Tar Village, the project centers around a cluster of upscale hotel units, a state-of-the-art 72-slip marina, and a palm-flanked beach.

The resort's core consists of nine two-story beach houses, each with between four and six living units inside. Spacious and breezy living quarters are outfitted in a Caribbean colonial style with a tropical country-club feel. Bathrooms are sheathed in marble, and each contains a shower/whirlpool tub combination and deluxe toiletries. A pair of restaurants—the **Dockside Grille** and **Aqua**—serve well-prepared Bahamian and international dishes.

This resort encompasses much more than just hotel accommodations. Its owners envision it as an entire village-in-the-making, relentlessly upscale and dotted with celebrity references. There's even an airplane landing strip less than a half-kilometer (⅓-mile) away. Plans will expand the marina and improve the beachfront. Building sites range from US$400,000 to US$1 million each; most are already sold, we were told. Investors have included John Travolta, who presently owns four of the beach-front hotel units. Celebrity sightings include Jack Nicklaus, Geraldo Rivera, and *Sex and the City* star Chris Noth.

West End, Grand Bahama, The Bahamas. © 800/444-9469 in the U.S. or 242/350-6500. Fax 242/346-6546. www.oldbahamabay.com. 73 units. Winter US$365–US$650 (£183–£325) suite, from US$910 (£455) 2-bedroom suite; off-season US$235–US$395 (£118–£198) suite, from US$700 (£350) 2-bedroom suite. Breakfast and dinner US$115 (£58) per person extra per day. AE, MC, V. **Amenities:** 2 restaurants; 2 bars; pool; 2 tennis courts; fitness center; watersports equipment/rentals; room service; massage; babysitting; laundry service; nonsmoking rooms (all). *In room:* A/C, TV, kitchenette, minifridge, beverage maker, hair dryer, iron, safe.

Viva Wyndham Fortuna Beach ★ *Kids*   The easternmost resort on Grand Bahama Island has some visitors arguing that the beachfront here is even better than the more extensively developed strands at Port Lucaya. The swimming pool, however, packs a lot less drama than those at the Westin and Sheraton at Our Lucaya. This place has made a name for itself by surviving more than one destructive hurricane. During the midsummer months, the staff welcomes an almost exclusively Italian clientele, the result of an exclusive arrangement with a tour operator. Because of that arrangement, you might have difficulty getting a room here between May and September. Through-out the rest of the year, a mostly North American clientele vacations here, and the property is an all-inclusive venue where all meals, drinks, lodgings, and most water-sports are included in your price.

The setting is a sprawling compound of 10 hectares (25 acres) of remote and breezy beachfront property, loaded with sports activities that are covered by the price. Estab-lished in 1993, Viva Fortuna lies 9.5km (6 miles) east of the International Bazaar along the island's southern coast, amid an isolated landscape of casuarinas and scrub-land. Comfortably furnished, stylish, midsize bedrooms lie in a colorful group of two-story outbuildings, some of which are technically classified as timeshares but are added to the resort's rental pool whenever they're not occupied. About three-quarters have ocean views; the others overlook the surrounding scrublands. Most have a private balcony and two queen-size beds; a small bathroom offers a shower stall but no tub in almost every unit.

All meals, which are included in the rates, are served buffet-style in three restaurants. In addition to an ongoing series of all-you-can-eat feasts, you'll find an Italian restaurant and an Asian restaurant, the latter centered around an appealing Buddha statue. Know in advance that if you stay here, you'll be far from Port Lucaya (though a shuttle bus brings guests to the International Bazaar in downtown Freeport twice each day). For clients who appreciate the all-inclusive format where there's not a lot of incentive for straying very far from the property, it's a worthwhile choice. Note, however, that singles pay 40% more than the per-person double-occupancy rate.

1 Dubloon Rd., Freeport, Grand Bahama, The Bahamas. (℃ **800/898-9968** or 242/373-4000. Fax 242/373-5555. www.wyndham.com. 276 units. Winter US$297–US$400 (£149–£200) double; off-season US$297–US$380 (£149–£190) double. US$78 (£39) extra person. Rates are all-inclusive. AE, DC, MC, V. **Amenities:** 3 restaurants; 3 bars; disco; pool; 2 tennis courts; gym; Jacuzzi; sauna; watersports equipment/rentals; kids' club; babysitting; non-smoking rooms; rooms for those w/limited mobility. *In room:* A/C, TV, fridge, coffeemaker, hair dryer, iron, safe.

4 Where to Dine

Foodies will find that the cuisine on Grand Bahama Island doesn't match the more refined fare served at dozens of places on New Providence (Nassau/Paradise Island). However, a few places in Grand Bahama do specialize in fine dining; the others get by with rather standard fare. The good news is that the dining scene is more affordable here.

FREEPORT
MODERATE
Silvano's ℛ ITALIAN   This 80-seat restaurant with Mediterranean decor serves worthy but not exceptional cuisine. A competently prepared repertoire inspired by Italy's culinary favorites incorporates quality ingredients, most of them shipped in from the U.S. Service is polite and helpful. The grilled veal steak is one of the genuinely commendable dishes, as are the homemade pastas served with a variety of freshly made sauces. The chef also works his magic with fish and shrimp. Other traditional Italian dishes round out the menu.

Ranfurley Circle. (℃ **242/352-5111.** Reservations recommended. Lunch specials US$7–US$14 (£3.50–£7); main courses US$16–US$30 (£8–£15). AE, DISC, MC, V. Mon–Sat noon–3pm and 5:30–11pm.

INEXPENSIVE
Beckey's Restaurant BAHAMIAN/AMERICAN   Near a busy landlocked traffic artery midway between Port Lucaya and downtown Freeport, this unpretentious yellow-and-white restaurant offers authentic Bahamian cuisine prepared in the time-tested style of the Out Islands, offering a welcome dose of down-to-earth, non-casino reality to locals and visitors who appreciate more modest lifestyles. Breakfasts are either all-American or Bahamian and are available all day. Also popular are minced lobster, curried mutton, fish platters, baked or curried chicken, and conch salads. Stick to the local specialties instead of the lackluster American dishes.

E. Sunrise Hwy. and E. Beach Dr. (℃ **242/352-5247.** Breakfast US$5–US$11 (£2.50–£5.50); main courses US$9–US$25 (£4.50–£13). AE, MC, V. Daily 7am to 8–10pm, depending on the season and on business.

Geneva's BAHAMIAN/SEAFOOD   To eat where the locals eat, head for this unpretentious local venue, where food is made the old-fashioned way. This restaurant is one of the best places to sample conch, which has fed and nourished Bahamians for centuries. The Monroe family will prepare it for you stewed, cracked, or fried, or as part of a savory conch chowder that makes an excellent starter. Grouper also features largely, prepared in every imaginable way. The bartender will get you in a good mood with a rum-laced Bahama Mama.

Kipling Lane and E. Mall, at W. Sunrise Hwy. ℂ **242/352-5085.** Lunch sandwiches and platters US$10–US$12 (£5–£6); dinner main courses US$12–US$28 (£6–£14). DISC, MC, V. Daily 7am–11pm.

The Pepper Pot BAHAMIAN   This might be the only place on Grand Bahama that focuses exclusively on Bahamian-style takeout food. It's popular throughout the day and evening, but it's especially mobbed on weekends after midnight, when night-clubbers descend upon it to squelch those after-disco munchies. (It's the only 24-hr. eatery we know of on the island.) Don't expect glamour, as it's in a cramped and very ordinary-looking modern building within a shopping center a 5-minute drive east of the International Bazaar. Order takeout portions of the island's best guava duff (a Bahamian dessert specialty that resembles a jelly roll), as well as pork chops, fish dishes (usually deep-fried), chicken souse (an acquired taste), sandwiches, hamburgers, and an array of daily specials.

E. Sunrise Hwy. (at Coral Rd.). ℂ **242/373-7655.** Breakfast US$3–US$8 (£1.50–£4); main courses US$11–US$18 (£5.50–£9); vegetarian plates US$7–US$9 (£3.50–£4.50). No credit cards. Daily 24 hr.

The Pub on the Mall INTERNATIONAL   Located on the same floor of the same building and under the same management, three distinctive eating areas lie across the boulevard from the International Bazaar and attract many locals. The **Prince of Wales** serves such Old English staples as shepherd's pie, fish and chips, platters of roast beef or fish, and real English ale. One end of the room is devoted to the **Red Dog Sports Bar,** with a boisterous atmosphere and at least four TV screens (including one that's a whopping 244cm/96 in. wide) blasting away for dedicated fans. **Silvano's** (p. 153) is an Italian restaurant serving lots of pasta, usually with verve, as well as chicken, beef-steaks, seafood, and tiramisu.

Ranfurley Circle, Sunrise Hwy. ℂ **242/352-5110.** Reservations recommended. Main courses US$15–US$36 (£7.50–£18). AE, DISC, MC, V. Prince of Wales and Red Dog Mon–Sat noon–midnight. Silvano's Mon–Sat noon–3pm and 5–11pm.

IN THE INTERNATIONAL BAZAAR
INEXPENSIVE
China Temple CHINESE   This battered-looking Chinese joint also does takeout. Over the years it's proved to be the dining bargain of the bazaar, surviving in a venue that hadn't been profitable for many of its (now-defunct) competitors. The menu is familiar, standard, and a bit shopworn: chop suey, chow mein, and sweet-and-sour chicken. It's certainly not gourmet Asian fare, but it's cheap, and it might hit the spot when you're craving something different.

International Bazaar. ℂ **242/352-5610.** Lunch US$8–US$10 (£4–£5); main courses US$10–US$14 (£5–£7). AE, MC, V. Mon–Sat 10:30am–10pm.

AT OUR LUCAYA AND TAÍNO BEACH
EXPENSIVE
China Beach ⏶ ASIAN FUSION   Within its own stone-and-stucco building on the seafront grounds of Our Lucaya, this restaurant proffers a culinary passport to the Pacific Rim. Exotic delights include the spicy hot cuisines of Vietnam, Thailand,

Korea, Indonesia, and Malaysia. The menu changes every month, but some dishes appear with regularity. Our favorites among those are a savory Hong Kong roast duckling and a zesty Thai chicken. The beef marinated in soy sauce is served with fresh spring onion, and the grouper filet appears with fresh ginger and scallions. Other Far East specialties include a seafood teppanyaki and stir-fried conch. The decor is particularly imaginative, with scarlet parasols doubling as ceiling chandeliers, and architecture that seems to float above one of the resort's serpentine-shaped swimming pools.

At the Westin and Sheraton at Our Lucaya resorts, Royal Palm Way. ℂ 242/373-1444. Reservations recommended. Main courses US$15–US$29 (£7.50–£15). AE, DC, DISC, MC, V. Tues–Sat 6–10pm, with occasional variations in hours based on resort occupancy.

Churchill's ℛℛ AMERICAN   One of the island's most elegant and formal restaurants is imbued with a sense of the faded grandeur of the British Empire. Surpassed only, we believe, by the Ferry House and Luciano's, both of which are listed in this section, Churchill's lures diners from other parts of the island to a dining room that opens onto the lobby of the Westin at Our Lucaya. The venue includes a British colonial-style bar with dark-wood flooring and trim, potted plants, ceiling fans, a grand piano, and big-windowed views over the sea. The island's best chophouse, it features succulent steaks flown over from the mainland and locally caught seafood. The manor-house setting is an appropriate foil for the finely honed service and top-quality ingredients. Regrettably, it's open less frequently than we'd like, sometimes operating only on weekends during low and shoulder seasons.

At the Westin and Sheraton at Our Lucaya resorts, Royal Palm Way. ℂ 242/373-1444. Reservations required. Main courses US$30–US$68 (£15–£34). AE, DC, DISC, MC, V. Usually Mon–Sat 6–10pm, but during off-season, hours vary according to occupancy levels of the hotel.

Iries ℛ CARIBBEAN   This is one of the newest restaurants at Our Lucaya. As such, a team of food and beverage experts threw tons of money and research into developing the appropriate blend of Caribbean tradition and postmodern methods of sales and marketing. The result will remind you of the dining room of a massive, colonial Jamaican manor house. Decor is replete with replicas of pineapples (the region's traditional symbol of hospitality), Rastafarian paintings, and elaborately carved mahogany furniture similar to what might have graced the home of a 19th-century Caribbean planter. You'll get a sense of spaciousness and old-fashioned dignity and restraint. Menu items include cracked conch with spicy sauce and sweet potato wedges, grilled sirloin steak with cumin and thyme, blackened grouper with fire-roasted peppers and pineapple sauce, and tamarind-glazed hen. On your way in, check out the Bahamian Junkanoo costume, which hangs like a permanent museum exhibition. Replete with sequins and mystical references, it's one of the most elaborate, outrageous, and costly examples of its kind.

The Westin and Sheraton at Our Lucaya resorts, Royal Palm Way. ℂ 242/373-1444. Main courses US$26–US$48 (£13–£24). AE, MC, V. Sat–Wed 6–10pm, though hours can vary.

MODERATE

Prop Club AMERICAN/INTERNATIONAL   This is one of our favorite informal restaurants in the Our Lucaya/Port Lucaya compound. Set within its own low-slung building, it's the kind of place that raffish-looking crew members from charter yachts moored nearby seek out during their time in port. Despite its location on the grounds of the most upscale resort on Grand Bahama Island, it manages to remain fun, funky, laid-back, and bemusedly entertained at its own Rastafarian references. Looking for a bar, a cafe, a restaurant, a dance hall, or a pickup joint? This place can be (and has been) all things to all kinds of people. It evokes a battered airplane hangar where mail planes might have been repaired during World War II. Many of the industrial parts hanging from the ceiling, including semi-antique airplane propellers and ship hulls, evoke a low-tech age when an airplane engine might actually have been repaired by a pilot wielding a monkey wrench and some copper wire. When the weather's right, which it is most of the time, large doors open to bring the outdoors in, and the party overflows onto the beach. The all-Bahamian staff is good-looking, the drinks are stiff, and the music is fine. Dig into a mountain of ribs or savor blackened grouper, a grilled margarita chicken sandwich, a juicy oversize burger, fajitas, or spicy conch chowder. Many dishes are at the lower end of the price scale, making it an affordable choice.

At the Westin and Sheraton at Our Lucaya resorts, Royal Palm Way. ✆ 242/373-1444. Main courses US$12–US$24 (£6–£12). AE, DC, MC, V. Restaurant daily 11:30am–10pm. Bar Sun–Thurs 11:30am–1am; Fri–Sat noon–2am.

INEXPENSIVE
Willy Broadleaf ✪ INTERNATIONAL   Set on the street level of the Westin at Our Lucaya, facing one of its S-shaped swimming pools, this imaginatively decorated restaurant focuses on one of the most lavish buffet breakfasts we've ever seen in The Bahamas. The decor fits the cuisine, with various sections evoking a Mexican court-yard, a marketplace in old Cairo, the dining hall of an Indian maharajah (including tables that are cordoned off from neighbors with yards of translucent fabric), and an African village. Food stations serve cold and hot breakfast foods—try the omelets, pancakes, and French toast, the best version of which is laced with coconut.

The Westin and Sheraton at Our Lucaya resorts, Royal Palm Way. ✆ 242/373-1444. Breakfast buffet US$15 (£7.50) for cold foods, US$20 (£10) for both hot and cold foods; buffet dinner US$38 (£19). AE, DC, DISC, MC, V. Daily 6:30–11am and 6–11pm.

AT PORT LUCAYA MARKETPLACE
EXPENSIVE
Ferry House ✪✪ *Finds* FRENCH/CARIBBEAN   This restaurant serves the island's most celebrated and fussed-over cuisine. Designed to look like the mostly brown inte-rior of a wood-trimmed ferryboat, it faces the ocean just at the edge of Bell Channel. Lunches are relatively simple affairs, consisting of pastas, the catch of the day, and meal-size salads. Dinner might feature a seafood platter laden with calamari, fish, and shrimp; a delectable filet mignon with potatoes and vegetables; fresh salmon with hol-landaise sauce; and savory grilled rack of New Zealand lamb. But our favorite meal here is the seared yellowfin tuna steak with veggie couscous. Many of the herbs used here are grown in the restaurant's own garden.

Beside Bell Channel, Port Lucaya. ✆ 242/373-1595. Dinner reservations recommended. Lunch platters US$18–US$38 (£9–£19); set-price lunch US$28 (£14); dinner main courses US$34–US$44 (£17–£22). AE, MC, V. Mon–Fri noon–2:30pm; Tues–Sun 6–9pm.

Luciano's ✪ FRENCH/CONTINENTAL   With its tables usually occupied by local government officials and dealmakers, Luciano's is the grande dame of Freeport restaurants, with a very European atmosphere. It's the only restaurant in Port Lucaya offering caviar, foie gras, and oysters Rockefeller, all served with a flourish by a for-mally dressed waitstaff, who, fortunately, have a definite sense of charm and humor. There's a bar inside and elegantly decorated tables set in the kind of socially correct dining room you might find in Paris. Additional seating on a breezy upstairs veranda overlooks the marina. For a good opener, opt for the lightly smoked and thinly sliced salmon, seafood crepe, or snails in garlic butter. Fresh fish and shellfish are delicately prepared, allowing natural flavor to shine through without heavy, overwhelming sauces. Good examples include local grouper topped with toasted almonds and a lemon-flavored butter sauce, and broiled Bahamian lobster tail. Steak Diane is one of Luciano's classics, along with an especially delectable veal medallion sautéed with shrimp and chunks of lobster.

Port Lucaya Marketplace. ⓒ 242/373-9100. www.portlucaya.com/lucianos. Reservations required in winter. Main courses US$29–US$44 (£15–£22). AE, MC, V. Daily 5:30–9:45pm (last order).

MODERATE

Giovanni's Cafe ⟨ʀ⟩ ITALIAN/SEAFOOD   Tucked into one of the pedestrian thoroughfares of Port Lucaya Marketplace, this cream-colored clapboard house provides the setting for a charming 38-seat Italian trattoria. The chefs serve Italian-influenced preparations of local seafood, highlighted by seafood pasta and a lobster special. Giovanni stamps each dish with his Italian verve and flavor, whether it be Bahamian conch, local seafood, or scampi. Dishes showing off his precision and rock-solid technique include sirloin steak with fresh mushrooms, delectable shrimp scampi, and fattening but extremely good spaghetti carbonara.

Port Lucaya Marketplace. ⓒ 242/373-9107. Reservations recommended. US$14–US$37 (£7–£19). AE, MC, V. Mon–Sat 4–10pm; Sun 5–10pm.

The Harbour Room ⟨ʀ⟩⟨ʀ⟩ (Kids) EUROPEAN/CARIBBEAN   The only member of the prestigious *Chaîne des Rotisseurs* on the island, this is one of Port Lucaya's best restaurants. It offers a definite continental flair; a creative kitchen; a polite, hardworking staff; and a sense of *gemütlichkeit* in the Tropics. Tucked away into one corner, its bar is the most lavish part, with esoteric liqueurs and an upscale, stylish decor that recalls a chic hideaway in Berlin. The dining room is simpler. Designed as a counterpart for the cuisine, and not an architectural statement in its own right, it's outfitted with dark-wood trim and a nautical decor that's especially charming when the Atlantic winds outside blow hard and cold. Its owners are not shy about publicizing their culinary ambitions. They serve one of the few white (that is, New England-style) conch chowders we've seen in The Bahamas. Jumbo cheeseburgers are appropriately juicy, but more appealing might be the Delmonico steaks, veal chops with Provençal herbs, and shrimp Alfredo with marinara-flavored pasta. Chilean sea bass poached in Irish butter and chardonnay sauce is a specialty, as is the lobster St. Jacques, wherein chunks of lobster are spooned over a bed of garlic-flavored mashed potatoes, then covered with cheese, and broiled.

Port Lucaya Marketplace. ⓒ 242/374-4466. Reservations recommended. Main courses US$25–US$42 (£13–£21); children's platters US$6–US$11 (£3–£5.50); Sun brunch US$30 (£15). AE, MC, V. Wed–Sun 5–11pm; Sun brunch 11am–4:30pm.

La Dolce Vita ⟨ʀ⟩ ITALIAN   Next to the Pub at Lucaya (p. 158), this small, upscale Italian trattoria has modern decor and traditional food. Enjoy freshly made pastas on a patio overlooking the marina or in the 44-seat dining room. Start with portobello mushrooms with fresh mozzarella, tomatoes, and a vinaigrette, or else carpaccio with arugula and spices. Homemade ravioli has fillings such as cheese, lobster, or spinach. There's also an excellent squid ink-flavored risotto, a roast pork tenderloin, and a crisp, aromatic rack of lamb.

Port Lucaya Marketplace. ⓒ 242/373-8652. Reservations recommended. Main courses US$23–US$38 (£12–£19). AE, MC, V. Daily 5–11pm. Closed Sept.

Mediterranean Restaurant & Bar ("Le Med") ☆ *Value* FRENCH/GREEK/ BAHAMIAN   This is a simpler and more cost-effective version of nearby Luciano's (p. 156), with which it shares its management. Decor includes a hardworking, almost indestructible combination of sand-colored floor tiles and refrigerated display cases loaded with pastries and salads. Devoid of linen, tables are so simple and angular-looking that they might have appeared within a coffee shop or a diner. Don't let this simplicity fool you: The place serves well-flavored and surprisingly sophisticated food that attracted many of the actors filming the sequel to *Pirates of the Caribbean,* as well as rock star Jon Bon Jovi and a gaggle of hangers-on. It's crowded during the breakfast hour, when omelets (including a feta-and-spinach-laden Greek omelet), eggs and bacon, and Bahamian stewed fish and steamed conch are crowd-pleasers. Lunch and dinner feature assorted Greek- and Turkish-style *mezes* and Iberian-influenced *tapas* that include marinated octopus and grilled calamari. Crepes, priced from US$8 to US$10 (£4–£5) each, come in both sweet and savory varieties. Other tempters include a seafood combo piled high with lobster, shrimp, conch, fish, and mussels; Delmonico-style steaks; *shashlik* (marinated kabobs redolent with herbs); and braised lamb shank cooked in red wine.

Port Lucaya Marketplace. ✆ 242/374-2804. Breakfast US$6–$10 (£3–£5); main courses US$13–US$28 (£6.50–£14). AE, DC, MC, V. Daily 8am–11:30pm

Pisces ☆ INTERNATIONAL   This ranks high among our favorites in the Port Lucaya Marketplace—and we're seconded by the locals and sailors who pack it every weekend. The place is outfitted with a quirky mixture of nautical accessories and dark-varnished wood, with a prominent bar where more gossip is exchanged the later it gets. Tabletops contain laminated seashells, fake gold coins, and sand. The place has a charming all-Bahamian staff outfitted in black and white. Pizzas are available in 27 different varieties, including a version with conch, lobster, shrimp, and chicken, as well as one with Alfredo sauce. Dinners are more elaborate, with a choice of curries of all kinds, fish, shellfish, and several kinds of pasta.

Port Lucaya Marketplace. ✆ 242/373-5192. Reservations recommended. Pizzas US$12–US$30 (£6–£15); dinner main courses US$9–US$37 (£4.50–£19). AE, DISC, MC, V. Mon–Sat 5pm–2am.

Pub at Lucaya ENGLISH/BAHAMIAN   Opening onto Count Basie Square, and reminiscent of the days when the Royal Navy might have hauled some of its sailors out to The Bahamas from a home base in, say, Liverpool, this restaurant and bar lies near the center of the Port Lucaya Marketplace. Returning visitors might remember the joint from when it was called Pusser's Pub, named after that popular brand of rum.

Many patrons visit just for the drinks, especially rum-laced Pusser's Painkillers. You can order predictable pub grub such as shepherd's or steak-and-ale pie. Juicy American-style burgers are another lure. There's also a scattering of more substantial Bahamian fare, especially lobster tail, cracked conch, herbed chicken breast, or the freshly grilled catch of the day. The tables outside overlooking the water are preferable, or else you can retreat inside under a wooden beamed ceiling, where the rustic pinewood tables are lit by faux Tiffany lamps.

Port Lucaya Marketplace. ✆ 242/373-8450. Sandwiches and burgers US$8–US$11 (£4–£5.50); main courses US$13–US$35 (£6.50–£18). AE, MC, V. Daily 11am–11pm (bar until 1am).

Shenanigan's Irish Pub IRISH/INTERNATIONAL   Dark and beer-stained from the thousands of pints of Guinness, Harp, and Killian's that have been served and spilled here, this pub and restaurant is the premier Irish or Bostonian-Irish hangout on Grand Bahama. Many visitors come just to drink, sometimes for hours at a time, soaking up the suds and perhaps remembering to eventually order some food; the menu here recently took a noticeable swing toward the more upscale. They still serve steak-and-kidney pie, burgers, and surf and turf, but newer items include French-style rack of lamb for two, seafood Newburg, and chicken Connemara drenched in whiskey sauce.

Port Lucaya Marketplace. (242/373-4734. Main courses US$10–US$49 (£5–£25). AE, DISC, MC, V. Mon–Thurs 5pm–midnight; Fri–Sat 5pm–2am (last order at 9:45pm).

INEXPENSIVE

Georgie's BAHAMIAN/AMERICAN   This laid-back, informal restaurant provides a harborside perch at Port Lucaya for breakfast, lunch, or dinner. It gets particularly busy during the late-afternoon happy hour, when drink prices are dropped. Service shows more effort than polish, but dishes do arrive and they are quite flavorful time-tested recipes, a repertoire of old favorites like cracked conch served with tasty coleslaw. The catch of the day is usually pan-fried grouper or snapper served with peas 'n' rice. The chef almost daily prepares hot roast beef, serving it with mashed potatoes and mixed vegetables. For lunch, try one of the island's better chef's salads, which comes loaded with turkey, ham, fresh tomatoes, cheese, and other good things. Other favorites include lobster, conch fritters, and barbecue chicken.

Port Lucaya Marketplace. (242/373-8513. Breakfast US$5–US$9 (£2.50–£4.50); main courses lunch US$11–US$13 (£5.50–£6.50), dinner US$9–US$24 (£4.50–£12). DC, MC, V. Thurs, Fri, Mon–Tues 10am–8pm; Sat–Sun 8am–9pm.

Outrigger's Native Restaurant/White Wave Club BAHAMIAN   Cement-sided and simple with a large deck extending out toward the sea, this restaurant was here long before the Port Lucayan Marketplace, which lies 4 blocks away. It's the domain of Gretchen Wilson, whose kitchens produce a rotating series of lip-smacking dishes such as lobster tails, minced lobster, steamed or cracked conch, pork chops, chicken, fish, and shrimp, usually served with peas 'n' rice and macaroni. Every Wednesday night, from 5pm to 2am, the restaurant becomes the venue for **Outrigger's Famous Wednesday Night Fish Fry,** when as many as 1,000 diners line up for platters of fried or steamed fish (US$10–US$15/£5–£7.50). A DJ and dancers provide entertainment. Almost as well attended are the establishment's **Bonfire Nights,** where set-price all-you-can-eat barbecue dinners, in addition to a la carte offerings, go for US$30 (£15) per person every Tuesday and Thursday evening. Drinks are served at the restaurant, but you might consider stepping into the nearby ramshackle bar called the **White Wave Club,** which serves only drinks. *Note:* If you make reservations for a Bonfire Night through your hotel, you may pay an extra US$20 (£10).

Smith's Point. (242/373-4811. Main courses US$10–$16 (£5–£8). No credit cards. Sat–Thurs noon–8pm.

Zorba's (Value BAHAMIAN/GREEK   If you've ever been captivated by Greece, this place might bring back happy memories and will certainly provide some of the best food value at Port Lucaya Marketplace. A narrow outside veranda overlooks a relatively uninteresting pedestrian alleyway outside, and the pale-blue-and-white Formica-clad interior might remind you of a diner. A TV set blasts out a Greek-language news broadcast. Big photos of Alan Bates and Anthony Quinn (playing Zorba, get it?) dancing on a beach add a touch of nostalgia for ouzo and *retsina*. The cuisine is a quirky and idiosyncratic mixture of Greek and Bahamian, and if you don't remember exactly what *taramasalata* or baklava is, the good-looking Bahamian staff will rattle off the ingredients like Peloponnesian pros. First thing in the morning, you'll see locals standing in line for the Bahamian breakfasts, with dishes that include chicken souse, corned beef and grits, and an array of pancakes, waffles, and omelets. Lunch could be a fat gyro, a burger, a salad, or a souvlakia. Dinner can begin with a Greek salad and then move on to moussaka, grilled chicken on a bed of spinach, or any of several different pasta dishes, and end with baklava, those honey and nut-studded pastries, for a sweet finish. We won't pretend the food here is a substitute for a trip to the Greek isles, but it's satisfying and filling.

Port Lucaya Marketplace. ⓒ 242/373-6137. Main courses lunch US$4–US$13 (£2–£6.50), dinner US$11–US$24 (£5.50–£12). AE, DISC, MC, V. Daily 7am–10:30pm.

OUTSIDE FREEPORT/LUCAYA
Bishop's Restaurant 🐸 *Finds* BAHAMIAN   This eatery, known mainly to East End locals, is patronized for its real down-home cooking. Just more than 50km (31 miles) east of Lucaya, it opens onto views of the sea. Far from the high-rise hotels, in a small residential community utterly devoid of casino-inspired glitz, this little restaurant and lounge looks as it would have if it existed in The Bahamas of the 1920s and 1930s. Some of the best cracked conch we've sampled on Grand Bahama is served here, rolled in a light batter and fried in piping-hot oil so that its crust is slightly crunchy. Another favorite, always on the menu, is fried grouper with classic peas 'n' rice. Or, for a savory dish, order the chicken barbecued in zesty sauce. However, don't set out on a trek to the East End with this place envisioned as your final destination without calling in advance, since opening hours have been erratic since the hurricanes of 2005.

High Rock. ⓒ 242/353-4515. Main courses US$10–US$20 (£5–£10). MC, V. Daily 9am–7pm, though hours may vary.

5 Beaches, Watersports & Other Outdoor Pursuits
HITTING THE BEACH
Grand Bahama Island has enough beaches for everyone. The best ones open onto Northwest Providence Channel at Freeport and sweep eastward for some 97km (60 miles) to encompass Xanadu Beach, Lucaya Beach, Taíno Beach, and others, eventually ending at such remote eastern outposts as Rocky Creek and McLean's Town. Once you leave the Freeport/Lucaya area, you can virtually have your pick of white sandy beaches all the way. Once you're past the resorts, you'll see a series of secluded beaches used mainly by locals. If you like people, a lot of organized watersports, and easy access to hotel bars and rest rooms, stick to Xanadu, Taíno, and Lucayan beaches.

Though there's fine snorkeling along the shore, you should book a snorkeling cruise aboard one of the catamarans to see the most stunning reefs.

Xanadu Beach 🐸🐸 is one of our favorites, immediately east of Freeport and the site of the famed Xanadu Beach Resort. The 1.6km-long (1-mile) beach may be crowded in winter, but that's because of those gorgeous, soft, powdery white sands, which open onto tranquil waters. The beach is set against a backdrop of coconut palms and Australian pines. In theory, at least, you can hook up here with an assortment of watersports, including snorkeling, boating, jet-skiing, and parasailing.

Immediately east of Xanadu is little **Silver Point Beach,** site of a timeshare complex where guests are out riding the waves on water bikes or playing volleyball. You'll see horseback riders from Pinetree Stables (p. 164) galloping along the sands.

Moments **Private White Sands**

Once you head east from Port Lucaya and Taíno, you'll discover so many splendid beaches that you'll lose count. Though these beaches do have names—directly east of Taíno is **Churchill's Beach,** followed by **Smith's Point, Fortune Beach,** and **Barbary Beach**—you'll never really know what beach you're on (unless you ask a local) because they are unmarked. If you like seclusion and don't mind the lack of facilities, you'll find a string of local beauties. Fortune Beach is a special gem because of its gorgeous waters and white sands.

Despite the allure of other beaches on Grand Bahama, most visitors go to **Lucaya Beach,** right off Royal Palm Way and immediately east of Silver Point Beach. This is one of the best strands in The Bahamas, with long stretches of white sand. In the vicinity of the Westin and Sheraton hotels, you'll also encounter a worthy scattering of beach bars. At any of the resorts along this beach, you can hook up with an array of watersports or get a frosty drink from a hotel bar. It's definitely not for those seeking seclusion, but it is a fun beach-party scene.

Immediately to the east of Lucaya Beach, and separated from it by a saltwater canal, **Taíno Beach** is a family favorite and a good place for watersports. This, too, is a fine, wide beach of white sands, opening onto usually tranquil waters.

Another choice, not too far east, is **Gold Rock Beach,** a favorite picnic spot for weekending locals; you'll usually have it to yourself on weekdays. A 19km (12-mile) drive from Lucaya, it's at the doorstep of **Lucayan National Park** (p. 166), a 16-hectare (40-acre) park filled with some of the island's longest, widest, and most fabulous secluded beaches.

BIKING

A guided bike trip is an ideal way to see parts of Grand Bahama that most visitors miss. Starting at **Barbary Beach,** pedal a mountain bike along the southern coast parallel to the beach. Stop for a snack, lunch, and a dip. Finally, you reach **Lucayan National Park,** some 19km (12 miles) away. Explore the cave in which the natives, centuries before the coming of Columbus, buried their dead. Crabs here occasionally come up through holes in the ground carrying bits of bowls once used by the Lucayans. **Grand Bahama Nature Tours** (also known as Kayak Nature Tours; ⊘ 242/373-2485; www.grandbahamanaturetours.com) runs these bike trips and transports you home to your hotel by van so you don't exhaust yourself in the heat while cycling back. The same company offers variations on this itinerary, with more time spent kayaking and snorkeling. All tours last about 5 hours and cost US$79 (£40) for adults, US$40 (£20) for children 11 and under. All equipment, sustenance, and round-trip transportation from your hotel is included.

BOAT CRUISES

Ocean Wonder, Port Lucaya Dock (⊘ 242/373-5880), run by Reef Tours, is a gargantuan 18m Defender glass-bottom boat. Any tour agent can arrange for you to board this vessel. You'll get a panoramic view of the beautiful underwater life off the coast of Grand Bahama. Cruises depart from Port Lucaya behind the straw market on the bay side at 9:30am, 11:15am, 1:15pm, and 3:15pm, except Friday, when only the earlier two tours happen. The tour lasts 1½ hours, costs US$25 (£13) for adults and US$15 (£7.50) for children 6 to 12, and is free for kids 5 and under. During high season (midwinter), arrange for reservations a day or two in advance, as the boat does fill up quickly.

Superior Watersports (Freeport; © **242/373-7863;** www.superiorwatersports. com) offers trips on its *Bahama Mama,* a two-deck, 22m catamaran. Its **Robinson Crusoe Beach Party** is offered four times a week and costs US$59 (£30) per adult and US$39 (£20) for children 11 and under. Schedules vary with the season: from 11am to 4pm from October through March, but from noon to 5pm from April through September. There's also a shorter sunset **booze cruise** that goes for US$45 (£23). (Apr–Sept cruises are on Tues, Thurs, and Sat night 6:30–8:30pm, and Oct–Mar the same nights, but 6–8pm.)

For an underwater cruise, try the company's quasi-submarine, the *Seaworld Explorer.* The sub itself does not descend; instead, you walk down into the hull and watch the sea life glide by. It departs daily at 9:30am, 11:30am, and 1:30pm, and the 2-hour ride costs US$45 (£23) for adults and US$25 (£13) for children age 2 to 12.

THE DOLPHIN EXPERIENCE

A pod of bottle-nosed dolphins is involved in a unique dolphin-human familiarization program at **Dolphin Experience,** located at Underwater Explorer Society (UNEXSO), next to Port Lucaya, opposite the entrance to the Westin and Sheraton at Our Lucaya (© **800/992-DIVE** [3483] or 242/373-1244; www.unexso.com). This close-encounter program allows participants to observe these intelligent, friendly animals and hear an interesting talk by a member of the animal-care staff. At the world's largest dolphin facility, the conditions aren't cramped. In addition, dolphins can swim out to sea, passing through an underwater gate that prevents their natural predators from entering the lagoon; the dolphins later return of their own free will to their protected marine habitat. After a 25-minute ferryboat ride from Port Lucaya, you'll step onto a shallow wading platform to interact with the dolphins. At press time, the dolphin colony had 17 members. The experience costs US$75 (£38) and is an educational, fun adventure for all ages. Children under 3 participate free, and it costs US$50 (£25) for those aged 4 to 12. If you like to document your life's unusual experiences, bring your camera. For certified divers, UNEXSO offers a **dolphin dive,** wherein a school of dolphins swim out from their marine habitat in Sanctuary Bay for a closely supervised diver-to-dolphin encounter. The cost is US$169 (£85). If business warrants, the dolphin dive is offered daily.

Swimming with dolphins has its supporters as well as its highly vocal critics. For insight into the various points of view surrounding this issue, visit the Whale and Dolphin Conservation Society's website at www.wdcs.org. For more information about responsible travel in general, check out www.ecotourism.org.

FISHING

In the waters off Grand Bahama, you can fish for barracuda, snapper, grouper, yellowtail, wahoo, and kingfish, along with other denizens of the deep.

Reef Tours, Ltd., Port Lucaya Dock (© **242/373-5880** or 373-5891; www. bahamasvg.com/reeftours), offers one of the least expensive ways to go deep-sea fishing around Grand Bahama. Adults pay US$110 (£55) if they fish, US$50 (£25) if they go along only to watch. Four to six people can charter the entire 13m craft for US$650 (£325) per half-day or US$1,250 (£625) per whole day. The 9.6m boat can

---

Moments Land & Sea Eco-Tours

If you're a nature lover, escape from the casinos and take one of the bush and sea safaris offered by **East End Adventures** (© **242/373-6662**), whose guides take you through dense pine forests and along deserted beaches, going inland on hikes to blue holes, mangrove swamps, and underground caverns. You may even learn how to crack conch. A native lunch is served on a serene beach in Lightbourne's Cay, a remote islet in the East End. Most of the tour is laid-back; you can snorkel in blue holes or shell hunt. The safaris happen Sunday to Friday between 9:30am and 5pm, costing US$120 (£60) for adults and US$60 (£30) for kids ages 2 to 12.

---

be chartered for US$440 (£220) for a half-day and US$825 (£413) for a full day. Departures for the 4-hour half-day excursions are daily at 8:30am and 1pm, while the 8-hour full-day excursions leave daily at 8:30am. Bait, tackle, and ice are included in the cost.

GOLF

Since two of the island's older courses, the Ruby and the Emerald, closed after the hurricane damages of the early millennium, Grand Bahama is not as richly accessorized with golf courses as it used to be. But golf on the island recently experienced a resurgence, thanks to the improvements to the courses described below. They're open to the public year-round; their pro shops can rent you clubs.

Fortune Hills Golf & Country Club, Richmond Park, Lucaya (© **242/373-2222**), was originally intended to be an 18-hole course, but the back 9 were never completed. You can replay the front 9 for 18 holes and a total of 6,916 yards from the blue tees. Par is 72. Greens fees are US$36 (£18) for 9 holes, US$48 (£24) for 18; carts are included. Club rental costs US$20 (£10) for 18 holes and US$16 (£8) for 9 holes.

The island's best-kept and most-manicured course is **Lucayan Golf Course,** Lucaya Beach at Our Lucaya (© **242/373-1333**). Made over after 2004's Hurricane Jeanne, this beautiful course is a traditional golf layout with rows of pine trees separating the fairways. Greens are fast, with a couple of par-5s more than 500 yards long, totaling 6,824 yards from the blue tees and 6,488 from the whites. Par is 72. Greens fees are US$120 (£60) for 18 holes, including a mandatory shared golf cart.

Its sibling golf course, with an entirely separate clubhouse and staff, is the slightly older **Reef Course** ❀❀, Royal Palm Way, at Our Lucaya (© **242/373-1333**). Designed by Robert Trent Jones, Jr., who called it "a bit like a Scottish course but a lot warmer," the course boasts 6,920 yards of links-style playing grounds. It features a wide-open layout without rows of trees to separate its fairways and lots of water traps—you'll find water on 13 of the 18 holes and various types of long grass swaying in the trade winds. Play requires patience and precise shot-making to avoid the numerous lakes.

At either of the above-mentioned golf courses, guests at either the Westin or Sheraton hotels, with which the courses are associated, pay between US$90 and US$120 (£45–£60), depending on the season, for 18 holes. Nonguests are charged between US$110 and US$160 (£55–£80) for 18 holes. Rates include use of an electric-powered golf cart.

Finds **The Ultimate in Relaxation**

The ideal place to relieve the stresses of everyday life can be found at Our Lucaya's **Senses Spa**, boasting an exercise facility with health checks, personal trainers, and yoga classes. A cafe serves fresh, natural food and elixirs. During one of their signature treatments, the Total Senses Massage, two massage therapists work in sync to relieve your tension. Throughout the Salt Glo body polish treatment, a therapist buffs away dead skin cells and polishes your body with natural, locally derived elements. Note that residents of either the Westin or the Sheraton can use the health and exercise facilities without charge, but spa, health, massage, and beauty treatments must be scheduled in advance and require additional payment.

HORSEBACK RIDING

Pinetree Stables, North Beachway Drive, Freeport (© **242/373-3600** or 305/433-4809; www.pinetree-stables.com), has the country's best and—with a boarded inventory of more than 50 horses—biggest riding stables, superior to rivals on New Providence Island (Nassau). Pinetree offers trail rides to the beach Tuesday through Sunday year-round at 9 and 11:30am. The cost is US$85 (£43) per person for a trail ride lasting 2 hours. No children under 8 are allowed. The weight limit for riders is 200 pounds.

SEA KAYAKING

To explore the waters off the island's north shore, call **Grand Bahama Nature Tours** (© **866/440-4542** or 242/373-2485; www.grandbahamanaturetours.com) and go on kayak excursions through the mangroves, where you can see wildlife as you paddle along. The cost is US$79 (£40) per person (children 11 and under pay US$40/£20), with lunch included. Double kayaks are used on these jaunts, and children must be at least 3 years old. For the same price, you can take a 30-minute kayak trip to an offshore island, with 1½ hours of snorkeling included along with lunch. Call ahead for reservations for either of these tours. A van will pick you up at your hotel between 9 and 10am and deliver you back at the end of the tour, usually sometime between 3 and 4pm. A popular variation on this tour, which operates during the same hours and at the same prices, includes more time devoted to snorkeling above a series of shallow offshore reefs and slightly less time allocated to kayaking.

SNORKELING & SCUBA DIVING

Serious divers are attracted to Grand Bahama sites like the **Wall,** the **Caves** (one of the most interesting of which is **Ben's Cavern**), **Treasure Reef,** and the most evocative of all, **Theo's Wreck** *⟨⟨*, a freighter that was deliberately sunk off Freeport to attract marine life. Today it teems with everything from horse-eyed jacks to moray eels. Other top locales include **Spit City, Ben Blue Hole, Pygmy Caves, Gold Rock, Silver Point Reef,** and the **Rose Garden.**

    Underwater Explorer Society (UNEXSO) *⟨⟨⟨* (© **800/992-DIVE** [992-3483] or 242/373-1250; www.unexso.com), one of the premier dive outfitters in the

Caribbean, offers seven dive trips daily, including reef trips, shark dives, wreck dives, and night dives. Divers can even meet dolphins in the open ocean here—a rare experience offered by very few facilities in the world (see "The Dolphin Experience," p. 162).

A popular 3-hour learn-to-dive course, the **Mini-B Pool and Reef Adventure,** is offered daily. Over UNEXSO's 30-year history, more than 50,000 people have successfully completed either this course or its similar predecessors. For US$85 (£43), students learn the basics in UNEXSO's training pools and dive the beautiful shallow reef with an instructor.

A nearby competitor, **Reef Tours** (© 242/373-5880; www.bahamasvacation guide.com/reeftours), offers highly recommended snorkeling tours. Lasting just less than 2 hours each, they depart from Port Lucaya thrice daily. Tours are priced at US$45 (£23) for adults and US$25 (£13) for children aged 6 to 12, with all equipment included. A variation on that program is a 3-hour sail-and-snorkel-tour. Departing daily at 9:30am and 1:30pm, it's priced at US$45 (£23) for adults and at US$25 (£13) for children aged 6 to 12.

TENNIS

The island's best tennis facilities are part of the **Ace Tennis Center** at Our Lucaya (© 242/350-5294), where four tennis courts feature different playing surfaces. They include a grass court (US$100/£50 per hour) that's often favored by players from the U.K., a clay surface (US$50/£25 per hour), a surface made from Nike rubber that's equivalent to the norm at the Australian Open (US$35/£18 per hour), and a hard deco-turf (US$25/£13 per hour) that's similar to what U.S. Open players compete on. Advance reservations are necessary, and there is no discount of any kind for resort guests. A resident pro offers individual 1-hour tennis lessons for US$90 (£45) per person, or US$130 (£65) for a couple.

WATERSPORTS IN GENERAL

Ocean Motion Water Sports Ltd., Sea Horse Lane, Lucaya Beach (© 242/374-2425; www.oceanmotionbahamas.com), is one of the island's largest watersports companies. It offers a wide variety of activities daily from 9am to 5pm, weather permitting, including snorkeling, parasailing, Hobie Cats, banana boats, water-skiing, jet skis, windsurfing, and other activities. **Parasailing,** for example, costs US$70 (£35) per person for 5 to 7 minutes in the air. **Snorkeling trips** cost US$35 (£18; US$18/£9 for kids under 12) for 1½ hours; **water-skiing,** US$40 (£20) per 3.2km (2-mile) pull, US$60 (£30) for a 30-minute lesson; **Hobie Cats,** US$50 (£25) for the 4.2m, US$75 (£38) for the 4.8m, US$20 (£10) for a lesson; **windsurfing,** US$30 (£15) per hour, US$100 (£50) for a 2-hour lesson; **kayaking,** US$20 (£10) for a single kayak, US$25 (£13) for a double; **water trampoline,** US$20 (£10) full day, US$10 (£5) half-day; and **banana boating,** US$15 (£7.50) per person for a 3.2km (2-mile) ride along a white-sandy beach. Call for reservations, especially for windsurfing.

Lucaya Watersports, Taíno Beach (© 242/373-6375), also offers options for fun in the surf, including **WaveRunners** for US$60 (£30) per 30 minutes and double kayaks costing US$20 (£10) per hour for two passengers. The outfitter also offers **paddle boats** that hold four people, for US$20 (£10) per hour. The **sunset cruises**— a 2-hour sailboat ride offered every Wednesday between 5 and 7pm—are especially popular and cost US$45 (£23) per person.

6 Seeing the Sights

Several informative tours of Grand Bahama Island are available. One reliable company is **H. Forbes Charter Services Ltd.,** at West Sunrise Highway, Freeport (② **242/352-9311;** www.forbescharter.com). From its headquarters in the International Bazaar, this company operates half- and full-day bus tours. The most popular option is the half-day Super Combination Tour, priced at US$25 (£13) per adult and US$15 (£7.50) per child age 5 to 12. It includes drive-through tours of residential areas and the island's commercial center, stops at the island's deep-water harbor, shopping, and a visit to a wholesale liquor store. Departures are Monday through Saturday at 9am and 1pm; the tour lasts 3½ hours. Full-day tours, conducted whenever business warrants, last from 9am to 3:30pm. In addition to everything included in the half-day tours, they bring participants in a bus or van, with guided commentary, all the way to the Caves, near Grand Bahama Island's easternmost tip, for US$40 (£20) per adult, US$30 (£15) per child.

See also "Beaches, Watersports & Other Outdoor Pursuits," on p. 160, for details about UNEXSO's Dolphin Experience, and "Shopping," below, for descriptions of the International Bazaar and the Port Lucaya Marketplace.

Lucayan National Park This 16-hectare (40-acre) park is filled with mangrove, pine, and palm trees. It also contains one of the island's loveliest, most secluded beaches—a long, wide, dune-covered stretch reached by following a wooden pathway that winds through the trees. Bring snorkeling gear with which to glimpse the colorful creatures living beneath the turquoise waters of the offshore coral reef. As you wander through the park, you'll cross Gold Rock Creek, fed by a spring from what is said to be the world's largest underground freshwater cavern system. There are 36,000 entrances to the caves, some only a few feet deep. You can explore two of the caves because they became exposed when a portion of ground collapsed. The pools in them (accessible via spiral wooden steps) are composed of 2m (6½ ft.) of fresh water atop a heavier layer of saltwater.

The freshwater springs once lured native Lucayans, those Arawak-connected tribes who lived on the island and depended on fishing for their livelihood. They would come inland to get fresh water for their habitats on the beach. Lucayan bones and artifacts, such as pottery, have been found in the caves, as well as on the beaches.

Settlers Way, eastern end of E. Sunrise Hwy. ② **242/352-5438.** Admission US$3 (£1.50); tickets available only at the Rand Nature Centre (see below). Daily 9am–5pm. Drive east along Midshipman Rd., passing Sharp Rock Point and Gold Rock.

Rand Nature Centre This 40-hectare (99-acre) pineland sanctuary, located 3km (2 miles) east of Freeport's center, is the regional headquarters of The Bahamas National Trust, a nonprofit conservation organization. Nature trails highlight native flora, including bush medicine plants, and provide ample opportunities for seeing the wild birds that abound here. As you stroll, keep your eyes peeled for the lush blooms of tropical orchids or the brilliant flash of green and red feathers in the trees. You can join a bird-watching tour on the first Saturday of every month at 8am. Other highlights include native animal displays, an education center, and a gift shop selling nature books and souvenirs.

E. Settlers Way. ② **242/352-5438.** Admission US$5 (£2.50) adults, US$3 (£1.50) children 5–12, free for children 4 and under. Mon–Fri 9am–5pm.

7 Shopping

Shopping hours in Freeport/Lucaya are generally Monday to Saturday 9am to 6pm. However, in the International Bazaar, hours vary widely, with shops usually closing a bit earlier. Most places are open Monday through Saturday.

PORT LUCAYA MARKETPLACE

Port Lucaya and its Marketplace took precedence over the International Bazaar (p. 168) in the mid-1990s, when it became clear that the future of merchandising on Grand Bahama had shifted. Today, Port Lucaya Marketplace on Seahorse Road rocks and rolls with a spankingly well-maintained plant set within a shopping, dining, and marina complex on 2.4 hectares (6 acres) of low-lying seafront land. Regular free entertainment, such as steel-drum bands and strolling musicians, as well as recorded music that plays throughout the evening hours, adds to a festival atmosphere.

The complex emulates the 19th-century clapboard-sided construction style of the Old Bahamas, all within a short walk of the island's most cutting-edge and desirable hotel accommodations, including the Westin and Sheraton at Our Lucaya. It's also within a minute's walk of the island's only casino, the Isle of Capri. The development arose on the site of a former Bahamian straw market. Today, in addition to dozens of restaurants and upscale shops, it incorporates rows of brightly painted huts out of which local merchants sell handicrafts and souvenirs.

The waterfront location is a distinct advantage. Lots of the business that fuels this place derives from the expensive yachts and motor craft that tie up at the marina here. Most of those watercraft are owned by Floridians. You might get the sense that many of them just arrived from the U.S. mainland, disgorging their passengers out onto the docks here.

Here is a listing of the most recommended shops at Port Lucaya Marketplace:

Animale   Trendy fashionistas would define this as a hot boutique with the kind of clingy, sophisticated tropical fashion that makes any reasonably shaped woman look good. Come here for long cotton dresses that make the female form look more-than-usually provocative, and the kind of fashion accessories—oversized straw hats, chunky necklaces, animal-print scarves—that emphasize the feline, the *animale,* and perhaps, the seductress. © 242/374-2066.

Bandolera   The staff can be rather haughty here, but despite its drawbacks, the store carries a collection of chic women's clothing that's many cuts above the T-shirts and tank tops that are the norm for many of its competitors. © 242/373-7691.

Colombian Emeralds International   This branch of the world's foremost emerald jeweler offers a wide array of precious gemstone jewelry and one of the island's best watch collections. Careful shoppers can get significant savings over U.S. prices. The outlet offers certified appraisals and free 90-day insurance. © 242/373-8400.

Corporate Casual Boutique   Positioned close to Giovanni's Restaurant, this women's clothing store is owned and operated by a sophisticated Bahamian press and public relations agent, Earnestine Moxyz, who's intimately familiar with dressing for success. Equally acquainted with the corporate climates of Nassau, London, and New York, she's made it a point to carry the kinds of clothing that a female executive would need on her climb up the corporate ladder. All of this is done with flair and an undeniable sense of style. Popular colors, at least at press time, included hot pink, white, aquamarine, and creative combinations of black and gold. Sizes on hand (sizes 2–24 are in stock) could dress virtually anyone. ℂ **242/373-5626.** Additional location at #2 Millennium Mall on West Atlantic Dr. in downtown Freeport. ℂ **242/351-5620.**

Flovin Gallery II   This branch of the art gallery located in the International Bazaar (p. 168) sells a collection of oil paintings by Bahamian and international artists, along with lithographs and posters. In its limited field, it's the best in the business. Also for sale here are a number of gift items, such as handmade Bahamian dolls, decorated corals, and Christmas ornaments. ℂ **242/373-8388.**

Les Parisiennes   This outlet offers a wide range of fine jewelry and watches. It also sells crystal, Versace wear, and perfumes, including the latest from Paris. ℂ **242/373-2974.**

UNEXSO Dive Shop   The nation's premier dive shop sells everything related to the water—swimsuits, wet suits, underwater cameras, video equipment, shades, hats, souvenirs, and state-of-the-art divers' equipment. ℂ **800/992-3483** or 242/373-1244.

THE INTERNATIONAL BAZAAR

The older and less glamorous of Grand Bahama Island's two main shopping venues, the International Bazaar has steadily declined since the collapse of the mega-resort Crowne Plaza Hotel, immediately next door. Originally conceived as a warren of alleyways loaded with upscale, tax-free boutiques, and still plugging away valiantly at its location at East Mall Drive and East Sunrise Highway, it encompasses 4 hectares (10 acres) in the heart of Freeport.

Today it's a pale shadow of what it was during its peak in the mid-1980s, when it boasted 130 purveyors of luxury goods, when the Marketplace at Port Lucaya was still a dream, and when busloads of cruise-ship passengers would be unloaded in front of its gates at regular intervals. With many shops permanently closed and cracks in its masonry, its aggressively touted role as an "international" venue seems a bit theme-driven and tired. Even worse for the retailers here, its rising competitor, the Port Lucaya Marketplace, is looking better every day.

Buses at the entrance of the complex aren't numbered, but those marked INTERNATIONAL BAZAAR will take you right to the entrance at Torii Gate on West Sunrise Highway. The fare is US$1 (50p). Visitors walk through this much-photographed gate, a Japanese symbol of welcome, into a miniature World's Fair setting (think of it as a kitschy and somewhat run-down version of Epcot). The bazaar blends architecture and cultures from some 25 countries, each re-created with cobblestones, narrow alleys, and a layout that evokes a somewhat dusty casbah in North Africa.

In the approximately 34 shops that remain in business today, you might find something that is both unique and a bargain. You'll see African handicrafts, Chinese jade, British china, Swiss watches, Irish linens, and Colombian emeralds. Many of the enterprises represented here also maintain branches within the Port Lucaya Marketplace. Various sections evoke the architecture of the Ginza in Tokyo, with merchandise—electronic goods, art objects, luxury products—from Asia. Other subdivisions evoke the Left Bank of Paris, various regions of India and Africa, Latin America, and Spain.

Some merchants claim their prices are 40% less than comparable costs in the U.S., but don't count on that. If you're contemplating a big purchase, it's best to compare prices before you leave home. Most merchants can ship your purchases back home at relatively reasonable rates.

A **straw market** next door to the International Bazaar contains items with that special Bahamian touch—colorful baskets, hats, handbags, placemats, and an endless array of T-shirts, some of which make worthwhile gifts. Be aware that some items sold here were actually made in Asia, and expect goodly amounts of the tacky and tasteless.

Here is a description of the best shops that remain in the bazaar:

ART
Flovin Gallery   This gallery sells original Bahamian and international art, frames, lithographs, posters, decorated coral, and Bahamian-made Christmas ornaments. It also offers handmade Bahamian dolls, coral jewelry, and other gift items. Another branch is at the Port Lucaya Marketplace (p. 156). © **242/352-7564.**

FASHION
Cleo's Boutique   This shop offers everything from eveningwear to lingerie. A warm and inviting destination, Cleo's prides itself on capturing the Caribbean woman in all her moods. There's also a wide array of costume jewelry beginning at US$25 (£13) per piece. © **242/351-3340.**

Unusual Centre   Where else can you get an array of items made of walrus skin or peacock feathers? There's another branch at the Port Lucaya Marketplace (© 242/373-7333). © **242/352-2333.**

PERFUMES & FRAGRANCES
The Perfume Factory Fragrance of The Bahamas   This is the country's top fragrance producer. The shop is housed in a re-creation of an 1800s mansion, in which visitors are invited to hear a 5-minute commentary and see the mixing of fragrant oils. There's even a "mixology" department where you can create your own fragrance from a selection of oils. The shop's well-known products include Island Promises, Goombay, Paradise, and Pink Pearl (with conch pearls in the bottle). The shop also sells Guanahani, created to commemorate the 500th anniversary of Columbus's first landfall, and Sand, the leading Bahamian-made men's fragrance. © **242/352-9391.**

8 Grand Bahama After Dark

Many resorts stage entertainment at night, and these shows are open to the general public.

ROLLING THE DICE
Grand Bahama maintains only one casino, the **Isle of Capri,** at Our Lucaya. Set within its own free-standing building on the grounds of Our Lucaya, this is the big draw for anyone looking to gamble on Grand Bahama Island. Outfitted in a neutrally modern, not particularly ostentatious design, it contains a crescent-shaped bar, a restaurant, and games that include baccarat, Caribbean stud poker, blackjack, roulette, and some 400 slot machines. It's open daily from 10am to 2am or later, and entrance is free. © **242/373-1333.**

THE CLUB & BAR SCENE
Located in the center of Port Lucaya Marketplace, **Count Basie Square** contains a vine-covered bandstand where the island's best live music is performed several nights a week, usually beginning around 7:30 or 8pm. And it's free! The square honors the "Count," who used to have a grand home on Grand Bahama. Steel bands, small

---

Finds **Bahamian Theater**

Instead of one of those Las Vegas leggy-showgirl revues, call the 450-seat **Regency Theater,** West Sunrise Highway (© 242/352-5533), and ask what performance is scheduled. This is the home of two nonprofit companies, the Freeport Players' Guild and the Grand Bahama Players. The season runs from September to June, and you're likely to see reprises of such Broadway and London blockbusters as *Mamma Mia!,* as well as contemporary works by Bahamian and Caribbean playwrights. Some really intriguing shows are likely to be staged every year by both groups, which are equally talented. Tickets cost US$10 to US$25 (£5–£13).

Junkanoo groups, even gospel singers from a local church are likely to be heard here, their voices or music wafting across the marina and the nearby boardwalk and wharves. Sip a beer or a tropical rum concoction while tapping your feet.

Club Amnesia This is one of the most popular discos and pickup joints on Grand Bahama Island, a local spot that seems a world away from the somewhat sanitized version of nightlife at the island's tourist hotels. Positioned across the street from the Best Western Castaways Hotel, it features an interior outfitted with big mirrors, strobe lights, and Junkanoo colors that are psychedelic. Recorded music grooves and grinds, and live bands are often imported either from the mainland of Florida or from nearby Caribbean islands. Crowds range in age from 18 to 35, and the cover charge, depending on who's playing that night, costs from US$10 to US$24 (£5–£12) per person (concerts cost up to US$50/£25 per ticket). Open nights vary with the season, but it's a good bet that the place is operating Thursday to Saturday from 8:30pm till around 2am. E. Mall Dr. © 242/351-2582.

Margaritavilla Sand Bar Arguably the hottest bar on the island is this lively "jump-up" place opening onto an isolated stretch of Mather Town Beach, about a 15-minute drive southeast of Lucaya. It's really a one-room sand-floor shack, but a lot of fun. Before this bar opened, this part of Grand Bahama used to be relatively sleepy. No more. A weekly bonfire cookout is staged Tuesdays from 6:30 to 9:30pm, with fish or steak on the grill along with a DJ. Main courses cost US$10 to US$16 (£5–£8) if you'd like to stick around to eat. The place rocks on Wednesday night with younger Bahamians; Sunday is for an older crowd that prefers singalongs. The bar swings open at 11am. As for closing times, the owner, Jinx Knowles, says it "might be 7 at night if it's quiet or 7 in the morning if it's jumpin'." Millionaire's Row, Mather Town Beach. © 242/373-4525.

Prop Club Previously recommended in "Where to Dine" (p. 153), this sports bar and dance club flourishes as a singles venue that rocks at high intensity, fueled by high-octane cocktails. A lot happens here, including occasional bouts of karaoke, cultural showcasing of emerging Bahamian and Caribbean bands, and both Junkanoo and retro-disco revival nights, depending on the season. You can also expect a "get down with the DJ" night on Sundays and game nights on slow Mondays. The DJ arrives at 10pm every night. Our Lucaya, Royal Palm Way. © 242/373-1333.

9 A Side Trip to West End

If you crave a refreshing escape from the plush hotels and casinos of Freeport/Lucaya, head to West End, 45km (28 miles) from Freeport. At this old fishing village, and along the scrub-flanked coastal road that leads to it, you'll get glimpses of how things used to be before tour groups began descending on Grand Bahama.

To reach West End, head north along Queen's Highway, going through Eight Mile Rock, to the northernmost point of the island.

A lot of the old village buildings had become seriously dilapidated even before the destructive hurricanes of 2004 and 2005, but those that remain hint at long-ago legends and charm. Old-timers remember when rum boats were busy and the docks buzzed with activity day and night. This was from about 1920 to 1933, when Prohibition rather unsuccessfully held America in its grip. West End was (and is) so close to the U.S. mainland that rum-running became a lucrative business, with booze flowing out of West End by day and into Florida by night. No surprise, then, that Al Capone was supposedly a frequent visitor here.

Villages along the way to West End have colorful names like **Hawksbill Creek.** For a glimpse of local life, try to visit the **fish market** along the harbor. You'll pass some thriving harbor areas, too, but the vessels you'll see will be oil tankers, not rumrunners. Don't expect too many historic buildings en route.

Eight Mile Rock is a hamlet of mostly ramshackle houses that stretches along both sides of the road. At **West End,** you come to an abrupt stop. By far the most compelling developments here are associated with **Old Bahama Bay** (p. 152), a good spot for a meal, a drink, and a look at what might one day become one of the most important real-estate developments in The Bahamas.

7

Bimini, the Berry Islands & Andros

In this chapter, we begin a journey through the Out Islands—a very different place from the major tourist developments of Nassau, Cable Beach, Paradise Island, and Freeport/Lucaya.

Bimini, the Berry Islands, and Andros are each unique. Bimini is famous and overrun with tourists, particularly in summer, but visitors will have the Berry Islands practically to themselves. These two island chains to the north and west of Nassau could be called the "westerly islands" because they, along with Grand Bahama, lie at the northwestern fringe of The Bahamas. They are the closest islands to Florida.

In contrast, much larger Andros is southwest of Nassau and is, in many ways, the most fascinating place in The Bahamas. The story goes that mysterious creatures once inhabited this series of islands laced with creeks and dense forests.

Each of the three island chains attracts a different type of visitor. **Bimini,** just 81km (50 miles) off Florida's east coast, and the setting for Hemingway's *Islands in the Stream,* lures big-game fishermen, yachters from Miami, and drug dealers from elsewhere in Florida. (The proximity to the U.S. mainland helps make drug smuggling big business here.) Bimini is home to world-famous sportfishing, excellent yachting and cruising, and some good scuba diving. Anglers will find seas swarming with tuna, dolphinfish, amberjack, white and blue marlin, swordfish, barracuda, and shark, along with many other varieties. Bonefish are also plentiful around the flats off the coast of Alice Town, the capital, but the blue marlin is the prize—Bahamians think so highly of this fish that they even put it on their $100 bill. Scuba divers can see black coral trees over the Bimini Wall and reefs off Victory Cay.

The **Berry Islands** might attract the weary Bill Gates or Steve Forbes types. It also draws fishermen, but this string of islands, which has only 700 residents, is mainly for escapists—*rich* escapists. The islands' very limited accommodations (some of which used to be private clubs) lie near the Tongue of the Ocean, home of the big-game fish.

Andros, the nation's largest island, is largely uninhabited. If The Bahamas still has an unexplored wilderness, this is it. The island's forest and mangrove swamps are home to a wide variety of birds and animals, including the Bahamian boa constrictor and the 2m-long (6½-ft.) iguana. The Bahamian national bird, the West Indian flamingo, can also be spotted during migration in late spring and summer. The waters off Andros are home to a wondrous barrier reef, the third largest in the world and a diver's dream. The reef plunges 167km (104 miles) to a narrow drop-off known as the Tongue of the Ocean.

Andros's mysterious blue holes, another diver's delight, are formed when subterranean caves fill with seawater, causing the ceiling to collapse and expose clear, deep pools. Few come here anymore looking for Sir Henry Morgan's pirate treasure, said to be buried in one of the caves off Morgan's Bluff on the north tip of the island. But Andros does attract anglers, mostly because it is known for its world-class fishing.

1 Bimini ★

Bimini is still known as the big-game fishing capital of the world, and fishermen come here throughout the year to fish in flats, on reefs, and in streams. Ernest Hemingway came to write and fish. It was here that he wrote much of *To Have and Have Not,* and his novel *Islands in the Stream* put Bimini on the map. Regrettably, fishing isn't what it used to be in Papa's day, and such species as marlin, swordfish, and tuna have been dangerously overfished.

Located 81km (50 miles) east of Miami, Bimini consists of a number of islands, islets, and cays, including North and South Bimini, the main tourist areas. You'll most often encounter the word "Bimini," but it is more proper to say "The Biminis," since North Bimini and South Bimini are two distinct islands, separated by a narrow ocean passage. Ferries shuttle between the two. The majority of the region's development took place on North Bimini, mostly in **Alice Town.** North Bimini's western side is a long stretch of lovely beachfront.

Off North Bimini, in 9m (30 ft.) of water, are some large hewn-stone formations that some people say came from the lost continent of Atlantis. Divers find the reefs laced with conch, lobster, coral, and many tropical fish.

Bimini's location off the Florida coast is where the Gulf Stream meets the Bahama Banks. This fact has made Bimini a favorite cruising ground for America's yachting set, who follow the channel between North and South Bimini into a spacious, sheltered harbor, where they can stock up on food, drink, fuel, and supplies at well-equipped marinas. From here, they can set off to cruise the cays that begin south of South Bimini. Each has its own special appeal, beginning with Turtle Rocks and stretching to South Cat Cay (the latter of which is uninhabited). Along the way, you'll pass Holm Cay, Gun Cay, and North Cat Cay.

Hook-shaped North Bimini is 12km (7½ miles) long and, combined with South Bimini, it makes up a landmass of only 23 sq. km (9 sq. miles). That's why Alice Town looks so crowded. Another reason is that much of Bimini is privately owned; despite pressure from the Bahamian government, the landholders have not sold their acreage, and Bimini can't "spread out" until they do. At Alice Town, the land is so narrow that you can walk "from sea to shining sea" in just a short time. Most of Bimini's population of some 1,600 people lives in Alice Town; other hamlets include Bailey Town and Porgy Bay.

Although winter is usually high season in The Bahamas, visitors flock to Bimini's calmer summer waters, which are better for fishing. Winter, especially from mid-December to mid-March, is quieter, and Bimini has never tried to develop a resort structure that would attract more winter visitors. If you go to Bimini, you'll hear a lot of people mention **Cat Cay** (not to be confused with Cat Island in the Southern Bahamas). You can stay overnight at Cat Cay's marina, which lies 13km (8 miles) off South Bimini; transient slips are available.

Bimini

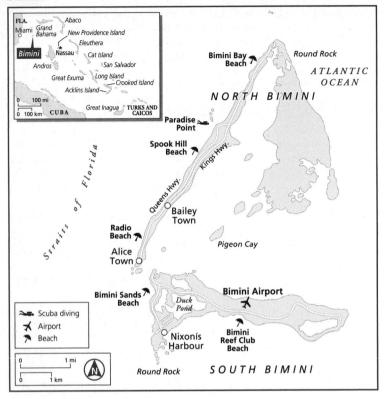

The island is the domain of **Cat Cay Yacht Club** (© **242/347-3565;** www.catcay club.com), whose initiation fee is a cool US$25,000 (£12,500). This privately owned island—attracting titans of industry and famous families—is for the exclusive use of Cat Cay Club members and their guests. At their leisure, they can enjoy the golf course, tennis, a large marina, white-sand beaches, and club facilities such as restaurants and bars. Many wealthy Americans have homes on the island, which has a private airstrip.

GETTING THERE

Note: A passport or an original birth certificate or a voter's registration card with a government-issued picture ID is required for entry to Bimini (bring your passport to be on the safe side), and an outbound (return) ticket also must be presented to Bahamian Customs before you will be permitted entry.

BY PLANE   The island's only airstrip is at the southern tip of South Bimini, a time-consuming transfer and ferryboat ride away from Alice Town on North Bimini, where most of the archipelago's hotels and yacht facilities are.

The best way to avoid this transfer is to fly for 20 to 30 minutes via **Chalk's International Airlines** (© **877/924-2557;** www.flychalks.com). The airline has a small fleet of 17-passenger amphibious aircraft that depart from Ft. Lauderdale/Hollywood International Airport and land in the waters near Alice Town. The baggage allowance per passenger is 30 pounds; if you're carrying heavy gear, you'll be hit with overweight charges. *Note:* Chalk's doesn't allow any hand luggage on board—every piece must be weighed and checked in.

Also, **Island Air** (℃ **800/444-9904** or 954/359-9942; www.islandaircharters.com) flies four times a week from Fort Lauderdale to South Bimini. Finally, **Western Air** (℃ **242/347-4100;** www.westernairbahamas.com) wings in from Nassau's domestic air terminal to South Bimini.

BY BOAT   In the old days, the way to get from Nassau to Bimini was by a slow-moving boat. You can still do it, but it'll take you 12 hours on the MV *Sherice M,* which leaves from Potter's Cay Dock in Nassau and stops at Cat Cay and Bimini. The vessel leaves Nassau Thursdays at 2pm. For details about departure, call the dock master at **Potter's Cay Dock** in Nassau (℃ **242/393-1064**).

GETTING AROUND

If you've taken our advice and traveled lightly to Bimini, you can walk to your hotel from where the seaplanes land in Alice Town. If not, a small minibus will transport you for US$2 (£1) per person.

If you arrive at the small airport on South Bimini, you'll need to pay for a US$5 (£2.50) taxi and ferry ride to Alice Town.

You won't need a car on Bimini—and you won't find a car-rental agency here. Most people walk to where they want to go (though your hotel may be able to arrange a minibus tour or rent you a bike or golf cart). The walk runs up and down **King's Highway,** which has no sidewalks. It's so narrow that two automobiles have a tough time squeezing by. Be careful walking along this highway, especially at night, when drivers might not see you.

This road, lined with low-rise buildings, splits Alice Town on North Bimini. If you're the beachcombing type, stick to the side bordering the Gulf Stream so that you can find the best beaches. The harborside contains a handful of inns (most of which are reviewed in this chapter), along with marinas and docks where supplies are unloaded. You'll see many Floridians arriving on yachts.

FAST FACTS: Bimini

Banks **The Royal Bank of Canada** has a branch office in Alice Town (℃ **242/ 347-3031**) with an **ATM,** open Monday to Thursday 9:30am to 3pm, Friday 9:30am to 4:30pm.

Clothing If you're going to Bimini in winter, take along a windbreaker for those occasional chilly nights.

Customs & Immigration The Chalk's flight from Miami stops right near the Alice Town office of **Customs and Immigration** (℃ **242/347-3100** for Customs, **242/347-3446** for Immigration) for The Bahamas. There's only one Immigration officer, plus another Customs official.

In Miami, you will have been handed a Bahamian Immigration Card to fill out, and you must carry a passport.

Drugs The rumrunners of the Prohibition era have now given way to those smuggling illegal drugs into the U.S. from The Bahamas. Because of its proximity to the mainland, Bimini, as is no secret to anyone, is now a major drop-off point for drugs, many on route from Colombia. If not intercepted by the U.S. Coast Guard, these drugs find their way to Florida and eventually to the rest of America.

Both buying and selling illegal drugs, such as cocaine and marijuana, is an extremely risky business in The Bahamas. You may be approached by dealers on Bimini, some of whom are actually undercover agents. If caught with illegal drugs, you face immediate imprisonment.

Emergencies To call the **police** or report a fire, dial ⓒ **919**.

Medical Care Nurses, a doctor, and a dentist are on the island, as is the **North Bimini Medical Clinic** (ⓒ **242/347-2210**). However, for serious medical emergencies, patients are usually airlifted to either Miami or Nassau. Helicopters can land in the well-lit baseball field on North Bimini.

Visitor Information There's a branch of **The Bahamas Ministry of Tourism** in Bimini's Government Building, Queens Highway, Alice Town (ⓒ **242/347-3529**). It's open Monday to Friday 9am to 5pm.

WHERE TO STAY

Accommodations in Bimini are extremely limited, and it's almost impossible to get a room during one of the big fishing tournaments unless you've reserved way in advance. Inns are cozy and simple; many are owned and operated by a family (chances are, your innkeeper's surname will be Brown). Furnishings are often timeworn, the paint chipped. No one puts on airs here; the dress code, even in the evening, is very simple and relaxed. From wherever you're staying in Alice Town, it's usually easy to walk to another hotel for dinner or drinks.

Big John's Conch Shell Bar & Hotel *Value*   Get a whiff of local life by staying atop this bar in one of the attractively furnished and remodeled bedrooms, most of which have ocean views. Filled with local flavor, Big John's employs part of the staff that used to work at the Compleat Angler, which was so beloved by Hemingway. Even the local band, the Hypnotics, moved to Big John's after the big fire that felled the Compleat Angler.

Downstairs is a laid-back lounge serving the island's best rum punches. Upstairs, you live in comparative luxury (at least for Bimini). Sliding glass doors open onto the view of the bayfront, and part of the decor consists of antique nautical furniture or closets fashioned from cargo netting.

King's Hwy. Bimini, The Bahamas. ⓒ 242/347-3117. www.bigjohnshotel.com. 7 units. Year-round US$125–US$150 (£63–£75) double. No credit cards. **Amenities:** Bar. *In room:* A/C, TV, no phone.

Bimini Bay Resort 🌴🌴   This is the first luxury resort to have emerged in years (it opened in 2007) to give the Bimini Big Game Resort (see below) some serious competition. When it settles in and realizes all its goals—one of them being to have 1,700 rooms by 2013—it should be the finest resort Bimini has ever seen. Other plans call for a state-of-the-art casino, with a full complement of slots, roulette, blackjack, and baccarat keno, plus an up-to-the-minute sports book that allows wagers on international contests.

Life here is like residing in a tropical condo, with rattan furnishings, Bahamian art, and contemporary kitchenettes. If that weren't enough, you can patronize the island's best restaurant (Casa Lyon; see p. 178) or sail your yacht into a 780-slip marina. Lunch is taken at the grill by the infinity pool.

King's Hwy. (north of Bailey Town), Bimini, The Bahamas. © 242/347-2900 or 305/513-0506. Fax 242/347-2312. www.biminibayresort.com. 300 units. Year-round US$350–US$550 (£175–£275) 1-bedroom unit, US$500–US$550 (£250–£275) 2-bedroom unit, from US$850 (£425) 3-bedroom unit. AE, MC, V. **Amenities:** 2 restaurants; 2 bars; beachfront; outdoor pool; watersports; bikes; Internet in lobby; laundry service. *In room:* A/C, TV, kitchen.

Bimini Big Game Resort & Yacht Club 🦀🦀   The chosen watering hole of big-game fishermen since the 1950s, this resort is better than ever following multimillion-dollar renovations. Its 81-slip marina often makes it a favorite stopover with the yachting crowd from Florida's east coast. The resort's restoration has been called a rebirth, and its patrons—mainly boaters, divers, eco-adventurers, and the deep-sea and bonefishing elite—have remained loyal. The resort and marina facilities have been improved, with the guest rooms and dining and drinking facilities getting a complete overhaul. Accommodations are now well-furnished, both the guest units in the main building and those in surrounding cottages. All rooms have patios or porches opening onto the marina and the club's swimming pool; the ground-floor cottages are more spacious than the standard bedrooms and have tiny kitchenettes and refrigerators.

If you want to charcoal-broil your catch at the end of the day (hotel staff can arrange all sorts of fishing charters), you can use one of the outdoor grills. This hotel is also the island's best place for food and entertainment (see "Where to Dine" and "Bimini After Dark," below).

King's Hwy., Alice Town, Bimini, The Bahamas. © 800/737-1007 in the U.S. or 242/347-3391. Fax 242/347-3392. www.biminibiggame.com. 51 units. Year-round US$150–US$205 (£75–£103) double, US$175–US$250 (£88–£125)

Island in the Stream

Nevil Norton Stuart, a Bahamian, came to Bimini in the late 1920s and purchased the Fountain of Youth, a Prohibition-era bar, and renamed it the **Bimini Big Game Resort & Marina.** In 1940, Stuart reclaimed land in Bimini Harbor, constructed a marina, and added several cottages along with a desalination plant. Thus began the legend of one of the world's most highly publicized sportfishing meccas.

Film stars, including Judy Garland and Sir Anthony Hopkins, have lodged at the club; Martin Luther King, Jr., visited twice. Of course, no one immortalized the island as much as Ernest Hemingway, who called it "my island in the stream."

Today, the complex boasts more than 50 rooms, including cottages and penthouses, and it's owned by the rum maker Bacardi International. In the 100-slip marina are enormous sportfishing boats, worth more than several million dollars each, proudly standing alongside simple outboard-powered runabouts.

cottage. Extra person US$25 (£13). AE, MC, V. **Amenities:** Restaurant; 3 bars; pool; all nonsmoking rooms. *In room:* A/C, TV, kitchenette (in some), minibar (in some), fridge (in some), hair dryer.

Bimini Blue Water Resort Ltd. ✺ *Finds* This is essentially a resort complex for sportfishermen, with complete dockside services and 32 modern slips—one of the country's finest places of its kind. The main building is a white-frame, waterfront Bahamian guesthouse, the Anchorage, where Michael Lerner, the noted fisherman, used to live. It's at the top of the hill, with a dining room and bar from where you can look out to the ocean (see "Where to Dine," below). The midsize bedrooms contain double beds, wood-paneled walls, white furniture, and picture-window doors that lead to private balconies.

The Marlin Cottage, although much altered, was one of Hemingway's retreats in the 1930s. He used it as a main setting in *Islands in the Stream.* It has three bedrooms, three bathrooms, a large living room, and two porches.

King's Hwy., Alice Town, Bimini, The Bahamas. ✆ 242/347-3166. Fax 242/347-3293. 14 units. Year-round US$90 (£45) double, US$190 (£95) suite, US$285 (£143) cottage. MC, V. **Amenities:** Restaurant; bar; pool; babysitting. *In room:* A/C, TV, fridge, iron, no phone.

Sea Crest Hotel & Marina *Kids* Built in 1981 and upgraded every year since, this hotel lies right on the main highway and was the first place to give the Bimini Big Game Resort (p. 177) some real competition. It's still not as good as that traditional leader, but the price is right. Rooms in this three-story hotel, which looks like a motel, are best on the third floor due to better ocean or bay views. Rooms don't have phones, and many are small, with rather cramped bathrooms (though each does have a shower stall), but they're comfortably furnished in a simple, traditional way. Accommodations open onto small balconies. Much better, larger, and more comfortable are the units in the new building beside the marina. Since the location is right in the heart of Alice Town, you can generally walk where you want to go. The Sea Crest is a family favorite, and children under 12 stay free. There's an on-site restaurant, Captain Bob's, which is independently operated and serves good seafood. The hotel is also a favorite of the boating crowd because it offers an 18-berth marina.

King's Hwy., Alice Town, Bimini, The Bahamas. ✆ 242/347-3071. Fax 242/347-3495. 14 units. Year-round US$99–US$135 (£50–£68) double, US$230 (£115) 2-bedroom suite, US$329 (£165) 3-bedroom suite. Extra person US$15 (£7.50). MC, V. **Amenities:** Marina. *In room:* A/C, TV, fridge, no phone.

WHERE TO DINE

Anchorage Dining Room SEAFOOD/BAHAMIAN/AMERICAN This dining room overlooks Alice Town's harbor; you can see the ocean through picture windows. The modern, paneled room is filled with captain's chairs and Formica tables. You might begin your dinner with conch chowder and then follow with one of the tempting seafood dishes, including spiny broiled lobster or perhaps a cracked conch. They also make a good fried Bahamian chicken and a tender New York sirloin. The cooking is straightforward and reliable, and never pretends to be more than just that.

In Blue Water Resort, King's Hwy., Alice Town. ✆ 242/347-3166. Main courses US$14–US$29 (£7–£15). AE, MC, V. Wed–Mon 6–10pm.

Casa Lyon ✺ AMERICAN/BAHAMIAN This is Bimini's best restaurant. It's associated with the huge Bimini Bay Resort (p. 176). The dining venue is divided between a covered outdoor veranda with views of the sea and an enclosed, all-white, air-conditioned dining room with big windows. Starters include shrimp dijonnaise with a brandy-and-mustard-flavored cream sauce, jumbo lump crab cakes, tuna tartare, and skewered beef satay with a coconut-flavored curry sauce. Main courses include steamed Nassau grouper with Bahamian peas 'n' rice, blackened mahimahi with tropical salsa, and jerk-flavored New York strip steak. The perfect dessert? Consider guava duff a la mode.

In Bimini Bay Resort, King's Hwy., North Bimini. ℂ **242/347-2900.** Reservations not necessary. Main courses US$27–US$46 (£14–£23). AE, DC, DISC, MC, V. Daily 6–10:30pm.

The Tackle Box BAHAMIAN/INTERNATIONAL   Set in the Bimini Big Game Resort (p. 177), this restaurant is perhaps the island's most popular. Expect fine views, as it's located directly adjacent to the marina, which is filled with dozens of world-class fishing boats. Don't expect grand or even particularly esoteric cuisine, as the menu might remind you of what's available at a bar and grill in neighboring Florida. Lunches are simpler than dinners, with salads, simple grilled dishes, burgers, chicken fingers, soups, and stews. If lunches are leisurely, then dinners are even more so, but with a wider choice of steaks, lobster dishes, pastas, and fresh fish, especially wahoo, mahimahi, swordfish, and tuna. You also have a choice of dining at a slightly more expensive on-site restaurant, **The Clubhouse,** in a building of its own a few paces away.

In Bimini Big Game Resort, King's Hwy., Alice Town. ℂ **242/347-3391.** Reservations recommended. Main courses lunch US$5–US$9 (£2.50–£4.50), dinner US$19–US$30 (£9.50–£15). AE, MC, V. Sun–Thurs 7am–10pm; Fri–Sat 7am–1am.

WATERSPORTS & OTHER OUTDOOR ACTIVITIES
BEACHES

Bimini's beaches are all clearly marked and signposted from the highways. The one closest to Alice Town, **Radio Beach,** is the only one on Bimini with toilets, vendors, and snack bars. It's set adjacent to Alice Town's piers and wharves; consequently, it's the island's most popular and crowded beach.

About 3km (2 miles) north of Alice Town, facing west, is **Spook Hill Beach.** Both it and its cousin, **Bimini Bay Beach,** about 4km (2½ miles) north of Alice Town, offer sparser crowds, worthy snorkeling, and lots of sunshine. Both are sandy-bottomed and comfortable on your feet. Many local residents prefer **Bimini Bay Beach,** which is wider than any other on the island.

On South Bimini, the two favorites are the west-facing **Bimini Sands Beach,** a sandy-bottomed stretch that's immediately south of the channel separating North from South Bimini; and **Bimini Reef Club Beach,** south of the airport, where offshore snorkeling is especially worthwhile, thanks to very clear waters.

Finds Ruins of the Roaring Twenties

A major attraction for both snorkelers and divers, not to mention rainbow-hued fish, is the wreck of a ship called *Sapona,* which has lain hard aground in 4.5m (15 ft.) of water between South Bimini and Cat Cay ever since it was blown here by a hurricane in 1929. In the heyday of the Roaring Twenties, the ship, which was commissioned by Henry Ford, served as a private club and speak-easy. You'll have to take a boat to reach the site, which is shallow enough that even snorkelers can see it. Local dive operators generally include the site in their repertoire.

Fire Guts Hemingway's Favorite Bar

A fire in January 2006 destroyed the Ernest Hemingway Museum and the Compleat Angler Bar, Bimini's number-one tourist attraction. The early morning blaze leveled the wood structure in Alice Town and destroyed photographs and other Papa memorabilia. Hemingway made the Compleat Angler his headquarters on and off from 1935 to 1937 when he was fishing for marlin. He penned parts of *To Have and Have Not* on the site.

FISHING

Ernest Hemingway made fishing here famous, but Zane Grey came this way too, as did Howard Hughes. Richard Nixon used to fish here aboard the posh cruiser of his entrepreneurial friend Charles "Bebe" Rebozo. In Hemingway's wake, fishermen still flock to cast lines in the Gulf Stream and the Bahama Banks.

Of course, everyone's still after the big one, and a lot of world records have been set in this area for marlin, sailfish, swordfish, wahoo, grouper, and tuna. But these fish are becoming evasive, and their dwindling numbers are edging them close to extinction. Fishing folk can spin cast for panfish, boat snapper, yellowtail, and kingfish. Many experts consider stalking bonefish, long a pursuit of baseball great Ted Williams, the sport's toughest challenge.

Five charter boats are available in Bimini for big-game and little-game fishing, with some center-console boats rented for both bottom and reef angling. At least eight bonefishing guides are available, and experienced anglers who have made repeated visits to Bimini know the particular skills of each of these men who will take you for a half- or full day of "fishing in the flats," a local term for bonefishing in the sea-level waterways and estuaries that cut into the island. Most skiffs hold two anglers, and part of the fun in hiring a local guide is to hear his fish tales and other island lore. If a guide tells you that 16-pound bonefish have turned up, he may not be exaggerating—catches that large have really been documented.

Reef and bottom-fishing around Bimini are easier than bonefishing and can be more productive. Numerous species of snapper and grouper can be found, as well as amberjack. This is the simplest and least expensive boat-fishing experience because you need only a local guide, a little boat, tackle, and a lot of bait. Sometimes you can negotiate to go bottom-fishing with a Bahamian, but chances are, he'll ask you to pay for the boat fuel. That night, back at your inn, the cook will serve you the red snapper or grouper you caught that day.

Most hotel owners will tell you to bring your own fishing gear. A couple of small shops do sell some items, but you'd better bring major equipment with you if you're really serious. Bait, of course, can be purchased locally.

At **Bimini Big Game Resort & Yacht Club,** King's Highway, Alice Town (© **242/ 347-3391**), you can charter a 10m Hatteras at US$1,100 (£550) for a full day of fishing, or US$600 (£300) for a half-day. Although this outfitter is your best bet, you can also pick up a list of locals whose boats are available for charter at **Bimini Blue Water Marina,** King's Highway, Alice Town (© **242/347-3166**). Rates for bonefishing are US$300 (£150) per half-day. For deep-sea fishing, charges range from US$500 to US$600 (£250–£300) for a half-day. Full-day experiences start at US$800 (£400), but most experienced fishers choose the half-day option because of the widely spread belief that fish are most abundant and hungriest in the morning.

SCUBA DIVING & SNORKELING

Explore the black-coral gardens and reefs here, plus wrecks, blue holes, and a mysterious stone formation on the bottom of the sea that some claim is part of the lost continent of Atlantis (it's 457m/1,499 ft. offshore in Bimini Bay, under about 6m/20 ft. of water). Bimini waters are known for a breathtaking drop-off at the rim of the continental shelf, an underwater mountain that plunges 600m (1,969 ft.) down.

The finest and most experienced outfitter is **Bimini Undersea,** King's Highway, Alice Town (© **242/347-3089;** www.biminiundersea.com). The people to see here are Bill and Nowdla Keefe. Scuba enthusiasts pay US$59 (£30) for a one-tank dive, US$99 (£50) for a two-tank dive. Snorkelers are charged US$39 (£20) for a single trip, including use of mask and fins. All-inclusive dive packages are also available. For reservations, call © **800/348-4644** or 305/653-5572.

Bimini Undersea also gives you the chance to swim with dolphins in the wild two or three times a week, depending on demand. Most excursions take from 3 to 4 hours and cost US$119 (£60) for ages 13 and up or US$99 (£50) for ages 8 to 12. Before you go, though, know that this activity has its critics. To learn more about that controversy, visit the Whale and Dolphin Conservation Society's website at www.wdcs.org.

EXPLORING BIMINI

At North Bimini's southern tip, ramshackle **Alice Town** is all that many visitors ever see of the islands, since it's where the major hotels are. You can see the whole town in an hour or two. **Bimini Big Game Resort & Yacht Club,** on King's Highway, offers some of the town's best duty-free liquor buys. If you're a souvenir collector, ask at the front office for T-shirts, sunglasses, coffee mugs, and hats logoed with the resort's catchphrase—Big Game.

As you're exploring the island, you may want to stop off at the **Bimini Straw Market,** next door to the Bahamas Customs Building, where you'll usually find two dozen vendors. Strike up a conversation with some islanders, and perhaps pick up a souvenir.

If you're curious, drop into the little **Bimini Museum** (© **242/347-3038**) on King's Highway, a sort of grab bag of mementos left behind by visiting celebrities. The museum owns the 1964 immigration card of Martin Luther King, Jr., a domino set left by frequent visitor Adam Clayton Powell (the former New York congressman),

---

Fun Fact Myths of Bimini

These islands have long been shrouded in myths, none more far-fetched than the one claiming that the lost continent of **Atlantis** lies off North Bimini's shore. This legend grew because of the weirdly shaped rock formations that lie submerged in about 6m (20 ft.) of water near the coast. Pilots flying over North Bimini have reported what they envisioned as an undersea "lost highway." This myth continues, attracting many scuba divers interested in exploring these rocks.

Ponce de León came to South Bimini looking for that celebrated **Fountain of Youth.** He never found it, but people still come here to search. In the late 19th century, a religious Christian sect reportedly came here to take the waters—supposedly a bubbling fountain or spring. If you arrive on South Bimini and seem interested enough, a local guide (for a fee) will be happy to show you "the exact spot" where the Fountain of Youth once bubbled.

(*Moments*   **A Drink at the End of the World**

Everybody eventually makes his or her way to the **End of the World Bar** (no phone number) on King's Highway in Alice Town. When you get here, you may think you're in the wrong place—it's just a waterfront shack with sawdust or sand on the floor and graffiti everywhere. The late New York congressman Adam Clayton Powell put this bar on the map in the 1960s. Between stints in Washington battling Congress and preaching at Harlem's Abyssinian Baptist Church, the controversial politician could be found sitting here. While the bar doesn't attract the media attention it did in Powell's heyday, it's still a local favorite. Open daily from 9am to 3am.

---

and Ernest Hemingway's fishing log and vintage fishing films. Also on exhibit are other island artifacts such as rum kegs. The location in a two-story 1920s house is a 4-minute walk from the seaplane ramp. The museum is open Monday to Saturday 9am to 9pm, Sunday noon to 9pm. Admission is US$2 (£1), but elementary-school-age children get in for free.

Queen's Highway runs up North Bimini's western side, and as you head north along it, you'll see that it's lined with beautiful beachfront. **King's Highway** runs through Alice Town and continues north. It's bordered by houses painted gold, lime, buttercup yellow, and a pink that gleams in the bright sunshine.

At some point, you may notice the ruins of Bimini's first hotel, **Bimini Bay Rod and Gun Club,** sitting unfinished on its own beach. Built in the early 1920s, it flourished until a hurricane wiped it out later that decade. It was never rebuilt, though developers once made an attempt.

To visit **South Bimini,** hire a taxi for about US$5 (£2.50) per person to see the island's limited attractions, which, at least to our knowledge, do not include Ponce de León's legendary Fountain of Youth. There's not a lot to see, but you're likely to hear tall tales worth the cab fare. You can also stop off at some lovely, uncrowded beaches.

BIMINI AFTER DARK

In Bimini, you can dance to a Goombay drumbeat or try to find some disco music. Most people have a leisurely dinner, drink (a lot) in one of the local watering holes, and go back to their hotel rooms by midnight so they can get up early to continue pursuing the elusive "big one" the next morning. Every bar in Alice Town is likely to claim that it was Hemingway's favorite. He did hit quite a few of them, in fact. There's rarely a cover charge anywhere unless some special entertainment is being offered.

Beginning at midmorning and lasting at least until midnight, the bars at **Bimini Big Game Resort & Yacht Club** (p. 177) are where to be; tall fish tales fill the air. **The Tackle Box** (p. 179) starts serving its famed conch pizza at noon. Play a hand of cards here or watch your favorite sports program on one of the TVs; this is the best place to entertain yourself during a lazy day in Bimini. The poolside **Barefoot Bar,** open from midmorning to late afternoon, serves favorite island drinks and ice-cold beer. Off the main dining room is the **Clubhouse,** featuring live bands on occasion.

2 The Berry Islands (⋆

A dangling chain of cays and islets on the eastern edge of the Great Bahama Bank, the unspoiled and serene Berry Islands begin 56km (35 miles) northwest of New Providence (Nassau), 242km (150 miles) east of Miami. This 30-island archipelago is known to sailors, fishermen, yachtspeople, Jack Nicklaus, and a Rockefeller or two, as well as to devoted beachcombers who love its pristine sands.

As a fishing center, the Berry Islands are second only to Bimini. At the tip of the Tongue of the Ocean (aka TOTO), it has world-record-setting big-game fish and endless flats where bonefish congregate. In the "Berries," you can find your own tropical paradise islet and enjoy—*sans* wardrobe—totally isolated white-sand beaches and palm-fringed shores. Some of The Bahamas' best shell-collecting spots are on the Berry Island beaches and in their shallow-water flats.

The main islands are, from north to south, Great Stirrup Cay, Cistern Cay, Great Harbour Cay, Anderson Cay, Haines Cay, Hoffmans Cay, Bond's Cay, Sandy Cay, Whale Cay, and Chub Cay. One of the very small cays, north of Frazev's Hog Cay and Whale Cay, has, in our opinion, the most unappetizing name: Cockroach Cay.

The largest island is **Great Harbour Cay,** which sprawls over 1,520 hectares (3,756 acres) of sand, rock, and scrub. Development here received a great deal of publicity when Douglas Fairbanks, Jr., was connected with its investors. It became a multimillion-dollar resort for jet setters who occupied waterfront town houses and villas overlooking the golf course or marina. Cary Grant, Brigitte Bardot, and other stars have all romped on the 12km (7½ miles) of almost solitary beachfront.

Bond's Cay, a bird sanctuary in the south, and tiny Frazer's Hog Cay (stock is still raised here) are both privately owned. An English company used to operate a coconut and sisal plantation on Whale Cay, also near the southern tip. Sponge fishermen and their families inhabit some of the islands.

BERRY ISLANDS ESSENTIALS

GETTING THERE   Great Harbour Cay is an official point of entry for The Bahamas if you're flying from a foreign territory such as the U.S. You can get here only via charter flights from South Florida, making these some of the most inconvenient islands to reach in all of The Bahamas. **Island Express** (✆ **954/359-0380**) operates charters from Fort Lauderdale, winging in to **Chub Cay Airport.**

If you're contemplating the **mail-boat** sea-voyage route, the **MV** *Captain Gurthdean* leaves Potter's Cay Dock in Nassau once a week on Tuesday at 7pm, heading for the Berry Islands. Inquire at the **Potter's Cay Dock** for an up-to-the-minute report (contact the dock master at ✆ **242/393-1064**).

FAST FACTS   The **Great Harbour Cay Medical Clinic** is at Bullock's Harbour on Great Harbour Cay (✆ **242/367-8400**). The **police station** is also at Bullock's Harbour (✆ **242/367-8344** or 367-8104).

GREAT HARBOUR CAY

An estimated 700 residents live on Great Harbour Cay, making it the most populated island of the Berry chain. Its main settlement is **Bullock's Harbour,** which might be called the capital of the Berry Islands. The cay is about 2.5km (1½ miles) wide and some 13km (8 miles) long. A grocery store and some restaurants are about all you'll find in town. Most visitors arrive to stay at **Great Harbour Inn** (see below).

Great Harbour Cay lies between Grand Bahama and New Providence. It's 97km (60 miles) northwest of Nassau and 242km (150 miles) east of Miami, about an hour away from Miami by plane or a half-day by powerboat. Unlike most islands in The Bahamas, the island isn't flat, but is comprised of rolling hills.

Deep-sea fishing possibilities abound here, with billfish, dolphinfish, king mackerel, and wahoo. Light-tackle bottom-fishing is also good; you can net yellowtail, snapper, barracuda, triggerfish, and plenty of grouper. Bonefishing here is among the best in the world. Great Harbour Cay's marina is an excellent facility, with some 80 slips and all the amenities. Some of Florida's fanciest yachts pull in here.

When you tire of fishing, relax on 13km (8 miles) of gorgeous beaches, play the 9-hole golf course designed by Joe Lee, or try your backhand on one of four clay tennis courts.

WHERE TO STAY

Great Harbour Inn   Opening onto the water, this all-suite inn offers private verandas from which to take in the views. This is a rather casual place, as the furnishings have seen a bit of wear and tear, but if you're staying on island, this is your choice. Each rental unit is furnished with a small kitchen, and each comes with a private bathroom, a luxury in this part of the world. Two of the suites are much larger than the others. Don't expect a lot of frills or pampering, but come here just to enjoy the fishing and beaches and you should be fine. The inn is located for convenient access to the main marketplace and a few local eateries.

Bullock's Harbour, Great Harbour Cay, Berry Islands, The Bahamas. ℂ 242/367-8117. www.greatharbourinn.itgo.com. 4 units. US$75–US$125 (£38–£63) double. No credit cards. **Amenities:** Laundry service. *In room:* Ceiling fans, no phone.

CHUB CAY

Named after a species of fish that thrives in nearby waters, Chub Cay is well-known to sport-fishing enthusiasts. A self-contained hideaway with a devoted clientele, it's the southernmost of the Berry Islands, separating the Florida mainland from Nassau's commercial frenzy.

Chub Cay's development began in the late 1950s as a strictly private (and rather spartan) enclave of a group of Texas-based anglers and investors. It was originally uninhabited, but over the years, a staff was imported, dormitory-style housing was built, and the island's most famous man-made feature (its state-of-the-art 90-slip marina) was constructed in the 392-hectare (969-acre) island's sheltered lagoon.

Chub Cay is today a tranquil, scrub-covered sand spit with awesome amounts of marine hardware, a dozen posh private homes, the marina, and a complex of buildings devoted to the **Chub Cay Resort & Marina** (p. 185). Today, membership in this club begins at around US$2,500 (£1,250) per year and grants reduced rates for marina-slip rental, boat repairs, and hotel-room and villa rental. Nonmembers, however, are welcome to use the facilities and rent rooms at the rates listed below.

A liquor store and a yachters' commissary are on the island, as well as a marine-supply store and a concrete runway for landing anything up to and including a 737. Most visitors reach Chub Cay by private yacht from Florida, but if you prefer to charter your fishing craft on Chub Cay, you'll find a mini-armada of suitable craft at your disposal. **Island Express Airlines** (ℂ **954/359-0380**) flies charter flights to Chub Cay from Fort Lauderdale. Chub Cay Resort & Marina's desk staff can help book charter flights for you. If you do opt to fly here, travel light; no more than 40 pounds of baggage is allowed per passenger.

The water temperature around Chub Cay averages a warm 80° to 85°F (27°–29°C) year-round, even at relatively deep depths. There's only a small tidal change and, under normal conditions, no swell or noticeable current in offshore waters. The waters are incredibly clear, making for great snorkeling.

WHERE TO STAY & DINE
Chub Cay Marina & Resort ⓐ   This is a far better and more luxurious choice than Great Harbour Inn (p. 184). Some of Florida's greatest yachts pull into the 110-slip marina where immigration services are available, as is fuel. New for 2008 is a luxurious clubhouse, plus an infinity pool and a tiki bar. Sportsmen from the East Coast flock here because of the resort's location at the Tongue of the Ocean and the Great Bahama Bank, lying at the archipelago's southernmost tip near sandy beaches.

The resort is still in transition, with more improvements likely to occur during the life of this edition. But currently, you can stay in luxuriously furnished villas or marina town houses. When completed, Chub Cay should be the most opulent property that the Berry islands have ever seen. Villas, when completed, will include two-, three-, four-, and five-bedroom homes built in authentic British colonial style.

There's a restaurant, the **Harbour House,** with its own bar, and the **Hilltop Bar,** which sits at the island's highest elevation. The latter has pool tables and a TV for sports broadcasts.

Chub Cay, Berry Islands, The Bahamas. ⓒ 877/234-2482 or 242/325-1490. Fax 242/325-7086. www.chubcay.com. 16 units (subject to change). US$650 (£325) 2-bedroom villa; US$945 (£473) 3-bedroom cottage. AE, MC, V. **Amenities:** Restaurant; 3 bars; 2 pools; 2 tennis courts; babysitting; laundry service. *In room:* A/C, TV, kitchenette (in some), beverage maker (in some), hair dryer, iron (in some), no phone.

3 Andros ⓐⓐ

The largest island in The Bahamas, Andros is an excellent budget destination. One of the Western Hemisphere's biggest unexplored tracts of land is still quite mysterious. Mostly flat, its 5,957 sq. km (2,300 sq. miles) are riddled with lakes and creeks, and most of the local residents—who still indulge in fire dances and go on wild boar hunts on occasion—live along the shore.

Andros is 161km (100 miles) long and 64km (40 miles) wide. Its interior consists of a dense tropical forest, really rugged bush, and many mangroves. The marshy and relatively uninhabited west coast is called "the Mud," and the east coast is paralleled for 193km (120 miles) by the world's third-largest underwater barrier reef, which drops more than 167km (104 miles) into the Tongue of the Ocean, or TOTO. On the eastern shore, this "tongue" is 229km (142 miles) long and 1,000 fathoms (2.9km/1¾ miles) deep.

Lying 274km (170 miles) southeast of Miami and 48km (30 miles) west of Nassau, Andros is actually comprised of three major land areas: North Andros, Middle Andros, and South Andros. In spite of its size, Andros is very thinly populated (its residents number only around 5,000), although the tourist population swells it a bit. The temperature range here averages from 72° to 85°F (22°–29°C).

You won't find the western side of Andros written about much in yachting guides because tricky shoals render it almost unapproachable by boat. The east coast, however, offers kilometers of unspoiled beaches and is studded with little villages. Lodgings that range from simple guest cottages to dive resorts to fishing camps have been built here. "Creeks" (we'd call them rivers) intersect the island at its midpoint. Also called "bights," they range in length from 8 to 40km (5–25 miles) and are dotted with tiny cays and islets.

The fishing potential at Andros is famous, spawning records for blue marlin catches. Divers and snorkelers find that the coral reefs here are among Earth's most beautiful, and everyone loves the pristine beaches.

Warning: Be sure to bring along plenty of mosquito repellent.

ANDROS ESSENTIALS

GETTING THERE   Reaching Andros is not too difficult. **Western Air** (© 242/377-2222 in the U.S.; www.westernairbahamas.com) has twice-daily 15-minute flights from Nassau to the airport at Andros Town in Central Andros (© 242/368-2759). Airports are also at San Andros in the north (© 242/329-4000), at Mangrove Cay (© 242/369-0003), and at Congo Town in South Andros (© 242/369-2222 or 954/772-9808). **Lynx Air International** (© 888/596-9247; www.lynxair.com) flies from Fort Lauderdale to Congo Town three times per week.

Make sure you know where you're going in Andros. For example, if you land at Congo Town on South Andros and you've booked a hotel in Nicholl's Town, you'll find connections nearly impossible at times (involving both ferryboats and a rough haul across a bad highway).

Andros's few available **taxis** know when the planes from Nassau land and drive out to the airports, hoping to pick up business. Taxis are most often shared, and a typical fare from Andros Town Airport to Small Hope Bay Lodge is about US$30 (£15).

Many locals, along with a few adventurous visitors, use **mail boats** to get to Andros; the trip takes 5 to 7 hours across beautiful waters. North Andros is serviced by the **MV Lisa J. II,** which departs Potter's Cay Dock in Nassau heading for Morgan's Bluff, Mastic Point, and Nicholl's Town on Wednesday, returning to Nassau on Tuesday. The **MV Captain Moxey** departs Nassau on Monday, calling at Long Bay Cays, Kemps Bay, and The Bluff on South Andros; it heads back to Nassau on Wednesday. The **MV Mangrove Cay Express** departs Nassau Wednesday night for a 5½-hour trip to Lisbon Creek, sailing back to Nassau on Monday afternoon. Finally, **MV Lady D** departs Nassau on Wednesday for Fresh Creek, stopping at Spaniard Creek, Blanket Sound, and Browne Sound. The trip takes 5½ hours, and the return voyage to Nassau is on Sunday. For details about sailing and costs, contact the dock master at **Potter's Cay Dock** in Nassau (© 242/393-1064).

A far more luxurious way to go over the waters is aboard *Sea Link* or *Sea Wind* (© 242/323-2166; fax 242/393-7451; www.bahamasferries.com). The *Sea Link* carries 250 passengers, while the *Sea Wind* seats 180, with another 100 seats available on the open-air decks of both vessels. Depending on where you dock on Andros, trip time from Nassau to Fresh Creek takes 1 hour and 45 minutes. From Nassau to Driggs Hill, however, takes 2½ hours.

ORIENTATION   Chances are, your hotel will be in **North Andros,** in either Andros Town or Nicholl's Town. North Andros is the most developed of the three major Andros islands. **Nicholl's Town** is a colorful old settlement with some 600 people and several places serving local foods. Most visitors come to Nicholl's Town to buy supplies at its shopping complex. Directly to the south is **Mastic Point,** which was founded in 1781. If you ask around, you'll be shown to a couple of concrete-sided dives that serve up spareribs and Goombay music. North of Nicholl's Town is **Morgan's Bluff,** namesake of Sir Henry Morgan, a pirate later knighted by the British

Andros

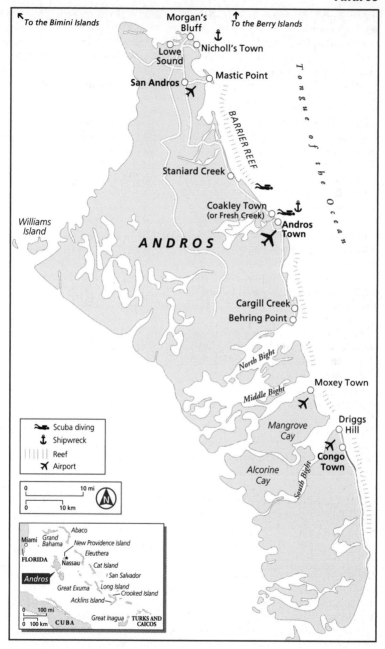

To the Bimini Islands

To the Berry Islands

Morgan's Bluff

Nicholl's Town

Lowe Sound

Mastic Point

San Andros

Staniard Creek

Tongue of the Ocean

BARRIER REEF

Coakley Town (or Fresh Creek)

Andros Town

A N D R O S

Williams Island

Cargill Creek

Behring Point

North Bight

Middle Bight

Moxey Town

Driggs Hill

Mangrove Cay

Congo Town

Alcorine Cay

South Bight

Scuba diving

Shipwreck

Reef

Airport

| 0 | 10 mi |
| 0 | 10 km |

N

Abaco

Miami

Grand Bahama

New Providence Island

Eleuthera

FLORIDA

Nassau

Cat Island

Andros

San Salvador

Great Exuma

Long Island

Crooked Island

Acklins Island

Great Inagua

TURKS AND CAICOS

| 0 | 100 mi |
| 0 | 100 km |

C U B A

monarch. **Andros Town,** with its abandoned docks, is another village, about 47km (29 miles) south of Nicholl's Town. Most visitors come to Andros Town to stay at **Small Hope Bay Lodge** (p. 191) or to avail themselves of its facilities. The biggest retail industry, Androsia batik, is in the area, too (p. 196). The scuba diving—minutes away on the barrier reef—is what lures most visitors to this tiny place; others come here just for the shelling. On the opposite side of the water is **Coakley Town.** If you're driving, before you get to Andros Town, you may want to stop to spend some restful hours on the beach at **Staniard Creek,** another old settlement that feels like it drifted over from the South Seas.

Moving south to the second major landmass, **Central Andros** is smaller than either North or South Andros. The least developed of the three, the island is studded with hundreds upon hundreds of palm trees. The Queen's Highway runs along the eastern coastline, but the only thing about this road that's regal is its name. In some 7km (4⅓ miles), you can see practically the whole island. It's truly sleepy, and for that very reason, many people come here to get away from it all. You won't find much in the way of accommodations—but you will find some (they're listed below).

The third and last major land area, **South Andros,** is the home of the wonderfully named **Congo Town,** where life proceeds at a snail's pace. The Queen's Highway, partially lined with pink-and-white conch shells, runs for about 40km (25 miles) or so. The island, as yet undiscovered, has some of the best beaches in The Bahamas, and you can enjoy them almost by yourself.

Another tiny island, undeveloped **Mangrove Cay,** is an escapist's dream, attracting naturalists and anglers, as well as a few divers. It's separated from Andros's northern and southern sections by bights. The settlements here got electricity and a paved road only in 1989. Mangrove Cay's best place for snorkeling and diving is **Victoria Point Blue Hole** (any local can point you there). Another village (don't blink as you pass through or you'll miss it) is **Moxey Town,** where you're likely to see fishermen unloading conch from fishing boats. Ferries, operated for free by the Bahamian government, ply back and forth over the waters separating Mangrove Cay from South Andros. At the end of the road in North Andros, private arrangements can be made to have a boat take you to Mangrove Cay.

GETTING AROUND   Transportation can be a big problem on Andros. If you have to go somewhere, try to use one of the local **taxis,** though this can be a pricey undertaking.

The few **rental cars** available are in North Andros. These are scarce, owing to the high costs of shipping cars here. The weather also takes a great toll on the cars that are brought in (salty air erodes metal), so no U.S. car-rental agencies are represented. Your best bet is to ask at your hotel to see what's available.

Anyway, it's not really recommended that you drive on Andros because roads are mainly unpaved and in bad condition, and gas stations are hard to find. Outlets for car rentals come and go faster here than anybody can count. Renting a car is less formal, and less organized, than you might be used to.

The concierge at Andros's most upscale hotel, Kamaleme Cay, will arrange a cab or a rental car for you, but frankly, it's all word of mouth and terribly unlicensed and informal, with no options for purchase of additional insurance. Taxi drivers and owners of a handful of battered cars that can be rented will be at the airport in time for the landing of most major flights. You can negotiate a car rental on-site or—perhaps more safely and conveniently—you can hire one of the local taxis to take you around.

Rates run between US$85 and US$100 (£43–£50) per day, plus gas. Be warned that signpostings and road conditions are horrible, but it's hard to get lost because the only road is the north-south, much-rutted thoroughfare known as Queen's Highway.

You may want to rent a **bicycle,** but you'll experience the same bad roads you would in a rental car. Guests of Small Hope Bay Lodge, Chickcharnie, and Mangrove Cay Inn can rent bikes at their hotels.

VISITOR INFORMATION   The **Ministry of Tourism** is located in Andros Town (℃ **242/368-2286**) and is open Monday to Friday 9am to 5pm.

FAST FACTS   Banks are rare on Andros. There's one, **ScotiaBank** (℃ **242/329-2700**), in Nicholl's Town, with an **ATM,** open Monday to Thursday 9:30am to 3pm, and Friday 9:30am to 4:30pm.

The island's post office (℃ **242/329-2034**) is in Nicholl's Town on North Andros. Hours are Monday through Friday from 9am to 4:30pm. Hotel desk staffers will sell you Bahamian stamps. Make sure to mark cards and letters as airmail; otherwise, you'll return home before they do. Each little village on Andros has a store that serves as a post office.

Government-run **medical clinics** are at Nicholl's Town on **North Andros** (℃ **242/329-2055**), at Mangrove Cay on **Central Andros** (℃ **242/369-0089**), and at Kemp's Bay in **South Andros** (℃ **242/369-4849**). To reach the **police,** call ℃ **919** in North Andros, ℃ **242/368-2626** in Central Andros, and ℃ **242/369-4733** in South Andros.

WHERE TO STAY & DINE

At the hotels listed below which have no phones in the guest rooms, phone service is available only at the front desks.

IN STANIARD CREEK

Kamalame Cay ★★★ *Finds*   In 1995, a group of international investors created one of the most exclusive resorts in the Out Islands from the scrub-covered 38-hectare (94-acre) landscape of a private cay off the east coast of Andros Island. Since then, it has discreetly and quietly attracted a clientele of banking moguls and financial wizards from Europe and North America, all of whom come for the superb service, escapist charm, 5km (3 miles) of beaches, and waterborne adventures that are among the best of their kind in The Bahamas. A staff of 30 to 50, some of whom were brought in from other parts of The Bahamas, includes six full-time gardeners, an army of chambermaids and cooks, and a sporting-adventure staff that's ready, willing, and able to bring groups of urban refugees out for scuba, windsurfing, snorkeling, plus deep-sea and bonefishing excursions above one of the world's largest barrier reefs.

Accommodations include a few smaller rooms, tasteful and very comfortable, next to the marina. More opulent are the cottages and suites, all of which lie adjacent to the beach; these are mainly crafted from local coral stone, cedar shingles, tropical-wood timbers, tiles, and, in some cases, thatch. Each is outfitted in a breezy but stylish tropical motif that evokes a decorator's journal. Food is superb, focusing on fresh fish, lobster, local soups, homemade breads, and surprisingly good wines.

Staniard Creek, Andros, The Bahamas. ℃ **242/368-6281** or 236-6279. www.kamalame.com. Winter US$840–US$1,190 (£420–£595) double, US$1,380 (£690) suite, from US$1,480 (£740) 1-bedroom villa; off-season US$840–US$950 (£420–£475) double, US$1,100 (£550) suite, from US$1,180 (£590) 1-bedroom villa. Rates all-inclusive, including a boat ride from Kamalame Cay. Discounts of up to 20% June–Oct. MC, V. **Amenities:** Restaurant; bar; pool; tennis court;

watersports equipment/rentals; room service (upon request); babysitting; laundry service. *In room:* A/C, minibar, beverage maker, hair dryer, iron, safe, no phone.

Love at First Sight   This little inn is for serious fishermen attracted to its location at the mouth of Stafford Creek. It may not be love at first sight when you see the place, but anglers find it suits the bill, especially if they want to spend most of the day in the vast bonefish flats of North Andros. When you come back in the late afternoon, a cold beer awaits along with some rum punches and delectable locally caught seafood. When you tire of fishing, you can dive along the coral reefs, bird-watch in the wetlands, or kayak to explore Stafford Creek—or just hang out by the pool. The rooms are utterly basic, like a roadside motel.

Staniard Creek, Andros, The Bahamas. ℂ **242/368-6082.** Fax 242/368-6083. www.loveatfirstsights.com. 10 units. Winter US$107 (£54) double; off-season US$97 (£49) double. No credit cards. **Amenities:** Restaurant; bar; outdoor pool; public Internet; laundry service. *In room:* Fridge, no phone.

IN ANDROS TOWN
Andros Lighthouse Yacht Club & Marina   At the mouth of Fresh Creek with an 18-slip marina, this complex is a favorite of the yachting crowd. The hotel rents comfortably furnished villas, each with a flair enhanced by Caribbean fabrics and ceiling fans. Accommodations open onto private patios and come with well-maintained private bathrooms with shower units. Scuba divers, snorkelers, and fishermen make ample use of the beach and the offshore waters because of the hotel's location near one of the world's largest barrier reefs and the deep Tongue of the Ocean.

The hotel has a good restaurant serving Bahamian and American dishes. Fishing charters are readily available, and scuba diving and snorkeling can easily be arranged through the hotel. The hotel's package rates include airport pickup, lodging, and meals.

Andros Town, Andros, The Bahamas. ℂ **242/368-2305** or 368-2306. Fax 242/368-2300. www.androslighthouse. com. 20 units. Winter US$120–US$145 (£60–£73) double, from US$150 (£75) villa; off-season US$115–US$130 (£58–£65) double, from US$145 (£73) villa. MAP (breakfast and dinner) US$40 (£20) per person. Ask about dive packages. AE, DISC, MC, V. **Amenities:** Restaurant; 2 bars; pool; 2 tennis courts; limited room service; coin-operated laundry; nonsmoking room; rooms for those w/limited mobility. *In room:* A/C, TV, kitchenette, fridge, hair dryer, iron, safe.

IN CARGILL CREEK
Andros Island Bonefish Club ✶ *Finds*   If Hemingway were around today and wanted to go bonefishing, we'd invite him here. This rustic lodge lies at the confluence of Cargill Creek, the Atlantic Ocean, and North Bight's eastern end. It fronts a small protected creek, a short distance from a wadeable flat, and fishing boats can dock directly in front of the lodge. Constructed in 1988, this is a modern but rather bare-bones facility that draws more repeat guests than any other hostelry in The Bahamas. The Bonefish Club recently merged with the nearby Creekside Lodge, adding 18 more rooms to the complex. More than two dozen fishermen can stay here at a time in accommodations with queen-size beds, ample dresser and closet space, bathrooms equipped with tub/showers, and ceiling fans. The club is the domain of Captain Rupert Leadon, who knows more fishing stories than anybody else in Andros.

Hearty and plentiful food, with an emphasis on fresh seafood, including Bahamian lobster and conch, is served at communal tables.

Cargill Creek, Andros, The Bahamas. ℂ **242/368-5167.** Fax 242/368-5397. www.androsbonefishing.com. 30 units. Year-round US$1,235 (£618) per person for 3 nights and 2 days of fishing. Rates include tax, all meals, all-day fishing w/boat and guide, and transportation to and from Andros Town. Room only US$205 (£103) per person. MC, V. **Amenities:** Restaurant; bar; pool; babysitting; laundry service; rooms for those w/limited mobility. *In room:* A/C, ceiling fan, fridge.

IN FRESH CREEK

Hanks Place Restaurant & Bar BAHAMIAN   This local eatery and bar lies on Fresh Creek's northern tier, near the bridge. It's in a tropical setting, with coconut palms shading diners who sit at tables with views over the water. In "The Green-Eyed Lady Bar," patrons feed leftovers to fish waiting under the deck. The signature drink is the Hanky Panky (don't even ask what's in it—it'll put you under the table).

Most diners start their meal with conch fritters, following with more conch, either steamed or cracked, or else the catch of the day which can be either steamed, fried, or baked. Chicken and ribs are also served, but the main-course specialty is the seafood platter with conch, fresh fish, lobster, turtle, or shrimp (you have a choice of three). The most elegant offering is the lobster dinner, which is only offered at certain times of the year.

If you'd like to stay over, Hank rents four basic but air-conditioned bedrooms for US$95 (£48) per night in a double.

Fresh Creek, Andros, The Bahamas. ℂ 242/368-2447. www.hanks-place.com. Reservations not accepted. Main courses US$8–US$18 (£4–£9). MC, V. Mon–Sat 5–10pm.

Small Hope Bay Lodge 🏖🏖 (Kids)   This is the premier diving and fishing resort of Andros, and one of the best in the entire country, with a beach right at its doorstep. Its name comes from a prediction (so far, accurate) made by a pirate named Henry Morgan, who claimed there was "small hope" of anyone finding the treasure he'd buried on Andros.

The resort is an intimate beachside cottage colony where tall coconut palms line a lovely beach. A laid-back atmosphere always prevails. And because this place is all-inclusive, your rate includes all accommodations, meals, drinks, taxes, service charges, airport transfers, and even the use of kayaks, windsurfers, and other boats, as well as bicycles and scuba lessons.

Large cabins, cooled by ceiling fans, are made of coral rock and Andros pine, and are decorated with Androsia batik fabrics. Honeymooners like to order breakfast to be served in their waterbed.

For groups of three or more, the resort has a limited number of family cottages, featuring two separate rooms connected by a bathroom. Single travelers have a choice of staying in a family cottage with private accommodations (which costs the same as per-person double occupancy) or staying in a regular cottage with a private bathroom. All bathrooms are neatly kept.

For conversations and meals, guests congregate in a spacious living and dining room. The bar is an old boat, the *Panacea*. Food here is wholesome, plentiful, and good—including island favorites such as conch chowder, lobster, and hot johnnycake. The chef will even cook your catch for you or make you a picnic lunch. Generally, though, lunch is a buffet; dinner, a choice of seafood and meat every night. Children under 10 dine in the game room. Drinks are offered on a rambling patio built out over the sea. Nightlife is spontaneous, with dancing in the lounge or on the patio, and water slides. Definitely do not wear a tie at dinner.

Diving is the lodge's specialty. The owners have been diving for more than 3 decades, and their well-respected dive shop has sufficient equipment, boats, and flexibility to give guests any diving experience they want, including a course for beginners. If you'd rather fish, the lodge can hook you up with an expert guide.

Andros Town Airport is a 10-minute taxi ride from the lodge.

Fresh Creek, Andros, The Bahamas. (C) **800/223-6961** in the U.S. and Canada, or 242/368-2014. Fax 242/368-2015. www.smallhope.com. 21 units. Winter US$229 (£115) per person adult; off-season US$209 (£105) per person adult; year-round US$95 (£48) ages 2–12. Dive packages available. Rates include tax, all meals, drinks, tips, airport transfers, and most activities. AE, MC, V. **Amenities:** Restaurant; bar; Jacuzzi; kayak; children's programs; massage; babysitting; laundry service; nonsmoking rooms. *In room:* Ceiling fan, no phone.

IN NICHOLL'S TOWN

Green Windows Inn   Kenny Robinson and her husband, Patrick, run this small, laid-back hotel set in a landscape of fruit trees and palms, where guests like to take after-meal walks. The small rooms are over the restaurant and bar on the second floor of the two-story inn. One recent improvement here is the installation of tiny private bathrooms with tub/showers in every bedroom, along with both ceiling fans and air-conditioning. The restaurant caters only to hotel guests, with mainly seafood and local food cooked to order. The beach is a 10-minute walk from the inn, and the Robinsons can arrange bonefishing and snorkeling trips.

Rawfon St., Nicholl's Town, Andros, The Bahamas. (C) **242/329-2515.** Fax 242/329-2016. 10 units. Year-round US$65–US$100 (£33–£50) double. No credit cards. **Amenities:** Weekend bar; nonsmoking room. *In room:* A/C, TV, beverage maker, iron, no phone.

ON SOUTH BIGHT

Tiamo (F) *(Finds*   One of the most ecologically aware places in the entire Bahamas, this lodge was built in stages between 1999 and 2003. It's nestled on 4.8 hectares (12 acres) of land that's studded with unusually large trees, directly beside the bight (inland waterway) that runs along the midsection of Andros. About 30% of the guests here come to fish; a boat rental (without fishing equipment included) goes for US$400 (£200) per day. Accommodations are within wood-framed, plank-sided bungalows, each with a screened-in wraparound porch, a sense of privacy, and a handful of "rustically elegant" amenities that are limited by the resort's eco-sensitive nature. This lack of plush hugely appeals to the nature-loving clients who come here. Days are spent reading, swimming off the white-sand beach that flanks one side of the resort, and generally reflecting on life. It's strongly advised that you bring company to this place, since many of the activities are engineered for couples.

Drigg's Hill, South Bight, Andros, The Bahamas. (C) **242/471-8087.** Fax 305/768-7707. www.tiamoresorts.com. 11 units. Winter US$415 (£208) per person based on double occupancy; off-season US$315–US$330 (£158–£165) per person based on double occupancy. Rates include meals, airport transfers, and almost all activities. AE, DISC, MC, V. **Amenities:** Restaurant; bar; kayaking; snorkeling; hiking; laundry service. *In room:* No phone.

ON MANGROVE CAY

Mangrove Cay Inn   This pleasant, well-managed inn belongs to a native son, Elliott Greene, who returned with his wife, Pat, after years of cold-weather life in Syracuse, New York, to establish this breezy motel. It's a short walk from the center of Grants, Mangrove Cay's third-largest village (Moxey Town and Burnt Rock, though tiny, are still larger). Positioned amid scrubland in the geographic center of the 14km-long (8¾-mile) island, the hotel was built in the early 1990s, 2 years after the inn was established as an easygoing and affable restaurant.

Separated from Grant's Beach by a brackish lake that's stocked with fish, the inn has a mysterious blue hole positioned beside the path connecting the hotel to the beach. Accommodations have cozy but unpretentious furnishings. Each unit contains a small bathroom with a tub/shower.

How do guests spend their time here? Sitting on a veranda that runs the length of the building and overlooks the water, riding on one of the bicycles that the hotel rents for around US$10 (£5) per day, snorkeling with the hotel's equipment on the outlying reef (waters offshore are particularly rich in natural sponges and spiny Caribbean lobster), hiking, hill climbing, and looking for chickcharnies (mythical red-eyed, three-toed, birdlike creatures). For fishing excursions, the Greenes can hire a local guide for a full-day outing (about US$300/£150 per day for up to four).

The wing that contains the bedrooms is attached to a restaurant that serves Bahamian and American food with specialties of cracked conch, grilled grouper and snapper, burgers, and steaks.

Mangrove Cay, Andros, The Bahamas. ⓒ 242/369-0069. Fax 242/369-0014. www.mangrovecayinn.net. 14 units. Year-round US$125 (£63) double, US$175 (£88) 1-bedroom cottage, US$300 (£150) 3-bedroom cottage. No credit cards. **Amenities:** Restaurant; bar; bike rentals; limited room service; laundry service; nonsmoking rooms; rooms for those w/limited mobility. *In room:* A/C, ceiling fan, TV (in some), kitchen (in some), beverage maker (in some), hair dryer, iron, no phone.

Seascape Inn ⊛ *(Finds* Joan and Mickey McGowan are some of the most welcoming innkeepers in the Andros chain. They took several cottages with private decks opening onto the ocean and turned them into secluded retreats for discerning guests. The cabins here are handsomely furnished with handmade mahogany pieces and original Bahamian art. Each cottage is spacious and well maintained, with tidy shower-only bathrooms. Included in the price is one of the best breakfasts you'll get on Andros: Joan is an excellent baker, turning out such early morning delights as banana bread. Fellow guests meet in the elevated dining room to dine on excellent American and Bahamian cuisine. The McGowans will arrange scuba diving and snorkeling trips, if you wish.

Mangrove Cay, Andros, The Bahamas. ⓒ/fax 242/369-0342. www.seascapeinn.com. 5 cottages. Year-round US$110–US$150 (£55–£75) double. Rates include breakfast and use of kayaks and bikes. AE, MC, V. **Amenities:** Restaurant; bar; watersports equipment/rentals; bikes; kayaks; laundry service; all nonsmoking rooms. *In room:* Ceiling fan, free Wi-Fi, no phone.

SOUTH ANDROS

Emerald Palms Resort ⊛ Lodging at this laid-back place, 3km (2 miles) from the Congo Town airport, is like staying at a beachside ranch. The accommodations are set on 8km (5 miles) of beachfront on an island that contains roughly 10,000 palm trees. The hotel is casual—a place to get away from urban life and rest your jangled nerves on a lovely beach. Guests are treated like family members.

Guest rooms are large and comfortable, with well-laid-out bathrooms providing adequate shelf space and shower stalls. All in all, it's a relaxed, tropical ambience.

Scattered over the palm-studded property are hammocks and a freshwater swimming pool. The dining room features Bahamian seafood, and sometimes puts on outdoor steak barbecues and seafood buffets.

South Bight marina is 2.5km (1½ miles) away, serving as a yacht anchorage for anyone who arrives by boat. The hotel will also rent you a car or bike if you need one.

Driggs Hill, South Andros, The Bahamas. ⓒ 800/504-1794 or 242/357-2713. Fax 242/369-2711. www.emerald-palms. com. 42 units. Winter US$155–US$295 (£78–£148) double, US$245–US$495 (£123–£248) 1-bedroom villa, US$445–US$695 (£223–£348) 2-bedroom villa; off-season US$105–US$245 (£53–£123) double, US$195–US$395 (£98–£198) 1-bedroom villa, US$395–US$595 (£198–£298) 2-bedroom villa. AE, MC, V. **Amenities:** Restaurant; 2 bars; pool; Jacuzzi; car-rental desk; limited room service; nonsmoking rooms; rooms for those w/limited mobility. *In room:* A/C, TV, kitchenette (in some), minibar, beverage maker, hair dryer, safe.

WHERE TO DINE

Andros follows the rest of The Bahamas in its cuisine. Conch, in its many variations, is the staple of most diets, along with heaping portions of peas 'n' rice, johnnycake, and pig or chicken souse.

If you're touring the island during the day, you'll find some local spots that serve food. If business has been slow at some of these little places, however, there might be nothing on the stove.

On Mangrove Cay, try **Dianne Cash's Total Experience,** Main Road (© **242/369-0430**), where you can sample Dianne's version of baked crab backs served with peas 'n' rice. Don't plan on dropping by without some kind of advance notification, though.

Emerald Palms Resort, outside Congo Town (© **242/369-2713**), is the best place to dine in South Andros. Even if you're not an overnight guest, you can make a reservation for dinner, which costs US$25 to US$45 (£13–£23) per person.

BEACHES, WATERSPORTS & OTHER OUTDOOR PURSUITS

Golf and tennis fans should go elsewhere, but if you're seeking some of the best bone-fishing and scuba diving in The Bahamas, head to Andros.

HITTING THE BEACH

The eastern shore of Andros, stretching for some 161km (100 miles), is an almost uninterrupted palm grove opening onto beaches of white or beige sand. Several dozen access points lead to the beach along the eastern shore. The roads are unmarked but clearly visible, and the clear, warm waters offshore are great for snorkeling.

FISHING

Andros 🏵🏵🏵 is often called the bonefishing capital of the world, and the epicenter of this activity is at **Lowe Sound Settlement,** a tiny one-road hamlet that's 6.5km (4 miles) north of Nicholl's Town. Anglers come here to hire bonefish guides. **Cargill Creek** is one of the island's best places for bonefishing; nearby, anglers explore the flats in and around the bights of Andros. Some excellent ones, where you can wade in your boots, lie only 68 to 113m (223–371 ft.) offshore.

Whether you're staying in North, Central, or South Andros, someone at your hotel can arrange a fishing expedition with one of the many local guides or charter companies.

Tips Saving Andros for Future Generations

The **Andros Conservancy and Trust** might be called the guardian angel of Andros. This nongovernmental organization was created to preserve and enhance the island's natural assets. In 2002, The Bahamas National Trust began to take on their concerns. Today, nearly 120,000 hectares (296,526 acres) of Andros have been preserved as wetlands, reefs, and marine-replenishment zones—doubling the size of the country's national park system.

All this development falls under the general authority of the **Central Andros National Park** 🏵🏵🏵. A great deal of self-policing is involved there, with bone-fishermen keeping watch over the flats, crabbers protecting local breeding grounds, and divers helping to preserve the reefs.

This park is only emerging, so there are no organized tours, no guides, no nature walks—yet. It is still a national park in the making.

Fun Fact **The Bahamian Loch Ness Monster**

When the Atlantic Undersea Testing and Evaluation Centre (AUTEC) first opened, Androsians predicted that the naval researchers would find **"Lusca."** Like the Loch Ness Monster, Lusca had reportedly been sighted by dozens of locals. The elusive sea serpent was accused of sucking sailors and their vessels into the dangerous blue holes around the island's coastline, but no one has captured the beast yet.

In particular, **Small Hope Bay Lodge,** in Andros Town (© **242/368-2014**), is known for arranging superb fishing expeditions for both guests and nonguests. They also offer fly-, reef-, and deep-sea fishing, and provide tackle and bait.

SCUBA DIVING & SNORKELING

Divers from all over the world come to explore the **Andros Barrier Reef** 👍👍👍, which runs parallel to the island's eastern shore. It's one of the world's largest reefs, and unlike Australia's Great Barrier Reef, which is kilometers off the mainland, the barrier reef here is easily accessible, beginning just a few hundred yards offshore.

One side of the reef is a peaceful haven for snorkelers and novice divers. The fish are mostly tame. A grouper will often eat from your hand, but don't try it with a moray eel. The water here is from 2.5 to 4.5m (8¼–15 ft.) deep.

On the reef's other side, it's a different story. The water plunges to a depth of 167km (104 miles) into the awesome **Tongue of the Ocean (TOTO)** 👍👍👍. One diver claimed that, as adventures go, diving here was tantamount to flying to the moon.

Myriad multicolored forms of marine life thrive on the reef, attracting nature lovers from all over the world. The weirdly shaped coral formations alone are worth the trip. This is a living, breathing garden of the sea, and its caves feel like cathedrals.

For many years, the U.S. Navy has conducted research at a station on TOTO's edge. **The Atlantic Undersea Testing and Evaluation Centre (AUTEC),** as the station is called, is devoted to underwater weapons and antisubmarine technologies. It's at Andros Town and is a joint U.S. and British undertaking.

Among other claims to fame, Andros is known for its **blue holes,** which drop into the brine. Essentially, these are narrow, circular pits that plunge as far as 60m (197 ft.) straight down through rock and coral into murky, difficult-to-explore depths. Most of them begin below sea level, though others appear unexpectedly—and dangerously—in the center of the island, usually with warning signs placed around the perimeter. Scattered at various points along the coast, you can get to them either in rented boats or as part of a guided trip. The most celebrated one is **Uncle Charlie's Blue Hole,** mysterious, fathomless, and publicized by the legendary underwater explorer Jacques Cousteau. The other blue holes are almost as incredible.

Another of these, called **Benjamin's Blue Hole** 👍, is named after George Benjamin, its discoverer. In 1967, he found stalactites and stalagmites 360m (1,181 ft.) below sea level. What was remarkable about this discovery is that stalactites and stalagmites are not created underwater. This has led to much speculation that The Bahamas are actually mountaintops and all that remains of a mysterious continent that has long since sunk beneath the sea (perhaps Atlantis?).

Most of the blue holes, like most of the island's surface, remain unexplored. Tour boats leaving from Small Hope Bay Lodge will take you to them.

For good snorkeling, head a few kilometers north of Nicholl's Town, where you'll find a crescent-shaped beach, along with a headland, **Morgan's Bluff,** honoring the notorious old pirate. If you're not a diver and can't go out to the Andros Barrier Reef, you can do the second-best thing and snorkel near a series of reefs known as the **Three Sisters.** Sometimes, if the waters haven't turned suddenly murky, you can see all the way to the sandy bottom. The outcroppings of elkhorn coral are especially dramatic.

Since **Mangrove Cay** is underdeveloped, rely on the snorkeling advice and gear rentals you'll get from the dive shop at **Seascape Inn** (© 242/369-0342; www.seascapeinn. com). A two-tank dive costs US$125 (£63) for hotel guests; nonguests are not served.

Small Hope Bay Lodge (p. 191) lies not far from the barrier reef, with its still-unexplored caves and ledges. A staff of trained dive instructors at the lodge caters to beginners and experienced divers. Snorkeling expeditions can be arranged, as well as scuba outings (visibility underwater exceeds 30m/98 ft. on most days, with water temperatures ranging 72°–84°F/22°–29°C). You can also rent gear here. To stay at the all-inclusive hotel for 7 nights and 8 days (rates include meals, tips, taxes, airport transfers, and three dives per day), you'll pay US$1,943 to US$2,083 (£972–£1,042) per person. For children 10 to 12, the cost is US$1,145/£573; kids 9 and under go for free. All guests are allowed, at no extra cost, to use the beachside hot tub and the sailboats, windsurfers, and bicycles.

EXPLORING ANDROS

Andros is largely unexplored, and for good reason—getting around takes some effort. With the exception of the main arteries, the few roads that exist are badly maintained and full of potholes. Sometimes you're a long way between villages. If your car breaks down, all you can do is wait and hope that someone comes along to give you a ride to the next place, where you'll hope to find a skilled mechanic. If you're heading out on your own, make sure you have a full tank of gas because service stations are few and far between.

At present, not all of Andros can be explored by car. We hope that as Andros develops, roads will be constructed so that it will be easier to get around. Most of the driving and exploring is currently confined to North Andros; even there, roads go only along the eastern sector past Nicholl's Town, Morgan's Bluff, and San Andros.

If you're driving on Central or South Andros, you must stay on the rough **Queen's Highway.** The road in the south is paved and better than the one in Central Andros, which should be traveled only for emergency purposes or by a local.

Near Small Hope Bay at Andros Town, you can visit the workshop where **Androsia batik** is made (the same textiles sold in the shops of Nassau and other towns). Here, artisans create designs using hot wax on fine cotton and silk fabrics. The fabrics are then crafted into island-style wear, including blouses, skirts, caftans, shirts, and accessories. All are hand-painted and hand-signed, and the resort wear comes in dazzling red, blue, purple, green, and earth tones. You can visit the factory (© 242/368-2080; www.androsia.com) Monday to Friday 8am to 5pm, and Saturday 9am to 2pm.

Morgan's Bluff, at the tip of North Andros, lures people hoping to strike it rich. The pirate Sir Henry Morgan supposedly buried a vast treasure here, but it has eluded discovery to this day, though many have searched.

Moments   What Would Tennessee Have Thought?

One custom in Andros recalls the Tennessee Williams drama *Suddenly, Last Summer:* catching **land crabs,** which leave their burrows and march relentlessly to the sea to lay their eggs. The annual ritual occurs between May and September. However, many of the hapless crabs will never have offspring, since both visitors and Androsians walk along the beach with baskets and capture the crustaceans before they reach the sea. Later, they get cleaned, stuffed, and baked for dinner.

Bird-watchers are attracted to Andros for its varied avian population. In the dense forests, in trees such as lignum vitae, mahogany, Madeira, horseflesh, and pine, dwell many **birds,** including parrots, doves, marsh hens, and whistling ducks.

Botanists are lured by the **wildflowers** of Andros. Some 40 to 50 species of wild orchid are said to thrive here, some of which can be found nowhere else. New discoveries are always being made, as more botanists study the land's rich vegetation.

Red Bay Village is the type of place that continues to make Andros seem mysterious. In the 1840s, Seminoles and people of African descent fleeing slavery in Florida fled to Andros and, miraculously, remained hidden until about 50 years ago, when an explorer "discovered" their descendants, who remain a very small, virtually self-sufficient tribe, living just as the Seminoles did in the Florida Everglades some 2 centuries ago. You should be polite and ask permission before indiscriminately photographing them.

Located off the northwestern coast of Andros, Red Bay Village is connected by a causeway to the mainland, and tourists can get here by road from Nicholl's Town and San Andros.

8

The Abacos

Called the "top of The Bahamas," the Abacos comprise the northernmost portion of the nation. This boomerang-shaped mini-archipelago is 209km (130 miles) long and consists of Great Abaco and Little Abaco, as well as a sprinkling of cays. The islands are about 322km (200 miles) east of Miami and 121km (75 miles) north of Nassau.

People come here mainly to explore the outdoors. The **sailing** 𝑘𝑘 and **fishing** 𝑘𝑘 are spectacular, and the **diving** is excellent, too. There are also many lovely, uncrowded beaches. The Abacos are definitely a world apart from the glitzy pleasures of Freeport/Lucaya, Nassau, or Paradise Island.

Many residents descend from Loyalists who left New England after the American Revolution. Against a backdrop of sugar-white beaches and turquoise water, their pastel-colored clapboard houses and white picket fences retain the Cape Cod architectural style of the area's first settlements. One brightly painted sign in Hope Town says it all: SLOW DOWN. YOU'RE IN HOPE TOWN. The same could be said for all the Abacos.

The weather is about 10 degrees warmer here than in southern Florida, but if you visit in January or February, remember that you're not guaranteed beach weather every day—it can get chilly at times, and when winter squalls hit, temperatures can drop to the high 40s (high single digits Celsius) in severe cases. Spring in the Abacos, however, is one of the most glorious and balmy seasons in all the islands. In summer, it gets very hot around noon, but if you act as the islanders do and find a shady spot in which to escape the broiling sun, the trade winds will cool you off.

Some yachters call the Abacos the world's most beautiful cruising grounds. Excellent marine facilities, with fishing guides and boat rentals, are available here; in fact, Marsh Harbour is the bareboat-charter center of the northern Bahamas. There, you can rent a small boat, pack a picnic, and head for one of many uninhabited cays just big enough for two.

Anglers from all over the world come to catch blue marlin, kingfish, dolphin-fish, yellowfin tuna, sailfish, wahoo, amberjack, and grouper. Fishing tournaments abound at Walker's Cay.

Finally, scuba divers can plumb the depths to discover caverns, inland blue holes, coral reefs, and underwater gardens, along with marine preserves and long-ago shipwrecks. Some scuba centers offer night dives.

ABACOS ESSENTIALS
GETTING THERE
BY PLANE   There are three airports in the Abacos: **Marsh Harbour** (the major one, on Great Abaco Island), **Treasure Cay,** and **Walker's Cay.** The official points of entry by water are at Marsh Harbour, Treasure Cay, Walker's Cay, and Green Turtle Cay

The Abacos

WALKER'S CAY

GRAND CAY

STRANGER'S CAY

Carter's Cay

The Abacos

Miami
Grand Bahama
New Providence Island
FLORIDA
Eleuthera
Nassau
Cat Island
Andros
San Salvador
Great Exuma
Long Island
Crooked Island
Acklins Island
Great Inagua
CUBA
TURKS AND CAICOS

100 mi
100 km

Little Abaco Island

SPANISH CAY

PENSACOLA CAYS

LITTLE CAVE CAY

CROSS CAYS

Cooperís Town

GREEN TURTLE CAY

New Plymouth

Treasure Cay Airport

TREASURE CAY

GREAT GUANA CAY

MAN O' WAR CAY

Marsh Harbour

Tahiti Beach

THE MARIS

Marsh Harbour Airport

Hope Town

Elbow Cay

MOORE'S ISLAND

Great Abaco Island

Pelican Cays Land and Sea Park

Pelican Harbour

Casaurina Point

Little Harbour

Cherokee

Eight Mile Bay

GORDA CAY

Crossing Rocks

Sandy Point

Cross Harbour

Bahamas National Trust Sanctuary

Hole-in-the-Wall

✈ Airport
Scuba diving
⚓ Shipwreck

0   15 mi
0   15 km

(New Plymouth). The latter doesn't have an airstrip, but yachters can clear Customs and Immigration there.

Many visitors arrive from Nassau or Miami on **Bahamasair** (© **800/222-4262** or 242/377-8451; www.bahamasair.com). Flight schedules change frequently, but usually include two to three flights out of Nassau on Fridays and Sundays, going first to Marsh Harbour, and then on to Treasure Cay. From West Palm Beach, there's often a direct morning flight to Marsh Harbour and Treasure Cay.

Other connections include **American Eagle** (© **800/433-7300** or 242/367-2231; www.aa.com), with flights from Miami to Marsh Harbour once daily, and **Continental Connection** (© **800/231-0856** or 242/367-3415 in Marsh Harbour, 242/365-8615 in Treasure Cay; www.continental.com), which flies to Marsh Harbour and Treasure Cay two to three times daily from several Florida locales. A smaller carrier is **Twin Air** (© **954/359-8266;** www.flytwinair.com), flying from Fort Lauderdale to Treasure Cay on Mondays, Wednesdays, and Fridays.

BY BOAT   The mail boat **MV *Legacy*** sails on Tuesday from Nassau to Hope Town, Marsh Harbour, Turtle Cay, and Green Turtle Cay. It returns to Nassau on Friday. Trip time is 12 hours. For details on sailings (subject to change) and costs, contact the dock master at **Potter's Cay Dock** in Nassau (© **242/393-1064**).

Bahamas Ferries (www.bahamasferries.com) operates a direct service from Nassau aboard the *Sea Wind.* A round-trip passage costs US$110 (£55) for adults and US$70 (£35) per child. For bookings and more information, call © **242/323-2166.** The trip from Nassau to Sandy Point in the Abacos takes 1 hour and 50 minutes.

GETTING AROUND

BY TAXI   Unmetered taxis, which you often have to share with other passengers, meet all arriving flights. They will take you to your hotel if it's on the Abaco "mainland"; otherwise, they will deposit you at a dock where you can hop aboard a water taxi to one of the neighboring islands, such as Green Turtle Cay or Elbow Cay. Most visitors use a combination taxi and water-taxi ride to reach the most popular hotels. From Marsh Harbour Airport to Hope Town on Elbow Cay, the charge is about US$13 (£6.50). From Treasure Cay Airport to Green Turtle Cay, it's is about US$15 (£7.50), and US$12 (£6) to Elbow Cay.

It's also possible to make arrangements for a taxi tour of Great or Little Abaco. These, however, are expensive, and you don't really see much.

BY FERRY   Mostly, you'll get around on **Albury's Ferry Service** (© **242/367-0290;** www.alburysferry.com), which provides several ferry connections between Marsh Harbour and both Elbow Cay (Hope Town) and Man-O-War Cay, a 20-minute trip to either destination. The one-way fare is US$16 (£8) adults, US$8 (£4) for children 11 and younger. (Ferries also go to Guana Cay.) The ferry docks aren't far from Marsh Harbour Airport; it's about a 10-minute, US$13 to US$15 (£6.50–£7.50) cab ride for two passengers (plus US$3/£1.50 for each additional passenger).

For car-ferry service to Green Turtle Cay, see "Green Turtle Cay (New Plymouth)," later in this chapter. Ferries go from Great Abaco Island to Green Turtle Cay, but those docks are a 35-minute, US$70 (£35) cab ride for up to four passengers from Marsh Harbour Airport. It's better to fly to Treasure Cay than Marsh Harbour to do this and then take a taxi to the ferry docks.

1 Marsh Harbour (Great Abaco Island)

The largest town in the Abacos, and the third largest in The Bahamas, Marsh Harbour lies on Great Abaco Island and is the major gateway to this island group.

Marsh Harbour is also a shipbuilding center, but tourism accounts for most of its revenues. A number of good inns are located here. Although the town doesn't have the quaint New England charm of either New Plymouth or Hope Town, it does have a shopping center and various other facilities not found in many Out Island settlements. Good water-taxi connections, too, make this a popular place from which to explore offshore cays, including Man-O-War and Elbow. Several hotels will rent you a bike if you want to pedal around town.

MARSH HARBOUR ESSENTIALS

GETTING THERE   See "Abacos Essentials," above. Marsh Harbour is the most easily accessible point in the Abacos from the U.S. mainland, served by daily flights from Florida.

GETTING AROUND   You won't need a car to get around town, but if you want to explore the rest of the island, you can rent a car for US$70 to US$80 (£35–£40) per day or US$350 to US$400 (£175–£200) per week (be prepared for bad roads, though). In Marsh Harbour, call **A&P Rentals** at © **242/367-2655** to find out whether any vehicles are available.

Rental Wheels of Abaco at Marsh Harbour (© **242/367-4643**) rents bicycles for US$10 (£5) per day or US$45 (£23) per week, and mopeds for US$45 (£23) per day or US$200 (£100) per week.

VISITOR INFORMATION   The **Abaco Tourist Office** is on Queen Elizabeth Drive in the commercial heart of town (© **242/367-3067**). It's open Monday to Friday 9am to 5pm.

FAST FACTS   There's a **First Caribbean International Bank** on Don MacKay Boulevard (© **242/367-2152**), plus several other banks and a **post office** (© **242/367-2571**).

For medication, go to the **Chemist Shop Pharmacy,** Don MacKay Boulevard (© **242/367-3106**), open Monday to Saturday 8:30am to 5:30pm.

Dial © **911** if you need the **police.**

SPECIAL EVENTS   In early July, Marsh Harbour hosts **Regatta Week,** the premier yachting event in the Abacos, attracting sailboats and their crews from around the world. Many of the yachters participating in this event stay at the Green Turtle Club (p. 221). For registration forms and more information, write to Regatta Time, Marsh Harbour, Abaco, The Bahamas, or call Ruth Saunders at © **242/367-3202.**

WHERE TO STAY

Abaco Beach Resort & Boat Harbour ⋇   This beachfront resort—Marsh Harbour's biggest and best—is a good choice, especially if you're serious about diving or fishing. Extending over sprawling acreage at the edge of town and fronting a small, lovely beach, it's a business with several different faces: the hotel, with handsomely furnished rooms that overlook the Sea of Abaco; the well-managed restaurant and bar; the Boat Harbour Marina, which has slips for 180 boats and full docking facilities; and a full-fledged dive shop.

Angler's Restaurant (see below), which is on-site, offers one of Marsh Harbour's best dining experiences. A swim-up bar and a beachfront bar serve snacks and grog.

To reach the resort from Marsh Harbour Airport, take a taxi (US$15/£7.50, but be sure to agree on the price first with the driver; 6.5km/4 miles).

Marsh Harbour, Abaco, The Bahamas. ℂ 800/468-4799 in the U.S., or 242/367-2158. Fax 242/367-4154. www.abaco resort.com. 82 units. Year-round US$280–US$420 (£140–£210) double, from US$550 (£275) suite. AE, DISC, MC, V. **Amenities:** Restaurant; 2 bars; 2 pools; 2 tennis courts; fitness room; free use of watersports equipment; boat rentals; bike rentals; dive shop; gift shop; massage; coin-operated laundry; nonsmoking rooms; rooms for those w/limited mobility. *In room:* A/C, TV, free Wi-Fi, kitchen (in some), minibar, beverage maker, hair dryer, iron, safe.

Conch Inn Hotel & Marina

At the harbor's southeastern edge, this is a casual one-story hotel leased on a long-term basis by one of the world's largest yacht-chartering companies, the Moorings. A number of small, sandy beaches are within walking distance. Its motel-style, midsize bedrooms are small, each with two double beds (rollaways are available for extra occupants). Bathrooms are small but neatly kept with tub/showers. All units overlook the yachts bobbing in the nearby marina.

On the premises is an open-air swimming pool fringed with palm trees, and nearby is a branch of the Dive Abaco scuba facility. The on-site restaurant and bar, called Curly Tails, is independently managed and serves standard, recommendable fare.

E. Bay St., Marsh Harbour, Abaco, The Bahamas. ℂ 242/367-4000. Fax 242/367-4004. www.conchinn.com. 9 units. Feb–July US$160 (£80) double; Aug–Jan US$120 (£60) double. Extra person US$20 (£10) per day. AE, MC, V. **Amenities:** Restaurant; bar; pool; nonsmoking rooms. *In room:* A/C, TV, fridge, coffeemaker, iron.

Lofty Fig Villas

This family-owned bungalow colony across from the Conch Inn overlooks the harbor. It doesn't have the services of a full-fledged resort, but it's good for families and self-sufficient types. Built in 1970, it stands in a tropical landscape with a freshwater pool and a gazebo where you can barbecue. Rooms have one queen-size bed, a couch that pulls out into another queen-size bed, a dining area, a kitchen, a private screened-in porch, and a fully tiled bathroom with a shower stall. Maid service is provided Monday through Saturday.

You're about a 10-minute walk from a supermarket and shops; restaurants and bars sit just across the street. Marinas, a dive shop, and boat rentals are also close at hand. From here, you can walk, bike, or drive 1.5km (1 mile) east to a point near the ferry-boat docks for access to a sandy beach and a snorkeling site, or you can take a ferryboat to Guana Cay for your day at the beach.

Marsh Harbour, Abaco, The Bahamas. ℂ 242/367-2681. Fax 242/367-3385. www.loftyfig.com. 6 villas. Dec 15–Sept 15 US$160 (£80) double, extra person US$20 (£10) per day; Sept 16–Dec 14 US$120 (£60) double, extra person US$10 (£5) per day. DISC, MC, V. **Amenities:** Outdoor pool. *In room:* A/C, TV, free Wi-Fi, kitchen, beverage maker, hair dryer, no phone.

WHERE TO DINE

If you'd like to go really casual, try **Island Bakery,** on Don McKay Boulevard (ℂ **242/ 367-2129**), which has the island's best Bahamian bread and cinnamon rolls, often emerging fresh from the oven. You might even pick up the makings for a picnic. It's open Monday to Saturday 7am to 6pm.

Angler's Restaurant ⭐ BAHAMIAN/INTERNATIONAL

At the Boat Harbour, overlooking the Sea of Abaco, this is the main restaurant of the town's major resort (p. 201). The interior features a nautical theme and Bahamian decor. Within a few steps of your seat, dock pilings rise from the water, yachts and fishing boats come and go, and the place is open and airy. The menu changes daily, but there's always fresh seafood, which the chef prepares with finesse, and a well-chosen selection of meat dishes. Begin with crab cakes served with a Caribbean salsa and garnished with mesclun greens, or perhaps the sesame seed-encrusted tuna steak with sweet soy sauce. Main dishes dance with flavor, especially the cracked conch marinated in a coconut-lime sauce.

In the Abaco Beach Resort & Boat Harbour, Marsh Harbour. ✆ **242/367-2158.** Reservations recommended for dinner. Main courses US$8–US$22 (£4–£11). AE, DISC, MC, V. Daily 6am–2:30pm and 6–10pm.

Curly Tails Restaurant & Bar BAHAMIAN   Adjacent to the Conch Inn and the Moorings facilities, this eatery attracts a lot of yachties and visiting pro athletes. The cooks use local ingredients, such as freshly caught grouper and snapper, whenever they can. They also know every conceivable way to prepare conch. The regulars don't even have to consult the menu; they just ask, "What's good?" Fish and seafood are always on the menu. Diners also look for daily specials, such as curried or steamed chicken. If you're frittering away a few hours, drop in for a Conch Crawl, a potent rum-based drink made with secret ingredients. The bar, set beneath an octagonal gazebo near the piers, is a fine place to meet people.

At the Conch Inn (the Moorings), Bay St. ✆ **242/367-4444.** Reservations not required. Main courses US$22–US$50 (£11–£25). MC, V. Daily 7am–10pm.

The Jib Room BAHAMIAN/AMERICAN   This funky restaurant and bar is a hangout for locals and boat owners who savor its welcoming spirit. If you want the house-special cocktail, a Bilge Burner, get ready for a head-spinning combination of apricot brandy, rum, coconut juice, and Kahlúa. Saturday night brings Jib's steak barbecue, when as many as 300 1-pound New York strip steaks are brought out. The only other night dinner is served is Wednesday, when grilled baby back ribs might be the featured dish. Other choices include a seafood platter, grilled chicken, and broiled lobster—and yes, you've probably had it all before in better versions, but the dishes are well prepared. Go for the convivial atmosphere rather than the food.

Marsh Harbour Marina, Pelican Shores. ✆ **242/367-2700.** Reservations required for dinner. Lunch platters US$8.50–US$14 (£4.25–£7); fixed-price dinners US$20–US$28 (£10–£14). MC, V. Wed–Sat 11:30am–2:30pm; dinner Wed and Sat 7–11pm.

Mangoes Restaurant 🔾 BAHAMIAN/INTERNATIONAL   Near the harbor in one of the town's most distinctive buildings, Mangoes is the best, and certainly the most popular, restaurant on the island, attracting both yachties and locals. It boasts a cedar-topped bar and a cathedral ceiling that soars above a deck jutting over the water. Chefs seem to try a little harder here, offering a typical menu along with a hint of island spirit. On the menu, grilled grouper gets dressed up a bit with mango and tomato, and cracked conch makes an appearance as well. Your best bet, as in nearly all Bahamian restaurants, is usually the fresh catch of the day. At lunch you can sample the restaurant's locally famous conch burger.

Front St. ✆ **242/367-2957.** Reservations recommended. Main courses lunch US$13–US$17 (£6.50–£8.50), dinner US$14–US$33 (£7–£17). MC, V. Mon–Sat 11:30am–2:30pm; daily 6:30–10pm.

Sapodilly's Bar & Grill BAHAMIAN   This restaurant occupies an open-air pavilion across the road from the harbor, in an area of town known as "the tourist strip." Even if you eventually head into the high-raftered interior dining room, take time for a drink or two on the covered open-air deck, surrounded by vibrant Junkanoo colors and a crowd of local hipsters, yacht owners, marina workers, and businessmen visiting from other parts of The Bahamas. Lunch might consist of grilled fish sandwiches, burgers, salads, quiche, or the island's best pizza. Dinners are more elaborate, with 12-ounce New York strip steak, a flavorful shrimp kabob in teriyaki sauce, and zesty curried grouper filets. A happy hour with live music happens every Friday from 5:30 to 7:30pm.

E. Bay St. © 242/367-3498. Reservations recommended. Lunch platters and sandwiches US$8–US$18 (£4–£9); dinner main courses US$20–US$37 (£10–£19). MC, V. Daily 11:30am–3pm and 6–10pm.

Wally's BAHAMIAN/INTERNATIONAL   Across the street from the water, this eatery occupies a tidy pink, colonial-style villa on a hibiscus-dotted lawn. It's got an outdoor terrace, a boutique, and an indoor bar and dining area filled with Haitian paintings. The drink of the house is Wally's Special, which contains four kinds of rum and a medley of fruit juices. The chef prepares Marsh Harbour's best Bahamian cracked conch, as well as tender filet mignon, lamb chops, tarragon chicken, and an excellent version of smothered grouper. Main dishes come with a generous portion of house salad and vegetables. The place really shines at lunchtime, when things get very busy as hungry diners devour dolphinfish burgers, several kinds of chicken platters, and some well-stuffed sandwiches. Sisters Barbara and Maureen Smith head to Paris every fall and bring culinary discoveries back to their enterprise in Marsh Harbour. Live music performances take place on Wednesday and Saturday nights.

E. Bay St. © 242/367-2074. Reservations recommended for dinner. Lunch sandwiches and platters US$9–US$18 (£4.50–£9); dinner main courses US$27–US$45 (£14–£23). AE, DISC, MC, V. Tues–Sat 11:30am–3pm and 6–9pm. Closed 6 weeks Sept–Oct.

BEACHES, WATERSPORTS & OTHER OUTDOOR PURSUITS

Whatever sport you want to pursue—whether it be **snorkeling** or **fishing**—Marsh Harbour's innkeepers can set you up with the right people and equipment. You can also take the ferry over to Hope Town and check out the facilities and outfitters there.

Of the major Out Islands towns, Marsh Harbour has some of the least appealing shores. You can try one of three private beaches, but none is very enticing, and none really wants outsiders. The easiest to get into is at Abaco Beach Resort, but it's small, not fabulous, and, again, private. Buy a drink for a local at the hotel bar, and you're in, but that, at best, is a somewhat uncomfortable arrangement.

To compensate, beach seekers head south of Marsh Harbour. Once south of Little Harbour after 15 to 20 minutes of driving, lots of good options begin to appear. The beaches near the hamlet of **Casuarina Point** benefit from some battered, all-Bahamian restaurants in the vicinity.

Some **swimmers** heading south from Marsh Harbour make it a point to go eastward from the main highway whenever an offshoot road appears, usually at points south of Little Harbour.

None of the beaches on Great Abaco Island has facilities or lifeguards. Guard your valuables and stay alert.

BOAT CHARTERS

If you'd like to try bareboating (seagoing without captain or crew), **Abaco Bahamas Charters,** Hopetown, Abaco (© **800/626-5690;** fax or local phone 242/366-0151; www.abacocharters.com), can set you up. Weekly charters with a choice of eight boats begin at US$1,925 (£963) and can go as high as US$9,000 (£4,500) during winter, with a US$2,000 (£1,000) deposit required. Only experienced sailors can rent.

The Moorings (© 888/952-8420 or 242/367-4000; www.moorings.com) is one of the world's leading charter sailboat outfitters. It operates from a perch behind the Conch Inn Resort and Marina, overlooking intersecting piers and wharves—at least 80 berths, with more on the way—where hundreds of upscale watercraft are tied up (many of them are for rent). With one of its vessels, you can enjoy short sails between the islands, stopping at white-sand beaches and snug anchorages. Yacht rentals generally range from US$2,000 (£1,000) per day, with a skipper costing another US$190 (£95) per day, and an onboard cook (if you want one) for an additional US$175 (£88) per day.

For the more casual boater, **Sea Horse Boat Rentals,** at Abaco Beach Resort (© 242/367-2513), offers some of the best rentals. A 4.5m Boston Whaler goes for US$145 (£73) per day, and a 5.4m Privateer costs US$165 (£83) per day. Other vessels are for rent, too, and all boats are equipped with a Bimini top, coolers, a compass, a swimming platform, life jackets, a paddle, docking lines, and other equipment. Sea Horse is open daily from 8am to 5pm.

SNORKELING & SCUBA DIVING

The strangest dive site of all is the **Abacos Train Wreck,** 4.5 to 6m (15–20 ft.) deep. This unusual wreck consists of two locomotives lying on their sides. During the U.S. Civil War, they were reportedly part of a Union train captured by Confederate troops and then sold to Cuba. The barge transporting the train ran aground on the reef during a storm in 1865. Enough of the train still exists to make it an interesting shore dive. Another nearby wreck, the *Adirondack,* lies in shallow water some 3 to 7.5m (10–25 ft.) deep. Many divers come here to explore the government-protected **Sea Preserve and Fowl Cay Land,** which teems with multicolored sea life in shallow reefs.

The best place to snorkel is **Mermaid Reef and Beach,** with its colorful reef, moray eels, and plethora of beautiful rainbow-hued fish. The reef and beach lie on Pelican Shores, the northernmost edge of the Marsh Harbour waterfront directly west of the Marsh Harbour Marina. From the center of Marsh Harbour at East Bay Street, walk east along the harbor, and then head northwest until you reach the marina. Once there, continue walking west to Pelican Shores across the stretch of scrub and sand until you reach Mermaid Reef, where you can enjoy the beach or snorkel in the clear waters. **Sea Horse Boat Rentals** at Abaco Beach Resort & Boat, Harbour Marina (© 242/367-2513), rents snorkel gear.

Scuba divers should check out the nearby **Pelican Cays Land and Sea Park** 🐾. You won't find any organized excursions here, but Dive Abaco (see below) is the best source of information and might arrange a trip. You can also drive down to the park by following the road immediately south of Marsh Harbour and then turning east at the sign leading you toward the park. Several small beaches are suitable for swimming. The easiest jumping-off point is at Pelican Harbour.

Dive Abaco, Marsh Harbour (© 800/247-5338 in the U.S., or 242/367-2787; www.diveabaco.com), rents snorkel gear and offers dive trips to tunnels and caverns along the world's third-longest barrier reef. Resort courses for uncertified novice divers are all-inclusive at US$175 (£88). Two-tank dives for certified divers cost US$95 (£48), including tanks and weights, and depart daily at 9:30am; afternoon times are dictated by demand. Shop hours are daily from 8:30am to 5pm; ask for owner-operator Keith Rogers.

ATTRACTIONS ON LAND

Marsh Harbour is the best central point for exploring the nature-created attractions of Great Abaco and Little Abaco.

A fully graded and tarred main highway links all the settlements, with such colorful names as Fire Road, Mango Hill, Red Bays, Snake Cay, Cherokee Sound, and, our favorite, Hole-in-the-Wall, which lies at the "bottom" of Great Abaco.

Driving south for 40km (25 miles) from Marsh Harbour along Great Abaco Highway, you come first to **Cherokee Sound,** set at the end of a jutting peninsula. The 150 residents are descended from Loyalists who fled mainland U.S. in 1783 to remain faithful to the British Crown. These people faced a lack of hospitality for 2 centuries and have tried to make a living as best they can. The men dive for lobsters or go out at night "sharking"; the sharks' jaws are sold in Marsh Harbour. They also hunt down tiniki crabs, as well as pigeon and wild boar in the remote pinelands of the Abacos.

The unhurried routine around here is in the process of major change. Entrepreneur Peter de Savary has opened the most exclusive club in The Bahamas. Called the **Abaco Club on Winding Bay** (*©* **800/303-2765** or 242/367-0077; www.theabacoclub. com), it is deluxe living personified, but only for the super rich. The first time you stay, a cabana suite costs between US$650 and US$800 (£325–£400) per night; two- to four-bedroom units range from US$1,200 to US$3,500 (£600–£1,750) per night. If you return, you'll have to pay a hefty membership fee.

Forty-eight kilometers (30 miles) south of Marsh Harbour, to the immediate east of Cherokee Sound, is **Little Harbour,** a circle-shaped cay with a white-sand beach running along most of its waterfront. Here, you can visit **Pete Johnston's Foundry** (*©* **242/366-3503**), the only bronze foundry in The Bahamas. Settling here in 1951, the Johnston family achieved international fame as artists and sculptors. They use an old "lost-wax" method to cast their bronze sculptures, many of which are sold in prestigious art galleries in America; you can also buy them here. Margot Johnston creates porcelain figurines of island life such as birds, fish, boats, and even fishermen. The Johnstons welcome visitors to their studio daily from 10 to 11am and 2 to 3pm. You can also purchase a remarkable book here, *Artist on His Island,* detailing the true-life adventures of Randolph and Margot Johnston, who lived a *Swiss Family Robinson* adventure when they first arrived at Little Harbour with their three sons. Sailing in an old Bahamian schooner, the *Langosta,* they stayed in one of the local caves until they eventually erected a thatched dwelling for themselves.

After a visit to the foundry, stop in for a drink at laid-back **Pete's Pub and Gallery** (*©* **242/477-5487;** www.petespubandgallery.com), where decor evokes *Gilligan's Island.* The pub was constructed in part from the timbers of the *Langosta* and opens daily at 11am, staying that way "until everyone leaves at night" (it's closed Sept and Oct). The beer is cold and the art on the walls is for sale. You can also order lunch here daily, costing around US$20 (£10). Fresh seafood such as mango-glazed grouper or lemon-pepper mahimahi is served along with burgers. A boar roast happens every Saturday from April to July. In the evening, Pete Johnston might sing a medley of sea chanteys, accompanying himself on his guitar.

After leaving Cherokee and Little Harbour, you can return to Great Abaco Highway, heading south once again to reach the little fishing village of **Casuarina Point** west of Cherokee Sound, where you'll find a lovely stretch of sand and some jade-colored flats (low-water areas where bonefish are plentiful). If you keep going south, you'll come to **Crossing Rocks,** another little fishing village. This one's 64km (40 miles) south of Marsh Harbour and is noted for its kilometer-long beach of golden sand. This hamlet, where locals barely eke out a living, takes its name from the isthmus where Great Abaco Island narrows to its thinnest point.

If you continue traveling south from here, you'll come to a fork in the road. If you take the southern route, you'll be heading toward **Abaco National Park** (also called Bahamas National Trust Sanctuary; (C) **242/393-1317**) and the aptly named **Hole-in-the-Wall,** a poor little hamlet with few settlers; it marks the end of the line for drives along the Abacos.

Protected by the government, the 8,296-hectare (20,500-acre) Abaco National Park, established in 1994, sprawls across Grand Abaco Island's southeastern portion. Some 2,023 hectares (4,999 acres) of it is pine forest, with a lot of wetlands that are home to native bird life, including the endangered Bahama parrot. Hardwood forests, sand dunes, and mangrove flats fill the area. Rangers, under the sponsorship of the Bahamas National Trust, lead occasional tours of the sanctuary and protect the area.

SHOPPING

Bahama Dawn, Engar Gottlieb Boulevard, next to the public library ((C) **242/367-4648**), carries Androsia batik clothing and some local crafts. For souvenir items, try **Iggy Biggy,** on Main Street, across from Conch Inn ((C) **242/367-3596**).

MARSH HARBOUR AFTER DARK

Sand Bar, opening onto the Sea of Abaco at Abaco Beach Resort ((C) **242/367-2158**), is the most popular gathering spot in town. The yachting crowd, often from Miami, hangs out here, swapping tall sea tales while downing strong rum punches. Another good hangout is **Wally's,** on East Bay Street ((C) **242/367-2074**), where drinkers enjoy the special punch on an outdoor terrace or inside the cozy bar. On Wednesday and Saturday, live entertainment is often presented. **Sapodilly's Bar & Grill,** on East Bay Street ((C) **242/367-3498**), attracts a blend of locals and visitors, some of whom play at its pool table while others prefer to mix and mingle at the bar.

2 Elbow Cay (Hope Town) ✶

Elbow Cay is known for its spectacular beaches. One of The Bahamas' best, **Tahiti Beach** lies in splendid isolation at the far end of Elbow Cay, with sparkling waters and powdery white sand. Access is possible only on foot, by riding a rented bicycle across sand and gravel paths from Hope Town, or by private boat.

The cay's largest settlement is **Hope Town,** a scenic little village with a candy-striped 36m (118-ft.) lighthouse—the most photographed attraction in the Out Islands. Hope Town seems frozen in time. Like other offshore cays of the Abacos, it was settled by Loyalists who left the new United States to remain subjects of the British Crown. Its clapboard saltbox cottages are weathered to a silver gray or painted pastel colors, with white picket fences setting them off. The buildings may remind you of New England, but this palm-fringed island has South Seas flavor.

The island is almost free of cars. While exploring Hope Town, you can take one of two roads: "Up Along" or "Down Along," which both run along the water.

ELBOW CAY ESSENTIALS

GETTING THERE   You can reach Elbow Cay in about 20 minutes via regularly scheduled ferry service from Great Abaco's Marsh Harbour. One-way fare is US$16 (£8), same-day round-trip costs US$22 (£11), and service goes three times daily.

For details, call **Albury's Ferry Service** at ℭ **242/367-0290** or visit www.alburys ferry.com.

GETTING AROUND   Many visitors rent **boats** to get around the island, snorkel, fish, and explore nearby cays. But if you're not interested in playing sea captain, you can still move easily around Elbow Cay. Hope Town's quiet, narrow streets are reserved for pedestrians and you can walk to many other parts of tiny Elbow Cay. You can't rent a car on the island, but that's not a problem, as Hope Town has banned all motor vehicles. If you'd like a golf cart delivered to your hotel, call **Island Cart Rentals** (ℭ **242/366-0448** in U.S.; www.islandcartrentals.com); these gas or electric carts cost US$45 (£23) per day or US$270 (£135) per week. Hotels provide **shuttle vans** to and from town. Some dining rooms offer pick-up and drop-off service at dinnertime if you call ahead. **Bicycles**—the use of them is often free for hotel guests—are available at or near most accommodations. **Taxis** meet incoming flights at Marsh Harbour airport, and arriving ferries as well. The staff at your hotel can call for one when you need it.

FAST FACTS   If you need **medical attention,** go to Marsh Harbour.

A local **post office** (ℭ 242/366-0098) is at the head of the upper public dock, but expect mail sent from here to take a long time. Hours are Monday to Friday from 9am to noon and from 1 to 5pm.

WHERE TO STAY

Elbow Cay's long, secluded white-sand shores, some backed by dunes, are some of The Bahamas' most stunning. Though accommodations are on or near beaches, the strands remain virtually vacant because the hotels are small and few in number.

Abaco Inn 𝒦 *Finds*   A sophisticated little hideaway about 3km (2 miles) south of Hope Town, Abaco Inn faces a lovely beach on White Sound. Compared to its main rival, Club Soleil (see below), Abaco Inn is more of a resort. An informal barefoot elegance and a welcoming spirit prevail here. The inn is located on Elbow Cay's narrowest section, between the jagged east coast's crashing surf and the sheltered waters of White Sound and the Sea of Abaco to the west. From the cedar-capped gazebo, you can gaze out over the Atlantic's rocky tidal flats. Excellent snorkeling is nearby.

The midsize accommodations are arranged in a crescent facing the beach. They're set amid palms and sea grapes, and each has its own hammock placed conveniently close for quiet afternoons of reading or sleeping. Each comfortable unit has a ceiling fan, a bathroom with a tub/shower, white-tile floors, sliding-glass doors, and traditional furniture.

A modern, rambling clubhouse with a fireplace is the social center and the island's most appealing restaurant (p. 210). Shuttle service is available from the airport, and boating and fishing can be arranged through the hotel.

White Sound, Hope Town, Elbow Cay, Abaco, The Bahamas. ℭ **800/468-8799** in the U.S., or 242/366-0133. Fax 242/ 366-0113. www.abacoinn.com. 22 units. Year-round US$126–US$240 (£63–£120) double. Extra person US$50 (£25) per day. AE, DISC, MC, V. **Amenities:** Restaurant; 2 bars; pool; bike rentals; babysitting; laundry service; nonsmoking rooms; rooms for those w/limited mobility. *In room:* A/C, beverage maker, hair dryer, iron, no phone.

Club Soleil Resort   Abaco Inn (see listing above) may have better accommodations, but nothing surpasses this inn's tranquility. Because of its isolated position near the lighthouse on the west edge of Hope Town's harbor, the only way to get to this Spanish-style resort is by boat. Once there, you're just a short walk from some lovely beaches. If you bring your own boat, you can moor it at this hotel's marina—but if you just happen to have left your boat at home, call the owners, who will arrange a complimentary waterborne transfer from any nearby coastline you designate.

Midsize rooms with shower units are set in a two-story, Mediterranean-inspired annex, overlooking a swimming pool and the boats in the harbor. Each room contains two double beds and clean, tasteful decor.

Western Harbourfront, Hope Town, Elbow Cay, The Bahamas. ✆ **888/291-5428** or 242/366-0003. Fax 242/366-0254. www.clubsoleil.com. 7 units. Year-round US$130–US$150 (£65–£75) double, US$149 (£75) triple, US$150 (£75) quad, US$160 (£80) 2-bedroom apt. AE, MC, V. Closed Sept. **Amenities:** Restaurant; bar; pool; laundry service; all nonsmoking rooms. *In room:* A/C, TV, kitchen (in apt), minibar, coffeemaker, hair dryer, no phone.

Hope Town Harbour Lodge ★★   This much-expanded former private home lies

near Hope Town's beach and harbor. It was the home of Brigadier Thomas Robbins, a British army officer who constructed the original core as his retirement house in 1948. After hurricane damage from Floyd in 1999, the property lay dormant until its recent renovation. Hurricane-strength windows and doors were implemented, along with new furnishings. Possibly the best addition was the installation of private balconies in all the rooms in the main building, each opening onto a water view. Boardwalks and artful landscaping added other grace notes. The best way to stay here is to rent the luxurious century-old Butterfly House. In addition to six independent cottages, each with terra-cotta tile floors and French doors opening onto private decks with a view, the hotel offers six cabanas.

Upper Rd., Hope Town, Elbow Cay, The Bahamas. ✆ **866/611-9791** or 242/366-0095. Fax 242/366-0286. www.hopetownlodge.com. 25 units. Year-round US$175–US$225 (£88–£113) double, US$190–US$195 (£95–£98) cabana, US$255–US$275 (£128–£138) cottage, US$425 (£213) for 4 or US$550 (£275) for 6 in Butterfly House. DC, MC, V. **Amenities:** 2 restaurants; 2 bars; outdoor pool; laundry service; nonsmoking rooms. *In room:* A/C, TV in Butterfly House only, free Wi-Fi, kitchenette (in some), minibar, hair dryer, iron, no phone.

Hope Town Hideaways   Staying here is like living in your own second home in

The Bahamas. Five gingerbread-style villas lie across from where the ferryboats arrive from Marsh Harbour. Located on 4.5 hectares (11 acres) of grounds and reached by boat, this hideaway lives up to its name. The accommodations are part of a larger complex of privately owned homes, surrounded by grounds handsomely landscaped with orange and mango trees and flamboyant bougainvillea. One or two couples—the maximum is six guests—can sleep comfortably in the units, each of which includes a large kitchen, a dining room, a living area with two single daybeds, and two bedrooms. Furnishings are custom-built, and each private bathroom comes with a tub/shower. You won't be on the beach, but you can enjoy the freshwater pool here. Hideaways is also a management company maintaining more than 75 privately owned rental cottages and villas on the island.

1 Purple Porpoise Plaza, Hope Town, Elbow Cay, Abaco, The Bahamas. ✆ **242/366-0224.** Fax 242/366-0434. www.hopetown.com. 5 villas. Year-round from US$1,000 (£500) per week cottage for up to 4 guests. DISC, MC, V. **Amenities:** Freshwater pool. *In room:* A/C, kitchen, no phone.

Sea Spray Resort & Marina ★   On 2.4 hectares (6 acres) of landscaped grounds,

5.5km (3½ miles) south of Hope Town and near Elbow Cay's southernmost tip, these beachfront villas are owned and operated by Ruth Albury, who runs them in a welcoming, personal way.

Accommodations are spacious and comfortably furnished, each with a small bathroom containing a tub/shower. Villas include full kitchens and decks that overlook the water. The Alburys and their hardworking staff are happy to share their vast knowledge of what to see and do around here; you can bike, sail, fish, snorkel, or explore nearby deserted islands.

Sea Spray also operates a restaurant serving well-prepared food at all three mealtimes, and diners enjoy a view of the crashing surf and a weathered gazebo. Nonguests are welcome, too; if you call in advance for a reservation, management will send a van to collect you from Hope Town.

White Sound, Elbow Cay, Abaco, The Bahamas. ℭ 242/366-0065. Fax 242/366-0383. www.seasprayresort.com. 5 units. Year-round US$180–US$260 (£90–£130) 1-bedroom unit, US$350 (£175) 2-bedroom unit, US$430 (£215) 3-bedroom unit. AE, MC, V. **Amenities:** Restaurant; bar; pool; watersports equipment/rentals. *In room:* A/C, TV, kitchen, no phone.

Turtle Hill Vacation Villas ℰ   On the outskirts of Hope Town, a trio of luxury villas (each housing two rental units) lies just steps from a vast secluded beach where sea turtles return to nest. Fruit trees and other tropical foliage make this a secluded getaway. Each house comfortably sleeps six in two large bedrooms, with a queen-size sleeper sofa in the living room, a full bathroom, a well-equipped kitchen, a spacious room for living and dining, central air-conditioning, and ceiling fans. Linens are provided, and a Caribbean-style cabana bar serves drinks and finger foods.

Between Abaco Sea and Hope Town, Abaco, The Bahamas. ℭ **800/339-2124** in the U.S., or 242/366-0557. Fax 242/366-0557. www.turtlehill.com. 6 units. Winter US$380 (£190) daily for 4 guests, US$420 (£210) for 5–6 guests; off-season US$270 (£135) daily for 4 guests, US$310 (£155) for 5–6 guests. AE, MC, V. **Amenities:** Bar; 2 pools; babysitting; laundry service; dry cleaning; nonsmoking rooms. *In room:* A/C, ceiling fans, TV, kitchen, beverage maker, hair dryer (in some), iron, no phone.

WHERE TO DINE
Abaco Inn ℰ BAHAMIAN/INTERNATIONAL   Flavorful food is served in a breezy, almost elegant waterfront setting. The chef prepares lunch dishes such as conch chowder, pasta primavera, and salads with delectable homemade dressings featuring tarragon and other herbs. The dinner menu changes frequently but usually offers seafood, vegetarian, and meat dishes, each expertly seasoned and well-prepared. Typical meals are likely to begin with seafood bisque or vichyssoise, followed by coconut grouper (a house specialty), spinach fettuccine Alfredo, roasted lamb with herbs and mint sauce, or, our favorite, broiled red snapper with a light salsa. The crème brûlée and Key lime, coconut, and chocolate-silk pies are delectable. The inn will send a minivan to pick you up from other parts of the island if you phone in advance.

About 4km (2½ miles) south of Hope Town. ℭ 242/366-0133. Dinner reservations required. Lunch sandwiches, salads, and platters US$8–US$13 (£4–£6.50); dinner main courses US$15–US$40 (£7.50–£20). AE, DISC, MC, V. Daily 8–10:30am, noon–3pm, and 6:30–9:30pm.

Cap'n Jacks BAHAMIAN   Depending on when you come, you may find turtle burgers or crayfish on the menu at this casual alfresco dining spot at the harbor's edge. Any time of year, the grouper and conch are well prepared and are the menu's freshest options. Landlubbers gravitate toward the more routine fried chicken and burgers. The Key lime and chocolate-silk pies are justifiably popular dessert choices. Try the bar's version of the omnipresent Goombay Smash. Come on Wednesday or Friday for live local music between 8 and 11pm.

On the harbor in Hope Town. ℭ 242/366-0247. Main courses US$9–US$19 (£4.50–£9.50). MC, V. Mon–Sat 8:30am–9pm.

Harbour's Edge ℰ BAHAMIAN   Hope Town's best and most popular restaurant is set above the water in a clapboard house. It's the island's lighthearted social center.

The bar has an adjacent waterside deck where you can moor if you arrive by boat, as many visitors do. Here and in the dining room, the crackle of VHF radio is always audible, since boat owners and locals often reserve tables over shortwave radio, channel 16.

Lunch includes typical yet flavor-filled dishes like hamburgers, sandwiches, conch fritters, conch chowder, and conch platters. In the evening, dinners are also well-prepared—entree options include generous portions of chicken in white wine with potatoes, Greek or Caesar salad, pan-fried pork chops, char-grilled grouper, New York strip steak, fish in coconut milk, and more.

Hope Town, next to the post office. © 242/366-0087. Reservations recommended. Main courses lunch US$10–US$18 (£5–£9), dinner US$23–US$40 (£12–£20). MC, V. Wed–Mon 11:30am–11pm. Bar Wed–Mon 10am–2am. Closed mid-Sept to mid-Oct.

Hope Town Harbour Lodge ✿ BAHAMIAN   One of the first lodgings ever built in Hope Town, this hotel's dining options are still winning it new friends. At night, romantic couples opt for a table on the cozy terrace with views of the harbor and yachts' lights. Begin the evening with a rum punch in Wrecker's Bar, which also overlooks the water. The menu here is hardly inventive, but it's good, featuring the usual array of chicken, steak, and pork chops. Occasionally, a fisherman will bring in a big marlin that the chef then grills to perfection. Bahamian lobster appears delightfully in a creamy fettuccine and the local grouper is fashioned into Chinese-style spring rolls served with a mustard-laced chutney sauce. In the main dining area are picture windows, rattan chairs, and nautical prints. During lunch, diners gravitate to the Reef Bar and Grill fronting the water.

Don't overlook the lodge as a possibility for rooms, either. Twenty comfortably furnished and air-conditioned doubles go for US$150 to US$195 (£75–£98). Accommodations come with a patio or balcony, sliding-glass doors, a small bathroom with shower stall, and wicker furnishings.

Hope Town. © 242/366-0095. Reservations recommended for dinner. Main courses lunch US$9–US$15 (£4.50–£7.50), dinner US$25–US$38 (£14–£19). MC, V. Daily 11:30am–3pm; Tues–Sun 6:30–8pm.

BEACHES, WATERSPORTS & OTHER OUTDOOR PURSUITS

In Hope Town, you'll find sandy beaches right at your doorstep, and more beaches are only a 15-minute ride south. **Garbanzo Beach,** near Sea Spray Resort, lures many surfers. Isolated **Tahiti Beach** ✿✿, at the island's southern end (a little more than .6km/1 mile from Sea Spray), got its name from its thick wall of palms. At low tide, the shelling can be excellent along this gorgeous curve of sand, and the shallow waters make for good bonefishing, too. Across the way, you can see uninhabited **Tilloo Cay** and the Atlantic's crashing waves in the distance. Tahiti Beach is about a 10-minute bike ride from Sea Spray and about 20 minutes from Abaco Inn, in the **White Sound area.** To get here, you have to walk your bike up and down a few small but rocky rises.

Traveling along, you'll pass sea-grape trees, fluffy long-needled pines, and other varied roadside vegetation. Turn left when you come to the first major place to do so (by the white house on the bluff) and then turn right when you see two stone pillars. Go downhill and turn left at the end of the road at the wire fences. Take this path to the end. Walk along the dense palm grove to the beach. Because you're heading for the shore, which is public, ignore the PRIVATE—NO TRESPASSING signs.

Irresistible deserted beaches lie south of Elbow Cay on pencil-thin Tilloo Cay and the tiny **Pelican Cays,** excellent targets for a day's sail. The waters here, packed with

Kids Exploring the Abacos by Boat

The ideal way to explore the Abacos is by boat. **Island Marine,** Parrot Cay in Hope Town (© **242/366-0282;** fax 242/366-0281; www.islandmarine.com), will set you up with one of its rentals. You can then cruise to the boat-building settlement of Man-O-War Cay, to artist Pete Johnston's bronze foundry/gallery/pub in Little Harbour (p. 206), and to many uninhabited cays and deserted beaches where you can go shelling, exploring, and picnicking in peace. Small-boat rentals range from a 5.1m Boston Whaler to 7m Man-O-War boats. Prices run from US$125 to US$250 (£63–£125) per day or US$625 to US$1,100 (£313–£550) per week.

grouper and conch, are particularly good for fishing and swimming. In Pelican Cays Land and Sea Park, **Sandy Cay Reef** is one of the most colorful dive sites around. Line fishing, spear fishing, and shelling, however, are all taboo in this protected area.

The waves and breezes at **Garbanzo Beach,** also in the White Sound area, make it prime hang-ten territory. If you didn't bring a surfboard, the staff at nearby **Sea Spray Resort** (© **242/366-0065**) can help you get one.

The waters off the coast of Elbow Cay are popular for boating and fishing. Head to the marina to join the fun.

About 20 steps south of Hope Town's post office, **Froggies Out Island Adventures,** on Harbour Road (© **242/366-0431;** www.froggiesabaco.com), is the largest dive outfitter in the Abacos, with three boats (ranging 9–17m in length) that owner Theresa Albury uses to take divers to local sites. A certified scuba diver is charged US$95 (£48) for an outing and gear rental. Snorkeling excursions cost US$55 (£28) for adults and US$40 (£20) for children.

The company also organizes dolphin-watching trips. A full-day cruise out to Great Guana Cay costs US$45 (£23) per person. An equivalent tour to Little Harbour, near the southernmost point of the Abacos, including visits to selected restaurants, bars, and an art gallery, also costs US$45 (£23) per person.

LAND ATTRACTIONS

No cars are allowed in the heart of **Hope Town,** so bikers and pedestrians have the narrow paved streets, with names like Lovers' Lane, to themselves. As you wander through town, you'll see harborside restaurants and pastel-painted cottages with purple and orange bougainvillea tumbling over stone and picket fences. Amid the usual island fare at the handful of souvenir shops is resort wear made from Androsia fabric (see "Shopping," below).

To find out why Malone is such a common surname here, stop by the **Wyannie Malone Museum** (officially open most days 10am–noon, but unofficially open "whenever"). This small collection of island lore is in tribute to the South Carolinian widow and mother of four who founded Hope Town around 1783.

Before Hope Town's red-and-white-striped **lighthouse** was erected in 1838, many locals made a good living luring ships toward shore to be wrecked on the treacherous reefs and rocks, and then turning the salvaged cargo into cash. To protect this livelihood, some people tried in vain to destroy the beacon while it was being built. Today, you can climb to the top of the 36m (118-ft.) tower for panoramic views of the harbor and town. Most weekdays between 10am and 4pm, the lighthouse keeper will be happy to give you a peek. The lighthouse is within walking distance of Club Soleil and Hope Town Hideaways. If you're staying elsewhere, make arrangements through your hotel for a visit.

SHOPPING

Of course, no one comes to Hope Town just to shop, but once you're here, you might want to pick up a souvenir. The **Ebb Tide Gift Shop** (② 242/366-0088) is the town's best-stocked boutique. It's in an aqua-trimmed white clapboard house 1 block from the harbor. Inside, you'll find many treasures, including Androsia batiks (p. 196), costume jewelry, T-shirts, original watercolors, and fabrics sold by the yard. Hours are 9am to 5pm Monday to Saturday.

ELBOW CAY AFTER DARK

On Saturday nights, a young party crowd gathers at **Harbour's Edge** (② 242/366-0087), a Hope Town bar and restaurant with the island's only pool table. On Monday night, Bahamian barbecues draw many people to **Sea Spray Resort** (② 242/366-0065), about 4.8km (3 miles) from Hope Town. The food is good, considering the low prices, and you can hear live music. Other evenings, people hang out at the bars of hotels and restaurants—or they turn in early to rest up for yet another day of exploring.

3 Man-O-War Cay

Visiting here is like going back in time. The island has lovely beaches, and many visitors come here to enjoy them—but it's best to leave more daring swimwear at home, as the people who reside on this island are deeply religious and conservative. You won't find any crime—unless you bring it with you. No alcoholic beverages are sold on the island, although you can bring your own supply.

Like New Plymouth on Green Turtle Cay or Hope Town on Elbow Cay, Man-O-War is a Loyalist village, with resemblances to a traditional New England town. The pastel clapboard houses, built by ships' carpenters, are set off by freshly painted white picket fences intertwined with bougainvillea.

The people here are shy, but they do welcome outsiders to their isolated island and are proud of their heritage, which includes a long boat-building tradition. Many locals, especially the old-timers, have known plenty of hard times. Like Key West's Conchs (pronounced "conks"), whom they're related to, these are a tough, insular people who have exhibited a proud independence for many years.

Tourism has only just begun to infiltrate Man-O-War Cay. Because of the relative lack of hotels and restaurants, many visitors come just for the day, often in groups, from Marsh Harbour. If you do stay for a while, stop by the **Man-O-War Marina** to arrange your boat rentals and watersports; there's also a dive shop there.

GETTING THERE & GETTING AROUND

To reach Man-O-War Cay, you must cross the water from Marsh Harbour. **Albury's Ferry Service** (② 242/367-3147 in Marsh Harbour or 242/365-6010 in Man-O-War; www.alburysferry.com) leaves from a dock near Abaco Beach Resort. The round-trip same-day fare is US$25 (£13) for adults and US$12 (£6) for children ages 6 to 12. The ride takes about 20 minutes.

Except for a few service vehicles, Man-O-War Cay has almost no cars. If you want to explore farther than your feet will carry you, ask around to find out whether one of the locals will rent you a golf cart.

WHERE TO STAY

Schooner's Landing   Set in isolation on Man-O-War Cay's northeastern edge, this four-unit apartment complex is the island's only official place to stay. A sea wall separates its lawns and hibiscus shrubs from the crashing surf, so swimmers and snorkelers meander a short distance down to the sands of a nearby beach. Each two-story unit contains a kitchen, ceiling fans, two private bathrooms, a TV, and a summery decor of wicker and rattan furniture. Each comes with a small, tidily kept bathroom with a tub/shower. There's no bar or restaurant, but either of the island's two grocery stores will deliver. Most visitors opt to cook in anyway.

Man-O-War Cay, Abaco, The Bahamas. (✆) **242/367-4469** or 365-6072. Fax 242/365-6285. www.schoonerslanding. com. Year-round US$275 (£138) daily, US$1,850 (£925) weekly. MC, V. **Amenities:** Pool; laundry service; nonsmoking rooms; rooms for those w/limited mobility. *In room:* A/C, ceiling fan, TV, kitchen, microwave, barbecue grill, beverage maker, iron.

WHERE TO DINE

Hibiscus Café (✦) *Finds* AMERICAN/BAHAMIAN   The sides of this wooden pavilion are open to the breezes and a view of boats bobbing at the nearby harbor. A crowd of loyal boat owners and local residents is always here, enjoying simple but savory cuisine. Monday to Thursday, the focus is on such time-favored staples as roasted chicken fingers, grilled fish, burgers, fried conch with peas 'n' rice, and steaks. On Friday and Saturday nights, however, many locals arrive for grilled lamb, fish, steaks, or chicken, and the place is practically transformed into a neighborhood block party. Though liquor isn't served, you can bring your own.

Man-O-War Marina, Man-O-War Cay. (✆) **242/365-6380.** Main courses lunch US$5–US$12 (£2.50–£6), dinner US$15–US$32 (£7.50–£16). No credit cards. Mon–Thurs 11am–2pm; Fri–Sat 5:30–9pm.

SHOPPING

A most unusual store and studio, **Albury's Sail Shop,** at the eastern end of Man-O-War Marina (✆ **242/365-6014**), occupies a house overlooking the water. The floor space is devoted to the manufacture and display of brightly colored canvas garments and accessories. The 8-ounce cotton duck fabric they're made from once served as sailcloth for the community's boats. When synthetic sails came into vogue, four generations of Albury women put the cloth and their talents to use. Don't stop in without chatting with them. It's open Monday through Saturday from 7am to 5pm.

4 Great Guana Cay (★)

The longest of the Abaco cays, Great Guana, on the chain's east side, stretches 11km (6¾ miles) from tip to tip and lies between Green Turtle and Man-O-War cays. The spectacular beachfront running the length of the cay is one of the loveliest in The Bahamas. The reef fishing is superb here, and bonefish are plentiful in the shallow bays.

The settlement stretches along the beach at the head of the palm-fringed **Kidd's Cove,** named after the pirate. Ruins of an old **sisal mill** near the western end of the island make for an interesting detour. The island has about 150 residents, most of them descendants of Loyalists who left Virginia and the Carolinas to settle in this remote place, often called "the last spot of land before Africa." The islanders' traditional pursuits include boat-building, carpentry, farming, and fishing.

As in similar settlements in New Plymouth and Man-O-War Cay, houses here resemble those of old New England. It won't take you long to explore the village; it has only two small stores, a one-room schoolhouse, an Anglican church—and that's about it.

GETTING THERE & GETTING AROUND

Albury's Ferry Service, Marsh Harbour (© 242/365-6010; www.alburysferry.com), runs four times a day to Great Guana Cay. A round-trip ticket costs US$22 (£11) for adults, US$11 (£5.50) for children under 11.

Instead of driving on the island, most people get around in small boats. Boats are available to charter for a half- or full day (or a full month, for that matter). A 7m (23-ft.) sailboat, fully equipped for living and cruising, is also available for charter, and deep-sea fishing trips can be arranged. Try **Island Marine Boat Rentals** (© 242/366-0282; www.islandmarine.com), which rents 5m Boston Whalers at US$125 (£63) per day, US$100 (£50) per day for 3 days, or US$625 (£313) per week. **Sea Horse Boat Rentals** (© 242/367-2513; www.sea-horse.com) rents 5.4m Privateers at US$165 (£83) per day (for rentals of 7 days or more, the cost is US$105/£53 per day or US$735/£368 for the week). Both establishments are open Monday to Saturday 8am to 5pm. Island Marine is also open on Sunday 8am to noon.

WHERE TO STAY

Dolphin Beach Resort ⚓   Set directly astride one of the best beaches in The Bahamas, a 15-minute walk north of Guana Cay's largest settlement (Guana Village), with miles of powder-soft sand, this resort offers informal but very comfortable lodgings. Four of the units are in the main house and have queen-size beds and ceiling fans, TVs, small refrigerators, and microwaves; three have private screened-in decks with teakwood furniture. The oceanfront cottages (nine in all) also have queen-size beds, ceiling fans, air-conditioning, and full-size kitchenettes with stoves and charcoal grills. Cottages can accommodate between two and four guests. The showers are outside, but are secluded and screened off by island flora. The entire place is private, intimate, and laid-back.

There's a restaurant on the premises, Bluewater Grill, with a "conch crawl," a Bahamian take on a lobster tank. Nippers, a beachfront bar and grill (see below), is within a 5-minute walk.

Great Guana Cay, Abaco, The Bahamas. © 800/222-2646 or 242/365-5137. www.dolphinbeachresort.com. 13 units. Winter US$200–US$290 (£100–£145) double, US$350–US$400 (£175–£200) 2-bedroom unit, US$360–US$440 (£180–£220) 3-bedroom unit; off-season US$135–US$205 (£68–£103) double, US$290–US$325 (£145–£163) 2-bedroom unit, US$300–US$330 (£150–£165) 3-bedroom unit. MC, V. Closed Sept to mid-Oct. **Amenities:** Restaurant; bar; pool; watersports equipment/rentals; limited room service. *In room:* A/C, TV, kitchen, microwave, beverage maker, hair dryer, no phone.

Flip Flops on the Beach ⚓*Finds*   The name alone suggests how laid-back and casual this little colony of upscale one- and two-bedroom cottages is. It opens onto one of the best sandy beaches in The Bahamas, stretching for 5 miles. Picnic tables are set out for guests who often lunch here, and there's also a private beach pavilion if you'd like a "sundowner." The well-furnished bungalows are breezily decorated with Bahamian handmade art prints and accented by thoughtful extras such as canvas beach chairs, a mahogany four-poster bed, and a charcoal grill. Kitchens are fully equipped.

Great Guana Cay, Treasure, Cay, Abaco. © 800/222-2646. www.flipflopsonthebeach.com. 4 units. Winter US$330 (£165) 1-bedroom cottage, US$400 (£200) 2-bedroom cottage; off-season US$235–US$310 (£118–£155) 1-bedroom cottage, US$330–US$350 (£165–£175) 2-bedroom cottage. Minimum 3-night stay. MC, V. Closed Sept to mid-Oct. **Amenities:** Beachfront. *In room:* Ceiling fans, kitchen, no phone.

WHERE TO DINE

For fun on the beach, head for **Nippers Beach Bar & Grill** (© **242/365-5143;** www.nippersbar.com), a dive where visitors hang out with locals. Right on the sand, you sit in split-level gazebos and take in the most stunning seascape in the Abacos, with a snorkeling reef just 11m (36 ft.) offshore. Burgers and well-stuffed sandwiches satisfy your hunger at lunch. But the best time to go is on a Sunday afternoon, for a pig roast attended by 900 to 1,000 people who gather for food, drinks, and dancing on the beach. One guest is said to have consumed five "Nipper Trippers"—and lived to tell about it. This is the bartender's specialty, a mix of five rums along with tropical juices. It's lethal. The Sunday pig roast is from 12:30 to 4:30pm and costs US$18 (£9); other menu items range from US$9 to US$16 (£4.50–£8). The grill is open daily 11:30am to 10pm, the bar 7am to 10pm. American Express, MasterCard, and Visa are accepted.

5 Treasure Cay ⊛

Treasure Cay now contains one of the most popular and elaborate resorts in the Out Islands. On Great Abaco's east coast, it boasts not only 5.5km (3½ miles) of spectacular sandy beach, widely recognized as being among the top 10 beaches in The Bahamas, but also one of the finest marinas in the Commonwealth, with complete docking and charter facilities.

Before the tourist complex opened, the cay was virtually undeveloped. As a result, the resort has become the "city," providing its thousands of visitors with everything they need, including medical supplies, grocery items, liquor (naturally), and bank services. But don't count on having these services when you need them. There are no ATMs on the island, and the bank is open only Tuesday and Thursday (and Thurs is payday on the island, so it's impossibly overcrowded). Medical supplies, even contact-lens solution, aren't available on the weekends. The real-estate office peddles condos, and the builders predict that they will one day reach a capacity of 5,000 owners. They're hoping that many visitors will like Treasure Cay enough to buy into it.

See "Getting There" under "Abacos Essentials," at the beginning of this chapter, for details on flying to Treasure Cay. Some direct service is available to the island from Florida. You could also fly into Marsh Harbour and take a 32km (20-mile) taxi ride north along the paved but bumpy Sherben A. Boothe Highway.

Treasure Cay hosts one of the most popular fishing tournaments in The Bahamas: the **Treasure Cay Billfish Championship** in May.

GETTING AROUND

Renting a car isn't necessary. To get where you're going, you can walk, bike, or take a golf cart or a taxi. Some restaurants outside the resort will send a shuttle to pick you up from your hotel. Except for moving between the airport or ferry dock and your hotel, you won't need a cab. For details about taxi fares, call the **Treasure Cay Airport Taxi Stand** (© **242/365-8661**). For a special occasion, call **Elegante Limo Service** (© **242/365-8248** or 365-8053; US$120/£110 per hour for up to 10 passengers); this company also rents golf carts.

The only real reason to rent a car is for the 35-minute drive to Marsh Harbour to catch the ferries to Elbow Cay and Man-O-War Cay. If you decide to do so, you can rent a car for about US$75 (£38) per day at **Cornish Car Rental** (© **242/365-8623**) at Treasure Cay Airport.

Through **Wendell's Bicycle Rentals** (© **242/365-8687**), across from the bank in the Treasure Cay shopping center, you can rent beach cruisers (single-gear bikes with wide wheels) or mountain bikes for US$8 (£4) per day or US$43 (£22) per week. Four-seater electric golf carts go for US$40 (£20) per day or US$245 (£123) per week through Wendell's or **Claridge Golf Carts** (© **242/365-8248** or 365-8053), just outside town.

WHERE TO STAY

Rooms can be scarce in May, when the place is packed with anglers trying to achieve fame in the Treasure Cay Billfish Championship.

Bahama Beach Club 🏖 Lying right off Treasure Cay Beach, this luxurious condo complex, the most idyllic spot in the Abacos for families, maintains elegantly furnished accommodations with two to four bedrooms. Most of the condos, though individually decorated, are filled with rattan furnishings and bold, colorful fabrics, along with a well-equipped kitchen and a spacious living room. Each accommodation opens onto a private patio or balcony overlooking the ocean. Daily housekeeping services are provided, and eateries are nearby.

Treasure Cay, Abaco, The Bahamas. © 800/284-0382 or 242/365-8500. Fax 242/365-8501. www.bahamabeachclub. com. 45 condos. Year-round US$350 (£175) 2-bedroom, US$400 (£200) 3-bedroom, US$500 (£250) 4-bedroom. 3-night minimum stay. AE, MC, V. **Amenities:** Outdoor pool; Internet access; laundry service. *In room:* Ceiling fans, kitchen.

Treasure Cay Hotel Resort & Marina 🏖 One of the biggest of the Out Island resorts, this property attracts boaters, golfers, fishermen, and divers, as well as yachties and escapists seeking a remote yet luxurious retreat. The foundation for this resort was laid in 1962, when a group of international investors recognized its potential. The vast majority of the peninsula, as well as the marina facility, all the villas, 80 privately owned condominiums, the tennis courts, and several blocks of other housing, remains under the ownership of the original investors. Guests can rent electric golf carts (around US$35/£18 per day) or bicycles to explore the sprawling compound's far-flung palm and casuarina groves.

Along with architecture that looks like it jumped off the pages of *House & Garden,* the setting here includes tropical plants, a spectacular beachfront, an excellent golf course, and marina facilities. Furnished simply in conservatively modern tropical motifs, most accommodations overlook the dozens of sailing craft moored in the marina. The renovated rentals are very attractive, with full kitchens, two bedrooms, and washer/dryers, plus a midsize bathroom with a tub/shower.

A restaurant, the Spinnaker (p. 218), serves standard fare, while two bars dispense tropical drinks.

Treasure Cay, Abaco, The Bahamas. © 800/327-1584 or 954/525-7711. Fax 954/525-1699. www.treasurecay.com. 96 units. Aug–Feb US$150–US$190 (£75–£95) double, US$240–US$290 (£120–£145) 2-bedroom suite, US$390 (£195) 3-bedroom suite; Mar–July US$170 (£85) double, US$290 (£145) 2-bedroom suite, US$390 (£195) 3-bedroom suite. Full board US$60 (£30) per person per day. US$20 (£10) extra per person per day. AE, DISC, MC, V. **Amenities:** Restaurant; 2 bars; pool; golf course; 6 tennis courts; watersports equipment/rentals; nonsmoking rooms; rooms for those w/limited mobility. *In room:* A/C, TV, kitchenette, beverage maker, hair dryer, iron.

WHERE TO DINE

Many vacationers opt to stay in accommodations with kitchens or kitchenettes. However, if you know you're not going to feel like cooking, consider purchasing your hotel's meal plan or dine at Spinnaker (see below). You might also sample a local dive called **Coconut's** on Queen's Highway (© **242/365-8885**), which serves typically Bahamian fare such as grouper and conch, plus a few Italian specialties. Main courses range from US$12 to US$25 (£6–£13), and it's open daily from 6 to 9:30pm.

Spinnaker Restaurant & Lounge AMERICAN/BAHAMIAN   Serving reliable seafood, steak, pasta, and Bahamian specialties, this restaurant at the Treasure Cay Hotel Resort (p. 217) occupies a prime waterside spot. For lunch, the cracked conch makes a good choice. At night, the portions of meat and potatoes or fresh fish (prepared in a variety of ways, from steamed to blackened) are generous. Guests of the Banyan Beach Club, about a half-mile away, usually arrive by golf cart.

In Treasure Cay Marina. © **242/365-8469**. Reservations recommended for dinner. Main courses US$17–US$32 (£8.50–£16). MC, V. Daily 7am–10pm. Limited hours in autumn and early winter.

BEACHES, WATERSPORTS & OTHER OUTDOOR PURSUITS

The **beaches** here are blissfully tranquil. Watersports in Treasure Cay are lots of fun, especially during the Treasure Cay Billfish Championship each spring. And although this area is far less developed than the more popular islands, golfers don't have to head to Nassau or Freeport for a great game. The course here is a big draw.

If you're seeking a beach with some of the softest, whitest sand you can imagine and water in some of the most amazing shades of blue and green, then **Treasure Cay Beach** is it. What's especially alluring is that—unlike eye-catching stretches on busier, more built-up islands—this 5.5km (3½-mile) shore is never crowded.

Treasure Cay Golf Club (© **242/365-8535**), designed by Dick Wilson, offers 6,985 yards of fairways, though it's hardly the best course the famed golf architect ever designed. Greens fees for hotel guests are US$45 (£23) for 9 holes and US$65 (£33) for 18 holes; for nonguests, it's US$60 (£30) for 9 holes and US$95 (£48) for 18 holes. This is the only golf course in the Abacos, and it lies 1km (⅔ mile) from the center of the resort.

Treasure Cay Marina (© **242/365-8250**) offers full-service facilities for a variety of watersports. Fishing boats with experienced skippers guide anglers to tuna, marlin, wahoo, dolphinfish, barracuda, grouper, yellowtail, and snapper. You can also rent a sailboat, a Hobie Cat, windsurfing boards, and snorkeling gear. The marina provides shower stalls, fish-cleaning facilities, daily laundry service, and water and electricity hookups.

Deep-sea fishing is set up through the reception desk of the Treasure Cay Hotel Resort (© **242/365-8535**), which can also arrange for you to hire a bonefishing guide. The same resort has six of the best **tennis** courts in the Abacos, four of which are lit for night games. Fees are US$14 (£7) hourly.

Treasure Cay Hotel Resort (© **954/525-7711**) also offers six tennis courts—three clay surfaces (US$16/£8 per hour) and three hard surfaces (US$14/£7 per hour)—all lit for night play. Check with the hotel to make arrangements.

The best **diving** is provided by **J.I.C. Boat Rentals & Treasure Divers** (© **242/365-8582**), which rents equipment and takes scuba divers to some of the best sites in the Abacos, where they see spectacular marine life in all its rainbow-hued glory. Guana Cay, Whale Cay, and No Name Cay are some of the best sites for viewing Bahamian marine life. Divers can also visit the underwater wreck of **San Jacinto,** a steamship freighter that sunk in 1865. The cost for any dive is US$90 (£45) for one tank, US$110 (£55) for two tanks.

TREASURE CAY AFTER DARK

Fishermen, yachties, and hotel guests head to the **Tipsy Seagull Bar** (© 242/365-8535), which presents live music sometime after 8pm in winter (off-season on Fri–Sat nights only). The setting is an A-frame and the decor is nautical memorabilia. When there's a fishing tournament on the island, this bar is jam-packed. Bar patrons can order pizza and lobster from the resort's adjoining Spinnaker restaurant. Happy hour is nightly from 5 to 7pm. It's closed in autumn and early winter.

6 Green Turtle Cay (New Plymouth) ★ ★

Five kilometers (3 miles) off Great Abaco's east coast, Green Turtle Cay is the archipelago's jewel, a little island with an uneven coastline, deep bays, sounds, and good beaches, one of which stretches for 1,080m (3,543 ft.). You can roam through green forests, gentle hills, and secluded inlets. The island is 5.5km (3½ miles) long and 1km (⅔ mile) across, lying some 274km (170 miles) due east of Palm Beach, Florida.

Water depths seldom exceed 4.5 to 6m (15–20 ft.) around here, and coral gardens teem with colorful sea life, making for fabulous snorkeling. The shells you'll find on the lovely beaches and offshore sandbars are among The Bahamas' finest. If you have a boat, you can explore such deserted islands as Fiddle Cay to the north, and No Name Cay and Pelican Cay to the south.

New Plymouth, at the cay's southern tip, is an 18th-century settlement that has the flavor of an old New England sailing port. Much of the original masonry was fashioned from lime that was produced when conch shells were broken up, burned, and sifted for cement (records say that the alkali content was so high that it would burn the masons' hands). Clapboard houses with pretty trimmings line the little town's narrow streets. New Plymouth, which once had a population of 1,800 people, now has 400. Parliament is the village's main street, and you can walk its length in just 10 minutes, passing only by a few clucking hens. Many of the houses have front porches, on which locals sit in the evening to enjoy the breezes.

Green Turtle Cay became known for the skill of its shipbuilders, though the industry, like many others in the area, failed after slaves were emancipated in 1838.

GREEN TURTLE CAY ESSENTIALS

GETTING THERE   Fly to **Treasure Cay Airport,** where a taxi will take you to the ferry dock for departures to Green Turtle Cay (New Plymouth). At the dock, you may have to wait a while for the ferry; the crossing takes about 15 to 20 minutes to Green Turtle Cay and will take you to the Green Turtle Club, if you're staying there, or to New Plymouth. This land-and-sea transfer costs US$16 (£8) per person round-trip.

GETTING AROUND   Though you can walk to many parts of Green Turtle Cay, the most common mode of transportation is by water. Some hotels provide water transport to town or to weekly hotel parties. Many vacationers **rent boats,** but if you'd rather not, you have other choices for getting around. Most of the island is accessible by foot. The virtually car-free streets of New Plymouth, the quiet 18th-century village by the sea, are prime walking territory. On Green Turtle Cay, **golf carts** stand in for rental cars. **D & P Rentals** (© 242/365-4655) at Green Turtle Club rents theirs for

US$45 (£23) for 8 hours or US$55 (£28) for 24 hours. You can **bike** all over the island, and pedaling is especially scenic in historic New Plymouth.

FAST FACTS   First Caribbean International Bank, which has an **ATM,** operates a branch (© **242/365-4144**) open only from 10am to 2pm on Tuesday and Thursday.

If you need **medical attention,** visit the government clinic (© **242/365-4028**), run by a nurse.

You enter Green Turtle Cay's **post office** (© **242/365-4242**), also the site of a **public telephone,** through a pink door on Parliament Street. Its hours are Monday to Friday from 9am to 5pm.

There's no crime in New Plymouth, so the little stone **jail** here makes visitors chuckle. No one can remember when, if ever, it held a prisoner.

SPECIAL EVENTS   One event that draws visitors in droves is the **Green Turtle Club Fishing Tournament, held in May. In 1984, the winner hooked a 226kg (498-lb.) blue marlin; it was so heavy that the competing participants from other boats generously climbed aboard the winning craft to reel the fish in. For more information, contact one of the Bahamian tourist offices or the **Green Turtle Club** (© **866/528-0539** or 242/365-4271), which more or less becomes the island's official headquarters when the tournament is held.

WHERE TO STAY

The Bluff House Beach Hotel ⟨★★⟩   One of the most famous and legendary hotels in the Out Islands, Bluff House originated in the 1950s when it was the private home of C. Pearce Cody III and his wife, Kitty. When friends of their friends asked if they could pay for a few days' stay, the Codys reinvented their home as the region's first hotel. In the years since, they've welcomed some extremely famous guests, including a well-heeled "same time next year" group.

Bluff House occupies one of the country's most desirable pieces of real estate: 4 hectares (10 acres) on the highest point in the Abacos with panoramic views. The property fronts the Sea of Abaco on one side and the sheltered harbor of White Sound on the other. A romantic spot, it has a lovely nautical charm with British colonial overtones. Against a backdrop of palm, oak, and pine-forested jogging trails, it lies within a 5-minute boat ride from New Plymouth (p. 219).

The hotel offers villas and hotel rooms in a variety of configurations and sizes, either set beside the beach or cantilevered into the steep hillside facing the sheltered harbor; all have lovely views and some have kitchens. The best accommodations are the spacious colonial-style suites, with cathedral ceilings and balconies that overlook the Sea of Abaco. Inside, decor includes floral bedcovers and tropical furniture.

Meals are served in the main Club House (p. 222), where drinks and fresh hors d'oeuvres are offered before a candlelit dinner that features local conch, grouper, snapper, and lobster, as well as roasted duck à l'orange. The bar in the hotel's main building is one of our favorite rooms in The Bahamas, with vistas sweeping across Green Turtle Cay. The blue-and-white cypress-paneled interior is cozy and comfortable, with the benefit of simple good taste. Peacefulness and prosperity prevail among nautical memorabilia and a flickering fire within an iron stove as slow-whirling tropical fans, wicker furnishings, and polished wooden floors create an upscale and highly appealing ambience. The grill, called the Jolly Roger Bistro, specializes in light meals. On

Tuesday evenings, there's an elaborate beachfront barbecue that's accompanied by music from a live local band.

Green Turtle Cay, Abaco, The Bahamas. ℂ **800/745-4911** or 242/365-4247. Fax 242/365-4248. www.bluffhouse. com. 30 units. Year-round US$200–US$306 (£100–£153) double, US$188–US$332 (£94–£166) suite, US$282– US$569 (£141–£285) villa, from US$625 (£313) cottage. Meal plan (breakfast and dinner) US$20 (£10) per person. AE, MC, V. **Amenities:** 2 restaurants; 2 bars; pool; tennis court; nonsmoking rooms. *In room:* A/C, beverage maker, hair dryer, no phone.

Cocobay Cottages

On the north end of Green Turtle Cay, where 150m (492 ft.) of land separate the Atlantic from the Sea of Abaco, this complex opens onto one beach on the island's Atlantic side and another sandy beach on the more tranquil bay. It's ideal for those who'd like to anchor in for a while. In fact, lots of folks arrive by private boat, which you can moor here for free. Otherwise, guests arrive by water taxi from the airport dock. The management welcomes a 70% repeat clientele. Set on 2 hectares (5 acres) dotted with some 50 tropical fruit trees, the spacious cottages here, which have improved over the years, feature Caribbean furnishings and refreshing pastel colors. The smallest accommodation, the honeymoon cottage, sleeps only two in one bedroom. The largest lodging is a two-bedroom, two-bathroom unit, which can comfortably sleep five. It offers a living room, a dining room, and a fully equipped kitchen with microwave. Linens and kitchen utensils are also provided (you can stock up on food at one of New Plymouth's three grocery shops), and air-conditioning, ceiling fans, and trade winds cool the rooms. A 1-week minimum stay is required.

Green Turtle Cay, Abaco, The Bahamas. ℂ **800/752-0166** or 242/365-5464. Fax 242/365-5465. www.cocobaycottages. com. 6 cottages. Year-round US$400–US$550 (£200–£275) daily cottage for 6 guests or US$2,700–US$3,600 (£1,350– £1,800) weekly, US$275–US$400 (£138–£200) daily cottage for 2 guests or US$1,700–US$2,700 (£850–£1,350) weekly. MC, V. **Amenities:** Exercise equipment; laundry service; nonsmoking rooms. *In room:* A/C, kitchen, beverage maker, hair dryer, no phone.

Green Turtle Club Resort & Marina 🐢🐢

An outstanding place for laid-back luxury, this resort attracts honeymooners and snorkelers. The excellent full-service marina and dive shop on-site draw serious anglers, boaters, and divers. The waters around the resort are shallow enough to spot schools of fish from the shore—sometimes you'll even see a green turtle paddling above the sandbanks.

Spread across 32 hectares (79 acres) of low-lying scrubland, the inn feels very much like a country club. The courteous staff members offer assistance yet don't intrude on peace or privacy.

The resort's yacht club, host of the prestigious Bahama Cup Around the Island Race, is associated with Florida's Palm Beach Yacht Club and England's Birdham Yacht Club. Members have their own villas right on the water, often with private docks.

Temporary guests lodge in spacious bungalows (usually two accommodations to a building) set within a gently sloping, carefully landscaped garden. Rooms are among the region's most upscale and luxurious—think England in the Tropics. Bedrooms boast Sheraton-style mahogany furniture, four-poster beds, French-inspired draperies, oak floors, terra cotta-tiled patios, and wicker or rattan furniture. Each comes with an immaculate midsize bathroom, and almost all contain tub/showers plus generous shelf space.

The flag-festooned bar is the resort's social center, where there's occasionally live music. There's an unmistakably British tone to evenings here, beginning with pre-dinner cocktails beside a roaring fire in the bar's iron stove (in chilly weather only, of course) before everyone adjourns to the pine-paneled dining room for well-prepared dinners. Breakfast and lunch are usually served on the veranda.

Green Turtle Cay, Abaco, The Bahamas. ✆ 242/365-4271. Fax 242/365-4272. www.greenturtleclub.com. 34 units. Year-round US$180–US$280 (£90–£140) double, US$495 (£248) 2-bedroom unit, US$635 (£318) 3-bedroom unit. Children under 12 stay free in parent's room. Extra person US$25 (£13) per day. Meal plan (breakfast and dinner) US$48 (£24). AE, MC, V. Take a taxi from Treasure Cay Airport to the ferry dock, transfer to a water taxi to the club for about US$15 (£7.50) each way. **Amenities:** Restaurant; 2 bars; pool; watersports equipment/rentals; bike rentals; Internet access; babysitting; coin-operated laundry; nonsmoking rooms. *In room:* A/C, TV, fridge, beverage maker, hair dryer, iron, no phone.

WHERE TO DINE

The previously recommended hotels have the island's best food, but consider one of these local spots as well.

The Club House Restaurant ⍟ INTERNATIONAL　Drop in here midday for a burger, sandwich, or salad. Dinner has an elegant note—start an evening meal with the cocktail hour at the bar, which we think is one of the most beautiful and appealing in the Out Islands. Lined with limed cypress, trimmed in cerulean blue, and beautifully proportioned, it includes sweeping views out over two shorefronts from the highest point in the Abacos. Dinner is served in a Queen Anne-style dining room. It's always a set menu, with items that change every night, but the cuisine is invariably excellent. Start with something like Waldorf salad or smoked salmon, followed by grilled and mango-flavored chicken breast, or lobster tail that's simply broiled with lemon and butter. Triple chocolate cheesecake or Key lime pie are soothing desserts.

At Bluff House Club Beach Hotel, Green Turtle Cay. ✆ 242/365-4247. Reservations required. Lunch platters US$10–US$20 (£5–£10); fixed-price dinners US$35 (£18) per person. AE, MC, V. Daily 11:30am–2:30pm; hors d'oeuvre service (included in dinner price) begins at 6:30pm, dinner begins at 7:30pm.

Laura's Kitchen BAHAMIAN/AMERICAN　On the town's main street, across from the Albert Lowe Museum, this family-owned spot occupies a well-converted white Bahamian cottage. Laura Sawyer serves up lunch and dinner amid her simple, homey decor. The menu changes nightly, depending on what's at the market, but she always serves the old reliables her family has eaten for generations: fried grouper, fried chicken, and a tasty cracked conch. The eatery is mainly known for its burgers: fish burgers, conch burgers, hamburgers, cheeseburgers, and bacon-and-cheese burgers.

King St. ✆ 242/365-4287. Reservations recommended for dinner. Lunch US$4–US$11 (£2–£5.50); dinner US$13–US$25 (£6.50–£13). MC, V. Mon–Sat 11am–3pm and 6–9pm; Sun 5:30–8pm. Closed Sept and Christmas Day.

Plymouth Rock Liquors & Café BAHAMIAN/AMERICAN　This place has New Plymouth's best selection of wines and liquors, including at least 70 kinds of rum; it also carries Cuban cigars. Part of its space is set aside for a pleasant and attractive luncheonette run by hardworking co-owners Kathleen and David Bethell. They serve up tasty sandwiches, split-pea soup, beef souse, and cracked conch with cucumber slices and potato salad. There's also an on-site art gallery, featuring works by about 50 artists, many of whom specialize in local themes.

Parliament St. ✆ 242/365-4234. Sandwiches and platters US$4–US$8.50 (£2–£4.25). DISC, MC, V. Cafe Mon–Sat 9am–3:30pm. Liquor store Mon–Thurs 9am–6pm, Fri–Sat 9am–7pm.

Rooster's Rest Pub & Restaurant BAHAMIAN　This local dive just beyond the edge of town serves good Bahamian food, including lobster, conch, and your best bet, fresh fish. It's casual through and through, the way The Bahamas used to be; nouvelle cuisine hasn't washed up on these shores yet. All main courses in the evening are served with peas 'n' rice, coleslaw, and potato salad. The cook also prepares some tasty ribs. Live music is offered at least 2 nights a week.

Gilliam's Bay Rd. *C* **242/365-4066.** Reservations recommended for dinner. Lunch burgers and snacks US$8–US$12 (£4–£6); main courses US$10–US$23 (£5–£12). MC, V. Mon–Sat 11:30am–9:30pm.

The Wrecking Tree Bar & Restaurant BAHAMIAN   This funky place is recognized by its coral and terra-cotta colors, and by the much-mangled casuarina tree that grows next to its foundation. The hearty menu is as simple as can be, featuring mostly peas 'n' rice, conch, grouper fingers, chicken souse, and burgers. Come here for lunch, a midday beer, and a view over the boats in the nearby harbor.

The Harbourfront. *C* **242/365-4263.** Main courses US$13–US$19 (£6.50–£9.50). No credit cards. Mon–Sat 11am–9pm.

BEACHES, WATERSPORTS & OTHER OUTDOOR PURSUITS

Along with sampling Green Turtle Cay's aquatic diversions, you can visit a museum and wander the streets of New Plymouth, the historic waterfront village.

About a 10-minute walk from **Bluff House** and 5 minutes from the **Green Turtle Club, Coco Bay** 🐠🐠 is one of the most beautiful crescents in The Bahamas. Shaded by casuarina pine trees and lapped by lazy waves, this long beach is often empty. The rougher **Ocean Beach,** about a 10-minute stroll from either Bluff House or the Green Turtle Club, is another stunner. Frothy waves thrash the starkly white sand, set off by the Atlantic's intense blue.

You can take a boat trip to one of the nearby uninhabited islands that are ringed with even more pristine beaches. On **Manjack Cay,** for example, the expanse of sugar-white sand seems to go on forever, and the shallow, clear water is a brilliant shade of turquoise. There's no regular service from the ferry dock; negotiate with one of the local boatmen. The staff at your hotel will be helpful in this regard.

With one of the world's largest barrier reefs, **the Abacos** offers some of The Bahamas' best snorkeling and diving sites. You can get an eyeful at reefs starting in depths of just 1.5m (5 ft.) and ranging to more than 18m (59 ft.). Like sheets on a clothesline, sprawling schools of fish billow by coral caverns, huge tube and barrel sponges, and fields of elk and staghorn coral. Sea turtles and large groupers are common sights. In fact, the waters are so clear that you can often see farther than 30m (98 ft.).

Scuba divers can poke around the wreck of the *San Jacinto,* an American steamship that was built in 1847 and sank 2 decades ago. Here, you can feed the resident bright-green moray eels. Rates run about US$140 (£70) for a scuba course, US$500 (£250) for full certification, US$85 (£43) for a one-tank dive, and US$110 (£55) for a two-tank dive.

If you like small groups and big fun, try **Brendal's Dive Center** (*C* **242/365-4411;** www.brendal.com) at the **Green Turtle Club Marina.** Whether you're an experienced diver or snorkeler or you're just getting your feet wet, the personal attention makes the difference here. Originally from Acklins, a small Bahamian island to the south, Brendal has more than 20 years of underwater experience. A special treat for snorkelers is the wild dolphin encounter trip ($75/£38 per person), which includes stops at undisturbed islands. This company also rents kayaks ($10/£5 per hour for singles, US$20/£10 per hour for doubles, or US$199/£100 per week for the single, US$250/£125 for the double). You can also try **Green Turtle Divers** (*C* **242/365-4271**), which has a full-service dive shop right at the hotel. Divers and snorkelers who are guests of the hotel get a 15% discount.

Call Lincoln Jones at *C* **242/365-4223,** and he'll arrange a snorkeling adventure for you—probably on some deserted beach that only he knows about. Prices are to be negotiated, of course, but a lunch of fresh conch or lobster is a fine addition to any day.

If you've had enough of sitting on the beach and relaxing, you can explore the ocean. From boat rentals to fishing expeditions, Green Turtle Cay offers an array of things to do.

Based at the Green Turtle Club, **Brendal's Dive Center** (© **242/365-4411**) can take you on a group sunset cruise (complete with rum punch) on an 8.8m sailboat for US$75 (£38) per person (up to eight passengers).

Contact **Donny's Boat Rentals** (© **242/365-4119**) in **Black Sound** for speed-boats. This company rents Whalers and Makos (types of motorboats) starting at US$82 (£41) per day for a 4.2m boat. Or try **Reef Rentals** (© **242/365-4145**), directly across from the ferry dock in **New Plymouth.** This fleet includes a sleek motorboat made on **Man-O-War Cay,** the nearby island long known for its excellent boat craftsmanship. Rentals start at US$265 (£133) for 3 days for a 5.7m Wellcraft.

Reserving a boat when you make your hotel and airline reservations is a good idea, particularly during the busy spring and summer months.

Fishermen from all over the world visit Green Turtle Cay, seeking yellowfin, dolphinfish, and big-game wahoo, among other catches. If you want to go deep-sea fishing, check with the two cousins in the Sawyer family. Referrals are usually made through the **Green Turtle Club** (© **242/365-4070**), or you can call directly at © **242/ 365-2461.**

The annual **Green Turtle Club Fishing Tournament** (© **800/688-4752** or 242/365-4271) was on hold at press time, but if you're planning to visit in May, call to find out whether it's back on. There's a tennis court at **Bluff House** (© **242/ 365-4247**), where guests play free.

EXPLORING THE ISLAND: A JOURNEY TO THE 18TH CENTURY

New Plymouth celebrated its bicentennial in 1984 by establishing the **Memorial Sculpture Garden** to honor Loyalists and some of their notable descendants, including Albert Lowe, a pioneer boat-builder and historian, and African-Bahamian Jeanne I. Thompson, the second woman to practice law in The Bahamas. At the memorial, across from New Plymouth Inn on Parliament Street, you can read about some of the Loyalists who came to The Bahamas from New England and the Carolinas. Statues are also dedicated to those people who were enslaved in these islands. This garden is laid out in the pattern of the Union Jack flag.

There isn't much shopping here, but consider a visit to **Ocean Blue Gallery,** adjoining Plymouth Rock Café on Parliament Street (© **242/365-4234**). This two-room outlet has one of the best collections of local artwork in the Abacos, including original sculptures and paintings.

Albert Lowe Museum ★★   More than anything else we've seen in The Bahamas, this museum, set in a beautifully restored Loyalist home, conveys the rawboned and sometimes difficult history of the Out Islands. You could easily spend a couple of hours reading the fine print of the dozens of photographs that show the hardship and the valor of citizens who changed industries as often as the economic circumstances of their era dictated.

The caretaker will give you a tour of the stone kitchen, which occupants of the house used as a shelter when a hurricane devastated much of New Plymouth in 1932. Inside the house, a narrow stairway leads to three bedrooms that reveal the simplicity

Finds **Miss Emily's Blue Bee Bar**

Our favorite bar in the Out Islands is **Miss Emily's Blue Bee Bar,** on Victoria Street in New Plymouth (© **242/365-4181**). This simple bar is likely to be the scene of the liveliest party in the Out Islands at any time of day; even normally buttoned-up types find themselves flirting or dancing before long. You never know what will be going on here. Until rising waters from the 1999 hurricanes washed some of them away, most of its walls were covered with the business cards of past guests and celebrities. Stop by and see how many replacements have been plastered up. The Goombay Smash, a specialty here, has been called "Abaco's answer to atomic fission." Its recipe includes proportions of coconut rum, "dirty" rum, apricot brandy, and pineapple juice. Miss Emily (Mrs. Emily Cooper) was a legend in these parts. She's gone now, but her memory lives on: Her daughter, Violet Smith, knows her secret recipe for the Goombay Smash and makes a potent rum punch. Tips go to St. Peter's Anglican Church. No food is served, but the bar opens Monday to Saturday from 11am until late.

of 18th-century life on Green Turtle Cay. Amid antique settees, irreplaceable photographs, and island artifacts, you'll see a number of handsome ship models, the work of Albert Lowe, for whom the museum was named.

The paintings of Alton Lowe, son of the museum's namesake, are also on display. Cherub-faced and red-haired, Alton is—and has been for a while—one of the best-known painters in The Bahamas. His works are part of collections all over the world; some appear on Bahamian postage stamps, blowups of which are displayed here. Your tour guide might open the house's basement, where some of Alton's paintings are for sale alongside work by other local artists. There's also a garden in the back of the house.

Parliament St. © **242/365-4094**. Admission US$5 (£2.50) adults, US$3 (£1.50) students, free for children 5 and under. Mon–Sat 9–11:45am and 1–4pm.

GREEN TURTLE CAY AFTER DARK

Ask at your hotel if the local Junkanoo band, the **Gully Roosters,** are playing their reggae- and calypso-inspired sounds. They're the best in the Abacos and often appear at various spots on the island. Also make sure to visit **Miss Emily's Blue Bee Bar** (described in the box below). You might catch a live band, and you'll certainly enjoy a wonderful setting for a drink, in the bars at the **Bluff House** and the **Green Turtle Club** (see "Where to Stay," earlier). **Rooster's Rest Pub & Restaurant** (p. 222) is yet another option.

A much more upscale bar than Miss Emily's is the **Yacht Club Pub** (© **242/365-4271**), at the Green Turtle Club. Along with sailors and fishermen, some of the captains (and owners) of the world's most expensive yachts stop here to enjoy the lively atmosphere and the bartender's special, a Tipsy Turtle, made by the gallon (it's got orange juice, pineapple juice, vodka, coconut rum, banana rum, and grenadine). Appetizers are served nightly from 6:30 to 7:30pm. Live bands perform on Monday, Wednesday, and Friday nights.

7 Spanish Cay

Set 19km (12 miles) northwest of Green Turtle Cay, this island was named after a pair of Spanish galleons that sank offshore in the 17th century. Originally owned by Queen Elizabeth II, the island was purchased in the 1960s by Texas-based investor (and former owner of the Dallas Cowboys) Clint Murchinson. After his death in the early 1980s, two successive Florida conglomerates poured time, money, and landscaping efforts into developing the island as a site for upscale private homes. Today, visitors and locals putter along the island's paved roads in electric golf carts.

Most visitors arrive by private boat or chartered aircraft from Fort Lauderdale. You can also fly to Treasure Cay from West Palm Beach on **Bahamasair** (℃ **242/377-8451;** fax 242/377-7409; www.bahamasair.com) and have the inn arrange water transportation. Two daily flights arrive from Nassau.

WHERE TO STAY & DINE

Spanish Cay Resort & Marina ⟨★⟩   Renovations and improved transportation have made this property better and more accessible than ever. Bedrooms have been completely refurbished to accommodate more than two guests per room. All the suites are roomy and spacious, with a double bed, a foldout sofa bed, and a small refrigerator, plus a tidy bathroom with a shower stall. The apartments are even more spacious, with both king-size beds and twins in their two bedrooms, plus a full kitchen, living room, dining room, and deck overlooking the marina. A one-bedroom apartment can sleep up to four people; a two-bedroom accommodates six.

Two on-site restaurants, **Point House,** open daily, and **Wrecker's Bar,** open in high season, serve conch, chicken, fresh fish, steak, and, occasionally, lobster. Dinners are reasonably priced. You can also get food and drinks at the poolside bar.

Cooper's Town, Abaco, The Bahamas. ℃ **242/365-0083.** Fax 242/365-0453. www.spanishcay.com. 22 units. Sept 16–Feb US$165–US$195 (£83–£98) double, US$295 (£148) 1-bedroom unit, US$390 (£195) 2-bedroom unit, US$875 (£438) 4-bedroom unit; Mar–Sept 15 US$215–US$275 (£108–£138) double, US$375 (£188) 1-bedroom unit, US$475 (£238) 2-bedroom unit, US$875 (£438) 4-bedroom unit. MC, V. **Amenities:** 2 restaurants; bar; freshwater pool; 4 tennis courts; spa; watersports. *In room:* A/C, TV, fridge, no phone.

8 Walker's Cay

At the edge of the Bahama Bank, this is the northernmost, the outermost, and one of the smallest islands in the Abaco chain. Coral reefs surround it, dropping off to depths of some 300m (984 ft.). It's known around the world as one of the best deep-sea fishing resorts. The cay produces its own fresh water and electricity.

Ponce de León reportedly stopped here in 1513 in search of fresh water—just 6 days before he "discovered" Florida. From the 17th century, this was a place known to pirates, who stored their booty here. It became a bastion for blockade-runners during the American Civil War; later, it was a hideout for rumrunners in the days of U.S. Prohibition.

To get here, prospective guests should call the Walker's Cay Hotel and Marina at ℃ **800/WALKERS** (925-5377) to make arrangements for a flight from Fort Lauderdale.

WHERE TO STAY & DINE

Walker's Cay Hotel & Marina ⟨★⟩   Established in the 1930s and a legend among fishermen ever since, this resort occupies all 41 hectares (101 acres) of a private island that contains the largest and most elaborate full-service marina in the Abacos. Each year, it runs at least two of the country's biggest deep-sea fishing tournaments. Come here for the fishing, for the marina and its charter boats, and for the way that sports permeate the air—but not necessarily for the luxury of the accommodations. Although they benefited from a renovation, these are rather standard motel-style units. Each accommodation contains a small bathroom with a shower stall. Meals are generally adequate, served in the **Lobster Trap** and **Conch Pearl** restaurants, both of which have a bar and offer American and Bahamian fare, chiefly steak and fresh fish.

Walker's Cay, Abaco, The Bahamas. © **800/WALKERS** (925-5377) in the U.S. and Canada, or 954/763-6025 or 242/353-1252. Fax 954/462-4100. www.walkerscay.com. Year-round US$130–US$170 (£65–£85) double, from US$425 (£213) villa. Meal plan (breakfast and dinner) US$40 (£20) per person. AE, MC, V. **Amenities:** 2 restaurants; 2 bars; tennis court; babysitting. *In room:* A/C, no phone.

9

Eleuthera

A sort of Bahamian Plymouth Rock, Eleuthera Island (pronounced Ah-*leu*-thra) was the first permanent settlement in The Bahamas, founded in 1648. A search for religious freedom drew the Eleutherian Adventurers from Bermuda here, to the birthplace of The Bahamas. The long, narrow island they discovered and colonized still bears the name Eleuthera—Greek for "freedom." Locals call it Cigatoo.

These adventurers found an island of white- and pink-sand beaches framed by casuarina trees; high, rolling green hills; sea-to-sea views; dramatic cliffs; and sheltered coves—and these beautiful sights are still here, unspoiled, waiting for you to discover them. More than 161km (100 miles) long but a mere 3km (2 miles) wide (guaranteeing that you'll never be far from the beach), Eleuthera is about 113km (70 miles) east of Nassau (a 30-min. flight). The population of 11,000 is largely made up of farmers, shopkeepers, and fishermen who live in old villages of pastel-washed cottages. The resorts are built around excellent harbors, and roads run along the coastline, though some of them are inadequately paved.

Eleuthera and its satellite islands, **Spanish Wells** and **Harbour Island,** offer superb snorkeling and diving amid coral gardens, reefs, drop-offs, and wrecks. Anglers come to Eleuthera for bottom-, bone-, and deep-sea fishing, testing their skill against dolphinfish, wahoo, blue and white marlins, Allison tuna, and amberjacks. Charter boats are available at Powell Point, Rock Sound, Spanish Wells, and Harbour Island. You can also rent Sunfish, sailboats, and Boston Whalers for reef fishing.

Eleuthera rivals the Abacos in popularity among foreign visitors, though boaters are more drawn to the Abacos and the Exumas. Along with the Abacos, Eleuthera has the largest concentration of resort hotels outside of Nassau/Paradise Island and Freeport/Lucaya. It's also got a wealth of sandy beaches.

With the exception of Andros Island (which has four airports), Eleuthera has more airports (three) than any other island in The Bahamas, ensuring that most points along its surface are relatively easy to access. Best of all, it has one long, completely interconnected highway, stretching 110 miles from the island's northern to southern tip, thereby avoiding the complicated ferryboat crossings that hinder developments in, say, Andros and the Abacos. There's not a traffic light anywhere on the island, a fact which makes locals inordinately proud. An offbeat adventure involves driving the island's entire length, along a sometimes bumpy road with nary a dividing line. Everywhere, you'll confront a landscape of rocks, sand, scrub, and sea views.

We love gorgeous **Harbour Island,** with its charming Dunmore Town, even more than New Plymouth or Hope Town in the Abacos; it's almost a Cape Cod in the Tropics. Of the 10 destinations recommended in this chapter, Harbour Island gets our vote as the number-one choice.

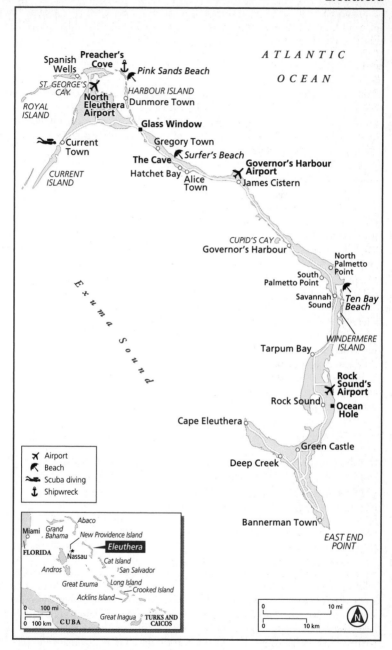

Spanish Wells is another small island just off Eleuthera's north end. Spanish galleons put sailors ashore to fill the ships' casks with fresh water after long sea voyages—hence the island's present-day name.

ELEUTHERA ESSENTIALS
GETTING THERE
BY PLANE   Eleuthera has three airports. **North Eleuthera Airport** (© 242/335-1068), as its name implies, serves the island's northern portion, along with two major towns on offshore cays, Harbour Island and Spanish Wells. **Governor's Harbour Airport** (© 242/332-2321) serves the center of the island, and **Rock Sound Airport** (© 242/334-2177) services the island's southern tier.

Bahamasair (© 800/222-4262; www.bahamasair.com) provides daily flights between Nassau and the three airports.

In addition, several commuter airlines with regularly scheduled service fly in from Florida with either nonstop or one-stop flights. Many private planes land on North Eleuthera Airport's 1,350m (4,429-ft.) paved runway. It is an official Bahamian port of entry, and a Customs and Immigration official is on hand. **Continental Airlines** (© 800/525-0280; www.continental.com) flies once daily from Miami and twice daily from Fort Lauderdale. **Delta** (© 800/221-1212; www.delta.com) flies in twice weekly from Atlanta.

Other small carriers include **Twin Air** (© 954/359-8266; www.flytwinair.com), flying from Fort Lauderdale three times a week to Rock Sound and Governor's Harbour, and Thursday to Tuesday to North Eleuthera.

BY FERRY   An inter-island link, **Bahamas Ferries** (© 242/323-2166; www.bahamasferries.com) launch from Potter's Cay, beneath the Paradise Island Bridge, and go to daily points, including Harbour Island, North Eleuthera, and Governor's Harbour. Round-trip fares are US$110 (£55) for adults, US$70 (£35) for children under 12.

BY MAIL BOAT   A mail boat visits Eleuthera from Nassau, leaving from Potter's Cay Dock every Monday afternoon at 5pm. Weather conditions and the vagaries of the Bahamian postal system sometimes causes this schedule to change. For details about sailings, consult the dock master at **Potter's Cay Dock** in Nassau (© 242/393-1064).

Every Thursday, the **MV Current Pride** goes from Nassau to both Lower and Upper Bogue on Current Island. It returns to Nassau from Current Island every Tuesday.

The **Bahamas Daybreak III** departs every Monday, weather permitting, for South Eleuthera, stops at Rock Sound and Governor's Harbour, and then returns to Nassau on Tuesday. On Thursday, it leaves Nassau for The Bluff (a small village in North Eleuthera) and Harbour Island, returning on Sunday. The **Eleuthera Express** sails from Nassau to Spanish Wells and Governor's Harbour on Monday and Thursday, and returns to Nassau on Sunday and Tuesday.

GETTING AROUND
It's virtually impossible to get lost on Eleuthera—there's only one road that meanders along the entire length of its snake-shaped form, and you'll stray from it only very rarely. Most visitors take a **taxi** only right after arriving at the airport or when they have to return to that airport to go home. Taxis meet all incoming flights and are also available at ferry docks. Because cabbies are independent operators, you can't call one central number. Your hotel staff can summon a taxi for you, but you may have to wait

a while, so plan ahead. Know, too, that taxis on Eleuthera are battered and expensive; the cost to haul you and up to two companions plus your luggage from North Eleuthera airport, in Eleuthera's far north, to Cape Eleuthera, near the island's southern tip, is around US$170 (£85), and it's a long, monotonous ride. As such, we advise you to select the airport on Eleuthera that's the closest, within reason, to wherever you'll be staying.

You can easily traverse all the settlements—really, hamlets, in most cases—on foot. With little traffic on the island, walking is an enjoyable experience here.

You won't find any American car-rental agencies on the island. Usually, your hotel can arrange for a **car rental** (prices are US$70–US$100/£35–£50 per day). You might end up driving a car that belongs to a local looking for extra cash. The three top contenders for car rentals on Eleuthera include **Highway Service Station** (✆ 242/ 332-2077), **Hilton Johnson's Car Rentals** (✆ 242/335-6241), and **Frederick "Fine Threads" Neely Car Rentals 2** (✆ 242/359-7780), whose owner's nickname was begotten because he wears great clothing.

1 Rock Sound/Cape Eleuthera

Rock Sound, in South Eleuthera, is a small, shady village, the island's main town and once its most exclusive enclave. The downsizing of a major touristic landmark, the Windermere Club, has, at least for now, halted the flow of famous visitors, who once included everybody from Princess Diana to a parade of CEOs. No reopening of that semi-private club is yet in sight, but at least that means that you can have many of South Eleuthera's best beaches practically to yourself.

Rock Sound opens onto Exuma Sound and is south of Tarpum Bay. The town is at least 200 years old and has many old-fashioned homes with picket fences out front. Once notorious for wreckers who lured ships ashore with false beacons, it used to be known as "Wreck Sound."

After leaving Rock Sound, head south, perhaps with a detour for a view of the re-inaugurated, all-new **Cotton Bay Club** (p. 232), and continue through the villages of Green Castle and Deep Creek. At this point, take a sharp turn northwest along the only road leading to **Cape Eleuthera.** Locals call this byway Cape Eleuthera Road, though you won't find any markings other than a sign pointing the way. If you continue to follow this route northwest, you'll reach the end of the island chain, jutting out into Exuma Sound.

⸜Fun Fact⸝ A "Bottomless Hole" in the Ocean

The **Ocean Hole,** in a sparsely populated neighborhood about 2km (1¼ miles) east of the heart of Rock Sound, is said to be bottomless, though modern depth soundings have defined it as being an astonishing 100 fathoms (about 600 feet) deep. This saltwater lake, whose waters, through uncharted underground channels, eventually meet the sea, is one of Eleuthera's most ecologically unusual spots. As such, it's closely monitored by geologists, zoologists, and botanists. Many birds and tropical fish can be seen through the greenish filter that seems to hover above the waters here; they seem to like to be photographed—but only if you feed them first.

Cotton Bay's Comeback

In the heyday of Pan American Airlines and its founder, Juan Trippe, Cotton Bay Club was The Bahamas' chicest enclave. Once a household name in the U.S., Trippe was a relatively forgotten figure until his character appeared in *The Aviator,* Martin Scorsese's film about Howard Hughes. Cotton Bay Club was where the Who's Who of America went barefoot in the sand. But since it folded it has been a ghost of itself, despite of its picture-perfect beaches.

Change, however, is on its way. Despite a series of setbacks, the infrastructure for a radically new series of private homes and villas, **Cotton Bay Estates,** was being excavated at press time, and 18 out of an eventual 25 imposing poured-concrete structures were at least halfway done. And though the potential for delay is high, developers expect to open a hotel, **Cotton Bay Villas,** in 2009. Although the first stage of development incorporates 200 acres of isolated beachfront land, eventual plans for this place will encompass 2,000 acres and will include a golf course designed by Robert Trent Jones, Jr.

At press time, Cotton Bay Villas promised a management team directed by Starwood, a company which has imposed many of its restrictions upon the site during early development phases. For more information about the hotel development or how to buy a condo, call ✆ **242/334-6520** or go to www.cottonbayeleuthera.com.

ROCK SOUND ESSENTIALS

Rock Sound has a **shopping center** and a **bank** (with an **ATM**) in addition to its airport, but not a lot else. Many residents who live in South Eleuthera come here to stock up on groceries and supplies.

A doctor and four resident nurses form the staff of **Rock Sound Medical Clinic** (✆ **242/334-2226**). Office hours are Monday to Friday 9am to 4pm; after that, the doctor is always available to handle **emergencies.**

If you need the **police,** call ✆ **242/334-2244.**

WHERE TO STAY

Powell Pointe at Cape Eleuthera Resort & Yacht Club 🏆🏆   During an earlier incarnation, this resort attracted some major American movers and shakers, including Richard Nixon. Some of the top U.S. golfers played its Bruce Devlin–Bob van Haage 18-hole course, which now, in a much-upgraded format, winds its way along the water. In 2007, the resort was reopened as part of a sweeping real-estate development plan which incorporated a roster of ultra-upscale private homes and condos, a hotel, and the most up-to-date and best-accessorized marina on "mainland" Eleuthera. Everything is perched on the tip of a sun-flooded peninsula that juts toward Nassau and the prevailing sea lanes, and is flanked with a trio of splendid white-sand beaches. Locals claim the deep-sea fishing is as fine as it ever was.

Accommodations are plusher and more state-of-the art than anything else in Eleuthera, easily rivaling the best lodgings on Harbour Island. A string of custom-built two-bedroom apartments lines the edges of the harbor. Each is owned by a different absentee investor but rented out as a hotel lodging. Expect spectacular kitchens with polished-stone countertops, lots of state-of-the-art lighting, and supremely comfortable furniture. Depending on the floor plan, units are either all on one level, or arranged as a duplex. Each has an outdoor balcony that's wide and broad enough for a private reception, and if you're tired of either the also-recommended **Barracuda's Restaurant** (unlikely) or the on-site coffee shop, modeled on a Starbucks, you can have the resort's cooks make you a private dinner within your suite. This resort is expected to expand during the life of this book's edition.

Cape Eleuthera, Rock Sound, Eleuthera, The Bahamas. ⓒ 242/422-9977 (resort) or 359-7208 (marina). www.cape eleuthera.com. 19 units. Winter US$800 (£400) 2-bedroom apartment for up to 4 occupants; off-season US$600 (£300) 2-bedroom apartment for up to 4 occupants. AE, MC, V. **Amenities:** 2 restaurants; coffee shop; bar; heated outdoor pool; easy access to nearby golf; wide array of watersports; bicycle and golf-cart rentals; fishing excursions and boat rentals; full-service marina. *In room:* A/C, TV, free Wi-Fi, separate living and dining areas.

WHERE TO DINE

Sammy's Place BAHAMIAN   Hot gossip and cheap, juicy burgers make Sammy's the most popular hangout in Rock Sound—come here for a slice of local life. Sammy's is northeast of Rock Sound, in a neighborhood that even the owner refers to as "the back side of town." Sammy Culmer (assisted by Margarita, his daughter) serves drinks (including Bahama Mamas and rum punches), conch fritters, Creole-style grouper, breaded scallops, pork chops, and lobster. If you drop in before 11am, you might be tempted by the selection of egg dishes.

This is primarily a restaurant and bar, but Sammy does rent four rooms with air-conditioning and cable TV, plus two efficiency cottages containing two bedrooms and a kitchen. The double-occupancy accommodations can be yours for US$66 (£33) per night; cottages cost US$100 (£50) per night.

Albury's Lane, Rock Sound, Eleuthera, The Bahamas. ⓒ 242/334-2121. Breakfast US$5–US$12 (£2.50–£6); lunch US$6–US$14 (£3–£7); main courses US$11–US$25 (£5.50–£13). No credit cards. Daily 7:30am–10pm.

2 Tarpum Bay

For an affordable vacation on high-priced Eleuthera, head here. This charming waterfront village, some 15km (9⅓ miles) north of Rock Sound, is good for fishing and has a number of simple, inexpensive guesthouses. Tarpum Bay, a tiny settlement with many pastel-washed, gingerbread-trimmed houses, is a favorite of artists, who have established a small colony here, complete with galleries and studios. **Gaulding's Cay,** north of town, has a lovely beach with great snorkeling.

WHERE TO STAY

Cartwright's Ocean Front Cottages   Cartwright's is a cluster of simple cottages right by the sea, with fishing, snorkeling, and swimming at your door. This is one of Tarpum Bay's few places where you can sit on your patio and watch the sunset. The small cottages are fully furnished, with utensils, stove, refrigerator, pots and pans; maid service is provided. Each unit comes with a small bathroom containing a shower stall. The property is within walking distance of stores and local eateries.

Bay St., Tarpum Bay, Eleuthera, The Bahamas. ⓒ 242/334-4215. 3 units. Year-round US$120 (£60) 1-bedroom cottage, US$150 (£75) 2-bedroom cottage, US$180 (£90) 3-bedroom cottage. No credit cards. **Amenities:** Babysitting; laundry service. *In room:* A/C, TV, kitchenette, coffeemaker, iron, no phone.

3 Windermere Island

Windermere is a very tiny island, connected somewhat haphazardly by ferry to "mainland" Eleuthera. It lies midway between Governor's Harbour and Rock Sound.

Even during its heyday, this enclave of private homes couldn't be more discreet. "We like to keep it quiet around here," a former staffer at the now-closed **Windermere Island Club** once told us. Regrettably, that wasn't always possible for this once-deluxe and snobbish citadel. When Prince Charles first took a pregnant Princess Diana here in the 1980s, she was photographed by paparazzi in her swimsuit. Much to the club's horror, the picture gained worldwide notoriety.

At press time, the hotel once associated with this cluster of private homes was closed, and many of its once-elegant private homes were occupied only a few weeks per year (if at all) by their mostly absentee owners. Wracked with inner dissent and an increasing state of disrepair, it's been the subject of many rumors about a rebirth. Stay tuned for more news about Windermere Island's on-again, off-again re-development plans (future editions of this book will keep you updated).

Meanwhile, if the ferryboat is operational by the time you visit, visit this island for its sandy, sheltered beaches and outstanding snorkeling opportunities, even though you'll have to bring your own gear. Be warned that in its present isolated, virtually uninhabited state, absolutely none of the beaches has anything even approaching supervision, so swim and cavort at your own risk.

4 Palmetto Point

On the east side of Queen's Highway, south of Governor's Harbour, **North Palmetto Point** is a little village where visitors rarely venture (though you can get a meal there). This laid-back town will suit you if you want peace and quiet off the beaten track.

Ten Bay Beach 🎯🎯 is one of the best beaches in The Bahamas, with sparkling turquoise water and a wide expanse of soft, white sand. The beach is a 10-minute drive south of Palmetto Point and just north of Savannah Sound. There are no facilities, only idyllic isolation.

WHERE TO STAY

Unique Village   Located on a steep rise above Eleuthera's Atlantic coast, this hotel is the creative statement of a Palmetto Point businessman who also owns the local hardware store (Unique Hardware). Built in 1992, the hotel offers accommodations in several configurations, including conventional single or double rooms, a one-bedroom apartment with a kitchenette, and two-bedroom villas with full kitchens. Each comes with a small bathroom with a tub/shower. A flight of wooden steps brings you to the beach, where a reef breaks the Atlantic surf, creating calm waters on this sandy cove. There's a bar and restaurant on-site (p. 235), but few other luxuries. Though there aren't any sailing, scuba, or tennis amenities on-site, the staff can direct you to other facilities that lie within a reasonable drive (you'll probably want a car here).

N. Palmetto Point, Eleuthera, The Bahamas. ⓒ **242/332-1830.** www.uniquevillage.com. 15 units. Winter US$138–US$150 (£69–£75) double, US$161 (£81) mini-suite, US$185 (£93) 1-bedroom apt, US$219 (£110) 2-bedroom apt; off-season US$104–US$115 (£52–£58) double, US$126 (£63) mini-suite, US$150 (£75) 1-bedroom apt, US$185 (£93) 2-bedroom apt. Meal plans US$55–US$70 (£28–£35) per person. MC, V. **Amenities:** Restaurant; bar; free snorkeling equipment; laundry service. *In room:* A/C, TV, free Wi-Fi, kitchenette, coffeemaker, iron.

WHERE TO DINE

Mate & Jenny's Pizza Restaurant & Bar BAHAMIAN/AMERICAN   This restaurant, known for its conch pizza, has a jukebox and a pool table. It's the most popular local joint, completely modest and unassuming. In addition to pizza, the Bethel family prepares pan-fried grouper, cracked conch, and light meals, including snacks and sandwiches. Lots of folks come here just to drink. Try their Goombay Smash, Rumrunner, a piña colada, or just a Bahamian Kalik beer.

S. Palmetto Point, right off Queen's Hwy. © 242/332-1504. Pizza US$8–US$29 (£4–£15); main courses US$6–US$22 (£3–£11). MC, V. Wed–Sun 11am–3pm and 5:30–9pm.

Muriel's Bakery *Finds* BAHAMIAN   Muriel Cooper's operation runs a bakery and a takeout food emporium. Her rich, moist pineapple and coconut cakes and tarts, as well as her lemon pies, are some of the best in the Out Islands.

N. Palmetto Point. © 242/332-1583. No credit cards. Mon–Sat 10am–6pm.

Unique Village Restaurant & Lounge BAHAMIAN/AMERICAN   This is the area's best place for food, and it offers the widest selection. Drop in for a Bahamian breakfast of boiled or stewed fish served with johnnycake, or steamed corned beef and grits ("regular" breakfasts, including hearty omelets, are also available). Lunch offerings include a zesty conch chowder and an array of salads. Burgers are served, along with what the kitchen calls "Bahamian belly pleasers," including the steamed catch of the day. At night, the options grow, and you'll find the best New York sirloin available in mid-Eleuthera, ranging in size from 8 to 16 ounces. Cracked conch fried in a light beer batter is one of the better renditions of this dish on the island.

In Unique Village, N. Palmetto Point. © 242/332-1830. Main courses US$24–US$45 (£12–£23). MC, V. Daily 7:30–11am, 11:30am–5pm, and 6–9pm.

5 Governor's Harbour

With a British colonial heritage that goes back at least 300 years, Governor's Harbour is the island's oldest settlement and is reportedly the Eleutherian Adventurers' first landing place. The largest town on Eleuthera after Rock Sound, it lies midway along the 161km-long (100-mile) island. A few of its clapboard-sided houses evoke the gracious elegance of Harbour Island to the North, and the town's sleepy harborfront carries memories of the town's role as a provider of black pineapple to the supermarkets of England, Canada, and the U.S. Today, however, things can get very sleepy indeed here. This is Out Island living at its most peaceful and uneventful.

The town today has a population of about 1,500, with some bloodlines going back to the original settlers, the Eleutherian Adventurers, and to the Loyalists who followed some 135 years later. A scattering of fine old homes lines the streets uphill from the harbor, amid trailing bougainvillea and coppices of casuarina trees. **James Cistern** is a little hamlet north of the Governor's Harbour Airport.

GOVERNOR'S HARBOUR ESSENTIALS

GETTING THERE   See "Eleuthera Essentials: Getting There," at the beginning of this chapter, for details. The town airport is one of the island's major gateways, with daily flights arriving from Nassau and Florida.

VISITOR INFORMATION   The friendly and welcoming **Eleuthera Tourist Office** is on Queens Highway (© 242/332-2142) in modern, contemporary-looking premises about 2 blocks uphill from the harbor. It's usually open Monday to Friday 9am to 5pm.

FAST FACTS   If you're staying outside the town in a cottage or apartment, you can find services and supplies in Governor's Harbour or at nearby Palmetto Point.

Governor's Harbour has a branch of **First Caribbean International Bank** on Queen's Highway (© **242/332-2300**) with an **ATM** dispensing Bahamian (but not U.S.) dollars. Hours are Monday to Thursday 9:30am to 3pm and Friday 9:30am to 4:30pm.

The **Governor Harbour's Medical Clinic** (© **242/332-2774**) is the island's largest and most comprehensive healthcare facility. Located on Queen's Highway, it's open Monday to Friday from 9am to 5:30pm and fills prescriptions. The clinic is also the site of a **dentist's office** which operates from 9am to 1pm Monday, Tuesday, and Friday. Call for an appointment before going.

Check with your hotel for **Internet access,** which can also be gotten on the second floor of the Haynes Library (© **242/332-2877**) at Governor's Harbour. The charge is US$5(£2.50) per hour, and the library is open Monday to Friday 9am to 5pm, Saturday 10am to 4pm.

If you need the **police,** call © **242/332-2111.**

There's a **post office** on Haynes Avenue (© **242/332-2060**); hours are Monday to Friday 9am to 4:30pm.

WHERE TO STAY

Duck Inn Cottages *(★) (Finds)*   The accommodations you'll rent here are larger, plusher, cozier, more historic, and more charming than what you'd expect in a conventional hotel. All come with kitchenettes and access to a menagerie of friendly dogs and cats who will, if you're an animal lover, quickly insinuate themselves into your heart. Within a garden surrounded by a high wall, the complex consists of three masonry-sided houses, each built between 90 and 200 years ago, and each almost adjacent to another, midway up a hillside overlooking the sea. The finest of these is Floris Cottage, with four bedrooms which can sleep eight comfortably. Nassau-born Johnson "J. J." Duckworth and Katie, his Exuma-born wife, are the resident owners and managers. Much of their time is spent nurturing a sprawling collection of orchids cultivated for export to Europe and the U.S. Their collection of orchids is one of the country's largest.

Queen's Hwy., Governor's Harbour, Eleuthera, The Bahamas. © **242/332-2608.** Fax 242/332-2106. www.duckinn cottages.com. 3 units. Winter US$150 (£75) double; off-season US$125 (£63) double. Year-round US$300 (£150) for Floris Cottage. AE, DISC, MC, V. **Amenities:** Babysitting; nonsmoking rooms. *In room:* A/C, TV, kitchenette, coffeemaker, iron, no phone.

Pineapple Fields *(★★) (Finds)*   Offering some of Eleuthera's most comfortable accommodations, this condominium complex sits across a quiet coastal road from the spectacular sandy beach. Isolated and very quiet, this retreat ranks alongside the (better-accessorized) Powell Pointe (p. 232) as our favorite resort on "mainland" Eleuthera. Built on the grounds of the once-fabled and very exclusive Potlatch Club, it occupies a meticulously landscaped 32-hectare (79-acre) site on the Atlantic just minutes south from the center of Governor's Harbour. Rooms sit within carefully landscaped gardens, a very short walk from 305m (1,001 ft.) of beach. Bedrooms are spacious, well-maintained, and furnished in a style you'd expect from an upper-middle-bracket condo complex in Florida, with both one- and two-bedroom units offered. There are also outdoor showers for when you're coming in from the beach, and a free-form swimming pool. To read about Tippy's, the resort's independently managed bistro, flip to p. 238. At press time, most, but not all, of the units had been sold to investors who rent them out to visitors.

Banks Rd., Governor's Harbour, Eleuthera, The Bahamas. © **877/677-9539** or 242/332-2221. Fax 242/332-2203. www.pineapplefields.com. 32 condo units. Winter US$275–US$310 (£138–£155) 1-bedroom unit, US$365–US$400

(£183–£200) 2-bedroom unit; off-season US$195–US$230 (£98–£115) 1-bedroom unit, US$296–US$330 (£148–£165) 2-bedroom unit. 5-night minimum stay required over Christmas, New Year's, and Easter. AE, MC, V. **Amenities:** Restaurant; bar; outdoor pool. *In room:* A/C, TV, kitchen, safe.

Quality Inn Cigatoo Resort *Value*   Built in 1976 and virtually reconstructed in 2000, this low-rise, concrete-sided hotel has a faded style, evoking the kind of motel you might find in a small town somewhere in Florida. It's on the crest of a steep hill overlooking the town, within a 7-minute walk to the beach. The hotel is small-scale, intensely local, and unpretentious. It consists of one two-story central core (where the in-house restaurant is) and three one-story buildings, each painted white, with doors to each room painted a different primary color. The buildings are clustered around a swimming pool, the resort's focal point. Management is cordial, albeit a bit blasé.

Governor's Harbour, Queen's Hwy., Eleuthera, The Bahamas. © **242/332-3060.** Fax 242/332-3061. www.choice hotels.com. 22 units. US$109–US$149 (£55–£75) double. AE, MC, V. **Amenities:** Restaurant; bar; outdoor pool; tennis court; room service (7am–10pm); babysitting; laundry service. *In room:* A/C, TV, free Wi-Fi, hair dryer, iron.

WHERE TO DINE

Charlie's Bar & Grill BAHAMIAN   Established in 2005 within a cement-block building directly across the quiet street from Eleuthera's central tourist office, this is the town's most likable local hangout. Its coterie of amiable, mostly middle-aged male clients is headed by the bar's gregarious owner, Charles Curry. Since there aren't a whole lot of dining and drinking options in this small town, it's likely to attract some unexpected celebrities, one of whom was Lenny Kravitz. Lunches consist of platters of stewed chicken or fish, grilled steaks, and burgers. Wash your food down with Kalik beer, cans of which sell for between US$3 and US$3.50 (£1.50–£1.75), depending on the time of day you happen to show up. Don't expect gastronomy or anything particularly urbane, as things around here are down-home, local-centric, and, if you take the time to savor it, occasionally charming.

Queen's Hwy. © **242/332-347.** Reservations not necessary. Lunch platters US$8–US$12 (£4–£6). No credit cards. Grill daily noon–3pm. Bar daily 11am–midnight.

Cigatoo Restaurant BAHAMIAN   Set beside the swimming pool within the also-recommended Quality Inn Cigatoo Resort, this is one of the more reliable and substantial dining places in a town that isn't known for its variety of choices. Expect a mixture of Bahamian food with what you'd expect from an American steakhouse or luncheonette, with a choice of sandwiches, salads, and meat and fish platters.

In the Quality Inn Cigatoo Resort, Queen's Hwy. © **242/332-3060.** Reservations not necessary. Sandwiches and salads US$8–US$15 (£4–£7.50); main courses US$16–US$24 (£8–£12). AE, MC, V. Daily 7am–3pm and 6–10pm.

Lee's Café BAHAMIAN   A hardworking local matriarch, Leona Johnson, established this down-home restaurant in 2001 and has conducted a roaring business with local residents ever since. Don't expect an orchestrated decor; you'll enter a long, low, endlessly efficient dining room where the day's specials are written on a large paper pad. If no one appears to immediately take your order, poke your head inside an impossibly small opening for a view of the kitchen, where Leona might be whipping up what we think is the best souse on Eleuthera: Even the Bahamian Minister of Tourism has complimented it and hauled some back to Nassau with him. Other menu items include conch salad, conch fritters, conch burgers with salad, grouper fingers either steamed or grilled, lobster, chicken, steak, and morning omelets. Most diners opt for takeaway; a smaller percentage dine in. Leona, incidentally, is related to many dozens of relatives within James Cistern, and at any time during your experience here might greet one or another of them with grandmotherly affection.

Spencer St., James Cistern. ⟨ 242/335-6444. Reservations not accepted. Lunch platters US$10–US$15 (£5–£7.50); dinner platters US$18–US$35 (£9–£18). No credit cards. Mon–Sat 6:30–9pm.

Pammy's Takeaway BAHAMIAN   Tile-floored and Formica-clad, this is just a little cubbyhole with a few tables. Lunchtime brings sandwiches or platters of cracked conch, pork chops, and either broiled or fried grouper. Don't expect anything fancy because this definitely isn't. Run by hometown matriarch Pammy Moss, it's a true local joint serving up generous portions of flavor-filled food.

Queen's Hwy. at Gospel Chapel Rd. ⟨ 242/332-2843. Reservations accepted only for dinner. Breakfast US$4–US$8 (£2–£4); light lunch US$6–US$11 (£3–£5.50); main courses US$15–US$21 (£7.50–£11). No credit cards. Mon–Sat 8am–5pm.

Tippy's Restaurant, Bar & Beach ⟨⟨ CONTINENTAL   By anyone's standards, this is the most urbane, international, and sophisticated restaurant on mainland Eleuthera, easily matching the flair of Harbour Island's best restaurants. It's set within a wood-and-masonry pavilion in an eerily isolated spot uphill from a spectacular beach. Established by a culinary team from Austria, it evokes the kind of bistro you'd have expected in an Austrian ski resort, albeit with a greater emphasis on fresh fish, sea breezes, and touches of island sizzle and spice. Those items which aren't recited to you orally by the staff are recorded on a blackboard. Examples include pistachio-studded paté, an ultra-fresh version of fish and chips, lobster ravioli, pan-fried grouper, veal chops with a mushroom cream sauce, snapper served either *en papillote* or as part of the above-mentioned fish and chips, seared sesame tuna with papaya chutney, and a roulade of smoked salmon layered with goat cheese.

Across the coastal rd. from Pineapple Fields. ⟨ 242/332-3331. Main courses US$20–US$29 (£10–£15). MC, V. Daily noon–2:30pm and 6–9:30pm.

HITTING THE BEACH

Near the town center are two beaches known locally as the **Buccaneer Public Beaches;** they're adjacent, appropriately enough, to the Buccaneer Club, on the island's sheltered western edge, facing Exuma Sound. Snorkeling is good here—it's best where the pale turquoise waters near the coast deepen to a dark blue. Underwater rocks shelter lots of marine flora and fauna. The waves at these beaches are relatively calm.

On Eleuthera's Atlantic (eastern) side, about 1km (⅔ mile) from Governor's Harbour, is a much longer stretch of mostly pale pink sand, similar to what you'll find in Harbour Island. Known locally as **French Leave Beach** (or less frequently, as the Club Med Public Beach), it's good for bodysurfing and, on days when storms are surging in the Atlantic, even conventional surfing.

Don't expect any touristy kiosks selling drinks, snacks, or souvenirs at any of these beaches because everything is pristine and undeveloped.

GOVERNOR'S HARBOUR AFTER DARK

Ronnie's Smoke Shop & Sports Bar, Cupid's Cay (⟨ 242/332-2307), is central Eleuthera's busiest and most popular nightspot, drawing folks from miles away. It's adjacent to the cargo depot of Cupid's Cay, in a connected cluster of simple buildings painted in combinations of black with lots of natural-stained wood. Most folks come here just to drink Kalik beer and talk at either of the two bars. But if you want to dance, there's an all-black room just for disco music on Friday nights. There's also

Eleuthera's only walk-in cigar humidor. If you get hungry, order some barbecue, a pizza, chicken wings, or popcorn. The place is open Monday to Friday 10am until midnight. On weekends, it often stays open until about 3am.

6 Hatchet Bay

Forty kilometers (25 miles) north of Governor's Harbour, Hatchet Bay was once known for a British-owned plantation that had 500 head of dairy cattle and thousands of chickens. Today that plantation is gone, and this is now one of Eleuthera's sleepiest villages, as you'll see if you veer off Queen's Highway onto one of the town's ghostly main streets, Lazy Shore Road or Ocean Drive.

WHERE TO STAY & DINE

Rainbow Inn *Three kilometers (2 miles) south of Alice Town, near a sandy beach, the Rainbow Inn is a venerable survivor in an area where many competitors have failed. Quirky and appealing to guests who return for quiet getaways again and again, it's an isolated collection of seven cedar-sided octagonal bungalows. The accommodations are simple but comfortable, spacious, and tidy; each has a kitchenette, lots of exposed wood, a ceiling fan, a small bathroom with a shower unit, and a porch. A sandy beach is just steps away.

One of the most appealing things about the place is its bar and restaurant, which make it a destination for residents far up and down the length of Eleuthera. It's an octagon with a high-beamed ceiling and a thick-topped woodsy-looking bar where guests down daiquiris and piña coladas amid nautical trappings. It has live Bahamian music twice a week and a relatively extensive menu. The owners take pride in the fact that the menu hasn't changed much in 20 years; this suits its loyal fans just fine. Local Bahamian food includes conch chowder, fried conch, fresh fish, and Bahamian lobster. International dishes feature French onion soup, escargot, and steaks, followed by Key lime pie for dessert. Table no. 2, crafted from a triangular teakwood prow of a motor yacht that was wrecked off the coast in the 1970s, is a perpetual favorite.

Governor's Harbour, Eleuthera, The Bahamas. © **800/688-0047** in the U.S. or 242/335-0294. Fax 242/335-0294. www.rainbowinn.com. 5 units. Winter US$140 (£70) double; off-season US$115 (£58) double. Year-round US$200 (£100) for 2-bedroom villa, US$225 (£113) for 3-bedroom villa. MAP (breakfast and dinner) US$45 (£23) per person. MC, V. **Amenities:** Restaurant; bar; pool; tennis court; watersports equipment/rentals; car-rental desk; babysitting; laundry service. *In room:* A/C, free Wi-Fi, kitchenette, fridge, coffeemaker.

7 Gregory Town

Gregory Town stands in the center of Eleuthera against a backdrop of hills, which break the landscape's usual flat monotony. A village of clapboard cottages, it was once famous for growing pineapples. Though the industry isn't as strong as it was in the past, the locals make good pineapple rum out of the fruit, and you can visit the **Gregory Town Plantation and Distillery,** where it's produced. You're allowed to sample it, and we can almost guarantee you'll want to take a bottle home with you.

WHERE TO STAY

The Cove Eleuthera *Although it isn't as plush or well-accessorized as either Pineapple Fields or Powell's Pointe, this is among Eleuthera's most upscale and luxurious resorts. Positioned on rocky terrain above a pink-sand cove 2.5km (1½ miles) northwest of Gregory Town and 5km (3 miles) southeast of the Glass Window, this

Note: Crash Pad for Surfers

A short walk from Surfers Beach, the **Surfers Beach Manor** (© 242/335-5300; www.surfersmanor.com) is a restored, laid-back inn offering nine air-conditioned bedrooms, with either twin or queen-size beds. In winter, doubles range from US$109 to US$129 (£55–£65), with summer rates lowered to US$89 to US$99 (£45–£50). A rental car can also be arranged for between US$70 and US$80 (£35–£40) per day, depending on its size. There is a restaurant and a lounge on-site serving Bahamian cuisine. Swimming, surfing (of course), and doing nothing are the pastimes here. American Express, MasterCard, and Visa are accepted. Peter and Rebecca are your congenial hosts.

year-round resort is set on 11 hectares (27 acres) partially planted with pineapples; it consists of a main clubhouse and eight simple, cement-sided bungalows, each containing four units nestled on the ocean side. Each unit was upgraded and is comparable to an isolated motel you might have found, say, somewhere along the Florida or Alabama Gulf Coast. They all have a spacious living area, tile floors, a relatively plush bathroom, a porch, and no TV or phone to distract you.

The restaurant (below) carries hints of island posh, with an amiable bar area and a commitment to serving three meals per day. The lounge and poolside patio are open daily for drinks and informal meals. Kayaks, bicycles, two tennis courts, and a small freshwater pool compete with hammocks for your time. There's fabulous snorkeling right off the sands here, with colorful fish darting in and out of the offshore reefs. Some clients here hail from Europe, including a surprising number of French honeymooners celebrating the debut of their second marriages.

Queen's Hwy., Gregory Town, Eleuthera, The Bahamas. © **800/552-5960** in the U.S. and Canada or 242/335-5142. Fax 242/335-5338. www.thecoveeleuthera.com. 26 units. Year-round US$235–US$285 (£118–£143) double, US$395 (£198) 1-bedroom suite, US$450–US$475 (£225–£238) 2-bedroom suite, US$995 (£498) Point House. AE, MC, V. **Amenities:** Restaurant; bar; outdoor hilltop pool; 2 tennis courts; watersports equipment/rentals; laundry service; nonsmoking rooms. *In room:* A/C, kitchenette (in some), hair dryer, no phone.

WHERE TO DINE IN GREGORY TOWN

Cambridge Villas BAHAMIAN   One of the few dining choices in town occupies a cement-sided room on the ground floor of a battered hotel (the accommodations aren't as appealing as the restaurant). Harcourt and Sylvia Cambridge, the owners, serve conch burgers, conch chowder, and sandwiches, usually prepared by Sylvia herself. It's just a simple spot, where you might be entertained by the continually running soap operas broadcast from a TV over the bar.

Main St. © **242/335-5080.** Reservations not required. Sandwiches and platters US$3.50–US$9 (£1.75–£4.50). MC, V. Mon–Sat 8am–9pm; Sun 10am–9pm.

The Cove ✦✦ BAHAMIAN/CONTINENTAL   In the previously recommended eponymous hotel 2.5km (1½ miles) north of Gregory Town, this spacious dining room is your best bet in the area, featuring gourmet continental cuisine with surprising amounts of local flair. The restaurant is decorated with pastel colors in a light, tropical style. Lunch begins with the inevitable conch chowder. Follow it with a conch burger, a generous patty of ground seafood blended with green pepper, onion, and spices. Conch also appears in the evening, and we think this is the best cracked conch in town, having been tenderized, dipped in a special batter, and fried to golden perfection. Other menu items include char-grilled tenderloin steak with skewered prawns and filed mushrooms, seared ahi tuna with pounded ginger sauce, and grilled chicken breast with papaya salsa and spicy coconut sauce.

Queen's Hwy. (℃) 242/335-5142. Breakfast US$8–US$14 (£4–£7); lunch main courses US$9–US$24 (£4.50–£12); main courses US$26–US$38 (£13–£19). MC, V. Daily 8–10:30am, 11:30am–2:30pm, and 6–8:30pm.

EXPLORING THE AREA: THE GLASS WINDOW & BEYOND

Behind a colorful facade on Queen's Highway in the heart of Gregory Town, the **Island Made Gift Shop** (℃ 242/335-5369) carries an outstanding inventory that owes its quality to owner Pamela Thompson's artistic eye and good taste. Look for one-of-a-kind paintings on driftwood or crafted on the soles of discarded shoes, handmade quilts from Androsian fabrics, Abaco ceramics, and jewelry made from pieces of glass found on the beach. There are extraordinary woven baskets made by the descendants of Seminole Indians and escaped slaves living in remote districts of Andros Island. Especially charming are bowls crafted from half-sections of conch shells.

Dedicated surfers have come here from as far away as California and Australia to test their skills at **Surfers Beach,** 4km (2½ miles) south of town on the Atlantic side. The waves are at their highest in winter and spring; even if you're not brave enough to get out there, it's fun to watch.

South of town on the way to Hatchet Bay are several caverns worth visiting, the largest of which is simply called **The Cave.** It has a big fig tree out front, which Gregory Town's people claim was planted long ago by pirates who wanted to conceal the cave because they had hidden treasure in it.

Local guides (to get one, ask around in Gregory Town or Hatchet Bay) will take you into the cave's interior, where the resident bats are harmless even though they must resent the intrusion of tourists with flashlights. At one point, the drop is so steep—about 3.5m (11 ft.)—that you have to use a ladder to climb down. Eventually, you reach a cavern ornamented with stalactites and stalagmites. A maze of passageways leads off through the rocky underground recesses. The cave comes to an abrupt end at the edge of a cliff, where the thundering sea crashes around some 27m (89 ft.) below.

After leaving Gregory Town and driving north, you come to the famed **Glass Window,** Eleuthera's chief sight and narrowest point. Once, a natural rock arch bridged the land, but it's gone now, replaced by an artificially constructed bridge. As you drive across it, pay attention to the contrast between the deep blue ocean of the sound's windward side and the emerald-green shoal waters of its leeward side. The rocks rise to a height of 21m (69 ft.).

Finds For a Drop-Dead Pineapple Tart

Follow the smell of fresh-baked goods to **Thompsons Bakery**, Johnson Street (℃ 242/335-5053), open Monday to Saturday 8:30am to 6pm. Run by two local sisters, Monica and Daisy Thompson, this simple bakery occupies a wooden lime-green building near the town's highest point. Although it churns out lots of bread—including raisin, whole-wheat, and coconut—the best reason to stop by are the fresh pineapple tarts, priced at US$1 (50p) each. They're among the best we've ever tasted. You might also find freshly baked doughnuts and cinnamon rolls.

Often, as ships in the Atlantic are being tossed about, the crew looks across the narrow point to see a ship resting quietly on the other side, hence the name Glass Window. Artist Winslow Homer was so captivated by this spot that he captured it on canvas.

FISHING TRIPS

Your best bet is **Capt. Z Fishing and Dive Charters,** located at the Cove House on Bay Street in Gregory Town. (Cove House is not to be confused with the entirely separate Cove Eleuthera resort described above.) Both half- and full-day fishing trips are offered aboard their custom-built boats. This charter outfit offers some of the Caribbean's best spearfishing. Phone © **242/335-5185** for details or bookings, or go to www.fisheleuthera.com.

OUTDOOR ADVENTURES

A particularly popular outfitter for anyone interested in exploring the Eleutherian great outdoors is Gregory Town–based **Bahamas Out Island Adventures** (© **242/335-0349;** www.bahamasadventures.com). Depending on demand, it can be all things to all outdoors enthusiasts. Come here for activities as diverse as surfing or kayaking lessons, birdwatching tours, and treks through the scrub and low trees of the island's windswept terrain. Full- and half-day tours can be custom-organized for your individual preferences, abilities, and needs.

GREGORY TOWN AFTER DARK

The place to be in Gregory Town, especially on a Saturday night, is **Elvina's,** on Main Street (© **242/335-5032**). Owners Ed and Elvina Watkins make you feel right at home and practically greet you at the door with a cold beer. Surfers and locals flock here to chow down on burgers, Bahamian dishes, and Cajun grub, served daily from 10am to "whenever we close." Elvina's husband, "Chicken Ed," is from Louisiana and makes great jambalaya. Bands play on Tuesday and Friday nights.

8 The Current

The inhabitants of the Current, a settlement in North Eleuthera, are believed to have descended from a tribe of Native Americans. A narrow strait separates the village from Current Island, where most locals make their living from the sea or from plaiting straw goods.

This is a small community that often welcomes visitors. You won't find crowds or artificial attractions. Everything focuses on the sea, a source of pleasure for the visiting tourists, but a way to sustain life for the residents.

From the Current, you can explore some sights in North Eleuthera, including **Preacher's Cave,** northeast of North Eleuthera Airport. In this barren and isolated backwater, the Eleutherian Adventurers found shelter during the mid–17th century when they were shipwrecked with no provisions.

Note that your taxi driver may balk at being asked to drive there; the road is hard on his expensive tires. As such, his round-trip asking price from, say, the ferryboat wharves servicing Harbour Island might be as much as US$80 (£40).

If you do opt for a detour here, you'll find yourself within one of the most historically important sites in The Bahamas—the point from which the origins of the country emerged. Set amid scrub and bush, the cave looks something like an amphitheater, with niches carved into its walls for seating for the community's elders, and a central boulder allegedly used as either a pulpit or an altar. The devout Eleutherian Adventurers held religious services inside the cave, which is pierced by natural holes in the roof, allowing light and rainfall to intrude.

For several years after they were stranded on reefs near this site, the settlers developed an elaborate series of religious and cultural codes and bylaws which in some ways factored into the legal and social codes of The Bahamas. The landscapes around this cave are rich with buried workaday artifacts from that early impromptu community, and much excavation work remains to be done, a project of ongoing interest to the Bahamian government. DNA tests of skeletons unearthed from the cave have drawn distinct links between the Eleutherian Adventurers and the modern-day residents of Spanish Wells (p. 254).

Another sight of interest to ecologists and marine scientists is **Boiling Hole,** part of a shallow bank on the island's Atlantic side that seems to boil and churn during changing tides.

WHERE TO STAY

Sandcastle Apartments   For escapists seeking a location far removed from the usual tourist circuit, this utterly plain but airy accommodation is a good bet. Its on-site kitchen, easy access to a simple grocery store within a 5-minute walk, and self-contained nature often appeal to families. Each modest bedroom, just across the road from the sea, has a double bed, a queen-size pullout bed in the living room, a small bathroom with a shower stall, and a view over shallow offshore waters, where children can wade safely for a surprisingly long distance offshore. If you want to explore, bicycles are available for US$5 (£2.50) per day.

The Current, Eleuthera, The Bahamas. ℂ 242/335-3244. Fax 242/393-0440. 2 units. Year-round US$85–US$90 (£43–£45) double. No credit cards. **Amenities:** Nonsmoking rooms. *In room:* A/C, coffeemaker.

9 Harbour Island ✶✶✶

One of the oldest settlements in The Bahamas, founded before the United States was a nation, Harbour Island lies off Eleuthera's northern end, some 322km (200 miles) from Miami. It is 5km (3 miles) long and 1km (⅔ mile) wide. The media have hailed this pink-sand island as the new St. Bart's, a reference to how chic it has become. Beware: If you're jogging along the beach, you might trip over a movie star.

Affectionately called by its original name, "Briland," Harbour Island is studded with good resorts. The spectacular **Pink Sands Beach** ✶✶✶ runs the whole length of the eastern side of the island and is protected from the ocean breakers by an outlying coral reef, which makes for some of the country's safest swimming. Except for unseasonably cold days, you can swim and enjoy watersports year-round. The climate averages 72°F (22°C) in winter, 77°F (25°C) in spring and fall, and 82°F (28°C) in summer. Occasionally, evenings are cool, with a low of about 65°F (18°C) from November to February.

To the amazement of even the island's most reliable repeat visitors, its clientele has gotten almost exponentially richer and more famous since the turn of the millennium. There's a building boom of ultra-upscale villas and a migration into the island by some staggeringly wealthy billionaires who have included Ron Perlman (CEO of Revlon) and India Hicks (a relative of England's royal family and former fashion model). Colin Farrell, Sylvester Stallone, and Sarah Ferguson, the Duchess of York, along with various titled aristocrats from the old houses of Europe make discreet but strategic appearances throughout the winter months. This new influx of the mega-wealthy has led to prices going far upward and caused something of a run on building sites along "zillionaire's row," a deliberately rutted and potholed byway north of the town center. No one is thrilled with these changes, especially the deeply entrenched owners of the island homes, and any attempt at expansion by any of the local hotels is rigorously opposed by increasingly politicized contingents of local residents and homeowners.

HARBOUR ISLAND ESSENTIALS

GETTING THERE   To reach Harbour Island, take a flight to the **North Eleuthera airstrip,** which is only a 1½-hour flight from Fort Lauderdale or Miami, and a 30-minute flight from Nassau (see "Eleuthera Essentials," at the beginning of this chapter, for details on which airlines provide service). From there, it's a 1.5km (1-mile) taxi ride to the ferry dock. The taxi costs about US$5 (£2.50) per person if you share the expense with four or five other passengers. From the dock, you'll take a 3km (2-mile) motorboat ride to Harbour Island. There's usually no waiting because a flotilla of high-powered motorboats makes the crossing whenever at least two customers show up, at a cost of around US$5 (£2.50) per person. If you're traveling alone and are willing to pay the US$8 (£4) one-way fare, the boat will depart immediately, without waiting for a second passenger.

Another way to get to Harbour Island is to board a speedy 177-passenger catamaran in Nassau. Contact **Bahamas Ferries** (✆ 242/323-2166; www.bahamasferries.com). You can begin this 2-hour trip at **Potter's Cay Dock,** which is under the bridge leading from Paradise Island to downtown Nassau. The fare for one of these daily excursions is US$110 (£55) round-trip or US$65 (£33) one-way for adults, and US$70 (£35) round-trip or US$45 (£23) one-way for children ages 2 to 11. This ferry pulls up to Harbour Island's Government Dock, where taxis wait to take you to your hotel.

GETTING AROUND   Once they reach Harbour Island, most people don't need transportation. They walk to where they're going, rent a **bicycle** (check your equipment carefully before renting because some bicycles rented to tourists are way past their prime), or putt-putt around the island on an electric **golf cart.** Most hotels offer these for rent or at least will arrange for a cart or bicycle; usually, they'll be delivered directly to your hotel.

Michael's Cycles, on Colebrook Street (✆ 242/333-2384), is the best place to go if you want some mobility other than your own two feet. The shop is open daily from 8am to 6pm. Bikes rent for US$12 (£6) per day, and you can also rent two-seater motorbikes for US$30 (£15) per day, or a four-seater golf cart for US$48 (£24) per day. You can also rent kayaks for US$40 (£20) per day, paddleboats for US$40 (£20) per day (or US$10/£5 per hour), and jet skis for US$85 (£43) per hour.

VISITOR INFORMATION   The **Harbour Island Tourist Office** on Dunmore Street (✆ 242/333-2621) is generally open Monday to Friday 9am to 5pm.

FAST FACTS   The **Royal Bank of Canada** is on Dunmore Street (✆ 242/333-2250) and has an **ATM.** Hours are Monday to Thursday 9:30am to 3pm and Friday 9:30am to 4:30pm.

The **Harbour Island Health Centre,** South Street, Dunmore Town (✆ 242/333-2225), handles routine medical problems. Hours are Monday to Friday 9am to 5pm. The on-call doctor can be reached at ✆ 242/333-2822.

Resorts usually provide Internet access. Arthur's Bakery, located in the center of town, also offers it. You can use the computer there or bring your own laptop. Hours are Monday to Saturday 8am to 2pm, and the cost is US$10 (£5) for 15 minutes.

You can get prescriptions filled at Briland's Pharmacy (© **242/333-3427**), at Johnson's Plaza on Dunmore Street. Hours are Monday to Saturday 9am to 5pm.

The post office (© **242/333-2215**) is on Gaol Alley; it's open Monday to Friday 9am to 5:30pm.

The police can be reached at either © **919** or © **242/333-2111.**

WHERE TO STAY
VERY EXPENSIVE

Dunmore Beach Club ⚜   This formal and exclusive colony of cottages is the quintessentially elegant hideaway, with 3.2 hectares (8 acres) of well-manicured grounds along the island's legendary 5km (3-mile) pink-sand beach. It's not as elaborate or sleek as its nearest rival, Pink Sands, but it's cozier, although in a bit of a state of decline, though extensive renovations did bring some of the units up to standard with huge showers and whirlpool tubs. The Bahamian-style bungalows attractively combine traditional furnishings and tropical accessories, with no phones or TVs to distract you. The Dunmore's heyday may have come and gone, but the feeling here is still dignified, comfortable, and pleasant.

Breakfast is offered on a garden terrace under pine trees with a view of the beach. Dinner is served at one sitting between 7 and 8:30pm; men should wear jackets (ties are optional). Bahamian and international cuisine is served in a formal dining room with a high ceiling, louvered doors, expensive china, and windows with views over the blue Atlantic. A clubhouse is the focal point for socializing, while a living room, library, and ocean-view bar provide additional cozy nooks.

Colebrook Lane, Harbour Island, The Bahamas. © **877/891-3100** or 242/333-2200. Fax 242/333-2429. www. dunmorebeach.com. 15 units. Nov–Apr US$499–US$599 (£250–£300) double, US$669–US$789 (£335–£395) suite for 2; May–Aug US$265–US$300 (£133–£150) double, US$350–US$420 (£175–£210) suite. Rates include all meals. MC, V. Closed Sept–Oct. **Amenities:** Restaurant; bar; tennis court; bike rentals; babysitting; laundry service; nonsmoking rooms. *In room:* A/C, minibar, hair dryer, safe, no phone.

Pink Sands ⚜⚜⚜   Posh and sophisticated, this hideaway is just the place to sneak away to with that special (wealthy) someone, located adjacent to a 5km (3-mile) stretch of pink-sand beach sheltered by a barrier reef. Yes, that was Julia Roberts in a bikini we spotted leaving the cottage next door. The elegant, relaxed retreat occupies an 11-hectare (27-acre) beachfront estate. Although it feels a bit like a pricey private club, it's less snobbish and a lot more hip than the Dunmore Beach Club. The resort's outrageous clubhouse is the most beautifully and imaginatively decorated room in the Out Islands.

The airy, spacious bedrooms occupy cement-sided cottages scattered throughout the grounds and gardens. Depending on the configuration and size, each cottage contains between one and two separate accommodations, with either an ocean or a garden view, mahogany furniture, and elaborate tile work. Each has a kitchen or kitchenette, pressurized water systems, walk-in closets, CD players and a CD selection, wet bars, and private patios with teak furnishings. The interior design features marble floors with area rugs, oversized Adirondack furnishings, local art, and batik fabrics. Fax machines and cellular phones can be supplied if you need them.

Hotel guests get some of the best meals on the island, an "A-B-C" fusion of Asian, Bahamian, and Caribbean cuisine. Dinner is an elegant four-course nightly affair. Lunches are much less formal, served in the Blue Bar, a postmodern beachside pavilion.

Chapel St., Harbour Island, The Bahamas. (C) **800/407-4776** or 242/333-2030. Fax 242/333-2080. www.pinksands resort.com. 25 units. Winter US$750–US$850 (£375–£425) 1-bedroom cottage for 2, from US$1,300 (£650) 2-bedroom unit; off-season US$600–US$700 (£300–£350) 1-bedroom cottage for 2, from US$1,100 (£550) 2-bedroom unit. Minimum stay of 3–7 nights required, depending on season. AE, MC, V. **Amenities:** 2 restaurants; 2 bars; pool; 3 tennis courts; health club; room service; babysitting; laundry service; nonsmoking rooms. *In room:* A/C, TV, kitchenette or kitchen, minibar, wet bar, coffeemaker, hair dryer, iron, safe.

EXPENSIVE

Coral Sands ★★ (Kids)   When it was built in the late 1970s, everyone wondered how this concrete behemoth would fit into a community otherwise composed of clapboard-sided houses and historic Out Island charm. Its present owners spent barrels of money skillfully concealing its angular structure, painting the outside a soft shade of pink, improving the gardens, and spiffying the place up to a family-friendly hideaway of enormous charm.

It stands on 3.6 hilly hectares (9 acres) overlooking the beach and within walking distance of British colonial-style Dunmore Town. This is one of the island's most consistently reliable hotels on the island, avoiding the glitter of some of the more volatile properties. It also opens onto one of the best beach locations and is a favorite of families, whereas some of the more posh resorts don't really cater to children.

Built with an airy design that features big-windowed loggias and arcades, it opens directly onto the 5km (3-mile) pink-sand beach for which the town is famous. Casual elegance, with ample doses of charm and friendliness, permeates every aspect of this hotel. Improvements have revitalized the property and freshened up the decor. Many rooms have private verandas or terraces; all are eminently comfortable, allowing you to fall asleep to the soothing sounds of waves breaking on the shore. The most recently restored rooms are on the Caribe building's second floor; these have been converted into deluxe one-bedroom ocean-view suites, some with two bathrooms, others with one, and have a bedroom facing the ocean, plus a separate living room with sofa.

The hotel's Terrace restaurant offers fine cuisine. Less elaborate food is also offered at the Beach Bar & Restaurant, which is dramatically cantilevered high above the pale-pink sands.

Chapel St., Harbour Island, The Bahamas. (C) **800/468-2799** in the U.S. and Canada or 242/333-2350. Fax 242/333-2368. www.coralsands.com. 37 units. Year-round US$315–US$395 (£158–£198) double, from US$585 (£293) suite. 3-night minimum stay. AE, MC, V. Closed Sept 5–Oct 18. **Amenities:** Restaurant; bar; pool; tennis court; nonmotorized watersports equipment/rentals; babysitting; laundry service; nonsmoking rooms; rooms for those w/limited mobility. *In room:* A/C, TV (in some), kitchen, coffeemaker, hair dryer, safe.

Rock House Hotel ★★★ (Finds)   This hotel, originally an unpretentious B&B, is now one of Harbour Island's most glamorous and stylish lodging properties. The forces behind the restoration were two partners, J. Wallace Tutt, an Alabama-born contractor who had designed buildings for clients such as Cher and Versace, and his Canada-born associate Don Purdy, who's responsible for the inn's restaurant (p. 251). More than any other hotel in The Bahamas, Rock House brings to mind a stylish and trend-conscious hideaway on Miami's South Beach, with a surprisingly posh repeat clientele.

Painted a pale yellow, with a white roof that's visible from Harbour Island's ferryboat terminal, the hotel sits on a low bluff above the harbor in the center of the island's only village. The property combines the original 1940s-era B&B with an adjoining site that had functioned for several decades as a Catholic schoolhouse.

Each of its nine whimsical accommodations is outfitted with a unique name and decorative style. Examples include the Reef Room, the Palm Room, the Asian Room, the Nautilus Room, the Pineapple Room, and the Parrot Room. Social life centers on the bar and the lavishly landscaped swimming pool, whose edges are lined with the kind of tentlike cabanas that you might expect along the coast of Sardinia.

Bay and Hill sts., Harbour Island, Eleuthera, The Bahamas. © **242/333-2053.** Fax 242/333-3173. www.rockhouse bahamas.com. 9 units. Year-round US$380–US$495 (£190–£248) double, US$575 (£288) junior suite, US$725 (£363) 2-bedroom unit. Rates include continental breakfast. AE, MC, V. Closed Labor Day–Nov 1. No children under 18. **Amenities:** Restaurant; bar; pool; exercise room; room service; laundry service; all nonsmoking rooms. *In room:* A/C, TV, minibar, safe.

Romora Bay Club & Resort 🐞🐞

Despite an ongoing series of management upheavals and continuing conflicts over its expansion plans, this cluster of cottages on the island's bay side is up and running, welcoming visitors to its oft-changing premises. The inn was originally developed as a private club for reclusive millionaires, but today is open to all. Built on a sloping hillside, a short golf-cart ride away from Pink Beach, its clusters of cottages and gazebos are scattered about the landscaped grounds.

Rooms have tiled floors and are cozily furnished with comfortable beds (with plush pillows) and a private patio. The junior suites and water-view rooms are the most desirable, opening onto panoramic vistas of the bay. Within an open-sided pavilion overlooking the harbor, an intimate, informal restaurant, Sunsets on the Bay, serves cheeseburgers, salads, and grilled lobster and grouper along with stiff drinks and the promise of memorable sunsets.

Colbrooke St., Dunmore Town, Harbour Island, Eleuthera, The Bahamas. © **800/688-0425** or 242/333-2325. Fax 242/333-2500. www.romorabay.com. 25 units. Winter US$285–US$350 (£143–£175) double, US$465 (£233) suite; off-season US$145–US$225 (£73–£113) double, US$350 (£175) suite. AE, DC, MC, V. **Amenities:** 2 restaurants; 2 bars; pool; dock; kayaking; snorkeling; diving; boat rental. *In room:* A/C, TV, free Wi-Fi, hair dryer.

Runaway Hill Inn

Small and intimate, within a 1938 masonry building with rambling verandas and porches, this conservative, comfortable hotel overlooks acres of pink-sand beach. It has a huge lawn and is separated from Colebrook Street by a wall. Owned by members of the Messier family, the building retains its English colonial-style dormers and many other original features, including a black-and-white checkerboard-tile floor which, we're told, was installed to emulate a sophisticated Cuban resort during the heyday of that island's pre-Castro tourism. In winter, a crackling fire sometimes burns in the hearth near the entrance. The social center is a cheerfully decorated, pastel-painted lounge/dining room/bar/reception with a sense of Bahamian whimsy.

As for bedrooms, each one is different, giving the impression that you are in a private home—as indeed this used to be. Only two of the guest rooms are in the original house, and these are accessible via the building's original 18th-century staircase. The others are within comfortable annexes built during the '70s and '80s. Bathrooms are small but well-maintained, and seven contain tub/showers (the rest just have showers).

Dinners are served on the breeze-filled rear porch overlooking the swimming pool, and nonguests are welcome to eat here (p. 251).

Colebrook St. at Love Lane, Harbour Island, The Bahamas. © **242/333-2150.** Fax 242/333-2420. www.runaway hill.com. 11 units. November–May 15 US$375–US$450 (£188–£225) double, US$450 (£225) villa; May 16–Sept 1 US$325–US$400 (£163–£200) double, US$400 (£200) villa. MC, V. Closed Sept–Oct. **Amenities:** Restaurant; bar; pool; watersports equipment/rentals; bike rentals; laundry service. *In room:* A/C, hair dryer, safe, no phone.

Valentines Resort & Marina ⭐ If Harbour Island has a mega-hotel, this is it. Since its inception as a small-scale haven for yachties in the 1980s, it has survived major shifts in both its ownership and its priorities. What you'll see today is a corporate-minded and somewhat anonymous enterprise that has survived many years of squabbling among its partners and with local homeowners. Some locals have objected—almost violently—to the construction of the resort's marina, which is Harbour Island's biggest and best-accessorized. Much of the new construction associated with this place has been sold as condominiums to mostly absentee owners. They're rented out as hotel accommodations whenever possible.

Don't expect a candy-colored confection in tones of Valentine pink. The predominant colors here are tangerine and coral, all in a low-rise venue just across the sleepy harborfront road, a 10-minute golf-cart ride from Harbour Island's ferryboat piers. Whereas the resort's airy, sunny bar and restaurant lie on the piers directly above the harbor, its accommodations are within Neo-Georgian two-story structures on a sloping lawn uphill from the harbor. Each evokes a government ministry, each is painted a different pastel color, and each contains between 8 and 10 separate accommodations.

Harbour Island, North Eleuthera, The Bahamas. ⓒ 242/333-2142. www.valentinesresort.com. 45 units. Winter US$350–US$600 (£175–£300) suite for up to 4, US$400–US$700 (£200–£350) 1-bedroom villa w/kitchen for up to 4, US$500–US$800 (£250–£400) 2-bedroom villa w/kitchen for 6–8; off-season US$300–US$350 (£150–£175) suite for up to 4, US$350–US$400 (£175–£200) 1-bedroom villa w/kitchen for up to 4, US$400–US$500 (£200–£250) 2-bedroom villa w/kitchen for 6–8. AE, MC, V. **Amenities:** Restaurant; bar; full-service marina; watersports; laundry service. In room: A/C, TV, fridge, safe.

MODERATE

The Landing ⭐⭐ This intimate inn is understated, tasteful, and lovely. Virtually destroyed by a hurricane in 1999, it was restored well by its former part-owner, India Hicks, daughter of the famed London decorator David Hicks, the granddaughter of Lord Mountbatten of Burma (grandson of Queen Victoria), and a bridesmaid to Princess Diana at her wedding to Charles. Although a few of the decor statements she made are still in place, new owners run the place primarily as a sophisticated restaurant, with bedrooms coming as a rustically upscale afterthought.

Harbour Island's first doctor built the house in the 1850s as his private residence. It's a few paces from the piers where ferryboats arrive from Eleuthera.

Accommodations are breezy, airy, high-ceilinged, and artistically old-fashioned, opening onto wraparound verandas, which seem to expand the living space within. Expect bold, cheerful island colors mixed with tones of muted gray, and design touches that evoke the seafaring days of old Harbour Island. The bathrooms are large and tiled, with tubs and showers.

Bay St., Harbour Island, The Bahamas. ⓒ 242/333-2707. Fax 242/333-2650. www.harbourislandlanding.com. 8 units. Winter US$275–US$385 (£138–£193) double, US$465 (£233) 2-bedroom unit; off-season US$250–US$340 (£125–£170) double, US$410 (£205) 2-bedroom unit. Rates include breakfast. AE, MC, V. **Amenities:** Restaurant; bar; babysitting; nonsmoking rooms. In room: A/C, hair dryer, no phone.

INEXPENSIVE

Bahama House Inn ⭐ *Finds* This is Harbour Island's only authentic B&B, with the owners living on-site. The setting is a pink-painted stone house that was built between 1798 and 1800 by the island's first justice of the peace, Dr. Thomas W. Johnson. In 1997, Denver-derived owners John and Joni Hersh expanded their property with the purchase of a 1970s-era house next door. Rooms are medium-size, artfully old-fashioned, low-key, and comfortable, and they are usually accessible via gracious verandas that wrap around the upper and lower floors. Bathrooms are tiled and beautifully maintained, and most come with shower stalls, except for three which have tub/showers. Everything shows a personal touch here, including the beautiful gardens. The beach is a 5-minute walk away, and the living room has satellite TV.

At the corner of Dunmore and Hill sts., Harbour Island, The Bahamas. © 242/333-2201. Fax 242/333-2850. www. bahamahouseinn.com. 7 units. Winter US$170–US$205 (£85–£103) double; off-season US$155–US$185 (£78–£93) double. Rates include breakfast. MC, V. Closed July–Sept. No children under 12. **Amenities:** Restaurant; bar; laundry service; rooms for those w/limited mobility. *In room:* A/C, hair dryer, safe, no phone.

Chef Neff's Getaway *(R)* *(Finds)*   Harbour Island's most respected chef, an Ohio-native gastronomic genius with a résumé which includes catering for Sarah Ferguson, Duchess of York, rents a duet of well-decorated rooms within her private home. Susan Neff, once the full-time chef at Coral Sands and now partially retired, offers good value within her neat-as-a-pin private villa, a short walk from Romora Bay Resort near the island's southern end. Surrounded with lush landscaping and flowering shrubs, the house, rebuilt to her specifications in 1999, boasts a panoramic cupola, comfortable beds, private bathrooms, and the benefit of Chef Neff's years of experience as a professional nurse, hospice counselor, and professional chef. Though it lacks the hands-on services of a private hotel, many guests return year after year at rates significantly less expensive than what's being charged for comparable accommodations in any of the island hotels. Each unit has a very small private patio. February sojourns are usually booked a full year in advance, so plan ahead.

Yellow Heron, off Queen's Hwy., Harbour Island, The Bahamas. © 242/333-3047 or 301/560-3166. 2 units. Year-round US$850–US$950 (£425–£475) weekly double. No credit cards. *In room:* A/C, free Wi-Fi, kitchenette.

Tingum Village   This is a simple, no-frills choice, but it does the trick at bargain prices, drawing loyal repeat clients. It lies just off the main street, a 3-minute walk over a forested ridge to the beach. Set in a steamy, low-lying, tropical garden, Tingum Village offers basic accommodations in small, somewhat cramped cement-sided bungalows. Each room has air-conditioning, ceiling fans, and a patio with plastic furniture, plus a small bathroom with a shower stall. Rooms aren't the most comfortable, and you'll wish they'd improve the wattage in the reading lamps. But the property has its charming aspects as well, such as the fact that it provides a good introduction to local life (in contrast to the more touristy places) and authentic Bahamian food. A cottage is meant for six to eight people. The hotel's restaurant, **Ma Ruby's,** named after this establishment's durable matriarch, overlooks the garden and offers standard Bahamian and American fare (see box below).

Colebrook St., Harbour Island, Eleuthera, The Bahamas. © 242/333-2161. Fax 242/333-2161. 19 units. Year-round US$135 (£68) double, US$140 (£70) triple, US$150–US$200 (£75–£100) suite, US$300 (£150) 2-bedroom suite or cottage. MC, V. **Amenities:** Restaurant; bar; limited room service; babysitting; laundry service; nonsmoking rooms; rooms for those w/limited mobility. *In room:* A/C, kitchenette (in suites), coffeemaker (in some), hair dryer (in some), no phone.

WHERE TO DINE

If you don't want to dress up for lunch, head for **Seaview Takeaway** (© 242/333-2542), at the foot of the ferry dock. Here you can feast on all that good stuff: pig's feet, sheep-tongue souse, and, most definitely, cracked conch. Everything tastes better with peas 'n' rice. Daily specials range from US$3 to US$9 (£1.50–£4.50), and service is Monday to Saturday 8am to 5pm.

Finds Ma Ruby's Conch Burger

If you'd like to sample some real local fare, head to **Ma Ruby's** on Colebrook Street (© 242/333-2161). Some dyed-in-the-wool locals claim you'll get the best down-home cooking in Harbour Island if Ma Ruby (the cook and owner) is in the kitchen herself. Her conch burger is certainly worthy of an award. She's been stewing chicken, baking grouper, and serving hearty meals in a trellised courtyard for a long time, and she's amassed a lot of devoted fans. The place is known for its cheeseburgers, which the manager says were ranked as one of the world's 10 best by "Mr. Cheeseburger in Paradise" himself, Jimmy Buffett. Prices range from US$6 to US$15 (£3–£7.50) for the a la carte menu; a four-course fixed-price Bahamian dinner costs US$26 to US$40 (£13–£20). The restaurant is open daily 9:30am to midnight.

Another casual drop-in spot for both visitors and locals is **Arthur's Bakery and Café,** Dunmore Street (© 242/333-2644), owned by Robert Arthur, the screenwriter for *M*A*S*H.* Artists, writers, media people, and what Arthur calls "international lollygaggers" hang out here. There are only a few tables, and they fill up quickly with those catching up on local gossip. Arthur's Trinidadian wife, Anna, bakes the island's best Key lime tart and is also praised for her croissants and banana bread. At lunch, drop in for fresh salads and sandwiches. Many guests come here to use the Internet.

EXPENSIVE

Acquapazza Wine Bar & Ristorante ★★ ITALIAN/MEDITERRANEAN Within marina-fronting premises, this is Harbour Island's newest and most talked-about restaurant. It's the culinary statement of two expatriate Italians, Hagmo (from Bolzano) and Manfredi (from Módena), who wax eloquent about the menu items of the day. (Both are refugees from the now-defunct kitchen of the Windermere Island Club on nearby Eleuthera.) Italian wines by the glass are appropriate foils for lunch platters which include seared tuna filets with onions and capers, grilled grouper with homemade tartar sauce and fries, burgers, and Mediterranean-style lobster salad. Dinner main courses are far more elaborate, including linguine with lobster and fresh tomatoes, roasted lamb chops with a balsamic reduction, beef tenderloin with sautéed wild mushrooms, and a signature version of poached grouper with herbs and tomato broth. Lighter appetites appreciate the antipasti, served only from 5 till 10pm. Examples include fried calamari, sea scallops poached in lentils with truffle broth, and kebabs of spicy "pil-pil" shrimp.

In the Harbour Island Marina. © 242/333-3240. Reservations not necessary. Lunch main courses US$9–US$22 (£4.50–£11); antipasti US$8–US$14 (£4–£7); dinner main courses US$16–US$37 (£8–£19). AE, DC, MC, V. Restaurant daily 11am–10pm. Bar daily 11am–11pm.

The Landing ★ INTERNATIONAL   This restaurant occupies the ground floor and most of the garden of the previously recommended hotel (p. 248), a stately building on the dock's right as your ferryboat pulls into Harbour Island. Built around 1850 with a combination of thick stone walls and clapboards, incorporating an annex that's 20 years younger, it's stylish and noted by virtually every local restaurant professional as one of the island's best restaurants.

The menu changes with the availability of fresh ingredients. You might begin with a salmon seviche with coconut, chili, lime, and cucumber-cilantro salad, or perhaps ravioli stuffed with goat cheese and shrimp and served with brown butter, pine nuts, and tea-soaked raisins. Among the more delectable main courses are char-grilled tuna steak with roasted tomatoes, spicy Thai-style green curry, or a New Zealand rack of lamb with saffron-flavored potatoes. Also worth trying are the pan-fried mahimahi, and the tuna with a salad of soba noodles.

Bay St. ℂ 242/333-2707. www.harbourislandlanding.com. Reservations recommended. Main courses US$39–US$45 (£20–£23). AE, MC, V. Thurs–Mon 6:30–10:30pm.

Rock House Restaurant ⓕⓕ INTERNATIONAL   Set on a covered terrace overlooking anchored boats bobbing in the harbor, this restaurant is the showpiece of Harbour Island's newest and perhaps most stylish hotel (p. 246). Inside, there's a hip-bodega feel, with decor that features lots of varnished mahogany, vanilla-colored walls, and ceiling fans. In addition to the tables for two and four, the restaurant offers a large chef's table (with 16 chairs), reputed to have been among the furnishings in the American Embassy in Paris and on which Winston Churchill signed lots of important documents during World War II's aftermath. Though lunches are charming, they're gastronomically simple affairs, with dishes that include burgers, rock lobster salad, sandwiches, conch chowder, and savory pasta variations. Dinners are more elaborate; the best menu items include curried "Junkanoo capellini with shrimp in a spicy arrabiata sauce with preserved lemons," cider-brined pork tenderloin, Colorado lamb chops with toasted couscous salad, seared yellowfin tuna, roasted lobster tail, and vegetarian arugula pesto pasta. Especially flavorful is a crispy pan-fried "almost deboned" chicken breast with a citrus-flavored herb sauce.

In Rock House Hotel, Bay and Hill Sts. ℂ 242/333-2053. www.rockhousebahamas.com. Reservations recommended. Main courses lunch US$15–US$24 (£7.50–£12), dinner US$36–US$55 (£18–£28). AE, MC, V. Nov–Apr daily noon–2pm and 6–10pm; May–Sept daily 7–10:30pm.

Runaway Hill Club ⓕ BAHAMIAN/AMERICAN/INTERNATIONAL   The dining room here presents a sweeping view over the beachfront. Inside, the decor is brightly painted in strong, whimsical colors, with wicker and rattan furniture and a fine collection of watercolors the owner has spent years collecting. The kitchen is known for such well-prepared dishes as conch marinara, tempura-crusted lobster with sweet Thai dipping sauce, curried mango prawns, crabmeat soup with scotch, spicy lobster bisque, blackened mahimahi, and many versions of local fish. An especially succulent dessert is the fresh pineapple-plum tart with cranberries and vanilla ice cream.

Colebrook St. ℂ 242/333-2150. www.runawayhill.com. Reservations required. Main courses US$33–US$40 (£17–£20). AE, MC, V. Mon–Sat dinner at 8pm. Closed Sept 5–Nov 15.

MODERATE

The Harbour Lounge INTERNATIONAL   This old clapboard-sided building dating from the early 1800s is the first place you're likely to see as you step off the ferryboat arriving from Eleuthera. Today, it's one of the island's most satisfying and authentic restaurants. Sometimes, eating here feels like attending an island dinner party. The menu has included at least three different preparations of grouper, fried scallops with a honey-pecan sauce, soft-shell or stone crabs, lobster tail, a variety of conch dishes, and a combination of feta cheese and shrimp marinara. Overall, it's an unpretentious, charming place, and the veranda provides a front-row seat for all the goings-on of Harbour Island. Some of the artifacts displayed on the walls here were salvaged from the local wreck of a ship called the *Vanaheim*.

Bay St. © 242/333-2031. Reservations recommended for dinner. Lunch salads, sandwiches, and platters US$11–US$20 (£5.50–£10); dinner main courses US$16–US$40 (£8–£20). MC, V. Tues–Sun 11:30am–3pm and 6–9:30pm.

Restaurant Sip Sip 𝕽 *Finds* BAHAMIAN/INTERNATIONAL   The only problem with this restaurant is that it's closed every evening (except for large parties), preferring to focus on lunch instead, when it gets extremely busy and crowded. Set at the top of a ridge overlooking Harbour Island's spectacular beach, it was built in 2003 in a traditional green-painted design (with louvered shutters) that's evocative of Harbour Island buildings that are a lot older.

Inside, the cuisine is the product of the Bahamian/American couple Jim Black and Julie Lightbourne, who met in Africa while Jim was working in the safari business. Within a brightly painted interior with mahogany doors, windows, and bar tops, you'll find a changing menu that, depending on the owners' whim, might highlight Bahamian, Italian, French, Thai, or Pacific Rim cuisine. The menu might include hummus with grilled pita bread, conch chili (a welcome variation on conch chowder), fresh salads, baba ganoush (a Lebanese eggplant specialty), seafood quesadillas, and a flavorful curried chicken salad with chunks of apple and mango chutney. Grouper filets, prepared at least two different ways, are usually available as well. The restaurant's name, incidentally, translates from local patois as "gossip."

Court St. © 242/333-3316. Reservations not necessary. Main courses US$15–US$30 (£7.50–£15). MC, V. Wed–Mon 11:30am–4pm. Closed Wed June–Nov.

INEXPENSIVE

Avery's Restaurant & Grill BAHAMIAN/AMERICAN   From the moment you enter, you get the sense that this is a simple, friendly, family-run restaurant. It occupies a tiny wooden house, painted in tones of orange and yellow, near Tingum Village. Inside you'll find a clean, white-tiled room with no more than four tables and a deck with six more. Maria Campbell and her daughter, Murieta, are the owners. Their breakfasts nourish city employees around town. The rest of the day, an unending stream of sandwiches and steaming platters of seafood and steaks emerge from the kitchen.

Colebrook St. © 242/333-3126. Reservations not accepted. Breakfast and lunch platters US$7–US$18 (£3.50–£9); dinner main courses US$25–US$35 (£13–£18). No credit cards. Daily 6:30am–3pm and 6–10pm.

BEACHES, WATERSPORTS & OTHER OUTDOOR PURSUITS

Pink Sands Beach 𝕽𝕽𝕽 is our favorite strand in all The Bahamas; its sands stretch for 5 uninterrupted kilometers (3 miles). Although the beach is set against a backdrop of low-rise hotels and villas, it still feels tranquil and pristine. The sun is best in the morning (afternoons become shadowy), and waves are generally gentle, owing to an offshore reef that breaks waves coming in from the Atlantic. It has many good snorkeling spots and is also the island's best place for a long, leisurely morning stroll.

The diving in this part of The Bahamas is among the most diverse in the region. The most spectacular site, judged among the 10 top dives in the world, is **Current Cut Dive** 𝕽𝕽𝕽, which is also one of the world's fastest (9 knots) drift dives. It involves descending into the water flow that races between the rock walls forming the underwater chasm between Eleuthera and Current Island. Swept up in the currents with schools of stingrays, mako sharks, and reef fish, divers are propelled 1km (⅔ mile) of underwater distance in less than 10 minutes. This dive may become one of the highlights of your whole life.

Valentines Dive Center, Harbourfront (© **242/333-2080;** www.valentinesdive.com), maintains a full range of dive activities and is centered in a blue-painted wooden building near the entrance to the marina at the Valentines resort. Lessons in snorkeling and scuba diving for beginners are given daily at 10am. Snorkeling trips cost US$50 (£25) per half-day, including equipment. A two-tank dive goes for US$85 (£43), with night dives costing US$95 (£48).

Lil' Shan's Watersports, Bay Street (© **242/422-9343;** www.lswatersports.com), offers everything from scuba diving to boat rentals and fishing trips. A two-stop snorkeling jaunt goes for US$55 (£28) per person, including gear. The staff here also offers special kids' programs.

Another worthy outfitter for exploring the watery depths around Harbour Island is **Ocean Fox,** Marina Road (© **242/333-2323;** www.oceanfoxdiving.com). A snorkeling expedition with two stops costs US$55 (£28) per person, including gear, and two-tank dives are competitively priced with what's charged at Valentines (see above).

You can rent a motorboat through **Michael's Cycles** (© **242/333-2384** or 464-0994), on Colebrook Street near Sea Grapes nightclub. Plan to spend about US$75 (£38) for a full day on a 4m boat, and US$100 (£50) for a half-day or US$150 (£75) for a full day on a 5m boat (rates do not include the gas charge). Kayaks go for US$40 (£20) per day.

You can book fishing guides and charters through your hotel or by contacting **Valentines Dive Center** (© **242/333-2142;** www.valentinesdive.com), on the harbor side of the island in Dunmore Town.

EXPLORING HARBOUR ISLAND

Dunmore Town, located on the island's harbor side, was named for the 18th-century royal governor of The Bahamas who had his summer home here. You can walk around the narrow, virtually car-free lanes in less than 20 minutes, or stroll slowly to savor the sight of the old gingerbread cottages lining the waterfront. Overhung with orange, purple, and pink bougainvillea, white picket fences enclose wooden houses painted pastel blue, green, and lilac. Wind chimes tinkle in front of shuttered windows while coconut palms and wispy casuarina pines shade grassy yards.

Americans and Canadians own some of these houses, which have whimsical names, such as Up Yonder and Beside the Point, instead of house numbers. One of the oldest, **Loyalist Cottage,** was built in 1797. It survives from the days when the original settlers, loyal to the British Crown, left the American colonies after the Revolutionary War.

The porches along the harbor make for prime sunset-watching. Lucky for you, some porches aren't connected to private homes. The terrace at Harbour Lounge Bar and Restaurant is an idyllic perch. Just across the road from Loyalist Cottage, you can browse through straw goods, T-shirts, and fruits and vegetables at vendor stalls.

On Sundays, dressed-up residents socialize in clusters outside churches before and after services. Two of The Bahamas' first churches are in Dunmore Town, still going strong: **St. John's,** The Bahamas' oldest Anglican church, established in 1768, and **Wesley Methodist Church,** built in 1846.

Spend some time wandering the streets—some hilly, some flat—away from the heart of town. You can see roosters doing their jerky marches through front yards and horses grazing in small fields. In this locals' area are unassuming but perfectly good Bahamian restaurants, bars, and nightclubs.

HARBOUR ISLAND SHOPPING

Miss Mae's, on Dunmore Street (② 242/333-2002), lives up to its billing as one of the island's finest clothing boutiques. **Briland's Androsia,** on King Street (② 242/333-2342), sells the best selection of bathing suits, with bright batik fabrics printed on the island of North Andros. **Blue Rooster,** in the center of town (② 242/333-2240), along with the Shop at the Landing (see below), offers what might be the island's most upscale and stylish collection of men's and women's clothing and casual eveningwear. Come here for something sporty and trim-looking to wear into a posh hotel's dining room, especially if the New England button-down look appeals to you. The **Shop at the Landing,** at the Landing Resort (② 242/333-2707), focuses on chic and wearable sportswear and items you might wear to a casual island cocktail party, a posh brunch, or a buffet dinner aboard a yacht.

Finally, check out **Princess Street Gallery** (② 242/333-2788), where owner Charles Carey has restored an ancestral home to become a showcase to display works by local artists.

HARBOUR ISLAND AFTER DARK

Unpretentious **Gusty's,** on Coconut Grove Avenue (② 242/333-2165), boasts sweeping sea and sunset views and a clientele that's drawn from every strata, top to bottom, of Harbour Island's complicated sociology. Inside is a sand-covered floor, while the outdoor veranda is sometimes the scene of fashion shows for local dressmakers. Live music is featured every night. Gusty's opens every night at 9:30pm and then goes on rocking virtually until dawn.

Sea Grapes, on Colebrook Street (no phone number), another favorite of locals, is where you can boogie down to the sounds of disco or catch a live band. Expect to be jostled and crowded on a Saturday night because everyone on the island comes here for a wild Bahamian hoedown.

Vic-Hum Club, on Barracks Street (② 242/333-2161), established in 1955, is the quintessential Harbour Island dive. Its walls are layered with the covers of hundreds of record albums and sports posters that music-industry and basketball buffs find fascinating. The Vic-Hum is open 24 hours a day, catering to breakfasting construction workers in the morning, and locals meeting friends for a beer all afternoon. Some of them play basketball on an indoor court that's transformed later in the evening into a dance floor (music begins at 10pm every Fri and Sat).

10 Spanish Wells

Called a "quiet corner of The Bahamas," Spanish Wells is a colorful cluster of houses on St. George's Cay, 1km (⅔ mile) off the coast of northwest Eleuthera. Here you'll find sparkling bays, white beaches, sleepy lagoons, excellent diving, and a fine fishing colony.

You can walk or bicycle through the village, looking at the houses, some of which are more than 200 years old. They have New England saltbox styling but bright tropical coloring. You'll also see handmade quilts in many colors, following patterns handed down from generations of English ancestors. Homeowners display these quilts on their front porches or out their windows, and they are for sale. No one locks their doors here, or removes ignition keys from their cars.

GETTING THERE

To reach the island, you can fly to the **North Eleuthera airstrip,** from which **taxis** will deliver you to the ferry dock. Regardless of the time of day you arrive, a ferryboat will be either waiting for passengers or be about to arrive with a load of them.

A ferry (© **242/554-6268**) runs between Gene's Bay in North Eleuthera to the main pier at Spanish Wells, departing whenever passengers show up. The cost is US$10 (£5) per person round-trip.

WHERE TO STAY

Adventurers Resort   This is Spanish Wells' only lodging option. It occupies a two-story, pale-lavender building in a well-tended garden about .5km (⅓ mile) west of the town center. A staff member will direct you to the beach, about 1km (⅔ mile) away. The small bedrooms have simple, durable furniture with tropical upholstery; six of the units are apartments with kitchenettes. Each comes with a tub/shower. Maid service is provided when you rent the regular double room.

Harbourfront, Spanish Wells, The Bahamas. © **242/333-4883**. Fax 242/333-5073. www.bahamasvg.com/adventurers. html. 22 units. Year-round US$125 (£63) double, US$152 (£76) 1-bedroom apt, US$250 (£125) 2-bedroom apt. MC, V. **Amenities:** Watersports; room service; coin-operated laundry; nonsmoking rooms. *In room:* A/C, TV, kitchenette, coffeemaker, iron, no phone.

WHERE TO DINE

Anchorage BAHAMIAN   Though you won't find Spanish Wells written up in any gourmet books, you can dine well here if you stick to locally caught fish and the like. Decent, unpretentious, and clean, this little eatery serves such home-cooked Bahamian-style items as cracked conch and grouper fingers. The island is known for its *langoustes* (Bahamian lobsters), so order this if it's on the menu. For dessert, try a mud pie.

Along the waterfront at the Spanish Wells port. © **242/333-4023**. Reservations required Sat–Sun. Main courses US$12–US$19 (£6–£9.50). No credit cards. Mon–Sat 9am–1:30pm; daily 5–10pm.

10

The Exumas

The Exumas are some of the prettiest islands in The Bahamas. Shades of jade, aquamarine, and amethyst in deeper waters turn to transparent opal near sandy shores; the water and land appear almost inseparable. Sailors and their crews like to stake out their own private beaches and tropical hideaways, and several vacation retreats have been built by wealthy Europeans, Canadians, and Americans.

A spiny, sandy chain of islands, the Exumas begin just 56km (35 miles) southeast of Nassau and stretch more than 161km (100 miles) from Beacon Cay in the north to Hog Cay and Sandy Cay in the south. These islands have not been developed like the Abacos and Eleuthera have, so they are relatively inexpensive to visit. But they still have much to offer, with crystal-clear waters on the west around the Great Bahama Bank, the 1,500m-deep (4,921-ft.) Exuma Sound on the east, rolling hills, ruins of once-great plantations, coral formations of great beauty, and uninhabited cays ideal for picnics. Although they're crossed by the Tropic of Cancer, the islands have average temperatures ranging from the mid-70s to the mid-80s (mid- to upper 20s Celsius).

Most of our resort recommendations are in and around George Town, the pretty pink capital of the Exumas, on Great Exuma. A community of some 900 residents, it was once considered a possible site for the capital of The Bahamas because of its excellent **Elizabeth Harbour** (see "Exploring George Town," p. 267).

Nearly all the other cays are uninhabited or sparsely populated. Over the years, remote accommodations have come and gone on these islands. Today, the only lodgings, which attract mostly the yachting set, are at Staniel Cay and Sampson Cay.

The cruising grounds around the Exumas, which are scattered over an ocean area of 233 sq. km (90 sq. miles), are among the finest in the Western Hemisphere—if not the world—for boating. The sailing rivals the Grenadines and the Abacos. If you don't come in your own craft, you can rent one here, from a simple little Daysailer to a fishing runabout, with or without a guide. Elizabeth Harbour's annual regatta in April has attracted such notables as Prince Philip and Constantine, Greece's former king. Yachters often say that the Exumas are "where you go when you die if you've been good."

Snorkeling and scuba-diving opportunities draw aficionados from around the world to the vast underwater preserve of **Exuma Cays Land and Sea Park** (p. 272) and to the island group's other exotic limestone and coral reefs, blue holes, drop-offs, and caves. Dive centers in George Town and Staniel Cay provide air fills and equipment.

The fishing, too, is superb here, and the "flats" on Great Exuma's west side are famous for bonefishing. You can find (if you're lucky) blue marlin on both sides of

The Exumas

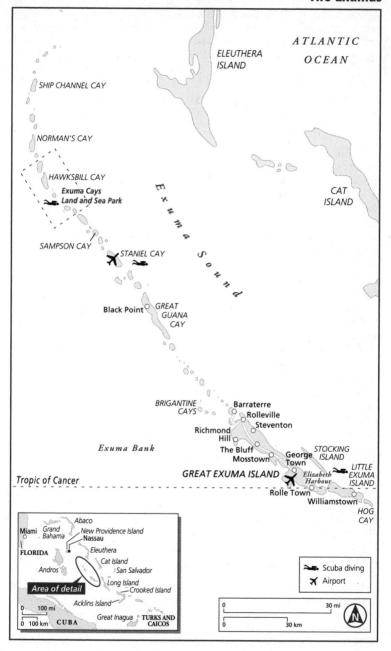

Exuma Sound, as well as sailfish, wahoo, and white marlin, plus others.

The Exumas are among the friendliest islands in The Bahamas; the people are warmhearted and not (yet) spoiled by tourism, seeming genuinely delighted to receive and welcome visitors. They grow a lot of their own food, including cassava, onions, cabbages, and pigeon peas, on the acres their ancestors worked as slaves. Many fruits grow on the cays, including guavas, mangoes, and avocados. At **Government Wharf** in George Town, you can watch these fruits being loaded for shipment to Nassau. The sponge industry is being revived locally; this product of the sea is found in shallow waters and creeks to the south side of the Exumas.

EXUMAS ESSENTIALS

GETTING THERE

BY PLANE   The region's major commercial airport, **Exuma International Airport,** is 16km (10 miles) from George Town, the capital. The most popular way to visit the Exumas is to fly there aboard **Bahamasair** (© 800/222-4262; www.bahamasair.com), which offers twice-daily service from Nassau to George Town. The first flight usually leaves Nassau in the morning sometime around 6:20am, depending on the day. The second flight is at 4pm. Be sure and call ahead because flight schedules are subject to change.

American Eagle (© 800/433-7300; www.aa.com) serves Exuma from Miami three times daily. **Delta** (© 800/221-1212; www.delta.com) has also recently begun service to George Town, flying from Atlanta four times a week.

Other minor carriers servicing the archipelago include **Lynx Air International** (© 888/596-9247; www.lynxair.com), on Thursdays, Fridays, and Sundays, with air links from Fort Lauderdale.

For flights to the private airstrip at Staniel Cay, see section 3 of this chapter.

BY BOAT   There is now a motorized catamaran making the 8-hour transit from Nassau. It arrives in George Town every Monday and Wednesday at 7:30pm and departs on Tuesday and Thursday. The cost of a round-trip fare is US$100 (£50) per person. Technically designed for transporting building supplies and freight, it nonetheless allows passengers as well, many of whom stretch out on the deck in sleeping bags. There are no sleeping compartments onboard. For information, call **Bahamas Ferry** at © 242/323-2166 or check www.bahamasferries.com.

Several **mail boats** leave from Potter's Cay Dock in Nassau, stopping at various points along the Exumas. Two mail steamers, the **MV *Grand Master*** and the ***Captain C,*** sail from Nassau several days a week, stopping at Big Farmer's Cay, Staniel Cay, Black Point, George Town, and Barraterre (stopovers last no more than a few

---

⌒Finds **Saddle Cay: The Perfect Beach**

For years, boaters have known of a special beach, **Saddle Cay,** whose horseshoe-shaped curve lies near the small archipelago's northern tip. The only way to reach it is by private boat; there are no organized excursions or tours (the Exumas are much too laid-back for that). However, if you own a boat, head for Saddle Cay, and you won't be disappointed when you see this totally unspoiled beach of white sand and tranquil water. The cay is perfect for beachcombers, bird-watchers, and snorkelers—but don't expect facilities.

hours). Passengers, as well as small amounts of freight, are allowed onboard. It usually takes about 21 hours for either of the ships to make the full-circuit itinerary described above.

Since sailing schedules are subject to change because of weather conditions, check times with the dock master at **Potter's Cay Dock** in Nassau (© **242/393-1064**).

GETTING AROUND

After arriving at the George Town airport, chances are you'll meet Kermit Rolle. Kermit, who runs things up in Rolleville, knows as much about the Exumas as anyone (maybe more). Stop in at **Kermit's Airport Lounge,** from 7am to 5:30pm, Exuma International Airport (© **242/345-0002**), which is just across from the airport terminal building. If you're lucky, Kermit will be available and you can negotiate a deal with him to take you in his car for a tour.

BY TAXI   If your hotel is in George Town, it will cost about US$25 (££13) to get there in a taxi from the airport. Rides often are shared. If you're going on to **Stocking Island,** an islet in Elizabeth Harbour, make prior arrangements with your hotel for boat transfers. The island has only a few taxis, and most of them wait at the airport. Hotels can usually get you a taxi if you need to go somewhere and don't have a car. Otherwise, for a taxi, call **Leslie Dames** at © **242/357-0405.**

BY CAR   It's also possible to rent a car during your stay, though the major North American companies aren't represented here. Try **Exuma Transport,** Main Street, George Town (© **242/336-2101**). They rent cars for US$60 (£30) and up per day or US$325 (£163) per week. A US$200 (£100) deposit is required. Your hotel can also usually arrange a rental car for you through a local firm.

The George Town area has two gas stations: one near Exuma International Airport and the other in Farmers Hill. They're generally open Monday to Saturday 8am to 5pm, Sunday 8am to noon, and 8 to 10am on holidays.

BY BOAT   For ferries between George Town and the beaches on Stocking Island, call **Club Peace & Plenty** at © **242/336-2551.** With departures twice a day, the ferries are complimentary to Club Peace & Plenty guests. If you're not staying at that hotel, the cost is US$10 (£5) round-trip and free for children under age 10.

BY FOOT   George Town is designed for strolling, but don't expect sights that scream "tourist attraction." This is a handsome little waterfront village where browsing at the tree-shaded straw market, sampling fresh conch salad at the dock, and mingling with residents and fellow vacationers over drinks and home-style meals are the big draws. The most idyllic walk is around **Lake Victoria.**

Shuttle service is provided to town from **Exuma Beach Inn,** or you can walk the scenic mile. If you don't succumb to wheels, you can enjoy leisurely glimpses of the turquoise and neon-blue water through the wispy casuarina pines and bushy coconut palms lining **Queen's Highway.** "Highway" is a serious overstatement, so walking here is fine, as traffic is sparse.

1 George Town

The Tropic of Cancer runs directly through George Town, the capital and principal settlement of the Exumas, located on the island of Great Exuma. This tranquil seaport village opens onto a 24km-long (15-mile) harbor. George Town, partly in the Tropics and partly in the temperate zone, is a favorite port of call for the yachting crowd.

If you need to stock up on supplies, George Town is the place to go, as it has more stores and services than any other spot in the Exumas. There are dive centers, marinas, markets, a doctor, and a health clinic. The town often doesn't bother with street names, but everything's easy to find.

GEORGE TOWN ESSENTIALS

GETTING THERE   Flights from Nassau and Miami come into nearby Exuma International Airport, 16km (10 miles) away. See the introduction of this chapter, above, for details on airlines and taxis.

FAST FACTS   A branch of the **Bank of Nova Scotia,** Queen's Highway (© 242/336-2651), is open Monday to Thursday 9:30am to 3pm and Friday 9:30am to 4:30pm. It has an ATM.

For information about the Exumas, go to the Ministry of Tourism Office in Exuma (© 242/336-2457) on Queens Highway, across from Exuma Market. It is open Monday to Friday 9am to 5pm.

If you come to the Exumas aboard your own boat, **Exuma Docking Services,** Main Street, George Town (© 242/336-2578), has slips for 52 boats with water and electricity hookups. Sam's Restaurant is on the premises, as are a laundromat, a fuel dock, fuel pumps, and a store with supplies for boats and people.

The government-operated **medical clinic** can be reached by phone at © 242/336-2088. Go here to have a prescription filled.

To call the George Town **police,** dial © 242/336-2666.

The **post office** is in George Town's government building and is open Monday to Friday 9am to 4:30pm. For **Internet access,** check with your hotel. You can also go to the **ABC Exuma Internet Café** at Exuma International Airport (© 242/345-6038).

SPECIAL EVENTS   In April, the **Family Island Regatta** (© 954/475-8315) draws a yachting crowd from all over the world to Elizabeth Harbour. It's a rollicking week of fun, song, and serious racing when the island sloops go all-out to win. It's said that some determined skippers bring along extra crewmen to serve as live ballast on windward tacks, and then drop them over the side to lighten the ship for the downwind run to the finish. The event, a tradition since 1954, comes at the end of the crayfish season.

The **Junkanoo Summer Festival** takes place in the hot months unlike the regular winter Bahamas' Junkanoo. The festival runs for 6 weeks (dates vary) at the peak of summer and takes place every Saturday night in George Town. Bands play rake-and-scrape music for street dancing, and small stands hawk fresh conch, grilled seafood, and plenty of rum punches. An onion-peeling competition celebrates Exuma's historic link to the cultivation of the bulb.

WHERE TO STAY

The most luxurious way to stay in the Exumas is to skip the properties recommended below (yes, even the Four Seasons) and rent a villa at **February Point Resort Estates** ☆☆ (© 877/839-4253 or 242/327-1567; fax 242/327-1569; www.february point.com) when the owners are away. This upscale resort community opens onto the Exumas' most coveted oceanfront property and lies on a private 32.4 hectare (80-acre) peninsula overlooking tiny cays, coves, and virgin beaches. These villas are luxuriously furnished with spacious bedrooms, dining rooms, and full kitchens, coming with two, three, four, or even five bedrooms. Villa rental in winter starts at US$800 (£400) to US$1,000 (£500) daily, but in summer, prices start at US$600 (£300).

VERY EXPENSIVE

Four Seasons Resort Great Exuma at Emerald Bay ☆☆☆ (Kids)   The quiet Exumas emerged from a centuries-long sleep with the official opening of this resort in late 2004. Its sweeping ocean vistas and tropical beauty frame an experience unique in this part of the world; the Out Islands have seen nothing like this in their history, and the resort is expected to change the archipelago's entire character.

All accommodations here open onto private terraces and balconies with scenic views of the bay. You're given a choice of rooms, from generously proportioned garden-view units to ocean-view rooms opening directly onto the bay. For the big spender, the resort also offers a series of executive suites and beachfront properties with one or two bedrooms.

So much goes on at this resort that you may never get around to exploring the surrounding islands. The most spectacular feature is a championship 18-hole golf course designed by Greg Norman. The full-service spa and health club is the finest in The Bahamas, and you can swim either at the hotel's crescent-shaped white-sand beach or in one of two pools. The best marina in the Southern Bahamas operates here. And the cuisine is among the best in the Out Islands, with both indoor and outdoor dining options and a selection of Italian, Caribbean, Bahamian, and international dishes. Since its "soft" opening, the hotel has worked out its kinks and is running smoothly with an improvement in food and service. The restaurant, Il Cielo, is perhaps the Southern Bahamas' finest, and it's accentuated by floor-to-ceiling panels and screens. Seating 180, it opens onto landscaped gardens or the stars overlooking Emerald Bay. On offer is a wide selection of Italian dishes, including locally caught seafood, and an impressive wine cellar. A children's menu is also available.

Emerald Bay, Great Exuma, The Bahamas. ✆ 800/819-5053 in the U.S. and Canada, or 242/366-6800. Fax 242/336-6801. www.fourseasons.com. 183 units. Winter US$520–US$1,045 (£260–£523) double; off-season US$375–US$795 (£188–£398) double; year-round from US$995 (£498) suite. AE, DC, DISC, MC, V. **Amenities:** 3 restaurants; 2 bars; 2 pools; golf course; 6 tennis courts; gym; spa; sauna; watersports equipment/rentals; children's programs; business center; salon; room service; babysitting; laundry service; dry cleaning; nonsmoking rooms; rooms for those w/limited mobility. *In room:* A/C, TV, Wi-Fi, minibar, coffeemaker, hair dryer, iron, safe.

Hotel Higgins Landing ☆   The beach at this resort is a major attraction. It is one of the first eco-resorts in The Bahamas and still the only hotel on undeveloped Stocking Island. Higgins Landing takes great care to preserve the natural beauty of its surroundings on this gorgeous island. It's bordered by Elizabeth Harbour and the Atlantic on one side and the crystal-blue waters of Turtle Lagoon and its colorful reefs on the other. This solar-powered hideaway bills itself as one of the great escapes of The Bahamas.

Cottages are exquisitely decorated with antiques, mirrors, and Higgins family heirlooms. Accommodations are furnished with queen-size beds, and each unit is given an island accent with cool tile floors and ceiling fans, plus a well-maintained private bathroom. The landscaped grounds are as colorful as your imagination, attracting many types of wildlife, from herons and hummingbirds to green sea turtles. Hotel ferry service from George Town provides access to the island.

Rates include a full breakfast and a first-rate candlelit dinner (nonguests are welcome too, with advance reservations). The open-air bar overlooks the cerulean Atlantic.

Stocking Island, George Town, Great Exuma, The Bahamas. ✆ 242/357-0008. Fax 866/289-0919. www.higgins landing.com. 5 units. Year-round US$425 (£213) 1-bedroom cottage, US$740 (£370) 2-bedroom cottage. Rates include dinner and transportation from George Town. Minimum stay of 4 nights required; 50% deposit required to secure reservation. MC, V. No children under 6. Closed Aug 1–Nov 25. **Amenities:** Restaurant; bar; watersports equipment/rentals; laundry service; nonsmoking rooms. *In room:* Kitchenette (in some), coffeemaker, hair dryer, no phone.

EXPENSIVE

Exuma Beach Inn ⚓ Early in 2008, what had previously been one of the trio of Peace & Plenty inns was purchased and radically renovated by North Carolina entrepreneur Brewer Ezzell and his wife, Bobbie. What has emerged is an all-new venue whose accommodations contain bathrooms and furnishings that are better and newer than those within either of its former siblings. The place's only drawback is that it lacks an on-site restaurant, although the breakfast room is still a daily feature (included in the price) and the bar does a thriving business serving simple appetizers and stiff drinks. Tranquil, and with a world-class reputation as a bonefishing resort, it opens onto 90m (295 feet) of sandy beach that's noted for its snorkeling. Bedrooms contain Italian tiles salvaged from the inn's earlier incarnation and marble vanities in 10 of the 16 units. Balconies overlook Bonefish Bay and Elizabeth Harbour. A separate building inspired by the country's British colonial heritage contains the above-mentioned breakfast room and bar.

Harbourfront, George Town, Great Exuma, The Bahamas. ℂ **242/336-2251.** Fax 242/336-2253. 16 units. Winter US$250–US$450 (£125–£225) double; off-season US$200–US$400 (£100–£200) double. Rates include breakfast. AE, MC, V. **Amenities:** Bar; pool; watersports equipment/rentals. *In room:* A/C, ceiling fan, TV, Wi-Fi, hair dryer, no phone.

Palm Bay Beach Club ⚓ *Finds* One of the archipelago's most tranquil accommodations, Palm Bay overlooks the waters of Elizabeth Harbour. This attractive resort offers beachfront villas featuring either a studio, a one-bedroom unit, or a more luxurious and spacious two-bedroom accommodation. The cottages are beautifully appointed, and most of them have kitchenettes, cable TV, and Internet access. Each villa is individually decorated and features queen- or king-size beds, ceramic tile flooring, and comfortable tropical-style furniture. A shuttle bus carries visitors to and from George Town. Kayaks and paddle boats are available.

Elizabeth Harbour, George Town, Great Exuma, The Bahamas. ℂ **888/396-0606** or 242/336-2787. www.palmbay beachclub.com. 38 units. Winter US$265–US$325 (£133–£163) double, US$380–US$455 (£190–£228) 2-bedroom unit; off-season US$220–US$275 (£110–£138) double, US$290–US$350 (£145–£175) 2-bedroom unit. AE, MC, V. **Amenities:** Beach bar; outdoor pool. *In room:* A/C, ceiling fan, TV, kitchenette (in some).

Peace & Plenty Bonefish Lodge ⚓ Eleven miles (18km) south of George Town, this is one of two Peace & Plenty properties in the Exumas—and the posher of the two. Established in 1990, it caters almost exclusively to fishermen (and their companions) who seek an all-inclusive holiday with three meals a day provided. The two-story inn, surrounded by young palms, is built of concrete and stone, and lies on a peninsula enveloped by crystal-clear waters and sandy flats. This is The Bahamas' most elegant bonefishing inn; you can fish all day and come back to be pampered in luxury.

The lobby is inviting, with tile floors and rattan pieces. From many of the midsize rooms opening onto the wraparound balcony, you'll have a great view of the turquoise waters, or perhaps you'd rather doze in a hammock. Accommodations are enlivened by bright floral spreads and prints, air-conditioning and ceiling fans, and spacious, immaculate bathrooms and tub/showers. You don't have to be an angler to stay here—but it helps. If you don't fish, you may be left out of the nighttime conversation.

The food served in the clubby dining room is excellent; it's made by a well-trained chef who not only knows how to grill steak to perfection but can whip up a mean vegetarian platter too. Of course, the finest way to dine here is on fish caught that day by the chef or one of the guests. After cleaning the fish, the kitchen staff toss scraps to the sharks in the adjoining waters. This is the chief evening entertainment, though there's an honor bar and a lobby lounge upstairs with a TV and VCR.

Queen's Hwy., George Town, Great Exuma, The Bahamas. ☏ **242/345-5555.** Fax 242/345-5556. www.ppbone
fishlodge.net. 8 units. Year-round US$900 (£450) per person for 3 nights/4 days. Rates include all meals, drinks, tips,
airport transfers, and most activities. MC, V. **Amenities:** Restaurant; 2 bars; pool; watersports equipment rentals;
laundry service; nonsmoking rooms; rooms for those w/limited mobility. *In room:* A/C, hair dryer, no phone.

MODERATE

Club Peace & Plenty   This attractive, historic waterside inn is a classic island hotel
in the heart of George Town. Once a sponge warehouse and later the home of a
prominent family, it was converted into a hotel in the late 1940s, making it the oldest in the Exumas. The two-story pink-and-white hotel has dormers and balconies
opening onto a water view. The grounds, planted with palms, crotons, and bougainvillea, front Elizabeth Harbour, making it a favorite of the yachting set, including England's Prince Philip.

The midsize units are all tastefully furnished, though a 1950s vibe lingers. A refur-
bishment has freshened things up a bit with bright print spreads and draperies, and
furnishings in white wicker or rattan. All rooms have queen, double, or twin beds, and
a tiled bathroom with a tub/shower. Many also sport balconies opening onto harbor
views; oceanfront rooms are the most desirable.

You can dine indoors or outside (see "Where to Dine," below), and calypso music
plays on the terrace. There are two cocktail lounges, one of which was converted from
an old slave kitchen and is now filled with nautical gear including lanterns, rudders,
and anchors. The hotel faces Stocking Island and maintains a private beach club there,
offering food and bar service, as well as kilometers of sandy dunes. A boat, free for
hotel guests ($10/£5 round-trip for nonguests), makes the run.

Queen's Hwy., George Town, Great Exuma, The Bahamas. ☏ **800/525-2210** in the U.S. and Canada or 242/336-2551.
Fax 242/336-2093. www.peaceandplenty.com. 32 units. Winter US$662 (£331) per person; off-season US$610 (£305)
per person. Rates include breakfast and dinner for 3 days/2 nights. AE, DC, MC, V. **Amenities:** Restaurant; 2 bars; pool;
laundry service; nonsmoking rooms; rooms for those w/limited mobility. *In room:* A/C, ceiling fan, TV, fridge, hair dryer,
safe, no phone.

Coconut Cove Hotel   Set about 1.6km (1 mile) west of George Town, this is the
most recent, much-renovated incarnation of a hotel that has stood here for at least 20
years. On a seafronting plot of land dotted with groves of coconut palms and palmettos and host to a brackish saltwater pond favored by bird life, the hotel was designed
with three wings radiating out from a central core, much like the shape of an airplane
propeller. It offers simple but well-cared-for rooms, a bar where the rum-based
Coconut Cove Specials are appropriately pink and heady, and a restaurant (see
"Where to Dine," below) whose cuisine is praised as among the best on the island.
The staff can arrange for island tours and watersports.

George Town, Great Exuma, The Bahamas. ☏ **242/336-2659.** Fax 242/336-2658. www.exumabahamas.com/
coconutcove.html. 11 units. Winter US$162–US$272 (£81–£136) double; off-season US$142–US$252 (£71–£126)
double. Add US$30 (£15) for extra person. AE, MC, V. **Amenities:** Restaurant; bar; pool; babysitting; laundry service;
nonsmoking rooms; rooms for those w/limited mobility. *In room:* A/C, ceiling fan, TV, fridge.

Regatta Point ⓕ *Kids*   This inn lies on a small cay just across the causeway from
George Town and opens onto a small, sandy beach. The cay used to be known as Kidd
Cay, named after the notorious pirate. Overlooking Elizabeth Harbour, the present
complex consists of six apartments, each with a full kitchen, making this a good choice
for families. The units are not air-conditioned, although the cross-ventilation is good
and ceiling fans help. Each of the pleasantly furnished, summery units comes with maid

service, plus a small bathroom containing tub/showers. Nearby grocery stores are fairly well stocked if you feel like cooking. Those who don't wish to cook can have dinner at one of the previously mentioned hotels in town or at a local restaurant. Bicycles are available at no extra charge. This colony hums in April during the Family Island Regatta.

Regatta Point, Kidd Cove, George Town, Great Exuma, The Bahamas. (℃ **800/688-0309** or 242/336-2206. www. regattapointbahamas.com. 6 units. Winter US$178–US$210 (£89–£105) double, US$264 (£132) 2-bedroom suite; off-season US$148–US$176 (£74–£88) double, US$216 (£108) 2-bedroom suite. Extra person US$20 (£10) per day. No credit cards. **Amenities:** Laundry service. *In room:* Ceiling fans, kitchen, games, books, no phone.

WHERE TO DINE

With a few exceptions (listed below), the best places to eat in George Town are in the hotels reviewed above.

There are several casual joints in George Town where you can grab a quick meal. **Towne Cafe,** in the Marshall Complex (℃ **242/336-2194**), serves one of the city's best breakfasts. It's really the town bakery. Drop in any day but Sunday for a sandwich or a lunch of Exumian specialties such as stewed grouper or chicken souse.

MODERATE

Club Peace & Plenty Restaurant CONTINENTAL/BAHAMIAN/AMERICAN
Come here for the finest island dining, with plentiful home-style cooking that leaves everyone satisfied. You might begin with conch salad or one of the salads made with hearts of palm or artichoke hearts, and then follow with local lobster. Bahamian steamed grouper regularly appears on the menu, simmered with onions, tomatoes, sweet pepper, and thyme. But you can also order such special dishes as an herb-flavored Cornish game hen that is juicy and perfectly roasted and flavored. Lunch options include homemade soups, conch burgers, a chef's salad, or deep-fried grouper. Breakfast offerings range from traditional French toast or scrambled eggs and sausage to truly Bahamian boiled fish and grits.

You sit under ceiling fans, looking out over the harbor. Windows on three sides and candlelight make the place particularly nice in the evening. And who knows who will be at the next table? It may be a celeb or two, or a crowd of yachters providing conversation and amusement.

In the Club Peace & Plenty, Queen's Hwy. (℃ **242/336-2551.** Reservations recommended for dinner. Breakfast US$9.25 (£4.65); lunch US$8–US$10 (£4–£5); dinner main courses US$18–US$35 (£9–£18). AE, DISC, MC, V. Daily 7:30–10:30am, noon–2:30pm, and 6:30–9:30pm.

Coconut Cove ITALIAN   Set on the premises of the Coconut Cove Hotel (p. 263), this dining room sits close to the sea, within a glassed-in, blue, white, and coral-colored dining room whose mahogany-and-glass doors slide open for maximum exposure to the breeze. American-born Pamela Chimento, in cooperation with her Bahama-born assistant, Shelia, churns out well-flavored versions of Italian and

---

Finds Fresh, Sexy Conch

The best conch salad is at **Big D's Conch Spot No. 2,** Government Dock (℃ **242/358-0059**). "Fresh, sexy conch," as it's called here, is served daily. They'll make it right in front of you, so you know what's going into your salad. The joint is open Tuesday to Sunday noon to midnight. Reservations are required only for parties of five or more.

Mediterranean dishes that are far removed from the usual Bahamian fare you might have expected. Starters include breaded calamari with oregano and parsley sauce, linguini marinara, jalapeño peppers, breaded mozzarella sticks, onion soup, and seafood salads. Main courses feature stone crabs, different shrimp preparations, crayfish, poached salmon served with a tropical fruit salsa, and "cowboy steaks." There's also a choice of pizzas from the "pizza bar." Most dishes, except for lobster, are priced at the low end of the scale.

In the Coconut Cove Hotel, George Town. © 242/336-2659. Reservations recommended. Main courses US$18–US$55 (£9–£28); pizzas US$12–US$30 (£6–£15). AE, MC, V. Thurs–Sun 6–9pm.

INEXPENSIVE

Kermit's Airport Lounge BAHAMIAN   Owned by Kermit Rolle, one of the island's most entrepreneurial taxi drivers, this simple but appealing place lies across the road from the airport's entrance. It's the semiofficial waiting room for most of the island's flights, and it might make your wait more convenient and fun. You can usually find Kermit hanging out here. The cook will fry you some fish, and there's always beans and rice around. Johnnycake and sandwiches are also available, along with burgers and an array of tropical drinks. Until an airplane flies you to a better restaurant, this place can come in handy.

Exuma International Airport. © 242/345-0002. Beer US$4.25 (£2.15); cheeseburgers US$6–US$9 (£3–£4.50); platters from US$8.50 (£4.25). No credit cards. Daily 6:30am–5pm.

BEACHES, WATERSPORTS & OTHER OUTDOOR PURSUITS

BEACHES

Stocking Island ☆, in Elizabeth Harbour, faces the town across the bay, less than 1.6km (1 mile) away. This long, thin barrier island has some of the most gorgeous beaches in The Bahamas. Snorkelers and scuba divers come here to explore the blue holes, and it is also ringed with undersea caves and coral gardens. Boat trips leave daily from Elizabeth Harbour at 10am and 1pm. The cost is US$8 (£4) per person round-trip. However, guests of Club Peace & Plenty ride free.

If you'd like to go shelling, walk the beach along Stocking Island's Atlantic side.

The island, which used to be a private enclave, has a marine-activity center run by **Dive Exuma** (© **242/336-2893;** www.dive-exuma.com) at February Point Resort Estates (p. 260). Visibility is great in these waters, and there are many rainbow-hued fish to see. For a 3-hour trip, snorkeling, including all equipment, costs US$65 (£33). A two-tank dive goes for US$150 (£75).

Yachting types and other island visitors like to drop in at Kenneth Bowe's **Chat & Chill** ☆ (no phone number), a laid-back place that manages to be both upmarket and a local dive. Many of the fresh fish dishes are grilled over an open fire, and the Sunday pig roasts are an island event. The conch burgers are the best in the Exumas. But the seasonings? They're secret.

BOATING

Landlocked **Lake Victoria** covers about .8 hectares (2 acres) in the heart of George Town. It has a narrow exit to the harbor and functions as a diving and boating headquarters.

If you come to the Exumas aboard your own boat, **Exuma Docking Services,** Main Street, George Town (© 242/336-2578), has slips for 52 vessels, along with water and electricity hookups. You can also stock up on supplies here, get fuel, and do laundry.

Through the **Starfish Exuma Adventure Center** (© 242/336-3033; www.kayak bahamas.com), you can rent Hobie Waves, high-performance sailboats that are easy to use. These stable, lightweight 4.5m catamarans are ideal for families, as they are simple to maneuver. Sailboat rentals, including Hobie Waves, cost US$75 (£38) per half-day or US$525 (£263) weekly. One-hour sailboat lessons cost US$70 (£35) for one to three participants.

If motorboats are more your speed, **Minns Water Sports** (© 242/336-3483 or 336-2604), based out of George Town, rents boats ranging from 4.5 to 6.6m for US$120 to US$210 (£60–£105) per day. With your boat, you can set out to sail some of the most stunning waters in The Bahamas, rivaled only by the Abacos. The best territory for recreational boating is the government-protected **Exuma Cays Land and Sea Park,** stretching south from Wax Cay to Conch Cay, which has magnificent sea gardens and coral reefs.

Getting around the archipelago of the Exumas is very difficult unless you're a yachtie or a skilled skipper of your own rented craft. If you're not a sailor, your best bet is to call Captain Steven Cole in George Town (© 242/524-0524), and book a half-day tour for US$400 (£200) or a full-day tour for US$700 (£350). His **Off Island Adventures** (© 242/524-0524; www.offislandadventures.com) takes you to remote spots in the archipelago, including such exotic locations as White Cay, where parts of the *Pirates of the Caribbean* movies were filmed. You can also opt for a sunset or moonlight cruise. Day cruises usually include a stopover at a remote beach bar for cocktails.

FISHING

Many visitors come to the Exumas just to go bonefishing. Arrangements for such outings can be made at **Club Peace & Plenty,** Queen's Highway (© 800/525-2210 or 242/336-2551), or at **Peace & Plenty Bonefish Lodge,** Queen's Highway (© 242/345-5555). The Exumas offer miles of wadeable flats (shallow bodies of water) where trained guides will accompany you. Fly-fishing instruction and equipment are also offered.

GOLF

The **Four Seasons Resort Emerald Bay Golf Club** 𝕬𝕬𝕬, Emerald Bay (© 242/366-6800 or 358-4185), is one of the great oceanfront courses in all of the Caribbean. The par-72 Greg Norman design features 6 oceanfront holes and stretches a challenging 7,001 yards, yet was laid out to accommodate golfers of various skill levels. The course uses environmentally friendly seashore paspalum grass and finishes on a rocky peninsula with a panoramic view of the sea. There's also a pro shop. Greens fees are a steep US$115 to US$165 (£58–£83) for 18 holes (US$145–US$175/£73–£88 for nonguests) and reservations are required.

KAYAKING

You can best appreciate some of the Exumas' most dramatic scenery from the peaceful perch of a sea kayak. In fact, many areas—including mangrove lakes, rivers, manta ray gathering spots, and bonefish flats—are too shallow for other boats. Don't worry if you haven't hit the gym lately. Anyone in at least average physical condition, from children to seniors, can kayak with a smile. **Starfish Exuma Adventure Center** (© 242/336-3033; www.kayakbahamas.com) rents sit-on-top kayaks for singles and doubles. Singles are US$75 (£38) per half-day, US$100 (£50) per day, and US$200 (£100) per week. Doubles run US$95 (£48) per half-day, US$150 (£75) per day, and US$225 (£113) per week.

For more adventure, book one of Starfish's daily guided kayak trips. You don't have to spend the whole time paddling. During half- and full-day excursions, lunch and beverages are served, and the price covers all gear, including snorkeling equipment. You may end up watching a blizzard of fish swarm a shipwreck, searching for sand dollars on a deserted beach, snorkeling into a sea cave, or finding out about bush medicine while you hike along a nature trail. Guided trips begin at US$70 (£35) per hour for adults and US$56 (£28) for children.

Another good outfitter is **Ecosummer Expeditions** (© 800/465-8884), whose guides are especially skilled at exploring **Exuma Cays Land and Sea Park** (p. 272).

SCUBA DIVING

Surrounding the Exumas, fields of massive coral heads, eerie blue holes, and exciting walls covered with marine life attract scuba divers. Many excellent reefs are just 20 or 25 minutes away from the George Town area, so long boat rides don't cut into your underwater time.

For scuba divers, the great attraction here is the **Exuma Cays Land and Sea Park** (p. 272). It draws scuba divers to its 453 sq. km (175 sq. miles) of sea gardens with magnificent coral reefs, flora, and fauna. Call your hotel to ask whether it offers a hotel/dive package, or try **Exuma Scuba Adventures** (© 242/336-2893) at Peace & Plenty Beach Inn for information about scuba-diving excursions. A two-tank dive costs US$150 (£75).

SHOPPING

In George Town, shopping is a very casual event, especially at the **Exuma Straw Market,** open Monday to Saturday 7am to 5pm. Here in the shade of a large Indian fig tree, local Bahamian women spend their day making straw baskets, colorful handbags, dolls, and other keepsakes. Bargaining is permissible, and prices go from US$25 (£13) for a hat to US$100 (£50) for an intricate basket.

SNORKELING

The best bet for snorkeling is found in the beautiful waters off the coast of **Stocking Island** (p. 265). Boat trips from George Town depart for the island twice daily. You can also rent snorkeling equipment for US$10 (£5) per day at **Minns Water Sports** (© 242/336-3483) in George Town. A US$50 (£25) deposit is required.

EXPLORING GEORGE TOWN

There isn't much to see here in the way of architecture except the confectionery-pink-and-white **Government Building,** which was inspired by the architecture of Nassau's Government House. Under an old ficus tree in the center of town, there's a **straw market** where you can talk to the friendly Exumian women and perhaps purchase some of their handicrafts.

George Town has a colorful history, despite the fact that it appears so sleepy today. (With so little street action, it doesn't even need a traffic light.) Pirates used its deep-water harbor in the 17th century, and those called the "plantation aristocracy," mainly from Virginia and the Carolinas, settled here in the 18th century. Over the next 100 years, **Elizabeth Harbour,** the town's focal point, became a refitting base for British man-of-war vessels, and the U.S. Navy used the port again during World War II.

There's not too much shopping here, but there are a few places where you can purchase souvenirs and gifts. **Exuma Liquor and Gifts,** Queen's Highway (© **242/336-2101**), is the place to stock up on liquor, wine, and beer.

The Sandpiper, Queen's Highway (© **242/336-2084**), stands across from Club Peace & Plenty. Its highlights are the original serigraphs by Diane Minns, but it also offers a good selection of Bahamian arts and crafts, sponges, ceramics, watches, baskets, jewelry, books, postcards, and Bahamian straw baskets and other handcrafted works. Diane designs and silk-screens T-shirts here in the shop, and she welcomes anyone to watch her work.

GEORGE TOWN AFTER DARK

The best place to head for some after-dark diversion is **Club Peace & Plenty** (© **800/525-2210** or 242/336-2093) in George Town. Though summer nights are slow, something is usually happening here in winter, from weekly poolside bashes to live bands that keep both locals and visitors jumping up on the dance floor.

EXPLORING FARTHER AFIELD

Queen's Highway, which is still referred to as the "slave route," runs the length of Great Exuma, and you can travel it in either a taxi or a rented car to take in the sights in and around George Town.

Forty-five kilometers (28 miles) north of George Town, **Rolleville** is named after Lord Rolle, a British plantation owner and, in his time, the chief employer on the island. The village is still inhabited by descendants of his freed slaves, as his will left them the land, which is never sold but passed from one generation to the next.

As you travel along the highway, you'll see ruins of plantations. This land is called "generation estates," and the major ones are **Steventon, Mount Thompson,** and **Ramsey.** You pass other such settlements as Mosstown (which has working farms), the Forest, Farmer's Hill, and Roker's Point. Steventon is the last settlement before you reach Rolleville, which is the largest of the plantation estates. There are several beautiful beaches along the way, especially the ones at **Tarr Bay** and **Jimmie Hill.**

You may want to head south of George Town, passing Flamingo Bay and Pirate's Point. In the 18th century, Captain Kidd is said to have anchored at **Kidd Cay.** You, however, can stay at the Regatta Point (p. 263).

Flamingo Bay, the site of a hotel and villa development, begins just 1km (⅔ mile) from George Town. It's a favorite rendezvous of bonefishers and the yachting set.

WHERE TO DINE

Iva Bowe's Central Highway Inn Restaurant & Bar BAHAMIAN   This roadside tavern, owned and operated by the Bowe family, specializes in very tender cracked conch, marinated in lime, pounded into tenderness, and then fried with Iva's own special seasonings. It's the best in the Exumas. The lobster linguini, garlic snapper, and shrimp scampi are also worth trying; this is good Bahamian cookery.

Queen's Hwy. (.5km/⅓ mile from the entrance to the International Airport and about 9.5km/6 miles northwest of George Town). © **242/345-7014.** Lunch US$8–US$10 (£4–£5); dinner main courses US$12–US$15 (£6–£7.50). No credit cards. Mon–Sat 8am–11pm.

2 Little Exuma ✩

This is a faraway retreat, the southernmost of the Exuma Cays. Despite the fact that it's in the Tropics, it has a subtropical climate and lovely white-sand beaches. The

Fun Fact **A Romantic Legend & a Movie Star**

On the road to Little Exuma, you come to the hamlet of **Rolle Town**. It was once, like Rolleville in the north, owned by Lord Rolle. Today, it is populated with descendants of his former slaves. This sleepy town has some 100-year-old houses.

In an abandoned field, where goats frolic, you can visit the Rolle Town Tombs, burial ground of the McKay family. Capt. Alexander McKay, a Scot, came to Great Exuma in 1789 after he was granted 161 hectares (398 acres) for a plantation. His wife joined him in 1791, and soon after, they had a child. However, tragedy struck in 1792 when Anne McKay, who was only 26, died along with her child. Perhaps grief-stricken, her husband died the following year. Their story is one of the romantic legends of the island.

The village also claims a more contemporary famous daughter: actress Esther Rolle. Her parents were born here (though they went to the U.S. before she was born). Rolle is best remembered for her role as the strong-willed mother on the '70s sitcom *Good Times*. She won an Emmy playing a maid in *Summer of My German Soldier;* Rolle's other film credits included *Driving Miss Daisy, Rosewood,* and *How to Make an American Quilt.* She died at the age of 78 in 1998.

waters are so crystal-clear in some places that you can spot the colorful tropical fish more than 18m (59 ft.) down. The island, about 31 sq. km (12 sq. miles), is connected to Great Exuma by a 182m-long (597-ft.) bridge. It's about a 16km (10-mile) trip from the George Town airport.

Less than a kilometer (⅔ mile) offshore is **Pigeon Cay,** which is uninhabited. Visitors often come here for the day and are later picked up by a boat that takes them back to Little Exuma. You can go snorkeling and visit the remains of a 200-year-old wreck, right offshore in about 2m (6½ ft.) of water.

On one of Little Exuma's highest hills are the remains of an old pirate fort. Several cannons are located nearby, but documentation is lacking as to when it was built or by whom. (Pirates didn't leave too much data lying around.)

Coming from Great Exuma, the first community you reach on Little Exuma is called **Ferry,** so named because the two islands were linked by a ferry service before the bridge was built. Ask around about visiting the private chapel of an Irish family, the Fitzgeralds, erected generations ago.

Along the way, you can take in **Pretty Molly Bay,** site of the now-shuttered Sand Dollar Beach Club. Pretty Molly was a slave who committed suicide by walking into the water. The natives claim that her ghost can still be seen stalking the beach every night.

Many visitors come to Little Exuma to visit the **Hermitage,** a plantation constructed by Loyalist settlers. The last surviving example of the many that once stood in the Exumas, it was originally built by the Kendall family, who came to Little Exuma in 1784. The family established their plantation at **Williamstown** and, with their slaves, set about growing cotton.

The Remote Darby Islands

There is an idyllic chain of five privately owned little islands in the Exumas, in the indigo waters of Exuma Sound to the east of Great Bahama Bank. They are called Big Darby (our favorite), Little Darby, Goat Cay, Bette Cay, and Guana Cay. These islands lie 458km (286 miles) southeast of Miami and 154km (96 miles) south of Nassau and are accessible only by boat or charter aircraft.

If you have time for only one, make it **Big Darby,** where you can hike to a decaying castle that's been abandoned for more than half a century. Talk about *Gone With the Wind.* You can see the ruins of **Darby Castle,** built as a working plantation in 1938 by an Englishman known as Sir Baxter. As a plantation, it became during World War II the largest employer in the southern Bahamas; its workers helped produce palm oil, fruit, cotton, and even goats. Today, the castle is the stuff of legend, with many tall tales told about the Englishman and his mistress. (Was he a Nazi sympathizer?) Though the so-called castle is in ruins, you can take a potentially dangerous walk to the second landing with its large stone-built balcony where you can take in one of the grandest panoramas in the Exumas.

Come to the Darby islands for some of The Bahamas' most beautiful beaches; the sand is the color and texture of sifted flour. On Little Darby and Big Darby, there are more than 10 good beaches. The best snorkeling and dive spot is the little harbor nestled between the two islands.

But they encountered so many difficulties having the cotton shipped to Nassau that in 1806 they advertised the plantation for sale. The ad promised "970 acres more or less," along with "160 hands" (referring to the slaves). Chances are, you'll be approached by a local guide who, for a fee, will show you around. Ask to be shown the several old tombs in the area.

At Williamstown (look for the seaside marker), you can visit the remains of the **Great Salt Pond,** a body of water in the center of the island that used to be the site of a flourishing salt-raking industry.

If you really have to see everything, you may be able to get a local to take you over to **Hog Cay,** the end of the line for the Exumas. This is really just a spit of land, and there are no glorious beaches here. It's visited mainly by those who like to add obscure islets at the very end of the road to their list of explorations. Hog Cay is privately owned, and it is farmed. The owner, whose house lies in the center of the island, seems friendly to visitors.

3 Staniel Cay ⟨⋆⟩

Staniel Cay lies 129km (80 miles) southeast of Nassau at the southern end of the little Pipe Creek archipelago. It's a 13km (8-mile) chain of mostly uninhabited islets, sandy beaches, coral reefs, and bonefish flats. There are many places for snug anchorages, making this a favorite yachting stopover in the mid-Exumas. Staniel Cay, known for years as "Stanyard," has no golf course or tennis courts, but it's the perfect island for "the great escape." It's home to just 80 full-time residents.

An annual bonefishing festival is sponsored here on August 5, during the celebration of Bahamian Independence Day. The **Happy People Marina** (② 242/355-2008) arranges guided sportfishing and snorkeling trips. There's a **straw market** where you can buy crafts, hats, and handbags.

The **Staniel Cay Yacht Club** (see below) arranges charter flights from Fort Lauderdale, costing US$260 to US$307 (£130–£154) per person one-way. Flight time is 3 hours. Call ② 954/771-0330 for flight information.

WHERE TO STAY & DINE

Staniel Cay Yacht Club   Staniel Cay is a great getaway, and the Staniel Cay Yacht Club—only a 5-minute golf-cart ride from the airstrip—is the place to get away to. Although once famous in yachting circles, drawing celebrities like the late Malcolm Forbes, the property became run-down and lost its chic clientele for several years.

Now it has bounced back. Fully restored and improved, it again welcomes the yachting world to its location near a white, sandy beach. Guest cottages, each with a small shower unit, have been completely remodeled and refurbished, and are quite charming. Each cottage is painted a different color with different decorative features. The cottages also have west-facing balconies, which make for unimpeded views of the sun setting over the water. This is one of the few guarantees each day on Staniel Cay. Since the island is only a kilometer (⅔ mile) wide, you can easily walk to the local village, which has a grocery store, straw market, church, and post office. A Boston Whaler docks outside each accommodation, and guests get a map of local waters and get invited to sail on their own. Many deserted islands surround Staniel Cay.

An on-site clubhouse offers American and Bahamian cuisine for breakfast, lunch, and dinner, with a menu that features steaks and seafood—nothing too foreign or experimental. The club can also rent you boats for activities, from a 4m Boston

---

⎛Tips An Insider's Guide for Sailors & Beach Buffs

If you want a beach to yourself, one of the uninhabited islands surrounding Staniel Cay could indeed become yours for the day. In the unlikely event that another yachting party arrives, just sail on to another nearby island—chances are, it'll be deserted.

The local map given out by Staniel Cay Yacht Club pinpoints the location of **Thunderball Grotto** ⦅⚑⦆, where part of the James Bond film *Thunderball* was filmed. This is one of the best places for snorkeling in the Exumas. To the north of Thunderball Grotto lies the curiously named **Big Major Cay,** where hungry pigs will even chase you down the beach for a handout. There are also stray cats on the island who appreciate a snack (they're especially fond of canned sardines), as well as some fresh water.

Believe it or not, **swimming pigs** will surround your boat here. They are harmless but do expect to be treated to food. At another point on your nautical map, about 6.4km (4 miles) beyond **Major Spot,** a tiny, uninhabited island directly northwest of Staniel Cay, you'll come across shallow waters where tame (at least, we hope so) nurse sharks like to have their pictures taken. Food makes them even less camera-shy.

Exuma Cays Land and Sea Park 🐟🐟🐟

In the northern Exumas, the best waters for private boating are found in the government-protected **Exuma Cays Land and Sea Park,** which stretches south from Wax Cay to Conch Cay—a distance of 35km (22 miles)—with magnificent sea gardens and coral reefs. The park is 13km (8 miles) wide and was inaugurated in 1958. The exact location is 35km (22 miles) northeast of Staniel Cay (p. 270).

As you wander these islands, you may see a glimpse of the endangered **Bahamian iguana.** The land below is also fascinating, a water world of coral reefs, mysterious caves, and scores of marine animals (take along your snorkeling gear). Fishing, incidentally, is prohibited, as is handling the coral—touching it will kill it.

The park is often called "The Garden of Eden," with its unspoiled beaches, safe anchorages, numerous islets, and endless cays. Wherever you go, expect to see tropical birds flying overhead.

The best place for hiking is **Hawksbill Cay** or **Warderick Wells,** which is the site of ruins of Loyalist settlements from the 18th century. Pioneers during that era tried to make a living out of farming these islands.

It's best to visit the archipelago between dawn and dusk. Note that there are no facilities and that you must bring your own water.

Whaler including fuel for US$110 (£55) to a 5.1m boat for US$235 (£118) per day, to something smaller. Scuba and snorkeling gear are also available.

Staniel Cay, the Exumas, The Bahamas. (For information, write to: 2233 S. Andrews Ave., Fort Lauderdale, FL 33316.) ℂ **954/467-8920** in the U.S., or 242/355-2024. Fax 242/355-2044. www.stanielcay.com. 9 units. Nov 20–Sept 9 US$165 (£83) double, from US$195 (£98) suite; off-season US$145 (£73) double, from US$178 (£89) suite. MC, V. **Amenities:** Restaurant; bar; marina; airstrip; outdoor pool; laundry service; nonsmoking rooms. *In room:* A/C, fridge, coffeemaker, hair dryer, no phone.

4 Sampson Cay

Tiny Sampson Cay, located directly northwest of Staniel Cay and just to the southeast of the Exuma Cays Land and Sea Park, has a certain charm, as well as a full-service marina and a small dive operation.

Besides Staniel Cay, Sampson Cay has the Central Exumas' only marina, so most visitors arrive in their own boats, and local guides taking out sportfishers for the day provide the chief entertainment.

Sampson Cay is 67 nautical miles southeast of Nassau and one of the safest anchorages in the Exumas. It is a natural "hurricane hole"—in other words, a fully protected anchorage with land all around. The cay lies near the end of Pipe Creek, which has been called a "tropical Shangri-La."

WHERE TO STAY & DINE

Sampson Cay Club 🐟   This is a rather remote outpost, but once you get here, you'll see that it's a gem. The resort has considerably improved in recent years and is now better than ever. Bedrooms, which are in two houses, are comfortable, well furnished, and generally spacious. Two of them have king-size beds; the others have queen-size beds. All accommodations have private bathrooms with showers, and two

Norman's Cay: A Shady Past

Throughout the Exumas, you'll see islands with NO TRESPASSING signs posted. In the early 1980s, on Norman's Cay, these signs were extremely serious: You could have been killed if you had gone ashore.

Fortunately, the drug smuggling that used to occur here has been cleaned up and the area is safe for travelers. However, private NO TRESPASSING signs should still be obeyed. Even without drug activity, privacy of individual property owners has to be respected, of course.

Once upon a time, you might have run into Ted Kennedy, Walter Cronkite, or William F. Buckley, Jr., enjoying the island's pleasures. The remote outpost enjoyed great popularity with the Harvard clique.

During the 1980s, however, all that changed when German-Colombian Carlos Lehder Rivas purchased most of Norman's Cay. According to experts, the island soon became the major distribution point for drug exportation to the U.S. Millions of dollars' worth of cocaine was flown from Colombia here before being smuggled onward to America.

Eventually, the U.S. applied strong pressure on the Bahamian government to clean up the island. Lehder fled for Colombia, where he was captured and extradited to the U.S. He is now in prison.

Norman's Cay may one day realize its ritzy tourist potential once again, but for now, it remains relatively quiet, visited only by stray yachting parties and the occasional cruise vessel.

of the units are right on the beach. Both houses are also equipped with outdoor showers and have their own dinghy docks.

Community life here revolves around the grocery store and commissary, the fuel and dockage facilities of the full-service marina, and a bar and restaurant favored by visiting yachters. The restaurant and bar serve drinks and sandwiches any time of day to anyone who shows up, but reservations are required before 4pm for the single-seating dinner, which is served nightly at 7:30pm. The staff will rent you a 3.9m or 5.1m whaler, as well as Hobie Cats and snorkeling equipment. Upon request, the hotel's staff will also point to walking trails that will link you up to one of seven beaches.

Sampson Cay, the Exumas, The Bahamas. (C) **877/633-0305** or 242/355-2034. Fax 242/355-2034. www.sampson cayclub.com. 10 units. Year-round US$250 (£125) double, US$350 (£175) villa. MC, V. **Amenities:** Restaurant; bar; coin-operated laundry service; nonsmoking rooms; rooms for those w/limited mobility. *In room:* A/C, kitchenette, fridge, coffeemaker, no phone.

11

The Southern Bahamas

This cluster of islands on the southern fringe of The Bahamas is one of the last frontier outposts that can be reached relatively quickly from the U.S. mainland. Their remoteness is one of the most compelling reasons to visit—that, and a chance to see life in The Bahamas the way it used to be. Some of the islands are proud to proclaim that "we are as we were when Columbus first landed here," an exaggeration, of course, but one that contains a kernel of truth.

The Southern Bahamas have a colorful history. In the 18th century, Loyalists from the Carolinas and Virginia came here with slave labor and settled many of the islands. For about 20 years, they had thriving cotton plantations until blight struck, killing crops and destroying the industry. In 1834, the United Kingdom Emancipation Act freed slaves throughout the British Empire. When the Loyalists moved on to more fertile ground, they often left behind emancipated slaves,

who then had to eke out a living as best they could.

With some notable exceptions, such as Long Island, tourism developers have stayed clear of these isles. However, they have enormous potential, as most of them have excellent beaches, good fishing, and fine dive sites.

If you're considering visiting any of these islands, be forewarned that transportation is inconvenient and that accommodations are rather limited. For these and other reasons involving the scarcity of tourist facilities, yachters and other boaters comprise the majority of visitors, since they can eat and sleep aboard their vessels.

Many changes are in the wind for the Southern Bahamas. Right now, however, there's almost no traffic, no banks, no lawyers. There are, however, mosquitoes, so bring a good insect repellent and a long-sleeved shirt for protection.

1 Cat Island ★★

Untainted by tourism, lovely Cat Island is the sixth-largest island in The Bahamas. The fishhook-shaped island—some 77km (48 miles) long and 1 to 6.5km (⅔–4 miles) wide—lies about 209km (130 miles) southeast of Nassau and 523km (325 miles) southeast of Miami. (Don't confuse Cat Island with Cat Cay, a smallish private island near Bimini.)

Cat Island, named after the pirate Arthur Catt (and not wild packs of marauding cats), is located near the Tropic of Cancer, between Eleuthera and Long Island. It has one of the country's most pleasant climates, with temperatures in the high 60s (low 20s Celsius) during the short winters, rising to the mid-80s (low 30s Celsius) in summer, with trade winds making the place even more comfortable. It is also home to some 2,000 residents, among the friendliest in all of The Bahamas.

The Southern Bahamas

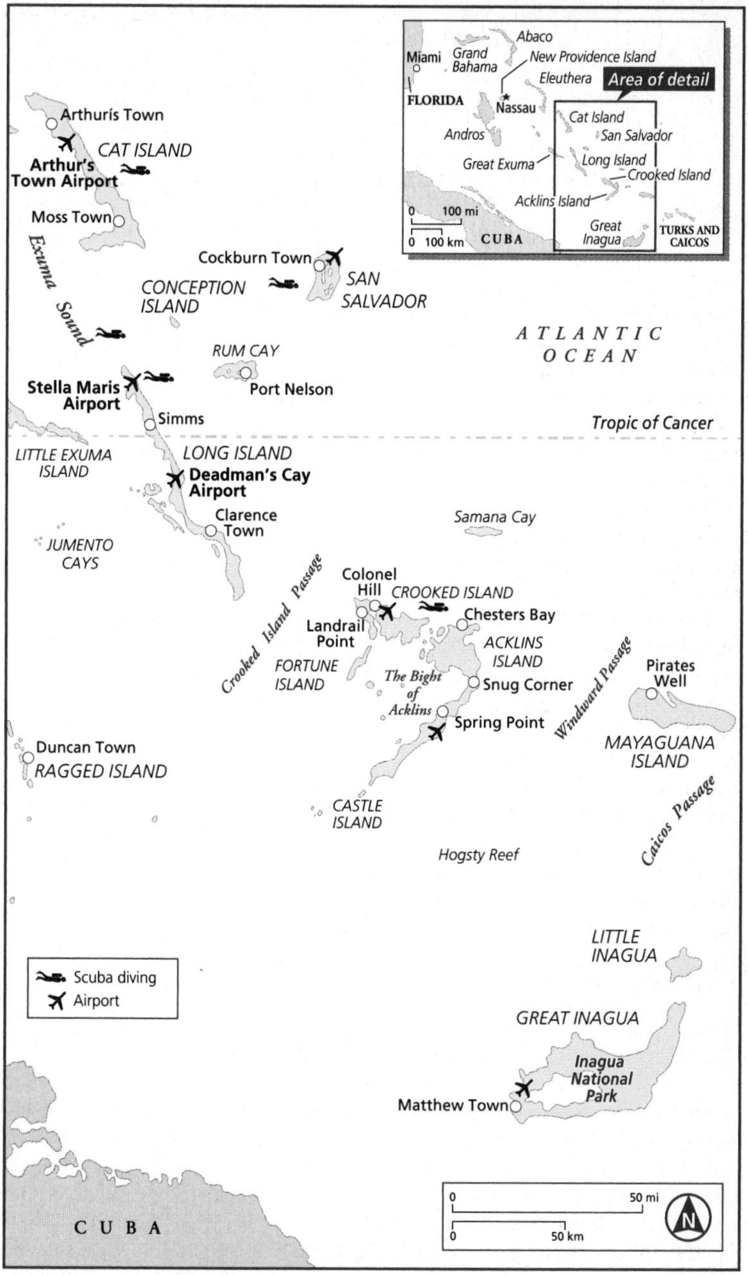

Abaco
Miami
Grand Bahama
New Providence Island
Eleuthera
Area of detail
FLORIDA
Nassau
Cat Island
San Salvador
Andros
Great Exuma
Long Island
Crooked Island
Acklins Island
0 100 mi
0 100 km
CUBA
Great Inagua
TURKS AND CAICOS
Arthuris Town
CAT ISLAND
Arthur's Town Airport
Moss Town
Exuma Sound
Cockburn Town
CONCEPTION ISLAND
SAN SALVADOR
ATLANTIC OCEAN
RUM CAY
Port Nelson
Stella Maris Airport
Simms
Tropic of Cancer
LITTLE EXUMA ISLAND
LONG ISLAND
Deadman's Cay Airport
Clarence Town
Samana Cay
JUMENTO CAYS
Crooked Island Passage
Colonel Hill
CROOKED ISLAND
Chesters Bay
Landrail Point
ACKLINS ISLAND
FORTUNE ISLAND
The Bight of Acklins
Snug Corner
Windward Passage
Pirates Well
Spring Point
MAYAGUANA ISLAND
Duncan Town
RAGGED ISLAND
CASTLE ISLAND
Caicos Passage
Hogsty Reef
LITTLE INAGUA
Scuba diving
Airport
GREAT INAGUA
Inagua National Park
Matthew Town
0 50 mi
0 50 km
N
CUBA

With its pristine virgin beaches, the island is beautiful to see, yet little-visited enough that it remains relatively inexpensive and untainted.

Many local historians claim that Cat Island residents were the first to see Columbus. Some believe that the explorer had been welcomed here by the peaceful Arawaks. Regardless of whether Columbus stopped here, the island has a rich history of adventurers, slaves, buccaneers, farmers, and visionaries of many nationalities. But even now, Cat Island remains mysterious to some. It's known as a stronghold of unfamiliar-to-most practices such as obeah (West Indian witchcraft) and of having miraculously healing bush medicines.

A straight asphalt road (in terrible shape) leads from the north to the south of the island. Along the way, you can select your own beach—and chances are you'll have complete privacy. These beaches offer an array of watersports, and visitors can go swimming or snorkeling at several places. **Fernandez Bay** is a fit-for-a-postcard white-sand beach set against a turquoise blue sea and lined with casuarina trees. The island's north shore is wild and untamed. Boating and diving are among the main reasons to go to Cat Island, and diving lessons are available for novices.

Arthur's Town, in the north, is the island's major hub. It's also the boyhood home of legendary actor Sidney Poitier. He has many relatives still living on the island, including a few amazing look-alikes. Poitier shares memories of his childhood home in his book *This Life.*

CAT ISLAND ESSENTIALS

GETTING THERE   A commercial flight on **Bahamasair** (℗ **800/222-4262** in the U.S.; www.bahamasair.com) leaves Nassau for Arthur's Town on Friday and Sunday at 11am. There is also an airport near **New Bight,** Cat Island's most scenic village. Flying to New Bight from Fort Lauderdale is **Lynx Air International** (℗ **888/596-9247;** www.lynxair.com), which also provides service between Fort Lauderdale and Cat Island on Wednesday, Friday, and Saturday.

Cat Island is also serviced by **mail boat.** The **MV *Worth Cat Island Special*** (℗ **242/393-1064**), which transports passengers for US$50 (£25) one-way and US$100 (£50) round-trip, departs Potter's Cay Dock in Nassau Thursday at 5pm, heading for Bennett's Harbour and Arthur's Town. Another vessel, the **MV *Lady Rosalind*** (℗ **242/393-1064**), departs Potter's Cay in Nassau on Thursday at 6pm, going to Old and New Bight.

GETTING AROUND   Limited, but quite adequate, taxi service is available on Cat Island. Hotel owners, if notified of your arrival time, will have someone drive to the airport to pick you up. You can, however, rent a car from **Bridge Inn Car Rentals,** Bridge Inn, New Bight (℗ **242/342-3014**). Prices begin at US$75 (£38) daily, with unlimited mileage. Hours are daily from 6:30am to 7:30pm.

FAST FACTS   There are three **medical clinics,** each of which is among the simplest in The Bahamas. They are in Arthur's Town, Old Bight, and Smiths Bay, and they're not always open. In case of an emergency, notify your hotel staff immediately. Someone will try to get in touch with a medical expert. Serious cases are flown to Nassau. If you're not in good health and might require medical assistance on vacation, Cat Island is not the island to choose, as there is no central number to call for help.

SPECIAL EVENTS   The island's annual **Three-Day Regatta** happens every summer, usually at the end of July. It attracts the largest collection of visitors to Cat Island;

the inns prove inadequate to receive them. Call your local Bahamas tourist office (p. 35) for more information.

WHERE TO STAY & DINE

Bridge Inn Lying 274m (899 ft.) from a beach, the relaxed, casual Bridge Inn is looking better than ever after the total overhaul it was treated to in 2008. The inn offers babysitting services (at an extra charge) so that parents can play tennis or go diving, sailboarding, snorkeling, jogging, bicycling, fishing, or sightseeing with the knowledge their youngsters are being carefully tended to. Bedrooms are modest and motel-style, but each unit can house three to four guests. Each of the high-ceilinged rooms comes with a private bathroom containing a shower stall. On the premises are a full bar and a restaurant that serves rather simple Bahamian and international cuisine. *Warning:* Confirm prices listed below; they may change over the life of this edition.

New Bight, Cat Island, The Bahamas. (✆ **242/342-3013.** Fax 242/342-3041. 15 units. Year-round US$150 (£75) double, US$200 (£100) villa. MC, V. Rates include breakfast. **Amenities:** Restaurant; bar; room service; laundry service. *In room:* A/C, TV, kitchenette (in some), iron.

Fernandez Bay Village (★ *Finds* Opening onto Fernandez Bay, this is Cat Island's best resort. Although rustic, it has a certain charm, mainly because of its position on a curvy beach set against casuarinas blowing in the trade winds. The beach is never crowded, so come here only if you *really* want to get away from it all; this place is far too laid-back for full hotel service. Things get done, but it takes time—and no one's in a hurry.

Fernandez Bay Village has been in the Armbrister family since it was originally established on a plantation in 1870. Its rusticity and seclusion are part of its charm. But if you wish, you can get acquainted with other guests whose interests match your own. Yachters, who moor in the water offshore—there are no marina facilities—often visit the resort to take advantage of the general store's fresh supplies. (Nearby Smith's Bay is one of the region's best storm shelters—even government mail boats take refuge there during hurricanes.)

The "village" consists of full housekeeping villas for guests who don't mind being responsible for their unit's upkeep. Each sleeps up to six people and contains a full kitchen and clothes washers and dryers. There are also five double-occupancy cottages, all built of stone, driftwood, and glass. All rentals here come with a private garden bathroom with a shower stall.

Meals are served in a clubhouse decorated with antiques and Haitian art. This clubhouse, which opens onto a view of the beach and sea, also features a sitting library area, a stone fireplace, and overhead fans. You'll eat dinners here on a beach terrace adjacent to a thatched-roof tiki bar that runs on the honor system. On many nights, guests gather around a blazing bonfire near the water to hear island music.

1.6km (1 mile) north of New Bight, Cat Island, The Bahamas. (✆ **800/940-1905,** 242/342-2018, or 954/474-4821. Fax 242/342-3051 or 954/474-4864. www.fernandezbayvillage.com. 16 units. Nov–May US$355–US$395 (£178–£198) villa, US$255–US$295 (£128–£148) cottage; June–Aug US$315–US$345 (£158–£173) villa, US$225–US$240 (£113–£120) cottage. AE, MC, V. Closed Sept–Oct. **Amenities:** Restaurant; bar; watersports equipment/rentals; bike rentals; car-rental desk; babysitting; laundry service. *In room:* Kitchen, fridge, coffeemaker, iron, no phone.

Greenwood Beach Resort & Dive Center (★ This resort's location on a 13km (8-mile) stretch of the Atlantic, bordered by pink sands, is idyllic, and there's good snorkeling right offshore. Since 1992, a German family has run this property, constantly making improvements. A group of modern buildings on the most isolated section of the island has a private beach and a freshwater pool. It's better run and more equipped than the Bridge Inn, and it attracts mostly divers. The small ocean-view double rooms are equipped with showers and their own terraces. There is a full bar and a dining room.

The hotel's dive center is the island's best, with a 7.5m and an 11m motorboat for diving excursions, plus complete equipment for 20 divers at a time. A two-tank dive costs US$95 (£48) per person, including equipment. A half-day snorkeling trip costs US$35 (£18), including equipment. The resort also has two boats available for bone-fishing. The staff greets each arriving Bahamasair flight.

Port Howe, Cat Island, The Bahamas. ✆ 242/342-3053. Fax 242/342-3053. www.greenwoodbeachresort.net. 22 units. Year-round US$99–US$130 (£50–£65) double. Breakfast and dinner US$48 (£24) per person. AE, MC, V. **Amenities:** Restaurant; bar; pool; watersports equipment/rentals; business center; babysitting. *In room:* A/C (in some), ceiling fan (in some), no phone.

Hawk's Nest Resort & Marina

This remote getaway lies on Cat Island's southwestern side, fronting a long beach and containing its own runway for charter flights and private planes, plus a 28-slip full-service marina that attracts yachters. This intimate resort is set near the village of Devil's Point, lying some 16km (10 miles) west of Columbus Point close to the ruins of two once-flourishing but now-abandoned plantations, Richman Hill and Newfield. Bedrooms, with either two queen-size beds or a king-size bed, are well-furnished and brightly decorated, each with a shower unit. Rooms have a patio for those late-afternoon toddies drunk while overlooking the sunset. If you bring the family, consider booking the two-bedroom house on the beach, which is separate from the other structures. The clubhouse, the rooms, and the main house are spacious and inviting. The resort serves full cooked-to-order breakfasts, sandwiches for lunch, and a buffet-style dinner, with the unannounced fare changing nightly. A one-tank dive costs US$60 (£30); a two-tank dive is US$80 (£40).

Devil's Point, Cat Island, The Bahamas. ✆ 800/688-4752 or 242/342-7050. Fax 242/342-7051. www.hawks-nest.com. 10 units. Year-round US$220 (£110) double, US$490 (£245) house. MAP (breakfast and dinner) US$55 (£28) per person. MC, V. **Amenities:** Restaurant; bar; pool; tennis court; marina, watersports equipment/rentals; bike rentals; laundry service; nonsmoking rooms. *In room:* A/C, TV, coffeemaker, hair dryer.

Island HoppInn ✪ *Finds*

This little all-suite resort is a real discovery. It overlooks the Atlantic with panoramic views over Fernandez Bay; from your front porch, you can see one of the island's best sandy beaches. The suites are spacious yet cozy, much like an upmarket B&B. Half the suites are large enough for three or four guests. Suites are furnished in a tropical style, with four-poster beds along with rattan furniture, well-equipped kitchens, and showers in the garden. Lunch can be delivered to your front veranda while you enjoy the ocean view, freshly baked bread, tasty main courses, and gourmet desserts. Your hosts are the best on the island for arranging watersports, including fishing charters; they'll also arrange a car rental upon request.

Fernandez Bay, Cat Island, The Bahamas. ✆ 216/978-8800 in the U.S. or 242/342-2100. Fax 242/342-2101. www.islandhoppinn.com. 4 suites. Year-round US$200–US$275 (£100–£138) double, US$225–US$300 (£113–£150) triple or quad. MC, V. **Amenities:** Restaurant; bar; private beach; watersports; room service; laundry service. *In room:* A/C, DVD in some, Wi-Fi, kitchenette, fridge, no phone.

Pigeon Cay Beach Club

This B&B fronts a tranquil bay at the island's north end, about a 15-minute ride from the airport. The main building consists of a trio of units and a small store. Each accommodation comes with a fully equipped kitchen, one to three bedrooms, and a shower stall. In addition, the property has some light-filled cottages built of stucco and coral stone, with beamed ceilings and Mexican tile floors.

North End, Cat Island, The Bahamas. ℂ/fax 242/354-5084. www.pigeoncay-bahamas.com. 11 units. Year-round US$160–US$180 (£80–£90) 1-bedroom unit, US$250–US$275 (£125–£138) 2-bedroom unit, US$375 (£188) 3-bedroom unit. AE, MC, V. **Amenities:** Room service; babysitting; laundry service; nonsmoking rooms. *In room:* Ceiling fan, kitchen, coffeemaker, hair dryer, iron, no phone.

Sammy T's Beach Resort ℛ *Finds*   Tucked away on a tiny cove opening onto an idyllic beach, this resort offers one- and two-bedroom villas individually designed with rattan furnishings and tiled floors resting under beamed ceilings. Picture it as your tropical home, with ceiling fans, Bahamian art, a DVD library, living room furnishings, and a well-equipped kitchen. Sammy T's is the most tranquil resort on the island.

For such a small place, the resort is well-equipped with recreational activities, including an excellent pool, a fitness center, even kayaks. Island tours can be arranged, as can fishing and snorkeling. Conch is likely to be sizzling on the grill at lunch, and a lobster dinner awaits.

Bennett's Harbour, Cat Island, The Bahamas. ℂ 242/354-6009. Fax 242/354-6010. www.sammytbahamas.com. 6 villas. Oct–Apr US$160–US$175 (£80–£88) 1-bedroom unit, US$265 (£133) 2-bedroom unit; off-season US$145–US$160 (£73–£80) 1-bedroom unit, US$245 (£123) 2-bedroom unit. MC, V. Closed Sept 1–Oct 15. **Amenities:** Restaurant; bar; outdoor pool; gym; watersports. *In room:* A/C, DVD player, kitchenette, no phone.

EXPLORING THE ISLAND: PLANTATIONS, PEAKS & A HERMITAGE

There's an interesting Arawak cave at Columbus Point on the island's southern tip. In addition, you can see the ruins of many once-flourishing plantations that saw their heyday during the island's short-lived cotton boom. Early planters, many of them British Loyalists, marked their property boundaries with stone mounds—some of which are now nearly 200 years old. The ruined plantations include **Deveaux Mansion,** built by Col. Andrew Deveaux, who led the fledgling U.S. Navy to recapture Nassau from the Spanish in 1783, and **Armbrister Plantation,** which lies in ruins near Port Howe.

You can also hike along nature paths through native villages and past exotic plants. Finally, you reach the peak of **Mount Alvernia,** the highest point in The Bahamas, at a mere 62m (203 ft.) above sea level. For your efforts, you'll be rewarded with a spectacular view.

The mount is capped by the **Hermitage,** a religious retreat built entirely by hand by the late Father Jerome, the former "father confessor" of the island, who was once a mule skinner in Canada. Interestingly, the building was scaled to fit his short stature (he was a very, very short man). Formerly an Anglican, this Roman Catholic hermit priest became a legend on Cat Island. He died in 1956 at the age of 80, but his memory is kept very much alive here.

Cat Island Dive Center at Greenwood Beach Resort (ℂ 242/342-3053) takes tourists out on diving or snorkeling excursions and rents out snorkeling gear and other water toys. A single boat dive costs US$75 (£38) per person, a double US$110 (£55), with half-day snorkeling trips going for US$35 (£18) per person. Our favorite diving spot is along the west coast, where **Dry Heads** is the finest reef. It gets its name because at low tide, a blanket of purple sea fans stands high and dry. The drop here is 7.6m (25 ft.), and as you plunge below, you'll meet butterfly fish and queen angels swimming over the coral heads.

2 San Salvador ⓕ★

This may be where the New World began. For some years, it has been believed that this is where Christopher Columbus left his first footprints in the Western Hemisphere, although some scholars strongly dispute this. The easternmost island in the Bahamian archipelago, San Salvador lies 322km (200 miles) southeast of Nassau. Much of its area—163 sq. km (63 sq. miles)—is occupied by water; there are 28 landlocked lakes on the island, the largest of which is 19km (12 miles) long and serves as the principal transportation route for most of the island's population of 1,200. A badly maintained 64km (40-mile) road circles the island's perimeter. The island's highest point is **Mount Kerr,** at 41m (135 ft.).

The tiny island keeps a lonely vigil in the Atlantic. At South West Point, **Dixon Hill Lighthouse,** about 50m (164 ft.) tall, can be seen from 145km (90 miles) away. The light is a hand-operated beacon fueled by kerosene. Built in the 1850s, it is the last lighthouse of its type in The Bahamas.

Except for the odd historian or two, very few people used to visit San Salvador. Then **Club Med–Columbus Isle** opened, and the joint's been jumping ever since—at least, at the Club Med property. Away from there, San Salvador is as sleepy as it ever was, though it's been known for years as one of the best dive sites in The Bahamas. The snorkeling, fishing, and lovely beaches are also excellent.

SAN SALVADOR ESSENTIALS

GETTING THERE   Club Med (p. 281) solves transportation problems for its guests by flying them in on weekly charter planes from Miami. In winter, charter flights from New York come in once a week. You can also rely on public transportation by air (Bahamasair flights) or sea (government mail boats), but if you do, you'll have to wait a long time before getting off the island.

Bahamasair (ⓒ 800/222-4262; www.bahamasair.com) provides flights 6 days a week from Nassau. Departure times constantly change, so check with the airline for a schedule.

From Nassau, the mail boat **MV *Lady Francis*** leaves Tuesday to head for San Salvador and Rum Cay. The trip takes 12 hours under uncomfortable conditions. For details about sailing on the mail boat, contact the dock master at **Potter's Cay Dock** in Nassau (ⓒ 242/393-1064).

GETTING AROUND   If you want to tour the island, ask your hotel's employees to help with arrangements and taxi service. If you have the staff at **Club Med** (p. 281) arrange an island tour for you, the cost is around US$30 (£15) per person for a half-day ramble.

On San Salvador, you don't need to rent a car unless you want to explore far-flung places on your own. If that's the case, **Riding Rock Inn Resort and Marina** (ⓒ 800/ 272-1492 or 242/331-2631; www.ridingrock.com) can arrange a rental for about US$85 (£43) per day.

Club Med guests also have use of bikes for cycling around the property and for guided tours around the island.

FAST FACTS   The San Salvador Medical Clinic (ⓒ 242/331-2105), a 5-minute drive north of Club Med, serves island residents, but serious cases are flown to Nassau. The clinic, which also fills prescriptions, is open Monday to Friday 8:30am to 4:30pm; only emergencies are handled on Saturday and Sunday.

Fun Fact **The Columbus Mystery**

In 1492, a small group of peaceful Lucayan natives (Arawaks) were going about their business on a little island they called Guanahani, where they and their forebears had lived for at least 500 years. Little did they know how profoundly their lives would change when they greeted three small, strange-looking ships carrying Christopher Columbus and his crew of pale, bearded, oddly costumed men. It is said that when he came ashore, Columbus knelt and prayed. Then he claimed the land for Spain and named it San Salvador.

Unfortunately, the event was not so propitious for the reportedly handsome natives. Columbus later wrote to Queen Isabella that they would make ideal captives—perfect servants, in other words. It wasn't long before the Spanish conquistadors cleared the island, as well as most of The Bahamas, of Lucayans, sending them into slavery and early death in the mines of Hispaniola (Haiti) in order to feed the Spanish lust for New World gold.

But is the island now known as San Salvador the actual site of Columbus's landing? Columbus placed no lasting marker on the sandy, sun-drenched island of his landfall. Hence, there has been much study and discussion as to just where he actually landed.

In the 17th century, an English pirate captain, George Watling, took over the island (there was no government in charge at the time) and built a mansion on it to serve as his safe haven. The island was listed on maps for about 250 years thereafter as Watling's (or Watling) Island.

In 1926, the Bahamian legislature formally changed the name of the island to San Salvador, feeling that enough evidence had been brought forth to support the belief that this was indeed the site of Columbus's landing. Then in 1983, artifacts of European origin (beads, buckles, and metal spikes) were found here together with Arawak pottery and beads and a shard of Spanish pottery. Though the actual date of these artifacts cannot be pinned down, they are probably from 1490 to 1560. The beads and buckles fit the description of goods recorded in Columbus's log.

National Geographic published two meticulously researched articles in 1986 that set forth the belief that Samana Cay, some 105km (65 miles) southeast of the present San Salvador, was actually Guanahani, the island Columbus named San Salvador when he first landed in the New World. The question may never be resolved, and there will doubtless be years and years of controversy about it. Nevertheless, history buffs still flock here hoping to follow in the explorer's footsteps.

To call the **police,** dial ℂ **919.** Phones are scarce on the island, but the front desk staff at Riding Rock Inn will place calls for you.

WHERE TO STAY

Club Med–Columbus Isle ᏘᏘ   This is one of the most ecologically conscious, and one of the most luxurious, Club Meds in the Western Hemisphere. Set at the edge of one of the archipelago's most pristine beaches, about 3km (2 miles) north of Cockburn

Town, this is the splashiest resort in the Southern Bahamas. Its promoters estimate that more than 30% of the island's population works here.

Most of the prefabricated buildings here were barged to the site in 1991. The resort is built around a large free-form swimming pool. The public rooms are some of the country's most lavish and cosmopolitan, with art and objects imported from Asia, Africa, the Americas, and Europe, and assembled by a battalion of adept designers. Bedrooms each contain a private balcony or patio, furniture that was custom-made in Thailand or the Philippines, sliding-glass doors, midsize bathroom with a shower stall, and feathered wall hangings crafted in the Brazilian rainforest by members of the Xingu tribe. Rooms are large (among the most spacious in the entire chain), and most have twin beds, though you might be able to snag one of the units with a double or a king-size bed if you're lucky. Dozens of multilingual GOs (guest relations organizers, or *gentils organisateurs*) are on hand to help initiate newcomers into the resort's many diversions. Unlike many other Club Meds, this one does not encourage bringing children and deliberately offers no particular facilities for their entertainment.

The main dining room, where meals are an ongoing series of buffets, lies in the resort's center. Two specialty restaurants offer Italian and grilled food. Nonfat, low-calorie, and vegetarian dishes are also available. Nightly entertainment is presented in a covered open-air theater and on a dance floor behind one of the bars.

3km (2 miles) north of Cockburn Town, San Salvador, The Bahamas. (€) **800/CLUB-MED** (258-2633) or 242/331-2000. Fax 242/331-2458. www.clubmed.com. 240 units. Winter US$1,450–US$3,328 (£725–£1,664) weekly per person double occupancy; off-season US$1,350–US$2,450 (£675–£1,225) weekly per person double occupancy. Weekly rates include all meals, drinks during meals, and most sports activities. AE, DISC, MC, V. Not recommended for children under 12. **Amenities:** 3 restaurants; 2 bars; disco; pool; 10 tennis courts; health club; watersports equipment/rentals; laundry service or coin-operated laundry; nonsmoking rooms. *In room:* A/C, TV, fridge, beverage maker, hair dryer, iron, safe.

Riding Rock Inn Resort & Marina   San Salvador's second resort is the motel-style Riding Rock Inn, which caters largely to divers. Its simple ambience is a far cry from the extravagant Club Med. Each accommodation faces either a pool or the open sea. The most recent improvement is an 18-room oceanfront building in which bedrooms are decorated in a tropical decor with two double beds, satellite TV, a refrigerator, a telephone, ceiling fans, and air-conditioning.

Many different dive packages are available—check with the hotel to find one that suits you. The resort specializes in weeklong trips that include three dives per day, all meals, and accommodations. Packages begin and end on Saturday. Although most guests are already experienced and certified divers, beginners can take a US$150 (£75) resort course on the first day of their visit and afterward participate in most of the daily dives. Full PADI certification can also be arranged for US$450 (£225).

An island tour is also included in the rates, but after that, most folks rent a bike or a scooter from the hotel. On the premises, a restaurant serves routine Bahamian specialties, and a bar features a seating area that juts above the water on a pier.

Cockburn Town, San Salvador, The Bahamas. (€) **800/272-1492** in the U.S., 954/453-5031 in Florida, or 242/331-2631 in The Bahamas. Fax 242/331-2020. www.ridingrock.com. 42 units. Year-round US$150–US$180 (£75–£90) double, US$165–US$200 (£83–£100) triple, US$210 (£105) quad. Children 11 or younger stay free in parent's room. MC, V. **Amenities:** Restaurant; bar; pool; tennis court; watersports equipment/rentals. *In room:* A/C, TV, fridge, hair dryer.

WHERE TO DINE
Rock Inn Restaurant BAHAMIAN/AMERICAN   Sit on the deck overlooking the water or eat inside; either way, you'll dine on hearty portions of comfort food. Pancakes make a good breakfast choice, and sandwiches are on the menu for lunch.

The fixed-price dinners include soup, salad, main course, dessert, wine, and soft, just-baked Bahamian bread. Launch your meal with the well-seasoned conch chowder or okra soup, and follow it up with steak, prime rib, chicken, or fresh fish. The Wednesday-night barbecues, featuring reggae music, are popular social events.

Cockburn Town. © 242/331-2631. Reservations recommended. Breakfast US$15 (£7.50); lunch US$18 (£9); dinner US$35 (£18). MC, V. Daily 7:30–9am, 12:30–2pm, and 6:30–9pm.

BEACHES, WATER ACTIVITIES & SPORTS

If you prefer finding a stretch of sand where the only footprints are your own, rent a car or bike at **Riding Rock Inn Resort & Marina** or call a taxi. Empty beaches are everywhere. Just remember to take plenty of water and, of course, sunblock; you won't find much shade. Along the way, look for the island's various monuments to Christopher Columbus.

On the northeast coast, **East Beach** stretches for some 10km (6 miles). Crushed coral and shells turned the shore a rosy pink. The deep-turquoise patches in the clear waters are coral heads, but the beach isn't good for snorkeling because of the presence of spotted sharks. Tall sea wheat or sea grass sprouts up from the sand. Off mile marker no. 24 on the main road, you can pick your way to the **Chicago Herald Columbus Monument** (p. 284).

Scuba divers flock to this remote island—a major destination with some 40 dive sites that lie no more than 45 minutes by boat from either of the two resorts. A major attraction here is **wall diving**—diving where the sloping shoreline suddenly drops off and plummets to the ocean depths.

Associated with Riding Rock Inn (p. 282), **Guanahani Dive Ltd.** (© 242/331-2631) offers dive packages, as well as snorkeling, fishing, and boating trips. Divers can book a getaway package year-round for 5 days and 4 nights that costs from US$875 to US$939 (£438–£470) per diver, including meals, transportation, diving, and rental gear. Prices are based on double occupancy.

Club Med–Columbus Isle (p. 281) should really be called an *almost*-all-inclusive resort because scuba diving is not covered by its rates. Diving courses at the resort run around US$200 (£100), and certification courses are US$450 (£225). A one-tank dive costs US$60 (£30) and a two-tank US$110 (£55).

With so many unspoiled and unpopulated kilometers of coastline, this area is ideal for swimming, shelling, and, of course, snorkeling. If you stay here a week, you've only begun to explore the possibilities. Places such as **Bamboo Point, Fernandez Bay,** and **Long Bay** all lie within a few miles of the main settlement of Cockburn Town on the island's more tranquil western side. At the southern tip of San Salvador are some of our favorite places for snorkeling: **Sandy Point** and nearby **Grotto Bay,** which has fine elkhorn coral reefs. Another wonderful spot for snorkeling is the wreck of the SS *Frascate,* which ran aground on January 1, 1902. Filled with such marine life as moray eels and grouper, it ranks as the area's best shallow wreck for snorkeling. Find it on the west coast, directly north of Riding Rock Inn (p. 282).

Club Med–Columbus Isle offers 10 tennis courts (three lit for night play) that are open to nonguests who buy a day pass. Riding Rock Inn has one (often empty) court.

Fishermen test their skill against blue marlin, yellowfin tuna, and wahoo on fishing trips, which you can arrange through Riding Rock Inn (© 242/331-2631). The trips run around US$500 (£250) for a half-day and US$800 (£400) for a full day. Bone-fishermen enjoy **Pigeon Creek,** where some record catches have been chalked up. Rent a boat from a local or get your hotel to set you up.

EXPLORING THE ISLAND: COMMEMORATING COLUMBUS

For such a small island, San Salvador offers a great deal of history as well as some sights that merit a look. Rent a bike, hire a taxi, or start walking, and see how many of the **Christopher Columbus monuments** you can hit. All of them are meant to mark the place where Columbus and his crew supposedly anchored the *Nina, Pinta,* and *Santa Maria* early that morning in 1492.

Just south of Cockburn Town, the **Tappan Monument,** a small four-sided stone pillar, stands on the beach at **Fernandez Bay** (mile marker no. 5 on the main road). The Tappan gas company embedded this monument here in 1951 in honor of Columbus.

The Chicago Herald Monument is located on the east coast at mile marker no. 24. To reach it, turn off the main road and drive 1.6 km (1 mile) to **East Beach.** Unless you meet a resident who can give you a ride in a four-wheel-drive car, you have to get out and walk. Turn right and hike 3km (2 miles) parallel to the beach until the sandy road ends. You'll see a cave to the left, at the water's edge. Follow the path to the right. Cupped by vegetation, a stone structure lies on the slice of land between the ocean and the bay. Although many historians dispute the claim, the marble plaque boasts, "On this spot Christopher Columbus first set foot upon the soil of the New World, erected by the *Chicago Herald,* June 1891." The only problem with the monument's claim is that the treacherous reefs here make this a dangerous—and thus highly unlikely—landing spot.

At Long Bay, the **Olympic Games Memorial** to Columbus, located 5km (3 miles) south of Cockburn Town, was erected in 1968 to commemorate the games in Mexico. Runners carrying an Olympic torch circled the island before coming to rest at the monument and lighting the torch there. The torch was then taken to Mexico on a warship. Another marker is underwater, supposedly where Columbus dropped the *Santa Maria*'s anchor.

Just north of the Olympic Games Memorial stands the **Columbus Monument.** On December 25, 1956, Ruth Durlacher Wolper Malvin—a leading U.S. expert on Columbus—established a simple monument commemorating the explorer's landfall in the New World. Unlike the spot marked by the *Chicago Herald* monument, this is actually likely to be the place where Columbus and his men landed.

Among the settlements on San Salvador are Sugar Loaf, Pigeon Creek, Old Place, Holiday Track, and Fortune Hill. **United Estates,** which has the largest population, is a village in the northwest corner near the Dixon Hill Lighthouse. The U.S. Coast Guard has a station at the island's northern tip.

Except for the party people at Club Med, San Salvador is mainly visited by the boating set who live aboard their crafts. If you're exploring for the day, you'll find one or two local cafes that serve seafood.

In the northeastern portion of the island, **Dixon Hill Lighthouse,** built in 1856, sends out an intense beam two times every 25 seconds. This signal is visible for 31km (19 miles). The oil-using lighthouse rises 49m (161 ft.) into the sky, and the keeper still operates it by hand. For permission to climb to the top, just knock on the keeper's door; he's almost always in the neighboring house.

After huffing and puffing your way up, you'll be surprised to see how tiny the source of light actually is. From the top of the lighthouse, take in the panoramic view of San Salvador's inland lakes, distant Crab Cay, and the surrounding islets. Ask the lighthouse keeper to show you the **inspector's log,** which has signatures dating back to Queen Victoria's reign. Be sure to leave at least a US$1 (50p) donation when you sign the guestbook on your way out. The lighthouse is about a 30-minute taxi ride from Riding Rock Inn and Club Med.

At French Bay, **Watling's Castle,** also known as Sandy Point Estate, has substantial ruins that are about 26m (85 ft.) above sea level. The area is located some 4km (2½ miles) from the large lake on the southwestern tip of the island. Local "experts" will tell you all about the castle and its history. The only problem is that each one we've listened to (three in all, at different times) has told us a different story about the place. Ask around and perhaps you'll get yet another version; they're entertaining, at least. One of the most common legends involves a pirate who made a living either by salvaging wreckage from foundered ships or by attacking ships for their spoils.

Once upon a time, plantations—all doomed to failure—were scattered about the island. The most impressive and best-known ruins of one are at **Farquharson's Plantation,** west of Queen's Highway, near South Victoria Hill. In the early 19th century, some Loyalist families moved from the newly established United States to this island, hoping to get rich from farmland tended by slave labor. That plan collapsed when the United Kingdom Emancipation Act freed the slaves in 1834. The plantation owners moved on, but the former slaves stayed behind.

A relic of those times, Farquharson's Plantation is where you can see the foundation of a great house, a kitchen, and what is believed to have been a jail. People locally call it "Blackbeard's Castle," but it's a remnant of slavery, not piracy.

COCKBURN TOWN

San Salvador's capital, Cockburn (pronounced "Coburn") Town, is a harbor village that takes its name from George Cockburn, said to have been the first royal governor of The Bahamas to visit this remote island (he stopped by in 1823). Look for the town's landmark: a giant almond tree. Major San Salvador events, like the Columbus Day parade held every October 12, generally take place here.

Holy Saviour Roman Catholic Church   The New World's very first Christian worship service was Catholic. It thus seems fitting that the Roman Catholic Diocese of The Bahamas in 1992, on the eve of the 500th anniversary of the Columbus landfall, dedicated a new church on San Salvador.

Cockburn Town. Free admission. Services Sun 10am.

New World Museum   This museum, 5.5km (3½ miles) north of Riding Rock Inn, has relics dating from pre-European times, but you'll have to ask around until you find someone with a key if you want to go inside. The museum lies just past Bonefish Bay in the little village of North Victoria Hill. Part of a large estate called Polaris-by-the-Sea, it's owned by a Columbus expert named Ruth Durlacher Wolper Malvin.

North Victoria Hill. No phone. Free admission. Open anytime during the day.

SAN SALVADOR AFTER DARK

Club Med (p. 281), just north of Cockburn Town, keeps its guests entertained every night, with musical revues and shows starring vacationers themselves. At **Riding Rock Inn** (p. 282), also north of Cockburn Town, the Wednesday-night barbecue features reggae music, and many locals come to party. The hotel's **Driftwood Bar** (© 242/331-2631) is hot on Friday nights. If you're still game for some fun after the lodgings' festivities, head to **Harlem Square Bar** (© 242/331-2777) in Cockburn Town. This friendly place is open daily from 7am "until food runs out."

SIDE TRIPS: DISCOVERING RUM CAY & CONCEPTION ISLAND

"Where on earth is **Rum Cay**?" Even many Bahamians have never heard of it. It's between San Salvador and Long Island, and is another cay, like Fortune Island (p. 293), that time forgot.

That wasn't always the case, though. The very name conjures up images of swash-bucklers and rumrunners. Doubtless, it was at least a port of call for those dubious seafarers, as it was for ships that took on supplies of salt, fresh water, and food before crossing the Atlantic or going south to Latin America. The cay's name is supposedly derived from a rum-laden sailing ship that wrecked upon its shores.

Like many other Bahamian islands, Rum Cay once attracted British Loyalists flee-ing the new United States. They hoped to establish themselves here as farmers and plantation overlords, but even those brave and homeless immigrants abandoned the island as unproductive. Salt mines were the mainstay of the island's economy before they were wiped out by a hurricane at the turn of the 19th century. After that, most of the inhabitants migrated to Nassau; by the 1970s, Rum Cay's population stood at "80 souls." Today, most of Rum Cay's 100 or so inhabitants live at **Port Nelson,** the island's capital.

The well-known underwater cinematographer Stan Waterman once described Rum Cay as the "unspoiled diving jewel of The Bahamas." For that reason, a diving club was opened here in 1983, but it closed, regrettably, in 1990.

Some maintain that Rum Cay was the next island where Columbus landed after he found and named San Salvador. He dubbed that second spot Santa María de la Con-cepción. However, many students of history and navigation believe that Columbus made this second landfall at the island today called **Conception,** which lies northwest of Rum Cay and northeast of Long Island. You'll have to travel here in a private boat.

Joseph Judge, a writer whose articles have appeared in *National Geographic,* believes that neither Rum Cay nor Conception was Columbus's second stop. He holds that, based on modern computer science and oceanography, the island the discoverer named Santa María de la Concepción has to be what's now called Crooked Island.

Still, the uninhabited Conception Island is under the protection of The Bahamas National Trust, which preserves it as a sea and land park; it's a sanctuary for migratory birds. The most secretive divers know of excellent scuba sites here, and endangered green turtles use the beaches as egg-laying sites. Park rules are strict about prohibiting littering and removing any plant or animal life—so don't do it.

With the Rum Cay Club's demise, tourist traffic to the island came to a halt except for the odd yachting party or two. It's gaining renewed interest, however, and you can arrange for boaters on San Salvador to take you to see Rum Cay and Conception, which remain frozen in time.

3 Long Island

Most historians agree that Long Island was the third island Columbus sailed to dur-ing his first voyage of discovery. The Tropic of Cancer runs through this long, thin sliver of land, located 242km (150 miles) southeast of Nassau. It stretches north to south for some 97km (60 miles) and is 2.5km (1½ miles) wide on average, and only 5km (3 miles) wide at its broadest point. Long Island is characterized by high cliffs in the north, wide and shallow sand beaches, historic plantation ruins, native caves, and Spanish churches.

The famed **diving sites** ✺ are offshore, including a blue hole of stunning magnitude that locals claim is bottomless.

Long Island's best beaches include **Deal's Beach, Cape Santa Maria Beach, Salt Pond Beach, Turtle Cove Beach,** and the **South End beaches,** the latter offering kilometers of waterfront scenery with powdery white or pink sands. Only recently has the island emerged as a minor tourist destination.

LONG ISLAND ESSENTIALS

GETTING THERE   There are two airstrips here, connected by a road. The **Stella Maris airport** is in the north, and the other, called **Deadman's Cay,** is in the south, north of Clarence Town. It's highly unlikely that you'll land at Deadman's Cay, and besides, it's a very expensive cab ride from most of the island's accommodations. **Bahamasair** (℡ 800/222-4262 in the U.S.; www.bahamasair.com) flies direct once daily (a 45-min. trip) from Fort Lauderdale, landing at Stella Maris, which is near most of the hotels.

From Nassau, the **MV** *Mia Dean* sails weekly to Clarence Town, leaving on Tuesday. Mail-boat trips take a grueling 10 hours. For information about how to board it, contact the dock master at **Potter's Cay Dock,** Nassau (℡ 242/393-1064).

GETTING AROUND   The **Stella Maris Resort Club** (℡ 242/338-2051; www.stellamarisresort.com) can arrange to have you picked up at the airport upon arrival or get you a rental car.

FAST FACTS   The **police** can be reached by calling ℡ 242/337-0999 or 337-0444.

Scotia Bank (℡ 242/338-2000) has an **ATM** and operates a small currency-exchange facility at Stella Maris Resort Club. Hours are Monday to Thursday 9am to 1pm, Friday 9:30am to 3pm.

SPECIAL EVENTS   In June, Long Island sailors participate in the big event of the year, the 4-day **Long Island Regatta,** held annually at Salt Pond since 1967. In addition to the highly competitive sailboat races, Long Island takes on a festive air with calypso music, reggae, and lots of drinking and partying. Many expatriate Long Islanders come home at this time, usually from Nassau, New York, or Miami, to enjoy not only the regatta, but rake 'n' scrape music. Call your local Bahamas tourist office (see chapter 3) for more information.

WHERE TO STAY

Cape Santa Maria Beach Resort ✺ *(Kids*   This cozy nest has become the island's most luxurious resort, taking over the position long held by Stella Maris Resort Club. Two-room cottages are centered around a clubhouse, and the entire complex opens onto a stunning 6.5km (4-mile) strip of white sand. All units are only 18m (59 ft.) from the beach, so the snorkeling is great. Though the accommodations don't have phones or TVs, each room is air-conditioned and also has ceiling fans, plus a small bathroom with a tub/shower. Bedrooms have an airy, tropical feel, with marble floors and tasteful rattan furniture. As part of a multimillion-dollar development, the resort in 2006 added eight beachfront villas, each with luxury appointments such as jetted tubs and Internet service. There's also a screened-in porch with ceiling fans so you can enjoy the outdoors without the mosquitoes (the curse of the southern Bahamas). The place is ideal for families, and several accommodations are configured so that children will have a separate room. The hotel's 65-seat restaurant is also good, serving tasty Bahamian, North American, and seafood dishes.

Cape Santa Maria, off Queen's Hwy., Long Island, The Bahamas. ℭ 800/663-7090 or 242/338-5273. Fax 242/338-6013. www.capesantamaria.com. 29 units. Winter US$325 (£163) double, US$795 (£398) 2-bedroom villa; off-season US$235 (£118) double, US$595 (£298) 2-bedroom villa. Breakfast and dinner US$65 (£33) per person extra. AE, MC, V. Closed Sept–Oct. **Amenities:** Restaurant; bar; health club; watersports equipment/rentals; bike rentals; car-rental desk; babysitting; laundry service; nonsmoking rooms. *In room:* A/C, ceiling fan, fridge (in some), coffeemaker, hair dryer, iron, safe (in some), no phone.

Chez Pierre ⍟ *Finds*   Just south of the Tropic of Cancer, Montreal expats Pierre and Anne Laurence found their little bit of heaven on 3.2 hectares (8 acres) of land opening onto a wide crescent beach. Here they built and attractively furnished a cluster of bungalows overlooking the sea, each with a screened-in porch. All the units come with private bathrooms with showers. A few steps from the beach cottages, an oceanfront restaurant serves the best food on the island. Dishes blend French, Italian, and Caribbean cuisines, incorporating island-grown fresh produce along with fresh fish and seafood from local waters. This is the most eco-sensitive resort in the southern Bahamas; it's powered by alternative energy, so the sun and wind keep it running. The location is halfway between Stella Maris and Deadman's Cay.

Simms, Long Island, The Bahamas. ℭ 242/338-8809. www.chezpierrebahamas.com. 6 units. Year-round US$150–US$170 (£75–£85) double. Rates include breakfast and dinner. AE, MC, V. **Amenities:** Restaurant; bar; bikes; fishing; kayaking; reef fishing; saltwater fly-fishing; snorkeling; island tours; babysitting. *In room:* Fans, no phone.

Gems at Paradise ⍟   This 15-acre complex of suites and condos stands on a hill that opens onto a pink beach and the bay at Clarence Town's harbor. Lying just south of town, the hotel is owned by Shavonne Darville, who welcomes guests to her pristine little place. In such a faraway place, there are quality furnishings, upmarket interior accessories, art, Italian tiles, and stained woodwork. In addition to its array of attractively furnished suites, the hotel offers one- and two-bedroom condos. Some of the suites open onto balconies, as do all the condos.

Clarence Town, Long Island, The Bahamas. ℭ 242/337-3016. Fax 242/337-3021. www.gemsatparadise.com. 15 units. Winter US$125–US$140 (£63–£70) suite, US$185 (£93) 1-bedroom condo, US$275 (£138) 2-bedroom condo; off-season US$100–US$125 (£50–£63) suite, US$165 (£83) 1-bedroom condo, US$225 (£113) 2-bedroom condo. AE, MC, V. **Amenities:** Bar; watersports; laundry service. *In room:* A/C, TV, no phone.

Lochabar Beach Lodge   One of the most remote retreats listed in this guide, this lodge offers escapist studios for those fleeing the civilized world. You step from your studio to a pristine beach 23m (75 ft.) away, surrounding a blue hole in a natural cove. The only acceptable lodgings in the southern part of Long Island, these guest studios measure 56 or 111 sq. m (603/1,195 sq. ft.) each. In lieu of ceiling fans, the studios were built to take advantage of the trade winds. Guests keep their Bahama shutters and double screen doors open to capture those breezes. Each studio comes with a kitchenette and a small bathroom containing a shower stall. If you like, a staff member will drive you to a nearby store to stock up on provisions.

Big Blue Hole, 1.6km (1 mile) south of Clarence Town, Long Island, The Bahamas. ℭ 242/337-3123. Fax 242/337-6556. www.bahamasvacationguide.com/lochabarbeachlodge. 3 units. Year-round US$138–US$180 (£69–£90) double. Extra person US$20 (£10) per day. MC, V. **Amenities:** Watersports equipment/rentals; car-rental desk; nonsmoking rooms; room for those w/limited mobility. *In room:* A/C, TV, kitchenette, fridge, coffeemaker, iron.

Stella Maris Resort Club ⍟   Situated on a ridge overlooking the Atlantic, this resort stands in a palm grove on the grounds of the old Adderley's Plantation. Though you can swim here, the beach isn't the best, so the hotel maintains a cabana at Cape Santa Maria, a gorgeous beach directly north, and offers shuttle service for its guests.

Accommodations vary widely—rooms, studios, apartments, and cottages with one to four bedrooms. Each accommodation has its own walk-in closet and fully equipped bathroom. Some are directly on the water. All of the buildings, including the cottages and bungalows, are set around a central clubhouse and a trio of pools. The resort makes a great honeymoon destination; everything is relaxed and informal.

The inn's on-site restaurant serves good Bahamian cuisine, as well as continental specialties. There are rum-punch parties, cave parties, barbecue dinners, Saturday dinners, dancing—and complete diving facilities. Divers and snorkelers can choose from coral head, reef, and drop-off sites along the island's protected west coast, north side, and all along the east coast, as well as around Conception Island and Rum Cay. Water-skiing and bottom- and reef fishing are also offered; there are three good bonefishing bays nearby. Hotel guests can use their 3.5m Scorpion and Sunfish sailboats at no cost.

Ocean View Dr., Long Island, The Bahamas. (℃) **800/426-0466** or 242/338-2051; 954/359-8238 for the Fort Lauderdale booking office. Fax 242/338-2052. www.stellamarisresort.com. 47 units. Winter US$175 (£88) double, US$200 (£100) 1-bedroom cottage, US$330 (£165) 2-bedroom bungalow, US$315 (£158) 2-bedroom villa; off-season US$170 (£85) double, US$195 (£98) 1-bedroom cottage, US$315 (£158) 2-bedroom bungalow, US$285 (£143) 2-bedroom villa. AE, MC, V. **Amenities:** Restaurant; bar; 3 pools; watersports equipment/rentals; laundry service; nonsmoking rooms; rooms for those w/limited mobility. *In room:* A/C, fridge, hair dryer, no phone.

WHERE TO DINE

All the inns listed above serve food, but you should call for a reservation. In addition, you can try local joints, such as the **Forest,** Queen's Highway, Miley's (℃ **242/ 337-3287**), south of Clarence Town. Its cracked conch is the island's finest, and you can also order the standard grouper fingers or barbecued chicken. The bar is made of seashells. On Friday nights, a live band plays and the Forest becomes an island hot spot, dancing and all. Another of our favorite stops is a little roadside dive called **Max's Conch Grill,** Deadman's Cay (℃ **242/337-0056**), which also serves some of the island's best conch. Daily specials are posted. At both eateries, lunch ranges from US$6 to US$10 (£3–£5), with dinners going for US$8 to US$12 (£4–£6).

FISHING, SCUBA DIVING & SNORKELING

Many savvy anglers come to Long Island to fish, eschewing more famous places such as Andros and Bimini. The secret of good fishing here: the major North Equatorial Current, which originates in the Canary Islands and washes Long Island's shores. The current transports huge schools of blue marlin, white marlin, sailfish, rainbow runners, yellowfin tuna, blackfin tuna, wahoo, and dolphinfish. Wahoo is best hunted from September through November. Catches weigh from 4.5 to 41kg (10–90 lb.), and some yellowfin have weighed up to 68kg (150 lb.). The small blackfin tuna (July–Dec) weigh from 4.5 to 14kg (10–31 lb.). In addition, there are kilometers' worth of reef fishing with hundreds of species including snapper or grouper that have been known to weigh 45kg (99 lb.). A jewfish caught here weighed 226kg (498 lb.). In-shore fishing for bonefish is also possible.

Though there are no watersports outfitters on Long Island, the two major resorts, **Stella Maris Resort Club** (p. 288) and **Cape Santa Maria Beach Resort** (p. 287), fill the void and offer more watersports than you can do in a week. Bonefishing goes at a rate of US$500 (£250) per day for up to two people; reef fishing costs from US$500 (£250) per day for up to six people; deep-sea fishing is US$800 (£400) per day for up to six people.

Snorkeling off the beach is complimentary at both resorts. However, boat excursions can be as little as US$15 (£7.50) per hour at Cape Santa Maria; on Wednesday and Saturday, these excursions are complimentary at Stella Maris. Both resorts offer scuba diving ranging from US$75 to US$110 (£38–£55) per person per day, with equipment rentals ranging from US$10 to US$50 (£5–£25). Both also offer kayaks, windsurfers, and bicycles. Cape Santa Maria also offers Hobie Cats and boogie boards.

EXPLORING THE ISLAND

At **Wild Tamarind** (© 242/337-0262), 1km (⅔ mile) east of Queen's Highway in the hamlet of Petty's, Denis Knight makes the best ceramics on the island. You might want to carry off one of his ceramic sculptures, or at least a bowl or vase.

Most islanders live at the unattractively named **Deadman's Cay.** Other settlements have equally colorful names: Roses, Newfound Harbour, Burnt Ground, Indian Head Point, and, at the island's northern tip, Cape Santa Maria, generally believed to be where Columbus landed and from where he looked on the Exumas (islands that he did not visit). Our favorite name, however, is Hard Bargain, located 16km (10 miles) south of Clarence Town. No one seems to know how this place (now a shrimp-breeding farm) got its name.

Try to visit **Clarence Town** ✿, 16km (10 miles) south of Deadman's Cay along the eastern coastline. It was here that Father Jerome, the priest who became known as the islands' "father confessor," built two churches before his death in 1956: **St. Paul's,** an Anglican house of worship, and **St. Peter's,** a Roman Catholic church. The "hermit" of Cat Island (you can visit his Hermitage there; see p. 279) was interested in Gothic architecture. He must also have been somewhat ecumenical because he started his ministry as an Anglican but embraced Roman Catholicism along the way.

Many ruins recall the days when local plantation owners figured their wealth in slaves and cotton. The remains of **Dunmore's Plantation** at Deadman's Cay stand on a hill surrounded by the sea on three sides. There are six gateposts (four outer and two inner), as well as a house with two fireplaces and wall drawings of ships. At the base of the ruins is evidence that a mill wheel was once used here. The property was part of the estate of Lord Dunmore, for whom Dunmore Town on Harbour Island was named.

In the village of Grays stand the ruins of **Grays Plantation,** where you'll see the remnants of at least three houses, one with two chimneys. One was very large, while the other seems to have been a one-story structure with a cellar.

Adderley's Plantation, off Cape Santa Maria, originally occupied all the land now known as Stella Maris. The ruins at this cotton plantation consist of three structures that are partially intact but roofless.

Two underground sites that can be visited on Deadman's Cay are **Dunmore's Caves** and **Deadman's Cay Cave.** You'll need to hire a local guide to explore these. Dunmore's Caves are believed to have been inhabited by Lucayans and later to have served as a hideaway for buccaneers. The cave at Deadman's Cay, one of two that lead to the ocean, has never been fully explored. There are two designs that were chiseled into the cavern wall by long-ago islanders.

4 Acklins Island & Crooked Island

These little tropical islands, approximately 386km (240 miles) southeast of Nassau, make up an undiscovered Bahamian frontier outpost. Columbus came this way looking for gold. Much later, Acklins Island, Crooked Island, and their surrounding cays became hideouts for pirates who attacked vessels in the Crooked Island Passage (the narrow waterway Columbus sailed), which separates the two islands. Today a well-known landmark, the **Crooked Island Passage Light,** built in 1876, guides ships to a safe voyage through the slot. Also known as the Bird Rock Lighthouse, it is a popular nesting spot for ospreys, and the light still lures pilots and sailors to the **Pittstown Point Landing Resort.** A barrier reef begins near the lighthouse, stretching down off Acklins Island for about 40km (25 miles) to the southeast.

Although Acklins Island and Crooked Island are separate, they are usually mentioned as a unit because of their proximity to each other. Together the two islands form the shape of a boomerang. Crooked Island, the northern one, is 181 sq. km (70 sq. miles) in area, whereas Acklins Island, to the south, occupies 311 sq. km (120 sq. miles). Both islands, which have good white-sand beaches and offer fishing and scuba diving, are inhabited mainly by fishermen and farmers.

In his controversial 1986 article in *National Geographic,* Joseph Judge identified Crooked Island as the site of Columbus's second island landing, and the island the explorer named Santa María de la Concepción.

Estimates say that by the end of the 18th century, more than three dozen working plantations were on these islands, begun by Loyalists fleeing mainland North America in the wake of the Revolutionary War. At the peak plantation period, there could have been as many as 1,200 slaves laboring in the 3,000 acres of cotton fields which were later wiped out by a blight. The people who remained on the island survived not only by fishing and farming, but also, beginning in the mid-18th century, by stripping the Croton cascarilla shrub of its bark to produce the flavoring for Campari liquor.

ACKLINS ISLAND & CROOKED ISLAND ESSENTIALS

GETTING THERE   There's an airport at **Colonel Hill** on Crooked Island and another airstrip at **Spring Point** on Acklins Island.

Bahamasair (© 800/222-4262 in the U.S.; www.bahamasair.com) operates two flights a week from Nassau, on Wednesday and Saturday, to Crooked Island and Acklins Island, with returns to Nassau scheduled on the same day.

Mail-boat service on the **MV *United Star*** leaves Potter's Cay Dock in Nassau and heads for Acklins Island, Crooked Island, Fortune Island (Long Cay), and Mayaguana Island each week. Check the schedule and costs with the dock master at **Potter's Cay Dock** in Nassau (© 242/393-1064).

A government-owned **ferry service** connects the two islands; it operates daily, about every hour, from 9am to 4pm. It links Lovely Bay on Acklins Island with Browns on Crooked Island. The one-way fare is US$5 (£2.50).

Once you arrive at Crooked Island, a **taxi service** is available, but it's wise to advise your hotel in advance of your arrival—they'll probably send a van to meet you.

FAST FACTS   There are several government-operated clinics. Phones are scarce on the islands, but your hotel desk can reach one of these clinics by going through the local operator. The clinic on Acklins Island is at Spring Point (© 242/344-3172). On Crooked Island, the clinic is at Landrail Point (© 242/344-2166).

The **police** station on Crooked Island can be reached by dialing © 242/344-2599.

WHERE TO STAY & DINE

Casuarinas Villas   A cottage by the beach or oceanfront sounds idyllic. Okay, these are basic motel caliber at best but well-maintained and reasonably comfortable in this remote part of the Americas. The property opens onto half a mile of pristine sands lying between Pittstown Point Landings and Landrail Point. Each of the cottages comes with a fully equipped kitchen and little verandas or decks facing westward. If you give the office sufficient notice, a Bahamian cook can prepare a dinner to be delivered to your cottage (wait until you try those pies). Snorkeling and scuba diving can be arranged, as can a rental car or fishing guide. At Landrail Point are such conveniences as a restaurant, a gas station, and a local market, which comes in handy if you want to cook in your cottage.

Landrail Point, Crooked Island, The Bahamas. (℮ **242/344-2197.** Fax 242/344-2197. 6 units. Year-round US$135 (£68) double in 1-bedroom cottage, US$220 (£110) 3-4 guests in 2-bedroom cottage. No credit cards. **Amenities:** Meals on request; watersports; laundry service. *In room:* A/C, TV, kitchen, no phone.

Crooked Island Lodge at Pittstown Point ⭐ *Finds*   Located on a beach at Crooked Island's extreme northwestern tip, this hotel is so isolated that you'll forget all about the world outside. For most of its early years, it was a well-guarded secret shared mostly by the owners of private planes who flew in from mainland Florida for off-the-record weekends. Even today, about 70% of the clientele arrives by one- or two-engine aircraft that they fly themselves as part of island-hopping jaunts around The Bahamas. The island maintains its own 690m (2,264-ft.) hard-surface landing strip, which is independent from the one used for the flights from Nassau on Bahamasair.

Surrounded by scrub-covered landscape at the edge of a turquoise sea, Crooked Island Lodge lies 4km (2½ miles) north of Landrail Point (pop. 50) on a sandy peninsula. Within easy access are some of The Bahamas' weirdest historic sites, including the sun-baked ruins of a salt farm, **Marine Farms Fortress,** which was sacked by U.S.-based pirates in 1812.

Spartan accommodations with tub/shower bathrooms occupy three low-slung, cement-sided buildings. They lie directly on the beach, usually with verandas facing the sea. Because of the constant trade winds, not all bedrooms have air-conditioning, but do contain paddle-shaped ceiling fans. The entire resort shares only one telephone/fax, which is reserved for emergency calls.

Guests usually opt for the full meal plan here. Repasts are served in a stone-sided building that was erected late in the 1600s as barracks for the British West Indies Naval Squadron and later served as the region's post office. The restaurant serves seafood, as well as North American and Bahamian specialties. You'll also usually find a scattering of yacht owners or aviators who drop in spontaneously for drinks and dinner.

Landrail Point, Crooked Island, The Bahamas. (For reservations and information, contact Pittstown Point Landing, 9274 SE Hawks Nest Court, Hobe Sound, FL 33455.) (℮ **242/344-2507.** www.pittstownpointlandings.com. 12 units. Year-round US$210 (£105) double. All meals US$75 (£38) per person extra. AE, MC, V. **Amenities:** Restaurant; bar; laundry service; nonsmoking rooms. *In room:* A/C (in some), no phone.

A PIRATE HIDEOUT & MORE

Crooked Island opens onto the **Windward Passage,** the dividing point between the Caribbean Sea and The Bahamas. When Columbus landed at what is now **Pittstown Point,** he supposedly called it Fragrant Island because of the aroma of its many herbs. One scent was cascarilla bark, used to flavor Campari as well as the native Cascarilla liqueur, which is exported. For the best view of the island, climb **Colonel Hill** ⭐— unless you arrived at Crooked Island Airport (also known as Colonel Hill Airport), which has the same vantage.

Guarding this island's north end is the **Marine Farms Fortress,** an abandoned British fort that saw action in the War of 1812. It looks out over Crooked Island Passage and can be visited (ask your hotel to make arrangements for you).

Finds **The Ghost Island of Fortune**

Lying off the coast of Crooked Island, **Fortune Island** is truly a place that time forgot. Your hotel can put you in touch with a boater who will take you here. Experts believe, based on research done for *National Geographic,* that Fortune Island (sometimes confusingly called Long Cay) is the one Columbus chose to name Isabella, in honor of the queen who funded his expedition. Its only real settlement is **Albert Town,** which is classified as a ghost town but officially isn't—some hardy souls still live here. **Fortune Hill,** visible from 19km (12 miles) away at sea, is the local landmark. Hundreds of Bahamians came here in the 2 decades before World War I, waiting to be picked up by oceangoing freighters, which would take them to seek their fortunes as laborers in Central America— hence the name Fortune Hill.

Hope Great House is also on the island, with orchards and gardens that date from the time of George V of England.

Other sights include **French Wells Bay,** a swampy delta leading to an extensive mangrove swamp rich in bird life, and the **Bird Rock Lighthouse,** built a century ago.

At the southern end of Acklins Island lies **Castle Island,** a low bit of land where an 1867 lighthouse stands. Pirates used it as a hideout, sailing forth to attack ships in the nearby passage.

Acklins Island has many interestingly named villages—Binnacle Hill, Delectable Bay, Golden Grove, Goodwill, Hard Hill, Snug Corner, and Lovely Bay. Some Crooked Island sites have more ominous names, such as Gun Point and Cripple Hill.

5 Mayaguana Island

The least visited Bahamian island, sleepy **Mayaguana,** across the Mayaguana Passage from Acklins Island and Crooked Island, seems to float adrift in the tropical sun at the remote extremities of the southeastern edge of The Bahamas, 564km (350 miles) southeast of Nassau. It occupies 285 sq. km (110 sq. miles) and has a population of about 400. It's a long, long way from the development of Nassau and Paradise Island.

Standing in the Windward Passage, Mayaguana is just northwest of the Turks and Caicos Islands. It's separated from the British Crown Colony by the Caicos Passage. Around the time of the American Civil War, inhabitants of Turks Island began to settle in Mayaguana, which before then had dozed undisturbed for centuries.

Mayaguana is only 9.5km (6 miles) across at its widest point, and about 39km (24 miles) long. Its beaches are enticing, but you'll rarely see a tourist on them, other than the occasional German. A few developers have flown in to check out the island, but to date, no new development has occurred.

Summer brings rain to Mayaguana. Combined with heat and mosquitoes, it can get a little rough here. However, summer is the best time to go fishing.

GETTING THERE

Bahamasair (© 800/222-4262 in the U.S.; www.bahamasair.com) flies in from Nassau Wednesday and Friday at 9:15am; the trip takes approximately 2½ hours.

From Nassau, a mail boat, **MV *United Star,*** makes a stop at Mayaguana. For information, check with the dock master at **Potter's Cay Dock** in Nassau (© 242/393-1064).

WHERE TO STAY & DINE

Few other outposts in The Bahamas are as remote as Mayaguana, which is the main reason many visitors come—to get away from everything. Tourists arrive by boat and just ask around for availability at one of the ultra-simple lodgings here. Some locals are willing to house you in one of their spare bedrooms for a rate that can be negotiated up or down to almost anything.

Baycaner Beach Resort   In operation since 1996, this is the island's only hotel that can even lay a claim to being that. Its owner, Ernal Brown, is called "Shorty" by all the locals, and he's the man to see if you're one of the rare visitors who ever makes it to this part of the world. You can literally jump from your simply furnished bedroom right into the water. Bedrooms contain a comfortable bed, a scattering of wicker furnishings, a small air conditioner, and a little, well-maintained bathroom. The lobby adjoins the dining room and bar (the latter is popular with locals). You might have the dining room to yourself, however. Dig into that Bahamian staple of brown pigeon peas 'n' rice. Most meals feature conch—perhaps in a chowder or freshly made salad—and the inevitable grouper, the most popular fish caught here. The cook bakes fresh bread daily.

Pirates Well, Mayaguana, The Bahamas. ✆ **242/339-3726.** Fax 242/339-3727. www.baycanerbeach.com. 16 units. Sept–Apr US$106 (£53) double; May–Aug US$88 (£44) double. MC, V. **Amenities:** Restaurant; bar; scuba diving; limited room service; laundry service. *In room:* A/C, TV.

EXPLORING THE ISLAND

Abraham's Bay is the south coast's main town, and it has an excellent harbor. The other little settlement on Mayaguana is **Betsy Bay,** secluded and lost in time. Wild corn and saucy hummingbirds share this spot along with some little sun-worn cottages. At **Pirate's Well,** goats are now the chief residents, although buccaneers used to roam past here. Locals still dream of finding buried treasure. The Mayaguana Passage's best views can be had from both Betsy Bay and Pirate's Well.

Fishing is good on the island. Locals will often take you out on one of their boats, but you've got to ask around. In summer and early autumn, temperatures can soar beyond 100°F (38°C). Winters, however, are ideal, and it never gets cold here as it can in the north Bahamas.

Mayaguana might be called The Bahamas' "great outback" or "wild west." It's a rugged, salty environment. Sailing, deep-sea fishing, scuba diving, snorkeling, swimming, and walking are the main pastimes. The island is still too laid-back to have many organized outfitters. If you want to rent gear or hire a guide for an organized outing, your best bet is to inquire at your hotel; the staff can usually hook you up with the right person.

6 Great Inagua ⭐

The most southerly and the third-largest island of The Bahamas, flat **Great Inagua,** some 64km (40 miles) long and 32km (20 miles) wide, is home to 1,200 people. It lies 527km (327 miles) southeast of Nassau.

This is the site not only of the **Morton Salt Crystal Factory,** here since 1800, but also of one of the Western Hemisphere's largest nesting grounds for **flamingos.** The National Trust of The Bahamas protects the area around **Lake Windsor,** where the birds breed and the population is said to number 80,000. Flamingos used to inhabit all of The Bahamas, but the birds have disappeared from most other places. The

Fun Fact **With Salt, Please**

Salt means a great deal to Great Inagua—not only because of the Morton Salt Company's extensive operations (the company produces more than 1 million tons of salt each year), but also for the unique local wildlife.

First, seawater is pumped into the island's interior and held by dikes. Great Inagua's salt ponds, about 80 of them, cover some 4,856 hectares (11,999 acres). As the water evaporates, it turns into heavy brine. The salt solidifies at night and melts during the heat of the day, and a crystallized bed forms at the bottom of the pond. During the final stage, any remaining water is drained and the salt is bulldozed into bleached-white mountains and then shipped around the world for processing.

As the water evaporates from these salt ponds, brine shrimp concentrate, providing hearty meals for the island's colorful pink flamingos.

reserve can be visited only with a guide. Besides the pink flamingo, you can see roseate spoonbills and other bird life.

Green turtles are also raised here, at **Union Creek Reserve,** and then released into the ocean to make their way as best they can; they, too, are an endangered species. (Tours of the reserve are not well organized, and the operation is very informal, but if you're here, inquire about getting a look.) This vast windward island, almost within sight of Cuba, is also inhabited by wild hogs, horses, and donkeys.

Matthew Town is the island's chief settlement, but it's not of any great sightseeing interest, though it does have an 1870 lighthouse. Other locales have interesting names, such as Doghead Point, Mutton Fish Point, and Devil's Point (which makes one wonder what happened there to inspire the name).

Little Inagua, 8km (5 miles) to the north, has no population and is just a speck of land off Great Inagua's northeast coast. About 78 sq. km (30 sq. miles) in area, it has much bird life, wild goats, and donkeys.

GREAT INAGUA ESSENTIALS
GETTING THERE   Bahamasair (℗ 800/222-4262 in the U.S.; www.bahamas air.com) flies to Matthew Town Airport from Nassau on Monday, Wednesday, and Friday at 9:15am. Flight time is approximately 2 hours.

You can also go by **mail boat, MV *United Star,*** which makes weekly trips from Nassau to Matthew Town. The schedule varies, so call the **Potter's Cay Dock Master** (℗ 242/393-1064) in Nassau for details.

GETTING AROUND   Taxis meet incoming flights from Nassau. If you need a car, check with one of the guesthouses, but don't expect the vehicles to be well maintained.

FAST FACTS   **Inagua Hospital** can be called at ℗ 242/339-1249. The **police** can be reached at ℗ 242/339-1263.

WHERE TO STAY
The choices of accommodations aren't great on this island, but most visitors are willing to forgo comfort to see the spectacular flamingos.

The Main House   This hotel is owned by Morton Bahamas Ltd., the salt people, so their employees often fill up all the rooms. Only five bedrooms are rented, and the furnishings are extremely modest, though everything is clean. Each unit comes with a small bathroom containing a tub/shower. Life here is casual and completely informal. You can order breakfast or lunch here—but no dinner. Unfortunately, it sits near a noisy power plant.

Matthew Town, Inagua, The Bahamas. ✆ 242/339-1267. Fax 242/339-1265. 5 units. www.inaguamainhouse.com. Year-round US$60–US$85 (£30–£43) double. No credit cards. **Amenities:** Nonsmoking rooms. *In room:* A/C, TV, fridge, iron, no phone.

Walkine's Guest House   Set 1km (⅔ mile) south of Matthew Town, this simple guesthouse has a blue exterior and rosy, shell-pink bedrooms. Your hosts are Eleanor and Kirk Walkine, who built their place in 1984 across the road from the beach. Rooms are very modest but spacious, with only racks to hang your clothes in lieu of a closet. Bathrooms are large, three containing a tub/shower.

Gregory St., Matthew Town, Inagua, The Bahamas. ✆ 242/339-1612. 5 units, 3 w/private bathroom. Year-round US$110 (£55) double. No credit cards. **Amenities:** Nonsmoking rooms. *In room:* A/C, TV, coffeemaker, no phone.

WHERE TO DINE

Cozy Corner BAHAMIAN/AMERICAN   The most consistently reliable restaurant besides those at the lodgings is this lime-green stone house 2 blocks from the sea. Your hosts, Rosemary Ingraham and her daughter Veronica, maintain a friendly bar where beer, rum punch, and gossip seem to be the staples. Menu items include a simple roster of mostly fried foods that are almost always accompanied by french fries. Dishes include fried conch, fried chicken, burgers, and "whopper burgers," plus whatever sort of fried seafood is available from local fishermen on the day of your visit.

William St., Matthew Town. ✆ 242/339-1440. Lunch and dinner US$7–US$15 (£3.50–£7.50). No credit cards. Daily 10am–5pm.

EXPLORING THE ISLAND: PINK FLAMINGOS & MORE

The island's vast number of **pink flamingos** ⟡⟡⟡ outnumbers its human population by far. They're so plentiful on Inagua that some of them even roost on the runway of the island's airport, as well as at thousands of other locations throughout the flat, heat-blasted landscape.

Dedicated bird-watchers who are willing to forgo comfort usually trek inland to the edges of the many brackish lakes in the island's center. About half the island is national park land, and the island's most viable industry involves distilling salt from the local salt flats.

To see the birds at **Inagua National Park** ⟡⟡ is reason enough to come here. Everyone entering the park must be accompanied by a warden, and reservations and a day pass (US$25/£13 for adults, US$10/£5 for students) must be obtained in advance. Get the passes either through The Bahamas National Trust in Nassau (✆ 242/393-1317; www.bahamasnationaltrust.org) or by contacting Henry Nixon, one of the local wardens, at ✆ 242/339-1616. In addition to the park fee, you're expected to offer the wardens a large tip. The usual payment is about US$50 (£25) per day. The best time to see the feathered beauties is from November until June.

One of the island's best panoramas can be taken in from **Southwest Point,** 2km (1¼ miles) south of Matthew Town. From here, you can see Cuba on a clear day because it lies just 81km (50 miles) west. The best view of Cuba can be gotten from the top of the **Inagua Lighthouse,** which dates from 1870 and is one of the quartet of hand-operated kerosene lighthouses left in The Bahamas. The reefs off this point are treacherous, as many a captain has fatefully learned.

Appendix:
Fast Facts, Toll-Free
Numbers & Websites

1 Fast Facts: The Bahamas

AMERICAN EXPRESS Representing American Express in The Bahamas is **Destinations,** 303 Shirley St. (between Charlotte and Parliament sts.), Nassau (© **242/ 322-2931;** www.destinations.com.bs). Hours are 9am to 5pm Monday to Friday. The travel department is also open Saturday 9am to 1pm. If you present a personal check and an Amex card, you can buy traveler's checks here.

AREA CODE The area code for The Bahamas is **242.**

ATMS See "Money & Costs," p. 46.

BUSINESS HOURS In Nassau, Cable Beach, and Freeport/Lucaya, commercial banking hours are 9:30am to 3pm Monday to Thursday, 9:30am to 5pm on Friday. Hours are likely to vary widely in the Out Islands. Ask at your hotel. Most government offices are open Monday to Friday from 9am to 5pm, and most shops are open Monday to Saturday from 9am to 5pm.

CAR RENTALS See "Toll-Free Numbers & Websites," p. 302.

CASH POINTS See "Money & Costs," p. 46.

CURRENCY See "Money & Costs," p. 46.

DRINKING LAWS Liquor is sold in liquor stores and various convenience stores; it's readily available at all hours, though not sold on Sundays. The legal drinking age is 18.

DRIVING RULES See "Getting There & Getting Around," p. 42.

DRUG LAWS Importing, possessing, or dealing unlawful drugs, including marijuana, is a serious offense in The Bahamas, with heavy penalties. Customs officers may at their discretion conduct body searches for drugs or other contraband goods.

DRUGSTORES Nassau and Freeport are amply supplied with pharmacies. However, if you're traveling in the Out Islands, it is best to carry your prescribed medication with you, since pharmacies are harder to find.

ELECTRICITY Electricity is normally 120 volts, 60 cycles, AC. American appliances are fully compatible; British or European appliances will need both converters and adapters.

EMBASSIES & CONSULATES The U.S. Embassy is on 42 Queen St., P.O. Box N-8197, Nassau (© **242/322-1181**), and the Canadian consulate is on Shirley Street Shopping Plaza, Nassau (© **242/ 393-2123**). The British High Commission is in Kingston, Jamaica, at 28 Trafalgar Rd. (© **876/510-0700**).

EMERGENCIES Throughout most of The Bahamas, the number to call for a medical, dental, or hospital emergency is © **911.** To call the **police** anywhere in The Bahamas, dial © **919.** In the Out Islands, the number is © **919.** To report a **fire,** however, call © **411.**

GASOLINE (PETROL) Gasoline is plentiful on New Providence (Nassau) and Grand Bahama Island (Freeport/Lucaya), but be prepared to pay almost twice the price you would in the U.S. In the Out Islands, stations are not plentiful, so plan accordingly. Also, watch out for those Sunday closings. Some islands are small, but others such as Eleuthera and Andros are very spread out with few stations.

HOLIDAYS Public holidays observed in The Bahamas are New Year's Day, Good Friday, Easter Sunday, Easter Monday, Whitmonday (7 weeks after Easter), Labour Day (the first Friday in June), Independence Day (July 10), Emancipation Day (the first Monday in August), Discovery Day (Oct 12), Christmas, and Boxing Day (the day after Christmas). When a holiday falls on Saturday or Sunday, stores and offices are usually closed on the following Monday too. For more information on holidays, see "The Bahamas Calendar of Events," p. 39.

HOSPITALS In Nassau, **Princess Margaret Hospital** (© **242/322-2861**), and in Freeport, **Rand Memorial** (© **242/352-6735**).

INSURANCE Medical Insurance For travel overseas, most U.S. health plans (including Medicare and Medicaid) do not provide coverage, and the ones that do often require you to pay for services upfront and reimburse you only after you return home.

As a safety net, you may want to buy travel medical insurance, particularly if you're traveling to a remote or high-risk area where emergency evacuation might be necessary. If you require additional medical insurance, try **MEDEX Assistance** (© **410/453-6300**; www.medexassist.com) or **Travel Assistance International** (© **800/821-2828**; www.travelassistance.com; for general information on services, call the company's **Worldwide Assistance Services, Inc.,** at © **800/777-8710**).

Canadians should check with their provincial health plan offices or call **Health Canada** (© **866/225-0709**; www.hc-sc.gc.ca) to find out the extent of their coverage and what documentation and receipts they must take home in case they are treated overseas.

Travelers from the U.K. should carry their European Health Insurance Card (EHIC), which replaced the E111 form as proof of entitlement to free or reduced-cost medical treatment abroad (© **0845/606-2030**; www.ehic.org.uk). Note, however, that the EHIC only covers "necessary medical treatment."

Travel Insurance The cost of travel insurance varies widely depending on the destination, cost, and length of your trip, your age and health, and the type of trip you're taking, but expect to pay between 5% and 8% of the cost of the vacation. You can get estimates from various providers through **Insuremytrip.com** (© **800/487-4722**). Enter your trip's cost and dates, your age, and other information to get prices from more than a dozen companies.

U.K. citizens and their families who make more than one trip abroad per year may find that an annual travel insurance policy works out cheaper. Check **www.moneysupermarket.com** (© **0845/345-5708**), which compares prices across a wide range of providers for single- and multi-trip policies.

Most big travel agents offer their own insurance and will probably try to sell you their package when you book a holiday. Think before you sign. **Britain's Consumers' Association** recommends that you insist on seeing the policy and reading the fine print before buying. The **Association of British Insurers** (© **020/7600-3333**; www.abi.org.uk) gives advice by phone and publishes *Holiday Insurance,* a free guide to policy provisions and prices. You might also shop around for better deals: Try **Columbus Direct**

(© **0870/033-9988;** www.columbus direct.net).

Trip Cancellation Insurance Trip-cancellation insurance will help retrieve your money if you have to back out of a trip or depart early, or if your travel supplier goes bankrupt. Trip cancellation traditionally covers such events as sickness, natural disasters, and State Department advisories. The latest news in trip-cancellation insurance is the availability of expanded hurricane coverage and the "any-reason" cancellation coverage—which costs more but covers cancellations made for any reason. You won't get back 100% of your prepaid trip cost, but you'll be refunded a substantial portion. **Travel-Safe** (© **888/885-7233;** www.travelsafe. com) offers both types of coverage. Expedia also offers any-reason cancellation coverage for its air-hotel packages. For details, contact one of the following recommended insurers: **Access America** (© 866/807-3982; www.accessamerica. com), **AIG Travel Guard** (© 800/826-4919; www.travelguard.com), **Travel Insured International** (© 800/243-3174; www.travelinsured.com), and **Travelex Insurance Services** (© 888/457-4602; www.travelex-insurance.com).

INTERNET ACCESS Internet access is limited on the islands, but it's available at **Cybercafe,** in the Mall at Marathon in Nassau (© **242/394-6254**), or in Freeport at **CyberClub** at Seventeen Center (© **242/351-4560**). Web access is increasingly common at hotels; even in the Out Islands, you can usually access the Web. But if this issue is especially important to you, check with specific accommodations before booking. Also see "Online Traveler's Toolbox" and "Staying Connected," p. 61 and 60.

LANGUAGE In The Bahamas, locals speak English, but sometimes with a marked accent that provides the clue to their ancestry—African, Irish, or Scottish, for example.

LOST & FOUND Be sure to notify all of your credit card companies the minute you discover your wallet has been lost or stolen and file a report at the nearest police precinct. Your credit card company or insurer may require a police report or record of the loss. Most credit card companies have an emergency toll-free number to call; they may be able to wire you a cash advance immediately or deliver an emergency credit card in a day or two. **Visa**'s U.S. emergency number is © **800/847-2911. American Express** cardholders and traveler's check holders should call © **800/221-7282. MasterCard** holders should call © **800/307-7309.** For other credit cards, call the toll-free number directory at © **800/555-1212.**

If you need emergency cash over the weekend when all banks and American Express offices are closed, you can have money wired to you via **Western Union** (© **800/325-6000;** www.westernunion. com).

MAIL You'll need Bahamian (not U.S.) postage stamps to send postcards and letters. Most of the kiosks selling postcards also sell the stamps you'll need to mail them, so you probably won't need to visit the post office. Sending a postcard or an airmail letter (up to ½ oz. in weight) from The Bahamas to anywhere outside its borders (including the U.S., Canada, and the U.K.) costs 65¢ (35p), with another charge for each additional half-ounce of weight.

Mail to and from the Out Islands is sometimes slow. Airmail may go by air to Nassau and by boat to its final destination. If a resort has a U.S. or Nassau address, it is preferable to use it.

MEASUREMENTS See the chart on the inside front cover of this book for details on converting metric measurements to non-metric equivalents.

NEWSPAPERS & MAGAZINES Three newspapers are circulated in Nassau and Freeport: the *Nassau Guardian,* the *Tribune,* and the *Freeport News.* Circulation in the Out Islands is limited and likely to be slow. You can find such papers as the *New York Times,* the *Wall Street Journal, USA Today,* the *Miami Herald,* London's *Times,* and the *Daily Telegraph* at newsstands in your hotel and elsewhere in Nassau.

PASSPORTS For U.S. residents: Whether you're applying in person or by mail, you can download passport applications from the U.S. Department of State website at http://travel.state.gov. To find your regional passport office, check the U.S. Department of State website or call the toll-free number of the **National Passport Information Center** (℃ 877/487-2778) for automated information.

For Canada residents: Passport applications are available at travel agencies throughout Canada or from the central **Passport Office,** Department of Foreign Affairs and International Trade Ottawa, ON K1A 0G3 (℃ 800/567-6868; www.ppt.gc.ca). *Note:* Canadian children who travel must have their own passport. However, if you hold a valid Canadian passport issued before December 11, 2001, that bears the name of your child, the passport remains valid for you and your child until it expires.

For Ireland residents: Apply for a 10-year passport at the **Passport Office,** Setanta Centre, Molesworth Street, Dublin 2 (℃ 01/671-1633; www.irlgov.ie/iveagh). Those under age 18 and over 65 must apply for a 3-year passport. You can also apply at 1A South Mall, Cork (℃ 021/494-4700), or at most main post offices.

For Australia residents: Pick up an application from your local post office or any branch of Passports Australia, but you must schedule an interview at the passport office to present your application materials. Call the **Australian Passport Information Service** at ℃ 131-232 or visit the government website at www.smarttraveler.gov.au.

For New Zealand residents: Pick up a passport application at any New Zealand Passports Office or download it from their website. Contact the **Passports Office** at ℃ 0800/225-050 in New Zealand or 04/474-8100, or log on to www.passports.govt.nz.

POLICE Dial ℃ **919.**

SAFETY See "Safety," p. 51.

TAXES A 6% to 12% tax is imposed on hotel bills; otherwise, there is no sales tax in The Bahamas.

TELEPHONES Though some of the Out Islands are still difficult to reach by phone, direct long-distance dialing is available between North America and Nassau, Grand Bahama, the Abacos, Andros, the Berry Islands, Bimini, Eleuthera, Harbour Island, Spanish Wells, the Exumas, and Stella Maris on Long Island.

To call The Bahamas:

1. Dial the international access code: 011 from the U.S.; 00 from the U.K., Ireland, or New Zealand; or 0011 from Australia.
2. Dial the country code: **242.**
3. Dial the seven-digit local number.

To make international calls from The Bahamas: First dial 00 and then the country code (U.S. or Canada 1, U.K. 44, Ireland 353, Australia 61, New Zealand 64). Next, dial the area code and number. For example, if you wanted to call the British Embassy in Washington, D.C., you would dial 00-1-202-588-7800.

For local calls within The Bahamas: Simply dial the seven-digit number. To call from one island to another within The Bahamas, dial 1-242 and then the seven-digit number.

For directory assistance: Dial ✆ **916** if you're looking for a number inside The Bahamas, 0 for numbers to all other countries.

For operator assistance: To reach an international or domestic operator within The Bahamas, dial ✆ **0.**

Toll-free numbers: Numbers beginning with **881** within The Bahamas are toll-free. However, calling a normally toll-free number within the U.S. (that is, one beginning with 800, 866, 887, or 888) usually involves a charge if made from The Bahamas. In fact, it usually costs the same as an overseas call unless the merchant has made arrangements with local telephone authorities. *Note:* Major airlines generally maintain toll-free 800, 866, 887, or 888 provisions for calls made to them within The Bahamas. If you dial what you think is a toll-free phone number and it ends up costing the long-distance rate, an automated recording will inform you of this fact. In some cases, the recording will suggest a local toll-free alternative—usually one beginning with 881.

To reach the major international services of **AT&T,** dial ✆ **800/CALL-ATT** (225-5288), or head for any phone with AT&T or USA Direct marked on the side of the booth. Picking up the handset will connect you with an AT&T operator. These phones are often positioned beside cruise-ship docks for disembarking passengers.

MCI can be reached at ✆ **800/888-8000.**

Note that the old coin-operated phones are still prevalent in The Bahamas and do still swallow coins. Those old phones, however, are gradually being replaced by phones that use calling cards (debit cards) that come in denominations of US$5, US$10, US$20, and US$50. They can be bought from any office of **BATELCO** (Bahamas Telephone Co.). BATELCO's main branch is on Kennedy Drive, Nassau (✆ **242/302-7008**), although a popular local branch lies in the heart of Nassau, on East Street off Bay Street.

TIME ZONE Eastern Standard Time is used throughout The Bahamas, and daylight saving time is observed in the summer.

TIPPING Many establishments add a service charge, but it's customary to leave something extra if service has been especially fine. If you're not sure whether service has been included in your bill, don't be shy—ask.

Bellboys and porters, at least in the expensive hotels, expect a tip of US$1 to US$2 (50p–£1) per bag. It's also customary to tip your maid at least US$2 (£1) per day—more if she or he has performed special services such as getting a shirt or blouse laundered. Most service personnel, including taxi drivers, waiters, and the like, expect 15% (20% in deluxe restaurants).

USEFUL PHONE NUMBERS Sources of information include:

U.S. Dept. of State Travel Advisory: ✆ 202/647-5225 (manned 24 hr.)

U.S. Passport Agency: ✆ 202/647-0518

U.S. Centers for Disease Control International Traveler's Hotline: ✆ 404/332-4559

WATER Technically, tap water is drinkable throughout The Bahamas. But we almost always opt for bottled. Resorts tend to filter and chlorinate tap water more aggressively than other establishments; elsewhere, bottled water is available at stores and supermarkets, and tastes better than that from a tap. On many of the Out Islands, rainfall is the main source of water—drink bottled water there.

2 Toll-Free Numbers & Websites

MAJOR U.S. AIRLINES

An asterisk (*) indicates that the airline flies internationally as well.

American Airlines*
☏ 800/433-7300 (in U.S. or Canada)
☏ 020/7365-0777 (in U.K.)
www.aa.com

Continental Airlines*
☏ 800/523-3273 (in U.S. or Canada)
☏ 084/5607-6760 (in U.K.)
www.continental.com

Delta Air Lines*
☏ 800/221-1212 (in U.S. or Canada)
☏ 084/5600-0950 (in U.K.)
www.delta.com

JetBlue Airways
☏ 800/538-2583 (in U.S.)
☏ 080/1365-2525 (in U.K. or Canada)
www.jetblue.com

Northwest Airlines
☏ 800/225-2525 (in U.S.)
☏ 870/0507-4074 (in U.K.)
www.nwa.com

US Airways*
☏ 800/428-4322 (in U.S. and Canada)
☏ 084/5600-3300 (in U.K.)
www.usairways.com

MAJOR INTERNATIONAL AIRLINES

Air Jamaica
☏ 800/523-5585 (in U.S. or Canada)
☏ 208/570-7999 (in Jamaica)
www.airjamaica.com

American Airlines
☏ 800/433-7300 (in U.S. and Canada)
☏ 020/7365-0777 (in U.K.)
www.aa.com

Bahamasair
☏ 800/222-4262 (in U.S.)
☏ 242/300-8359 (in Family Islands)
☏ 242/377-5505 (in Nassau)
www.bahamasair.com

British Airways
☏ 800/247-9297 (in U.S. and Canada)
☏ 087/0850-9850 (in U.K.)
www.british-airways.com

Continental Airlines
☏ 800/523-3273 (in U.S. or Canada)
☏ 084/5607-6760 (in U.K.)
www.continental.com

Cubana
☏ 888/667-1222 (in Canada)
☏ 020/7538-5933 (in U.K.)
www.cubana.cu

Delta Air Lines
☏ 800/221-1212 (in U.S. or Canada)
☏ 084/5600-0950 (in U.K.)
www.delta.com

US Airways
☏ 800/428-4322 (in U.S. and Canada)
☏ 084/5600-3300 (in U.K.)
www.usairways.com

CAR-RENTAL AGENCIES

Alamo
☏ 800/GO-ALAMO (462-5266)
www.alamo.com

Avis
☏ 800/331-1212 (in U.S. and Canada)
☏ 084/4581-8181 (in U.K.)
www.avis.com

Budget
☏ 800/527-0700 (in U.S.)
☏ 087/0156-5656 (in U.K.)
☏ 800/268-8900 (in Canada)
www.budget.com

Dollar
☏ 800/800-4000 (in U.S.)
☏ 800/848-8268 (in Canada)
☏ 080/8234-7524 (in U.K.)
www.dollar.com

Hertz
☏ 800/645-3131 (in U.S.)
☏ 800/654-3001 (for international reservations)
www.hertz.com

National
℡ 800/CAR-RENT (227-7368; in U.S.)
www.nationalcar.com

Thrifty
℡ 800/367-2277 (in U.S.)
℡ 918/669-2168 (international)
www.thrifty.com

MAJOR HOTEL & MOTEL CHAINS

Best Western International
℡ 800/780-7234 (in U.S. and Canada)
℡ 0800/393-130 (in U.K.)
www.bestwestern.com

Embassy Suites
℡ 800/EMBASSY (362-2779)
www.embassysuites.com

Hilton Hotels
℡ 800/HILTONS (445-8667; in U.S. and Canada)
℡ 087/0590-9090 (in U.K.)
www.hilton.com

Holiday Inn
℡ 800/315-2621 (in U.S. and Canada)
℡ 0800/405-060 (in U.K.)
www.holidayinn.com

Marriott
℡ 877/236-2427 (in U.S. and Canada)
℡ 0800/221-222 (in U.K.)
www.marriott.com

Radisson Hotels & Resorts
℡ 888/201-1718 (in U.S. and Canada)
℡ 0800/374-411 (in U.K.)
www.radisson.com

Sheraton Hotels & Resorts
℡ 800/325-3535 (in U.S.)
℡ 800/543-4300 (in Canada)
℡ 0800/3253-5353 (in U.K.)
www.sheraton.com

Westin Hotels & Resorts
℡ 800/937-8461 (in U.S. and Canada)
℡ 0800/3259-5959 (in U.K.)
www.westin.com

Wyndham Hotels & Resorts
℡ 877/999-3223 (in U.S. and Canada)
℡ 050/6638-4899 (in U.K.)
www.wyndham.com

Index

See also Accommodations and Restaurant indexes, below.

RESTAURANTS